An Introduction to

CHILD STUDY

THE MACMILLAN COMPANY
NEW YORK · CHICAGO
DALLAS · ATLANTA · SAN FRANCISCO
LONDON · MANILA

IN CANADA
BRETT-MACMILLAN LTD.
GALT, ONTARIO

The whole family goes to school. Thus schools contribute intimately and intensively to child development.

An Introduction to

CHILD STUDY

Ruth Strang

Professor of Education, Teachers College
Columbia University

FOURTH EDITION

Photographs by
Jean Williamson

New York
THE MACMILLAN COMPANY

Printed in the United States of America

PREFACE

Everyone in close contact with children and young people can contribute to their development. Among these very important persons are parents, grandparents and other members of the family, friends, teachers, doctors, dentists, nurses, social workers, pastors, policemen, recreation leaders, and many others. Often these people feel baffled by children's behavior. If they better understood human growth and development, they could contribute more to the welfare of children and thus to the building of a better world.

Some people just naturally have a constructive influence on children; they are therapeutic personalities. Many others have learned much through their own experience as children and adolescents and from their contacts with children as parents, teachers, and other workers. To clarify, verify, and supplement their basic understanding, they turn to published sources. Child-study groups usually reach a stage at which they need books to interpret the information they have obtained about particular children. Students in classes, seminars, practicums, and workshops in child psychology and human relations need facts and theory to guide and interpret their observation and practical work with children. Parents who want their children to achieve the best development or are baffled by a child's behavior turn to published material for understanding. From books and articles they can glean guiding principles that illumine experience and help them to fit facts into a meaningful pattern for the whole expanse of infancy, childhood, and adolescence. Understanding should not arouse anxiety or feelings of guilt on the part of parents or teachers. Rather, it should give perspective and acceptance of the ups and downs and normal problems of growing up.

For these purposes, the three previous editions of *An Introduction to Child Study* have proved so helpful that a fourth seems to be indicated. The present edition attempts to meet a need which has not been fully met by any single type of publication: the persuasive pamphlets and popular books which give a wealth of sound practical suggestions on child care and training; the books which consist largely of case studies; the technical type of child psychology organized around topics such as motor ability, language development, growth of intelligence, emotion, and personality; the theoretical books delving deeply into psychological and psychoanalytical points of view; or the highly technical encyclopedic volumes that review the tremendous amount of research in the field. Each type of publication has an important place in the field, and references to all types are included in the text and in the bibliographies at the end of each major division and at the end of the book.

Briefly, the main features of this revision of *An Introduction to Child Study* are these:

1. A picture of the child's sequential development, which shows the continuity, trends, interrelations, and overlap of aspects of growth at different ages. An ascending spiral form of organization, or developmental approach by age, is used; the same aspects of development are treated repeatedly, each time with additional information and appropriate applications. Important points of view and principles are repeated for emphasis and as an aid to learning.

2. Explanations of and more emphasis on the dynamics of children's behavior: Why do they behave as they do? What dynamics of growth, concepts of themselves, personal relations, cultural influences, and conflicts are affecting their behavior and the way they perceive their world?

3. Description and explanation of how children learn. Since school is such an important part of the experience of middle and later childhood, it seemed desirable to relate information about school learning to child development as a whole during these years.

4. Description of conditions in home, school, and community that are conducive to wholesome child development. Since a child is constantly interacting with his environment, the central task of those who work with children is to create a favorable environment and guide the child in that environment.

5. Suggestions for child study and guidance including practical experience in observing and helping children.

6. References to books, articles, and films, including references to recent research mentioned in the text plus a short bibliography, which students should read to supplement the content of each chapter.

A positive emphasis is maintained throughout the book. The family is viewed as a positive factor with emphasis on the potentialities of parents rather than on their faults. Problems are viewed as the child's effort to meet life situations. The distinction is made between "problems of growing up" and "problems that interfere with growing up." Independence, stubborn-

ness, and other behavior often annoying to parents and teachers are recognized at certain ages as manifestations of maturity. The emphasis is on
"developmental tasks" rather than on "problems," in the negative sense.

Especially helpful in preparing this revision were the specific suggestions and comments made by the following persons in the field of child
development, some of whom had used the book as a text in their child-study
classes:

Dr. M. Arline Albright, Marquette University, Department of Education,
   Milwaukee, Wisconsin
Dr. K. S. Bernhardt, University of Toronto, Institute of Child Study,
   Toronto, Canada
Miss Ethel Kawin, Director, Parent Education Project, University of Chi-
   cago, Chicago, Illinois
Dr. G. Lawrence Kibler, Waynesburg College, Department of Education,
   Waynesburg, Pennsylvania
Dr. Harriet L. Rheingold, National Institute of Mental Health, Bethesda,
   Maryland
Dr. Olive Woodruff, Head of Kindergarten-Primary Education, Kent State
   University, Kent, Ohio.

The author is also greatly indebted to many persons: to the authors of
published books and articles, listed in the bibliographies, from which many
facts and points of view included in the text were obtained; to her students
who have contributed anecdotal records included throughout the book,
among whom are Dorothy Adams, Eleanor Barry, Rose Maria Guerra,
Lavonia Houseworth, Norman J. M. Murray, Joseph W. Smith, Rhoda U.
Yearwood; to John Antrobus for his critical reading of much of the manuscript; to Mrs. Alma Fogarty, for her intelligent typing of the manuscript;
to Mrs. George MacLeod of Glasgow, Scotland, for her observations of the
development of two children; and to other parents and teachers who have
contributed points of view and illustrations from their firsthand experience
in bringing up children.

RUTH STRANG

SUGGESTIONS TO STUDENTS
FOR STUDY

1. Look through the table of contents to find out what you can learn from the book. Note the organization of the book as a whole.

2. Before beginning to read a chapter:
   a. Recall what you already know about children of the age to be described.
   b. Observe infants or children, or look at pictures or films of children of that age.
   c. Raise questions you would like to have answered.
   d. State your purpose in reading the chapter.
   e. Decide on the best method of reading for that purpose.

3. Read the questions and problems at the end of the chapter or others prepared by the instructor. Which can you work on before reading the chapter? Which help to guide your reading of the chapter and stimulate you to think and to evaluate?

4. Skim through the chapter to find out what the author is trying to do and where you can find the answers to your questions. Keep the questions in mind as you read the chapter.

5. Read each paragraph to grasp its main idea, and note the illustrations or evidence offered in support of the idea.

6. Keep these main ideas in mind and relate them to one another and to your experience. Thus your understanding of children will grow as you read.

7. Use the index to get a more complete picture of any aspect of development, such as growth in vocabulary.

8. Select from the bibliography books and articles. Read these to increase your understanding of children. Read critically newspaper columns and articles in current magazines on how to bring up children. You may want to make your own child-study scrapbook of sound clippings and your own observations. Compile your own bibliography from different types of journals on at least one important topic.

CONTENTS

Part Four

MIDDLE CHILDHOOD

Part Five
FROM THE PRIMARY PERIOD TO ADOLESCENCE

Part Six
PREVIEW OF ADOLESCENCE

FIGURES

An Introduction to

CHILD STUDY

Chapter 1

INTRODUCTION

Adults, in general, are friendly to childhood. They delight in the child's spontaneity; they are amused at his wide-eyed wonder about everything; they marvel at the rapidity of his development in wisdom and stature and social relations. Yet many adults have vague, inaccurate ideas about children and are often awkward at entering into a child's world. Failing to understand the meaning of his behavior, they do not respond to him as helpfully as they might. They lack the wizardry which De la Mare (9, p. xvi, 1935)* likened to the born gardener's "green thumb"—the gift of being able to bring into flower that most delicate plant, the infinitely complex personality of a child.

UNDERSTANDING NEEDED

Although parents and teachers cannot acquire this intuitive gift merely by reading child psychology, they can increase their understanding in several ways:

1. Through an appreciation of basic principles: that the child grows; that the way he grows depends on the kind of child he is and the experiences he has; that parents and teachers can influence his growth by the way they feel and act toward him; that while it is of the utmost importance that the child be loved, trusted, understood, and accepted in his early years, the fact remains that the personality can be strengthened or weakened at any stage of life.

2. Through knowledge of how children grow—the stages, phases, or epochs of development through which they pass, the developmental tasks that they accomplish year by year.

3. Through an understanding that, though the individual child is like other children of his age in some ways, in many ways he is like no one else.

The adult who is familiar with the guiding principles and general sequences of child development, and who has taken the trouble to study the unique characteristics of individual children, is in a position to help each

* The first number in parentheses refers to references at the end of Part One, pp. 45-47; the second number, to pages quoted within the reference; the third number (or second where only two are given) is the year of publication.

1

child make the best progress possible for *him*. A child needs teachers and parents who neither ignore his potentialities nor push and prod him to achieve the impossible.

HOW CHILDREN DEVELOP

A child's many-sided development is the result of his interaction with his physical and social environment as he perceives it. An infant's repertory of reactions is relatively simple. As he develops and the environment exerts an increasing influence on him, the range of his possible responses becomes wider. For example, once the child has learned to walk and run, a whole new environment opens up to him. He no longer has to wait for the environment to come to him; he goes to it; he makes changes in it. As the preschool years advance, the possible variations in his behavior are multiplied. During adolescence, his responses become still more unpredictable. This increasing complexity of behavior may be suggested by the following diagram, representing at the left the child at birth and, moving to the right, his expanding capacities.

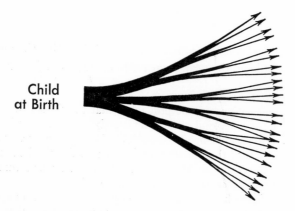

Child at Birth

Each child develops according to an orderly sequence that is common to human beings in general, but capable of countless unique variations. The baby sits up before he creeps, creeps before he stands, stands before he walks. In walking, he progresses by increasing the length of his stride, keeping his feet closer together, taking more steps, having fewer falls. As he progresses through recognizable stages or phases during a lifelong sequence of growth, his patterns of behavior are somewhat similar to those of other people; however, he goes ahead at his own rate, he sets his own timetables.

Developmental sequences can be defined most reliably as they pertain to bodily changes and the development of motor abilities. Even these basic aspects of development can be modified in individual cases by illness, privation, and other environmental conditions. Social and emotional sequences are greatly modified by such factors as social acceptance or rejection in the home and the school, the character of the neighborhood, and the influence of younger or older brothers and sisters.

DEVELOPMENTAL NORMS AS SIGNPOSTS

Although psychologists recognize certain stages or epochs of development that occur through life, they disagree as to the value of age norms or timetables. One side of this controversy is represented by Gesell and his associates, who have published detailed descriptions of sequences of development from birth through sixteen years. These year-by-year descriptions of sequences are fairly reliable for infants but they become far less applicable as children grow older. Gesell repeatedly warns that the behavior outlined for each age simply illustrates the kinds of behavior which tend to occur under contemporary cultural conditions. Yet the major part of his book consists of specific statements, such as, "Six is an active age," "Nine is rather positive in his food likes and dislikes." In opposition to this approach, Senn (35, 1955) maintains that these age norms are based on unrepresentative samplings of children, some of whom were studied more than twenty years ago when conditions of life and child-rearing practices were different than they are today. Moreover, individual differences among children in their rate of growth and age of maturing make the age-norm approach unsound. Much more research is needed to know how much variation in different aspects of development a parent may normally expect of a two-year-old or a seven-year-old under different conditions, and which deviations are desirable, allowable, or pathological.

This controversy results partly from the way in which timetables are interpreted:

As rigid age norms to which all children are expected to conform.
As midpoints in a broad range of frequency of behavior with which a child of a given age may be compared.
As developmental sequences, stages, or epochs which may serve as signposts for adults' observation and guidance of individual children.

Developmental summaries or norms may be misused, as when, instead of accepting a certain range of differences as normal and even desirable, some parents become anxious about them, prematurely apply remedial measures, put pressure on the slow child to come up to average. On the other hand, by accepting these averages as normal, parents or teachers may overlook the potentialities of a gifted child; neglect his abilities; and let him mark time, lose interest, and become bored.

It is useful, however, to have some idea of the changes in children as they grow up. By having a "ground plan of growth" based on physical development and taking into account the influence of common characteristics of the culture, parents and teachers can gain perspective on their own children and help them to accomplish the developmental tasks appropriate to each stage of growth. Such knowledge gives perspective and helps the adult to "look before and after," to observe trends in a child's development over a period of time, and to view it as a process that has its ups and downs and yet, ideally, always continues to spiral upward toward maturity. Parents and teachers who realize that the behavior of a child or adolescent may be expected to show fluctuations will not be disturbed by his occasional lapses into less acceptable behavior. At such times they will not take the fatalistic attitude, "He'll always be like this."

It is also important for parents and teachers to know what is the best time to teach children various knowledges and skills. If a skill is introduced too early, learning is slow and laborious, and consequently apt to be accompanied by dissatisfaction, resistance, or failure. If, on the other hand, the child is allowed to pass the peak of his readiness for acquiring a certain skill, an opportunity for effective learning is lost. By being alert to a child's sequences of development, the adult can be ready to provide the experiences he needs when he needs them. Summaries of child development are useful, but always in combination with the individual approach. Developmental norms are milestones on the common path of child development. They raise questions as to whether adults are providing conditions for the child's optimum development.

WHY CHILDREN BEHAVE AS THEY DO

In the beginning, children are inherently active and insatiably curious. These two qualities account for much of their remarkable progress in learning. The more things they do, the more skills they acquire; the more skills they possess, the more effectively they attack and solve new problems. They are essentially self-motivated. It is satisfying for any individual to function as he was intended to function.

As a result of their experiences, especially their interpersonal relations, their concept of themselves becomes clearer. This self-concept, in turn, does much to determine their subsequent behavior. The self-concept is likely to show a high degree of self-consistency and self-persistency.

Children's behavior also is influenced by other people's expectations. The nature of this influence is affected by the quality of the child's relations with these people. If a parent toward whom the child feels hostile expects him to reach a high level of scholastic achievement, the child may develop a conscious or unconscious determination not to learn. On the other hand, a much-loved person, adult or chum, may bring out the best in a child—may even help to correct certain warps that have resulted from unfavorable early experiences.

In addition to the child's emotional relations with his family and friends, other conditions play a part in determining his behavior. Among these are illness and the way the ill child is treated, physical defects, diet, play opportunities, and school experiences. Neighborhood conditions, the socioeconomic status of the family, and national and world affairs may have an indirect influence on even a young child's behavior.

The way in which a child uses his environment depends on the initial quality of his nervous system and its subsequent development through interaction with his social and physical environment. His distinctively human ability to use abstract symbols makes it possible for expectations of the future as well as recollections of the past to influence his present behavior.

Scientific child study does not end with the description of behavior; it aims to discover what a given instance of behavior means to the child, and what conditions have given rise to his unique behavior patterns. Varied causes underlie seemingly identical acts. It is therefore necessary to be alert to the significance of clues and subtle impressions, as well as to be closely observant of the child's overt behavior against the background of his family, school, and neighborhood setting. The ideal case study of a child is one that shows the dynamics of his many-sided development from birth on.

HOW TO HELP CHILDREN GROW

Children do not "just grow." They need guidance. Everyone who lives with children has been in situations that have made him aware of the need for more understanding on the part of both child and adult. Suppose that a child of three or four years says "I won't" or "No" to every request, reasonable or unreasonable. What should the parent do? Suppose that a child of five screams and kicks when he has to come in from play.

Why does he behave in this way? Or perhaps a six-year-old is exceedingly docile; he does everything he is told to do, but nothing on his own initiative. How can the teacher help him to develop independence and self-reliance? Why is a third-grade child, though equal in intelligence to other children in his class, the only one who has not learned to read? What should be done about it? If an older girl is timid and seclusive, what can a teacher do to further her best development? There are no short, easy answers to questions like these, which continually arise in the process of bringing up children.

We need to learn how to help children, at different levels of maturity, to learn to read, to work and play constructively with others, to develop skill in living in groups. How do children develop values? How can we help them translate values into action? How can we teach them the arts of learning, and of solving problems? All this and more is involved in helping children grow. What basic points of view should guide our efforts in this direction?

Much is gained by "accentuating the positive." The emphasis in child development seems to be shifting from *problems* to *progress*; parent education aims to give reassurance rather than arouse anxiety. This sound attitude of positive expectancy should be applied to both children *and* parents. It is based on the belief that the individual has inner resources for developing in his own best way. It avoids focusing a child's attention on a defect or a fault, with the possible result that he may assign it undue importance in his concept of himself. The positive point of view is exemplified by counselors in the "client-centered approach," by pediatricians in the "self-selection" schedule, and by physicians in their reliance upon "the wisdom of the body."

Further, our attention should be focused on creating a favorable environment in which the child can develop his growth potential. The element regarded as most essential in the child's environment is "a pair of good parents who love him truly." In early infancy parental love is expressed through warm, relaxed, secure physical contact; later, affection may be conveyed in many ways, as by trusting the child, accepting him as a person, helping him to learn without unnecessary failure or frustration, giving him words of genuine specific praise. When the child or adolescent needs firmness, strictness, or control, and knows that these are needed for his best development, he accepts these restrictions as signs that his parents care. One youngster said, "I'd rather have my father punish me than not care what happens to me." "Whom the Lord loveth he chasteneth."

It is obvious that the child needs suitable experiences in each epoch of his development. At every age the child needs appropriate equipment and materials, freedom to explore, someone to listen to him, someone to answer his questions. He needs encouragement to work out problems for himself. Help must be skillfully timed—if given too early, it deprives him of the satisfaction of accomplishment or makes him feel inadequate as a person; if it is delayed too long, he may feel frustrated and helpless.

PREVIEW OF THE BOOK

This book will describe the familiar stages of development that have been recognized by poets, parents, and teachers. Each of these periods will be discussed in turn: the prenatal period and birth; the first two years of life; the preschool period, ending with the fifth year; the primary or middle childhood period, including years six to eight; the later childhood and pre-adolescent period, comprising years nine to the appearance of puberty; and the adolescent period, from about the twelfth or thirteenth to the end of the eighteenth year or later. Each period, of course, merges imperceptibly into the next, and it can be explained only by what has gone before.

In infancy and young childhood many ways of feeling and acting are initiated. "Well begun is half done." Children do not easily outgrow their early experiences—especially vivid emotional crises—as they do their dresses and shoes. These experiences sometimes exert a persistent influence on their adult behavior. An extreme view of the importance of the first years of life was expressed by Alfred Adler, an Austrian psychiatrist. He was of the opinion that a child's behavior pattern is formed by the time he is four years old. Thereafter, Adler said, the child is not appreciably changed by his environment; on the contrary, he twists and reshapes his experiences to conform to his preconceived pattern. Although this view exaggerates the influence of the early years on children in general, there is no doubt about their importance. Since teachers and parents need to understand the whole expanse of childhood as well as the segment with which they are particularly concerned, and since more accurate knowledge is available about the early years than about any other, we shall devote considerable space to this period.

During the elementary school years the child's development can be enhanced or impeded. The skills he learns and the understanding he acquires contribute greatly to his growth. By means of friendships formed during this period, he may correct earlier fault lines. Certainly this is a period that deserves more scientific study.

Adolescence is seen as a distinctive phase, as well as a continuation of the individual's personality development. Even though the influences of early life tend to persist, the attitudes and habits precipitated by sexual maturity and changes in his sex role and by his imminent adult status may facilitate or hinder life adjustment. Although this period can only be briefly introduced in a general book on child study, it seemed important to include some reference to this often turbulent period between childhood and adulthood.

The aim of the following chapters is to describe some of the known features of desirable development, to state some of the conditions that make it possible, to facilitate understanding of individual children and of threats to their development, and to suggest methods of correcting personality fault lines at each stage of life. The statements made should be considered as tentative. The quest for certainty is still going on. All we can say at present is: This *seems* to be the answer; this *seems* to be the truth.

A HIGH CALLING

Bringing up children is being recognized as one of the most important tasks in the world today. The world of tomorrow will be shaped by the children now growing up. Improvements in child care and education can change society for the better. What lifework, therefore, is more important than that of parent, teacher, pediatrician, child psychologist, guidance worker, or anyone else who helps children develop their potentialities, especially their capacity for love? Parents and teachers engaged in this task are laying the foundation of peace and good will among men. What other kind of work can yield deeper satisfactions? Surely understanding of the psychology of infancy, childhood, and adolescence has world-wide significance. In the words of the International Committee for Mental Hygiene: "In the mental health goal—harmonious living—lies a concrete hope for a frightened world."

Questions and Problems

FOR CLASS DISCUSSION OR STUDY GROUPS*

1. In what ways may the word *timetable* be interpreted? Which interpretation is the soundest and why?

* The questions suggested are merely samples of types of questions that may be raised. Many teachers prefer to formulate their own questions, or have a given class suggest questions and problems.

2. Which of the following uses of growth tables do you think are desirable and which may be undesirable or detrimental?

To suggest the question: "Why is my child's behavior out of line with that of children described in the studies? Are there home conditions that can be improved?"

To justify prodding a child who is below the developmental level for his age, regardless of any consideration of the child's capacity and environmental conditions.

To guide one's study of the sequences of behavior in an individual child.

To imply that something is wrong with a child who does not conform to the common pattern.

To suggest that each child is unique and that there is a wide range of developmental patterns, any of which may be appropriate for an individual child.

3. One father said, "I leave the reading of books on child care and child psychology for my wife. She was pleased when our children were up to par according to the book." Should these parents have been pleased? Or should they have been stimulated to inquire whether their children showed any sign of strain or anxiety as a result of trying to conform; or whether, under favorable conditions, they would be reaching a higher stage than other children of their chronological age?

What was commendable in this mother's attitude: "I found my children ahead of the average in some ways and lagging behind in others. I guess they can't grow on all fronts at once and will zigzag up to maturity eventually."

4. Summarize the view of child development presented in this chapter. How does it compare with the viewpoint of one of the reference books listed at the end of Part I?

5. What kind of understanding of children do parents and teachers need? What is the difference between understanding children and trying to "psychiatrize" them?

6. What conditions influence a child's development?

7. "Children must do their own growing." "Children do not 'just grow'; they need guidance." Are these two statements necessarily conflicting? Discuss the meaning of each.

THE ROOTS OF

BEHAVIOR

Time, that renews the tissues of this frame,
That built the child and hardened the soft bone,
Taught him to wail, to blink, to walk alone,
Stare, question, wonder, give the world a name,
Forget the watery darkness whence he came,
Attends no less the boy to manhood grown. . . .

Wine from These Grapes
(New York: Harper & Bros., 1934), p. 25.
With permission of Harper & Bros.

Chapter 2

CONSTITUTIONAL INFLUENCES

Much happens in a child's development before he is born. Constitutional tendencies are determined; body structures are built; behavior begins; preparation is made for responses that will occur at birth.

HOW LIFE BEGINS

Life begins with a single cell. This cell is so small that "one hundred could ride on an inch-long spider web." Yet in this single cell are the makings of a person. All the elements that heredity can give to the new individual are there, brought together by the union of one cell (the sperm) from the father with one cell (the ovum) from the mother. Within this fertilized cell are twenty-four different pairs of chromosomes, one of each pair given by the mother, one by the father. Within the chromosomes are invisible particles called *genes*. These genes, together with other gene-like substances, are handed down from the parents to the child; they determine the individual's hereditary tendency (36, 1949).

If a healthy sperm cell and an ovum come together during a period of one to two days in approximately the middle of the menstrual cycle, the chances are that the sperm will enter and fertilize the ovum. However, if the sperm cells are weak or defective in some way, they may not be active enough to travel up the Fallopian tube, down which the ovum is being pushed; or if they do, they may not have sufficient vigor to enter the outer wall of the ovum. It takes a healthy sperm cell to reach and fertilize the ovum. On the other hand, if the woman is in ill health or subject to some nutritional or glandular deficiency, the ovum may be too feeble to fulfill its function. Even if both sperm cell and ovum are healthy, their union may be prevented by an obstruction in the Fallopian tube or an acid secretion in the female reproductive organs that kills the sperm. Childless couples can obtain medical treatment which, in many cases, overcomes these conditions.

NO TWO ALIKE

Human inheritance is somewhat like a grab bag. Half of the potential characteristics of each male and each female cell are discarded. This fact helps to explain the marked differences, as well as the similarities, among children of the same family. One child may resemble his mother; another child, his father; a third child, one of his grandparents. Only identical twins have the same hereditary pattern. Since each of the forty-eight chromosomes contains about three thousand genes, which are combined by chance, a child may inherit, according to one estimate (33, 1950), any one of between sixteen and seventeen million potential patterns. Consequently, no two babies will be exactly alike.

Once conception, or fertilization of the ovum by the sperm cell, has occurred, the hereditary nature of the individual is determined. Under favorable environmental conditions, the fertilized cell will mature in its own broadly predestined and unique way. At conception the foundation is laid for biological structure and its manner of functioning. Sex is likewise determined at this decisive moment. If the single cell splits at this crucial time, two or more separate eggs may be formed, from which twins, or even quintuplets, may develop. According to one report, twins occur about once in every ninety-two white births in the United States; quadruplets, once in every 570,196 white births (8, 1956). A greater frequency of multiple births occurs among Negroes.

Yet, even in the case of identical twins,

> "every man is in certain respects
> like all other men
> like some other men
> like no other man." (23, p. 53, 1955)

MATURATION AND BEHAVIOR

The fertilized ovum then divides into two cells. Eventually these two will increase, according to one estimate, to twenty-six billion cells. As this division of cells that are at first all alike is repeated over and over, increasing differentiation takes place. It is a chemical called "the organizer" (15, 1957) which determines whether a group of cells becomes the head or the arm, the eye or the ear. Each part of the body begins its development at a different time. Consequently special stresses to the mother at different periods of the prenatal period can influence the development of different parts of the body (18, 1957; 19, 1955).

Each advance in development influences its subsequent course of growth. For example, once sex is determined, certain lines of development will have to be followed.

This increasing differentiation of body structures and growth in size is called *maturation*. As maturation increases, new kinds of behavior are available to the child. He can do things that were previously impossible for him, no matter how hard he tried or how persistently he was taught. The role of maturation is well illustrated in development of the lower animals. Small water animals make swimming movements at the appropriate time in their development, even though they have had no previous practice or training. Chicks spontaneously begin to peck; canaries sing without being taught. One human twin who was given special practice in climbing and other motor activities was, in the long run, not much ahead of the other twin who had had no special practice in these skills. At the human level, however, much less of the infant's behavior is built in—i.e., dependent on maturation. In contrast to the lower animals, much of a human's behavior must be learned and can be acquired only after considerable practice. A potentially gifted child who receives little stimulus to use his intellectual capacity may turn out to be quite mediocre. The way an individual matures depends upon his inherited capacities and his opportunities to use them.

Inherited dispositions cannot play their role except under favorable conditions (23, pp. 53-110, 1955). The physical, biological, and social environment may facilitate or thwart the course of development. This process is not a mere unfolding of inherited tendencies. It is rather the continuous reordering of patterns of structure and function in a continually changing environment. "Environment plays a part in all 'maturation,' and maturation plays a part in all learning." (7, p. 160, 1954)

QUESTIONS ABOUT INHERITANCE

Among the questions that parents, teachers, and young people ask about heredity are these: What determines the sex of a baby? What physical and mental tendencies are inherited? Are diseases heritable? Will a child inherit his parents' bad habits?

Is it a boy or a girl?

This is an important question because the parents' preferences influence their attitude toward the child from the day he is born. If their present children are all of the same sex, most parents would prefer that the next baby be of the other sex. Young college students, when asked about their preferences as to the sex of their future children, had definite ideas: 92 per cent of the men and 66 per cent of the women said they wanted a boy, if they were to have only one child. If there were to be more than one child, about half of those questioned said they would prefer to have about the same number of each sex (10, 1954). Actually there are more boys born than girls—a ratio of 105 or 106 males to every 100 females; however, the mortality rate for boy babies is higher than that for girls.

Whatever preferences parents may have, there is nothing they can do to insure having a baby of the preferred sex. That is determined by chance. The father produces two kinds of sperm in equal numbers: one with a large X sex chromosome, the other with a small Y sex chromosome. The mother's sex chromosomes are all of one kind—the large X. If the sperm with the large X chromosome enters the ovum, it pairs with the mother's X chromosome. The result is a girl—XX = girl. If the sperm with the Y chromosome enters the ovum, it cannot match up with a similar Y chromosome. The result in this case is a boy—XY = boy. Once this has happened the child's sex is determined; there is nothing the parent can do to change it.

Many attempts have been made to predict whether the unborn baby will be a boy or a girl. The fetal heartbeat was once used as an index—if it's slow it's a boy; fast, a girl. State of ossification was also used—bones ossify later in boys than in girls. But individual differences made these tests quite unreliable. Likewise unreliable is the saliva test, which at first seemed promising. In any case, foreknowledge would have little use except in giving parents time to adjust if the child were not to be of the preferred sex. The important thing is that parents lovingly accept the baby, whether it is a boy or a girl.

What is the resemblance between parents and their children?

Members of a family usually resemble one another more than they resemble their neighbors. The intelligence of children in foster homes was found to resemble that of their real parents more closely than that of their foster parents. Identical twins (those who develop from a single sperm fertilizing a single egg, having the same genes, and who are always of the same sex) show the closest resemblance of all, even when reared apart (6, 1958; 21, 1955). From an extensive study of identical twins, of whom twenty-one were reared apart; two-egg, or nonidentical, twins reared together, siblings, some of whom were reared apart; and foster children,

Burt (6, 1958) tentatively concluded that differences in tested intelligence, like difference in stature, depend more largely on the action of numerous genes, than on environmental conditions.

Bayley reported that the older a child grows, the more his mental test scores resemble those of his parents. During the first year of the child's life the correlation* is zero, or negative, but it rises to 0.50 at two years and to 0.60 or more in the teens. In similiar fashion, resemblance in height tends to increase with age (2, 1954). Comparing two developmental studies, Honzik (16, 1957) concluded that parent-child resemblance in mental ability, which becomes manifest during the child's fifth or sixth year (even though the child is being reared in an institution or by foster parents), reflects individual differences in heredity.

Hidden in the germ cells of the parents are potentialities that they themselves do not show. Exceptionally intelligent parents can expect their children to be more intelligent than the average, but less intelligent than themselves. Exceptionally dull parents are likely to have children less intelligent than the average, but more intelligent than themselves.

Are physical and mental traits inherited?

Certain physical traits, such as color blindness, length of fingers, color of eyes, color of hair, curly or straight hair, appear to be determined by heredity. Under ordinary conditions environment does not modify these characteristics. But with a few rare exceptions every characteristic is the product of the interaction of heredity and environment.

However, there are hereditary *tendencies*—toward long life, toward emotional stability, toward high intelligence. If a parent has a good ear for music, it is likely that some of his children will have this characteristic. A certain tempo and intensity of responsiveness seem to be inborn. For example, some babies laugh easily—a characteristic that tends to evoke favorable responses.

Certain types of feeble-mindedness tend to run in families. Low mentality occurs when some factor that ensures normal development is lacking in both parents. Difficulty arises in the diagnosis of true mental deficiency. There is no conclusive evidence that all cases of feeble-mindedness are clearly hereditary. Some may be congenital, i.e., acquired during prenatal life. At birth severe lack of oxygen may cause brain damage. Other cases may be intensified by an impoverished social environment.

* A coefficient of correlation shows the relation between factors in the same individuals. Perfect agreement is represented by +1.0; lack of agreement, by 0.0; complete disagreement, by −1.0.

In experiments with rats, clear evidence has been obtained that selective breeding can produce more intelligent, more aggressive, or more timid strains. However, the results of these experiments cannot be applied, without further proof, on the more complex human level, where it is not feasible to control choice of mates and environmental conditions. There is little evidence at present of the biological inheritance of specific personality traits.

Are diseases inherited?

Several diseases, notably syphilis and gonorrhea, which were at one time thought to be inherited, are actually transmitted to the newborn through early infection. Syphilis may be transmitted by the mother to the unborn child. A mother with gonorrhea may infect the child while it is being born. Gonorrheal blindness results in about 80 per cent of the cases that are not given the simple protection that is possible at birth. Treatment of the syphilitic mother early in her pregnancy will protect the child. Tuberculosis, too, is not directly inherited, although there is some evidence that heredity may be a contributing factor in that it may cause constitutional weakness.

People display differing degrees of susceptibility to such other diseases as diphtheria, diabetes, and cancer. Certain kinds of cancer, for example, seem to be more prevalent in some families than in others, but direct inheritability has so far been demonstrated only in certain rare types. A "genetic predisposition to many of the psychosomatic diseases" has also been demonstrated (23, p. 79, 1955). Individual differences in susceptibility may be accounted for in part by environmental factors such as conditions causing emotional stress and strain, and in part by structural weakness, certain types of inherited constitution, and predisposition to the disease. For actual contraction of these diseases, there must be both susceptibility and exposure to the infectious agent and/or the environmental pressures. From the field of animal experimentation has come evidence that mice known to have inherited susceptibility to cancer do not develop this disease when environmental conditions are properly controlled.

In the case of most mental disorders as well, the causes are complex and uncertain. One obtains a variety of clinical pictures in any type of childhood psychosis. The interaction between hereditary and environmental influences is diverse and devious. An important part is played by constitutional factors such as unusual sensitivity and functional disturbances during the process of maturing. Moreover, a disturbed mother-child relationship is almost always involved.

Only one or two kinds of insanity are known to be inherited. Huntington's chorea, an extremely rare disease, is one of these. However, there is evidence that genetic elements are involved in the predisposition to and development of schizophrenia and the neuroses (11, 1952; 22, 1953). And it is probable that certain children inherit temperamental tendencies that may make them susceptible to mental disorders. This is one explanation of the fact that certain kinds of insanity tend to run in families. More conclusive research is needed.

If a child's parents can detect some of his organic weaknesses, they may so arrange the environment as to reduce certain stresses and strains. Many kinds of weakness are intensified by emotional disturbance. Individuals differ in their resistance to strains; some have slight resistance, others possess remarkable "emotional tensile strength." A favorable environment will counteract predispositions toward certain disorders. Without the environmental stimulus, the child may entirely escape the predisposition; even when a mental disease has started, its progress is ordinarily determined by factors other than heredity. No disorder is incurable because of its hereditary components (22, 1953). A follow-up study (31, 1945) of children of alcoholic and psychotic parents twenty years after they had been placed in foster homes, showed no child of psychotic parents who became psychotic and none of alcoholic parents who became alcoholic. Practically all were leading useful lives, although 30 per cent showed evidence of emotional disturbances.

Are acquired characteristics inherited?

Little evidence has been offered in support of the inheritance of characteristics acquired during a parent's lifetime. Mothers who sew beautifully have daughters who do no kind of needlework. Parents who have attained a high degree of scholarship may have children who are not scholars. If the father is a murderer, his child is not predestined to a criminal career. It is fortunate that children do not directly inherit their parents' bad habits. It is unfortunate that children of parents who have achieved a good life do not directly inherit habits of healthful living, honesty, industry, and courage. However, a child may unconsciously imitate his parents, and thus create the impression that he has inherited their characteristics.

We should not take a fatalistic attitude toward heredity. Learning is possible at every stage of life. Behavior patterns may be changed by experience. We should have a dim, discouraging view of man if we thought that he was helplessly driven by his innate predispositions or unresistingly molded by his culture. Man has more nobility when he feels responsible for what he is and what he becomes.

RELATION BETWEEN HEREDITY AND ENVIRONMENT

The interplay of hereditary dispositions, previous experiences, and present environments is revealed in studies of family trees, of children growing up in the same family, and of identical twins.

In the study of family trees, heredity, at first glance, seems to play the leading role. One family has a long line of illustrious descendants, while another family shows an equally long line of criminals and paupers. The first family, however, had social advantages, while the other had the disadvantages of an unfavorable environment.

Brothers and sisters growing up in the same family may be alike or very different. One is musical; the other cannot carry a simple tune. One is ambitious; the other lackadaisical. They respond in different ways to what seems to be the same environment. However, the environment, especially that part of it that comprises the emotional relations in the home, is not the same for any two children. Each child is influenced by the way in which relatives and friends feel toward him, speak to him, and act toward him. Each has different experiences that interact with his unique hereditary pattern.

Long ago Galton observed that identical twins were alike and tended to stay alike in many respects, even though their environments differed. More recent studies have shown that identical twins brought up in different homes and schools may differ considerably in certain respects (4, p. 20, 1950). Of four twins reared apart, the two who had markedly superior education made higher scores on intelligence tests; the differences were from 8 to 45 IQ points (26, pp. 1-6, 1947). The average difference in scholastic achievement was more than twice as great for twins reared apart as for those reared together. Differences in health were also noted in twins who had been living under different conditions.

Evidence is accumulating from the study of identical twins that a radically different environment may affect social characteristics (4, p. 11, 1950). One pair of identical twin sisters were brought up in widely different cultural environments. The one who had the advantage of a home characterized by cultural opportunities and by sociability was poised, affable, and self-confident; the other, reared in a home of meager cultural and social advantages, was somewhat awkward, diffident, and restrained

—she felt herself to be inferior. Wide differences in environment appear to account for more variations in these personality traits than do differences in heredity. Nevertheless, there may still be "biological substrata" that subtly modify an individual's response to his environment.

It is agreed that "heredity and nature always operate together" as complementary forces. They are "mutually inclusive." Hereditary tendencies find expression and are discovered through the environment; the environment enables the development of the child's hereditary tendencies; it is a circular response. Heredity sets the limits within which an individual can develop; the environment determines the development that actually takes place. Heredity appears to create dispositions to react in certain ways, if certain environmental conditions are provided. The influence of heredity is most clearly seen in the infant as he learns the basic essentials of living. The influence of environment is more obvious in the diversity of personality patterns found among adolescents.

PRACTICAL APPLICATIONS

There are many practical applications of the scientific facts about inheritance. By choosing a mate who is healthy and intelligent and whose ancestors and relatives have attained some degree of eminence, one improves one's chance of becoming the parent of superior children. Men do not "gather grapes of thorns, or figs of thistles." It is true, to be sure, that human beings are not "wholly grapes or wholly thistles." They represent a complex combination of potentialities. A genius may spring from an obscure or even a disreputable family. But why take a chance when choice is possible? Every child has a right to have parents who are not mentally deficient, who have no diseases that might prevent his best development, who really want him, and who are able and willing to provide for his basic needs.

Eugenists hope to improve the human race by seeing that the right children are born. In several communities this has been attempted. A province in northern Italy was burdened for many years with a certain type of feeble-mindedness. In 1890 the feeble-minded were by law prevented from marrying. By 1910 this type of person had almost disappeared from the province. Science, which has done so much to improve farm animals, can also do much more to build a better human race.

Euthenists hope to improve the race by modifying the child's environment. They would provide a favorable home, an adequate diet, and suitable recreational and educational facilities for every child. Without doubt these measures would raise the intellectual and social level of the community.

Few persons realize their inherited potentialities. A schematic representation may make this point clearer. In the diagram (Fig. 1) the larger circle represents the limits within which an individual may develop. The pattern within the circle represents the extent to which he actually does develop. The margin between the actual and the potential development represents the area of individual responsibility. The problem of growing up is to use hereditary tendencies as fully as possible, and to accept unalterable limitations.

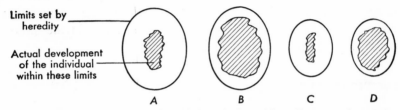

Fig. 1. Schematic representation of the relation of heredity to environment.
A illustrates an individual with large native capacities who is not realizing them. B illustrates an individual with large native capacities who has realized them more fully. C illustrates an individual with small native capacities who has not developed the small amount he has. D illustrates an individual with small native capacities who has made much of them.

In all children there are unrealized potentialities for growth. However, pushing and nagging tend to make the slow child feel inferior and insecure. Parents and teachers can gently help every child to develop his capacities; they can give social approval to all who do their best, regardless of how their achievement compares with others. The parable of the talents presents this truth. The commendation of "good and faithful servant" is bestowed on each person who uses to good advantage the talents given him.

Questions and Problems

FOR CLASS DISCUSSION OR STUDY GROUPS

1. Note ways in which you are like your father, your mother, your brothers and sisters. Which of these characteristics seem to be most clearly inherited? Which would probably not have developed in a different kind of environment?

2. Recall someone you have known well, and who did not turn out so well as you were led to expect by your observations of his parents and of him as a child. What are some of the possible reasons why this child became so different from his parents?

3. If parents are above average in some characteristics, what would you expect of their children in this respect?

4. Are all men created free and equal? Discuss.

5. Are qualities that parents develop during their lifetime transmitted to their children? Find evidence to support your statement.

6. How do teachers profit by knowing the characteristics of a child's parents? What cautions should be observed in using such information? For a given expenditure of time, which would yield the larger returns in understanding a particular child: a direct study of the child, or a study of his heredity? Why?

7. The following comments about children were made by adults. Tell why you agree or disagree with them:

"George, who is a behavior problem, is like his mother used to be in school. He evidently inherited her lack of responsibility and her ability to lie himself out of an awkward situation."

"Charles, who is overweight, has probably inherited this tendency from his father."

"Harry is not very bright. He is also bad tempered and easily discouraged if things do not go as he wishes. His mother says he takes after his father."

"Patricia is very bright because her father is a judge and her grandfather was a governor. Unfortunately, tuberculosis runs in her mother's family, so Patricia is doomed to have a short life."

8. As an example of an excellent research article, study Cyril Burt's "The Inheritance of Mental Ability" in *The American Psychologist*, January 1958. Note how he first gives a brief historical survey, then raises various hypotheses and questions, and presents, with critical comments, evidence pro and con with respect to each. Note also his caution in making generalizations and drawing conclusions, and his emphasis on further research, especially intensive studies of children by psychologists and of pure strains of animals by geneticists.

Chapter 3

PRENATAL INFLUENCES

ON DEVELOPMENT

.

> Mary had a little cat
>> Which ate a ball of yarn
> And when her baby cats were born
>> They all had mittens on.

Though the above rhyme is a striking illustration of alleged prenatal influence, it is no more wonderful than some of the stories one hears about the prenatal influence of the human mother upon her child. From early times people have believed that the mother's thoughts and experiences directly influence the developing unborn child. What are the scientific facts?

Does the food the mother eats affect the development of the child during the nine months before birth? Are birthmarks due to some experience that the mother has during this period? Can a mother make the child more intellectual by reading serious books? What changes should the mother make in her daily life during the prenatal period? These are some of the questions frequently asked.

INFLUENCE OF THE MOTHER

Apart from mechanical injury, whatever influence the mother has upon the prenatal development of her child is exerted, after the second week, chiefly through her circulatory system. Food and oxygen filter through the mother's blood vessels into the walls of special blood vessels and are carried by a twisted cord of vessels—the umbilical cord—into the circulatory system of the embryo. (From the end of the second week to the end of the second month, the unborn child is called an *embryo*. From that time until birth, it is called a *fetus*.) Endocrine secretions, such as insulin and adrenalin, may also filter through from the mother's circulatory system. Waste products are removed through the same channels.

24

Toxins and drugs ingested by the mother may be carried to the unborn child by the same route. It has been found, for example, that during the last six months of pregnancy there is an increase in the fetal heart rate a few minutes after the mother begins to smoke a cigarette. Apparently the toxic products of tobacco smoke pass into the fetal circulation (38, 1938). It is probable that alcohol or any other chemical substance constantly introduced into the bloodstream, if detrimental to the mother, will also affect the fetus. The same is true of excessive use of barbiturate sleeping pills, aspirin, and other sedatives. These may reduce the oxygen in the blood, and a normal supply of oxygen is of the utmost importance for the welfare of the child. For the same reason, it may also be wise for the expectant mother, especially during the first three months of pregnancy, to avoid long airplane trips which involve radical changes in altitude.

Anything that seriously affects the nutrition of the mother may affect the physical development of the child (5, 1949). The prospective mother should have a well-balanced diet even before pregnancy; otherwise she will have to augment her nutrition during pregnancy. Experiments have shown that optimum diets before and during pregnancy were associated with less toxemia, healthier babies, better teeth, and with fewer premature births, stillbirths, and congenital abnormalities (28, 1957). Severe deficiency of vitamins may cause congenital scurvy; in animal experiments lack of vitamin E has resulted in abortion. Very low reserves of vitamin A in the mother may also endanger the development of the offspring. Endemic cretinism seems to be associated with iodine deficiency. Calcification of the deciduous teeth begins about four or five months before birth; insufficient calcium in the mother's food may seriously impair development of both teeth and bones. There is an old saying that the mother loses "a tooth for every child." Mothers can avoid this loss by consuming plenty of milk and vegetables and taking good care of their teeth before and during pregnancy. Except when there is a severe shortage of food elements, the fetus usually manages to get what it needs, even at the expense of the mother's health.

Certain diseases have particularly serious effects on the prenatal development of the child. By injuring the germ cells before fertilization, or by infecting the fetus before or at birth, the toxins of syphilis frequently cause stillbirth, miscarriage, congenital mental deficiency, blindness, or deafness. Gonorrhea is responsible for much sterility in men and women. In the past it has also been a common cause of blindness in the child. There is a simple preventative for this type of blindness: drops of a solution of silver nitrate are placed in each eye at birth. A small pamphlet published by the Association for the Prevention of Blindness, *Eyes . . . Right!*, describes this simple treatment, which is now required by public health laws.

German measles or rubella may have serious effects if the mother contracts the disease during the first four months of pregnancy. It may produce deafness, defective teeth, mental deficiency, and other malformations in the child. This is only one example of the varied effects that any disturbance may produce, depending upon the time it occurs. Mumps, chicken pox, whooping cough, and influenza viruses are also suspect. Wasting diseases such as tuberculosis and diabetes may have effects similar to those of poor nutrition.

Endocrine disorders in the mother would also seem to affect the child's development, although scientific proof is meager. For example, a thyroid deficiency, especially during the earlier stages of pregnancy, may impair development of fetal bone and cartilage. In its most pronounced form, thyroid deficiency results in cretinism.

Recent research on blood of various types has revealed the role played by the Rh blood factor in abortions, stillbirths, and mental deficiency. X-ray or radium treatment of the mother early in pregnancy has been found to produce abnormal head and brain development in the child. Exposure to radiation from an atomic bomb apparently heightens the incidence of stillbirths and malformations.

By protecting herself from toxic substances, maintaining a diet adequate in every respect, and otherwise keeping herself in good health and good spirits, the expectant mother is doing her best to further her child's development. In calling attention to the hazards of childbirth, we should not lose sight of the fact that it is a normal and natural process. In view of all the modern aids afforded by medical science and technology, the prospective mother should feel little anxiety.

There are many fanciful stories of alleged influences on prenatal development. That they are fallacious becomes apparent when one considers that no direct nervous connection exists between the mother and the child. Instances which seem to show causal connections are merely coincidental. One mother, who desired her child to be musical, and decided to study and listen to music during the prentatal period, found her attention diverted to religious books. "It didn't make any difference after all," she said after the child had grown up, "for my daughter did turn out to be musical, and she is not specially religious." Wishing that the child be beautiful, or looking at beautiful things, will not alter the child's features.

The fact that the expectant mother was once amused by the clowns at a circus cannot be offered as the reason why the child acts foolishly when he grows up.

Birthmarks often suggest curious connections with something the mother has thought or done. However, it is simply coincidence that a birthmark resembling a crab appears on a child whose mother was frightened by a crab at some time during the prenatal period. In *Little Pierre*, Anatole France makes the following entertaining comment:

Madame Morin informed the company that I had a red spot on the left hip due to a longing for cherries which had come upon my mother in Aunt Chausson's garden before I was born. Whereat old Dr. Fournier, who had a great contempt for all such popular superstitions, remarked that it was lucky Madame Noziere had kept her desires within such modest limits during the period of gestation, since, if she had allowed herself to hanker after feathers, trinkets, a cashmere shawl, a coach and four, a town house, a country mansion and a park, there wouldn't have been skin enough on the whole of my poor body to hold the record of such inordinate ambitions.*

Nevertheless, it is true that if the mother's anxieties and fears are intense or prolonged, the resulting changes in the composition of her blood, glandular secretion, and metabolism can affect the unborn child. Fear and anger are not merely states of mind; they have physiological effects, and the chemicals produced can enter the baby's bloodstream. Infants who at birth are overactive and irritable, who do not digest their food well, or who show a high fluctuation in heart rate "often have a history of such disturbing prenatal environment." (37, 1946) If a mother rejects the unborn child, resents having a baby, or dreads the ordeal of birth, these emotions may in some way influence the development of the fetus and the difficulty of labor. Emotional disturbances occurring late in pregnancy seem to be detrimental to the child for weeks or, in some instances, for months. If prenatal influences such as these make the newborn baby irritable, nervous, and prone to cry, they may affect his mother's feelings toward him. She may reject the child in part because he is less desirable than she had hoped. Thus the infant's prenatal environment may influence his initial adaptability to his new world and the consequent responses that he evokes.

* Anatole France, *Little Pierre* (translated by J. Lewis May; New York: Dodd, Mead & Co., 1925), p. 12. Quoted by permission of Dodd, Mead & Co. and The Bodley Head, London.

LENGTH OF PRENATAL PERIOD

Although nine calendar months is usually given as the duration of the prenatal period, some babies are born much sooner, some later. The range in age of newborn babies may be from twenty-six to forty-six weeks; the span of prenatal life may, in extreme cases, vary from the normal period by as much as five months. The shortest period at which a baby may be delivered alive from the mother's body is about 180 days; the longest period, about 330 days. Variations of three months in the gestation period are relatively normal.

GROWTH DURING THE PRENATAL PERIOD

Marked changes in body proportions occur during the fetal period. In the second month the head is half the length of the embryo as a whole. At the end of eight weeks the embryo is only about an inch in length; by the end of the fifth month the fetus is approximately a foot in length and a pound in weight. Its nervous system already contains its full quota of nerve cells—as many as twelve billion. By twenty-eight weeks the machinery for breathing is developed to such a degree that the child

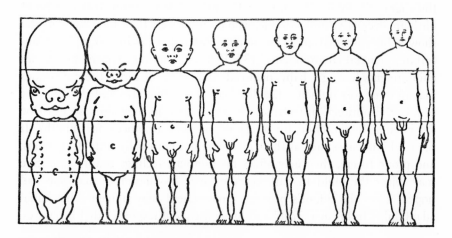

2 mo. (fetal) 5 mo.   Newborn   2 yr.   6 yr.   12 yr.   25 yr.

Fig. 2. Changes in form and proportion of the human body during fetal and postnatal life.

(From "Some Aspects of Form and Growth" by C. M. Jackson. In *Growth*, p. 118, by William J. Robbins, S. Brody, A. G. Hogan, C. M. Jackson, and C. W. Green. New Haven: Yale Univ. Press, 1928. 189 pp.)

could survive if he were born prematurely. Nowhere is "the wisdom of the body" so clearly shown as in this early development. At the end of the prenatal period, the fundamental structures of bones and nerves and muscles, and the systems of circulation, respiration, and digestion are ready for functioning in the world outside the womb.

In fact, most of these organs have begun to function in a preparatory way before birth. Among these early movements are the heartbeat, the peristalsis of the digestive tract, and the premature expansion and contraction of the chest similar to breathing, which may be preparatory to true lung-breathing. Before birth the fetus may make specific responses, such as opening and closing of the mouth. In late fetal life even the mechanisms for taste and smell are ready to function, under appropriate stimulation. Most of the reflexes present at birth, plus some sensitivity and response to pressure, heat, cold, loud sounds, and severe pain, are also present before birth. For example, thirty-one days before her delivery a pregnant woman reported that a sharp clang on the metal bathtub in which she was lying caused a sudden jump of the fetus unlike the usual movements to which she was accustomed. Music may also increase activity in the unborn child. Controlled experiments have shown that the human fetus has a tendency to respond to sound stimuli—a response that becomes more pronounced as the time of birth approaches. The eye, too, seems to be sufficiently developed before birth to make possible a differentiation between light and dark. All of these developments of function are gradual.

DEVELOPMENT OF BEHAVIOR

The roots of behavior have many intricate branches. It is in vain that we look for a single cause. Jennings expressed this basic point of view as follows:

Natural phenomena—and most emphatically is this true of biological phenomena—merely arise out of the complex situation in which they occur. Many elements of that situation affect them; and all that experimental science can do is to determine what difference is made by altering one or more of these elements; none is "the" cause to the exclusion of the others. [20, p. 208, 1930]

Behavior develops along with structure and can best be understood if one knows both the previous stages and the present environment. From a record of responses made to stimuli at each stage of development, the progress of behavior can be traced.

Knowledge that movement occurs in the fetus is as old as mankind. There are frequent references to fetal activity, commonly called "quickening," in ancient, classical, and medieval writings. The physician can note fetal movements at about the fifteenth week. According to mothers, some fetuses are more than ten times as active as others. From the first time when movement is noted, activity increases up to about the eighth calendar month. From then on the movement may be restricted by increasingly close quarters. It has been observed that fetal activity seems to increase toward the close of the day and whenever the mother is severely fatigued. It tends to decrease when the mother is eating and immediately after she has been exercising. Very active fetuses tend to be underweight, but well advanced in motor performance. Much fetal activity may be stimulated by changes in its internal environment—temperature, and concentration of oxygen, carbon dioxide, glucose, sodium, and other substances. The secretion of the suprarenal gland may be a factor in initiating fetal movement.

Research has shown the once irrefutable generalization that behavior proceeds from a generalized, diffuse pattern of the fetus to the specific responses of the adult to be an oversimplification (7, p. 138, 1954). A fetus can early make quite specific responses to some stimuli. The fact that many of its responses are diffuse, involving the whole body, may be attributed in part to the intensity and subsequent spread of the stimuli required to elicit a response. Although the older fetus has acquired a larger repertory of quite specific responses, some of these are lost soon after birth—e.g., the grasping reflex; others persist throughout life. The complexity and the independent rate of growth of the various structures of the human organism require that we consider integration or the combination of specific responses, as well as individuation or the refinement of diffuse responses, in explaining the development of behavior patterns. Carmichael gives a significant technical treatment of prenatal development and relates experimental findings to psychological theory (7, pp. 125-139, 1954).

PRENATAL CARE OF THE MOTHER

One eminent specialist recommended that the mother simply follow her usual way of living, if this way is reasonably hygienic.

Many tragedies of childbearing could be prevented. An early medical examination may reveal conditions that make childbearing unsafe for the mother, or conditions that can be corrected if treated in time. The physician should continue his supervision during the entire prenatal period. A careful program of maternal and infant hygiene, including postnatal supervision of the infant, results in a significant lowering of infant mortality and an increased chance for happy childhood. The mother-child division of a health center should offer services covering the whole period from the beginning of pregnancy to the end of adolescence, including prenatal service, preschool service, school hygiene clinics, and pediatric, dietetic, and vaccination clinics.

MENTAL HEALTH OF THE FAMILY

The mother often has a difficult adjustment to make, especially with the first child. Writing of the emotional factors in pregnancy, Menninger (25, 1943) gave the following interpretation: a woman's dread of becoming pregnant may stem from having rejected in some degree her feminine role. Even when a woman achieves complete acceptance of her role as mother, the changes in her body size, her relations with her husband, and her social activities may make it difficult for her to escape emotional stresses. In some cases, the decision to become pregnant may reflect the woman's desire to bind her husband more closely to her. Attitudes may be changing: in one carefully conducted study (34, pp. 32-50, 1957) it was found that three fourths of the mothers were pleased or delighted when they became pregnant.

During her first pregnancy the mother has time to relinquish her idea of herself as a girl free to come and go as she pleases, and replace it with the more deeply satisfying self-concept of wife and mother. She can get a long-range view of her life and the importance of her new role. She should view realistically what this role involves, considering its effect on her career, and asking herself whether she really wants the baby for itself, without expecting that a child will solve personal problems of loneliness, insecurity, unfulfilled desires, or marital unhappiness; and without counting on any magical change in personality as a result of motherhood. Motherhood not only gives satisfactions; it also demands sacrifices—considerable drudgery is often involved. The mother cannot expect to have the freedom she knew before she had a baby to care for. Yet she should not go to the extreme of devoting herself exclusively to the baby. It is better for the expectant mother to take a realistic view in advance than to be completely disillusioned after the baby is born. On the mother, more than on anyone else, depends a healthy fabric of family relationships in which each member develops as a person in his own right, in which no one is the boss, in which each plays his special role in his own appropriate way.

The prenatal months are a period of preparation for the whole family as well as for the mother and for the unborn child. When the baby comes, he will somewhat change the way of life of everyone in the family. All should be psychologically prepared for this. The father as well as the brothers and sisters must be ready to expect less of the mother's time and attention and to share in the home duties. Both parents should love the baby and care for him. Neither should feel guilty about taking needed rest. In every way possible each member of the family group should be prepared to welcome the baby, whether it turns out to be a boy or a girl, quick or slow, beautiful or homely.

Questions and Problems

FOR CLASS DISCUSSION OR STUDY GROUPS

1. Talk with several pregnant mothers. How does each one feel about having a child? How might their several attitudes influence the development of the children during the prenatal period? How might their attitudes affect the children's welfare during the birth process itself?

2. What help can an expectant mother get in your community from family doctors, prenatal clinics, maternity welfare centers, guidance centers, home-demonstration agents, hospitals, public health nurses? Describe these services and write an article about them for the local newspaper or for a talk at a parent study group.

3. Give illustrations of the alleged influence of the prospective mother's experiences on the unborn child.

4. What can the mother do to promote the well-being of the child during pregnancy?

5. What emotional adjustments must be made by the expectant mother and father?

6. How may the prenatal months be used to help all the members of the family to make a good adjustment to the new baby?

7. Read the appropriate sections in Hurlock, Stone and Church or in Carmichael to increase your grasp of the technical details of prenatal development (see bibliography at the end of book).

Chapter 4

THE BABY AT BIRTH

At birth the baby already has a past. He has been growing for about nine months. He has built structures that are ready to begin their work; he has the minimum essentials of living. He brings into the world the potential ability to take his first breath, to satisfy his hunger, to move more freely, and to make his needs known. He begins to learn at a rapid rate from the moment he is born.

THE BIRTH EXPERIENCE

Birth means changing from one type of environment to another. From the baby's point of view it is a most uncomfortable move. He has been suddenly transferred from a soft, warm resting place that requires almost no effort on his part into a relatively cold, hard, uncomfortable, exacting world. He has emerged from an environment which presented few stimuli into one that offers many confusing stimuli. During a difficult delivery the baby may suffer lack of oxygen, or even sustain physical injury—brain damage, injury to the sense organs, or bone fractures. It is no wonder that a good case history requires information about the conditions of birth.

Birth is the individual's first step toward gaining independence, the first stage in the process of psychological weaning that continues through adolescence. It is now up to him to breathe for himself and to make sucking movements that will appease his hunger. He is still very dependent on his mother, yet not as directly and completely as before. To this bewildering situation he responds in a hit-and-miss way. By trying out his repertory of responses he happens on some that are useful to him.

A child's experiences during the first few weeks of life affect his future development. According to some psychologists—Rank and Jung, for example—the birth experience itself is a basic cause of future anxiety and has a profound influence on the child's personality. However, there is little evidence to support this theory of the birth trauma (41, pp. 403-20, 1956). No clear evidence has been reported to show that the birth experience as

33

such has a lasting effect—provided it has involved no physical injury. Fortunately, the incomplete development of the newborn's nervous system makes him relatively insensitive to pain. He has great capacity for withstanding the stress and strain of being born, and for effecting self-repair thereafter. He may also be insensitive to fear, anxiety, and other emotions (27, p. 30, 1949; 29, 1950). This is another example of the "wisdom of the body"; it is difficult indeed to conceive the extreme pain and anxiety that might be experienced if one were to come into the world with a fully developed nervous system.

PERSONAL RELATIONS

Of the greatest importance is the attitude of the mother. If she has been fearful and anxious about the birth experience, her attitude may increase the duration and painfulness of the labor. If the birth process proves to be difficult for the mother and possibly damaging to the child, it may affect the attitudes of both parents toward the child. Resentment, conveyed to the baby by nonverbal means, may profoundly influence his emotional development (24, 1952).

Emotional patterns and interpersonal relations in the family play a role in the drama of birth. Strained marital relations can make the situation very difficult. In other cases the father may have mixed feelings of anxiety—for the mother, for the child, and for his own position in the family.

Separating the newborn from his mother, a practice still too common in hospitals, may have psychological effects of more significance than the possible infections that are thereby avoided. Such scientific aloofness does not meet the newborn baby's need for warm, secure, satisfying contact with his mother. For this, and other reasons, more and more hospitals are now letting each baby sleep in a crib in his mother's room, if the mother so desires; some are advocating that the baby be born at home. This enables the mother to learn how to care for the baby and to minister to his needs, dispel his vague feelings of loneliness and fear, and help him build a sense of trust and security. Certainly the nature of the psychological world into which parents bring the child is an important factor; it may account for the happy, trustful personality of some children and the emotional disturbances evident in others.

WHAT TO EXPECT OF THE NEWBORN

Scientific experiments and clinical study are answering many questions about the newborn baby: What is his physical appearance? What are the signs of good development? What movements may he be expected to make? What does he see and hear and feel? Does he have a unique personality? If one has had experience with newborn babies, or has seen certain films, which are the best substitute for firsthand observation (see pages 47-48), then information from books will be more interesting and meaningful.

Physical appearance and size

Anatole France thus described the birth of Little Pierre:

Meanwhile I set up such a yelling that they all thought I was going to choke. I was as red as a tomato and unanimously pronounced an ugly little creature. [12, p. 12, 1925]*

A newborn baby does not look "mighty like a rose" to anyone but his parents or a poet. To unprejudiced eyes he is usually an incredibly small creature, wet, coated with a protective chalky substance, and often red and wrinkled. His head and abdomen look much too large; his legs are short and bowed. His smoky blue eyes wander about independently of each other and often cross.

Babies who arrive a little after the nine-month period are more likely to resemble the chubby, rosy, doll-like creatures that advertisers picture to appeal to prospective parents. Yet even the most unprepossessing specimens are complete in almost every detail—delicately formed fingers that can grasp your finger, toes complete with nails, facial features that have survived the hardships of the birth process.

At birth some babies are more fully developed than others. One newborn baby may weigh three times as much as another. They grow at different rates before birth as well as after birth. The majority weigh between 6 and 9 pounds and are between 15 and 24 inches in length. At birth, male full-term babies are, on the average, larger than female, and weigh more.

Babies are classified as premature if their weight is under $5\frac{1}{2}$ pounds for boys or $5\frac{1}{4}$ pounds for girls, and if the pregnancy has lasted less than

* Anatole France, *Little Pierre* (translated by J. Lewis May; New York: Dodd, Mead & Co., 1925), p. 12. Quoted by permission of Dodd, Mead & Co. and The Bodley Head, London.

260 days (14, 1945). Premature babies are approximately three times as frequent as postmature babies. A premature infant has three ages: his chronological age registered on his birth certificate, his true age as reckoned from conception, and his developmental age. Babies weighing less than four pounds need expert medical care and special feeding. During infancy, prematurely born children are usually more frail than full-term children; they require especially favorable environmental conditions. Since the premature infant is actually younger than the full-term infant, he may appear to be retarded. If urged to do things characteristic of full-term children of the same chronological age, he may become irritable and unhappy.

Learning to live

Within thirty minutes after birth, or as soon as the umbilical cord is cut, the baby begins an independent existence. However, he takes from two to five weeks to get completely born. So complex a machine cannot immediately begin running smoothly. During this period of adjustment to an independent existence, the baby, or *neonate*, as he is now called, may vomit easily, breathe irregularly, sleep fitfully. Immediately after birth his pulse is rapid—120 to 150 beats per minute as compared with 68 to 71 for the average adult. The range for the neonate pulse may be from 100 to almost 200 beats per minute. When the baby is crying, his pulse has been found to be as much as 95 beats higher than during deep sleep (30, 1954).

Since the newborn's heat-regulating mechanisms are not yet working well, he is easily chilled. His temperature at birth may vary normally from 96 to 101.6 degrees, the average being about 99 degrees (30, 1954). It is easily deflected from normal by illness, or even by a sudden change in room temperature. Healthy newborn babies can maintain a certain stability in body temperature by means of crying and other variations in muscular activity. With premature infants, maintaining body temperature is a more serious problem.

The newborn has to learn to breathe with his own lungs. The first breath seems to be produced by conditions within the body, such as an increase of carbon dioxide tension in the blood, and by external conditions, such as the stimulus of cold air. His breathing is more rapid than that of adults; it averages thirty-five to forty-five respirations a minute as compared with the adult rate of sixteen to eighteen. Like the heartbeat, the respiration rate is also extremely variable. During sleep the average rate of respiration may be thirty-two per minute; in crying, it may rise to 133 respirations per minute (30, 1954). Especially when he is disturbed, the newborn's breathing may be irregular, noisy, and rapid. Slow and regular breathing movements seem to indicate a pleasant, satisfied feeling.

The newborn is ready to digest food even from the first day. Most of the digestive juices are ready for action, except those that digest starches. His mother's milk is usually not available until eighteen or twenty hours after birth. Hunger contractions have been observed in babies who have not yet been nursed. Even before he takes food, the neonate may have bowel movements which get rid of accumulated glandular secretions, mucus, and other wastes.

While he is learning to take and digest food, he tends to lose weight; the loss may amount to several ounces during the first few days. This loss may be due merely to loss of water or to the fact that breast-feedings of colostrum—the early form of mother's milk—do not meet the newborn child's energy requirements. With a milk mixture high in protein and low in fat, infants thrived better and showed less loss in weight. Between the seventh and the tenth day they are likely to recover their original birth weight.

Although the mother has given the neonate an immunity to many diseases that lasts for several months, he needs special protection from colds and from digestive and skin infections. During the first four weeks, the mortality of boys exceeds that of girls by 40 per cent among full-term babies and by 50 per cent among prematures (32, 1958).

The activity of the newborn

What may a mother expect her baby to do at birth? She should certainly expect him to cry. The organs of speech are ready to produce sounds at birth, or even before. The first cry is not a wrathful protest against enforced entrance into this cold, uncomfortable world nor "an expression of an overwhelming sense of inferiority." It is merely a muscular response to both internal and external stimuli.

For many weeks after birth, the baby controls his environment, to some extent, by crying. By this means he summons adults to minister to his needs. Although the baby's cries do not clearly indicate his specific feelings and needs, the mother, by observing the situation in the light of her previous experience, can usually distinguish between rage or pain and hunger. She will not attempt to feed him every time he whimpers or anxiously respond to *every* indication of discomfort. He may even get satisfaction from a certain kind and amount of crying.

However, the baby's continued crying is likely to make the mother anxious, and her anxiety, in turn, may be conveyed in subtle ways to the baby. If the crying becomes intense and the anxiety of mother and infant mounts, it may eventually interfere with his breathing, and thus anxiety may be transformed into terror (40, pp. 53-54, 1953). Under these circumstances there is only one thing for the mother to do—remove the cause of the crying and try to substitute tenderness for her own feeling of anxiety.

Some babies, it has been reported, have sneezed themselves into the world. A few, as though bored from the beginning, start life with a yawn. Crying, sneezing, coughing, yawning—all these responses have been observed at birth.

The newborn usually knows how to make sucking movements, but he often dillydallies. Sometimes it is difficult to induce him to take his first meal, even when he is hungry. It may be several days before the baby learns to keep the nipple in his mouth and suck long enough and hard enough to get the milk he needs. Some fall asleep before they have taken enough food. The role of the mother is to accept the baby's ineptitude and be patient. During the first month the sucking response increases in vigor. While it holds the center of the stage, general activity tends to disappear, even crying is quite difficult to excite.

Even shortly after birth, when lying face down in a pillow, a baby can usually turn his head far enough to permit free breathing. Babies do not smother themselves easily, as some old wives say. There are cases of suffocation due to glandular causes, but tales of accidental suffocation should not frighten mothers. By the end of the first month, the baby can lift his head enough to raise his chin off the pillow.

The mechanism for walking, too, is present. The baby held erect may make stepping movements. In some instances he makes a primitive kind of creeping motion. A baby lying prone on a table was observed to kick so vigorously against hands placed on the soles of his feet that he propelled himself several inches across the table. These, however, are not true creeping and walking movements.

The Moro response—the spreading out of arms and legs often followed by hugging himself—is also one of the earliest. During the first three months of life this response, as well as a startled movement, may be provoked by a sudden loss of equilibrium, a sudden loud noise, or a sudden jar. Almost all babies will also make a foot-grasping response when the soles of their feet are touched.

The newborn can also grasp a rod placed in his hands and hold on to it. This reflex persists up to about three weeks or longer. It tends to disappear altogether around the fourth month as the hand movements become better co-ordinated.

In addition to these and other specific unlearned reactions, there are more general movements, apparently involuntary. These spontaneous movements, as well as other behavior, seem to be stimulated by the "hunger drive"—by contractions of the stomach and intestines. From birth the baby tends to move in an apparently aimless way—bringing the hands to the head, beating the bed coverings, making grimaces which sometimes seem like real smiles and sometimes are as grotesque as the expressions of gargoyles. He makes many jerky, kicking movements, which may arise from neurological immaturity, from the rapid growth of nerve centers, or from other internal stimuli. In response to a specific stimulus, such as a light pinch on the knee, the newborn is likely to squirm and show general restlessness. If he is hungry, the same stimulus may produce sucking movements. Intense stimuli tend to evoke both general and specific movements.

Even within the first two weeks, the baby has learned to use his repertory of specific and general responses in adjusting to his new environment. He seems to try everything until he hits on at least one response that brings the desired results. Sucking satisfies his hunger; crying or sighing brings relief from discomfort; kicking and stretching relieve muscle tension; sneezing and yawning help to clear nose and throat. Out of his many apparently unco-ordinated movements, he learns to select those that meet his needs. For example, his first response to hunger is a vigorous crying and thrashing of arms and legs. If he is picked up, he calms down for a few minutes and then seems to go about his food-seeking business in a more purposeful way. Being picked up has suggested a change from multiple response to more specific behavior.

Particularly significant are movements that are directed toward the stimulus or the area that receives the stimulus, as for example the opening of the mouth and the turning of the head toward the side where the cheek is touched. Defensive movements when pressure is continued are even more significant for future development. These evidences of interrelation between perception and movement are the first manifestations of problem-solving.

Activity is a rough index of discomfort. It increases just before feeding time and subsides when hunger is appeased. When the newborn is content—in physiological equilibrium—he sleeps, or stares blankly in whatever direction his head is turned. When he is hungry or in pain, he springs into multiple action.

The newborn's basal energy requirement increases at birth and continues to increase during the first four or five months. When he cries, his expenditure of energy is approximately three times as great as when he sleeps.

Individual differences in the activity of the newborn are very great. At birth some babies are almost three hundred times as active as others. These differences in muscular activity may be related to tempo and temperament, to mother-child relations, to bodily conditions, and to stimuli in the external environment.

The baby's sensations

All the newborn desires is physical comfort and food when he is hungry. It is difficult to discover what he sees and hears and feels; impossible to know what he thinks. One can get clues to his sensations only by observing his activity. Careful experimenters have used the method of presenting a stimulus and observing the resultant changes in the baby's action.

Babies differ in their sensitivity toward and readiness to respond to light, noise, restraint, and other stimuli. Auditory and visual sensitivity may be decreased by a long and difficult birth experience. To evoke any response from the newborn, most stimuli have to be fairly strong, or to occur in combinations. He tends to ignore ordinary stimuli, and to make an all-out response to stimuli that distress him. He may, at different times, respond differently to the same stimulus. And different babies respond differently to the same stimulus.

Sight. Vision is one of the easiest sensations to study. Movement or fixation of the eyes gives the observer a clue as to the newborn's awareness of a light stimulus. At birth, the baby has only a vague consciousness of light, and a dim awareness of blurs of darkness. It is difficult to evoke any responses that show whether he can see anything at all. Shortly after birth, he is disturbed by intense light and shuts his eyes against it. During the first two weeks of life he begins to learn to follow a moving object up and down, sideways, and around.

The newborn is not capable of seeing, as we understand the word. Even the mother's face or a bright pink rattle has no meaning to him. A little later, he becomes visually aware of certain objects, but he does not attach meaning to what he sees.

Hearing. The newborn's responses to sound are less clearly indicated than are his responses to light. He may show that he has heard something by a movement or by a change in respiration. He may hear without giving any sign that he has heard, just as adults often ignore familiar street noises. After the first shock of the birth experience is over and after the middle ear is free from the fluid which filled it, the infant probably hears many sounds, though he does not know their meaning.

Some babies are very responsive to sounds; others are not. Marked individual differences in auditory sensitivity have been observed during the first few days of life. During this period some infants seem impervious to sounds that later evoke a prompt reaction. Under carefully controlled conditions the response appears to be related to the intensity and duration of the sound, to the infant's age, and to his total bodily state. If the sound is of short duration but strong intensity, a variety of responses may appear. Some of these disappear as the sound is repeated. An intense sound of long duration generally produces less activity than would normally be expected (30, 1954).

Taste. The newborn is likely to increase his general activity and to make a grimace when a drop or two of a weak solution of sugar, citric acid, quinine, or salt is placed on his tongue. Sugar solutions encourage sucking; salt solutions discourage it. Unlike adults, very young infants appear to find the bitter taste of quinine not unpleasant. As the baby grows older, he begins to suck longer on the sweet substances and a shorter time on the bitter and acid substances; he even tries to push away the unpleasant substances or pull his head away from them. But he does not yet appear to distinguish milder flavors. Cod-liver oil, castor oil, and olive oil seem to be equally palatable. He takes turnip juice as eagerly as orange juice.

Thirst and hunger. Thirst is present at birth and demands satisfaction more frequently than many mothers realize. A thirsty baby will cry as lustily as a hungry one. The newborn's stomach contracts in hunger just as the adult's does, but at more frequent intervals.

Sleep. Sleep is the newborn's major activity, usually occupying more than eighteen hours a day—if he is comfortable. His sleep is probably somewhat different from that of the adult. It is lighter, and is broken by short waking periods about every two hours, instead of being concentrated in one long period. As the baby grows, he spends more time in comfortable awareness of the world about him.

Comfort and discomfort. The infant experiences general feelings of comfort and discomfort—comfort when he is warm and fed and free in his movements; discomfort when he is cold and hungry and restricted in some of his movements. At birth he is sensitive to cold and warmth. A lowering of the room temperature makes him shiver and increases his muscular activity. When protected from the cold air of his new environment, he will frequently stop crying. Normal newborn infants are sensitive to pressure. The newborn's discomfort comes chiefly from hunger, colic, discomforts of skin and muscles, cold, and possibly from swift, startling changes in his familiar world. Sensations of pleasantness and unpleasantness are the earliest form of drive, or motivation. Sensitivity to pain is present during the first month.

Conditions influencing sensitivity. The same stimulus does not elicit an invariable response. The response varies with several factors: the inherited constitution of the individual, the severity of the birth ordeal, the general bodily condition, and previous as well as present competing stimuli. Much of the insensitivity of the newborn to various sensations is related to the difficulty and duration of labor. The condition of the organism as a whole, and the impressions left by previous stimulation, cause variations in the immediate response to sound and light. In one experiment infants who were crying showed the least response to the stimuli introduced, while those who were awake and inactive showed the greatest response.

Although the newborn baby's repertory of responses is not very useful in its random, unmeaningful state, it represents his capacity for maturing and learning; for meeting his needs through action; for finding more and more meaning in the world about him; for making connections between what happens to him and what he does; and, later, for modifying his actions by thought.

Emergence of mental ability

Does the baby at birth have some dim ideas? Nobody knows, because no evidence can be obtained on this question. The baby cannot tell us. However, the level of his mental development may be reflected in the nature of his physical response to various stimuli.

The genesis of personality

During these first weeks of life, under favorable conditions, the baby builds basic attitudes. He begins to develop a sense of trust. If he is warm and comfortable, if his hunger and thirst are satisfied, and if his other developmental needs are met, he tends to feel secure.

Every infant has many potentialities. He may become friendly and co-operative, timid and withdrawing, hostile and aggressive, depending in large measure on his experiences following birth. Erich Fromm (13, pp. 217-18, 1947) compared child development with the growth of an oak tree. In his view an acorn has as its primary potentiality to grow into an oak—if conditions are favorable. If they are not, the acorn has a secondary potentiality for "badness," i.e., it becomes rotten. Its environment determines which of these two lines of development it will follow. In a similar though vastly more complex way, man has the potentialities for calm assurance or gnawing anxiety, for love or hate, for feelings of satisfaction and accomplishment or for inferiority and frustration. Any of these may develop, depending largely upon the parental figure who provides the setting for this maturing process (1, 1953). The child's constitution and his total environment, especially his personal relations, are more important for personality development than any single factor such as breast-feeding or bottle-feeding.

Individuality manifests itself during the first few weeks of life. One may observe characteristic differences in babies at birth—differences in activity, muscle tone, amount of muscular energy, tempo, drive or dynamic force, degree of co-ordination, and responses to various stimuli. These differences appear to be fairly constant for an individual infant, even though his patterns of behavior are in a state of flux. His characteristic tendencies, or "nucleus of personality," determined partly by his sex, the functioning of his glands, and his nervous plasticity, seem to persist through the first weeks of life. Such are the earliest beginnings of personality!

PHYSICAL CARE OF THE BABY

The physical care of the neonate has psychological significance. In fact, it comprises the only language he understands during the first weeks of life. Good physical care also plays an important role throughout infancy in preventing serious illness and all its psychological complications. It influences the baby's future disposition and outlook on life.

The first twenty-four hours of a baby's life are usually supervised by the doctor or nurse rather than by the mother. The first bath, the first feeding, the first dressing are the work of an expert.

Before the baby is born, the mother should learn exactly how to diaper him skillfully and quickly, how to lift and carry him, how to bathe him with ease, how to dress him properly, how to tuck him in to be warm and comfortable at night, and how to avoid and treat attacks of colic. Knowing what to do gives the mother a feeling of security. This is important because the emotional state of the mother is quickly sensed and reacted to by the infant.

A child who is nursed by a loving mother has a good start in life. Nursing is one of the baby's most satisfying experiences. It lays the foundation for a warm, secure mother-child relation. It may relieve nervous tension for both mother and child. It gives the baby the feeling that he is loved and wanted. In instances in which breast-feeding is difficult or impossible, essentially the same values may be gained if the mother holds the baby while he is having his bottle and treats him in the same way that a fond mother treats her nursing infant. There is no conclusive evidence that breast-feeding as such is invariably superior to artificial feeding.

Many elements in the total situation should be considered. A mother who is calm, happy, and relaxed is a more wholesome influence than an overanxious mother. Differences in the personality of first- and second-born children may be due in part to the greater confidence the mother has acquired by the time her second child is born. Many a new mother is unduly anxious and worried. She has learned too many rules, too few basic principles. The mere physical routine is exhausting. Add to this her worry over not doing all the things she has been told she ought to be doing, and you have a tense and insecure mother. She would begin to relax, Hymes (17, 1948) says, if she heard "the voice of authority" say: "Watch your baby, don't bother to train him now; enjoy your baby, don't wear yourself out with unnecessary details of child care; love your baby, don't worry about spoiling him."

Questions and Problems

FOR CLASS DISCUSSION OR STUDY GROUPS

1. Observe a newborn or very young baby. Describe as accurately as possible all the cries and movements he makes. What seem to be the causes of the movements? What conditions modify them? For example, if you think his restlessness and crying are caused by hunger, note whether they cease when he is fed.

2. Talk with mothers of very young babies. How do they feel toward their babies? How do their attitudes seem to affect their treatment of the babies?

3. If possible, see the films on how life begins and on the baby at birth listed on page 48.

4. What responses are present at birth? How do they vary with the situation?

5. What can the nurse or mother do to make the baby comfortable? What instruction should the trained nurse give to the mother before she leaves the care of the baby to her?

6. What evidences of personality are present in the newborn baby? What potentialities are there? In what ways can the mother contribute to the infant's personality development? How can doctors, nurses, and teachers relieve the young mother's anxiety and help her to enjoy and feel warmly toward her baby?

Bibliography*

1. ALLEN, FREDERICK H. "Special Problems of Infancy and Childhood," *Annals of the American Academy of Political and Social Science,* CCLXXXVI (March, 1953), 63-73.

2. BAYLEY, NANCY. "Some Increasing Parent-Child Similarities During the Growth of Children," *Journal of Educational Psychology,* XLV (January, 1954), 1-21.

3. BLEWITT, D. B. "An Experimental Study of the Inheritance of Intelligence," *Journal of Mental Science,* C (October, 1954), 922-933.

4. BURKS, BARBARA S., and ANNE ROE. *Studies of Identical Twins Reared Apart.* ("Psychological Monographs: General and Applied"; Vol. 63, No. 5, 1950.) Pp. 1-62.

5. BURKE, BERTHA S., STUART S. STEVENSON, JANE WORCESTER, and HAROLD C. STUART. "Nutrition Studies During Pregnancy. V. Relation of Maternal Nutrition to Condition of Infant at Birth," *Journal of Nutrition,* XXXVIII (August, 1949), 453-467.

**6. BURT, CYRIL. *The Subnormal Mind* (3d ed.). London: Oxford Univ. Press, 1955. 391 pp. *See also* "The Inheritance of Mental Ability," *The American Psychologist,* XIII (January, 1958), 1-15.

**7. CARMICHAEL, LEONARD. "The Onset and Early Development of Behavior," in Leonard Carmichael (ed.), *Manual of Child Psychology* (2d ed.), pp. 60-187. New York: John Wiley & Sons, Inc., 1954. 1295 pp.

8. "Chances of Twins; Frequency of Multiple Births," *Science News Letter,* LXIX (April 28, 1956), 258.

*9. DE LA MARE, WALTER. *Early One Morning in the Spring; Chapters on Children and on Childhood as Revealed in Particular in Early Memories and in Early Writings.* New York: The Macmillan Co., 1935. 605 pp.

10. DINITZ, SIMON, RUSSELL R. DYNES, and ALFRED C. CLARK. "Preferences for Male or Female Children: Traditional or Affectional?" *Marriage and Family Living,* XVI (May, 1954), 128-134.

**11. EYSENCK, HANS J. *The Scientific Study of Personality.* New York: The Macmillan Co., 1952. 320 pp.

* All references referred to in the text are included in the bibliography. The single-starred references (*) are specially recommended for their practical suggestions; those double-starred (**) are specially recommended for their technical and research emphasis.

*12. FRANCE, ANATOLE. *Little Pierre*. Translated by J. Lewis May. New York: Dodd, Mead & Co., 1925. 297 pp.

13. FROMM, ERICH. *Man for Himself: An Inquiry into the Psychology of Ethics*. New York: Rinehart & Co., Inc., 1947. 254 pp.

14. GESELL, ARNOLD, and CATHERINE S. AMATRUDA. *The Embryology of Behavior: The Beginnings of the Human Mind*. New York: Harper & Bros., 1945. 289 pp.

15. GRAY, GEORGE W. "The Organizer," *Scientific American*, CXCVII (November, 1957), 79-88.

16. HONZIK, MARJORIE P. "Developmental Studies of Parent-Child Resemblance in Intelligence," *Child Development*, XXVIII (June, 1957), 215-228.

*17. HYMES, JAMES L., JR. *Enjoy Your Child—Ages 1, 2, and 3*. ("Public Affairs Pamphlet," No. 141.) New York: Public Affairs Comm., Inc., 1948. 32 pp.

18. INGALLS, THEODORE H. "Congenital Deformities," *Scientific American*, CXCVII (October, 1957), 109-114, 168.

19. ———. "Environment and Heredity," in I. Galdston, *Society and Medicine*. New York: International Universities Press, 1955. 131 pp.

20. JENNINGS, HERBERT S. *The Biological Basis of Human Nature*. New York: W. W. Norton & Co., Inc., 1930. 384 pp.

21. JONES, HAROLD E. "Perceived Differences among Twins," *Eugenics Quarterly*, II (June, 1955), 98-102.

22. KALLMANN, FRANZ J. *Heredity in Health and Mental Disorder*. New York: W. W. Norton & Co., Inc., 1953. 315 pp.

**23. KLUCKHOHN, CLYDE, and HENRY A. MURRAY (eds.). *Personality in Nature, Society and Culture* (2d ed.). New York: Alfred A. Knopf, 1953. 701 pp.

24. LEVY, DAVID M., and AUDREY HESS. "Problems in Determining Maternal Attitudes toward Newborn Infants," *Psychiatry*, XV (August, 1952), 273-286.

25. MENNINGER, WILLIAM C. "The Emotional Factors in Pregnancy," *Bulletin of the Menninger Clinic*, VII (January, 1943), 15-24.

26. NEWCOMB, THEODORE M., and EUGENE L. HARTLY (eds.). *Readings in Social Psychology*, pp. 1-6. New York: Henry Holt & Co., 1947. 672 pp.

**27. ORLANSKY, HAROLD. "Infant Care and Personality," *Psychological Bulletin*, XLVI (January, 1949), 1-48.

**28. PECKOS, PENELOPE. "Nutrition During Growth and Development," *Child Development*, XXVIII (September, 1957), 273-285.

29. PINNEAU, SAMUEL R. "A Critique on the Articles by Margaret Ribble," *Child Development*, XXI (December, 1950), 203-228.

**30. Pratt, Karl C. "The Neonate," in Leonard Carmichael (ed.), *Manual of Child Psychology* (2d ed.), pp. 215-291. New York: John Wiley & Sons, Inc., 1954.

31. Roe, Anne, Barbara S. Burks, and Bela Mittelman. "Adult Adjustment of Foster Children of Alcoholic and Psychotic Parentage and the Influence of the Foster Home." ("Memoirs of the Section on Alcohol Studies, Yale University," No. 3.) New Haven, Conn.: *Quarterly Journal of Studies on Alcohol*, 1945. 164 pp.

32. Scheinfeld, Amram. "The Mortality of Men and Women," *Scientific American*, CXCVIII (February, 1958), 22-27.

33. ——— *The New You and Heredity*. Philadelphia: J. B. Lippincott & Co., 1950. 616 pp. *See also* the author's supplement, *The Human Heredity Handbook, ibid.*, 1956. 276 pp.

*34. Sears, Robert R., Eleanor E. Maccoby, and Harry Levin. *Patterns of Child Rearing*. Evanston, Ill.: Row, Peterson & Co., 1957. 549 pp.

*35. Senn, Milton J. E. "The Epoch Approach to Child Development," *Woman's Home Companion*, LXXXII (November, 1955), 40-42, 60, 61, 62. *See also* "Fads and Facts as the Bases of Child-Care Practices," *Children*, IV (March-April, 1957), 43-47.

36. Sonneborn, Tracy M. "Beyond the Gene," *American Scientist*, XXXVII (January, 1949), 33-59.

**37. Sontag, Lester W. "Some Psychosomatic Aspects of Childhood," *Nervous Child*, V (October, 1946), 296-304.

38. ———, and Thomas W. Richards. *Studies in Fetal Behavior. I. Fetal Heart Rate as a Behavioral Indicator*. ("Monographs of the Society for Research in Child Development," Vol. 3, No. 4, 1938.) 72 pp.

39. Spitz, René A. "Hospitalism. An Inquiry Into the Genesis of Psychiatric Conditions in Early Childhood," in *The Psychoanalytic Study of the Child*, Vol. I, pp. 53-74. New York: International Universities Press, 1945. 423 pp.

**40. Sullivan, Harry Stack. *The Interpersonal Theory of Psychiatry*. New York: W. W. Norton & Co., Inc., 1953. 393 pp.

41. Wile, Ira S., and Rose Davis. "The Relation of Birth to Behavior," in Clyde Kluckhohn and Henry A. Murray, *Personality in Nature, Society, and Culture* (2d ed.), pp. 403-420. New York: Alfred A. Knopf, 1956. 701 pp.

Films for Child Study

The films on page 48 are recommended to students of child development. More detailed information about their rental and purchase, as well as about films which will follow them in the future, may be obtained by consulting the *Educa-*

tional Film Guide,* by getting in touch with local film libraries, or by writing to the visual instruction department of the nearest state university.

At Home with Your Child (12 films). NET Film Service, Indiana Univ. Audio-Visual Center, Bloomington, Indiana. Sound. 1956. A series of twelve films discussing various problems that arise in the course of the baby's growth.

Baby Meets His Parents. Encyclopaedia Britannica Films. 11 minutes. 1948. Points out how differences in personality can be accounted for, not only by heredity, but also by the human relationships and environmental factors experienced during the first years of life.

Biography of the Unborn. Encyclopaedia Britannica Films. 16 minutes. 1956. Traces the life of the human fetus from conception to birth.

Human Beginnings. Eddie F. Albert Productions in co-operation with Lester F. Beck of the Univ. of Oregon. 22 minutes. Color. 1950. Attitudes of children toward the coming of a new baby.

Human Heredity. Churchill-Wexler. 18 minutes. 1956. A color, sound film that shows how heredity and culture influence the development of human characteristics.

Mother Love. New York Univ. Film Library. 20 minutes. Silent. 1952. Produced by René Spitz. The happy relationship of a baby to his mother during the nursing period and after weaning is contrasted with the behavior of children who are deprived of a mother's love. (*See also* other films in this series by René A. Spitz, produced by the Psychoanalytic Research Project on Problems in Infancy.)

Some Basic Differences in Newborn Infants During the Lying-In Period. New York Univ. Film Library. 23 minutes. 1944. Produced by Margaret E. Fries and Paul J. Woolf. Accents individual differences in newborn infants.

---

* Published annually, with monthly supplements, by the H. W. Wilson Co., New York.

Part Two

EARLY PRESCHOOL

PERIOD:

THE FIRST TWO YEARS

I do not want to MAKE *you anything: I want to know what Nature has made you, and to perfect you on her plan.*

DR. JOHN GREGORY
in A *Father's Legacy to His Daughter*, 1775

The task of child care is not to mould the child behavioristically to some pre-determined image, but to assist him step by step, guiding his growth.

ARNOLD GESELL and FRANCES L. ILG
in *Child Development*, 1949

Chapter 5

DEVELOPMENT DURING
THE FIRST TWO YEARS

During the first two years of life the child lays the foundation for his future. Although change is possible at any age, early trends and patterns tend to persist. Competent students of child psychology were able to match personality sketches of fifteen children written before they were two years old with sketches of the same children written after fifteen years (70, 1948). There is an element of psychological predestination in the past. New patterns of action evolve out of previous structure and behavior, and in response to new patterns of relationship. Beginning with his present level each child needs to pass gradually through a sequence of development during his first two years.

NATURE OF CHILD DEVELOPMENT

Development is a dynamic process which influences what a child perceives and the way he responds to it. Almost everything in a child's environment has a strong attraction for him.

Development is gradual. For example, the trend toward psychological independence actually begins at birth, increases as the child masters motor skills, and makes significant advances when he leaves home to go to school, when the opinion of his gang comes to mean more to him than adult opinion, when he shows increasing resentment of adult supervision in early adolescence. Parallel with this trend is the quality of dependence, always present throughout life.

The rate of a child's development is uneven. There are spurts of growth and accomplishment between periods of relatively slow progress. Certain behavior becomes prominent for a time and then gives place to other preoccupations.

A child's development during the first two years of life is fascinating. He changes every day. His energy is enormous. When he begins to walk

51

and run, he can wear out a sturdy adult. He gets repeated practice in doing all the things he attempts to do. His curiosity is insatiable and he loves to satisfy it. He also has a great need to learn. As he acquires new abilities, he experiences his first sense of independence and a new relationship with his parents.

Even before his second year the child is faced with the fact that he is not omnipotent, that his parents do not have to meet his every need as in infancy, that they are beginning to make demands on him to conform to the culture. His first reaction is usually a period of negativism. Eventually he must cope with the situation in one of two ways—moving toward becoming an independent person or clinging to the comforts and security of infancy. How he handles this dilemma may determine his characteristic responses not only during this phase of development but also in later years (6, 1952).

Naturally there are marked individual differences in the pattern of development of children even in the same family. One mother described the differences in her two boys as follows:

Teddy as a small baby was intensely energetic and enterprising, and walked sturdily at 11 months. He made no attempt to talk until 20 months, but never knew a moment's shyness and made friends with anybody at the drop of the hat, or before it. Sammy, on the other hand, has been an enthusiastic chatterbox ever since he began at about one year. But although he has always been strong and healthy, he was so long in making any effort to sit or stand that in alarm we consulted the doctor—who laughed at us. It seemed as though Sammy wanted to be sure of himself before taking any chances. And Sammy is not nearly so sociable as Teddy. He is not shy, but makes few advances to strangers, and unless visitors make a specific effort to be friendly with him he gives them a careful once-over and then amuses himself with very little reference to them. Now that he is well established on his legs there is nothing *under*-active about him. He trots tirelessly around the garden, but finds more time to "stand and stare" than Teddy did at the same age; and other people and their activities don't stimulate him (visibly) to the same extent.

The parents' role is to accept the child as he is and as he can become, provide a favorable environment for him, and encourage him to go through the normal stages of childhood, however immature they may seem. Although they cannot hurry their child's development, they can often change or remove conditions that are hampering it.

PHYSIOLOGICAL CONDITIONS

The mean pulse rate and variation in pulse rate, taken under conditions of quiet and relaxation (41, 1952), decreased greatly during the first two years and more slowly until about fifteen years. At ages one to two the mean pulse rate for boys and girls was almost the same—105 and 104 per minute.

Mean respiratory rates of boys and girls at ages one to two were approximately the same—twenty-six and twenty-seven per minute—and showed a gradual decrease after the second year to sixteen at ages seventeen to eighteen.

The body temperature, however, did not show such a difference in the rate of decrease during childhood and youth. At ages one to two the mean temperature was approximately ninety-nine for both boys and girls, as it had been during the first year.

PHYSICAL GROWTH AND HEALTH

The child who shows vigorous and well-proportioned growth and has the radiant appearance that comes from good health tends to elicit a favorable response from adults. On the other hand, a small, immature physique may hinder a child's social adjustment, and lower his sense of personal adequacy. Muscular growth, with the accompanying motor facility and strength, makes possible many new activities. Development of the brain and nervous system affect not only the child's intelligence but also his emotional and social adjustment. The reciprocal relation between physical and psychological factors may show up in psychosomatic disturbances.

Height and weight

Never again during his whole life will the child grow as fast as he does in these first two years. Even so, his rate of growth is already much slower than it was during the prenatal period. It has been roughly estimated that there is a 5,000,000 per cent increase in bulk from conception to birth; a 200 per cent increase during the first year; and a slightly less than 30 per cent increase during the second year. A baby may be expected to double his weight during the first five or six months, treble it by the end of the first year. At eighteen months he is likely to weigh three to four times as much as at birth, and he may gain two to four pounds more before the end of the second year. During the first two years there is also a rapid increase in height, from about 20 inches to 34 inches, on the average.

Although growth is rapid, changes in bodily proportion are relatively small during the first half year. But from birth to adulthood, however, the head size doubles; the trunk increases in length three times; the arms, four times; and the lower extremities, five times (38, 1954).

Weight is one indication of nutrition. Infants from poor homes weighed less and were shorter than those from good homes; however, those underweight children might have been brought up to par if their diet had been effectively supervised in a pediatric clinic. Body build must also be considered. The weight-gaining of the tall, slender individual may follow a different pattern from that of the short, stocky person. In fact, the optimum height-weight relation may be different for each child. Accordingly, parents should not worry if their child does not reach the average weight for other children of his age. However, if he loses weight, fails to gain for several weeks, is markedly overweight, or does not grow in height for six months, they should have him examined by a doctor. They should also consider whether there is anything in his diet, daily schedule, or home relations that may be affecting his health and growth. Overweight is commonly a problem of overfeeding. Occasionally it is related to unsatisfied psychological needs, which make food unduly important.

Among the factors that have a favorable influence on growth are (1) a wholesome parent-child relationship, (2) a daily schedule satisfying to both child and parents, (3) a diet that is adequate in every respect, (4) an optimum amount of sunlight, and (5) freedom for the child to be active and to rest as he feels the need.

Death and illness

The death rate is high in infancy. The largest number of deaths of children under one year is caused by premature birth, congenital malformations, pneumonia and influenza, and birth injury. During the first year of life the male death rate is 33 per cent greater than that among females. The rate of illness declines to its minimum at one month of age. It then increases up to six months, and from that age remains fairly constant for the remainder of life. In the second year, pneumonia, influenza, and accidents tend to be the most frequent causes of death. If the child becomes ill, his illness should not be made so disproportionately pleasant that he learns to resort to it in order to gain attention or other satisfactions.

Physical defects

During these two years of rapid growth, physical defects should be corrected as soon as possible. It is not wise to neglect defects in the hope that the child will outgrow them. For example, a club foot can usually be made normal if it is treated early enough.

By having regular health examinations and following the advice of the physician, parents may be able to spare the child serious physical or psychological consequences of a physical defect or illness. This they can do without calling the child's attention to the defect or making it seem of grave importance to him.

Teeth

At birth, hidden under the gums, are the first set of teeth and the beginning of all the permanent teeth except the second and third molars. By the end of the first year, the calcification of the crowns of the first, or temporary, set of teeth is completed. Calcification of the roots continues into the third year.

Once in a great while, a baby is born with one or more teeth. About 1 per cent get their first tooth by the fourth month; about the same percentage do not get it until the end of the first year. In the large majority of babies, the first tooth is likely to appear during the seventh month. The remaining three front teeth, upper and lower, usually appear two or three months after the first tooth. When the baby is one and a half years old, he usually has one molar on each side of his jaw and a total of eight teeth in sight. At two years he may be the proud possessor of sixteen teeth.

It is obvious that the child must be provided with building material during these first years as well as during the prenatal period. The addition of vitamin D to the standard diet of children has greatly reduced the amount of decay in the first set of teeth. Evidence is also accumulating on the relation of psychological factors to dental caries.

Sleep

Sleeping is the newborn's main business. During the period of infancy sleeping habits show these characteristics: fluctuation in the daily duration of sleep, decrease in the total sleeping time, and variation among individual children. As the infant matures the daily amount of sleep may fluctuate, but the total amount gradually diminishes—an illustration of "the principle of self-regulatory fluctuation." (35, p. 364, 1954)

As children grow older they spend different amounts of time in sleeping. As the child's activity increases, he tends to sleep less. As he becomes more sociable he wants to put off his bedtime. At around four months he may sleep the whole night through; a little later he may amuse himself for a while when he wakes up, instead of immediately demanding to be fed. Because individuals differ in the amount of sleep they require, the parent may safely follow the child's own pattern, *if* the child:

1. has been active and out of doors during the day,
2. is not being overstimulated socially, and
3. is not in a noisy or very warm room.

Sometimes, as many parents have found, a romp before bedtime, provided it is not *too* exciting, will use up the baby's excess energy and be conducive to sleep.

MOTOR ABILITIES AND SKILLS

Muscular activity has psychological as well as physical aspects. According to Mittleman (66, 1954, 1955), motility is the dominant source of pleasure during the second year of life. She postulates a motor drive or urge based on the random movements of the child, i.e., movements that are not clearly purposive or expressive; movements that accompany joy, fear, and other emotions; well-organized, vigorous, rhythmic patterns such as rocking and bounding; and skilled motor patterns.

The two-year-old has already made great gains in body control and locomotion. At birth he was a helpless, squirming, fumbling bit of humanity. Subsequently he has tried out many movements and obtained a tremendous amount of practice by interminably repeating those that give him satisfaction. His body structure makes various activities possible; his activities, in turn, stimulate further growth. What he lacks in skill, he makes up for in effort.

Many motor abilities dovetail into one another. Thus we have several orderly developmental sequences. Studies of groups of children show that they tend to follow a general pattern of postural control that sweeps from head to foot: first, they are able to control head and neck; then chest, back, and lower trunk; and finally, legs.

Although all children tend to follow this general pattern of motor development, each progresses in his own way and at his own rate. If a baby is slow in sitting up and creeping, he is likely to be slow in walking. The time-range for the appearance of a particular motor ability may be from ten to twenty weeks; with standing or walking, the range may be from twenty to thirty weeks.

Postural control and locomotion

The following is a common sequence of postural control and locomotion, beginning at the age of four to six months:

Holds head erect and steady;
Learns to sit alone;

Creeps, pulls himself up to a standing position, edges alongside a bed or couch;

Walks unsteadily, legs wide apart, arms flying out to maintain balance;

Climbs stairs;

Runs on his toes, often in preference to walking;

Stands on one foot;

Plays ball with a person who is only a few feet away.

All these activities are carried on in an awkward, intent way. The child manages to get where he wants to go by whatever mode of locomotion seems most effective. Walking, even in his jerky, trotting way, gives the child a new perspective on the world. It broadens his horizons. When the active explorer begins to get into everything, he is not being naughty but normal. This is his way of learning.

Hand movements

Paralleling these large-muscle activities is a gradual increase in the effective use of the hands. From the aimless hand movements which he makes at birth, the baby progresses to squeezing an object, then to grasping it with his hand, and finally to using his thumb and forefinger. By the end of the sixth month, the majority of children who have been studied can grasp an object of suitable size, hold it, and let go of it. By the end of the ninth month, practically all babies can accurately reach for and pick up an object. "Give and Take" becomes a favorite game.

During the second year the child becomes more skillful with his hands. He may learn to pull off his cap and stockings, open boxes, unscrew the lids of jars, put pegs into holes, scribble, draw a straight line on paper, turn the leaves of a book one at a time, build a tower four or five blocks high. A child of this age is highly distractible; if his play world is *too* "full of a number of things," he becomes confused, even to the point of tears.

Hand preference

During the first two years most children fluctuate between using one hand and both hands and between using the right or the left hand. A right-handed child may start off using the left hand, then both hands, then the right hand. Even at two years of age he will often trot around with an object in each hand, wave bye-bye with both hands. He may, however, show preference for one hand in reaching for objects. This preference may be constitutional—a tendency toward greater activity in one side of the body. Or it may be explained psychologically. If the parent or nurse consciously encourages the baby to use his right hand, it will get a far greater amount of practice than the other. It is the adult's critical attitude toward left-handedness in children that causes the most difficulty. If a left-handed child is made to feel that he is queer or inferior, then left-handedness becomes a real handicap.

Work and play

For the little child any activity is play in the sense that it is engaged in wholeheartedly for its own sake. Babies find amusement in any pleasant social contacts and in every opportunity to explore. The two-year-old will really play with toys instead of just hustling things around. But he is easily distracted by objects and movement around him; he responds to these with action.

Some of his energy may be channeled into helpful activities. Even a two-year-old, if he shows readiness, can learn to help in dressing himself. He becomes eager to feed himself; though this process usually gives more satisfaction to him than to his mother. "Putting away your toys" can be made the last "game" of the play period. However, in general, he is interested, not in objective accomplishment, but in the activity itself—the feel of swinging, springing, pulling a wagon, carrying big blocks, using his big muscles. Play for him means responding to whatever delightful activity happens to suggest itself as he trots around here and there.

DEVELOPMENT OF VISUAL ABILITY

During the first two years the fine art of looking at things appears to develop somewhat in accordance with this sequence:

Awareness, shortly after birth, of a moving light in the field of vision.
Ability to follow a light with the eyes.
Ability to make the eyes work together so that they focus on the mother's face or hands, or some nearby object.
Preference for certain colors.
Eye-and-hand co-ordination which makes it possible to pick up a small object.
Ability to follow a more distant object such as a bird or an airplane (usually acquired by the end of the first year).

Any observed tendency for the eyes to pull inward or outward should be noted and reported to an eye specialist. Early care will prevent loss of vision due to disuse or improper use of the eye muscles.

DEVELOPMENT OF LANGUAGE

The motor abilities that the two-year-old has acquired have advanced him a long way toward his goal of being on his own. Language skills are of utmost importance: they aid in his social adjustment by helping him to express his feelings and desires; they enable him to satisfy his needs, and to understand and control his environment. Language skills also help the child to organize his experience, which would otherwise remain incommunicable.

Specific language abilities are described in anecdotal records and in more systematic reports of the observation of children in natural situations. These abilities can also be measured by standardized tests. One picture-vocabulary test (3, 1948) has the advantages of being quick to administer, and highly interesting and appropriate for children two, three, four, and five years of age. There are two comparable forms. The reliability of this test is fairly high. Its results are similar to those of the Stanford-Binet intelligence tests (4, 1949).

The latest revision of the Stanford-Binet test measures the following language abilities on the two-year-old level: naming familiar objects, identifying parts of the body, using word combinations spontaneously, and obeying simple commands (98, pp. 75-77, 1937). These test items require the ability to understand words; the last two test the child's ability to use words; all are passed by the majority of two-year-olds.

Sequences in language development have been reported by a number of investigators (58, 1954). Although, as McCarthy points out, their results are not comparable because of variations in subjects, definitions, methods of study, and interpretations, the general pattern appears to be somewhat as follows:

First   Vocalizes in different ways, beginning with vowel sounds.
year   Responds to human voice.
    Coos, babbles, vocalizes pleasure.
    Vocalizes in response to social stimuli.
    Vocalizes several syllables such as "da-da" as sound play, to express eagerness, displeasure, satisfaction.
    Imitates sounds.
    Shows recognition by vocalizing.
    Listens to familiar word.
    Imitates syllables and words.
    Says first word, usually a monosyllable repeated, such as "mama," "bye-bye."

Second   Understands simple commands and prohibitions.
year   Names objects or pictures in book.
            Adds a few words to his vocabulary, usually nouns and verbs, a single
                word often serving as a sentence, such as "Eat" for "I want to
                eat." Meaning depends on the situation, and on the gestures
                and facial expression accompanying the word.
            Comprehends simple questions.
            Uses words in combination such as "Water, drink"; "Baby, up";
                "See, clean," meaning, "See it is clean."

It will be noted that the child uses vocalization as a means of communication before he has learned words. He understands words before he can say them. By the end of the first year, the child can usually say several words. Then for a while progress is slow. But by the end of the second year he has learned many more nouns and verbs and is beginning to combine them or use one- or two-word sentences. For him, words first have a general meaning; they gradually take on more specific meanings. According to Piaget, thought precedes language, and later, language transforms thought.

Estimates of a two-year-old's vocabulary range from 6 to 1,127 words, depending upon the background and ability of the child and the method of estimating or recording the vocabulary. An average is between 250 and 300 words.

Children show wide differences in their ways of learning to talk. No two babies follow exactly the same developmental sequence. There are silent children who seem uninterested in language. There are children who chatter incessantly. Some just watch and listen to what is going on, and then rather suddenly begin to speak without going through all the usual stages. At every age, girls generally talk more than boys. Twins usually lag behind other children in their speech development; they often share a more or less private language of their own. Under favorable conditions bright children are usually more advanced in vocabulary than the mentally retarded. Each child seems to have a unique language pattern.

There are many reasons why speech may be delayed. Some children seem more concerned with becoming independent and acquiring motor skills. In institutions or homes where there are few playthings or playmates or perceptive adults, the child lacks the usual incentives to acquire language. Mental ability enters in, but parents should not conclude that their child is mentally retarded if he does not talk at one and a half years of age. Some superior children are late in learning to talk. For example, a child of professional parents, whose intelligence was far above average, could say only thirteen words at the age of two, and some of these she pronounced so crudely that the uninitiated could not understand them. At the age of four, though she passed the thousand mark in vocabulary, she was still below the average vocabularies reported for most children of that age. It was not until she started school at the age of six, under the guidance of an excellent primary teacher, that she began to make rapid progress and soon overcame her early vocabulary deficiency.

The child can understand many more words than he can use in conversation. He may respond correctly to "Go to the door," or "Shut the door," before he can say the words "door," "go," or "shut." If the mother has a good relationship with her two-year-old, she may expect him to "Put the ball in the box," "Put the plate on the table," and carry out other simple requests, spoken slowly and distinctly. Children of this age enjoy listening to nursery rhymes and simple stories, especially if they are accompanied by pictures.

Spoken words are only one means of communication. There is also a language of behavior. Ideas, feelings, and needs may be expressed by gestures and bodily movements, by drawings and other art forms. Laughing and crying are modes of expression by which we communicate our feelings to others all through life. The baby usually produces his first real smile during the second month; at about two years he laughs at his own or other children's antics and in response to grotesque social situations. Sensitivity to people's words, tones of voice, and gestures is an asset all through life.

The child's natural way of learning the language is psychologically sound. The social significance of the situation is of primary importance to him. Later he practices various speech sounds with great satisfaction. With the help of adults he associates some of these sounds with familiar objects and actions. He understands the meaning of words before he attempts to say them. From the clusters of meanings attached to certain key words, he later sorts out separate meanings. In addition to the sheer pleasure of making speech sounds, he finds that words have meaning, use, and purpose for him. He can use them to get what he wants. It is no wonder that a child's language development is so closely related to his mental and social development.

DEVELOPMENT OF UNDERSTANDING

At first the infant sees the world, as William James said, as "a great, big, bloomin', buzzing confusion." He notices first the objects that either threaten or give him satisfaction. From the beginning, feelings are related to perceptions—to the objects the child sees and the meanings they have for him. He recognizes objects by what he can do with them or what they do to him. "A hole is to dig"—is the way older children define it. The best way to help the young child distinguish one object from another is to be sure that it serves a different purpose for him.

The little child lives in the present. Objects and actions are part of the "here and now." Nevertheless, early in the first year, some children give evidence that previous experience has left some trace. The baby may associate being taken up in his mother's arms, or even hearing her voice as she announces feeding time, with being fed. He will stop crying and make sucking movements. Being placed on the bath table is a signal for gurgles or howls, depending on whether bathing has been pleasant or disagreeable. Before the end of the first year a child will look for a spoon he has dropped or a toy with which he has previously been playing. Babies one year old could remember a familiar plaything after it had been hidden for five minutes; babies two years old, after twenty minutes. Instances are rare in which a child of less than two years retains a memory for more than a month. Year-old babies often pain their parents by not recognizing them after they have been away for a few weeks; a two-year-old often remembers his father when he has been absent for several weeks.

Some two-year-old children are able to relate recent experiences such as a walk in the woods or a visit to grandma's. They also enjoy repeating bits of their favorite stories.

This kind of development is strongly influenced by the emotional responses of the parents. The parents' pleasures or displeasure, anxiety or optimism, fear or security, which may be conveyed in subtle ways, all have an effect on the child's responses to objects and actions. Even before the child acquires language, he learns a great deal from the language of behavior—an angry voice, an abrupt or tense manner may create the kind of anxiety that decreases learning; whereas a gentle voice, a reassuring and loving manner may encourage exploration and learning.

Intelligence and its measurement

According to the French psychologist, Piaget, the child is born with the ability to organize his experience (75, 1953). Children vary in the degree to which they possess this power to organize and relate. During the first year of life the child shows this ability largely through perceptual-motor activities; during the second year, he shows it through his comprehension of simple questions and problems, his language development, and his responses to other people. Intelligence is an evolving, dynamic succession of functions, each more complete, depending upon earlier simpler functions.

Interest in the measurement of an infant's intelligence has focused on the prediction of his intelligence at school age and during adulthood. However, intelligence during these latter periods depends largely upon verbal, reasoning, and other abstract abilities which have scarcely begun to develop during infancy. In fact, the only reliable measurements of intelligence available during the first year are largely measures of motor efficiency. Unfortunately, there is only a moderate correlation between motor and verbal abilities at any particular age (7, p. 17, 1935). The correlation falls almost to zero when one compares measures of intelligence obtained during the first year with those beyond age six (8, 1955). It is not until age two that individual differences can be obtained that carry on into childhood.

Obviously any important decision on which the child's future welfare depends, such as placement in a foster home, or home for retarded children, cannot be made on the basis of these early test results. Up to the age of two and one-half, the IQ of either parent is often superior to present tests as an indicator of a child's future intelligence. Parents should hold as tentative any opinion they have at this time about the intellectual ability of their child.

SOCIAL-EMOTIONAL DEVELOPMENT

Children have to learn to love. Their first concern is with themselves; the world revolves around them. Soon they begin to love the person who satisfies their physical needs, usually the mother. In time, this attachment becomes a genuine affection. The child who does not achieve a fairly early identification with a loved person may go through life without warm relations and without the ability to identify himself with other people. Older children and adolescents who are lacking in motivation for achievement, who show indifference toward themselves and others, or who engage in destructive acts are often found to have had unsatisfactory family relationships in these first years of life.

The child's responses to his world during the first two years stem from his concept of himself and determine the way he is perceived by others. A few children seem to be "set in their ways" by the time they have reached the age of two or three. These are the individuals who have had continuous, intense, blighting experiences of anxiety and loneliness. For example, babies in institutions, who have minimal social contacts with several persons instead of with their own mother, have been reported to be less socially sensitive and responsive to people and less interested in manipulating things in their environment than are babies who are being brought up in families. Spitz (90, 1954), in an orphanage in which children were given good physical care but little love or individual attention, reported that the babies became apathetic and were frequently ill. Malnutrition, a fixed expression, rocking and rolling, failure to respond as readily as most children do to outside stimulation, and outbursts of anger or excitement when their fantasy is interrupted have been observed in cases of severe maternal deprivation (79, 1957). An experiment with sixteen institutional babies (78, 1956) showed that those cared for by one person became more socially responsive, not only to that person, but also to strangers, than did those who were cared for by many different persons under institutional conditions.

Most children, however, have a resiliency that makes it possible for them to overcome the bad effects of some of their earlier experiences. We need to know much more about the *patterns* of parental motives, behavior, attitudes, and subtly conveyed feelings that help to determine childhood personality. We need to know more about what "mothering" means to an infant in his first months of life. We need to know more about the psychological effects that specific situations may exert upon infants and children with certain constitutions at various ages.

Persistent trends in personality that arise from early experiences may be reinforced by frequently recurring conditions in the environment. On the other hand, early conditions that may appear to be favorable can be counteracted by unfavorable conditions that occur later. Pueblo and Navaho Indians, although protected and indulged in infancy, show as adults a high degree of maladjustment and anxiety. Some children of lower socioeconomic status who are fed when they cry, weaned late, and not required to achieve bowel and bladder control until three or four years old, develop into insecure, egocentric adults. In both of these instances, later conditions appear to offset the sense of security and trust developed during infancy. With each experience, however, the child's personality becomes more organized and ideally more free from "the dominancy of the situation."

Development of social responsiveness

Some children have an initial advantage in social responsiveness. They seem to have been born happy. They smile easily. Constitutionally they are placid, happy-go-lucky. Chances are that they have been fortunate in being fed when they were hungry, held when they might otherwise have felt a vague or intense sense of loneliness, mothered by a person who was herself secure and relaxed. These happy babies evoke happy responses from the persons in their environment. A circular response is set in motion: The baby's smile calls forth smiles and tenderness on the part of the mother; she may even handle him more skillfully than she would otherwise do. The baby who has not been so fortunate in his heredity and first experiences needs more than the average amount of affection.

The baby's social development progresses rapidly. It begins with his solemn watching of his mother's face as he distinguishes it from its vague background. As early as the third week some babies begin to attend to human voices in preference to other sounds. Usually by the third or fifth month the infant will turn his head in response to a voice. The things that he pays most attention to are those that have emotional significance for him. By far the most important are his parents' responses to him; they give an emotional tone to everything he sees and does.

At about five weeks of age, the baby is smiling in response to an adult's overtures, and in the second month, he gives evidence of special responsiveness to his mother. A little later he may protest the presence of strangers by crying or withdrawing from them—he now distinguishes strangers from his familiar associates.

From the age of about four months, he needs to be with people, where things are going on. Shortly after the middle of the year he plays "peek" and "pat-a-cake" with obvious enjoyment; he shows a social interest in both children and adults.

Near the end of the first year his fear of strangers or indifference to them begins to decrease. His contacts broaden beyond the playpen, but he is still not what anyone would call sociable. Two-year-olds in nursery school bump into one another and sometimes congregate in one spot, but they are usually bent on their own private play enterprises. They express glee in activities that they initiate and that represent personal achievement.

During the last half of the second year, association with other children, even though the play remains parallel rather than co-operative, is important for language development. The desire to make an impression on someone or to get him to do what you want is a strong incentive to speech. Play with others also helps the child to learn to accept the natural consequences of interference with other children's activities or belongings.

Since other children and adults do not play the role of a solicitous mother, the child begins to learn that he cannot always get what he wants when he wants it.

The child's social behavior varies with his age and temperament, and with environmental factors such as the place, the company present, the activity going on, the adult guidance, and the quality of the child's relationships with grown-ups.

Sibling relationships

During the second year, the child may have to make an adjustment to a new baby. It is quite natural for the older child to have mixed feelings about his baby brother or sister. He enjoys petting and playing with the baby and making him laugh. But his love-pats sometimes become slaps, and his play gets so rough that his mother may have to tell him repeatedly, and sometimes emphatically, to "be careful." Even when the mother has done all she can to prepare the older child for the coming of the baby, and even when she lets him share her care of the littlest one, he may still feel jealousy. This is not serious if he soon learns that his parents still have a good measure of affection for him, and that life inevitably involves changes in human relations. If his resentment becomes so strong that he really intends to injure the baby, his parents should leave no doubt in his mind that this must not be done. However, even in forbidding specific behavior, they may still convey a general attitude of acceptance of the child.

Anxiety and loneliness

Pervasive anxiety that begins before the child has begun to talk is more devastating than specific fears. Through nonverbal channels the mother may somehow convey feelings of anxiety to the child. This may occur if she is stiff, tense, and awkward in her handling of the child; if she withdraws the nipple repeatedly; if she resents taking the time to nurse the baby. Feeding difficulties increase as the mother grows more and more insecure. When the baby refuses to eat, the mother's anxiety increases and her ability to show tenderness decreases.

The baby's first response to loneliness, pain, and hunger is to cry. If his need is not met, the crying becomes intense. Then he makes an adaptation to the situation and stops crying. But if the stress is too strong and persistent, he loses his ability to adapt to it and may become insecure, apathetic, or ill. The extent to which stress is tolerated varies with the age of the child and the cultural traditions of his environment (89, 1955).

Infants feel loneliness. When separated from their parents, or left alone, or in the dark, or with a strange person, or in any situation which the child associates with loss of love and insecurity in relation to his parents, infants have shown a pervasive and persistent anxiety and loneliness. Bowlby (18, 1953) presented evidence of the possible damage that may be done if certain children are separated from the mother before the age of four and a half years. He further described the emotional forces that may be generated, and that may produce such vicious cycles as the following:

1. An unloving mother is probably more likely to part with a child; the child may sense her lack of affection.

2. The child is not easy to love; in fretting for his mother he tends to reject others; if he does become attached to someone else, he is greedy and jealous in the relationship.

3. On his return to his mother, he may fail to recognize her, or reject her outright, or behave in a possessive and whining manner.

The responses learned under these circumstances are hard to overcome, especially when the stress is acute. As a result of these investigations and their own observation, some doctors think "mothering" is so important for the health and well-being of a baby that they prescribe it for babies in institutions.

Counterevidence was offered by Dennis (24, 1951). In his experiment, twin girls were given only the attention needed for feeding, bodily care, and testing. Never fondled or played with until they were seven months old, they seemed to have reached normal development both physically and socially. However, the testing itself offered frequent contacts and the total environment of these twins must have had many favorable features: Their parents showed genuine interest in the children, and amply met the twins' other needs.

Fear and anger

Fear, in contrast with anxiety, is localized; it is usually aroused by something that has the elements of strangeness, suddenness, or unexpectedness (43, 1954). A frog was found to be the most fear-provoking of the animals presented to one group of small children, probably because of its tendency to jump unexpectedly.

Fear may be "caught" from other people. If a mother shows fear of lightning, for example, the baby is likely to behave in the same way. If,

on the other hand, a fearful situation such as the air raids in World
War II is associated with reassurance and active efforts to do something
about it, the child is not so likely to be afraid. To the anxious child,
anything may be a possible danger, and the child's fear is quite disproportionate to its cause. He feels a pervasive insecurity when his mother is
away. The frightened child needs reassurance, not scolding or scoffing.
He needs to learn how to handle the situation himself. As he understands and gains control over his environment, some of his fears tend to
wane. His responses become more rational. A five-month-old child does
not know enough to be afraid of strangers; one or two months later he may
show fear of situations or persons that he recognizes as strange and new.
The nature of any emotional response depends upon many factors in the
total situation. As a child gains a deep sense of trust in his parents, security in their love, and confidence in himself, his fears subside.

It is natural and desirable for a baby to make positive or aggressive
responses to frustration. We see this kind of response in the newborn, as he
alternates between placidity and protest. In a frustrated two-year-old, anger
is unmistakable. It is expressed by kicking, stamping, and other aggressive
movements, or in crying, frowning, or pouting.

It is no wonder that the young child is often moved to anger. There
are many things he wants to do, for which he has not acquired the necessary skill; there are many times when he wants to communicate with an
adult, but does not have the words; there are many items in his daily
routine that he would like to avoid. During the first year the child's outbursts of anger are explosive and do not have much effect on the situation
that causes them. Gradually his anger comes to be focused on someone or
something. The way he expresses his anger varies with his age and with the
way in which adults respond to him.

ORIGINS OF THE SELF

A child's concept of himself is built on the chemistry of the body and
the structure and functions present at birth. At the start it evolves from a
certain sensitivity and quality of the nervous system—the ability to relate
and organize experience. Very soon after birth, the baby is influenced
by his experiences of approval and disapproval, praise and blame, acceptance and rejection, by the persons who are significant in his life.
According to Sullivan, an individual's personality is built out of the complex of interpersonal relations in which he lives (96, 1953). If the infant
does what is pleasing to the mother, she spontaneously shows increased

tenderness to him. She fondles, smiles at, and talks to him in endearing ways, making him feel that he is loved and cherished. If he does not respond, she may as unconsciously withhold tenderness. Whatever concept he is forming of himself and the world tends to persist and to influence his behavior.

At first an infant reacts soberly to his mirror image without sustained interest. Next he responds to it as to a playmate. Between six and seven months of age he begins to react toward his image as if he were attempting to relate the mirror image to himself. At about one year, his behavior suggests true self-recognition (26, 1957).

Interpersonal relations become increasingly important as the child begins to realize that everything will not always bend to his will. Pain cannot always be avoided or alleviated. Ways of civilized life must be learned. If this is done, while still retaining a sense of the affection of the persons most important in his life, the infant emerges into childhood with a sense of trust and security.

Well-adjusted children generally feel accepted, respected, and trusting, whereas disturbed children are more often motivated by feelings of hostility, fear, and anxiety. The negative attitudes of well-adjusted children are less frequently expressed, less intense, and more often focused on some specific thing than are the negative attitudes of disturbed children (67, p. 21, 1956). These tendencies observed in school children probably have their origin in individual differences in emotional sensitivities and responsiveness early in infancy. The responses children make evoke similar responses from others. Thus the maladjusted child's fear and hostility continue to be reinforced in his interaction with other children and adults.

The child's competency in daily activities likewise affects his personality and his personal relations. If he has opportunities to succeed in suitable tasks, if help is not offered so long as he can do the task himself, but is given before it becomes frustrating, he begins to think of himself as a competent person. There is then no serious gap between his idea of what he can do and his ability to accomplish it.

Questions and Problems

FOR CLASS DISCUSSION OR STUDY GROUPS

1. Observe a baby at any age between birth and two years of age. These observations should be objective—i.e., describe the child's behavior; do not label it. They should be recorded immediately and accurately. Apart from these

snapshots of behavior, also record your impressions of what the behavior may have meant to the child and what influence you might have had on him. Thoughtful observation of a situation or of a certain kind of behavior will give the adult clues as to why the child behaves as he does, how adults and other children are influencing the child, and how one may best deal with the situation. Such a study will enable the adult to see more clearly which responses he should encourage, what experiences he should supply, and what effects various kinds of treatment are having on the child.

The following is an example of a recorded observation of a bright two-year-old growing up in a loving, accepting, intellectually stimulating environment. Both father and mother enjoy their home and their child. Charlie is the only child at present, but his mother is expecting a baby soon. Note this child's language development, his negativism, the parent-child relations, the parents' guidance of the child.

One morning he woke up late—at eight o'clock crying for "Daddy." His mother ran to his bed and placed him in his highchair at the breakfast table. He saw an egg on his mother's plate and said, "Mommie, egg." His mother told him that she would cook him one. He sat quietly, rubbing his eyes until his egg was cooked. His father fed him. As soon as he was through eating his egg, he began pushing things around on the dining table. His father allowed him to touch all the things near him, after he had removed some breakable objects.

After breakfast he was put on his "toidey." He remained there for some time and then decided it was time for him to be taken off. He called, "Mommie, come take son . . . Daddy, come take son." His father took him off. . . .

He pushed his chair over to the window and looked out. After sitting there for some time he called out, "Mommie, Mommie." When his mother went over to him he said, "See man." He jumped off the chair and went over to the table lamp and tried to turn it on. His mother stopped him by raising her hand as if to hit him and he walked away from the table. Suddenly he started singing, "Twinkle, twinkle, little star," and then said, "Mommie, you sing it." After a few minutes of silence, he started singing "Kool days, kool days, gloria's kool days, readin' an' ritin' and 'ritmic." Jumping off the bed he went to the telephone and said, "Wan' talk a fone to Aunt Jenny, Aunt Mary, Grandpa, Daddy." His mother said, "Yes, you may make believe you are talking on the phone." He said, "Hello, Grandpa, how are you? Fine, hello, thank you very much. Bye." . . .

He turned on the radio and pushed several buttons until he heard music. Then he started dancing around. He went over to his mother and asked if she saw "man dancing." He then went into his room and took a book out of his toy box and asked his aunt to "read it." She pointed to the pictures, to which he responded correctly: "mommie bear," "Peter rabbit," "shicken," "cat," "doggie." Then he said, "You read it, Auntie." She read for about ten minutes when he said, "Nuf, no more." He seldom did anything for more than ten minutes.

In preparation for his bath in the late afternoon, his mother showed him how to take off his clothes, and he immediately took off his shirt. With his mother's help he took off both his shoes. When she attempted to help him with his socks he said, "No, no." He enjoyed his bath. When his mother pulled the stopper out, he replaced it. When she insisted on letting out the water, he put his foot over the drain. After seeing the water go out of the tub, he turned on the hot water faucet and said "Hot"; then he turned on the cold water and said, "Cold."

When his mother started putting on his night shirt he assisted by putting one arm in the neckhole. Finding this wasn't right he tried and tried until he got his hand in the sleeve and then his face lighted up.

After drinking his milk he said to his mother, "Mommie, records," and she got his records and played Mother Goose songs for him. . . .

When his mother said, "Say good night to Daddy," he kissed his father and said, "Good night." His mother took him to his crib. Before she could put him in, he started crying. She turned out the lights and patted him to sleep.

Discuss such questions as: Is this environment too permissive? Is it too early for a two-year-old child to begin to learn that there are some things he cannot have and some things he cannot do?

It would be enlightening to continue studying this child to see the kind of further development that results from this kind of early environment.

The most valuable observations are those that are made systematically and repeatedly, instead of casually, spasmodically, and irregularly. A modern baby book is a behavior diary-record kept over a period of years and including daily observations The best way to learn about an individual child is to study him directly, recording stages in his motor, intellectual, and social development, and taking into consideration the environmental forces which are influencing his development. The skilled observer knows what kind of responses may be expected of children at a given stage of development, under certain conditions. Thus he can note and appraise deviations in a particular child.

2. Parents will find it fascinating to make a careful study of their baby's vocabulary as talk grows word by word. A word may be considered a part of the child's vocabulary when it is used correctly in daily conversations; when it is spoken in reply to a question such as "What is this?"; when it is used spontaneously by the child in response to objects or events, or in his own interminable monologues. The following form of record is simple and convenient

Date	Word	What the Word Was Intended to Mean
Dec. 1	drink	I want a drink.
	shoe	[Name of the object]
Dec. 3	up	I want to get up on your lap.
	Dada	Father.
Dec. 4	shoe	[Forgotten when tested]
	dog	[Name of the animal]
	down	I want to walk.

3. Discuss each of the following modern emphases in bringing up children:

a. The child has growth potentials and an urge to grow that largely determine his development.

b. The parent's role is to provide favorable conditions for child development.

c. One essential is "unconditional love."

d. Ups and downs, fluctuations in growing, are to be expected.

4. Explain more fully this statement made by an eminent psychiatrist: "Infancy is the time for parents to be good and children to be bad."

5. What kinds of behavior make you think a baby is intelligent?

6. What can parents do to help a child acquire, during his first year of life, a "basic sense of trust"?

7. Give examples to support the statement that the two-year-old is in an "in-between stage"—wanting to explore the unknown boldly; yet still feeling an underlying dependency on his mother.

8. Study Piaget's *The Origin of Intelligence In Children* as an example of a productive type of research, similar to that employed in the biological sciences. What is his method of collecting data? Give examples of his critical thinking on the basis of the data collected.

Chapter 6

INFLUENCES ON

CHILD DEVELOPMENT

As the child grows, all of the abilities we have mentioned are carried forward despite occasional lapses, provided conditions are favorable. If any specific ability is to develop normally, it must have ample opportunity to function in a variety of situations (100, 1955). Growth in competencies is accompanied, in turn, by increased security and independence.

THE CHILD'S FOUR WORLDS

The child lives in four worlds: (1) the physicoeconomic world that affects the lives of its inhabitants by its climate, soil, and natural resources; and by its depressions, wars, and shifting values; (2) the culture— the patterned ways of living that are characteristic of a given society; (3) the personal-social world of relationships, beginning with the family group and widening as the child grows older; and (4) the private, personal world that is unique to each individual.

The physicoeconomic world

Geographical conditions influence child development both directly and indirectly. For example, people living in tropical countries where needs are easily met tend to develop characteristics different from those of residents of cold, barren regions where the necessities of life are obtained only by hard work, scrimping, and saving.

Unwholesome living conditions such as unsanitary homes, overcrowding, lack of play-space and equipment, and inadequate medical care may obviously affect the health of both mother and child. Migratory laborers find it hard if not impossible to maintain wholesome family life. A condition known as "secondary poverty" arises when parents who have an adequate income spend it without regard for the needs of their children. In the

73

year 1956, the people in the United States spent $71.3 billion for food, and more than a fifth as much—$15 million—for tobacco and alcoholic beverages. Approximately the same amount—$15.5 billion—was spent on public and private education. War has a particularly devastating effect, because it is accompanied by widespread malnutrition, disease, and maladjustment.

Too often the adult world projects its own hates and miseries into the lives of children. However, it is not always physical or social conditions as such that blight family life; the way in which the family perceives its conditions is also to be considered. It is practically impossible to establish a cause-and-effect relationship between the socioeconomic conditions in a child's home and his school achievement or emotional attitudes (42, p. 152, 1957).

The culture

"Patterned ways of behaving," of thinking and feeling, which we call *culture*, also influence a child's development by the time he can talk (10, 1949). In infancy the culture exerts its influence through the prevailing habits and customs of child care. For example, where custom demands that the expectant mother be confined to dark rooms and deprived of dietary essentials, the development of both mother and infant is seriously impaired. The parent is the agent of the culture; he transmits his version of it through what he says, and does, and feels. The favored patterns of conduct are built into the child by the responses which adults make to his daily behavior. Some things he does are rewarded; others are disapproved or punished. The parents' skill in helping the child to profit by what the culture offers in the way of order and stability, or design for living, has much to do with his later attitude toward society. Whiting and Child (104, 1953) found that the child-care patterns characteristic of a culture are related to the type of adult personality which it commonly produces.

The influence of the culture on child development is seen most clearly in studies of primitive societies that have differing child-care practices (51, 1947; 104, 1953). In some societies, affection for children predominates; in others, children experience indifference and other "anxiety-provoking" treatment. In one tribe, for example, the baby is a plaything, passed around from one person to another. This sort of teasing tends to develop withdrawn and detached personalities. In another tribe, children grow up with little or no need to be aggressive; they are treated affectionately by the adults, who feel responsible for all children and exercise a certain affectionate control over them.

In modern cultures, various methods are employed to socialize the

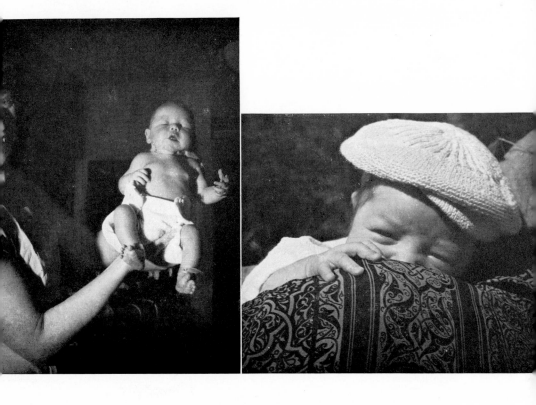

During the first year the baby grows dramatically—physically, intellectually, socially and emotionally.

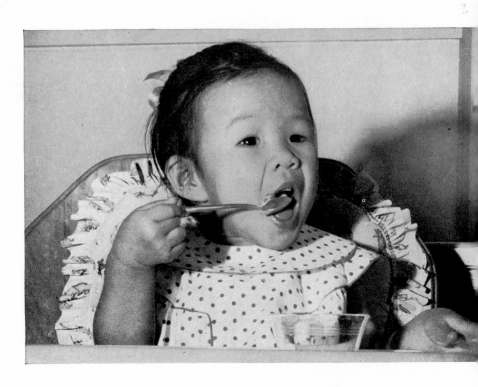

"Where there's a will there's a way."

child. In Lebanese culture, restrictions are imposed by the tradition. This impersonal authority has the advantage of protecting the mother-child relationship from the child's resentment of imposed restrictions. Although children are cherished, it is not a child-centered culture; the child is expected to fit into the adult world. Another feature in the Lebanese culture is the relatively large family circle, which may at once give the child greater indulgence and greater security. Parents are more casual and less self-critical with respect to their methods of child care.

During early childhood, Chinese children are much indulged. The mother is very permissive about feeding, weaning, and toilet-training. Close physical contact with the infant, and permissiveness in dealing with his physiological functions, are accompanied by a kind of character-training in which the parent tries to modify the present or anticipated behavior of the child through his personal influence. This method of child-rearing seems to result in the co-operative attitude characteristic of Chinese children.

In our own country there are significant differences in child-rearing among the diverse social groups. A teacher observed differences between the personality patterns of preschool children in Greenwich Village, New York, and those of children in the Tennessee mountains (53, 1946). A review of three important studies of child-rearing practices leads to the conclusion that middle-class mothers in the regions studied were generally more permissive and less punitive toward their young children than were working-class mothers. (84, p. 446, 1957) Each culture has its unique methods of child nurture, which are reflected in the personalities of both children and adults.

The effect of any child-care practice depends on the complex situation in which it occurs. An experience such as being strapped to a cradleboard or wrapped in swaddling clothes, which to us seems frustrating, may not be frustrating to the infant. For example, the Navaho infant, fastened to a cradleboard on his mother's back, has never known freedom of movement. However, this restraint protects him from the falls and bumps common to the active baby. Moreover, thus fastened to his mother, he is with people almost constantly from his earliest days.

During the second year the child not only learns the words spoken in his environment, but also something of the emotional implications with which his social group has invested them. Values, attitudes, expressive movements—all develop in subtle ways, according to the culture pattern. In place of simple primitive taboos, modern life has substituted a far more complex mesh of distracting strains and conflicts.

So far as possible, tension should be kept low enough so that the child can control it. This is the principle of "tempering the wind to the shorn lamb." There is a growing agreement that some kind of control is unavoidable in child-rearing; in fact, it is an essential part of the child's development. Unless he learns to handle frustration, no child can learn to accept the normal controls involved in living. It is not restrictions in themselves which cause stunted development; as a matter of fact, children accept reasonable limits. Damage occurs when restrictions are imposed without regard to children's feelings in the matter. Children of this age are very sensitive to their parents' attitudes; they fear loss of love.

A sensible middle way lies somewhere between the extremes of rigid adherence to cultural demands and complete surrender to the child's impulses. The infant needs a period in which his own rhythms are satisfied as they were before birth; he is not yet ready to understand and handle frustration. By cultivating and maintaining sensitivity to the baby's needs, the mother can gradually help him to meet cultural demands, to adapt to the requirements of outside reality, to accept normal and inevitable deprivations. Children who have enjoyed the satisfactions of infancy will be more ready to move on to the next stage of development, for which they can assume some responsibility themselves.

Moreover, institutions and customs can be changed. What man has invented, he can replace with a better invention. Adults as well as children can learn. It is important to work on all age levels and with all groups at once. While contemporary parents are bringing up their children in a more enlightened way, high-school pupils can be learning about family life and child care, and statesmen can manage national and international affairs in such a way as to ensure a good life for all people.

Personal relations

The pervasive attitudes and behavior of parents are more likely to affect the child's development than are specific child-care practices. Of all the influences on child development, human relations are the most important. In any family there is a constantly changing constellation of relationships, which influences the development of each of the children in a different way. Many forces may affect the parent-child relationship. The parents' health and attitudes, inconsistencies, and possible immaturity or psychological disorders; tensions and quarrels between them; the birth of a younger brother or sister; the child's position in the family; the presence of a grandparent or other relative or boarder in the home; and many other influences enter into the dynamics of family relations.

Underlying principles. There are four principles that are frequently emphasized as basic to parent-child relations:

1. The mother's loving care, based on understanding of the infant, helps the child to develop a basic sense of security and trust.

2. The period between two and three years of age seems crucial for the child in working out the dependency-independence relation.

3. Parent-child relations change as the child grows older. During the first five or six months of life the parent takes major responsibility for meeting the infant's needs. Later the child begins to desire independence. Somewhere between the fifth and eighth months, he reaches a stage where it is possible to "overmother" or "overprotect" him. If the mother recognizes these sequences in emotional development she can be ready to adjust her behavior accordingly.

4. Certain patterns of parental personality, behavior, and home atmosphere seem to be associated with certain patterns of child behavior and personality.

Influence of parents. Of all the human relations influencing a child's development, the personality of the mother is of central importance (84, 1957). Her attitudes toward pregnancy, toward her husband and other members of the family, toward her career and social life, toward her role as a mother, and, most of all, her attitude toward the child and his need for understanding, affection, acceptance, approval, and control, are vital.

The mother-child relationship is so crucial to the baby because he is almost entirely dependent on his mother. During the first two years he has few satisfactions other than his close relationship with her, and to a lesser extent with the rest of the family. He cannot turn to friends for solace because his social environment is limited. When his mother fails to give him the affection he needs he has nowhere to turn.

Some of the possible effects of severe maternal deprivation on young children have already been mentioned in Chapter 5. In one case the mother had been committed to the state mental hospital. A public health nurse, who had already had contact with this family of two parents and eight children, made the initial visit. The mother, apathetic and withdrawn, had neglected the children, especially the twins, who were the youngest. The father was staying away from the home more and more, and the oldest girl was assuming responsibility for the younger children, a task too heavy for her. The most serious and immediate problem was the physical and emotional condition of the twins. At the special community clinic concerned with problems of maternal deprivation, social worker, psychologist, pediatrician, nutritionist, psychiatrist, and nurse worked as a team, examining the children, making recommendations, and following up the case. The recommendations included (1) medical care for the children; (2) work with the father and older daughter in planning the budget; (3) work with the older daughter, who at first resented the nurse, when the latter offered to teach her food-buying and planning, and infant care; (4) with the school in securing consideration for all of the children, especially for the younger girl. Basic to this work was the need to establish a closer relationship with the mother and the eldest girl. The nurse was successful in carrying out these recommendations, with the result that the twins no longer showed the initial signs of physical and emotional retardation (79, 1957).

Individual cases, of course, do not prove the necessity of mothering, but the work of Spitz, Bowlby, and others, although open to certain criticism, presents evidence of the detrimental effects of institutional care where no mothering person is in contact with the child. "Social stimulation is itself a biological necessity." (94, 1954)

The importance of the father's role in child care is being increasingly recognized. While many writers lament the modern father's lack of contact with his children, Margaret Mead warns against going too far in the direction of domesticating either parent. What emerges from this controversy is a clearer recognition of the need for real co-operation between the sexes, which alone can foster optimum personal development for each. The 1957 summer issue of *Child Study* was devoted to a consideration of "the man in the family." (62, 1957) It was pointed out that children are growing up with little awareness of the role of the father, and only a dim understanding of their own masculine and feminine roles; that "fathering" has received very little attention in comparison to the emphasis on "mothering." We need to know much more about the potentialities of the father-child relationship for child development. The traditional conceptions of the good father as provider, disciplinarian, fount of wisdom, and good example are quite different from the concept of the father as a sharer in the child's total development and in all aspects of family life.

Despert (25, 1957) made an excellent analysis of the way children may be affected by the father's death, divorce, and temporary or prolonged absence. The age of the child, the emotional climate prevalent in the home preceding the child's separation from the father, and the mother's emotional maturity and understanding of the child are the most important factors in the child's adjustment to a fatherless home. We need to know much more about the meaning of separation to the child. For example, an only child whose mother sent him to a play group where he would have more contact with children of his own age, thought of the group as a means of "taking you away from your mommy for two hours."

A parent who is left with the sole responsibility for bringing up his children because of separation, divorce, or death, is likely to be anxious about whether he is acting in the best way. In some cases, the "only parent" may feel a guilty responsibility for breaking up the marriage, or even for causing the partner's death. Thus he feels in duty-bound to compensate to the child who has been deprived of the other parent. If he does sacrifice his own personal desires, as for example, to marry again, for what he considers the good of the child, he may come to feel an undercurrent of resentment against the child. Moreover, it is difficult for an "only parent" to have an adequate social life; married people prefer to invite couples to their social affairs, and single people do not share his interests as a parent. It has proved helpful for "only parents" to face the situation with others who have similar feelings, and who can help them to find successful ways of handling the problem (34, 1956).

Influence of persons other than parents. Persons other than parents, brothers, and sisters may have a major influence on the development of children. Since most fathers are away at work, and about half the mothers, too, are gainfully employed, grandmother and grandfather may take an active part in bringing up the children, especially if there is a housing shortage. Grandparents may help or hinder. They come in handy when there are no baby sitters. Sometimes they have a better relationship with their grandchildren than they did with their own children because they have the advantage of perspective on two or more generations. Many grandparents have supplied the love and care that children so sorely need. They relieve the mother of some of her housekeeping burdens. But they are a liability when they take over the role of the parents, alienate the child from them, use outmoded methods of child care, over-restrict the child's natural activity, or cause conflict and tension in the family (71, 1954).

Other relatives and guests staying in the home also exert diverse influences upon the development of children. They may contribute new standards, ideas, customs, rules of social behavior, intellectual stimulation, anecdotes and sayings, and occasions for changing family routine. They may also represent a source of conflict and family tension, or an intrusion against which the family unites in a mild conspiracy.

Nursemaids and governesses play an important role as parent surrogates. Unfortunately the persons so employed often fall far short, intellectually and emotionally, of meeting the needs of growing children. Parents should not leave a child with any person whose relations with the child they have not had a chance to observe.

Foster homes often supply conditions for child development that are not found in the children's own homes, if the foster parents are genuinely fond of the child. As one child said, when she was told that the woman whom she called mother was not her real mother, "It really doesn't matter." And the social worker with whom she was talking replied, "You're right, it really *doesn't* matter, for your mother loves you very much." However, the child should be given this information early. To wait until adolescence is to add to the many other problems the child has to solve during that period. In addition to this basic relationship, these other conditions are important: Children should be adopted at a very early age, preferably by foster parents whose age and mental ability are similar to their real parents. The foster parents should want the child for his own sake; they should not regard him as a possible means of improving their own unsatisfactory marital adjustment. They should give the adopted child the same social status and the same opportunities that they give, or would give, to their own children and stick by him through thick and thin.

Parental attitudes and behavior. Parents need reassurance, not criticism. They should not be blamed for unfavorable attitudes, which are often built unconsciously from their life experiences. Instead of blame, they need help with their problems. A sense of humor also helps; it prevents parents from taking child-rearing too seriously and is relished by the most obstreperous children.

Unfortunately, most of the early research in this area has been concerned with detrimental attitudes (47, 1949). Too little attention has been given to the positive approach (46, 1953). The attitudes most commonly mentioned are rejection and overprotection. Parents may quite unconsciously reject the child as a whole or in part. They may reject the child because he came at an inopportune time; because he is not of the desired sex; because he is "a little runt"; because he does not fit into the family pattern, as in the case of a mentally retarded child in a gifted family or a phlegmatic child with energetic parents. These attitudes make it very difficult for a child to accept himself. Such a parent does not want the child the way he is, emphasizes his faults and defects, has no faith in him. Loss of love is the most serious experience a child can have. It sometimes occurs when a new baby has become the center of attention or because the child himself has become disagreeable or disappointing to the parents. Children who lack affection may become independent but rather cold, unresponsive, defensive.

Overprotection, too, has many causes. Among these are overemphasis on the hazards of modern life, previous loss of children, distorted ambition, or an attempt by the parents to satisfy emotional lacks in their own lives. Overprotection may be manifested in many ways: the mother may be overanxious or oversolicitous; she may want the child to be perfect. Some extremes of overprotection may represent unconscious attempts to conceal rejection of the child. To all appearances the child is lovingly mothered, but a sustained atmosphere of true affection is lacking.

Other parents show a laissez-faire attitude, forgetting that limitations or bounds have positive value in providing a stable background for children's growth. The ideal is to give the child only as much freedom as he can handle.

Some parents view their child as a possession or an accomplishment, and try to realize in him their own unfulfilled ambitions. Others have never grown up themselves; they dislike the responsibility of having children, and childishly compete with a child for the affection of some other member of the family. Some mothers who have been happily employed prior to marriage feel frustrated by being tied down to the home. Some parents feel hostility because the child reminds them of a past they want to forget, reflects some of their weakness, or has fallen short of their expectations. They often allow their hostility to come out in unexpected ways that baffle and confuse the child.

Another factor influencing the parent-child relation is the existence of "unmatched tempos." An active baby may have a quiet mother, or vice versa—an incompatibility that may make it difficult for the two to adjust to each other.

Marital conflict has been frequently mentioned as a detrimental influence on the child. There have been recent attempts to devise ways of resolving marital conflicts—of helping husbands and wives to talk about their incompatibilities realistically and frankly. A certain amount of honest marital conflict is not necessarily detrimental to the child; it may further a child's growth in understanding human relations.

The parental attitude most favorable for child development is what Sanford has called "affectionate training," or acceptance plus "affectionate training." Children of affectionate parents are usually outgoing, confident, orderly, independent, and affectionate. They tend to yield to reasonable social pressure. They are not "spoiled." Children may become "spoiled" when they are given everything they want except their parents' affection. Yet, love is not enough (12, 1950). Affection should be combined with understanding and order. Parents who have this attitude realize that certain limits or bounds have a positive value in providing a stable background for growth. They maintain a certain firmness but do not dominate or supervise excessively. They encourage children to explore and experiment without too much supervision or criticism. They are judiciously permissive, steering a middle course between overstrictness and indulgence. They do not overpraise the child so that he becomes dependent on approbation, and tries to get it from others.

It takes time and thought to create the psychological climate in which a child grows best. Despite the many modern laborsaving devices, many young mothers are so busy doing things for the children that they have little time for doing things with them. Ideally, the home should meet the needs of all members of the family. It should be a place in which parents as well as children can realize their best potentialities. Understanding the child may lead to self-understanding. The child is only part of the family, not the hub about which everything else revolves. In the long run, the best development of the parents contributes to the best development of the child. It is not good for the child if one or both parents sacrifice too much for him. Parenthood should be rewarding, and it should not completely disrupt the parents' own way of living.

The family is a *group*; its members have common goals or purposes and work together to attain them. They talk things over. Each member must make adjustments to the group, just as the group must make adjustments to each individual. Each has his special needs. The family tries to figure out how these individual needs can be met.

Position in the family. The child's position in the family—whether he is the eldest, youngest, middle, or only child—has some influence on his development. Bossard and Boll (15, 1955) identified in large families eight general personality roles—responsible, sociable, socially ambitious, studious, isolate, irresponsible, ill, and spoiled. In their opinion, these roles seemed to be related to position in the family.

Contrary to popular opinion, it is the eldest, not the only, child who is likely to be at a disadvantage. The eldest child tends to be adult-oriented, less self-confident, showing sensitive seriousness, whereas the second child is more often peer-oriented with easy-going friendliness, according to McArthur (57, 1956). Perhaps this is partly because parents lack experience at the time they are bringing up their first child. As one child said, "My father's experience as a parent was all gained at my expense." The age difference between the first and second born may have an important influence on the mother's behavior toward the two children (50, 1954). By the time the third child comes, the parents have had time to work out their own marital adjustments. They have also become more expert in the techniques of child-rearing. Moreover, parents are usually less well off financially at the time when their first child is born. They are also likely to expect more of the eldest child, feel less warmly toward him, be more restrictive, and want him to follow in his father's footsteps. When the new baby comes, it is the older child who is likely to feel displaced in his parents' affection.

Psychologically, brothers and sisters do not have the same parents; no two siblings have exactly the same relation to their parents. It is not position in family by itself that is responsible for differences observed in eldest, youngest, or only children, but rather their position in the complex total family situation.

The child's private world

The newborn exists in a world of his own. The world of the one- and two-year-old child is different from that of the newborn and also different from the world of adults. His world of thought would seem to us distorted. Many objects and acts have not yet acquired the significance that experience alone can lend them; the words he hears and uses may have completely different meanings to him than to adults. Yet, if we viewed his world through his eyes, we would be surprised at the reasonableness in his thinking.

Lewin urged his readers to distinguish between "the situation which the teacher, the parents, or the experimenter sees and the situation which exists for the child as his life space" (52, p. 919, 1954). The child's perception of a situation will vary with his physical and emotional state: whether he is fatigued, insecure, hungry, or rested, safe, and content. His goals, needs, and social relations also influence his perceptions. To understand him it is indeed important to consider how he may view his world and feel about it.

Stimuli come from within as well as from without. The child's development is constantly influenced by such factors as the chemical composition of the blood, the secretion of the thyroid and other endocrine glands, the energy reserve stored in the tissues and liver, and the irritability of the nervous system. More obvious is the influence of illness. Pain is the earliest form of discipline. If severe and prolonged, pain may cause a child to withdraw from social contacts; it naturally makes him more self-centered. Information about the diseases a child has had and about his parents' treatment of him at such times contributes to an understanding of his development.

Although there are aspects of development common to all children, the way a particular child develops is influenced, not only by his inherited tendencies, but also by the state of the world, the culture in which he is brought up, and, most of all, by his personal relations. All these determine how he feels about his world and himself.

INFLUENCE OF CHILD-REARING PRACTICES

What about conflicting theories of child-rearing? Certainly they have a history of fluctuation—from great severity and almost complete disregard for the child as a person, to extreme permissiveness and a completely child-centered approach; from good old-fashioned fondling, to rigid schedules and "scientific" aloofness; and from a new intensity of emphasis on tender loving care to a reversion to coercive methods.

At present, authorities seem to have settled down to a reasonable point of view calculated to relieve parents of excessive anxiety about their competence in child care (105, 1957). In brief, they now say: "Enjoy your child." "Live the good life and love that baby"; "Watch the baby rather than the clock"; "See what is going on—be aware of the personal relations between mother and baby"; and be fairly consistent, gradual, and affectionate but firm in teaching him the ways of civilized life. There is general agreement that a basic security established in infancy and early childhood helps the child to meet the inevitable difficulties of later life. The child who has loved and been loved is better able to cope with life's disappointments than is the child who has never known security or love.

Child-rearing practices seem to stem as much or more from the personalities of the parents as from the prevailing tendencies in the culture. For example, the personalities of fathers who were restrictive in their attitude toward their children showed more than average constriction, submissiveness, and suggestibility, and less than average self-assurance; whereas the more permissive group of fathers were more self-reliant and competent (14, 1955).

Both Linton (55, 956) and Riesman and associates (80, 1950) have described the relationship between child-rearing practices and the personality patterns which the child evolves as he grows up. Differences in people's personality, according to Linton, are due "less to their genes than to their nurseries." Several considerations suggest caution in accepting this emphasis on the direct relation between the child's personality development and the parents' attitudes toward the child, the amount of mothering that he receives, and other specific child-care practices:

1. Clinical observations of these relations as cause and effect have not been satisfactorily confirmed by research.

2. The infant is more likely to be influenced by the feelings of comfort or discomfort that result from certain infant care practices and by deprivation of sensory experiences than by interpersonal relations only. (However, the mother's attitude may be reflected in the way she handles the baby, and these

physical impressions of tension or relaxation, of self-confidence or anxiety, may be conveyed to the infant in a vague but nonetheless real way (96, 1953)).

3. Infants who are treated in widely different ways show apparently good development.

4. A given general parental attitude does not necessarily manifest itself in consistent infant-care practices; for example, favorable practices do not invariably spring from positive acceptance of the child; unfavorable practices are not always the result of rejection or overprotection. "Permissiveness or severity in one phase of training may be associated with their opposites in other or later practices." (87, pp. 147-48, 1955)

The problems that are being presented by parents today seem to arise more often from misunderstood permissiveness than from strictness. This practical dilemma may be explained in several ways:

1. Although considerable permissiveness during infancy is essential to building a sense of trust, the baby should not be habituated to expect the parents to rush to him whenever he cries for any reason.

2. The parents may maintain an overpermissive attitude beyond the time when it is most appropriate—that is, beyond the months when the baby cannot understand the reason for any deprivation.

3. Methods appropriate to emotionally sick children have sometimes been applied to all children.

4. The meaning that the child attaches to parental permissiveness has not been understood.

Despite conflicting opinions, several guides to sound parent-child relationships can be offered:

During the first six months, the infant needs "mothering." He needs to be held tenderly, and comforted when in pain or afraid. The transition from his effortless prenatal existence to a relatively independent life should be made as easy and gradual as possible.

At about the middle of the first year, several weeks' separation from the "mothering one" should be avoided, if possible.

At no time during the first year should the infant be allowed to cry so long or hard that he reaches a crisis of fear and anxiety.

During the first and second years, the baby should be given increasing opportunities to co-operate with the mother in her daily care of him.

The ways in which specific child-rearing practices affect the development of personality are not entirely clear at present. Sears, Maccoby, and Levin (84, p. 456, 1957) summed it up as follows: "Mothers' practices and attitudes unquestionably have *some* importance, but with respect to many kinds of child behavior, they may not be the most important determiners. And we as yet know very little about their importance to the adult personality." But there is general agreement that a child's behavior at any given time is "a product of his native endowment, of his immediate situation, and of the qualities of personality he has developed up to that moment in his life." (84, pp. 453-454, 1957) Child-rearing is one of many factors.

RESOURCES FOR PARENTS

Many private and government agencies offer help to parents. The Children's Bureau, the Department of Agriculture, the Department of Labor, the Public Health Service, and the Office of Education have a major interest in child development. They disseminate knowledge (1) through directed work with children as in nursery schools, (2) through consultation services, and (3) through publications, radio programs, motion pictures, magazines, and letters (73, 1956).

Child welfare clinics

There is evidence that modern pediatric knowledge can be successfully applied to groups of children and parents in free clinics. A follow-up study of a group of children, most of whom had been under supervision in clinics for infant welfare since birth, showed them to have good health, low incidence of serious illness, low mortality, and absence of serious physical defects. Care counts.

According to Allen (2, 1948), parents and children come to clinics because they need help with their immediate problems. "They [parents] needed more than good advice and well-intentioned prescriptions, which pointed out their weaknesses and the way to correct them. It became increasingly clear that they needed help to attain a better understanding and to arrive at a healthier set of values about themselves." (2, p. 1202, 1948) This kind of help can be given only if the clinic really believes that child and parent have "capacities for responsible living." "Building on what parents and children have, rather than stressing their liabilities and mistakes, has been an approach that has been basic in working with parents and children." (2, p. 1209, 1948)

Counseling service and group therapy

The counseling service of the Child Study Association of America aims to accomplish in the realm of mental health what the well-baby clinics do with respect to physical health. By means of this service, parents who have a good basic relationship with their children but are troubled about some phase of their children's development, or about marital problems that might adversely affect the child, have an opportunity to talk with someone who is understanding. This service is especially effective with parents of children under six years of age. Many parents welcome this opportunity to discuss a variety of situations: how to help a child make the transition from home to school; how to prevent a child from feeling extreme jealousy when a new baby arrives; how to help the child accept the death of a beloved grandparent; how to prepare the child for a long separation from his father. The workers take care not to give pathological interpretations to essentially normal behavior.

Group therapy with parents has also proved helpful. In the permissive atmosphere created by the therapist, parents bring their feelings out into the open, and gain understanding of themselves and of problems common to early childhood. One pediatrician found mixed groups of fathers and mothers more responsive than groups of mothers alone.

Community programs

Progress is being made in community education in child development. Most effective is the community health program concerned with all phases of development—physical, mental, and emotional—with lectures, pamphlets, and seminars reaching the persons most concerned with child care and education—parents, doctors, nurses, and teachers. An important part of such a program is an excellent series of loose-leaf bulletins containing sound, simple, eminently practical suggestions organized chronologically to follow the baby's growth. By reading these bulletins while still in the hospital, the mother acquires sound information and attitudes before assuming the full responsibility of caring for the baby and the household.

A community mental hygiene program in Toronto, Canada, combines clinical service to parents and children with education of teachers and research (86, 1954). One aim of the Forest Hill Village Project was to describe child-rearing practices and their relation to the mental health of children. The counseling teams of workers helped with classroom discussions and with parent education.

Pamphlets, plays, and films

There is need for more evaluation of the large number of pamphlets and leaflets prepared for parents. Problems of receptivity, readability, and response enter into the preparation of material of this kind. Since parents are especially anxious about their firstborn, they are responsive to guidance at the time of his birth. In response to this need, a series of pamphlets was prepared as part of a mental health project of the Louisiana Society for Mental Health. Written with simplicity, humor, and a sound point of view, these leaflets were sent, one each month, to all parents of firstborn children in the state during the first year of the child's life.

The series of American Theatre Wing community plays (92, 1957) presents situations for parent groups to analyze and discuss. The hoped-for effect of such plays is to make parents less anxious about their mistakes, and to help them accept themselves as good parents and be less dependent upon experts. Emphasis should be placed on what parents do right, and on their privileges as persons, as well as on their obligations as parents.

Here is a great opportunity for movies, radio, television, newspapers, books, and magazines. Progress has been made. Films may help many people to gain a more sympathetic understanding of children, and of adults who are burdened with a "problem child." Professionally trained editors of women's magazines publish excellent articles on child care and education. Some of the syndicated newspaper columns are also of high quality. How to personalize these publications and to make connections with parents' immediate, specific needs and problems is a challenging task.

HOW TO FORM A CHILD-STUDY GROUP

Any parent or teacher can help to form a parent study group (48, 1952; 77, 1957). The plan may be introduced in a panel discussion conducted by parents who have heard about or have already participated in a successful study group. There should be a trained consultant to help the chairman and the group develop effective methods.

Enlist as members those who will come voluntarily and who are genuinely interested in learning to understand children. Limit the size of the group to about fifteen members and set a definite time and place for the meeting—one meeting every two weeks at a time when fathers can attend may be best. Once organized, the group selects a chairman who is willing to get special training for this job.

Following are some of the characteristics of effective discussion in parent study groups:

The members use simple, nontechnical language.

The chairman never probes deeper into the causes of a child's behavior than the parents want to go.

Each member has opportunities to initiate discussion on questions about which he is especially concerned, in case they are not raised as common problems.

The chairman tries to make the members feel that the group is to serve them, that each member is important and can help others by contributing to the discussion.

The chairman provides time for a general discussion of books, articles, and films.

The discussion aims to develop attitudes rather than to give answers, and to emphasize developmental stages and the causes of behavior.

There should be a recorder, and possibly an observer who briefly analyzes the group process at the end of each meeting.

At the meetings during the first year a parent may report his observation of a single child—the child's relationship with other children of his own age, with older and younger children, and with adults; variations in the child's behavior at home and at school; when the child seems happiest, and when he seems unhappy or annoyed. In the discussion, members pool their observations of similar behavior in other children. They note that apparently similar behavior may arise from different causes.

Having obtained this picture of the child, they may consider the forces that are at work within the child and in his home and school environment to make him as he is. They suggest and discuss possible reasons or hypotheses for the behavior observed. As they recognize the limitations of their own experience, they turn to books and magazines to gain further understanding of the dynamics of children's behavior. Some groups build up a file of classified current articles on child study. On the basis of their firsthand experience and study of individual children, they make generalizations and build concepts useful in solving problems such as "How can I help my child get along better with other children?" "How can I handle conflicts that arise when he plays with his friends?" "What can I do to help him gain acceptance in his group?" "What shall I do about giving him an allowance?"

Understanding is relative. It spirals upward with each successive year of study. After the first year, parents often begin to seek more scientific information.

A real problem in developing a parent study group is to find leadership. Child study requires know-how. Someone who can teach the technique is needed as a consultant. The Institute of Child Study at the University of Maryland under the direction of Dr. Daniel Prescott offers this consultant service. State departments of education and psychology and guidance departments of colleges and universities should develop this kind of expert consultant service, for rural as well as for urban groups.

The possible outcomes of a parent study group are many. First, of course, is the parents' increased understanding of children. They become acquainted with the developmental needs and problems of children at different stages of growth. They recognize certain behavior patterns as the child's way of meeting his needs; they become interested in "the language of behavior." Gradually they gain more insight into the possible causes of behavior. One parent said, "Even though I do not yet understand my child, at least I believe that he has a right to be understood." Moreover, in this kind of study group, parents may gain some understanding of themselves and other adults as well as of children. The study group represents a practical program of human development and human relationships.

Questions and Problems

FOR CLASS DISCUSSION OR STUDY GROUPS

1. Each member of a child-study or child-psychology class may select a hypothetical parent and write a pamphlet or playlet to help her understand some one aspect of child development. No longer than 1,800 words, it should be based on sound study and bibliographical research. The best of these pamphlets and plays should be chosen for use with parents in the community.

2. Explain how a child may learn about human nature and human relations from the way parents treat him.

3. Work out possible relations among the child's four worlds.

4. Assist in a survey of resources for child development and parent education in your community.

5. What is your "annoyance-quotient"? What kinds of behavior in a child bother you most? How do you account for this feeling?

6. Read Sears, Maccoby, and Levin's *Patterns of Child Rearing* (84, 1957), especially the direct quotations to be able better to appreciate the wide range of parental attitudes and their possible effect on children. This book represents another type of research. How were the data collected and treated? What is the special value of personal documents in research in this field?

7. If possible, have discussions of films or plays dealing with influences on child development, such as:

A Father's Role in a Happy Family. Produced for the Mental Health Film Board by Sun Dial Films; 16 mm., 25 min., black and white, sound; commentary in either English or Spanish. Available from the Mental Health Materials Center, Inc., 1790 Broadway, Room 713, New York 19, N.Y. Purchase $85; rental $5.00 per day plus transportation charges.

A Two-Year-Old Goes to the Hospital. Produced by James Robertson, Tavistock Clinic, London, British National Health Service; 16 mm., 50 min., black and white, sound. Distributed by New York Univ. Film Library.

The Room Upstairs, a play by Nora Stirling on how old people and young people learn to live together. Available from the Mental Health Materials Center, 1790 Broadway, N. Y. Producing Packets (6 scripts), $5.00; single copies, $1.00.

Chapter 7

HOW THE BABY LEARNS

After a lecture by the late Francis Parker, famous Chicago educator, a mother asked how early she could begin the education of her child.

"When will your child be born?" he asked.

"Born?" she exclaimed. "Why, he's already five years old!"

"My goodness, woman," he replied, "don't stand here talking to me. Hurry home. You have already lost the best five years." T. S. Eliot also expressed the importance of the first years of life in the line, "In my end is my beginning."

Learning begins when an active child reaches out and makes contact with his environment. Some learning may even take place before this time. The baby learns as he grows, and sometimes the two processes are inseparable. How does the baby learn? Why does he learn? What part do adults play in the process? These are important questions.

LEARNING THEORY

Modern learning theory, derived largely from animal experimentation, emphasizes the way in which our behavior is shaped by rewards and punishments. This appears to be true of the verbal behavior of human beings as well as nonverbal behavior of animals. Modern theory also points out that the mere opportunity for activity or change of scene may be rewarding. It would even agree with the psychoanalysts that some behavior is maintained by rewards that seem intrinsically painful or are "unconscious" for the person most concerned. Today it becomes more and more obvious that the necessary conditions for one's growth in wisdom, skill, and responsibility lie in the learning processes of childhood.

HOW THE BABY LEARNS: THE LEARNING PROCESS

At birth some response patterns seem already to have been established in the child. They are ready to function as soon as the appropriate stimulus

92

appears. The way a baby routs for his mother's nipple may be a case of this sort, although even here a little learning may be going on. Some improvement in his suckling may be observed.

As the baby grows older, he becomes ever more expert in finding the right action for the right situation. His repertory of appropriate responses increases with every new opportunity to investigate and manipulate the objects of his world. He comes also to respond effectively to familiar objects when seen from different angles, in different sizes, and at different distances.

A baby's readiness for further learning depends upon many factors: his stage of physical development; his health; his repertory of selective responses; and his personal relations. These factors all determine the way he will respond to his environment; they also determine the way he will respond to himself—to the stimuli from his own behavior.

Putting one and one together

Some learning takes place through conditioning. The baby associates certain stimuli, and eventually makes the response that was in the beginning attached to only one of them. For example, being held in a certain position may mean to him that his hunger is about to be relieved. Investigations of conditioning in infants have shown that responses such as sucking, crying, and general activity may be conditioned to tactual, visual, and auditory stimuli. These conditioned responses tend to become more stable as the infant grows older (69, p. 381, 1954), but they continue to be affected by need—principally hunger and other bodily conditions.

Readiness

The level of the child's neurological and physiological development determines the kinds of learning that can take place. Accordingly, the age at which a particular task should be taught to a child depends on the complexity of the skill, the degree of co-ordination and mental ability involved, and the rate of that particular child's development. A little practice at the appropriate stage of maturation is more effective than a lot when the child is too young.

Certain basic motor abilities appear to develop independently of any formal training. Both of the identical twins studied by Gesell and Thompson (37, 1929) developed skill in handling cubes, regardless of whether they had had special training. The twin who, at about one year of age, had been given six weeks' practice in climbing a short flight of stairs, later showed no superiority in this activity over the twin who had been given two weeks' training at a later time. McGraw (59, 1935) likewise found that the greater training given to Johnny did not make him permanently superior to his twin brother, Jimmy, in the ability to crawl and creep, to sit up, to reach and grasp objects. Little or no learning appears to be involved in the acquisition of these primitive abilities. In the more complex skills, however, such as swimming, diving, climbing up and down inclines, skating, jumping, or manipulating stools and boxes, training did make Johnny superior to untrained Jimmy. Instruction and practice begun with a maturity advantage produce more mature patterns of response than does premature training. On the other hand, readiness for a certain kind of learning often fades away if it is ignored. Accordingly, parents should be alert to detect individual readiness for learning to eat with a spoon, to comprehend words and simple directions, and to embark upon other accomplishments.

The role of satisfaction

The satisfaction that results from an activity plays an increasingly important role. The baby learns to repeat an activity that is accompanied or followed by an expression of maternal tenderness, a sense of comfort, a decrease of tension or anxiety, a relief from loneliness, or other satisfactions. At first, the baby expects satisfaction immediately. In time, he will anticipate satisfaction.

Emotional factors in learning

By the middle of the first year, emotional factors may have an acute effect on learning. The infant who, instead of actively reaching out to his environment, becomes passive and apathetic, ceases to learn. On the other hand, the infant who continues to grow up with a sense of being loved and cared for is, as Allport said, free to learn.

Failure to learn to walk, for example, may sometimes be traced to deprivation of affectionate relations. An eighteen-month-old boy, brought to the New York Foundling Hospital after the death of his father and the nervous breakdown of his mother, could neither walk nor talk. He did not even try. He was diagnosed as undernourished and retarded. The hospital's volunteer workers gave him a great deal of affection. They held him when he was being fed, put their arms around him and spoke to him as they passed by his crib. Within a few days his appetite improved. Two weeks later the diagnosis was much more favorable. Under this program of concerted loving care and approval, he began to walk and talk. Six months later he had gained nine pounds. In this case, fortunately, the initial deprivation had not been too extreme to be counteracted by tender loving care.

The self-system in learning

Underlying all other learning is the infant's growing awareness of himself. At first the infant does not distinguish between himself and the mother's breast. According to Linn (54, 1955), since the hand participates in a significant way in early feeding experiences, the infant first discovers the separateness of his hand and then learns to distinguish between his hand and his face. Through further experiences with his mother, he develops a concept of himself. Sullivan (96, pp. 161-164, 1953) has described the possible kinds of self-concepts as the *Good-me*, the *Bad-me*, and the *Not-me*. *Good-me* is "the beginning personification which organizes experience in which satisfactions have been enhanced by rewarding increments of tenderness, which come to the infant because the mothering one is pleased with the way things are going." (96, pp. 161-162, 1953) *Bad-me*, on the other hand, is the personification produced by tenseness instead of tenderness—by maternal behavior that is forbidding rather than accepting. *Not-me* is "a very gradually evolving personification"; it is poorly understood by the individual, and it involves dread and anxiety. When the self-system is involved, any individual tries to learn quickly in order to keep a feeling of security and to maintain his concept of himself.

INDIVIDUAL DIFFERENCES IN LEARNING

After unfavorable environmental conditions have been detected and corrected, the mother can settle down to accept certain individual fluctuations, lags, and lapses in her child's development. This was the attitude of the mother who thus described her child's fluctuations in learning to walk:

During Teddy's first two years, there was in almost everything he did a long gap between the time when he could manage with just a suggestion of help, and the time when he would venture unaided. For instance, he made no unaided attempts to sit up until 10 months, yet barely a month later he was taking long and enthusiastic walks down the road, with both hands held. The support he got was negligible, yet it was a long time before he would walk with only one hand held, and he didn't walk by himself until 17 months. Now at less than two years he is as steady as a rock on his feet, and whether walking or running rarely miscalculates or loses his balance.

Teddy took his own time about growing, and learned when he was good and ready. And his mother had been told there was something seriously wrong with a child who made no attempt to sit up at ten months!

There are sure to be ups and downs in learning, but the over-all trend is upward toward maturity. Progress in one activity, such as talking, may come to a standstill while the baby is learning another, such as walking. Young children tend to be completely absorbed in the activity of the moment. They also have a drive to use their newly acquired abilities—they babble interminably, creep assiduously, and put covers on boxes over and over again.

Sometimes infantile ways of behaving persist longer than desirable; sometimes a child reverts to baby ways that he abandoned some time ago. Such regressions often involve a consolidation and reorganization of behavior patterns and may signal the advent of an advanced stage of development.

WHY THE BABY LEARNS

The newborn seeks appropriate situations to which he can respond. He gets relief from discomfort by finding situations that offer him a maximum release of tension. Then he relapses into sleep. Before long, objects begin to take on meaning for the baby, not only because he can do something with them, but also because of the increase or decrease in tension which he associates with them. When he has gained more experience with the world of things, objects tell him what to do—a ball is to throw, stairs are to climb.

Some time during the middle of the first year the mother is almost certain to become anxious about her child's development and to feel he should be learning certain things. This attitude implies a certain amount of restriction. Thus the mother's tenderness takes on the nature of a reward for something learned or something done right. A slight increase of tension on the infant's part serves him as a warning or an indication that he had better change his behavior. This motivation to infant learning has been described by Sullivan (96, pp. 158-160, 1953) as comprising "gradients of anxiety." The child learns to do the things that reduce his anxiety and to avoid the activities that increase it. Thus, some important learning results from the child's attempt to cope with his anxiety. However, it should be noted that severe, unfocused anxiety disrupts learning.

Babies learn first those things that have emotional meaning for them. They learn to act in ways that bring them, first, relief from discomfort, then positive satisfaction or pleasure, and later, security in personal relations.

HOW TO FACILITATE LEARNING

There are three ways in which adults can help a baby learn the things appropriate for him during his first two years. The first is to establish and maintain the constructive personal relations which have already been emphasized. The second is to provide an environment in which he will find appropriate stimuli at each stage of his growth. During the first six months, the baby's crib, his carriage (for trips), his mother's arms, and a few safe and sanitary toys constitute a sufficiently stimulating environment. The third is to guide him in the use of this environment.

Outdoor play materials

When he begins to creep and walk and to grasp things, his environment expands. Suitable play material is an invitation to learning. The child's attention span increases with age; suitable toys also help to extend it. The closer a toy comes to satisfying the child's needs, the higher its developmental value will be (68, 1955). However, a brightly colored rolled-oats box or a pack of cards may have more appeal for a year-old baby than expensive toys (61, 1955).

The toddler who has fields and paths to wander about in, little hills and steps to climb, children and pet animals to play with, flowers, birds, trees, and farm animals to look at and feed and listen to, has a wealth of learning experiences. In the open country there are many objects the child can handle—rocks, pebbles, branches of trees, logs, chips, small sticks, milkweed pods, dandelions, and daisies. These play materials are not found on the neat, well-groomed lawn of a suburban house.

However, almost any backyard can be furnished with a few boxes of assorted sizes—apple boxes to crawl into and around, smaller boxes to build with. Satisfactory "wagons" can be made out of cans free from sharp ragged edges: punch a hole in one end and put a strong piece of string through it. An old bell or a can full of pebbles will furnish the noise so satisfying to two-year-olds. Some place can usually be found in which to hang a low, strong swing. Trains, fire engines, autos, kiddie cars, and other toys to pull or push or move about in are popular at this age. Wagons, doll carriages, and wheelbarrows are particularly helpful to children who are just beginning to walk, because they give a little extra support. A plank raised from the ground at one or both ends trains the sense of balance and provides the thrill of adventure. A box of beach sand, or a small plot of ground, well dug up, so that there is plenty of loose dirt for making mud pies, furnishes primitive, but very important, play material. What difference does it make if one corner of the yard looks disheveled? The child can eventually be taught to keep the rest of the yard tidy.

The same play materials may be used on the well-fenced-in roof of an apartment house. There are many flat city roofs which are going to waste as far as children are concerned. They would be ideal, convenient city play spaces—sunny, and free from some of the noise, dust, and dangers of the streets. One apartment house has organized its own roof nursery school where the preschool youngsters play together under the direction of one or two mothers who take turns supervising. The boxes, sand table, and other apparatus were bought co-operatively. There is a little house where the individual children's toys are kept, so that wagons, balls, pails, and the like do not have to be carried up and down each day. Each child learns to put his toys away each day in his own locker, and to respect the possessions of the other children. The mothers in charge seldom have to say "Don't" or otherwise interfere with the children's activities, because there is nothing on the roof that the children should not play with. The occasional squabbles that do arise over toys furnish opportunities for learning to get along with others and to take turns.

It is the freedom to explore and learn that is important, not the place itself. This freedom may be secured in cities and villages as well as in the open country.

Indoor play materials

Indoors, the two-year-old enjoys small household articles—a little broom, washtub, iron, and hammer. At this age he likes to play with doll's furniture. Irregular pieces of wood left by a carpenter are often more fun to play with than expensive blocks. Toys should be as large as the child can manage. They should be things that he can make a noise with, build with, cause to move, ride on, or manipulate in some way.

His nursery, or his own corner of a larger room, should contain low cupboards and shelves in which he puts away his toys, picture books, crayons, pencils, paper, blocks, and other belongings. He should have a low table and chair of just the right size, so that when he sits down his elbows are at the level of the table and his feet flat on the floor.

LEARNING MOTOR CONTROL

Beginning to walk

The child has a strong urge to walk. Even in countries where the baby's movements are hampered by swaddling children make progress as soon as they are free to use their bodies. This means that in learning to walk maturation plays an important role.

Environmental factors also enter in. For example, one twelve-month-old baby was making steady progress in learning to walk without help. One day he slipped on a small rug and fell on the slippery hardwood floor, hitting his head. This one painful experience delayed his progress. The fall made him unwilling to continue his attempts. As long as walking brought satisfaction, progress was made. When it produced more pain than pleasure, progress was interrupted. Some environments provide more incentives for walking than others—things to get hold of, children to play with, the pleasure of fond parents in the baby's first steps.

What can the mother or nurse do to help the baby learn to sit, stand, and walk? At least two things are essential—food, and freedom with safety. The child needs adequate food to build muscle and bone. He needs freedom for developing and learning to control his muscles. A clean sheet spread on a rug where there are no drafts is a safe place for the baby to turn and kick and squirm freely, unhampered by clothing. A little pen along the sides of which the child can pull himself up to standing position is helpful about the sixth or seventh month. Again the best policy is that of "adult guidance in line with the child's own pattern of growth." Adults provide conditions favorable to the child's learning to walk, but they let him take his own time in beginning to sit, stand, and walk. Thus they avoid the danger of strain from premature, forced attempts to sit up and to walk.

All babies tumble while learning muscular control, but mothers soon learn that babies are not breakable. They can bump around quite a bit without damage. Continual admonitions to be careful may check their emerging desire for independence and overemphasize their vulnerability in a dangerous world. Of course, there are situations in which a heedless little child might be seriously injured. To prevent these serious injuries the mother should never leave the inexperienced baby alone, except in a crib with raised sides, in a baby pen, or in some other place from which he cannot fall. One mother thought her four-month-old baby was safe on the bed because he had not yet learned to creep or crawl. But while the mother was out of the room, Bobby managed to wriggle to the edge of the bed and tumble over. To ensure the baby's safety while he is learning to creep, it is best to wait until he tries to get off a bed; then instead of picking him up and putting him on the floor, help him to learn to slide down himself, feet first. The baby should also be taught to slide downstairs in the same careful way, step by step, before serious accidents have a chance to occur. In these ways the baby learns to take care of himself.

Two-year-olds get "into everything." The problem is twofold: to provide enough things that they can "get into" without harming themselves or making trouble for others, and to remove from the house and surroundings as many things as possible that might harm them—poisonous substances, matches, and the like. At the same time they can be taught what to do in situations that might prove dangerous or annoying. For example, a father told his child that the stove was hot and would hurt. The child touched it anyway, and the father said, "See, stove is hot; it burns; Polly shouldn't touch."

Learning to pick up objects

The varied movements which the newborn makes are the capital he has to invest in new combinations of skills. At first his hands will fumble with the small rubber toy; finally, they will succeed in grasping it in an awkward manner. He should be allowed to "try, try again" without much help from adults. Left alone to solve the difficulties he meets in picking up objects, he will learn to work things out for himself. Overcoming difficulties gives even a baby a satisfying feeling of power. Occasionally he may be shown a more convenient way of grasping than the one he learns by chance. Although most infants follow the same general sequence in learning to pick up objects, they do not use any single method to the exclusion of other methods.

When the baby is in the fumbling stage, the mother can provide objects small enough to be grasped easily, but too large to be swallowed. At this stage of getting acquainted with his world, he needs things to handle, fit together, build with. To spank his hands before he can clearly understand what he is doing wrong or appreciate the reason for it, and to be constantly saying "No, no," will promote anxiety and confusion rather than learning.

At about six months of age, the tendency to put things in the mouth is very strong. That is natural; it is an important way of learning about objects. The hands will in time find other interesting things to do, and the hand-mouth pathway should slowly fade out. If the baby is left alone too much of the time with nothing to look at or to play with, he may amuse himself by sucking his thumb. Rattles, strong celluloid or rubber rings and animals, unbreakable dolls, blocks, untearable picture books, finger paints, nests of hollow blocks, spools, buttons and beads on strings that will not break, small lids and covers, and aluminum spoons and cups are all suitable toys for the first year. Each of these objects practically demands that the baby do something with it.

Learning to look

The toys suggested above supply experiences that the baby needs in learning to use and co-ordinate eyes and hands. At this stage the mother should introduce only one or two objects at a time and let him look at things as long as he likes. Moving from room to room, or from indoors to the street or garden, increases his interest in learning to look and see.

Learning to feed himself

Whenever the baby is ready to use a spoon like the rest of the family, he should be given an opportunity to learn to use one. Of course, teaching him to feed himself is at first more trouble than feeding him; but if the mother continues to feed him, he may lose his eagerness to learn to feed himself.

The mechanics of feeding should be made as easy as possible. The spoon should be of medium size. A piece of oilcloth on the table and another under the baby's chair, and even a bib made of the same material, will prevent worry and impatience when the baby spills a good deal, as he is sure to do at first. It is easier to fill the spoon from a bowl with deep sides than from a shallow plate. The top of the table should be at about the level of his waist. The child should be able to rest his feet flat on the floor, or on some firm support. Books, or a box of the right height, may be used as a footstool.

The mother may place the spoon in the correct position, guide the hand to the mouth a few times, and show approval of his effort. The step-by-step method brings best results. At first he should not be expected to feed himself during the entire meal. When he tires, the mother may help with the last few spoonfuls.

Learning to dress himself

Before the baby is a year old he can begin to help in the process of undressing. During the second year he should have plenty of practice in learning to dress himself, as soon as he shows readiness. Since taking off his clothes is easier than putting them on, that should come first. The next step may be putting his arms and legs through the proper openings. The mother may call the child's attention to armholes by games and songs. By two years of age he may learn to put on his stockings. Buttoning is one of the most difficult processes. Experiments suggest that between the second and third birthdays parents may expect their children to begin to button some of their own clothing part of the time. Unbuttoning is easier than buttoning, and buttons in front are easier to manage than buttons on the side or in the back.

The child is more likely to co-operate if the person dressing him is gentle and cheerful, chooses clothes that are easy to slip on, encourages him to help, and sees that he gets satisfaction from his attempts to learn.

The teaching of skills frequently has far-reaching effects even in the first two years. Acquiring one skill may change the child's general attitude. One three-year-old became restless and a little defiant—a noticeable change from his former co-operative self. The family paid little direct attention to his changed behavior, but reduced all possible demands. He had been nearly to the point of being able to dress himself, but still needed help at several points. They taught him some little tricks that helped him to dress himself more quickly. For example, he learned to spread his clothes out in order and to complete whole stages in the process for himself. He still asked for help but now he, instead of the adult, was in command of the situation. He was proud of this shift in responsibility and said, "I'm a big boy. I'm almost grown up. See, I can dress myself." Just getting enough control over the techniques of dressing so that he could care for himself seemed to be an important factor in overcoming his lapse into irritability. The acquisition of skills is an aid to independence and to personalty development.

LEARNING THE LANGUAGE

Even during the first months of life, a child's progress in the preverbal phase of language may be influenced by his personal relations. The baby's learning seems to depend to a considerable extent on the reassuring, loving quality of the mother's voice, especially as it is associated with pleasant experiences. Sex differences in children's language development may be related to differences in parent-child relations with boys and girls. Several important researches have shown that children deprived of personal attention, play activities, and interesting things to do show marked lacks in their language and mental development, as well as in their personality development (58, 1954). In a favorable emotional climate, children who have the ability learn to talk when it serves some need or interest.

Every baby at first has a language of his own. Babbling comes naturally to him. The sounds that come out surprise and delight him. He keeps on making them, babbling interminably. He needs this experience in trying out the many sounds he will use later in speaking a language. He imitates his own favorite sounds; he learns sounds in his native language through his own natural vocal play. If the adult repeats words that resemble some of the baby's sounds, the child will say them again with a little more of the adult's pronunciation and tone of voice.

From the babble stage a baby's language may develop in a number of directions—into "baby talk," careless, inaccurate speech, or cultured speech. The direction it takes depends partly upon the way in which people respond to his attempts.

Parents can facilitate a baby's language development in three main ways: (1) by maintaining a parent-child relationship in which the child is accepted as he is and allowed to develop at his own pace; (2) by providing an environment in which there are interesting experiences, frequent conversation, and good language usage on which the child can draw whenever he wants to; and (3) by associating a given word or phrase, at "teachable moments," with an object or action that is highly interesting to the child. Learning the language is part of a larger pattern—part of a happy association between parent and child.

Among factors that favor speech development are new experiences, picture books, songs, rhymes, and stories, as well as the constant stimulus of correct, distinct speech as used by adults and other children. Interesting sights and sounds, outdoor trips, looking out into a busy street—all sorts of experiences give the child new ideas, which he wants to talk about. Picture books about familiar animals, persons, and objects enlarge the child's experience still further.

There are many ways of encouraging language development within the framework of a satisfying relationship. By taking time to talk with the baby, to name and explain familiar objects and activities in which he is interested, to answer his questions, and to tell him stories about himself and his activities, parents can maintain a happy association with the baby, and, incidentally, increase his vocabulary. While the baby is dressing, the mother can name rhythmically the various articles of clothing as they are put on. Lucy Sprague Mitchell (65, 1921) has shown the poetic possibilities of such rhythmic enumeration. The words the child naturally learns first are those which he needs in his familiar environment, such as

"milk," "bread," "table," "chair," "coat," "hat," "shoe," "water," "drink."
Listening to the child's chatter is important, too. He needs to repeat words
over and over to gain control of the muscles of his tongue, mouth, and
throat. Some parents are afraid the child is stuttering when he makes
repetitious attempts to get words out. If they attach anxiety to this natural
repetition of sounds, it may become fixed as a habit. Some children have
too little stimulation toward learning new words; others have too much
supervision. Forced vocabulary drill sometimes causes the child to take a
negative attitude toward learning.

BUILDING EMOTIONAL PATTERNS

Emotional patterns, which are largely learned, influence all further
learning. The parents' attitudes toward themselves, toward each other,
and toward the child do most to create the emotional climate for the
baby.

The late Dr. Plant developed the important concepts of "whatness"
and "whoness." That is, some parents are only interested in *what* the
child can accomplish. They are primarily concerned that he be a credit
to them. This attitude may make them overanxious about his training, and
lead them to withdraw their affection when he is not so responsive, so
bright, or so cute as they had hoped.

If the basic emotions and attitudes of the parents are favorable, the
voice of experience and experiment may generally be followed with confidence. However, the situation may have different meanings for different
children and different meanings for the same child at different times.
Children's physical conditions vary; they feel varying degrees of security
and anxiety; they differ in previous knowledge and present ways of responding. There is no substitute for continuous sensitivity to the needs of the
individual child in his particular environment.

Learning not to be afraid

The child's unfamiliarity with the infinitely complex world around
him makes it difficult for him to know what to make of a strange face, a
sudden noise, or a novel situation. He cannot tell whether it be threatening or not; and if it were, he would have no effective way of responding
or defending himself. His difficulty is compounded by his inability to
use word symbols efficiently to help differentiate between threatening and
nonthreatening situations or objects. This lack of specificity in fears which

are learned during the preverbal stage is one reason why they are especially difficult to identify and eradicate in later years.

One of the child's greatest needs at this stage of development is a sense of basic trust. This can be promoted if parents introduce the child to a variety of situations—new faces, animals, and unusual sounds—in a manner in which the child can feel assured. The child can be encouraged to rely on the facial expressions and tone of voice of his parents as cues to aid discrimination. After a sudden bump, a six-month-old baby will often look at his mother as though to find out the appropriate response to the event. A hearty chuckle will often elicit a broad smile whereas profuse sympathy would provoke tears. A two-year-old on the beach who was about to cry as a wave came up around his feet, when he saw his sister enjoying it, laughed and splashed as she did.

New fears are acquired as new experiences are associated with earlier experiences that induced fears. Ignorant nurses may implant fears of policemen, burglars, animals, or ghosts in order to secure obedience. The temptation to use fear for this purpose is strong because it is such an easy way to control the behavior of little children. Shutting them in a dark closet after having created a fear of the dark, telling them the bears will get them, telling them the policeman will carry away bad children—such disciplinary devices belong to the Dark Ages. Use of fear as a means of controlling children's behavior is likely to produce two kinds of children: the defiant child who disbelieves the threats and refuses to be intimidated; and the nervous, timid child who is afraid of innumerable things.

Fear is part of a larger pattern. If a child continually shows timidity, the adult should examine the entire life of the child—his relations and satisfactions—and look especially for demands and pressures that need to be lessened. Fear which is understood and localized is less harmful to the child than severe anxiety, which is incomprehensible and vague (see Chap. 5).

Learning to handle anger

From an early age infants show differences in their tolerance of frustration. At first, this is evident chiefly in relation to being fed. Frequent intense outbursts of anger are destructive. It is therefore desirable to know how they may be prevented, and how treated when they occur. For example, a baby who is taking an active part in dressing himself is not so likely to get angry at his mother, who is now aiding his movements and desires, rather than thwarting them. If it is necessary to carry him away from some interesting activity, his attention may first be attracted to some little object which he may carry with him without interfering with his mother's plans. Nor should the baby have to experience continued failure to get the things he wants: his mother's presence, success in some physical activity, toys that are in another room. If he cannot reach something he desires, the object should be moved a little nearer so that he can get it with reasonable effort. Helping the baby just a little in these indirect ways, when he cannot yet understand the cause of his anger, gives him a sense of achievement in place of a sense of failure and frustration.

Physical irritations such as sore gums, chapped skin, mosquito bites, and indigestion predispose a child to anger. Parents should make allowances for these discomforts.

It is, of course, impossible and probably undesirable to prevent all outbursts of anger. There are some things a child cannot do and some objects he should not touch. His second year is not too early for him to learn what he can do and what he cannot do in certain situations. Limits can be set. Moreover, the child needs to learn that his angry crying is not something to be feared. Neither he nor the world has been destroyed by his anger.

When a temper tantrum does occur, the parent should recognize the bewilderment and anxiety which this profound organic disturbance is causing to the child himself. Certainly his intense feelings should not be aggravated by spanking or by deprivation. When a baby cries and his needs are not met, he grows more uncomfortable and cries more loudly. When he really yells, the parent gets worried and relieves his distress. If, on the other hand, his needs are met as soon as he begins to cry or even before, the feeling tone is not intense. Since learning is related to the intensity of the drive, the chances of his learning to get what he wants by crying are greatly reduced. If he also gets loving attention at other times, he will not learn to use crying as a sole attention-getting device; he will know that he can get attention in many other ways. Thus he will not get the notion that only fretfulness gets rewards. He will use crying only as a last resort. The frequency and intensity of the child's outbursts of anger, and the nature of the parents' response to them, influence the child's attitude toward himself and the way he handles his feelings in the future (30, 1954).

In the early weeks, persistently leaving the child to "cry it out" may have a detrimental effect. If his crying is always in vain he may feel a vague sense of hopelessness and futility. This may lower his general level

Toddlers pass through teething troubles.

Every activity is an adventure to the toddler.

of aspiration. If this attitude persists it may seriously affect his future learning and emotional adjustment.

When, during the first year, babies show anger, adults and baby sitters can help most by (1) recognizing that anger is the baby's response to being hurt or unsuccessful or disappointed, (2) relieving his discomfort and helping him to achieve what he has been vainly trying to do, (3) remaining calm and accepting the baby's rage.

DECREASING THE "DON'TS"

To remove from the baby's environment as many as possible of the things that call forth parental "don'ts" is a negative way of providing for positive learning. If the mother will write down for several days the reason for every "don't," she will have an interesting list to study. It is surprising how many dangerous and destructive things an active two-year-old can start to do! Still, the mother may discover that many don'ts are occasioned by objects in the room or on the grounds that might just as well have been removed from the baby's sight or reach. Heavy urns, breakable bowls, books, bric-a-brac, loose pins and buttons, knives, and forks should be put away until the baby has learned to use them properly. The mother will also learn how many of her don'ts are really spoken in the interest of the baby's safety, and how many are not. A stairway without a gate, an open window that he can reach, machines that are running, scalding water, a chair so placed that he may tip over backwards—these dangerous situations may be avoided by forethought.

The following is a list of the don'ts which one mother said to her nineteen-month-old baby during *one day*:

Don't throw dollie out of the bed. [One morning the baby threw her doll and hit her mother on the head.]

Don't put the powder-can top in the water. [The powder-can top was given to the baby to play with during her bath.]

Don't pull the washcloth away from mother. [She thinks this is a good joke, and laughs when mother tries to get it away from her.]

Don't upset the water.

Don't pull the bureau cover off.

Don't pull the highchair over on you.

Don't touch spoons, knives, and forks. [She likes to go around "unsetting" the table.]

Don't slap the spoon with food in it. [She likes to push the spoon and spill its contents as she is being fed.]

Don't put your spoon in sister's plate. [She likes to take a sly dip out of someone else's plate.]

Don't kick the table. [By kicking against the table she can push her high-chair over backwards.]

Don't stand up in the highchair.

Don't pull the highchair apart.

Don't put the pin in your mouth.

Don't touch the bread.

Don't break any more wall. [The baby tries to break off bits of plaster from a crack in the wall.]

Don't put the plaster in your mouth.

Don't scratch the chair with the plaster.

Don't break the cup.

Don't pull the flowers up.

Don't walk in the mud.

Don't climb on the cellar door.

Don't shake your highchair.

Don't reach for the corncobs.

Don't reach for the dish. [When on mother's lap.]

Don't put the safety pin in your mouth.

To be sure, many objects in the environment are not removable. Bureau drawers must be used by adults. Bookcases cannot be emptied. Matches are difficult to keep out of the climbing baby's reach. However, to most of these hazards the baby can eventually learn to respond in a satisfactory way. If he wants to pull everything out of his mother's bureau drawer, he can be given a drawer or basket full of scraps of material and various objects, and told: "This is baby's. He can take everything out of this. This [the bureau drawer] is mother's. Baby must not open this." If he is noisy while his grandfather is taking a nap, he should be told to run on tiptoe and speak in a low voice. Later, when there is no occasion to be quiet, he should be told, "Grandpa isn't sleeping now. Now you may run and shout." In order to avoid harm from autos and other sources of danger, the child must learn that an out-and-out command must be obeyed instantly. These are situations where immediate obedience is imperative.

The second year is a practice year. The child should have plenty of opportunities to look around him, to handle objects under supervision, to talk, to express his feelings, and gain independence. He will improve on everything he started to learn in the first year. During the second year he must learn the meaning of no. The "no-nos" should be definite, but as few as possible. Until the child has sufficient language ability and ex-perience to comprehend explanations, a short, decisive "No," or "Don't do that," is effective. Later, it is helpful to give the reasons for a request; older children and adolescents expect and appreciate it.

SUMMARY: HOW TO HELP THE BABY LEARN

For the baby, living is learning. Seen from his point of view, everything he learns is the result of trying to get something he wants or to do something he feels the urge to do. Life is one learning opportunity after another.

The role of adults is to try to understand the baby's behavior, provide a favorable environment, set the stage for success, and lend a helping hand when the baby cannot succeed without a little help. With just enough help, children can solve their own problems of growing up. It is facinating to watch a baby learn. Although it is impossible to generalize, a few specific suggestions—not prescriptions—are offered here to help bridge the gap between theory and practice:

1. Leave the baby free to grow, i.e., do not interfere unnecessarily with his activities; let him take his time.
   a. Leave him unhampered by unnecessary and unsuitable clothing.
   b. Allow him to look at things steadily and as long as he wishes to.
   c. Leave him free to kick and squirm and creep so that he will be ready to sit and to stand when the time comes for him to do so.
   d. Let him do things for himself; let him try to find a way out of his own difficulties, and let him make an effort to get the things he wants. Expect him to look out for his own needs as far as he is able.
   e. Encourage him to make his wants known through speech, and reward his successful attempts.
   f. Play with him, but avoid tiring him with too many unusual or exciting experiences.
   g. Plan the mechanical details of bathing and dressing so as to avoid unnecessary fear and irritation.
   h. Remove from the house as many things as possible that may harm the baby or give rise to many don'ts. Put away vases and dishes which the baby may break. Remember that he may pull down glass bowls and heavy ornaments if they are set on a tablecloth. Keep scissors and knives out of reach until the baby is old enough to learn to use them safely. Check the house for possible causes of accidents, such as low open windows, unprotected stairs, poisonous materials. By taking these precautions you will give the child a chance to explore without danger; you will make your house fit for a child to learn in. You will also relieve yourself of anxiety.
2. Provide an environment from which the child can select the experiences he needs at this stage of development. Give him opportunities for initiative and adventure. If he has suitable materials he may be expected to make

good use of them. Whatever the child does day by day becomes part of him.

   a. When he begins to want to handle things, place within his reach a few objects of convenient size.
   b. When he is learning to look for, reach for, and recognize special objects, place two or three things of interest near him.
   c. Provide colored balls and birds and other objects that are washable, nonbreakable, and colorfast for the baby to look at.
   d. Take him from room to room and outdoors on the street so that he will see new sights.
   e. Provide a little pen or something by which he can pull himself to a standing position when he feels so inclined.
   f. Talk to him with clear, slow, accurate articulation and varied inflections.
   g. Help him become acquainted with things that might harm him. For example, let him feel the heat of the stove for himself while you say, "Stove hot; hurts baby."
   h. Provide him with shoes and stockings that fit well, and roomy, easy-to-manage clothes that are durable and washable.

3. Provide, if possible, a pleasant, sanitary nursery with washable walls and floors, low shelves, a wicker wardrobe, homemade or ready-made toys, a box or cupboard in which to keep toys, a sunny window, a low rocking chair, a low, firm table. The colors in the room should be harmonious, and there should be one or two beautiful pictures, changed from time to time. If the baby cannot have a room of his own, a corner may be furnished for him.

4. Treat him consistently with respect to the fundamental routines, so that he knows what to expect. For example, maintain reasonable uniformity in the bedtime program. Do not hurry him to bed one night and permit people to frolic with him at bedtime another night.

5. At first follow his own physiological rhythms, but help him to settle down to reasonable regularity in feeding, sleeping, bowel movements, and exercise, as soon as he is ready and able to do so.

6. As far as possible, avoid situations that evoke undesirable responses; for example, offering him food that is slightly burned or spoiled may produce an aversion to that particular food.

7. Recognize and provide for individual differences. Temper the task to the child's ability. If the learning task is too difficult, he will give up and turn his attention to other things. Learning takes place when a child feels a need and recognizes that the knowledge and skill to satisfy it are within his power to acquire.

8. Try to do things *with* the baby, not *to* him. Wait for him to take part in an activity. For example, when you pick up a tiny baby, slide your hands under him, then wait until he curls up a little as an adjustment to being lifted. Let him be active rather than passive.

9. Enjoy the baby. Try not to be so careful and troubled about many details that you cannot enjoy him as well as love him. A consciousness that the

adults around him are confident and at ease is very comforting to the baby.
10. Make desirable behavior satisfying to the baby. Certain routine habits are most easily acquired if they are performed each day with satisfaction. It is satisfying to the baby to solve his own small difficulties.

In general, try to make pleasant the things that the baby ought to learn. Anatole France sums up this most important principle when he says: "I would make lovable to her everything I would wish her to love." (33, p. 198, 1918)

Questions and Problems

FOR CLASS DISCUSSION OR STUDY GROUPS

1. Observe a baby one or two years old in his attempt to learn something —to pick up an object, to use a spoon, etc. Note the processes he goes through and the conditions that seem to facilitate or retard his learning. Relate your observation to learning theory.

2. Record the don'ts spoken during a day to a one-to-two-year-old child of your acquaintance. Which of these were necessary? Show how the unnecessary don'ts could have been avoided. How did these unnecessary interferences with the child's activities seem to affect his relationship with the adult and his eagerness to learn?

3. Make a list of appropriate play materials for children between one and two, which even the poorest parents could afford. Describe safe places where babies might play in a given neighborhood. Pool these suggestions and have them mimeographed for parents in child-study groups, parent-teacher organizations, or other parent groups.

4. What changes take place in the learning process between birth and two years? What differences occur in drive or motivation? How do personal relations enter into a young child's learning?

5. Interview several mothers of children up to two years of age. What changes have there been in their attitudes toward their children, and in their methods of treating them, as the children grew older? What have the mothers done to facilitate their learning?

6. Read Fred S. Keller's *Learning Reinforcement Theory*, Garden City, New York: Doubleday and Company, Inc. 1954. What contribution has animal experimentation made to the understanding of the learning process? What principles of learning are stated and illustrated? Relate these principles to the specific suggestions for helping a child to learn that were given in this chapter.

7. Present a case or a description of a situation for analysis.

Chapter 8

PROBLEMS OF DEVELOPMENT

DURING THE FIRST TWO YEARS

By the word *problem* we mean a difficult step in the learning process, a troublesome but normal phase of development, or a deviation from the best development of a given child. Blatz has wisely said that what are commonly called problems or bad habits "are part and parcel of life, and that too much significance is attached to their seemingly *abnormal* aspect and too little to their value in the total learning scheme." (13, p. 731, 1933) More recently, Valentine (103, 1956) likewise has called attention to the fact that some of the instances of behavior that we call problems are a normal part of growing up. What adults call *problem behavior* is often the child's best way of meeting a situation.

This positive approach is taking precedence over the negative emphasis on problems. The Institute of Child Study of Toronto is concerned with ways of identifying and describing well children (102, 1956). Parents want to discuss the delights of rearing a family rather than the difficulties.

Even if a child has made a poor start, it may be corrected by later life experiences, with the help of an understanding adult or through association with a chum or a group of peers. For example, in a family limited in intelligence and income, but blessed with genuinely warm feelings toward one another, the development of one child took place as follows: At twenty months the child was unweaned, had temper tantrums, and was retarded in language development. At this time a clinical study of the child was made and discussed with the mother. Four months later the tantrums were less violent; he had begun to talk and was gradually giving up the bottle. At two years, four months, he ate well and talked well, but was jealous of the new baby. At three years, two months, his appetite was fine, and he had no tantrums or other difficulties that were not a normal part of the growing-up process. Here was a child who was getting off to a poor start. The parents recognized this and sought help in time. At the guidance clinic they gained knowledge of themselves and

112

of child development. They were able to change the child's environment, including their behavior toward him, in a few simple ways. Self-knowledge and knowledge of child development, in a setting of genuine affection for the child, are the keys to good parenthood.

"All God's chillun got problems." Vigorous living inevitably involves conflicts and difficulties. We should not want our children to achieve a pathological passivity. The healthy personality is characterized not by an absence of problems, but by a constructive manner of viewing and solving them. This is the viewpoint toward problems that is presented in the chapters of this book.

THE PROCESS OF SOCIALIZATION

It is obvious that the helpless, kicking, uninhibited infant must eventually be transformed into a responsible adult. The questions are: How soon? How gradually? By what methods? The child needs to learn the ways of civilized life in order to promote his own stability and a sense of security, as well as to ensure the comfort and convenience of others. Socialization involves gradually settling down to a three-meal-a-day schedule, with midmorning and midafternoon fruit juice, or crackers and milk, as recommended by the physician. It involves learning to eat solid food and use table utensils. Toward the end of the second year, socialization requires attention to bowel and bladder control. Psychologically, socialization means a gradual recognition of others' rights, and a realization that one is not the center of the universe. Learning the ways of civilized life also requires some modification of infantile ways of satisfying desires, and an understanding of the meaning of obedience to reasonable requests.

Many behavior problems arise from conflict between the child's growth impulses and the demands of the culture. In a survey of five hundred parents (44, 1949), difficulties with routine care of children were found to rank second in frequency among the problems of parenthood. Problems of feeding, sleeping, dressing, and elimination were mentioned, even in the case of children up to the age of twelve. In extreme forms, a child's rebellion against socialization, i.e., training to conform to social customs, may be expressed in enuresis, psychic vomiting, and other bodily manifestations, as well as in temper tantrums, negativism, and other psychological reactions.

In dealing with conflicts over socialization, parents and teachers have three choices: (a) to ignore the child's natural tendencies and insist on conformity to social standards and customs, (b) to modify social customs, bringing them into closer accord with the child's developmental needs, and (c) to give the child skillful and sympathetic help in moving gradually in his own best way in the direction of socialization. According to psychoanalytic literature it would seem that, the more abrupt the socialization process, and the greater the pain associated with it, the frequency of punishment, and the severity of the emotional conflict produced, the greater would be the consequent anxiety (104, 1953). Follow-up studies by Harris and his associates at the University of Minnesota indicate that children reared by extremely permissive methods may also show anxiety and often find it hard to settle on their objectives in adulthood (39, p. 28, 1957-1958).

The child should be helped to make these adaptations to society, without acquiring feelings of guilt or unworthiness, or of resentment or resistance toward the persons who have been responsible for the training. Socialization should be a gradual, gentle educational process in which the child takes as much initiative and responsibility as possible.

BASIC IMPORTANCE OF HEALTH AND SAFETY

Adequate progress in social development also requires a healthy physical constitution. Among the conditions conducive to good health are sun and clean, fresh air. Exposure to untraviolet rays should be for only a few minutes at first; it may be gradually increased. The amount of ultraviolet radiation increases as one approaches the equator; it is greater at high altitudes than at sea level, in the summer than during the other seasons, and between 10 A.M. and 2 P.M. than other hours of the day. Actually, the deep blue sky radiates about as much ultraviolet light as the sun itself. Unfortunately these rays do not pass through clothing, ordinary window panes, thick clouds or fog, or the dust and smoke of cities. Of course, the baby's eyes should always be shielded from direct sunlight.

The baby's diet should be adequate in every respect to build positive health and to prevent flabby muscles, weak bones, poor teeth, and rickets. The physician will prescribe the diet that seems best for a particular baby. He will supervise the gradual introduction of solid foods. He will avoid fads.

Great progress has been made in preventing illness and death among babies during the first two years. In some communities immunization alone has practically eliminated some of the most serious diseases—diphtheria, for example. Nevertheless, in many places diphtheria is still one of the most serious diseases of infancy. It is the baby's right to be immunized against diphtheria between the ages of six and nine months. Immunization is the ounce of prevention that is worth a ton of cure. Whooping cough vaccine, given at about the age of six months, helps protect many babies from a disease which is especially dangerous for children up to two years of age. Before the baby is a year old he should also be vaccinated against smallpox—unless the doctor advises against vaccinating a particular child. The doctor will be cautious about using new vaccines and drugs; he will wait for adequate experimental proof of their effectiveness. Parents should avoid becoming excited by popular appeals and mass hysteria; they should not try to sway the doctor's carefully considered judgment.

There is increasing recognition of the relation between illness and the tensions created by anxiety and hostility. Disturbances in family relationships may be reflected to some degree in a variety of physical difficulties.

Accidents kill more children than polio, heart disease, pneumonia, leukemia, and tuberculosis combined. The only immunization for accidents lies in taking preventive measures (see Pages 107, 109). The adult must keep potentially harmful things out of the baby's reach and keep the baby away from danger until he has learned to protect himself.

SOME BAFFLING SITUATIONS
IN THE SOCIALIZATION PROCESS

The whole business of growing up must be quite baffling to the child who has reached his first birthday. Growing up means giving up some of the pleasures and security of infancy. He is expected to do more things for himself, learn to handle a cup instead of getting his milk the easy way, exert himself to begin walking instead of being carried. Occasionally, special problems arise—he loses a toy, his mother or father is away from home, death claims a pet or a loved person, he is frightened by a thunderstorm or some other loud sudden noise, or he is knocked down by a large animal or another child. In addition, he often fails to accomplish something he sets out to do. He cannot bounce the ball as he sees other children do or get a toy before another child reaches it. Repeated failures decrease his self-confidence.

At these times, understanding parents try to show him that they appreciate the difficulty with which he is faced. They understand his disappointment and his occasional retreats to the security of infancy. At other times they will show appreciation of his achievements and help him to gain faith in himself. Realizing that to him the world is still a vast, uncharted place, they will not hesitate to say no to something he should not do or have. This firmness is helpful; it gives him boundaries to his behavior, when otherwise he might get out of bounds.

When specific suggestions are given on the following pages, it is only to bridge the gap between theory and practice. The suggestions will work only if they are appropriate to the individual child, and if they are used by parents who feel fairly confident, are genuinely fond of the child, and are concerned for, but not over-anxious about, his well-being.

Bowel and bladder control

Although it is gratifying to the mother to have the child take this responsibility early, it may not be physiologically or psychologically best for the child to do so. Observers have noted that premature and unsympathetic training often results in constipation, temper tantrums, or other resistant or defensive reactions. Whereas these emotional disturbances, as well as later personality problems, probably arise from the total parent-child relationship rather than from specific training per se, the achievement of bowel and bladder control is of particular importance because of its effect on the child's developing sense of autonomy, or, negatively, on his feelings of doubt and shame (28, pp. 80-81, 1950). If faultless functioning is expected of him before he has mastered the required co-ordination, the child will find satisfaction and control only by either returning to infantile patterns that deny any responsibility for his own functioning and demand full attention of his mother, or by attaching so much anxiety to the process of eliminating that he may be unable to "let go." Since either behavior usually elicits considerable attention from the parents it tends to be sustained as a habit. Only by allowing the child to attempt the gradual control of his bowels and other functions willingly and by free choice can he achieve a sense of control and autonomy.

There seem to be several ages when bowel training can be accomplished—not without transient difficulties. Before the child is a year old, he takes little interest in his bowel movements. Even though he can frequently anticipate his eliminations, they are still quite irregular, and he is not actively co-operative. By the beginning of the second year he takes a more positive interest and pride in using the toilet. Before the end of the year he can give some sign that a movement is coming. This awareness, sharpened by his recollection of how uncomfortable he feels when he is soiled, and by the pleasure that his parents show when he notifies them, leads him to give the signal in time. Imitation of another child may also play a part in successful bowel control. Sometimes the sense of independence that a child gains from learning to walk makes him more ready to tackle the problem of bowel control.

It is most important to recognize the child's feeling about the matter and encourage his active co-operation. He wants to feel that he can do it himself. The parent can help by taking a positive approach when he does not quite succeed: "Next time, you'll tell me in time; then you'll feel so nice and clean." (91, pp. 245-260, 1957) Any progress made should be reinforced immediately instead of waiting to reward the complete response.

The child usually achieves bowel control before bladder control, and daytime bladder control before control at night. The baby has to give his attention to one problem at a time. The mother notes his natural rhythm and anticipates his need. If he is picked up and taken to the toilet in time, he will feel pleased with the comfortable dry feeling, and with his mother's approval. The next step is his own recognition that he should go to the toilet. At first he speaks of his need too late—this is not naughtiness; it shows real progress. Soon he will be able to announce it far enough in advance. Still later he will go of his own accord. The majority of babies usually become dry in the daytime between one and a half and two and a half years. Keeping dry at night comes a little later—between two and three years.

To summarize, bowel and bladder control will be most easily gained if the parent can provide these favorable conditions:

Wait until the baby is sufficiently mature physically to control his movement.

Wait until the child can attach words to the objects or functions over which he seeks control.

Remove wet diapers promptly so that the baby learns to appreciate the comfortable, dry feeling.

Be gentle and understanding when the baby soils his diaper after he has begun to make progress. Control is difficult for him. Show pleasure when he succeeds; try not to show annoyance or disappointment when accidents occur.

Have a simple little toilet chair just the baby's size. Such a chair is comfortable and inexpensive. A father handy with tools can make it himself.

Try not to be tense, rigid, or anxious about getting control established, since this attitude may increase the child's need to defend himself against being changed.

Children need the parents' encouragement and guidance in gaining control; a three- or four-year-old child who has not achieved bowel or bladder control may have a feeling of inferiority if his peers have already achieved it.

Weaning

Giving up the pleasure of nursing is a real problem for the infant. Nursing contributes to the sense of "togetherness" between mother and child. Weaning disrupts an emotional relation that has been a source of satisfaction from infancy. However, many well-adjusted children have been fed from the beginning with a bottle, or even with a cup. The important factor is the parent-child relation in the situation as a whole, not in any single process such as weaning. If an affectionate relation has been established between child and mother, the child is likely to accept weaning as a somewhat unpleasant part of a generally satisfying relationship.

Weaning has a positive aspect; it gives the baby new satisfactions, such as greater independence and the chance to learn new skills; it is a step toward maturity. The weaning from the mother's breast in infancy has its counterpart in the psychological weaning that must occur at adolescence. From infancy to adulthood there is a gradual weakening of the infantile satisfactions that arise from close dependence upon other persons.

Weaning should be a gradual process. Many pediatricians introduce orange juice and tomato juice in small amounts during the first or second month. Then gradually, to accustom the baby to the taste of different foods, they give him water in which vegetables have been cooked, a half-teaspoon of sifted vegetables or fruit, cereal gruel, or other foods. Even after the ninth month, however, new foods should be introduced slowly. There is no need to hurry and no need to add new foods to the diet at a specified time if the weather is very hot, or the baby is not quite so well as usual. If the step-by-step method is used, the child will accept the gradual change.

Eating

Many mothers are putting their babies on what are variously called "self-demand," "self-regulation," or "self-selection" schedules. That is, they give the baby (within limits) what he wants to eat when he wants it. In other words, they are flexible and responsive to the child's bodily rhythms and needs for food, warmth, and comfort. Self-regulation in the feeding of babies has gained much support from Davis' studies (23, 1931). Although the number of children she studied was small, the results of her experiments with spontaneous food selection have had great influence on practice. Her newly weaned babies were offered trays which contained a large array of foods. Even though their diets were not balanced day by day, over a period of time the babies chose a balanced diet that seemed to meet their nutritional needs. The baby who is fed when he is hungry also tends, after many fluctuations, to settle down to a schedule very much like that recommended by pediatricians. This fact is reassuring to mothers. However, the self-selection program is not without its difficulties—difficulties of providing the proper variety of foods, of acquiring sufficient knowledge of nutrition to check the child's choices, of dealing with distorted appetites and habits, and of counteracting the child's occasional failure to select the foods that he needs.

Insofar as infants choose their food and their mealtimes in accordance with their bodily needs, the mother should not insist that every single meal be balanced, or that the child invariably eat all the food he is offered. If he refuses to eat cereal but likes bananas, the mother may give him bananas and milk. Children—like adults—seem to go through periods when they eat everything in sight and other times when they do not want much to eat. The self-demand method has put the emphasis on the child himself, rather than on prescribed amounts of food to be eaten, or precise times of day at which feeding is to take place.

A baby often refuses unfamiliar food. It is natural for him to spit it out. If he does so, it may not mean that he dislikes it. It may be merely that he is surprised by the new consistency or flavor or, perhaps, that he has not learned to swallow solid food. If food is well prepared and wholesome, if it is introduced gradually, and if the child feels free to choose whether he will eat it or not, he will learn to acquire a reasonable repertory of tastes. Among the thirty-six children at St. George's Nursery School, there were only 103 refusals of food out of a total of 7,438 opportunities over a period of six months. Twelve children never refused any food. The three dishes most frequently refused were rice, casserole of beef and tomato, and vegetable marrow (13, pp. 742-743, 1933).

Psychological and social elements often enter into the feeding situation—parental anxieties and desires, as well as the emotional needs of the infant. Refusing to eat or overeating are ways in which a child may express antagonism toward the parent; overeating may occur in some children who are alternately loved and rejected. The following sequence is quite common. Parents desire a child who will be a credit to them, will enhance their social status; they are much concerned with the child's nutritional condition; the child learns that he can gain privileges by refusing food; he does so, and shows signs of malnutrition. This increases the mother's anxiety and she goes to almost any lengths to "get food into him." Because of his poor nutrition the child has less energy and vitality to cope with daily situations. Consequently, he may show an inferior social adjustment as well as an inferior physical appearance. This makes him less acceptable to the parents and increases their frustration.

Escalona (29, 1945) reported examples of the influence of the adult on feeding disturbances in babies from ten days to twenty-four months in age. Babies refused tomato juice and orange juice when it was offered them by adults who showed dislike for the juice, or adults who were disliked by the babies. Babies commonly refused solid food when it was first presented. Refusals of solid food were less intense

if the infant was fed by a fairly relaxed person, if he was fed slowly, if his attention was directed to each approaching spoonful and he was allowed to touch it, if he was well supported in an upright sitting position, and if the person feeding talked to him in a quiet and encouraging manner. [29, pp. 78-79, 1945]

Infants who were fussy about food were generally unstable in other respects. Severe feeding problems arose in response to events not directly connected with the eating situation, such as loss of a loved person or even lack of success in learning to walk. When the person in charge of the baby is tense or unhappy there is likely to be an increase in mealtime tantrums, refusal of food, vomiting, and other eating disturbances. Eating behavior may serve as "an especially sensitive indicator of the infant's general adjustment," and of the status of the parent-child relationship.

In summary, the baby is more likely to get the food he needs if the adult fulfills the following conditions:

Gives him affection as well as food, relaxes and enjoys the baby while she is feeding him.

Watches the baby rather than the clock. Although a three-hour, and later a four-hour, schedule of feedings is satisfactory for many babies, the schedule should be changed if it does not seem to fit a particular baby. If he wakes up at 4 a.m. it is best to feed him then, before he cries hard and long, and gradually to let him work out a flexible schedule that seems best for him and not too hard on the rest of the family.

Introduces him to only one new food at a time, and this in very small amounts.

Gives him a new solid food at the beginning of the feeding period when he is hungry.

Tastes the food to see whether it has a burned, bitter, or otherwise unpleasant taste that might cause the baby to spit it out.

Does not force the baby to eat. The surest way to create a feeding problem is to force a child to eat when his physiological need for certain foods is low.

Does not begin weaning too early or too abruptly; waits for the baby to show a readiness to give up the breast or bottle. In fact, children tend to "resist anything suddenly introduced or anything that is too much at variance with the status quo." (13, p. 737, 1933)

Substitutes, in case of refusal, another food with similar values, and later tries the first food again.

Keeps the baby's mealtime quiet and pleasant. The baby is disturbed by fussing, coaxing, too much talk, the presence of many people while he is eating.

It is better and easier to create favorable feeding conditions from the beginning than to try to correct poor food habits later on.

Sleeping

Sleep is normal and necessary. The baby's natural rest rhythms can be gradually modified so as to conform to the convenience of adults. After the first month or two, most children gradually increase their waking hours until, at the end of the first two years of life, they are accustomed to a long nighttime sleep and a daytime nap of an hour or two. Although individual children vary in their sleep requirements, the bedtime of a particular child should be fairly regular, despite the many possible interferences. On the other hand, children should not be abruptly sent to bed. A happy pre-bedtime period following an active day should be the prelude to a sound night's sleep in a clean, airy, familiar room.

Why, then, do parents have so much difficulty in getting two-year-olds to go to sleep? At this age there are a number of reasons why a child may resist going to bed: He is giving up the fun of being with people and is being separated from them. Staying up with older children and adults may make him feel more grown-up. Or the dark may harbor frightening shapes he does not yet understand (see Chapter 7).

Overfatigue may also be a cause of wakefulness in young children. When a child first begins to creep and walk, he is fascinated by his own locomotion and uses up a tremendous amount of energy. Ordinarily, however, he will take short periods of rest of his own accord. If a child becomes so tired that he cannot sleep, the parent should examine conditions in the child's life as a whole. Such a child may be helped if the mother sings or talks to him, or plays some quiet game for a few minutes whenever she has time and he shows readiness. If they understand the reasons why a child refuses to go to sleep, the parents will not make the mistake of scolding him when he really needs comforting (27, 1956).

Thumb-sucking

Thumb-sucking and other forms of nonnutritive sucking are common to almost all infants between birth and one year. It tends to become rapidly more frequent up to three months, lets up between six and ten months, and often recurs toward the end of the first year. The parent need not be concerned about spasmodic thumb-sucking during the first two years. Fussing about it may make a habit out of what would otherwise have been a passing phase of development. Some of the most troublesome cases seem to have been caused by scolding the child or otherwise attaching emotional significance to the habit before the child has had a chance to outgrow it.

Thumb-sucking appears to be most directly an expression of hunger or loneliness, unhappiness, or overfatigue (81, 1957); it is therefore important to search for and do something about the basic disturbance. The effect of insufficient sucking at the breast or bottle on thumb-sucking (85, 1950) seems to depend upon the degree of acceptance or rejection experienced by the child, and thus indirectly upon parental attitude and the home environment—in fact, the whole personal-social situation. No single factor can account for thumb-sucking.

The most important remedy is the provision of a satisfying life situation—to see to it that the baby is happy and secure; that he has enough of the right kind of food to meet his nutritional needs; that he has playthings that use his hands in interesting ways; and that the adult does not get excited when the baby puts his thumb or fingers in the mouth.

As with all the problem situations described, the child's thumb-sucking causes the parents a great deal of anxiety. The greater the anxiety, the greater are the parents' attempts to correct the "problem behavior." However, if the child ordinarily gets little love and affection from his parents, he will be motivated to continue and even increase this behavior. Thus "problem behavior" for the parents becomes "attention-getting behavior" for the child. Since these parents often see problems in much of their child's behavior, the child learns a whole repertory of attention-getting devices.

Negativism

Nature of negativism. At some time during his second or third year the child frequently becomes "contrary." He says no even to reasonable suggestions. "Stubbornness," the mother may call it. He "wants what he wants when he wants it." He insists upon doing the opposite of what the mother or nurse tells him to do. With girls, this kind of behavior appears to reach a peak near the end of the second year; with the boys, near the end of the third year. It appears to last longer and to be more severe with boys. After the third year it tends to decrease.

Explanations of negativism. This resistance to authority is a sign of growing independence. It represents the child's effort to assert his newly discovered self, to prove that he has a mind of his own, to develop his own individuality. It may also represent the child's naïve attempt to make the world conform to his whim. Of course, this is a futile attempt. The world is indifferent and strong. The child has to learn this through his early experiments in resistance.

Negativism may also be explained partly by the child's lack of knowledge, experience, and competence in verbal expression. The two- or three-year-old is constantly confronted with situations that he does not understand, and is continually expected to do things for which he has not yet acquired the skill. His first reaction to these difficulties is resistance. His refusal to act is a defense against demands that are beyond his power. Later, if his environment is favorable, and if he receives skillful guidance from adults, he learns by experience that he can meet difficulties in more satisfying ways; he then gradually ceases to use his first infantile way out.

Sometimes a child responds in a negative way to a person whom he does not like. He refuses to do anything the person asks; he even rejects the person's praise. Toilet-training sometimes becomes a battleground where the child asserts his will against the wishes of his parents.

Negativism is probably an outcome of a complex situation into which the following factors may enter:

1. Overprotecting or "babying" the child at certain times and in certain aspects of his life, and applying undue pressure on him not to be a baby in other situations and at other times.

2. Being impatient with his slowness.

3. Giving the child unrealistic choices—asking him if he would like to eat, put on his hat, etc., when actually he has no choice. If he says no, the adult resents it.

4. Making unreasonable demands on him; saying "No, no" to him too frequently.

5. Tactlessly interfering with the child's activities.

Acute negativism seems to occur more often when parents lack real understanding of the child as a person, or lack interest in or respect for his rights, wishes, and feelings. Or it may arise when parents overindulge the child, so that he gets the idea that he is omnipotent and can have his own way in everything. Then he is unwilling to accept necessary restrictions.

A positive approach to negativism. Margaret McMillan, an English nursery school worker (60, 1927), described a case of negativism which was typical of those she frequently met:

The two-year-old comes into our open-air nursery school a very unhappy little person. . . . His first idea is that *he is not going to be coerced.* "No! No!

No!" cries a little voice. "No bath!" "No dinner!" "No clean pinafore!" Above
all, "No sleep!" A hundred times I have found one panacea for this wild and
multiple revolt. It is acquiescence, consent. . . . It is not coaxing he wants.
. . . This sense restored, it is wonderful to see how quickly an attitude of calm
and power to note or observe, follow. . . .

In time, he is attracted to the other children and their activities, and
makes some movement to join them. His approach is met, of course, with
welcoming smiles.

Ability to put oneself in the child's place is a valuable asset in dealing
with all kinds of behavior problems. Too frequently there is no common
ground between the child's world and the adult world. A certain activity is
pleasant and constructive to the child, but naughty to the adult. One two-
year-old was in the "me too" stage; she wanted to do everything her slightly
older sister did. One morning the older sister found an eggshell on the table, and crushed it as she had seen her mother do when making coffee. The
little one looked for another eggshell, but there was none. She then spied
a basket of fresh eggs, dropped one of them on the floor, and squashed it
with her heel, saying gleefully, "Me break egg, too." On such occasions, if
the mother stops to try to understand what the act means to the child, she
will seldom err in her treatment of the situation. One mother says that she
sometimes sits in the baby's place and tries to see things from his point of
view before acting.

Often mother and child get caught in a vicious circle of "naughtiness,"
impatience, and more "naughtiness." The daily routine may be a potential
source of upset. Insufficient sleep and similar mundane factors have a profound influence. They make the child more irritable, more demanding. A
feeling of discouragement on the part of the mother also makes the situation more difficult. A harrassed parent, a child with a difficulty or two—
and the stage is set for trouble. When a child is disturbed and exasperating,
it is most difficult for the parent to love, to be sympathetic, understanding,
patient. When an adult meets with bitterness, hostility, hatred, and abuse
from children whom he is trying to help, he should try to remember that
these children need love the most.

CONCLUDING STATEMENT

In dealing with any problems of development during the first two
years, firmness is required to help the child discriminate behavior appropriate to different situations. Yet his environment must support his attempts
at self-control to prevent feelings of shame or doubt.

It can readily be seen that the child's basic manner of reacting to his parents and to people in general is determined by what happens to him in early infancy. Naturally his way of behaving determines to a large extent how others react to him. The pattern thus becomes self-perpetuating.

Questions and Problems

FOR CLASS DISCUSSION OR STUDY GROUPS

1. Observe and record the interaction between a child and an adult; note ways in which the adult's behavior seems to evoke certain behavior on the part of the child, and the child's behavior seems to influence the adult's response.

2. Observe a child about two years of age and record in detail the situations in which he shows "stubbornness" or "contrariness." Try to discover the conditions that give rise to the resistant behavior and suggest the best method of acting in the situation. If a child a year and a half old is disobedient, which of these possible clues would you explore further:

a. He is just naturally stubborn.
b. He does not understand the requests made of him.
c. He is trying to break away from the dependency of infancy.
d. Objects that he sees demand action on his part.
e. His memory span is short.
f. He is expressing hostility toward his mother who has been harsh in her treatment of him.
g. He has a will of his own which must be broken.

Discuss each of these possible explanations.

3. What are the most common causes of infant deaths and illness in your community? What is being done to prevent them?

4. Describe the weaning process as you would recommend it to a young mother.

5. What factors that cause children to dislike certain foods may have their origin in the first year? How could these be avoided?

6. There is a difference of opinion about the extent to which a crying baby should be given attention. What plan would you recommend for dealing with a baby who cries in the night?

7. How should these so-called problems of early childhood—thumb-sucking, bowel and bladder control, etc.—be viewed?

8. Study the investigation reported by Bowlby (18, 1953) from the standpoint of its research design. Note particularly his theoretical interpretation of the data and its practical value.

9. To obtain perspective on the theory and research on parent-child relationships, read Percival M. Symonds' *The Dynamics of Parent-Child Relationships*. New York: Bureau of Publications, Teachers College, Columbia University, 1949. 197 pp.

Bibliography*

1. Aldrich, C. Anderson. "Techniques for Interesting a Community in Growth and Development of Children," *Child Development*, XIX (March-June, 1948), 35-39.

2. Allen, Frederick H. "Developments in Child Psychiatry in the United States," *American Journal of Public Health*, XXXVIII (September, 1948), 1201-1209.

3. Ammons, Robert B., and Helen S. Ammons. *The Full-Range Picture Vocabulary Test*. New Orleans: R. B. Ammons, 1948. 21 pp.

4. Ammons, Robert B., and James Clifford Holmes. "The Full-Range Picture Vocabulary Test: III. Results for a Preschool-Age Population," *Child Development*, XX (March, 1949), 5-14.

5. Anderson, Harold H., Charles Hanley, and John R. Hurley. "Personality Development in Infancy and Preschool Years," *Review of Educational Research*, XXV (December, 1955), 453-468.

6. Ausubel, David P. *Ego Development and the Personality Disorders*. New York: Grune & Stratton, 1952. 564 pp.

7. Bayley, Nancy. *The Development of Motor Abilities During the First Three Years*. ("Monographs of the Society for Research in Child Development, Vol. 1, No. 1.) Washington, D.C.: Society for Research in Child Development, National Research Council, 1935. 26 pp.

**8. ———. "On Growth of Intelligence," *American Psychologist*, X (December, 1955), 805-818.

9. Behrens, Margaret. "Child Rearing and the Character Structure of the Mother," *Child Development*, XXV (September, 1954), 225-238.

10. Benedict, Ruth. "Child Rearing in Certain European Countries," *American Journal of Orthopsychiatry*, XIX (April, 1949), 342-350.

11. Bernstein, A. "Some Relations between Techniques of Feeding and Training during Infancy and Certain Behavior in Childhood," *Genetic Psychological Monographs*, LI (February, 1955), 3-44.

12. Bettleheim, Bruno. *Love Is Not Enough: the Treatment of Emotionally Disturbed Children*. Glencoe, Ill.: The Free Press, 1950. 386 pp.

13. Blatz, William E. "The Physiological Appetites," in Carl Murchison (ed.), *A Handbook of Child Psychology* (rev. ed.), pp. 723-770. Worcester, Mass.: Clark Univ. Press, 1933. 956 pp.

14. Block, Jack. "Personality Characteristics Associated with Fathers' Attitudes toward Child-Rearing," *Child Development*, XXVI (March, 1955), 41-48.

* All references referred to in the text are included in the bibliography. The single-starred references (*) are specially recommended for their practical suggestions; those double-starred (**) are specially recommended for their technical and research emphasis.

15. Bossard, James H. S., and Eleanor Stoker Boll. "Personality Roles in the Large Family," *Child Development*, XXVI (March, 1955), 71-78.

16. ———. "Security in the Large Family," *Mental Hygiene*, XXXVIII (October, 1954), 529-544.

**17. Bowlby, John. "Maternal Care and Mental Health," *Bulletin of the World Health Organization*, III (1951), 355-538.

18. ———. "Some Pathological Processes Set in Train by Early Mother-Child Separation," *Journal of Mental Science*, XCIX (April, 1953), 265-272.

19. Brim, Orville G., Jr. "The Parent-Child Relation as a Social System: I. Parent and Child Roles," *Child Development*, XXVIII (September, 1957), 343-364.

20. Brody, Sylvia. *Patterns of Mothering*. New York: International Universities Press, 1956. 446 pp.

21. Burmeister, Eva. *Forty-Five in the Family; the Story of a Home for Children*. New York: Columbia Univ. Press, 1949. 247 pp.

**22. Cattell, Psyche. *The Measurement of Intelligence of Infants and Young Children*. New York: The Psychological Corp., 1940. 274 pp.

23. Davis, Clara M. "Self-Selection of Diets: An Experiment with Infants," *The Trained Nurse and Hospital Review*, LXXXVI (May, 1931), 629-634.

24. Dennis, Wayne, and Marsena G. Dennis. "Development under Controlled Environmental Conditions," in Wayne Dennis (ed.), *Readings in Child Psychology*, pp. 104-131. Englewood Cliffs, N.J.: Prentice-Hall, Inc., 1951. 624 pp.

*25. Despert, J. Louise. "The Fatherless Family," *Child Study*, XXXIV (Summer, 1957), 22-28.

26. Dixon, J. C. "Development of Self Recognition," *Journal of Genetic Psychology*, XCI (December, 1957), 251-256.

*27. Dybwad, Gunnar. "When Children Need Comforting," *National Parent-Teacher*, L (January, 1956), 14-16.

**28. Erikson, Erik H. *Childhood and Society*. New York: W. W. Norton & Co., Inc., 1950. 397 pp.

29. Escalona, Sibylle K. "Feeding Disturbances in Very Young Children," *American Journal of Orthopsychiatry*, XV (January, 1945), 76-80.

*30. ———. *Understanding Hostility in Children*. Chicago: Science Research Associates, Inc., 1954. 48 pp.

31. ———. Mary Leitch, and others. *Early Phases of Personality Development: A Non-normative Study of Infant Behavior*. ("Monographs of the Society for Research in Child Development," Vol. 17, Serial No. 54, Nov. 1, 1952.) 72 pp.

32. Eysenck, Hans J. *The Scientific Study of Personality*. New York: The Macmillan Co., 1952. 320 pp.

33. FRANCE, ANATOLE. *The Crime of Sylvestre Bonnard*. New York: Dodd, Mead & Co., 1918. 310 pp.

34. FREUDENTHAL, KURT. "A Class for 'Only Parents,' " *Understanding the Child*, XXV (October, 1956), 111-113.

35. GESELL, ARNOLD L. "The Ontogenesis of Infant Behavior," in Leonard Carmichael (ed.), *Manual of Child Psychology* (2d ed.), pp. 335-373. New York: John Wiley & Sons, Inc., 1954. 1295 pp.

36. ———. and CATHERINE S. AMATRUUDA. *Developmental Diagnosis* (2nd ed.). New York: Paul G. Hoeber, Inc., 1947. 496 pp.

37. GESELL, ARNOLD L., and HELEN THOMPSON. *Learning and Growth in Identical Infant Twins*. ("Genetic Psychology Monographs," VI, No. 1.) Worcester, Mass.: Clark Univ. Press, 1929. 124 pp.

38. GOFF, CHARLES W. (with N. M. Shutkin and M. R. Hersey). *Legg-Calvé-Perthe Syndrome*, Figure 29. Springfield, Ill.: Charles C. Thomas, 1954. 344 pp.

39. HARRIS, DALE B. "Science Says—," *Child Study*, XXXV (Winter, 1957-1958), 28, 30.

40. HOETLIN, RUTH. "Child Rearing Practices, Child Care Resources Used by Ohio Farm Families with Preschool Children," *Journal of Genetic Psychology*, LXXXIV (June, 1954), 271-297.

41. ILIFF, ALBERTA, and VIRGINIA A. LEE. "Pulse Rate, Respiratory Rate, and Body Temperature of Children between Two Months and Eighteen Years of Age," *Child Development*, XXIII (December, 1952), 237-245.

42. INHELDER, BÄRBEL. "Developmental Psychology," in Paul R. Farnsworth and Quinn McNemar (eds.), *Annual Review of Psychology*, Vol. 8, pp. 139-162. Palo Alto, Calif.: Annual Reviews, Inc., 1957. 502 pp.

**43. JERSILD, ARTHUR T. "Emotional Development," in Leonard Carmichael ed.), *Manual of Child Psychology* (2d ed.), pp. 833-917. New York: John Wiley & Sons, Inc., 1954. 1295 pp.

44. ———. ELLA S. WOODYARD, and CHARLOTTE DEL SOLAR. *Joys and Problems of Child Rearing*. New York: Teachers College, Columbia Univ., 1949. 235 pp.

45. JONES, MARY COVER. "A Laboratory Study of Fear; the Case of Peter," *Journal of Genetic Psychology*, XXXI (September, 1924), 308-315.

*46. KANNER, LEO. "Mental Health in Child Rearing," *Child*, XVII (March, 1953), 116-117.

47. ———. "Unwholesome parental attitudes and children's behavior," *Education*, LXIX (January, 1949), 263-270.

*48. KAWIN, ETHEL. *A Guide for Child-Study Groups*. Chicago: Science Research Associates, 1952. 72 pp.

49. LARKIN, MARTIN. *Personality Factors in Mothers of Excessively Crying (Colicky) Infants*. ("Monographs of the Society for Research in Child Development," Vol. 12, Serial No. 64, No. 1, 1957.) 48 pp.

50. Lasko, Joan Kalhorn. "Parent Behavior toward First and Second Children," *Genetic Psychology Monographs*, XLIX (February, 1954), 97-137.

51. Leighton, Dorothea, and Clyde Kluckhohn. *Children of the People.* Cambridge, Mass.: Harvard Univ. Press, 1947. 277 pp.

52. Lewin, Kurt. "Behavior and Development as a Function of the Total Situation," in Leonard Carmichael (ed.), *Manual of Child Psychology* (2d ed.), pp. 918-970. New York: John Wiley & Sons, Inc., 1954. 1295 pp.

53. Lewis, Claudia. *Children of the Cumberland.* New York: Columbia Univ. Press, 1946. 217 pp.

54. Linn, Louis. "Some Developmental Aspects of the Body Image," *International Journal of Psycho-Analysis*, XXXVI (January-February, 1955), 36-42.

**55. Linton, Ralph. *Culture and Mental Disorders.* Edited by George Devereux. Springfield, Ill.: Charles C. Thomas, 1956. 139 pp.

**56. MacFarlane, Jean W. *Studies in Child Guidance. I. Methodology of Data Collection and Organization.* ("Monographs of the Society for Research in Child Development," Vol. 3, Serial No. 19, No. 5, 1938.) 254 pp.

57. McArthur, Charles. "Personalities of First and Second Children," *Psychiatry*, XIX (February, 1956), 47-54.

**58. McCarthy, Dorothea. "Language Development in Children," in Leonard Carmichael (ed.), *Manual of Child Psychology* (2d ed.), pp. 492-630. New York: John Wiley & Sons, Inc., 1954. 1295 pp.

59. McGraw, Myrtle B. *Growth; A Study of Johnny and Jimmy.* New York: D. Appleton-Century Co., 1935. 319 pp.

60. McMillan, Margaret. "The Nursery School in Organic Education," *American Childhood*, XII (February, 1927), 5-7.

*61. McNulty, John. *My Son Johnny.* New York: Simon & Schuster, 1955. 174 pp.

*62. "The Man in the Family," 1957 Annual CSAA Conference Report. *Child Study*, XXXIV (Summer, 1957), 1-33.

63. Martz, Eugene W. "Phenomenal Spurt of Mental Development in a Young Child," *Psychiatric Quarterly*, XIX (January, 1945), 52-59.

64. Mead, Margaret, and Martha Wolfenstein. *Childhood in Contemporary Cultures.* Chicago: Univ. of Chicago Press, 1955. 473 pp.

65. Mitchell, Lucy Sprague. *Here and Now Story Book; Two-to-Seven-Year-Olds.* New York: E. P. Dutton & Co., Inc., 1921. 360 pp.

66. Mittleman, Bela. "Motility in Infants," and "Motor Patterns and Genital Behavior: Fetishism," *Psychoanalytic Studies of the Child*, IX (1954), 142-177; X (1955), 241-263.

*67. Moustakas, Clark E. *The Teacher and the Child: Personal Interaction in the Classroom.* New York: McGraw-Hill Book Co., Inc., 1956. 265 pp.

68. MOYER, KENNETH E., and B. VON HALLER GILMER. "Attention Spans of Children for Experimentally Designed Toys," *Journal of Genetic Psychology*, LXXXVII (December, 1955), 187-201.

69. MUNN, NORMAN L. "Learning in Children," in Leonard Carmichael (ed.), *Manual of Child Psychology* (2d ed.), pp. 374-558. New York: John Wiley & Sons, Inc., 1954. 1295 pp.

70. NEILON, PATRICIA. "Shirley's Babies after Fifteen Years; a Personality Study," *Journal of Genetic Psychology*, LXXIII (December, 1948), 175-186.

*71. OGG, ELIZABETH. *When Parents Grow Old*. ("Public Affairs Pamphlet," No. 208.) New York: Public Affairs Comm., Inc., 1954. 28 pp.

72. OLDEN, CHRISTINE. "On Adult Empathy with Children," *Psychoanalytic Study of the Child*, VIII (1954), 111-126.

73. "Parent Education in Perspective," *Child Study*, XXXIII (Fall, 1956), 1-48.

74. PIAGET, JEAN. *The Construction of Reality in the Child*. New York: Basic Books, 1954. 386 pp.

75. ———. *The Origins of Intelligence in Children* (2d ed.). New York: International Universities Press, Inc., 1953. 419 pp.

**76. PRATT, KARL C. "The Neonate," in Leonard Carmichael (ed.), *Manual of Child Psychology* (2d ed.), pp. 215-291. New York: John Wiley & Sons, Inc., 1954.

*77. PRESCOTT, DANIEL. *The Child in the Educative Process*. New York: McGraw-Hill Book Co., Inc., 1957. 502 pp.

78. RHEINGOLD, HARRIET LANGE. *The Modification of Social Responsiveness in Institutional Babies*. ("Monographs of the Society for Research in Child Development," Vol. 21, Serial No. 63, No. 2, 1956.) 48 pp.

79. RHODES, WILLIAM C., and PHYLLIS N. MATHEWS. "Combatting Maternal Deprivation," *Children*, IV (March-April, 1957), 54-60.

80. RIESMAN, DAVID, NATHAN GLAZER, and RUEL DENNEY. *The Lonely Crowd*. New York: Doubleday & Company, Inc., 1950. 386 pp.

81. ROSS, SHERMAN, ALAN E. FISHER, and DAVID KING. "Sucking Behavior: A Review of the Literature," *Journal of Genetic Psychology*, XCI (September, 1957), 63-81.

82. RUSSELL, DAVID H. *Children's Thinking*. Boston: Ginn & Co., 1956. 449 pp.

83. SEARS, ROBERT R., and others. "Some Child-Rearing Antecedents of Aggression and Dependency," *Genetic Psychological Monographs*, XLVII (April, 1953), 135-236.

*84. SEARS, ROBERT R., ELEANOR E. MACCOBY, and HARRY LEVIN. *Patterns of Child Rearing*. Evanston, Ill.: Row, Peterson & Co., 1957. 549 pp.

85. SEARS, ROBERT R., and GEORGE W. WISE. "Relation of Cup Feeding in Infancy to Thumb-Sucking and the Oral Drive," *American Journal of Orthopsychiatry*, XX (January, 1950), 123-138.

86. Seeley, John R. "The Forest Hill Village Project," *Understanding the Child,* XXIII (October, 1954), 104-110.

87. Sewell, William H., Paul H. Mussen, and Chester W. Harris. "Relationships among Child Training Practices," *American Sociological Review,* XX (April, 1955), 137-148.

88. Shirley, Mary M. *The First Two Years; A Study of Twenty-Five Babies. Vol. II: Intellectual Development.* ("Institute of Child Welfare Monographs," Series No. 7.) Minneapolis: Univ. of Minnesota Press, 1933. 513 pp.

89. Sontag, Lester W., Charles T. Baker, and Virginia L. Nelson. "Personality as a Determinant of Performance," *American Journal of Orthopsychiatry,* XXV (July, 1955), 555-562.

**90. Spitz, René A. "Infantile Depression and the General Adaptation Syndrome; On the Relation between Physiologic Model and Psychoanalytic Conceptualization," in Paul Hoch and Joseph Zubin (eds.), *Depressions.* New York: Grune & Stratton, Inc., 1954. 277 pp.

*91. Spock, Benjamin. *Baby and Child Care.* New York: Pocket Books, Inc., 1957. 627 pp.

*92. Stirling, Nora. *5 Scripts—"What Did I Do?"* ("Human Relations Aids") New York: Mental Health Materials Center, 1957. 40 pp.

93. Stolz, Lois Meek. *Father Relations of War-Born Children.* Stanford, Calif.: Stanford Univ. Press, 1954. 365 pp.

94. Stone, L. Joseph. "A Critique of Studies of Infant Isolation," *Child Development,* XXV (March, 1954), 9-20.

95. Stott, Leland H., and Rachel Stutsman Ball. "Consistency and Change in Ascendance-Submission in the Social Interaction of Children," *Child Development,* XXVIII (September, 1957), 259-272.

**96. Sullivan, Harry Stack. *The Interpersonal Theory of Psychiatry.* New York: W. W. Norton & Co., Inc., 1953. 393 pp.

97. Tasch, Ruth J. "Interpersonal Perceptions of Fathers and Mothers," *Journal of Genetic Psychology,* LXXXVII (September, 1955), 59-65.

98. Terman, Lewis M., and Maude A. Merrill. *Measuring Intelligence.* Boston: Houghton Mifflin Co., 1937. 460 pp.

**99. Thompson, Helen. "Physical Growth," in Leonard Carmichael (ed.), *Manual of Child Psychology* (2d ed.), pp. 292-334. New York: John Wiley & Sons, Inc., 1954.

100. Thompson, William R. "Early Environment—Its Importance for Later Behavior," in Paul Hoch and Joseph Zubin (eds.), *Psychopathology of Childhood,* pp. 120-139. New York: Grune & Stratton, Inc., 1955. 303 pp.

101. Thorpe, William H. "Some Implications of the Study of Animal Behavior," *Scientific Monthly,* LXXXIV (June, 1957), 309-320.

102. Toronto University, Institute of Child Study. *Well Children* (in Mary L. Northway (ed.), "A Progress Report on the Research Con-

ducted at the Institute of Child Study, 1953-1955.") University of Toronto, Toronto, 1956. 91 pp.

*103. VALENTINE, CHARLES W. *The Normal Child and Some of His Abnormalities*. Baltimore: Penguin Books, Inc., 1956. 290 pp.

**104. WHITING, JOHN W. M., and IRVIN L. CHILD. *Child Training and Personality*. New Haven, Conn.: Yale Univ. Press, 1953. 353 pp.

*105. WINNICOTT, D. W. *Mother and Child: A Primer of First Relationships*. New York: Basic Books, Inc., 1957. 210 pp.

Films for Child Study

A Long Time to Grow (Part I) Two- and Three-Year-Olds in Nursery School. New York Univ. Film Library. 35 minutes. 1951. Produced by the Dept. of Child Study at Vassar College. Shows the learning behavior and activities of two- and three-year-old children thorugh the day and various seasons of the year. (*See also* other films of the Vassar Series, *Studies of Normal Personality Development*.)

Karba's First Years. New York Univ. Film Library. Produced by Gregory Bateson and Margaret Mead. 19 minutes. One of a series of six films on *Character Formation in Different Cultures*. Shows development of a Balinese child.

Know Your Baby. National Film Board of Canada. 10 minutes. Color. 1947. Methods for caring for the new baby to insure his best development.

The Terrible Twos and Trusting Threes. National Film Board of Canada. 20 minutes. 1950. Shows the increasing maturity in social behavior as the child ages from two to three years.

Why Won't Tommy Eat?, National Film Board of Canada. 19 minutes. Color. 1948. The study of Tommy illustrates a common problem and through him looks for reasons for children's lack of appetite.

Yale Child Development Clinic series of films produced under the direction of Arnold Gesell, and distributed by the Encyclopaedia Britannica Films, Inc., 20 North Wacker Drive, Chicago, Illinois:

    Growth of Infant Behavior—Early Stages
    Growth of Infant Behavior—Later Stages
    Posture and Locomotion
    From Creeping to Walking
    36 Weeks Behavior Day
    48 Weeks Behavior Day
    Behavior Patterns at One Year
    Learning and Growth
    Early Social Behavior
    Life Begins
    Baby's Day at Twelve Weeks

Part Three

THE PRESCHOOL PERIOD:

YEARS THREE, FOUR,

AND FIVE

*In the mental health goal—harmonious living—
lies a concrete hope for a frightened world.*

*We need above all to renew our faith in human
beings—building on what they can do rather than on
what they cannot do.*

International Committee for Mental Hygiene, 1949

Chapter 9

DEVELOPMENT DURING

PRESCHOOL YEARS

Between two and three years of age, children usually move rapidly toward independence, toward autonomy, toward wanting to do things for themselves. That is why this period has sometimes been called "the first adolescence." They now have to give up being babies—though they still yearn sometimes for the advantages of infancy. In this "in-between stage," they shift back and forth between babyhood and self-reliant childhood. One youngster expressed this feeling in a soliloquy overheard by his mother: "Today I'm not going to be a big boy. I'm tired of being big. I want to be a baby, and you take care of me." However, they leave the helplessness of infancy far behind. Most preschool children want to grow up. They often object to being called babies and not being allowed to share in grown-up activities. One mother's statement is typical: "He does not like to be called a baby. He protests. He often puts his hand over his head and says proudly, 'This is how big I am.' "

DYNAMICS OF PRESCHOOL DEVELOPMENT

During the third, fourth, and fifth years the positive relationship between the child's rate of progress in physical growth and his progress in social, intellectual, and emotional maturity becomes increasingly evident. The significance of this relationship depends on the child's own concept of the acceptability of his physical status. This, in turn, depends on his experiences of success, and the positive appraisals he receives from others. These are the years of "the flowering of the self." The two-year-old toddler becomes more worldly-wise. Individuality emerges.

Day-to-day fluctuations in the preschool child's behavior may be expected as he wavers between the dependency of infancy and the growing independence of childhood. Neither excessive submissiveness nor defiant independence is the solution; instead, a balance between dependence and

135

independence should be encouraged. Overdependency may result from maternal overprotection or inconsistency; parents can carry their responsibility for the child's growth too far. A child's independence increases as he begins to take responsibility for what he is and for what he does. Accompanying this satisfaction in doing things for himself, should be the recognition and acceptance of his dependence on those who fulfill his needs. The role of the parent is to reinforce the child's growing independence but to hold steady in the face of his petulant protest.

Preschool children become more clever in handling adults. From their experiences they learn that it pays to respond to adults in certain ways. They have become nearly self-dependent in their daily home routines. They are fresh and honest in the expression of their emotions. They often ask why and, as they grow older, more often want a serious answer. By the end of the preschool years many children have gained enough independence and skill to hold their own in the kindergarten or first grade.

PHYSICAL GROWTH AND HEALTH

Height and weight

During these years growth in height and weight is still rapid, though somewhat slower than it was in infancy. Height depends chiefly on a child's growth potentials; weight is more easily influenced by diet, economic circumstances, and other environmental conditions. By five years, the child is usually about twice as tall as he was at two—around three feet, four inches. X-rays of his hands and wrists show his skeletal age. From this evidence, the child's adult height can be predicted quite accurately.

Weight varies much more from child to child than does height. In the first year the child often doubles his weight. At two and three he may gain about five pounds a year, and less than that for the next few years. At five years he is about five times his birth weight.

In asking the question, "Is my child the right weight?" parents should take into consideration his age, stature, and body build, as well as his nutritional condition. They cannot get the answer just by looking at average-height-and-weight tables. A child may be naturally short and slight like his parents. X-rays of bone development may show that a small child is relatively more mature physically than a large child of the same age. He may be as healthy, too, and resistant to disease as a child who looks more robust. However, if a child does not gain over a period of several months, a doctor should examine him to detect any physical or psychological causes.

It is well to be aware, too, of seasonal variations in growth. One can expect the greatest gain in height between April and June; the smallest gain between October and December. The greatest gain in weight usually takes place between October and December; the smallest gain between April and June. Growth differences between boys and girls are not so marked at this age as they are just before adolescence. Three biological factors—size, rate of maturation, and balance or harmony in the growth process (61, 1956)—enter into the child's concept of his growth pattern.

Changes in body proportions

The preschool child also changes in body proportions. This is because each part of the body has its own rate of growth. The growth of head and chest regions which was most rapid during the prenatal and infancy period has begun to slow down, whereas the development of the arms and legs now becomes rapidly accelerated. By age five, his proportions are more like those of adults. He has lost that top-heavy look of infancy. His chubby baby features take on more individuality.

Posture

Poor posture sometimes becomes a problem for the first time during the preschool years. Children often lose the good posture and natural grace that they had as two-year-olds. They slump rather than stand tall. They thrust their heads forward. If they are undernourished their shoulder blades stand out like wings; their abdomens sag and become more prominent. Nagging a child about his posture will not improve it. A child's posture is a symptom of his health and strength and self-confidence.

Energy requirement

Energy requirement, as everyone now knows, thanks to the many popular articles on reducing diets, is measured by calories. The average daily caloric requirement for preschool children, varying with their size and activity, is between 1,300 and 1,400. The more physically active a child is, the more calories he uses. Per pound of body weight, younger children require more fuel-food than do older children, provided their activity is similar.

Teeth

At about the age of two and a half, the last of the baby's first teeth—the second molars—should appear. He then has his full set of twenty baby teeth. Since it is hard for these later teeth to push through the gums, they often cause more teething trouble than the earlier teeth. Children seem to be particularly susceptible to tooth decay at about two and a half and at about five years. Brushing, or even rinsing, the teeth after each meal is a good habit, although it is no insurance against decay. Sweets seem to be associated with tooth decay, though not proven to be its cause.

Reduction of diseases

Children up to five years are especially susceptible to colds and other respiratory diseases—the outstanding cause of illness at all ages.

The best way to prevent the spread of communicable diseases among nursery-school children is to teach parents to detect the first signs of illness, such as a running nose, sneezing, a new cough, any sort of rash or skin eruption, a flushed face, or unusual paleness. However difficult it may be for some parents to keep a child at home, they should do so, both for his sake, and to protect others from communicable diseases. One sneezing child may spread colds to a half-dozen other children. An undetected case of diphtheria or scarlet fever is still more serious.

Illness may have many complications. A natural response in illness is to call for mother, like a very small child. If hospitalization is necessary, very young and dependent children may feel great anxiety at being separated from their families. An insecure child may learn to use illness as a means of getting the special attention he craves. The effect of any illness depends upon the way in which the personality of the child interacts in the particular situation.

Sleep

The number of hours a child sleeps decreases with age. For example, a two-year-old may sleep twelve hours out of the twenty-four; a three-year-old, eleven and one-third; and a four-year-old, eleven hours. The amount of sleep recommended by pediatricians is generally more than the actual sleeping hours reported in studies.

It is highly desirable that children should associate going to bed with going to sleep. This can be facilitated by planning a regular quiet, relaxing, pre-bedtime hour. An ideal sequence is a warm bath, followed by dressing for bed, and a not too exciting story. A serious problem in overcrowded homes is providing a quiet room out of range of the interesting television programs from which the child feels he is being excluded.

Daytime naps diminish during the preschool years. At two years practically all the children studied took naps; at four years only about half. At around two and a half years, the child begins to resist afternoon naps. By the time he is three he would rather play than sleep during the afternoon nap period. With the younger child, the afternoon nap aids sleep; with the older child, a nap longer than he needs tends to delay his falling asleep at night.

Different children need different amounts of sleep. A young Edison may actually need less sleep than another child of his age. Sturdy children seem to need less sleep than frail children; healthy children less than ill children. Fatigue, irritability, and loss of appetite may indicate that a child is not getting sufficient sleep. The "self-selection" theory applies to sleeping as well as to eating. Good sleep habits are most likely to develop when parents recognize and accept the natural sleep tendency of each child.

Many conditions may prevent children two years or older from getting the sleep they need. Teething difficulties may make a child restless. Some children are constitutionally overactive; it is hard for them to relax. Illness may disturb a child's sleep schedule. Fears, worries, tension, exciting play or stories, overstimulation from listening to the radio or looking at television—these and similar experiences leave a child so keyed up that he cannot go to sleep. A few children are afraid to go to sleep; to them, dreams are real events that happen right in their bedrooms.

Conditions conducive to growth and health

If conditions are favorable, children will attain the best health possible for them. They need, of course, an adequate diet. Mealtimes should be free from strain, pressure, nagging, and emotional disturbance. They need a well-balanced day of rest, indoor and outdoor activity, and sunshine in moderation. They should have playmates, and each child needs some time with his parents that is exclusively his. Incidentally, such a schedule would be good for the parents, too.

Children need a combination of freedom, reasonable restrictions, and guidance. As safeguards, they should have regular medical and dental examinations. An examination by a friendly doctor is a good learning experience for the child. If for any reason the child fears a visit to the doctor, play-acting about going to the doctor or dentist may be useful in preparing him.

DEVELOPMENT OF MOTOR SKILLS

During the second year of life, motor activity becomes a dominant source of satisfaction, reaching a peak around four or five years (76, 1955). The rapid maturation of complicated muscle systems opens doors to a wider world. Their newly acquired ability to walk, run, and climb give two-year-olds access to situations, experiences, and people that were hitherto not available to them. They flit from one thing to another. Objects demand their attention and action. They respond to all sorts of stimulus situations and thus learn the kinds of responses that bring them the greatest satisfaction. The nature of their development is best revealed in free play.

Several descriptions of the activity of three-year-olds in a nursery school will illustrate individual differences in motor skills:

Jane is riding a tricycle, very fast, up and down and around the room. She runs her tricycle into the doll carriage that Jimmy is pushing around. He pulls the carriage away and bangs it against her tricycle. She rides away, takes a turn around the room, runs her tricycle into a chair and then abandons it to join a group making finger paintings.

Ann is agile; she climbs the tower gym swiftly, shows good judgment of distance, handles a tricycle easily, puts puzzles together. She likes to use the slide, although she fell off the ladder twice on the first day and cut her lip the second day. The doll corner is her favorite spot.

Betty had learned to walk up and down the slanting board all by herself: Sue was afraid to try it. The teacher suggested that Betty take Sue's hand and walk beside her as she went up the plank. She went cautiously, laughing delightedly at the exciting experience she was having. Betty next turned her attention to blocks.

Large-muscle activities

During the preschool years motor skills multiply and improve. As time goes on children may be expected to make marked progress in the speed, accuracy, and strength of their muscular activity. The characteristic toddling walk of two becomes a rhythmic stride. The child goes upstairs one foot after another; learns to climb on whatever is available for climbing; can skip and hop; rides around on a tricycle. Four-year-olds run more quickly, climb higher and in more difficult places, and jump more skillfully than they did a year earlier. They enjoy playing ball. They have fewer falls. They get fewer bumps. They can walk and run longer distances. Around five years they become quite graceful at roller skating and bicycle riding. The hardest thing for them to do is to be inactive. To have to sit still is more fatiguing than to trot about all morning. They are more likely to "get tired sitting still" than to "get tired."

The sense of rhythm develops during these years. Children learn to keep time to music, to beat time with their hands, to walk to music, and, usually after four, to skip to music. Rather fast tempos are easier for them to follow than slower tempos.

With the parallel growth in mental alertness and social adjustment, the developing motor abilities of older preschool children become increasingly instrumental to imaginative play and other purposive activity rather than being engaged in for their own intrinsic pleasure. These children run for a purpose more often then they "just run."

Eye-hand co-ordination

Refined eye-hand and eye-finger co-ordination is gained more slowly. An especially joyful occupation for two- and three-year-olds is driving nails. One mother found her little girl of three driving large nails into the side of the house with remarkable accuracy of aim and intense satisfaction. She was equally content to drive them into a wood block which her mother hastened to provide. Between three and five years, children learn to use blunt scissors in following roughly the outline of a picture. Five-year-olds become skillful with tools of a suitable size. By the sixth year, some children will use their skill in carpentry to make a table, a wagon, or a boat. To be sure, these articles are crude, but making them has much more educational value than watching Father turn out a perfect product.

Helpful activities

The preschool child can help his mother in numerous ways. Cleaning the bathtub can be a pleasant form of water play. Wearing a rubber apron, he can clean the faucets with soapsuds and rub them shiny with a dry cloth. Mirrors are delightful to clean. Powders and oils are too difficult for little children to use. In the living room there are books and magazines to arrange neatly and plants to water. In the dining room there is the table to set. In the kitchen there may be a little bit of cookie dough to cut out with a thimble. There are dishes to dry, potatoes to scrub clean for baking, lettuce and spinach to wash leaf by leaf, and, in the country, there are chickens to feed.

The older preschool child can learn to put his toys away in a box, and wash his face and hands without getting his clothes very wet. He shows increasing ability to carry a glass or pitcher of milk without spilling it and to pour water from a pitcher. About three years of age children learn to button their clothes, i.e., the easy buttons. Acquiring these abilities does much to increase their self-esteem.

The mother should help the child to find satisfaction in these little tasks, and make him feel that he is really helping her. As E. L. Thorndike once remarked, "Children would rather make real pies than mud pies." They like useful activities suited to their capacities. They like to feel independent and can be depended on increasingly.

WRITING, DRAWING, PAINTING, AND MUSIC

Learning to write one's name is also part of a developmental sequence. In a study of handwriting of mentally superior children, it was found that they first made a meaningless scrawl—the zero point in name writing. Then they imitated adults' writing by making a hasty up-and-down scribbling across the page. At about four, they became interested in forming letters. After five, they showed ability to write their first names with increasing interest, care, and speed.

Between two and five years, children show improvement in their ability to make designs with blocks and build more stately towers. Gesell found that 85 to 100 per cent of the five-year-old children whom he studied were able to "fold paper diagonally," to "copy a square," and to trace around one or two diamonds drawn on a paper; 65 to 84 per cent could draw a triangle, a diagonal, and a recognizable picture of a man. However, only a small proportion of children—about a third—were able to draw another line-drawing of objects or animals just like the model given them. Graphic symmetry does not seem to be completely understood until nine or ten years of age. Children are likely to emphasize details that represent their special interests or difficulties. For example, when certain children were having difficulty in buttoning, they made buttons prominent in their drawings.

In drawing and painting, children tend to follow a sequence. They progress from single lines and single colors to combinations of colors and pictures of familiar objects and activities. In the early preschool years children seem to be more concerned with the use of the painting materials and the expression of what they feel than with the portrayal of what they see. Painting gives children an outlet for expressing their deeper feelings, wishes, anxieties. Rhythmic, moderately heavy brush strokes seem characteristic of the happy, easy-going child; crisscross lines and angles and heavy strokes suggest inner conflict; spotty painting with broken lines that get nowhere are commonly produced by easily distractible children who have a very short attention span.

In interpreting children's drawings and paintings, the adult will get the best understanding of the child's feelings by studying interrelations of color, form, content, and use of space; by observing the child's behavior in the painting situation, and by asking him to "tell me about the painting," or "tell me the story of the painting." For example, during World War II a little Japanese girl joined a group of boys playing soldiers. For a while she marched around with them gaily. Then they began an imaginary play in which they were fighting the enemy. They shouted, "There's a Jap, kill him." The little girl gradually withdrew from the group, went over to a table, and with black crayons and an intense expression drew a picture full of heavy crisscross lines.

Usually nothing will be gained by asking a child *what* he has been painting. The following is a description of a teacher's understanding approach to a child's painting:

Betty covered her ears as a huge truck rumbled by the school. Then she drew it—a black rectangle with lots of wheels underneath. Next she seized the red crayon and covered the whole with great, swirling red scrawls, almost obliterating the black. "See my truck I made," she said happily. "It has lots of wheels," her teacher commented, and paused to trace a red spiral or two with her finger, smiling inquiringly at Betty. "That's the noise,'" Betty volunteered.

The child who paints with wholehearted absorption is doing something important to him.

Encouraging children to express their feelings in drawing or painting builds a good basis for spontaneous, creative art work. Negative criticism stifles their interest. If one gives approval to their imitations of someone else's work, he may check their impulse to paint what they feel. The preschool years are not the time to emphasize mastery of the techniques of drawing and painting.

Without special instruction children do not usually learn to name colors correctly much before the age of five. Of the three primary colors, yellow seems to be preferred by infants. Red next becomes the favorite color, and blue and green are increasingly preferred by older children. Young children demonstrate a pronounced preference for saturated colors —the brighter the better. The more subtle, pastel shades preferred by older children are not usually chosen by young children (47, p. 399, 1956). A few children show sensitivity to color harmony as early as the fourth year. At all ages girls seem to be more sensitive to colors than are boys, but they are not always superior in color discrimination. Great individual differences are found in preschool children's responses to color.

Differences in musical ability are likewise great. Of a group of sixteen children between the ages of three and a half and four and a half years, some were wholly unable to reproduce a simple melody on a tin fife, while others gave an almost perfect performance. Those who were least capable were not at all interested. A more natural way for preschool children to express their interest in music is by singing, marching or skipping to rhythm, and by playing drums, cymbals, and other percussion instruments.

Unlike most of the earlier motor skills of walking, grasping objects, and so on, the developments just mentioned do not take place without training. The amount that the child learns depends largely on the opportunities provided in his environment, and the degree of encouragement and help that people give him. He still must do his own learning, but he will learn skills quicker and better if the adult gives him just the right help at just the right time. Given a favorable environment, it is astonishing how much a preschool child will learn.

COMMUNICATION ARTS

Man's ability to make use of his higher mental processes is largely dependent on his social experience. The use of language and other techniques of thinking are built on the discoveries of the past (32, 1950). As soon as the child acquires language, his opportunities for communication are increased. Children receive a great deal of social experience through putting words and sentences together in ways that help them solve their problems and reach their goals. Even sentences which the child learns from others can help him work out solutions on his own. Thus one little boy who was continually teased by a bully down the street, was told, "He's just trying to get you angry. If you didn't fight back, he wouldn't tease you." The next time the child met the bully, he repeated this to himself, acted accordingly, and after several trials succeeded in discouraging the bully.

The complex process whereby the child learns to associate patterns and chains of thought and action with words and sentences is the very foundation of social communication and the use of language as thought. The child learns to listen and talk so that he can satisfy his desires and needs, express his thoughts and feelings, and can communicate with others more effectively than through his earlier methods of crying and gesturing.

Preschool children often talk to themselves to explain what they are doing. Their talking and thinking go on simultaneously; they talk so that they will know what they think. "I'm going to put my dollie to bed. I'll wash her face first. I can wash my face, too." By means of these soliloquies adults can often gain insight into the way a child's mind is working. A change from what Piaget has called *egocentric speech* to social conversation is related to the child's perception of himself and others.

Growth in vocabulary and sentences

The understanding of other people's speech is accompanied by rapid expansion of the child's own vocabulary. At the age of two he may know only one or two hundred words; at six, around two thousand. Three-year-olds can be expected to give the right names to pictures of common objects, to obey simple commands, to talk about pictures presented to them, and to answer questions involving simple cause-and-effect relations. Children's knowledge of words varies in quality as well as in quantity. The meanings they attach to some words have grown out of firsthand experience, and are vivid and precise; their understanding of other words is vague or incorrect. Between these two extremes are all degrees of word knowledge. Individual differences in this respect are as wide as the ranges of childhood experiences that lie behind speech.

Beginning with single words, mostly nouns and verbs, and single-word sentences, preschool children's speech develops to complete sentences of six to eight words. At two years of age, children's sentences are often, on the average, about two words long; at four and a half years they tend to increase to five words. Sentences such as, "I'll come in when you call me," are occasionally used by three-year-old children. During the same period, their output of incomprehensible speech and incomplete sentences decreases.

Conversation

At about four years or earlier, children can carry on real conversations. In the following samples of the conversation of three-year-olds, four-year-olds, and five-year-olds, difference in quality may be noted:

Three-year-olds:

Don is sitting on his haunches in front of the water tank in which float several boats. He washes a boat with a cloth. "Too much, that's what makes dirty."

Betty holds the sprinkling can, and Ben fills it up for her.

BETTY: That's enough.

BEN: I can carry it.

BETTY: No, I can. (She carries can into bathroom, but comes right out and starts sprinkling water into tank.)

DON: You're getting me wet. Bad girl.

BETTY: I'm not a bad girl.

Four-year-olds:

Five four-year-olds were working around a table. They had taken some dough out of a jar and were going to make cookies. The teacher found the cookie cutters for them.

CHARLES: Look, I made a chicken.

JIMMY: I want the chicken cutter, please.

CHARLES: No!

SALLY: When he says *please*, it's nice to give it.

Five-year-olds:

Three girls were sitting around the clay table, each with a lump of clay. They carried on the following conversation, which fluctuated between childish and adult ideas, logical and illogical content:

JANE: My clay is like lotion.

ALICE: What are you making, Jane?

JANE: Nothing. Just something. (She rolls clay balls.) Now I'm going to smooth it and leave it that way. . . . Hi, the cups look tiny, like doll-house cups. (To Alice:) Do you know how to make cross-eyes? . . . I do. (Alice tries.)

JANE: Your eyes will stay like that. Won't you look silly if your eyes stay that way. If your eyes are cross-eyed, you can't make them cross-eyed.

DOROTHY: Just like if you get the chicken pox you can't get it any more.

At the end of the fifth year children differ greatly in their language ability. Some still use only very simple words and sentences. Others converse as fluently as many adults.

Sex differences

For a while girls have a slight edge over boys in language development. They have a larger vocabulary; they talk more; they begin earlier to use longer and more complex sentences. After six years of age this superiority is not so marked.

Content of children's speech

The lack of continuity and scope in children's speech is the result of the poverty of their experience, the brevity of their memory and the shortness of their attention span. Insofar as the child lives in the present, his speech is concerned with immediate objects and events. Although by the age of about four the child may begin to use the future tense, he is still concerned primarily with the present, and has almost no apparent interest in the past. His language reflects his attitude toward life.

Similarly, the little child's world centers upon himself. "I" and "me" are pronouns that recur frequently after the child has gained a certain amount of self-awareness. Other common words are those that have direct social significance to the child—"mother," "home," "father," "brother," and "sister."

Many words have a different meaning for a child than they have for adults. Four-year-olds use words like "kill" and "die" to dispose of persons they dislike or with whom they are temporarily annoyed. They do not seem to expect death to be final. One child said to a playmate, "Bang! Bang! Now you're dead," and the playmate nonchalantly replied, "I'm busy now, so I can't die." (One is reminded of the philosopher and poet Goethe's comment that one does not die until he consents to die.) These expressions of pseudo-hostility do not alarm the parent who realizes that four-year-olds talk that way. Some children of this age are bothered by words that sound the same but have different meanings. To them words are confusing enough anyway without having the same form but different meanings. Moreover, there is a startling variation in the meaning that different children give to the same words.

Children often play with words. One child leads off with some absurdity and the others try to go him one better. A group of four-year-olds had learned a new song, one line of which was: "I wish you a Merry Christmas." One child began to substitute all kinds of words for the word "Christmas." He said, "I wish you a merry gumdrop." Another child said, "I wish you a merry airplane." The rest joined in with other incongruous words. The children became hilarious over this word play. They also enjoyed inventing other expressions which had the humor of incongruity, e.g., "I'm going to take you to the circus in my pocket."

Preschool children vary in their loquacity. It has been estimated that some four-year-olds speak as many as ten thousand words a day; others vary in their chattering from zero to 1,100 words per hour.

Preschool children's questions

On the average, 10 to 15 per cent of preschool children's conversation consists of questions. When he started to climb up on one of the living-room chairs, one four-year-old was told, "Teddy, *your* chair is to climb on, but grownup chairs will get scratched or break." This simple statement evoked a veritable avalanche of questions: "Then what will you have to do?" "Why can't you fix it yourself?" "Will it cost a lot?" "If you have to pay for it, what else can't you get?" And so on. Another four-year-old seemed more scientifically inclined: "Mama, why are there two suns out?" (One was the moon.) "Why do worms dig tunnels?" "Was I ever really as little as that one?" (pointing to a newborn baby). A slightly older child riding in the subway asked, "What is that old man for?" Only children, and children in well-to-do homes tend to ask more questions than the average, perhaps because they get more satisfactory answers. Almost all their questions concern immediate situations. Sometimes when a child asks, "Why?" he is just wondering out loud. Sometimes he forgets the question by the time he has finished it, or a new question occurs to him before he can wait for the answer of the first one.

Sometimes children's questions are about things that no man knoweth (46, 1956). When children ask such questions as "Who made the world?" and "Why are there people?" and many other questions about God and heaven and the meaning of life, parents and teachers should reply with answers that do not belittle the eternal mysteries. Better an "I don't know," than a reply that bricks up with indifference or prejudice the first window a child opens toward the unseen.

Children ask questions for many reasons: to satisfy the natural curiosity of an inquiring mind, to get information or reassurance, to get attention, to solve a problem, to test their own judgment. Sometimes they ask questions just to be sociable—to prolong a personal contact. Adults should try to understand what a child's question means to him.

Errors in speech

In their spontaneous conversations, preschool children commonly omit an essential word or misuse a verb form. Immature speech should not be confused with speech defects. Even though a child seems slow in outgrowing his infantile speech patterns, it is usually better to provide social contacts that stimulate him to talk correctly than to correct his errors or drill him on the mechanics of speech.

Stimulation of language development

Experiences to talk about, people who will listen, play materials like dolls, blocks, and clay that stimulate conversation, chances to listen to stories told or read—all these experiences stimulate language development. At two years of age children are most fond of simple stories about themselves and familiar things. At four years, they enjoy longer stories about the mailman, milkman, and other familiar persons and things in their expanding environment. Books that appeal to children's awareness of sound, taste, smell, touch, and sight are especially attractive to four- and five-year-olds. Margaret Wise Brown has written for young children a number of books that make various sense appeals. For example, her "Noisy" series bring the child in contact with city noises, country noises, and seashore noises through the story of a small sightless dog, Muffin, who trots around hearing noises. Five-year-olds enjoy nonsense stories and rhymes, as well as realistic stories.

MENTAL DEVELOPMENT

Aspects of mental ability

Language ability is closely related to general mental ability. As a child grows older, his vocabulary and word usage become the best single indication of his intelligence as commonly measured. According to Piaget (88, 1955), sensory-motor ability is the basis of intelligence; it influences perception and leads to the formation of concepts on a higher level of thinking than perception alone. Other ingredients of intelligence are ability to perceive situations accurately, to see relations, to remember, to use good judgment, and to persist in solving problems.

Attention. Attention is a complex factor involving drive, memory, culturally imposed inhibitions, and other past experience. To learn anything, a child must first pay attention to it. His ability to attend to a particular thing increases with age. It was found that children three and four years old would wait attentively eight seconds for a jack-in-the-box to open; five-year-olds would wait twice as long; six-year-olds, more than three times as long. In spontaneous play two-year-olds stayed with a given activity only six to seven minutes, while five-year-olds maintained their interest in one kind of play about twice as long. In individual children, the length of the attention span ranged from one to forty-five minutes. In general, preschool children may be expected to sustain attention from seven to twenty minutes, according to their maturity and the appropriateness and interest value of the activity.

Perception. Perception involves sensory-motor activity, memory, and association. It involves exploration of the visual field, fixing the eyes successively on different parts, relating these parts, and anticipating parts that are not yet clearly perceived. The child tends to overestimate the part of the visual space on which the eyes focus and to underestimate the periphery. Thus visual space contracts or expands depending upon the point fixated by the eye. As the child grows older his good perceptual patterns become more fixed—three times more resistant to change at nine to ten years than at five to seven.

The development of perception in young children has been studied by analysis of repeated Rorschach tests given to the same children—fifty in all (8, 1953). At every age from two to nine years, their perception of the inkblots was predominately global, i.e., they perceived the blot as a whole and were more influenced by the total configuration of a visual stimulus than by specific details. They responded more frequently to large than to small details. Their response to form alone decreased from two to seven years. During the first three years the children's perception tended to be vague and inaccurate. By three years of age many children could point out accurately the parts of the blot they were identifying, but they tended to keep repeating a certain response rather than respond to each new visual stimulus. By three and a half years they introduced things which were not clearly present in the blot and appeared to confuse pictures of objects with actual objects, and animate with inanimate objects. During the fourth year children's perceptions were uncertain and either confused, or expressive of runaway imagination.

Studies such as those by Ames and her associates and Allen's records on single children (3, 1955) suggest certain developmental trends in perception: a change from the global approach to the ability to differentiate parts, an increase in creativity and imagination, and more control over emotionality without inhibiting a spontaneous reaction to environmental stimuli.

Seeing relations.   Still more advanced is the ability to see relations. After learning the names of objects and discovering what they are made of and what can be done with them, the child begins to note relations among them. One bright child slightly more than two years old wanted to know how everything was made. When he asked his mother, "How are cans made?" she said, "In a can factory." "How are my shoes made?" "In a shoe factory." Then he asked, "How is kitty made?" Before his mother had found an answer, he supplied it himself: "In a kitty factory." Although errors in judgment are common among preschool children, their ability to make simple rational deductions within the limits of their experience is frequently underestimated.

Between the ages of three and five, children show an increasing ability to put parts of a picture puzzle together, to match various forms, to distinguish two boxes of different weight and two lines of different length. Spatial relations—up and down, over and under, before and behind—are the first to be learned, usually not before the age of five. Between the third and the sixth years, children learn to judge distances. They become more precise in their use of such words as "over," "back," and "from." First, they recognize objects in relation to themselves; then they see the relations between objects; finally they begin to think of space more abstractly—and become at home in rocket ships. Children of five are often able to compare the speeds of two moving objects, even when they do not see them pass one another.

Time relations follow a similar pattern. Concepts of time develop slowly. A child in his second year may know the meaning of "now," but not of "soon." It may take six months' more experience to give him a real comprehension of "soon." Most children do not use "yesterday," "today," and "tomorrow" correctly until about their fifth year. Little children are helped by schedules, measurements, cues that show sequences, and statements such as, "It's time to put away your toys." "It's time for Grandpa to come home."

Children do not seem to have much sense of their own growth until about their fourth birthday; then they become interested in hearing stories about when they were "very young." They become aware that they are changing and growing, but they have difficulty in thinking of adults as having once been young or as growing older. Yet the will-to-grow, to-become-adult, although vaguely felt, may account for children's development quite clearly and convincingly.

Concept formation. The preschool child's ideas of space, form, and size are abstractions which develop through experiences with real objects. The precision of his concepts develops as he learns to associate the sensations of sight, touch, temperature, sound, smell, movement, and emotion with the object or event to which he is attending. It also depends on his ability to distinguish among the relevant and irrelevant sensations characteristic of one object but not of another. At first he calls everything with four legs a chair. A bunny may be to him any kind of soft furry animal. Later he sees differences between a bunny, a squirrel, a kitten, a puppy. It is not until he gives objects a name—begins to use language—that he sees ways in which an object is similar to another object having the same name, and different from an object having a different name. When a child forms such a concept, he can tell what the object's essential characteristics are; he can think and talk about it. This ability does not develop in most children until the later preschool years.

Useful ideas of number may be acquired in this period. Two-year-olds usually know the difference between "one" and "many." At three years "two" has real meaning. It is easier for a child to bring five apples than to tell how many apples are in the dish. Experience with things in series is good preparation for learning to count. Like primitive people, the child's first attempt at counting is a naming process. "One" is the name of the first flower in the row. "Two" is the name of the second. If a child is told he may pick four flowers, he will probably pick only the fourth flower. The task of counting four objects, in response to the question, "How many?" is placed on the revised Stanford-Binet scale at the five-year level. If children use rulers and measuring cups in their play, they will become familiar with the concepts of inch, pint, and quart, if someone is at hand to name these quantities for them. The number concepts acquired through experience in the later preschool years supply a valuable arithmetical background for the primary-school child.

Concept formation in children progresses by clarifying old concepts and reorganizing them into new patterns. Parents often expect children to comprehend highly abstract ideas before they have gone through the stages requisite to the formation of these concepts. This is often done with the concept of God. Parents and church-school teachers are likely to forget that the preschool child's world consists of the things and persons he can see and touch, the activities in which he engages day by day. God is a symbol that embraces the greater purposiveness of experience and life. It is an abstraction of the highest order. However, parents and teachers should be cautioned against introducing God as the reason or cause or purpose of everything for which they lack a simple naturalistic explanation. A better reply is, "I don't know." Otherwise, as the child develops and learns more about physical causation, he may completely reject his early conception of God.

The concept of God as a spirit can have little meaning to a little child. For example, a four-year-old who had been taught that God made the flowers and sunshine and rain, one day said, "God can do anything, can't He, Mummie? He makes cars run over people." After looking at pictures of the destruction caused by a hurricane a five-year-old said, "God made the hurricane. . . . If he makes the rain and snow, he must make the wind, too." (35, 1939) These children were thinking of God as a sort of superman who was doing things that to them seemed bad. The concept that God is everywhere is equally difficult for preschool children to grasp. If these ideas are introduced prematurely, children may get fantastic misconceptions of God.

Death is another concept difficult for preschool children to grasp. If there is a death in the family, it is usually better for the child to share the experience with the persons he loves than to be sent away until the funeral is over, only to return with unanswered questions. Children three to five years old do not think of death as final; to them it is more likely to mean "going away" for a longer or shorter time. Only when death has broken a relation that means much to them do they begin to understand its significance (117, 1958).

Problem-solving. Children have to think whenever they meet difficulties, whenever they want something they cannot immediately get. For example, if a child's playhouse of boxes tumbles down, he must invent a more secure way of placing them. If a tower grows beyond his reach, he must devise some means, such as climbing up on a chair, to add more blocks to the edifice. If he loses a ball under the piano, he may, after some trial and error, use a stick to push it out. A four-year-old boy in a swing saw that a wagon was in the way. If he swung higher he would hit it. When he saw the relation between the wagon and the swing he pushed the wagon away. A child two years and six months old, seeing his father picking peas, said, "Tom away?" Tom was the gardener who usually brought in the vegetables. Many of a child's errors in reasoning are due to inexperience.

Children like to find out things for themselves. They remember solutions that work and discard those that do not. Adults should not short-circuit this process by telling the child answers that he could find out for himself. One youngster who had a great desire to investigate everything discovered some dry ice in which ice cream had been packed. His mother said she was glad he had not touched it. He said soberly, "Well, I did touch it a little teeny bit, and it gave me a shock so I left it alone." When information is given it should be accurate, and errors in thinking can be tactfully corrected. Persistent misconceptions may hamper the child's school adjustment.

Memory. Memory is the child's response to a need to understand the past in relation to his present self. The abilities to receive, absorb, and clarify impressions are a prerequisite to memory. These abilities are essential to seeing relationships and behaving intelligently. Both develop with age. Two-thirds of a group of preschool children between the ages of two and five and a half could remember after three days under which of three plates a cookie was hidden (98, 1931). Less than half remembered after twenty-one to twenty-nine days. They used different memory aids: some used verbal symbols, others used color to identify the correct plate. The memory span varies with the methods used by the experimenter, the type of task and its emotional meaning, and the age and personality of the child.

Some preschool children seem to have a photographic kind of memory. They can look attentively at an object and then, after several years, "see" it again. This type of image has been found occasionally in children of all levels of intelligence, and appears to be more common in preschool years than in later life.

Intelligence tests for preschool children include a number of memory items, tied up with verbal ability and comprehension:

At three years:

To select a previously identified animal picture from among several on a different card.
To repeat three digits.

At four years:

To tell which of three objects is missing, after one has been hidden.
To repeat four digits.
To obey simple commands which involve keeping the directions in mind as well as comprehending them.

A four-year-old in a nursery school remembered all day the picture puzzle he wanted to take home with him. Pleasant experiences seem to be remembered more easily than disagreeable ones—"ice cream" lingers in the mind longer than "spinach."

Individual differences

There are marked differences in mental ability among preschool children, even among those in the same family. At one extreme is the feeble-minded; at the other extreme, the gifted child. For an accurate diagnosis of feeblemindedness, a thorough clinical study is essential. In estimating the intelligence of any child, we should take time to observe his learning behavior under favorable environmental conditions. Often his day-by-day performance is quite different from that which would be expected on the basis of a single intelligence test.

Definition and measurement of intelligence

Although psychologists have been testing intelligence for over 50 years they have as yet failed to reach agreement on the definition of what they are measuring. Most of the definitions proposed emphasize: (1) adjustment, or the adaptation of the individual to his environment; (2) the ability to learn; and/or (3) the ability to carry on abstract thinking (40, pp. 60-62, 1955). Wechsler includes all three categories in his definition of intelligence as "the aggregate or global capacity of the individual to act purposefully, to think rationally, and to deal effectively with his environment." (112, p. 3, 1944)

In constructing tests of intelligence the psychologist for practical reasons must discard such broad definitions. Instead, he makes up tests with many kinds of items, each of which can be passed by some persons and failed by others. These items tend to fall into clusters which he may call tests of perceptual speed, word fluency, or verbal ability; or if a variety of different tests are all highly intercorrelated, he will call such a cluster a general factor.

The psychologist also wants to know if this measured ability is important for getting along at school or work. To this end he correlates his test with performance of various kinds. If the correlations are high, the test is a useful one because it can predict how well a person will, or can be normally expected to, perform.

Intelligence tests and theoretical issues

In general, intelligence tests are constructed so as to minimize an advantage of environment, training, or role.

1. *Sex differences.* Girls tend to score highest on some items while boys score highest on others. Since these differences can be accounted for on the basis of exposure to different experiences, the test items are selected so that neither sex is favored over the other.

2. *Socioeconomic differences.* Early investigators have reported differences of about twenty IQ points between children of parents engaged in the professions and children of unskilled laborers. Terman argued for the predominant influence of heredity on the grounds that the differences found in early childhood, i.e., with six-year-old children, were also found with older children. Later studies showed that children from underprivileged homes may have an IQ of 100 at six but 85 at thirteen. It may be argued that the content of the older tests is biased in favor of middle-class children, but even when the content has been made more suitable for children of lower social status, there is still social class differences in scores (43, 1954). This difference may be due to the cumulative effect of poor environment, an inherent difference in rate of mental growth, or both. Better-educated parents are, in general, brighter than those who have dropped out of school, and tend to provide a more intellectually stimulating environment for their children. However, a "good" home as judged by its rating on a scale of socioeconomic status is not necessarily a "good" home psychologically.

3. *Emotional adjustment.* A clinical study of thirty nursery school children (30, 1946) showed a close relation in all of the cases between emotional adjustment and changes in IQ. In instances in which large gains

are made in IQ points, it is possible that an emotional block has prevented the child from performing at his optimum level. In some cases temporary, but severe emotional tension may disorganize a child's responses to intelligence test items.

4. *Home and nursery-school environment.* A large number of experiments have been carried out to determine the effect of an enriched nursery school environment on IQ change. Marked gains were obtained only when the children tested were initially from an extremely impoverished environment. Other gains from nursery school attendance may be attributed in part to familiarity with the testing situation and to an increased sense of personal worth and a greater security in social relationships, which favorably affect mental functioning.

5. *Constancy of IQ.* By the age of five or six, it is possible to classify children quite reliably into groupings of normal, defective, and bright (18, p. 808, 1955). The older the child grows, the more stable his IQ usually becomes. Variations in IQ from one year to another result from fluctuation in rate of general mental development and of various specific abilities as well as from changes in the nature of the abilities sampled by the test and other individual factors. It should be noted that differences in scores based on different kinds of intelligence tests cannot be interpreted as changes in IQ. Recognition of fluctuations in rate of growth are important to insure

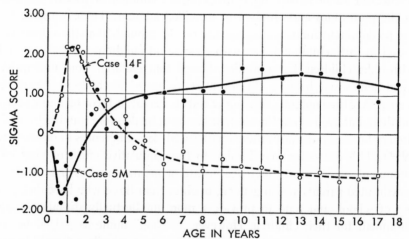

Fig. 3. Individual mental growth curves: two contrasting cases.

(From original data, Berkeley Growth Study, Harold E. Jones, "The Environment and Mental Development," in Leonard Carmichael, ed., *Manual of Child Psychology,* p. 642. New York: John Wiley & Sons, Inc., 1954.)

caution in interpreting a specific IQ score and to set limits to the confidence with which one can generalize.

Individual growth curves "will enable us to observe a child's periods of fast and slow progress, his spurts and plateaus, and even regressions, in relation to his own past and future" (18, p. 814, 1955). Many factors may explain the ups and downs in these individual curves: changes in the tests used at different ages; current conditions of motivation, health, or emotional well-being or disturbance; environmental influences. The mental growth curves in Figure 3 illustrate striking contrasts in growth pattern not often found in the usual sample.

It is extremely unwise to judge a child's mental ability on the results of a single test. Test results should be supplemented by systematic, accurate, daily observation of the child's way of learning. Psychological examinations should always be interpreted dynamically and in the light of all other information available about the child in his environment.

Functioning intelligence

A preschool child's mental alertness is expressed in action more often than in words. It shows up in his resourcefulness in meeting daily difficulties. His thinking is largely about concrete, familiar, and present experiences.

Even if the structure and quality of a child's nervous system cannot be altered, a few practical suggestions for helping every child to attain his intellectual potentialities may be offered:

1. Provide understanding and "affectionate training" in the home. Try to modify any emotional block, parental attitudes, or environmental deprivation that may be decreasing the child's learning ability.
2. Discover and correct any glandular or nutritional deficiency which may influence the child's ability to learn.
3. Put the preschool child in an environment favorable to the exercise of his ingenuity and the satisfaction of his curiosity, such as a nursery school rich in educational and social experience, but not overstimulating.
4. Put the orphaned or neglected child in a carefully selected foster home where he will receive an optimum amount of stimulation and personal care.
5. Avoid putting pressure on the child to achieve beyond his true ability.

PLAY ACTIVITIES

Most of the preschool child's learning about himself and his world is accomplished by means of play. Through making and doing things he develops motor skills. Through playing with other children, he learns how people respond when he does certain things. Through fantasy and dramatic play, he gets an idea of how other people feel—how it feels to be a teacher, a mother, a baby, a doctor, a policeman, a milkman. When he acts out experiences in play, he achieves successes that he may not have been able to achieve with real people in real situations. Some achievement of this kind is necessary to neutralize the young preschool child's feeling of inability to cope with increasingly complicated life situations.

Many children seem to follow a general sequence in their play. First they merely "hustle things around"—handle them, take them apart and put them together again, pick them up and put them down. These activities satisfy their desire for action per se. Later they become more interested in building things. Having acquired this skill, they use it to serve other ends and purposes. Readiness for certain play activities develops gradually. The father often wants to play games that are beyond his son's present phase of development. He finds it hard to wait for the baby to grow up enough to play the games he enjoys. Healthy children do not engage in one kind of activity exclusively; they move from one activity to another.

Make-believe and dramatization

Children often express their fantasies during free play. Adults can learn much by observing the child in free-play situations, by noting his responses to selected pictures, incomplete stories, and puppets, and by listening to what he says about them. A child's make-believe often yields insights into his home relationships, adult characteristics, or his social and emotional adjustment. In doll-play, he may express jealousy of his baby sister. Or he may reflect, very accurately, the attitudes which his mother has taken toward him, and which she thought she had concealed. Nursery-school children in a residential community of young mothers who were occupied with many social activities would often have the mother doll say to the little-girl doll, "You bad, naughty little girl to get up so early in the morning!"

However, such play responses are difficult to interpret. A child who is apparently docile at home may be violently aggressive in free-play situations or in play-therapy sessions. A child playing the role of mother or teacher may soundly spank her imaginary children, although she has never experienced spanking herself. In play the child may gain understanding of real life situations and how to cope with them; he may safely express his feelings of hostility, fear, and inadequacy. On the other hand, severe anxiety may interfere with constructive play.

Before the age of five, imaginative play most often involves constructing a house and supplying all the necessary details. A four-year-old may play that he is running an elevator with only a post to represent reality; or he may line up several children to form an imaginary train. There is little need for stage properties; imagination supplies them. Children are pleased when adults go along with them on some of these imaginary adventures. One four-year-old flung open the door of the nursery and announced excitedly, "Dr. C. [the family physician] is here." When his mother saw no evidence of the doctor's arrival, she said, "How do you know Dr. C. is here?" At once he grinned broadly and shouted, "Because I'm him." Then he produced a flashlight, a pair of pincers for a stethoscope, and a pencil for a tongue depressor. Preschool children also like to dramatize simple stories. There seems to be a period, somewhere between the ages of five and seven, when the actual world is no longer strange and frightening, but before it becomes matter-of-fact, when fairy tales delight the imaginative child.

Imaginary playmates are sometimes very real to children three years of age or older. From one-tenth to one-third of the children in various studies reported having had an imaginary playmate. These fantasies were not limited to lonely children. Imaginary companions serve different purposes for different children. For some, they represent a relief from loneliness; for others, a means of draining off resentment. In other cases the imaginary companion reproves the child or increases his sense of guilt and fear. Some companions seem to serve no special purpose, but they are nonetheless real until in time they fade away or die a dramatic death.

DREAMS

In the preschool child's mind, dreams are real events. There are no clear boundary lines between the world of facts, and his own world of imagination and dreams. Dreams are frequent among preschool children. Almost half of a group whose mothers kept daily records had some unpleasant dreams during the week.

Various interpretations have been given to dreams. At one extreme is the view that dreams are related to exciting or emotional experiences that have occurred during the day, especially just before bedtime. Some detail of the experience appears in the dream but is changed in character; for instance, a friendly dog seen in the afternoon may become a strange and fearful animal in the dream. At the other extreme is the psychiatric point of view that "through dreams children spontaneously express their hopes, fears, conflicts, wishes, needs, hostilities, and frustration." (29, 1955) So viewed, dreams become "one of the most fruitful sources for uncovering personality dynamics." De Martino mentioned several cautions in interpreting children's dreams: Young children (1) frequently confuse dreams with real experiences, if the dream is not recorded immediately on waking, (2) tend to fill in missing detail, (3) do not report occurrences contrary to their own experiences, and (4) are limited by lack of vocabulary.

Age, personality, socioeconomic status, intelligence, physical health, and the day's experiences seem to affect the frequency and content of children's dreams. Unpleasant dreams arise from fear-beliefs rather than from fear-experiences. Aggressiveness in dreams is related to anxiety over aggressiveness in life, and neurotic children have more dreams regarding death than do healthy normal children. Frequent dreamers are usually anxious, though the converse is not true.

SPIRITUAL DEVELOPMENT

The child and his concepts concerning religion should grow up to-gether; in childhood, religion should contribute to the child's social as well as spiritual development. It should supplement not supplant reality. Since many of the child's religious concepts are gained from experiences with his parent, family relations and methods of discipline are very important. The child's ideas of God, sin, guilt, and forgiveness grow out of his experiences with parental love, authority, and the parent's treatment of his successes and failures, accomplishments and mistakes, joys and sorrows. During the years when children think of everything in their environment as animate, God is near at hand and vividly alive to them (44, 1955).

We should also be careful not to brush aside brusquely children's "wonder of the world." Francis Thompson expressed it in this way:

> The angels keep their ancient places
> Turn but a stone and start a wing.
> 'Tis ye with your estranged faces
> That miss the many-splendored thing.

A great scientist recognized the limits of his knowledge of the physical world when he said, "In the beginning, God." This was his ultimate explanation. A great philosopher wrote an essay on "The Unknowable." Neither of these outstanding persons had ever lost their sense of spiritual forces in the world.

SOCIAL-EMOTIONAL DEVELOPMENT

Social development during the preschool years reflects the child's expanding world. From the first close ties to his mother he expands his relations to include his father and other persons in his immediate family, and then begins to reach out in contacts with children of his own size. His relations with the latter stem largely from his play activity. Desire for physical activity, for the company of others, for recognition and approval—all may enter into children's social behavior.

Social relations

Both individual differences and age differences are illustrated in the following examples of social behavior of mentally superior children.

Three-year-olds:

Two boys, Bert and James, are watching the water boil.

BERT (stands with the lid of the saucepan in his hand, looking at the water, and says): Put it on, not boiling, take it off, boiling.

TEACHER (joins them and watches): Let's turn the fire off and see what happens. See if the bubbles get bigger or smaller.

BERT: Bubbles become bigger, bigger.

TEACHER: If you want them to become bigger, you have to turn the fire on. Cover it up and see what happens. (She walks away and Bert immediately takes the lid off.) Bert walks away and when he comes back, James has the lid.

BERT: My cover, my cover. He won't give it back.

TEACHER: There are two covers and you can each use one.

BERT (tries the other cover and finds it too small): No, that's my one.

TEACHER: You must ask James, and when he's through, he'll give it to you.

BERT: My cover!

TEACHER: James, do you think it's time for Bert to have it?

JAMES: No!

TEACHER: James, you tell Bert when it's his turn.

BERT: It's my turn.

Teacher is busy elsewhere for a moment and then comes back.

TEACHER: James, you go along and help get your cot now, and then Bert can have the cover a little while.

BERT (to James and rest of group): You folks rest and when it's ready I'll call you. (To teacher): Leave it as it is, and nobody touch it so it can boil.

Four-year-olds:

Jane poured the juice and carried the paper cups to the table, serving each in turn.

BETTY: Jane comes last.

SALLY: You don't mind, Jane, do you?
Jane shakes her head.
SALLY: Jane is nice, she doesn't mind if she's last.
Jane offered the observer a cup of juice.
OBSERVER: Oh, one for me, too? Thank you very much, Jane.
JANE (smiling—an infrequent occurrence; she seemed surprised): How did
you know my name? Did teacher tell you?

Five-year-olds:

Two five-year-olds, a boy and a girl, are playing at the water tank—a long
square tub with boats, fish, wooden men floating in it, and a good-sized water
pump sturdily mounted on a wooden box at one end.
JEAN: I caught two fishes! (She takes them out of her net.) Look, bright colors,
red and yellow.
BOB: You put them in the pump. (She does so, and he pumps the water; the
fish cataract down. This is repeated several times—along with conversa-
tion.)
A second girl, Mary, joins them.
MARY: I'll play in the water but my Daddy doesn't want me to. (To Bob):
Will you play in the water if your Daddy doesn't want you to?
BOB: Sure!

Techniques of social behavior develop in response to the demands of
the situation. For example, the twin, Jimmy, who had not learned to
climb, became skillful in inducing Johnny to climb up and get the jam for
him.

The preschool child's first approach to other children is to look them
over, very much as he examines inanimate objects in his environment. In
general, the two-year-old likes to engage in parallel play, provided his companions do not interfere with his activities. Even when other children are
available, two-year-olds tend to play alone more than half the time. Children of this age do not always respond to friendly overtures.

Curiosity often brings them together in bunches. Imitation often
leads several children to do the same thing. Imaginative play encourages
real social interaction. Before the age of four neither competition nor co-
operation has real meaning for them. By the age of five, children more
frequently engage in common play projects. Even at five, however, children observed in nursery school engaged in individual play with materials
from one-third to one-half of the time.

Children grow in sociability if their social environment and guidance
are favorable. They tend to show development along these lines: (1) they
spend more time in social contacts with an increasing number of children,

(2) they show greater skill in relating themselves to others, (3) they make more active and constructive social use of materials and equipment, and (4) they become able to play with materials and with other children for longer periods of time. Children who have grown up in a family with other children, who have playmates at home, or who have had experience in nursery school are usually at an advantage in making social contacts. It is through the play experiences of the preschool years that children begin to learn the give-and-take that is fundamental to all social interaction.

Do girls engage in more social interaction of a friendly nature than do boys? There does not seem to be much difference between boys and girls in social acceptance and social interaction as observed by teachers. Girls, however, tended to seek satisfaction from dependency on adults rather than from participation with their peers more frequently than boys. Even at this early age boys seem to avoid a dependency relation with teachers and compensate for their lack of popularity with their peers in other ways (67, 1957).

Extreme dependency at the preschool age may be due to several causes—to unsatisfied needs for affection, to frustration in infancy, to overprotective parents, to lack of techniques for relating to other children. With two small groups of preschool children around four to five years of age in free play situations, over-dependence on adults "accompanied relatively low social status and group participation." (68, 1957) Pain and illness are often accompanied by the tendency to withdraw from social contacts.

The quality of children's social relations is more important than the quantity. How do they behave toward one another? Are they sympathetic or aggressive, forward or shy? Do they initiate activities or merely acquiesce or imitate? The same children may show sympathy, aggression, and leadership to a marked degree and with many variations. In a given environment, however, some are predominantly sympathetic; others predominantly aggressive (82, 1937).

Sympathetic behavior

Sympathetic behavior in a preschool child may merely indicate that he recognizes another child's distress, and feels sorry for himself also. Another child may merely imitate the behavior that members of his own family have expressed toward him in similar situations. With increasing social experience involving shared emotional reactions common to situations, comes the ability to understand how a playmate feels in elation or in anger. This quality of social sensitivity and a warm feeling toward others is related to the best kind of leadership—not dominating, not bossy, not showy, but a quiet and constructive influence.

In a favorable environment spontaneous co-operation is frequently noticed. When a three-year-old girl did not know where to hang her hat and coat, a little boy took her by the hand and showed her. Two children played together with the swing, one pushing and the other swinging. Two children set the table together without any supervision from the teacher.

The way in which a mother's casual comments may influence a child's social behavior is illustrated by the following incident:

David, two years and eight months old, was very generous and could not understand why his playmates did not share their toys with him. While he was visiting his grandmother a little girl, Mary Jane, came over into the garden with her rake and shovel. She would not let David touch them. After asking her "Please," he came crying to his mother.

DAVID: I want a rake.

MOTHER: Well, David, it costs a lot of money.

DAVID: I have big money.

MOTHER: All right, let's go to the store and buy one.

DAVID: When I get my pretty rake, I will not let Mary Jane play with it.

MOTHER: That's right, David, you show her.

DAVID: I will show her—she will not let me have her rake. She can't have mine.

(Later David is raking slowly when Mary Jane arrives on the scene.)

MARY JANE: Hi, Dave.

DAVID: Hello, Mary Jane.

MARY JANE: Let me have your rake, Dave.

DAVID: No.

MARY JANE: I don't have any rake, Dave.

DAVID: Yes, you have.

MARY JANE: It's broken, Dave.

DAVID: Mommy, Mary Jane's rake is broken.

MOTHER: Mary Jane's rake is not broken, Dave.

MARY JANE: Yes, it is.

DAVID (pointing finger at Mary Jane): My Mommy says it is not broken.

David continues to rake and does not talk to Mary Jane, who eventually goes home crying.

Aggressive behavior

The nature and frequency of aggressive behavior vary with the environment and the age of the child. Crowded conditions and lack of suitable play materials increase the frequency of conflict. Children left alone in a room with very few toys tend to become selfish and aggressive. Toys so big that two children are needed to play with them encourage social behavior.

It is no wonder that a two- to three-year-old child is frequently hard to manage. He is thwarted on every hand. His lack of physical skills prevents him from keeping up with older children; he wants to play with them but does not know how. Nor has he sufficient mastery of the language to explain his difficulties. As he becomes more competent he has fewer occasions for frustration. His methods of dealing with frustration also change. Primitive expressions of anger such as kicking, stamping, screaming, crying, throwing things, biting, and refusing to budge gradually disappear as they fail to bring the desired results. As their sense of cause and effect develops, children learn to focus their random expression of anger directly against the object or person that appears to prevent them from obtaining their wishes.

Younger children quarrel chiefly over toys; they try to get possession of the thing they want by sheer physical force. In three- to four-year-old children competitive behavior appears and is usually in a more intense form in children from a low socioeconomic background. Later they are likely to express resistance to interference by shouting angrily and by hurting the person or the property involved. But the aggressor is not always victorious, and even the victor cannot count popularity among his prizes. If the child is to learn how to both give and take, he must not be denied a reasonable number of such conflicts. To succeed in life each person needs to have a certain amount of aggressiveness, directed toward problems rather than against people.

Jealousy

Jealousy is a fear that something that means much to the child, especially the affection of a parent, will be transferred to a rival. Jealousy between brothers and sisters seems to occur most frequently when they differ in age from eighteen to forty-two months. When the age difference is greater, the relationship between siblings may be more free from jealousy. This seemed to be true of Teddy and Sammy. Teddy was ten and one-half years old when Sammy was born and, according to his mother, he was delighted when told they were going to have a baby, "and his pleasure in Sammy has never flagged. He very willingly takes care of him for me, enjoys playing with him. . . . Teddy has always been kind to smaller children. . . . People often ask me if Teddy wasn't jealous after being an only child for so long, but I am quite sure Sammy has been sheer gain for him."

Every child may be expected to feel both love and hate for his parents or for a new baby. If he is invariably affectionate toward the new baby, the mother should consider what need he has to behave in this way: Is he excessively dependent on her and afraid of losing her love? Is he trying to cover up a real feeling of intense hostility? Is he afraid that any expression of hostility toward the baby would result in punishment or deprivation for him? The preschool child may not have foreseen how hard it would be for him to share his mother with the new baby.

Children express jealousy in different ways. They may attack the rival physically—pinch or slap the baby when they get a chance. Or they may show a false, exaggerated affection for him. Jealousy may also appear as disobedience or obstinacy. It may lead to a relapse into bed-wetting, thumb-sucking, baby talk, or unreasonable demands for attention. Jealousy may be accompanied by self-pity and self-devaluation as a means of getting attention and affection.

Parents can try several methods to overcome a child's jealousy of a brother or sister: (1) the mother should show the older child that he, too, is loved and cherished; (2) the older child's desire for independence should be encouraged; (3) he should feel he is mother's partner in taking care of "their" baby.

Fears and anxiety

Fear is a form of withdrawal from a situation in which the child has no effective means of maintaining himself. Anxiety is more vague, more unconscious, more disproportionate to its apparent cause, more persistent and pervasive. At this age anxiety usually arises from the threatened loss of the approval of the person most important in his life. Another indirect cause of anxiety may be hostility aroused by restriction of the child's impulses and the resulting feeling of guilt over his hostility toward someone whom he loves.

The most serious fears seem to be associated with overdependence upon adults, emotional instability, insecurity in social relations, inability to protect one's rights, lack of skill in physical activities, and poor health. There are wide individual differences in children's responses to annoying or fear-provoking situations. The more intelligent children tend to develop certain fears earlier than do those of less intelligence. Girls tend to be more fearful than boys. Pervasive anxiety intensifies any fear-provoking situation.

Fears may increase with the child's self-awareness and his understanding of the real dangers in the world. For this reason children four and five years of age may become more fearful than they were earlier. They realize that some of the disasters they hear about may happen to them. Although most three-year-olds have outgrown their fears of high places, insecure footing, strangers, and loud noises, they may acquire other fears. They may people the dark with imaginary creatures.

Caution is quite different from intense, blind fear. There are real dangers to be recognized. The child should be encouraged to use caution in crossing the street, caution with strangers, and the like. But a preschool child's sense of security may be undermined by overstressing the dangers in his environment, the harmfulness of germs, the threat of insects and strange animals. Preschool children are influenced by a suspicious, cynical, negative attitude in the home.

When a child's fears are aroused by real dangers such as storms at sea, lightning and tornadoes, adults can help by accepting the child's feeling— "It's quite all right to feel afraid." It is also wise to let the child share in doing anything that can be done to minimize the danger. Adult and child are brought closer together by sharing a common fear and working together on a common problem. Talking beforehand about a possibly fearsome experience or acting it out sometimes helps to decrease the child's fear when it arises. The best antidotes to fear are a basic sense of trust, a feeling of being able to cope with situations, and a generally sound and stimulating environment.

Individual differences

Individual differences in the social habits acquired during the first five years are very great. Children differ in the relative amount of time they spend in solitary as compared with truly social play. Some approach strangers with the greatest friendliness and candor, while others refuse to speak in response to the most cordial greeting. In Marston's experiment (72, pp. 50-57, 1925) with children of two to six years, the experimenter, seated at a small table and playing with a teeter-totter, subjected each child in exactly the same way to six degrees of invitation:

1. He entirely ignored the presence of the child for sixty seconds.
2. He looked up at the child but "did not smile, or make other overtures of friendliness."
3. After another thirty seconds he looked up again and smiled.
4. After another thirty seconds he asked, "Do you like to teeter-totter?"
5. After thirty seconds more he looked up and asked cordially, "Would you like to play with this teeter-totter?"
6. He finally said reassuringly: "You may; come over and play with it."

Some children waited for no invitation, but ran immediately to the experimenter and began to play with the toy. Some children approached and began to play with the toy as soon as the experimenter recognized their presence with a smile. Some waited for the invitation, "Would you like to play with this teeter-totter?" Some needed additional assurance before they approached. Some required considerable urging, while others steadfastly refused to speak, smile, or touch the toy. It would be interesting to know *all* the details of the environmental conditions that may have produced these different social attitudes.

Fluctuations in behavior of an individual child are particularly baffling to parents. For example, when a child has passed his second birthday and seems to have become co-operative, outgoing, and amiable, it is disappointing and discouraging to parents when marked changes in his behavior occur. He may become more timid with strangers, less satisfied with himself and his environment. There are "seasons of calm weather" and periods of turmoil in the life of a child. Some children pass through a negative stage quite easily; others go all to pieces under stress.

As the child's awareness of his self develops, it is increasingly difficult to know what his observed behavior really means to him. When is sympathetic behavior an expression of genuine concern for the distress of another person, and when is it self-pity or desire to obtain approval? When is "resistance" not really resistance? When is "protective" behavior concealed hostility? What seems to be aggression may be nothing more than play-acting or experimentation on the part of the child. Unless there are deep-seated feelings of hostility, aggressive behavior tends to be transient. It is important to observe the kinds of situations that make a child happy, sad, angry, or afraid.

Ways of coping with social situations

The following glimpses of an unhappy, confused four-year-old, whose parents are divorced, show how mixed emotions not understood by the child influence his behavior. In turn, the child's negative behavior might well lessen the father's affection for him. His father is permitted to see David on Saturday afternoons for four hours.

November 3:

Another child, Laura, a ten-year-old cousin, goes up to David's father and says, "Here are some pictures—what do you think of them?"

DAVID (jumps off chair, jerks Laura's hand away roughly): He's my Daddy, you have your own Daddy.

LAURA: Oh, you're jealous. I'm going in to look at the television. (Does so and younger sister goes with her.)

DAVID: Good, now we're alone, huh, Daddy? (Puts his arm around father's neck.)

November 10:

On this day David and his nine-year-old cousin had returned from the theater, where the children had been refused admission unless David's father were with them throughout the performance.

DAVID (sobbing): That bad lady in the box. She won't let us in.

FATHER: Next week we'll all go together and I'll see the movie with you.

DAVID: No. (Pulls hand away from father.) I wanna go today.

UNCLE: Maybe next week, I'll go, too. There's a better picture showing next week anyway.

DAVID (runs into bedroom, jumps onto the bed and sobs).

FATHER (goes into room and stands by David): Now that's no way to act, is it, fella?

DAVID (pounds the pillow): I don't care. I don't care.

FATHER: But we're all going next week. Uncle David, too.

DAVID (turns over in bed, still crying): I don't wanna go next week. I hate next week.

November 17:

David was with his father and aunt in the kitchen.

AUNT: David, are you hungry?

DAVID: No. I just ate.

AUNT (offering him a piece of frankfurter): Wouldn't you like a little piece, David?

DAVID (just shakes his head negatively).

FATHER: You always liked hot dogs, David. What's the matter?

DAVID: Well, Mommy said I can't eat anywhere. (Hangs head.)

FATHER: Not even with me and your aunt?

DAVID: No. Mommy said I can't, only at home.

UNCLE (pats David on the head): Well, that's because your mommy wants to be sure you get the right foods and don't spoil your appetite.

DAVID (head still low—no reply).

This four-year-old child was not able to cope with his normal self-assertive tendencies which, at this age, usually reflect an increased consciousness of his own competence and capacity, because he was torn by conflicting parental attitudes and his own mixed feelings toward his father and mother.

Children find various ways of meeting situations that seem threatening to them. They use any hit-or-miss method that brings relief. If withdrawing, blaming others, or daydreaming brings satisfaction, they will continue to use this way of dealing with reality. However, if the child makes several unsuccessful attempts to escape from an unpleasant situation, and then meets the situation in a constructive way, adults should accept and approve the better way out. Dr. Leta S. Hollingworth gave an excellent illustration of the way in which an intelligent child may experiment with various mechanisms when he is in a "trap" situation. A little girl who had been told not to play with the electric light fuses inserted a metal object in one of the sockets one evening and blew out the fuse. Her first response was the rationalization, "Oh, we all like the nice dark." As the adults did not accept this statement, she said, "This is my house, I bought it with the money in my bank." When the fallacy of this statement was pointed out, she resorted to crying, which elicited no sympathy. Finally after trying out several other methods of escape from the unpleasant situation, she said, "I'm sorry I did it, and I'll not do it again." This way of meeting the situation was accepted and approved by the adults.

A child uses various evasive methods to maintain his self-respect. His need to use these methods should be recognized. What does the behavior mean to the child; how does he feel about it; what is he trying to accomplish through it; what conditions give rise to it—these are the questions adults should ask. For example, a feeling of insecurity may make one child excessively submissive. In another case insecurity may lead the child to tease and annoy other children. As the first child becomes more secure he may become more aggressive, more active in defending himself, may play alone less frequently. As the second child becomes more secure he may have fewer conflicts and be more content to play by himself part of the time. We can understand the meaning and appropriateness of a child's behavior only by getting perspective on his development in his total life situation.

Degree of socialization expected

During these later preschool years the child must become increasingly socialized.

Picture, if you can, an adult who is extremely destructive of property, insistent and demanding that every desire be instantly gratified, helpless and almost totally dependent on others, unable to share his possessions, impatient, prone to tantrums, violent and uninhibited in the display of all his feelings. Such behavior, normal to a two-year-old, would be monstrous in a man. Unless these qualities are markedly altered in the process of becoming we have on our hands an infantile and potentially evil personality. Hobbes well said that the wicked man is but the child grown strong. [5, pp. 28-29, 1955]

Property rights are very difficult for the little child to comprehend; they conflict with very strong desires; they hamper exploration of the world. The child best learns about property rights by being with other children. He learns to share the sand he is not using and to ask permission to use a pail and shovel that belong to another child. Other children gradually teach him that "findings" are no longer "keepings." As he comes to value the things he has made, he can be helped to realize that other children feel the same way about their possessions. Accepting appropriate responsibility is a form of behavior that can be learned; it is oriented to the future and involves attitudes toward oneself and others (37, 1955).

Honeymoon over

The permissiveness and solicitude the mother shows to the helpless infant gives way gradually to the necessity for some restrictions and control. Knowing that there are limits helps the normal child to gain self-control and to respect the rights of others. The confidence and security of children increases as they are helped to develop their potentialities, not as they are protected from all possible sources of fear and thwarting.

One of the most common concerns of parents today is to steer a middle course between nagging the child excessively about social conventions and the other extreme of fearing to restrict his spontaneity. The first tends to make the child priggish and self-conscious in his social relations, and the second to produce an exceedingly obstreperous youngster—a "Dennis the Menace." Adults certainly have a right to insist on a few rules to protect their own peace and comfort. At the same time, young children need to experiment—to experience the consequences of certain kinds of behavior and to learn by their mistakes. A child should have his own way whenever his way is a good one for all concerned.

If at the end of his fifth year a child has made progress in acquiring a few basic personal health habits and in eating quietly, using knife, fork, and spoon as a matter of course and resorting to fingers only rarely, and saying, "Please," and "Thank you," spontaneously when he really means it, his parents should be content. The aim of social education should be to develop the kind of person who desires to act in ways that are advantageous both to himself and others.

DEVELOPMENT OF THE SELF-CONCEPT AND PERSONALITY

Individuality flowers in the preschool period. The child becomes more aware of himself and other people. Between two and three he uses "I" as a symbol of his unique self. He begins to see that people are alike in certain ways and that he is a person in his own right. Children's responses to their environment become more and more characteristic of them. "The personality has a consistent, persistent, and pervasive quality that permits fairly accurate prediction of their behavior in new situations" (52, 1936). One mother recognized differences in her two children with respect to the predictability of their behavior:

> As for being able to predict how the children will behave under given cir-cumstances, I think that in the main I can—provided that the circumstances are not too unusual—but with Sammy the prediction is fairly easy, while with Teddy it is the result of hard-won experience. Sammy seems to have a strong natural desire to please. Approval and disapproval are very cogent arguments to him, which makes him very easy to teach. Teddy at the same age purred much louder under approval, but if it had to be gained at the expense of some other desire, it was a toss-up which would win. Teddy's notions are so deter-mined that it has always been difficult to find a workable control. And a con-trol which worked one day didn't necessarily work the next. . . .
>
> Never at any time has Teddy's mainspring been obvious. In fact, I think he has a half a dozen mainsprings, and I have never been enough of a mind reader to be sure that I was working on the right one at the right time. He has a very affectionate nature, and he does enjoy approval. But although he readily admits that when his behavior is acceptable to others life is very much pleasanter for himself, in a crisis that is beside the point!

During the third and fourth years of life initiative flourishes. The child's "reach exceeds his grasp" and often leads to imaginative activities that he sometimes confuses with reality. He is developing his self-concept through others' attitudes toward him, through experiencing approval and disapproval, reward and punishment. He is constantly learning what he can do and what he cannot do. Conscience begins to be active—overactive in some cases. The child's personality develops as he finds himself ac-cepted, meets with success in developing his capacities, and begins to un-derstand himself and his relations to others. If, on the other hand, he has come to think of himself as bad, weak, or stupid, he will have little stimu-lus to improve.

The child's development of personality consists of "organizing transi-tory impulses into a pattern of striving and interest" (5, p. 29, 1955) in accord with his developing self- concept. "With time there comes a diminu-tion in the preponderance and intensity of personal inclinations, and a growth and extension of other-regarding sentiments. . . . Self-love, it is obvious, remains always positive and active in our natures . . . it need not remain dominant." (5, p. 30, 1955)

If a child has had affection and security during infancy, he is better able to tolerate frustration, accept himself and others, give and receive love. These conditions are the groundwork for future learning. Such a child is "free to become." (5, p. 33, 1955) This is quite different from viewing "the character of healthy people, as well as the unhealthy, as fundamentally established by the age of three." (5, p. 33, 1955)

Many parents recall that their child has at some time undergone some severe emotional experience—a shocking or traumatic experience. Such an event does not produce permanent effects unless it is reinforced. A traumatic experience may be reinforced in a number of ways: members of the family may repeat the account of the event; the family or play group may continue to present the attitudes, expectancies, and roles that initially gave rise to the experience; because of its incompleteness, the child may repeatedly return in thought to the experience; he may come to use the experience as an attention-getting device. However, such an experience is often only part of a persistent problem of adjustment.

A child's personality development is influenced by his parents' methods of child care and discipline, and by the way of life prevalent in the society in which he grows up. When discipline is consistent and administered by an understanding, loving parent who seldom yields to anger, the child tends to be more sociable than the average, to do the right thing more often, to be more ready to face reality, and to develop a desirable degree of independence. Some parents who are confused about the best way to bring up their children need primarily to have their self-confidence restored.

At each stage of development children should learn to meet life's situations as adequately as possible; to enjoy events as they occur, moment by moment; to delight in their world, even though they recognize its difficulties and limitations.

Questions and Problems

FOR CLASS DISCUSSION OR STUDY GROUPS

1. To obtain more understanding of the development during this stage, read the section on preschool children in one of the recent references on child psychology listed at the end of this book.

2. Keep and analyze a stenographic record of the language used by one child during a day. How many words did he speak? How many different words did he use? What was the longest sentence? What was the average length of sentence? How many times did he use complex sentences? What pronouns did he use? What grammatical errors did he make? What kind of words occurred most frequently in his conversation? What practical use did he make of his language ability? What incentives did he have to speak effectively?

3. Note the helpful acts which a certain child performs during a day.

4. Play ball with preschool children of various ages and note the differences in their co-ordination and in their emotional and social reactions.

5. Devise a simple memory test, such as showing several objects, covering them up, and after certain intervals of time, asking children of different ages from two to six to name the objects seen.

6. Expand with explanation and illustrations the following brief statements of stages in character development:

The baby does what pleases him, takes what he wants, judges right or wrong by whether the act brings pleasure or pain.

His first ideas of right and wrong stem from his close personal relations. If treated consistently he learns that certain acts bring approval and other things bring disapproval.

By three or four years of age a child should know what kinds of behavior are socially acceptable.

From three to six he understands different degrees of seriousness of his acts even though he does not understand the reasons why they are serious.

Between four and six he tends to be self-centered but does not feel guilty about it. He often does not understand what a lie is.

By six years of age he should have learned to obey reasonable, consistent requests. He still does not question rules though he may try to evade them.

7. Read Part Two of *Child Development and Personality* by Mussen and Conger to obtain more details of research on how personality develops during the first two years. Note also how psychoanalytic and learning theories contribute to our understanding of the experimental literature.

Chapter 10

HOW PRESCHOOL
CHILDREN LEARN

Learning is fascinating to the preschool child. A child is usually interested in learning anything that contributes to his ongoing activity and is well enough within his capacity so that he can succeed at it.

Parents and teachers should be concerned with the process itself—when the child learns, under what conditions, from whom, and how a learning experience fits into the child's own scheme of things. The learning that takes place in a particular situation depends not only upon the child, but also upon the demands of the environment and the attitudes, expectations, and skill in guidance of parents and teachers. The emotional effect of the learning process itself leaves a trace that will influence the child's future behavior and his attitudes toward learning. Any learning takes place against a child's previous pattern of responses and is modified by it.

CHILDREN'S LEARNING AS A MOTHER SEES IT

The following description illustrates the selective nature of preschool children's learning:

On the generalized list of the things a two-year-old is able to do, Sammy has been proficient in some for a while and in others he hasn't even made a beginning. We have encouraged him to learn the things he obviously wanted to learn.

Is there really any great gain in trying to organize the under-twos, or even the under-threes? They are willy-nilly learning all the time. Sammy can't, for instance, feed himself. He has a good appetite and enjoys his meals, but he has no use for a spoon. He stirs it around in his food, takes a couple of half-hearted and badly-directed mouthfuls, and then puts the spoon down with an expression that is as expressive as a yawn. On the other hand, with very little effort on my part, he has been co-operative about dressing himself ever since he was a few months old. Laying face down on a table he used to ease himself on to one forearm as soon as I touched the other one to put it in a sleeve. He is now very

175

helpful indeed, and shoves arms and legs in and out so automatically that he doesn't even need to stop chattering about something quite different. Just this week he has developed an interest in putting his socks on himself.

Sammy's toys are kept in two long drawers which fit indifferently and stick if they aren't pulled carefully by both handles. I gave him no encouragement to open the drawers at all, but he hadn't been walking long before he was opening and shutting them more efficiently than I do myself. But he can't play ball, and he won't turn the pages of his books (though he loves looking at them with me). As long as he is interested and happy, does it matter? What I am really driving at so long-windedly is that there seems to me little point in trying to *induce* a desire for knowledge where there is more than enough existing spontaneously.

With unusual intuition, and from firsthand observation of her children, this mother arrived at the same conclusions about learning that have been emphasized in the modified "self-selection" point of view. Learning may take place incidentally as well as intentionally.

OBSERVATIONS OF CHILDREN'S LEARNING IN AN EXPERIMENTAL SITUATION

When preschool children were confronted with problem situations under controlled conditions they solved them in various ways. The following description (7, 1928) shows how a three-year-old's trial-and-error method culminated in a sudden solution:

The child was placed before a cage containing a doll which could be obtained only by fastening one stick to another. First she examined one stick and tried to reach the doll with it; then she used the other stick in the same way. Both were too short. She repeated "I can't" over and over.

Then she tried poking the stick downwards between the bars at the top of the cage, stretching and straining to reach the doll. Failing, she became angry and whined, "I can't." On three occasions she tried to reach the doll by these and similar methods. "Dolly doesn't want me to get him," she complained, and finally gave up.

The fourth time she was placed in the same situation, her behavior was the same as at first. Then she said, "Let's try big stick on little one." She picked them up, examined them, fitted them together, and with a shout of "Bang!" angled for the doll and reached it. She was so pleased with her solution that she repeated it several times; the learning process itself was of more interest than possessing the doll.

Children in this experiment seemed to attack a problem most frequently by exploring the situation and eliminating unsatisfactory responses until they gained insight into the relations involved. Children often hit on the solution of their simple problems without help.

However, well-timed suggestions and demonstration may hasten success in the learning process and result in better responses. Two-year-old children made substantial gains in learning to play a ring-toss game when they were shown how to hold and throw the ring. They made slight improvement when they were merely told how to do it. As children grow older they learn still more effectively if they verbalize the method demonstrated. For instance, Sammy at two years, two months, liked to carry the basket down to the vegetable garden and help his mother pick peas. At first he yanked enthusiastically, bringing away vines as well as peas. His mother told him he must pull just the peas, and showed him how to hold the vine in one hand and pull the pod with the other. He got the idea in a twinkling, and all he needed thereafter was an occasional reminder to "hold the vine." As they were carrying the basket up to the house he looked up at his mother earnestly and said, "Pull the peas, *not* the vines!"

MORE ABOUT THE PSYCHOLOGY OF LEARNING

Learning is a complicated process; it is not a *simple* matter of rewarding good behavior and punishing undesirable behavior. Although there are divergent theories of learning, psychologists tend to agree on certain elements in the process, which may be represented as follows:

DRIVE → CUES → RESPONSE → GRATIFICATION, i.e., REDUCTION OF DRIVE

Drive, or drive state, is a condition of the person that impels him to respond, e.g., hunger or avoidance of pain, an incomplete activity, fear or anxiety, habit or hope.

Cues are objects or events that help determine when and where a person will respond and which response he will make. As the child matures he learns to respond to patterns of cues or to some element of the cue, including cues within himself as well as in his environment.

Response is what the child does in the presence of a cue. If a response reduces the strength of the drive, the feelings of tension that arise from hunger or thirst, fear or a desire for affection, the response may become learned, i.e., attached to the cue or pattern of cues. According to Mowrer (78, 1956), the child responds in whatever way will lessen fear or reinforce hope.

Gratification or reward refer to the reduction in tension, or in strength of drive, that occurs when a person has made a satisfactory response. The more quickly a response is rewarded the more surely it is re-

inforced and hence learned. Since satisfaction is such an important de-
terminer of behavior it is important to know "what satisfies" at different
ages and under different individual and environmental conditions.

Punishment is a complicated process by which the child attaches the
response of fear to the original response that has now been forbidden.
Punishment becomes effective when the fear response attached to an act
is greater than the pleasure derived from carrying out the act. The influence
of approval, reward, disapproval, and punishment, or merely ignoring
the child can be accurately appraised only when their meaning to the
child is known; all have significance to the child only in the framework of
his personal relations. A child who had been punished by not being
kissed good-bye by his mother took a longer time that day to learn certain
words and made twice as many errors as in previous periods. In brief, a
child's learning is influenced by the child's capacity for learning and by
the whole psychological field in which it takes place.

INFLUENCE OF ENVIRONMENT

Some environments, such as that of the Virginia "hollow folk" (96,
1933), offer relatively little incentive to learn. Other environments encourage the most effective learning of which the child is capable. A child
grows mentally as his environment makes reasonable demands upon him.
In addition to the personal relations in his home, the most important
positive factors in the environment of children from two to six years of
age are appropriate play materials and equipment, playmates, instruction
and guidance, and tasks that are challenging but not too difficult.

Play materials and equipment

The basic raw materials for preschool children are space, unhurried
time, and suitable materials which they can use in their own way. From a
wealth of possible activities, children can choose those which best meet
their needs. Clay, large crayons, painting materials, blocks, and puzzles
evoke interest and creative responses. Tricycles, scooters, swings, and
places to dig satisfy children's desire for large-muscle activities or swift
motion. Standard tools—hoes, rakes, brooms, and other household-carpen-
ter and farm implements—of the smallest available size, cut down to a
length that the child can easily handle, are more satisfactory than poorly
constructed toy tools that look cute but do not work.

Some of the favorite play materials are the least expensive. Boxes of
all sizes, trees, fences, cellar doors, a swing, a seesaw, planks of different

widths raised at one end, rocks to climb, a little ladder firmly fastened to the barn or garage, the kitchen stepladder chair, tools for digging—all these provide opportunity for many-sided child development. The child may like to stand in the center of concentric circles drawn on the ground or painted on the floor of the barn or garage and see how many circles he can jump across. In general, materials requiring large-muscle activity are preferred.

Some mothers say, "I'm afraid he will fall and hurt himself if I let him climb." But the child who learns to climb first a low sturdy chair, a small fence, a firmly fastened ladder of two or three rungs, and gradually more difficult things is less likely to hurt himself than the child who was allowed no opportunities for climbing when he was three and four years old, and at six attempts to imitate the children who are doing difficult stunts.

Children love to play in the water and mud. If there are no little brooks or ponds out of doors to play in, the bathtub, the kitchen sink, or a wooden or tin washtub will help to supply this lack. The small child welcomes any opportunity to put on a rubber apron or a summer bathing suit and play with celluloid aquatic animals or the little boats he has made. On a rainy day, dressed in his waterproof coat, hat, and boots, or in a bathing suit if the weather is warm, the child can play out of doors in the rivulets and puddles. Rainy days, when spent in this way, are welcomed rather than resented by preschool children.

Wagons, dishes, dolls, doll furniture, and hollow blocks encourage co-operative play. Material for solitary play should also be provided because some children get worn out if they are with a group all the time. Rest periods and a quiet story time before lunch provide the relief children need from constant social contact.

If a separate room can be set aside for the children, it can be made attractive with a stained, shellacked wooden floor or a covering of smooth linoleum; a table and chairs just the right size, painted some favorite color; growing ferns or flowers, goldfish in a bowl, cupboards, and open shelves for books and toys. Detailed plans for a combination bedroom and playroom for a preschool child (107, 1949) would interest many parents. The minimum floor space considered adequate was eleven by twelve feet, and the essential features, free play area, storage space for toys and clothing, and space for bedroom furniture. If the child cannot have a separate room of his own, a corner with toy cupboards should be provided.

Attention should also be given to the esthetic aspect of the environment. Any home can furnish three elements of beauty—simplicity of line and form, a feeling of order, and harmony of color. Elimination of the superfluous is often the first step to take in making the home more beautiful. A wall space for just one picture which can be changed from time to time is a miniature art gallery for the child. Many children's picture books are works of art. A low easel by a window offers the child opportunity for self-expression. The phonograph, radio, and television offer possibilities for desirable influences.

Playmates

The child's socialization is advanced and his desire to learn stimulated through daily association with other children of approximately the same age. The desire to play an adequate part in a group of one's own age may be effective in developing self-discipline. The following is an example of discipline by the group: An aggressive five-year-old boy hit one of the little girls in the play group and made her cry. The other children did the disciplining. "Tommie, you go right away. You can't play with us if you hit Mary Jane. You go right home," they said. This was an effective learning situation for normal little Tommie. He found that he must modify his tactics in order to remain in the group.

Social interaction increases rapidly after three years of age. Before this age children lack both readiness and social experience. From three to five years of age Stott and Ball (102, 1957) found that preschool children doubled their interaction with other children, especially in degree of ascendancy behavior. At the same time they decreased in the frequency with which they played alone. When they entered kindergarten at age five, the percentage of ascendant behavior sharply decreased, whereas the percentage of submissive behavior remained practically the same.

Preschool children can be taught how to overcome shyness. The methods of doing this were experimentally demonstrated by several workers. Koch (58, 1935) increased the social interest of a group of unsocial children by letting each child play with a more sociable child, using toys that encouraged co-operation. Jack (48, 1934) worked with five four-year-old children who seldom took the lead, attempted to direct other children's behavior, or pursued their own purposes against interference. These nonascendant children were skillfully and sympathetically taught to make a mosaic design, solve a picture puzzle, and tell a story illustrated by pictures. They were then returned to the nursery school with children who had previously been the more dominant. Equipped with their new skills, the originally shy children began to take the lead; increasing self-confidence effected a marked change in their behavior. Page (86, 1936) obtained further proof that preschool children as young as three years could pass from submissive or moderately ascendant behavior to more ascendant behavior through an increase in self-confidence. They were taught to tell a story, to make plasticine and wood flowers, and to solve picture puzzles. The materials and instruction were graded to insure success from the beginning. The training was continued until each child had mastered the skills involved. During the training period the children's self-confidence increased. They showed an increase in directing behavior, but made fewer attempts than the other children to secure materials by force. Moreover, their newly acquired ascendant behavior seemed to carry over into other nursery school situations. More recently, Mummery (80, 1947) reported that, with training in self-confidence by the Jack method, three- and four-year-old children "increased in ascendant behavior," but their *methods* of achieving ascendance were no more socially acceptable than before. There are different kinds of shyness: destructive and constructive withdrawal. More study of accepted methods of treatment is needed to see which are really effective.

Instruction and guidance

In a favorable environment many children will find adequate natural stimuli for learning. However, with most children, the self-selection method requires some modification. Toys encouraging play with others may be placed near the child who is slow in developing social contacts. Toys that will keep him quiet may be suggested to the child who runs himself ragged. Equipment that requires active play may stimulate the slow or overweight child to greater activity. Thus adults can suggest activities to certain children who have not selected a suitable activity themselves or who seem reluctant to try anything new.

The manner in which directions are given also influences a child's response. Children from two and a half to seven years of age obey more willingly and persist longer in the tasks assigned when positive, specific, unhurried, and encouraging instruction is given than when the instruction is negative, general, hurried, and discouraging. Comment of any kind is usually more effective than none at all, and verbal approval superior to nonverbal. It is recommended, in general, that suggestions be used instead of commands and that commands or suggestions be positive rather than negative. For example, the instruction, "Blow this one [a balloon] up. It is easy. You can do it," induced more favorable performance than did the question, "Can you blow this one up? It may be too hard." Similarly, the encouraging comment, "You almost did it that time," was more effective than "You haven't done it yet." The experimenter's emphasis on an immediate objective, such as, "If you cut the ball out, you may take it home today," was clearly more potent than emphasis on a postponed objective, such as, "If you cut the ball out you may take it home next week." Suggestions such as, "When I was downtown yesterday I saw some pretty red balloons. I brought two home with me. They are in the paper sack on the table by the window," were more effective than direct commands such as, "Bring them over here." The appeal to competitiveness, "Look at the man that ——— drew. Can you draw a man as well as that?" elicited less response, especially with the younger children, than the simple command, "Draw another man." (69, pp. 279-284, 1936) Immediate approval of what children are doing right should be *far* more frequent than disapproval of what they are doing wrong.

Guidance is most effective when it is given in connection with specific learning situations. Its function is to help the child discover for himself better ways of doing things. At lunchtime, for instance, the teacher stays with the newly appointed child-housekeepers the first day to offer such suggestions as are necessary to prevent spilling and other accidents. A child who is speaking to a playmate in a whining, fussing voice may be told to "talk to him in a big voice." A child who is shouting indoors may be reminded, "Let's see if we can hear you just as well if you speak in a soft voice." Thus children can be helped to make acceptable responses in many everyday situations. These early years are a strategic time for setting up desirable patterns of response.

In brief, the role of the alert teacher or parent is to encourage the child when he is successfully solving his own problems, to make suggestions or to do part of the job when the child is becoming discouraged, and to share the responsibility when the child is about to evade it. One parent's patience was rewarded eventually when her child acquired excellent sleep habits:

As soon as Sammy was able to move about under his own steam, he declined to be put under the covers. He was no sooner under than he bobbed out again, so for months we put him on top of his bed, and when silence indicated that he was asleep somebody went up and bundled him under. Just after his second birthday we began finding when we went up that he was already tucked in, right side up with care. After two or three nights it became clear that Sammy was doing the job himself before going to sleep. Now, at 26 months when he is put to bed, he takes going under the covers for granted, and almost always stays there until he wakes up. He has never protested against taking his nap or going to bed at night, and in fact seems to consider bed an excellent idea.

Parents and teachers need to learn to take things easy—to relax. They can help the child to grow up step by step, starting with the simplest part of the developmental task. With each step learned, the rest comes easier. The young child needs one teacher at a time and one method at a time. If grandmother's method is sound, mother can use it; if there is a better method, mother will have to teach grandma.

There is a tide in children's learning, to paraphrase Shakespeare, which, taken at the flood, leads on to achievement. If the child is pushed to learn before he is physically and mentally able he may get a sense of failure that spreads to tasks not yet attempted. If he passes the crest of readiness for a certain skill without having had the opportunity to learn it he may want to skip it entirely. Practice given at the time of greatest readiness results in the most efficient learning. This is the way one mother does it:

First I employ studious diplomacy in choosing a moment to teach him to do something new for himself. Last week I made a start on getting him to put his toys away at night. I chose a wet day when he had been cooped up in his room most of the day and was enchanted to have company. I played with him for a bit, and then said I would stay while he put all his toys away in the drawers. There was the expected amount of putting things away and then snatching them out again and running giggling to hide behind the bed. I gave him plenty of time. When the toys were all put away he went off very happily for his bath, and was in the middle of supper when his father came in. The first thing Sammy said to him was, "Clever boy put away all a toy." So that was an easy beginning.

The same principle can be applied in the dressing and other situations.

The following conditions are conducive to learning in the early preschool years:

Provide many opportunities for the child to think things out for himself.

Allow the child plenty of time; do not hurry him, if it can be avoided. It is hard for a busy mother not to get impatient and finish the child's job herself. As Sammy's mother put it:

To say that you shouldn't try to hurry a child is advice which is almost guaranteed to produce congestion in the harassed housewife. But it is one of my few conscious policies never to try to make Sammy do anything for himself in a hurry. If I must hurry, I do it for him.

Sometimes it is possible for the mother to work along with the child: "I put on this shoe; you put on that one."

Help him to set definite goals which he can attain.

Let him make increasingly important decisions for himself and take as much responsibility for them as he is able. If parents always make decisions for their child, the child may grow up without confidence in his ability to make decisions for himself.

Give him only as much help as he needs to succeed.

Set the stage for success. "Nothing succeeds like observed success." Success maintains efficiency, whereas failure results in a decrease of efficiency. In Meek's study of learning (74, p. 82, 1925) two nursery school children who failed to recognize the words they were being taught showed a marked dislike for both the teacher and the activity. "I hate this. . . . I don't want to play," one said. The other said, after the third day of failure, "I'm tired of it. It makes me mad. This old game is no good." But when they were successful in recognizing the words, they liked everything about the situation. "I'd like to play today. Take me," they would say.

Accentuate the positive in his behavior.

Give him examples of considerateness and kindness to imitate.

Some children fear competition. If a parent considers a brother or sister superior in some respect, the other child is likely to think of himself as generally inferior and to accept his parent's judgment as final. An adult often says, "You can do it like your big brother if you try." A comparative approach like this is likely to make the younger child feel still more resistant or inadequate. It is better to encourage him to engage in the activity for its own sake and in his own way.

The attitudes of the persons in the child's environment have a subtle influence on his learning. A child's self-confidence is fostered not only by the acquisition of skills under favorable conditions of instruction but also by people's attitudes toward him. If parents keep obviously trying to improve the child's behavior, he may get the idea that he is unacceptable as a person.

LEARNING NOT TO FAIL

Learning difficulties arise when the individual's aspirations or the practical demands which he faces are out of line with his ability. If he does not reach his end goal immediately, the parent can point out signs of progress. The child should not get the feeling of having "failed, failed again." Repeated failure is a drag, not a spur, to his effort.

The child can be helped to view failure as an opportunity to learn— as a lesson in what not to do another time. Children who have acquired a reasonable degree of self-confidence are not upset by failure. The responses to failure of eighty-two children ranging in age from three years, two months, to five years, eleven months, were studied by Keister (57, pp. 429-440, 1943). Fifteen of these children showed undesirable responses to failure: retreat from the task, repeated requests for help, destructive behavior directed against objects or persons, rationalization, and "exaggerated emotional responses such as crying, sulking, yelling." Twelve of the fifteen were given special instruction and guidance for six weeks. In essence, this program consisted of a graded series of problems, beginning with some in which the child could readily succeed. As he successfully completed each one, he was given another one that required more persistence and effort. The role of the teacher, who worked individually with the children, was to encourage the child but not actually help him. If the child asked for help she made remarks such as: "I won't need to help you. You can do it all by yourself if you keep on trying," or "Try that piece of a picture puzzle some more different ways. You'll soon find out, by yourself, how it goes," or "Remember how you did the puzzles in the story about the horse? You kept right on trying until you got it right." (57, p. 435, 1943) When the child had difficulty the teacher would encourage him: "Now you have a chance to start over and build it straighter and steadier than before."

As each child left the room, the teacher usually remarked that he had done a good job and told him specifically why it was good. As the training period continued the children asked for less and less help, and made more and more remarks such as the following: "I'll try and try till I find out how it goes." "Oh, look, I finded the way! I tried and finded the way."

When tested at the end of the period of training, the children showed a measurable improvement. They no longer responded to difficulty by sulking and crying, and less often asked for help. Their improvement in general attitude was shown by such remarks as: "See, I'm almost gettin' this right. Pretty soon I'm gonna know how it goes." These changes were traceable directly to the special instruction and guidance that shaped and reinforced positive responses in the learning process. Children who experience success develop confidence in their own ability; they expect to succeed. Fluctuations are to be expected and accepted. The beginning stages in preschool children's learning are sometimes confused with bad habits.

LEARNING THE LANGUAGE

A child's language develops as his experiences broaden. The child's words are symbols of his most vital experiences. They make possible communication and the fine distinctions essential to social learning. It is through the use of words that intricate stimulus-response sequences can be carried out in his head instead of being acted out in behavior.

Social and emotional factors in the learning process

The child first learns to respond to words as commands and to use them as requests (32, p. 117, 1950). He is taught to relinquish mother's hair when she protests, "Let go!" and to call out for a toy that is out of reach. Imitation continues to play a major role in language development. In learning to obey commands and follow directions he is required to repeat phrases or short sentences. This verbal rehearsal seems to involve the association of the words and phrases with anticipated actions that he is to carry out or avoid.

As he learns to listen and obey, the child also learns to discriminate between cues or stimuli that are based on his own drives or needs and those that come from others, or the rehearsal of what others have said (32, p. 117, 1950). Suggestions from others that do not promise to satisfy his drives are not rewarded (and hence rejected). Thus when father says, "Jimmy, will you please get my slippers," and Jimmy wants to play in the sand pile, Jimmy learns to distinguish between the source of the two suggestions and chooses the most rewarding.

If a child makes an immediate, impulsive response to a stimulus in a problem situation, he does not allow sufficient time for the chain of internal verbal thinking to occur. A child learns to stop and think as he is consistently criticized for impulsive behavior and rewarded for actions that demonstrate the use of rational thought. Children who are under frequent pressure from their parents to think faster often fail to show the intelligence of which they are capable, because they cannot endure the anxiety that is aroused by the period of indecision during which action is suspended while they are thinking (32, p. 119, 1950).

The process of learning to talk involves continuous practice in matching the right words and sentences to the objects and events in the child's environment. He is corrected for calling a truck a car. He eventually learns to have anxiety about describing objects or events different than other people. He learns to distinguish between his own private dreams and phantasies, and perceptions that can be verified by his other senses and by other people. Likewise he learns to give an accurate account of social behavior and not blame others when he himself is responsible. Above all, he is taught to be self-critical and to reject comfortable but false ideas. It is of the utmost importance that he receive consistent guidance in making discriminations commensurate with his capacity. Parents who read meaning into a child's unclear speech tend to foster or reward lack of precision and clarity in their child's narration.

The child also receives considerable education in associating appropriate action and emotion to what he says. He must keep his promises and carry out his plans. He must match his words with deeds. Similarly he learns that he cannot say he is happy when he is crying nor laugh when he says he is sorry. The many subtle, and not so subtle, rewards associated with social conformity, and punishments with nonconformity provide strong motivation to make one's verbal behavior appropriate (32, p. 122, 1950). The quality of this early experience to a large extent determines the child's sense of reality and his ability to adjust to it.

Understanding of the child's capacity to learn

Preschool children sometimes appear to be stupid in remembering certain words and in making distinctions that seem easy to adults. Walter De la Mare describes a four-year-old who was sensitive about her missing "r's." Embarrassed at having to call Jerry, the dog, "Jellie," especially in the presence of her brother with his superior six-year-old language ability, she was delighted when her mother "in a moment of inspiration referred to the animal as *Jinks.*" Merely urging children to speak better without regard to their capacity to learn is almost certain to set up inhibitions and create friction. Still worse is holding the child responsible and punishing him for laziness or stubbornness when his failure to learn is due to immaturity, to lack of experience, or to inadequate mental ability.

Setting the stage

Learning the language is encouraged in an environment in which the child has a real need to talk and gets satisfaction from his efforts. When a child's interest in some object or animal is high, that is the best time to name it, thus associating the object with the spoken word and later with the printed symbols for it. Engaging in interesting activities increases his understanding and use of verbs. The child who has toys to use indoors and outdoors; who takes trips to the seashore, to the mountains, to the city;

who lives on a farm, or has a chance to visit one; who has his own little garden, even in a flower pot or window box; who goes to the zoo, to the circus, to a picnic, to a dairy; who listens to nursery rhymes and stories; and who has friends and pets to play with is thus stimulated to learn words to describe his experiences.

Learning that is embedded in the child'd daily living is meaningful and important to him, immediately useful, and likely to function in new situations. The five- or six-year-old can take a real part in the conversation at mealtime. He should have a turn in telling his experiences. The other members of the family should try to make their conversation of some interest to the children as well as to the adults. Talking *at* the child and talking *with* the child are two different things. The first should be avoided; the second, encouraged.

Stories

Stories contribute much to the development of a preschool child. Three- and four-year-olds enjoy stories rich in sense impressions and action—stories about the sights they see, the substances they touch, the activities in which they engage, the sounds they hear. They like to have the animals in the story make their characteristic noises. They like to hear and imitate the sound of the engine, of the steamboat whistle, of the wind, and of other familiar noises. Up to the age of six, a child is most alive to moving things—engines, boats, automobiles, animals, boys and girls in action. In telling a story to preschool children, one can notice the drop in interest during descriptive and explanatory passages, and the flare-up of interest when the action is resumed.

Rhythm and repetition also appeal to them. Rhythm makes Mother Goose popular before the meaning of the verses is clear. The repetition of refrains helps to divide a story into simpler units—to furnish a breathing space, as it were, for the child to catch up with the action of the story.

There should be humor in these simple stories. Children are amused by a thing in an unusual place, such as a cow in a wagon, a wig on a pig. They laugh spontaneously when characters bump into things, fall down, or encounter other surprises.

Since the young child's own activities and experiences are the most interesting to him, the first stories should be about familiar experiences. He is eager to understand his everyday world, which is still new and strange to him. In telling a story about a journey by train to one group of preschool children, the teacher observed slight interest. In telling the same story to another group of children of the same age, the teacher found keen interest. The first group had never been on a journey while the second group, who were refugees, had had experiences on trains similar to those described in the story.

Stories true to life foster sympathy and understanding of how others feel in certain situations. They show what kinds of acts are approved and what kinds are disapproved. They show ways in which situations can be met and suggest interesting things to do.

Children usually do not appreciate the unusual until they are acquainted with the usual. They do not see humor in the absurd until they are familiar with ordinary behavior. This does not mean that stories must do nothing more than recount familiar experiences. They should begin with children's experience and add an element of the dramatic or a new relationship among familiar facts. The child has many isolated experiences which stories can tie together. For example, he drinks milk; he has seen cows; he sees the milkman deliver bottles of milk. These separate experiences may be related in a story showing where his glass of milk comes from. He has seen seeds, plants growing in the field, and flowers and fruit. A story will show the sequence of events in the life of one plant.

Stories for preschool children do not need complicated plots. The children's own lives are a series of incidents, and their stories may be built on similar lines. Complicated sentence structure is unfamiliar and confusing to children who have only recently learned to combine words into a sentence, and whose own sentences are still simple in form.

Fairy and folk stories have their place. Certain fairy tales appeal to children in various developmental phases. For example, a five-year-old girl's identification with Cinderella was related to her problems of adjustment at that time. Some of these stories give many children a sense of awe and wonder, which is more lacking in the modern world than a sense of realism. Fanciful tales are not likely to cause emotional upsets if the child's total environment is satisfying and if the stories are not cruel or fear-inspiring.

Jacobs (49, p. 36, 1956) suggested the following criteria for the selection of books for the early preschool years:

1. Stories that give enjoyment—"enjoyment of plot and character, of image and rhythm, of language, of the exploration of life, of the extension of self-insight."
2. "Prose and poetry that charm them magically or tickle their funny bones."
3. Books that give information about the world around them—about liv-

ing things, transportation, communication workers, the earth and outer space about which they hear so much these days; "books that let them work in the shoes of others and thus come to know life intimately and well."

4. Books that "confirm and extend everyday experiences."

5. Books of great adventure that go beyond the real world and make children wonder and believe.

6. A wide variety of books—children's classics, new types of books being published, fiction and nonfiction, prose and poetry.

7. Books that capture the interest and enthusiasm of both the child and the adult who is reading to him.

The range of books for preschool children is so wide that only types of books and sources of information can be suggested here. The children's classics—*Mother Goose, Johnny Crow's Garden, Chicken World, Peter Rabbit*—and many others are perennial favorites. A wealth of modern juvenile literature has been coming out by such authors as Marjorie Flack, Margaret Wise Brown, Wanda Gág, Lois Lenski, Dr. Seuss, and others. Poetry of A. A. Milne, Dorothy Aldis, Rachel Field, Elizabeth Maddox Roberts, and others deserve part of the child's reading time.

Information about children's books may be obtained from (1) magazine reviews of children's books, such as *The Hornbook* and *Junior Libraries, The Saturday Review, Elementary English, Childhood Education* and *Child Study;* (2) book lists in pamphlet form—*Bibliography of Books for Children* (Association for Childhood Education International) and *Children's Books Too Good to Miss* (Western Reserve University); and (3) books about children's literature—Bess Porter Adams' *About Books* and *Children* (Holt), May Hill Arbuthnot's *Children and Books* (Scott Foresman), Josette Frank's *Your Child's Reading Today* (Doubleday), Anne T. Eaton's *Treasure for the Taking* (Viking), and Nancy Larrick's *A Parent's Guide to Children's Reading* (Doubleday).

LEARNING TO REMEMBER

"Oh, I forgot!" The preschool child is not the only one who has occasion to say this, but he does say it frequently. His forgetting to do what mother tells him may be due to a number of causes.

"What did you see when you were out walking today?" "Where did Grandfather take you?" "What did Aunt May do when the canary flew out of the cage?" Questions of this kind asked spontaneously as the child shows interest make him feel he is contributing to the family conversation, give him a chance to organize his material, and teach him how to interest others by presenting his experiences in an effective way. They are incentives to a discriminating use of memory.

By hearing nursery rhymes and stories again and again the child is encouraged to remember them. Pictures in story books suggest the events that they illustrate and thus give practive in recall. After one or two repetitions of a story children as young as two and a half years will supply the words when the storyteller pauses at certain points. After four years they show considerable ability in reproducing stories.

LEARNING TO LIVE WITH OTHERS

Learning does not consist only of book learning; it also includes learning to live happily with people, to keep healthy, to be kind, happy, and considerate. Learning to live with others on a basis of mutual satisfaction and a real appreciation is, for the majority of people, the most important of all learnings. Parents who are courteous and have a genuine friendly feeling toward people furnish examples from which the child himself can choose the forms that express his own feeling naturally and sincerely.

One mother described as follows the difficulty of developing social sensitivity in her child:

I presume that the chief objective is to produce an adult who can live happily with himself and others. The black-and-white virtues are relatively easy to inculcate, but, for instance, to teach a bossy child to consider the other children's point of view is difficult. There is always the danger of too much insistence becoming fruitless nagging. At what point with a child is it wiser to let nature take its course, even if it's not a very good course? I think this is something of a problem to most affectionate parents. Teddy's particular brand of egoism has always been a source of worry to us, for his own sake. He is a decent, honest child, with a good deal of charm; and I have almost never known him to do anything deliberately unkind. But within the limits of decency and honesty, he firmly believes that whatever he wants to do is right for him to do, and he is hell-bent on doing it in his own way. The results are frequently inconsiderate and irritating to others, but to Teddy it is always the objector who is being unreasonable! At the same time he is intensely sociable. We have talked ourselves hoarse trying to make him realize that he frequently defeats his own best interests, and in the past few years have often wondered if our persistent attacks have really helped or hindered.

Many children do work out their social relations quite successfully. Physical conflicts decrease as preschool children learn to settle their difficulties verbally.

Children meet their problems of social relations in various ways. One three-year-old boy formed a close friendship with another boy at the beginning of the year. Most of his social contacts were with this boy. Older children in the group ignored him. After several absences he returned to find his friend interested in another child. He did not know how to make an adjustment to his loss of follower and friend. His reaction took the form of aggressive behavior toward the entire group and attempts to get attention. Other children might react to a similar situation with shyness and timidity.

Another three-year-old, small for his age, was not accepted by the group. They told him he was too small to do various things with them. His first response was to cling to the teacher. When he later turned his attention to play materials that he could use by himself, this represented progress.

Widely different leadership patterns also develop during preschool years. One three-year-old attracted the attention of other children by shouting commands at them: "Bring me that board!" "Watch me do it!" But his control of the group through these tactics was only transitory. Another child in the same group used quite different leadership techniques. He was clever in finding jobs that appealed to the other children. While really directing the activity, he made the others feel that they were of importance. For instance, he asked another child to be captain on top of the boat of blocks while he was engineer below. "The captain is the biggest boss . . . ," he said. Then he went on to direct the activity with the other child's willing help (50, 1939). A five-year-old child achieved a leading position by sensing the common problems of other children and serving as spokesmen for them.

Although friendships are important in children's social development, it is best not to try to force friendships, but rather to let children make their own overtures toward each other. Even a friendship that seems to be harmful serves some need of the child. If this need can be discovered and met, the friendship may fade out in a natural way. The needs of both children should, of course, be considered and substitute satisfactions provided.

Some conditions under which a child learns to make friends are:

1. When he has a chance to be with other children and is not interfered with much by grownups. In some communities mothers take turns supervising small play groups for four- and five-year-olds, so that the isolated preschool child will have opportunity to learn more about himself and others through playing with other children.

2. When his first experiences with other children are happy—not with children who hurt him,

3. When he is taught the skills which other children of his age are acquiring—riding a tricycle, roller skating, swimming, playing ball, climbing—as soon as he shows readiness for learning a skill or a game. The acquisition of skill increases self-confidence and initiative.

Why does one child tend to move toward people, another to move away from people, and still another to move against people? So far as we can see, the baby who has had "unconditional love" from birth has no need to move against people or away from them. With affectionate training he will learn the difficult and sometimes cramping ways of civilized life without losing his good relations with people. He views persons important in his life as friendly and helpful, not hostile and dominating.

During the year or two following infancy, the child's social learning is largely motivated by his desire to keep or win the approval of the parent figure with whom he has identified. The child may go to either extreme—become excessively dependent and fearful of losing the parents' esteem or extremely and unrealistically independent. The ideal adjustment avoids extremes. Realizing that he is not omnipotent, the child welcomes the security that comes from being accepted and valued by the parents who are, to him, all powerful. Since it is important for him to obtain their approval, he tries to behave in appropriate ways and to accept their values and standards. The wise parent will encourage his independence in activities which he can handle successfully with his present abilities. Thus the self-centered baby develops into a more independent, socially inclined child.

LEARNING TO WAIT FOR SOMETHING HE WANTS

At the beach, about eleven o'clock Ralph went over to the lunch basket. "Mommy, I'm hungry. I want my lunch," he said.

"No, it's too early. We have to wait until 11:30 before we are all ready to eat."

"But I'm hungry now. I want to eat now."

"I'm sorry, but it's too early. Play in the sand or take another swim and then it will be time."

The mother handled this situation effectively: She recognized Ralph's feelings and was sympathetic, but consistently held to her original statement. At the same time she suggested an activity to make waiting easier for the child.

Willingness to defer satisfaction begins to take root in preschool years. In infancy, the child is not able to understand why his needs cannot always be met promptly. But there comes a time when he begins to learn that some disappointments, denials, limitations, and pain are an inescapable part of life. Stephen, age four, had formulated his philosophy in words: "I don't have to do anything I don't want to do." When his mother said no when he started to take a playmate's toy home with him, he staged a small temper tantrum, received a spanking from his father, and made an unhappy ending to what had been a pleasant visit. How could the parents have been reasonably permissive, without reinforcing a sense of unrealistic omnipotence in this little boy? In most areas of life Stephen could have been given freedom to explore and to act according to his wishes. But certain limits appropriate to his age should have been held to firmly. When a reasonable demand is made pleasantly, preschool children tend to respond with willingness to do as they are asked.

Though the child who grabs others' toys may resent adult interference, he has to learn sometime to face the reality that all attractive things are not his for the grabbing. On the other hand, preschool children should not be expected to share their cherished toys with other children. Generosity develops slowly and is meaningless unless it arises from a genuine feeling of pleasure in giving and getting.

LEARNING TO DO THE RIGHT THING

Social acceptance and approval of a little child's acceptable behavior are the surest ways to reinforce it. During the early years the home is in almost complete control of these conditions of learning (53, 1954). To the child, what is disapproved, blamed, or punished, is wrong; what is approved, praised, or rewarded is right. The more consistently the persons in his environment respond to him, the more easily he will learn to conform to social standards. He can learn to distinguish between different degrees of seriousness of his acts, though he cannot be expected to understand the reasons why they are disapproved or to generalize from specific experiences. During preschool years the child learns through concrete personal experiences, not through general moral concepts.

Personality and character traits also develop as the individual tries to cope with his fears, frustrations, and anxiety. The ways in which the child finds solutions for these conflicts and anxieties, satisfactory to himself, play a leading role in personality and character formation. Even in the best-regulated homes infancy and childhood include some frustrating experiences, which are part of growing up. They cannot be avoided. Therefore the child should learn how to handle them. He can be helped to find some element of satisfaction—some plus values in difficult situations.

Many parents pay little attention to the character development of their preschool children because they feel the child is too little to understand. They do not realize that from very early years the child is being conditioned by his parents' attitudes, precepts, and example. He is getting a preliminary orientation about the relative importance of persistence in a worthy purpose, respect for the feelings of others, and other kinds of desirable behavior. Identification with a loving person is an effective way of transmitting parents' values (95, 1954).

Parental attitudes determine the emotional atmosphere surrounding him before he even understands spoken words. If the atmosphere of the home radiates genuine affection and respect for and trust in people, then the children will assume that this is the way life is and will reflect these positive attitudes. Consistency in discipline conveys to the child a sense of moral orderliness in the world and an acceptance of a reasonable degree of social conformity. The most intense frustration and its consequent aggression seems to follow a sudden change from freedom to restraint, a clamping down on privileges previously permitted.

Approval as an incentive for learning may be misused. It may be overused; there is no need to approve everything a child does. Nor should the parent try to obtain conformity to many or to unreasonable demands. Disapproval should not mean rejection of the child himself. There is also a danger in making disapproval so personal as to arouse excessive feelings of guilt, fear, and anxiety, as in the following situation:

A three-year-old had taken his brother's toy and the mother was determined that he give it back.

MOTHER: Please give the toy back to brother. He was playing with it.
CHILD: No. I want it.
MOTHER: If you don't give the toy to brother, you'll make Mommy very unhappy. You'll make Mommy cry.
CHILD: No.
MOTHER (pretends to cry).
FATHER: You've made Mommy unhappy. She's crying.
CHILD (stands uncertainly for a few moments, then runs to mother and puts her arms around her): Please don't cry, Mommy. (When mother continues to pretend to cry, child clings to mother and begins to cry also.)
MOTHER: If you want to make Mommy happy, and have her stop crying, give the toy back to your brother.
CHILD (still crying, does so, then returns to mother, who immediately stops crying and smiles).
MOTHER: You've been a good girl and made Mommy happy.

This approach, while immediately effective, equates in the child's mind prompt compliance with intense dependence upon the approval of others. Adjustments motivated by anxiety may result in a compulsive need for approval, a submissive dependence, or a self-defeating conformity. This child evidenced much tension, insecurity, and anxiety at the threat of losing what she most needs, a feeling of complete confidence in the reality of her mother's constant and sustaining love and approval.

LEARNING NOT TO BE AFRAID

Conquering fear in the later preschool period involves active participation by the child. If possible, fear should be replaced by interest or enjoyment. This can be accomplished by bringing the child into successful encounters with the thing he fears. Learning not to be afraid is an active developmental process.

The usefulness of this method of directing and aiding the child toward ways of coping actively with certain fear situations was studied experimentally by Jersild and Holmes (51, 1939). As defined in the experiment, fear means "a complete refusal to enter into the situation" or a "refusal to enter the fear situation until the experimenter has offered either to accompany or help the child." (51, p. 13, 1939) The twenty children participating were between three and five years of age. The two situations to which the children were exposed were fear of height and fear of the dark. In the first situation the experimenter suggested that the child walk along an elevated board to get a box of brightly colored toys at the far end. If he hesitated, he was told he could do it. If he was afraid of falling, he was reassured that he could do it and would not fall. If the child still held back, the experimenter offered to take his hand while he walked across.

In the second setup a ball with which the child and the examiner had been playing rolled into a dark room. Similar directions were given (51, p. 181, 1939). Thus the child was gradually familiarized with the fear experience and left it each time with a feeling of satisfaction. The procedure used in helping children to overcome their fear of the dark was as follows: When the child and the experimenter came to the door, the experimenter explained to the child where the light was and how he could locate it by the small phosphorescent pendant at the end of the chain. If the child still refused to enter, she said, "Then I'll go in with you and show you how you can find the light." They entered the room together and the examiner showed the child how he could feel his way along the screen and look for the little shining pendant which would help him find the chain. When he had done so, she let him pull the chain and turn on the light. She then asked him to turn off the light and watch the "little light" that shone in the dark. Then he turned on the light again and they played, for a few minutes, with several puzzles which the child enjoyed. Just before leaving, the child again turned out the light and the examiner said, "Now you'll know where to find the light the next time you come in. You can remember that it hangs in front of the screen and you can look for the little light at the end of the chain." In this way the child was taught a method of finding his way in a dark room; he became familiar with being in the dark; he actively participated in making the room dark; and he left what had been a pleasant experience with the positive expectancy that in the future he would be able to cope with any difficulties. The same procedure was repeated with slight variations until the child entered the room alone. Whenever the child found the light for himself, the examiner made some encouraging comment: "That's fine. You found the light all by yourself, didn't you?"

The results of this procedure proved very satisfactory. The children showed an active interest and co-operation and made a definite attempt to utilize the instructions given. When they had acquired skill in dealing with the dark, they entered the room without hesitation or objection. Their pleasure in mastering the difficulties and in being themselves the cause of darkness and light was evident. A child whose parents had reported that he was afraid of the dark at home learned to enter the experimental dark room in three trials. After he had succeeded in finding the light, he later said with a wide smile, "I know where the light is." In the absence of desire to overcome the fear or of pleasure in accomplishing a previously difficult feat, aversion to the dark room was much more difficult to overcome.

Fear of sleeping in the dark can be diminished by helping the child to associate his bedroom with pleasant feelings and emotions, especially those which recall happy experiences with his toys, dolls, and especially his parents. By helping the child undress and reading him a story in his own bedroom, parents can prevent the child from associating the dark bedroom with separation from the parents.

The experience of parents has indicated that the method of helping the child to cope actively with the fear-stimulus is superior to such methods as avoidance of fear-arousing occurrences, warnings, escape from the situation, reassurance, and explanation. Knowledge of how to handle the situation tends to cast out fear. Skills help to minimize fear. In a case of severe fear the child's life situation as a whole needs to be evaluated.

THE RELATION OF LEARNING
TO PERSONALITY DEVELOPMENT

No fairy godmother can, at birth, give a child a winsome personality. Personality is shaped by the child's experiences. Children's personality is influenced most strongly by "emotionally toned experiences of interpersonal relations." The way each new experience is perceived depends upon what has gone before.

During preschool years the child's concept of himself is largely determined by his interpersonal relations with parents, brothers and sisters, playmates, nursery-school teachers, and other persons with whom he comes in contact. These persons either help him to find himself by giving him freedom to be himself and learn what he can do, or they contribute to his "loss of self" by constantly trying to change his ways of behavior and by maintaining a critical attitude, which gives him the impression that he is "bad, worthless, and unloved." Even the effect of physical handicaps depends upon the social or interpersonal meaning that these deviations have as perceived by the child.

For their best personality development children of this age need love, understanding, opportunities and materials to develop competence and express their ideas and feelings, and guidance in their activities.

Questions and Problems

FOR CLASS DISCUSSION OR STUDY GROUPS

1. Observe children of different ages to find out what uses language serves in their lives.

2. Spend as much time as possible in a nursery school or recreation center studying the interaction of teacher and preschool children and the way in which the teacher contributes to their development. Later, if possible, take care of two or more children for an hour or more a day, applying the principles and procedures you have learned.

3. In the light of the theory of learning, outline what you consider the best procedure in teaching a preschool child to (a) hit a target with a ball, (b) improve his language ability, (c) play co-operatively with other children. Show how the external environment, the child's native capacity, his previous experience, and instruction and guidance enter into each of the above learning situations.

4. Give an illustration of learning that took place apparently as a result of sudden insight rather than as a result of trial and error. Was repetition with

satisfaction a factor in this type of learning? Was any influence of previous experience observed?

5. What appears to be the most effective method of overcoming fears?

6. Find examples of ways in which parents or nursery-school teachers help children to solve their own problems.

7. Read the experiments described in Part Three of Mussen and Conger's *Child Development and Personality*, and summarize the kinds of experiments that have contributed to our knowledge of the personality development of children of preschool age, guidance in their activities, and reasonable limits set by a parent who speaks with authority.

Chapter 11

SPECIAL PROBLEMS

OF DEVELOPMENT IN THE

LATER PRESCHOOL PERIOD

The course of development does not always run smooth. Some-times the child seems to linger in one stage of development, or he may have setbacks. He fluctuates between the natural impulse to grow up and his impulse to maintain his comfortable *status quo*, or even to return to the satisfactions of earlier dependence on his mother. In the following fantasy a five-year-old expresses regressive desires: "The little girl feels like cry-ing." Examiner: "Why does she cry?" "Because then her mother loves her. When she cries Mother comes over and kisses her. Then the little girl feels like getting into baby's bed." (60, p. 32, 1949) Sometimes children retreat from present frustrations into infantile behavior. For example, a four-year-old child may begin to wet the bed or go back to infantile forms of play when a baby brother or sister seems to him to be usurping his mother's affection.

Certain behavior problems are not to be regarded as bad habits, but as a normal and necessary part of the process of growing up. MacFarlane and her associates (70, 1954) described the problems of normal children. These problems decline with age. Bowel and bladder control is one of the earliest. Later, speech problems, fears, thumb-sucking appear. Temper tan-trums, destructiveness, and overactivity reach peaks around three and five years. Nail-biting is the only problem that was found to increase with age. Irritability, temper tantrums, and destructiveness seemed to be related to poor health, but the correlation between intelligence and number of problems was insignificant during the early years, but increased to -0.41 by twelve to thirteen years.

CONDITIONS RELATED TO PROBLEM BEHAVIOR

The causes of children's behavior are complex and interrelated. No kind of problem can be explained on the basis of one, or even two or three, antecedent factors. A child's behavior can be understood only in the light of knowledge about the relations and experiences that have influenced him from birth and are influencing him in the present. "Behavior of the moment thus appears as the temporarily last scene of an uninterrupted plot or theme, during which a person has developed a certain readiness to perform in a . . . particular manner." (55, p. 264, 1949) Consequently, the remedy for a particular kind of problem behavior cannot be found simply by changing one single factor in a child's environment, i.e., one additional punishment, reward, deprivation, or restriction.

The child's immaturity

Many temporary difficulties arise out of the preschool child's inability to handle so many baffling situations. Much of children's behavior annoying to the adult arises from their lack of experience and skills. For example, dawdling may represent the two-year-old's attempt to explore his still-unfamiliar world. Anything in his environment may capture his interest for the moment and take his attention away from eating or dressing. Time means nothing to him. Given too much attention by parents and nursery-school teachers, these temporary difficulties may become real problems. Treated casually and constructively, they are soon outgrown. In moving about in his life-space, the child comes up against all sorts of barriers which he is not equipped to understand or tolerate.

In his no man's land between fact and fiction, he cannot be accused of telling lies. To be sure, what he says does not always correspond to adult ideas of the truth, but it seems true to the young child. In his magical world he really believes "saying makes it so." If he makes a mistake, he should be helped to understand why his behavior was disapproved.

Parent-child relations

Most problems of preschool children have their roots in the parent-child relation. They can be fully understood only if one knows the interaction in the family, and especially the emotional relation of child and mother. The child's failure to learn the language, feeding problems, failure in bowel and bladder control, lack of popularity with other children, fears, and tantrums often frustrate the parents. The child's nonconforming behavior is a threat to their self-esteem. From the child's standpoint, the parent appears to be forcing him into a way of life that is in conflict with his needs and capabilities. If carried to an extreme this treatment results in the child's loss of self-esteem.

Some parents keep trying to make the child over in their own image or in the image of the kind of person they wanted to become. For example, five-year-old Sydney had never been allowed to be a child; he was always being pushed beyond his capacities. His parents were partially rejecting him—rejecting the childish qualities in him. Underneath was his mother's resentment that the child was restricting her freedom to go and come as she pleased. When the father returned from the war, Sydney had to share her affection with his father. Later he was crowded out still further by the coming of a baby brother.

How often do parents of preschool children express disapproval of their children? How often do they say, "You're a naughty child," or "You'll be the death of me yet." Do they often tell him, "That was well done," "We are proud of you," or "You're a good boy"? The ratio of disapproval to condemnation is probably still high. A child hearing constant unfavorable appraisals comes to believe that he is inadequate and inferior. Favorable evaluation on the part of his parents tends to build a stable core of self-respect and self-acceptance (12, p. 59, 1952). Acceptance of a child, however, should not be confused with resignation—the attitude, "There's nothing we can do about it."

"Give children affection," the rule which some child psychologists state so glibly, is not so simple and easy as it sounds. Whether parents and teachers *can* feel genuine affection for a child depends on whether they, as children, have learned to love. "The difficult mothers of today are the difficult children of yesterday." Horney (45, 1945) showed how the parent who tends to move toward people in a compulsive way may want to do everything for the child, thus preventing him from using his own resources. The parent who moves away from people and maintains few social contacts may fail to give the child the normal human relations he needs. The parent who moves against people may develop in the child a sense of helplessness and anxiety.

The statements made by mothers in response to the question: "What are the most and the least enjoyable aspects of parenthood?" were most revealing.* Some frankly expressed their negative feelings:

* Anneliese Friedsam Korner, *Some Aspects of Hostility in Young Children* (New York: Grune & Stratton, 1949), pp. 67-68. Quoted by permission of Grune & Stratton.

MARIO'S MOTHER: I don't like to be a mamma. Being a mamma is too much work. I don't want any more children. (She had two.)

JACK'S MOTHER: I don't know how to explain this . . . (and then after pausing for over a minute) It was really a burden to have too many children. When I discovered that I was pregnant, I felt bad about it. Then I finally made up my mind saying to myself what's the use of grieving. And once I had made up my mind, I took it. [60, p. 67, 1949]

To some mothers their children were a personal possession:

STANLEY'S MOTHER (was quite explosive in the affirmation of her fondness): I have two nice children. I am happy about them. My kids mean everything to me; they are my life. I could throw myself out of a window for them. I love them. They are the best I have, and the only thing I have. I love them . . . even more than their father. [60, p. 68, 1949]

Other mothers showed a warm acceptance of their children:

RUDI'S MOTHER: . . . It's a natural feeling. . . . I always wanted children. When I had one child I was unhappy that it was only one. The only thing I ever regretted in relation to my children was that I could not be with them as much as I would like to. They were never in my way . . . we feel good about them. We both have the same feelings in regard to them [60, p. 68, 1949]

Especially with young children a certain consistency helps to prevent problems. But parents are human, and human beings have their ups and downs, their fluctuation of moods. We can go too far in expecting parents to be angelic. Overconscientious mothers, worried by the psychologist's emphasis on consistency, may achieve a forced and rigid uniformity. With normal children it is usually better for parents honestly to express the emotion they feel. Children need to learn how people feel when they behave in certain ways.

For most children it is important to set up a few definite, firmly established boundaries, to remove unnecessary barriers, and to make necessary restrictions clear-cut and understandable. This gives these children a sense of security and stability (114, 1957). If they give free rein to their aggression, even in a play situation, they are likely to feel guilty about it. The adult can accept the child's feeling of resentment against restrictions and at the same time remain very definite about those that are necessary. The child's problem is to adjust to the reasonable demands of his environment without loss of love or self-esteem. The way in which restrictions are introduced makes all the difference—whether gently with sympathy, understanding, support, and encouragement, or harshly with arbitrariness, exasperation, and threats.

Parents may play any one of three roles: (1) They may make demands upon the child that he is ready and able to meet at a given time; in this way they further his development. (2) They may make excessive and unsuitable demands that evoke the child's aggressive tendencies or cause him to feel paralyzed by constant failure. (3) They may become slaves to the child's wishes and thus deprive him of the training necessary for him to take his place in the social group. The overaggressive child is likely to have received too little attention; the dependent child, too much; and the child who is unco-operative and has emotional difficulties, to have come from a home characterized by tensions and conflicts.

Family atmosphere

Using the Fels Parent-Behavior Rating Scales, Baldwin (14, 1949) found significant differences in the behavior of children from two types of home atmosphere. The first, called "democracy," is characterized by joint planning and policy-making, verbal explanations to the child, absence of arbitrary decisions, and general permissiveness plus emotional restraint. This type of atmosphere tends to raise the child's activity level and to produce children who are aggressive and fearless, take initiative in planning, and are likely to be leaders in nursery-school situations; they are less likely to conform to cultural demands. The other type of home atmosphere, called "control," makes clear to the child, though without friction, the necessary restrictions upon his behavior. This type of atmosphere obtains conformity but "tends to decrease *quarrelsomeness, negativism,* and *disobedience;* at the same time, however, it tends to decrease *aggressiveness, planfulness, tenacity,* and *fearlessness.*"

Other kinds of family atmosphere are created when the home has been broken by death or divorce, or even when the mother goes out to work. In the first instance there may be bitterness and antagonism between the parents who still share the responsibility of bringing up the child. In the situation where the mother is away from home during the day, the effect on the child depends a great deal on the personality of the housekeeper, the co-operation of the husband, and the relationship the mother is able to establish with the child under these circumstances. For example, five-year-old Tom, whose mother was away at work during the day, often became petulant and hung onto her when she had to leave in the morning. For example, one day when she said good-bye, he said to her, "Why do you have to go? And why do I have to go to school?" After going to the door with her and saying good-bye in a mournful voice, Tom seemed to adjust to the situation and came running back into the kitchen eagerly responding when the housekeeper asked what he wanted for breakfast. His mood was happy and conversational.

His mother telephoned as Tom was leaving for school and his comment, after a brief conversation with her, was, "That was my mommy who called and it was all for me."

Another morning he got up only a few minutes before his mother had to leave and clung to her asking, "Why do you have to go now? I don't want you to go." She responded by explaining quietly, hugging and reassuring him.

At other times he made these remarks:

"Everyone does not live happy like my mother and me."

"My mother never scolds me; she's always nice to me."

"I guess I've got the best daddy there is."

In nursery school Tom shows initiative and independence. He is fortunate in having a mother and father who make the most of the limited time they have with him. He is also fortunate in having a housekeeper who is able to enforce necessary restrictions objectively without causing personal antagonism.

There is need for further detailed study of parent-child interaction in particular cultures (see Chapter VI). Such investigations would include a study of the kind of children parents want, descriptions of the methods of bringing up children, and their effect on the children as they grow older.

DEALING WITH PROBLEM BEHAVIOR

Problems do not occur singly or in isolation. In any comprehensive case study, the complexity of a child's adjustment is illustrated:

Sarah, four years and four months old, was referred to a child guidance clinic. The problem as stated by her mother was "refusal to eat." The child had "gone on a strike" and refused to eat for two or three days. The mother was also concerned about thumb-sucking.

In the interviews with the mother, the worker found it difficult to get beyond a façade of psychological sophistication. From her reading of books and articles on child psychology, the mother had learned certain theories and formulas. She said the child had had lots of affection. Actually the mother was lacking in self-esteem; she felt insecure in her relations with her husband; she was unable to set limits for herself or her child.

A thorough medical examination showed that the child had no serious health problem. However, her experiences with doctors had been unhappy, and she began to cry when "doctor" was mentioned. She had established bowel and bladder control early. It seemed as though she had never had a chance to be a baby and that her present resistance to eating might be an expression of hostility toward an ambitious parent who had subjected her to more frustration than she could handle. According to the Stanford-Binet test given a year earlier, her IQ was 140. In the play interviews, however, she did not give the impression of high intelligence; her play was repetitious rather than creative and original.

Recognizing that the child's problems were embedded in the whole family pattern, the workers tried to help the mother observe the child more accurately, more objectively, to analyze the situation out of which the child's problem arose, and to recognize her satisfactions and insights, as she did in such remarks as "I'm being more consistent than I was." As she talked about herself and her relations, she obtained a clearer self-concept and a greater willingness to accept her role as a mother, with its satisfactions and its annoyances.

The counselor believed that the mother had inner resources to solve her own problems and accepted her first hesitant attempts to look squarely at the situation. The mother was able to bring into the open the incompatibilities between her husband and herself, as, for example, the husband's desire for definite routine as contrasted with her own lack of time-sense and aversion to routine. She thought it might help to keep a daily schedule, not only of her activities, but also of her satisfactions and annoyances. This reorientation toward herself helped the mother to create a psychological environment in which the child's needs were more adequately met.

An ounce of prevention is worth a pound of scolding or punishment. In fact, the more parents focus on positive aspects of the child's behavior and the less on problems, the more likely they are to have well-adjusted children.

Family fun is an important part of a favorable environment for children. The whole family's playing together is an experience children never forget—sharing plans, plotting surprises, reading aloud, going on trips together, celebrating special days. The child often gives parents a chance to do some of the things they have always wanted to do—play with electric trains, do handicrafts and woodworking, take pictures. They can have fun learning with their children.

ACCIDENTS

Accidents in the home happen more often to children under five than to any other age except over sixty-five. Parents have been given much information on the kinds of accidents that frequently occur and ways of preventing them. They have selected safe toys; kept knives, poisons, and other harmful things out of children's reach; made stairways and windows safer; and supervised the children at play. But they have not yet solved the problem of "safety without fears for the active child." (15, 1957)

Safety habits are both "caught" and taught. Preschool children like to do things "the grown-up way," and will imitate adults in the way they cross the street, use tools, and handle other safety situations. Safety is best taught as part of the child's everyday activity. By showing the child why he is forbidden to fool with the electric light socket, his curiosity will be satisfied. By providing plenty of interesting, guided exercise on safe play apparatus, his desire to do dangerous things just to show off, will be reduced. Safety rules, too, have a place, especially if the child helps to make them, because an idea expressed in words is often a guide to action. For preschool children these rules should be simple and unequivocal.

Like other problems, playing safe is not simple. Some children are accident-prone; they have more than their share of accidents. These are usually impulsive, physically active children with unmet needs for affection, security, and recognition. Relatively few accidents occur in a home atmosphere of warmth and acceptance.

AGGRESSIVE BEHAVIOR

No kind of behavior is more disturbing to many parents and nursery school teachers than children's attempts to hurt other persons and to destroy things. The child's aggressive acts keeps the parent in a constant state of anxiety; he fears the possible danger to the child and to other children. The child's aggression also makes him more acutely aware of his own similar suppressed tendencies. According to mothers interviewed (27, 1955) on their attitudes and methods of developing self-restraint in children between three and four years, there is a general cultural emphasis on the suppression of aggressive behavior, especially that directed toward adults. The possible relation between the suppression of all aggressive tendencies and later passive nonco-operation, clinging dependency, and subservience to others should be considered.

The nature of aggression

Aggression in young children is not the destructive force so often described. It represents in the majority of cases an effort to achieve certain goals. The socialization of the child, with its many prohibitions, is a frustrating process, and it is natural for the child to react with acts of defiance. The child's strong drive toward independence, as he tries to maintain the omnipotence of infancy, between two and three years old and as he later begins to sense his growing competency, is a constructive and normal aspect of growing up. It is a mistake to try to eradicate it.

Children's responses to frustration vary with their previous and present experiences and needs (85, 1955). Those children for whom socialization has been achieved with affection and understanding tend to react to frustration with more constructive activities, while others react more destructively and with hostility (28, 1952). During frustration, children with a strong drive or need to dominate showed higher total aggression scores than those low in this need; whereas children high in need for affection showed lower aggression scores (85, 1955).

A child's aggression becomes harmful (1) when it exceeds the demands of the situation, (2) when it is so intense that it breaks out in destructive acts, (3) when it is directed against people with the intent to injure them rather than against things and conditions that should be changed, and (4) when it is turned inward and arouses strong feelings of guilt and anxiety in the child (90, 1957).

Aggressive behavior in preschool children

Preschool children express their feelings of hostility in various ways. They may direct aggression inward rather than outwardly, especially if the source of frustration is strongly feared. Some picture the parent as dead or ill. Some defy the parent and deliberately do the forbidden thing. Still others express their hostility verbally: "I don't like you any more." Preschool children's expressed attitudes toward aggression do not always correspond with their behavior. They may reflect their parents' attitudes and rules verbally, but on the playground use their aggressive impulses to maintain their rights.

Some evidence on the relation between children's expression of hostility and parental affection and warmth is given in Korner's study (60, 1949) of twenty children four to six years old attending nursery school. Individual differences were striking. In general, the children whose parents gave them affectionate care expressed strong hostility in the play situation and low hostility in life situations. This behavior suggests that they may have learned to repress their expression of hostility in order to keep the affection of their parents, but that their feelings of hostility, still strong, were given free rein in the permissive play atmosphere. The children whose parents did not give them affectionate care showed either strong hostility in all situations or low hostility in the play situation and strong hostility in life situations. Severe corporal punishment and lack of affectionate care tended to produce unruly children. Two children who showed low hostility in all situations seemed to be constrained by a deep anxiety. Stendler (100, 1954) reported a tendency for aggressive children to have rejecting mothers and for some dependent, timid children to have overprotective, oversolicitous, or overanxious mothers.

How to handle aggression

The child has to learn how to handle his aggressive impulses. Since his mother is the person who is most frequently associated with the frustration inherent in the process of socialization—with his sleeping, eating, and toilet habits—he most often directs his aggression against her. He feels guilty when he finds himself hating the person who loves him most. That is why a nursery-school teacher, or other children, may be more helpful than the parents; they can set limits that in the home would cause greater tension and anxiety.

It is obviously a mistake for adults to be so preoccupied with children's hostility that they ignore their co-operative, pleasant behavior.

As the child grows older, they can help him to understand his feelings of hostility. By expressing his anger in words in frustrating situations, the child keeps his aggressive tendencies on the level of conscious awareness and thus is better able to handle his conflicts and correct his misconceptions as they arise (62, p. 70, 1948).

Permissiveness in extreme form implies a denial of the need or desirability of training the child in the way he should go. Many parents and teachers have made the mistake of regarding methods of psychotherapy appropriate for emotionally sick children as applicable to their well children (20, 1956). It should be pointed out that although Freud concluded that there was a background of frustration in every neurosis, he did not justify the conclusion of some of his followers that all frustration was unhealthy and did not therefore advocate extreme permissiveness.

In brief, the child's aggressive impulses may be handled in four main ways:

1. By reducing frustrations and the conditions that provoke them. It is wise to prevent, as far as possible, the arousal of intense feelings when the child is too immature to control them.

2. By trying to replace some satisfaction of which a child must be deprived with another satisfaction that is more appropriate to his stage of development. The child needs an additional expression of tenderness when he gives up a socially disapproved habit or attitude.

3. By recognizing individual differences; some children have a low frustration tolerance; they are quick to wrath, oversensitive, and excitable; they have had previous blighting experiences.

4. By helping the child to recognize his feelings, to bring them out into the open, and to consciously direct the aggressive impulses into constructive

work and active play or into symbolic behavior like painting, imaginative play, or verbal expression (1, pp. 13-14, 1957).

TEMPER TANTRUMS

Anger is expressed in various ways. It may take the form of violent temper tantrums, destructiveness, attempted injury of others, surliness, refusal to co-operate, or ridicule and criticism of others. Temper tantrums, which are likely to begin at about age two, are the child's expression of helpless rage at conditions that he cannot handle. Instead of being directed against others, this emotional energy may turn inward and express itself in illness, self-injury, or self-depreciation.

The chief cause of anger in the preschool child is frustration of any kind: having an activity interfered with, failing in his attempts to make and do the things he wants to do, being harshly made to submit to physical routines. Often a temper tantrum is a child's reaction to the last straw in a series of demands and restrictions of which the parents were not even aware. From two and a half years on, the outbursts in connection with the establishment of routines tend to decrease, while conflicts with authority and frustration in social situations tend to increase. A temper tantrum now and then between the ages of two and three is part of growing up; it is nothing for parents to worry about. A child who is in good physical condition, who is not overfatigued, and who feels generally secure can learn to handle a considerable amount of frustration.

Adults have had sufficient experience with violent emotions to recognize to some extent the panic which a little child must feel when he is, as it were, seized by the overwhelming psychological and physiological disturbances of anger and fear. They will, accordingly, reassure him by their own steady calm and do nothing to aggravate the intensity of his emotion (34, 1954). The child needs help in learning to find effective substitute responses in the beginning when his energy can be harnessed to overcome it, rather than later when his energy is dissipated in chaotic responses.

To summarize, temper tantrums are discouraged by:

1. Helping the angry child to find outlets that are effective in dissipating the drive-energy, not self-destructive, and not destructive to others.

2. Showing that he is loved even though his behavior is disapproved.

3. Keeping as matter-of-fact and calm as possible when the child is excited and angry, thus setting him an adult example of self-control.

4. Including more relaxed fun in his life and avoiding unnecessary restraints on his activities, abrupt and arbitrary commands, tasks that are too

difficult for him, too high standards, too little rest, too little freedom to play in suitable places.

5. Helping him to acquire the knowledge and skills he needs in order to meet more effectively new situations that involve frustration.

6. Helping him to learn to turn his attention to other things when he cannot have something he wants.

7. If tantrums do occur despite the adult's best efforts to avoid them, repeatedly letting the child get what he wants by having a tantrum is likely to reinforce this kind of behavior. Dealing with a so-called spoiled child is not simple and easy. What appears to be the same behavior may arise from many causes; the parent needs perspective on the situation as a whole, including his own feelings and predispositions. Harshly and abruptly laying down the law increases the child's hostility and fans the fires of aggressiveness. A reasonable firmness on important issues, combined with genuine concern and affection for the child, is generally effective in the long run.

NAGGING

Parents and teachers are not the only ones who nag. Some preschool children become adept at nagging their parents for things they want. Such behavior is, of course, encouraged by the parent who at first holds out on the child, finally gives in, and lets him have the thing for which he was teasing. Nagging is discouraged by the parent who treats the child with respect, who listens attentively to his questions and comments, and who is willing to work toward reasonable compromises and so does not give the child occasion to nag. If the child is making "a perfect nuisance" of himself, the parent should be firm. Thus the child will learn that teasing is of no avail in getting what he wants. However, if a child suddenly starts to nag, the parent may well pause to ask why.

The child tends to become more demanding when he needs some kind of emotional reassurance, and when the parent shows favoritism to another child and seems indifferent, aloof, or even hostile to the first child.

SHOWING OFF

A child who "shows off" may merely want people to recognize his newly acquired competencies. This tendency may be reinforced intentionally or unintentionally. He has performed some little stunt, and people have exclaimed, "How cute!" "How bright!" "How cunning!" In this way his attention has been directed toward himself rather than toward the thing he is doing or the pleasure he is giving to the audience. After he has made his contribution to the gaiety of the party, the adults or children present should say, "Thank you, that was very interesting," or "That was lots of fun, thank you." Then the child should be willing to take his place as part of the audience and enjoy what someone else says or does. He should have practice in the roles both of performer and of member of the audience. Children who have been in the habit of playing games with adults and assisting them in their daily work are usually free from the tendency to seek the center of the stage in social situations.

• EXCESSIVE CRYING

Small children cry easily. Tears are sure to occur occasionally. But the normal state for a child is happiness and wholehearted absorption in his activities. If a child habitually weeps over "nothing at all," the mother should try to discover what situations make her child cry and what the underlying causes may be. Physical defects, irritation, fatigue, pain, or general weakness often account for excessive crying. Children frequently cry when their property is taken away, when they are left alone in a room, or when they are working at something too difficult for them. Sometimes children being given mental tests will suddenly push the testing materials from the table and burst out crying when the exercises become difficult. Sometimes they cry when other children or adults refuse to play with them or to look at what they have made or what they are doing. Occasionally the task of getting dressed or undressed, especially in winter clothing, annoys them to tears.

After the mother has discovered the probable causes of the child's crying, she may study the ways in which some of them can be eliminated. She should demonstrate how unavoidable pain and disappointment should be met, at the same time giving the child assurance of her sympathy and understanding. Accepting his feeling—"Yes, it does hurt and it's all right to cry"—and encouraging him to talk about it is far better than urging him to "be brave" and bottle it up inside.

Children also cry because they are afraid. One mother handled fear of dogs as follows:

Fear of dogs is so far the only fear that Sammy has displayed. When he was just an infant, twice within a short time a boisterous puppy rushed up, put his paws on Sammy's chest, and barked in his face. After that alarming experience he whimpered and wanted to be picked up whenever a dog came near him, though he was quite interested in them at a distance. We have largely ignored his fear and have made no attempt to persuade him out of it, except indirectly by our own friendly response to dogs. His whimperings in due course gave way to a somewhat apprehensive watchfulness, and that in turn to complete confidence as long as the dog made no overtures to him. A week ago he came back from a walk with his father and told me as an item of interest that he had "patted a dog." His father had stopped to speak to the dog, and patted it, and Sammy stretched out his hand and did likewise. The interesting thing is that he clearly feels he has achieved something. The rest of us haven't referred to the matter again, but Sammy has brought it up himself two or three times, "Patted a dog!"

In every case of excessive crying, it is important to study the child's relations to members of his family and to other persons close to him, as well as his ideas about himself and his ability to cope with life's situations.

MASTURBATION

The habit of masturbation (sometimes called self-abuse) is a source of much unnecessary worry. This habit is frequently found among three- and four-year-old children in nursery schools and in kindergarten. It should be treated casually and sympathetically. During the first years it accompanies the child's interest in exploring all parts of the body and his enjoyment of the ensuing sensation. If in later preschool years it is indulged in excessively, it may indicate that the child is tense or worried about something, that his days are dreary, or that he is not getting enough affection from the persons who count most in his life. The child should not be allowed to feel that he is "bad" because he resorts to this source of satisfaction. Instead, he should feel that he can count on his parents' help in overcoming the habit.

The child will quickly imitate the parent's attitude toward the functions of the body. A "hush-hush" attitude is likely to give him an unwholesome concern with the sexual parts, while disregard for privacy may overstimulate his curiosity. He can learn not to shock the excessive respectability of neighbors. "People are funny; they don't like it," is sufficient reason for him to conform to social conventions.

ENURESIS (BED-WETTING)

About the middle of the third year is early enough for the child to take full responsibility for bowel and bladder control. Because of possible lapses, three-year-olds at nursery school should have a complete change of clothing.

Children differ widely in the time at which they take responsibility for bowel and for bladder control. Enuresis should not be considered a problem until after the third or fourth year. Probably about 95 per cent of the causes of enuresis are of psychological origin.

When a child still wets in the later preschool years the cause may lie in general tension; too early or too strict training; a physical condition which might be discovered by medical examination; anxiety about the process of elimination; subjection to too high a standard in behavior, manners, and the like; or deeper psychological factors such as jealousy of a brother or sister, or hostility toward parents. Enuresis may be part of a general immaturity or resistance to growing up. Perhaps the child is easily excited and disturbed, or feels insecure. In some cases, the first days at school are enough of a strain to cause temporary loss of bowel or bladder control.

Parents should try to be casual about accidents and to make the child's entire day as happy and relaxed as possible. Doing anything that might increase his anxiety, fear, sense of guilt, frustration, or shame will aggravate the condition. A quiet period before bedtime and a cool bedroom are advisable.

The child's attention should be directed to the advantages of control. Having a dry bed is in itself an effective reward. He especially needs to feel he is taking responsibility himself for keeping it dry. When the child does wet, he may be given the responsibility of mopping the floor and changing his clothes, not as punishment but as a way in which he can co-operate.

RUNNING AWAY

Almost as soon as the toddler can run, he begins to run away. Between the ages of one and two, a child seems to develop a desire to go the other way when he is asked to come. If the child is in no immediate danger, he can be patiently called back. From the time he is two or two and a half years old, he becomes a source of constant anxiety to his mother, because running out into the streets or woods is dangerous for one of his limited experience of the world.

However, the child needs experience in exploration in order to develop ideas of spatial relationships and a sense of direction, and to satisfy his desire for adventure. One mother let her child trot off in safe places wherever he wanted to go and followed after, not in pursuit but just to see where he went. In a little over a week he had satisfied his curiosity and preferred to stay at home with his playthings, which proved more interesting than anything he had found in his wanderings.

"HE WON'T EAT THIS AND HE WON'T EAT THAT"

Feeding problems are of many kinds and degrees of severity. They are related to the culture as well as to individual needs. Many are emotional, not nutritional; many are problems from the standpoint of the parents rather than from the standpoint of the child. The following should not be considered feeding problems: when a child eats less as his rate of growth and food requirement decrease; refuses a certain kind of food but willingly eats other foods of equal cost and similar nutritional value; eats lightly sometimes but in the long run achieves a balanced diet; occasionally relapses into earlier habits of eating with his fingers or spilling food. Parents who continually nag a child about eating or otherwise arouse his resistance and hostility may have a serious feeding problem on their hands if the child realizes that his refusal to eat is an exceedingly effective means to control them.

Causes and prevention of feeding problems

Some of the possible causes of a child's refusal to eat are lack of hunger, unfamiliar taste or consistency of the food, desire for attention, defiance of authority, or incipient illness. The kind of diet itself may decrease a child's appetite, especially a diet low in vitamin B. In about 35 per cent of the cases there was a resemblance between the food aversions of the parents and those of the children; there was a still greater resemblance between the food dislikes of the children in the same family. More obscure psychological causes of feeding problems have been reported: parental overprotection may lead to overfeeding the child; deprivation of satisfying relations may cause the insecure child to use food as a solace; overeating may satisfy aggressive impulses. Lack of appetite is very common in certain well-to-do groups; relatively rare among country children who usually have a higher energy expenditure. Good appetite and good behavior at table occur most frequently in homes where parents are relaxed, consistent, and generous in their approval of the child.

Eating with other children in the nursery school often helps a child develop good food habits. Kurt Lewin demonstrated the influence of the group situation in a cracker-eating experiment. He succeeded in getting children to eat a large number of dry soda crackers shortly after breakfast, just by pointing out to the child, in an imaginary group situation, that Bobbie had only eaten seven but Jackie, for example, being a little fellow, would not be able to eat so many. Having created a goal and a challenge to Jackie's maturity, Lewin induced him to eat twelve crackers before giving up!

Overcoming bad feeding habits

The way in which feeding problems are created and intensified is illustrated in the following quotation from an interview with the mother of a four-year-old child:

Eating is my main problem with her. That is the origin of almost all troubles and scenes at home. She simply won't eat. When she was four months old I gave her a spoon full of Pablum and she spit it right into my face. Ever since I have had trouble with her. She will take one or two hours over a plate of food. Every day we have scenes on account of her eating habits, and she thoroughly enjoys her nuisance value. She fiddles around with food forever. I tried not to force her, hoping that she would get hungry by herself. She went three days without solid food and did not show the slightest signs of hunger. I am afraid that isn't the method, either. [60, p. 64, 1949]

Another mother reported:

He dislikes pea soup and custard. When I prepare these dishes I usually do so only for the two of us [the parents]. I feel I should not insist, since grown-ups don't like certain dishes either and that he has a right to dislike some of them. I don't make a fuss over it." [60, p. 64, 1949]

In the first case, the mother had an extreme feeding problem on her hands; in the second case, no problem at all.

The best practice in feeding preschool children is to provide a well-balanced diet and let the child's natural appetite guide his eating. When he is not *made* to eat, he is likely to feel it is up to him and he eats.

DISOBEDIENCE AND DISCIPLINE

The concept of obedience has changed. Fifty years ago obedience to authority was the first law of education. It also had the sanction of religion: "Children, obey your parents." "Spare the rod and spoil the child." Children were expected to do the tasks set for them whether or not they understood the reasons. Discipline was synonymous with punishment. Now it refers to the teaching of desirable behavior—to the guiding of a learning process. The goal of all discipline is self-discipline—where the child accepts the responsibilites associated with his freedom.

Positive view of discipline

What adults call "willfulness" is usually not intentional disobedience. Perhaps Lewis Carroll had this all too frequent parental attitude in mind when he wrote (25, p. 85, 1932):

> Speak roughly to your little boy,
> And beat him when he sneezes:
> He only does it to annoy,
> Because he knows it teases.

Resistance, as manifested by crying and later in more complex ways by speech and action, is often an expression of the child's desire to be an individual in his own right—to get a sense of autonomy.

It is important for parents to distinguish between these four conditions: immaturity, which makes it impossible for a young child to make the choice between yes and no; the reluctance of a bright child to conform to adults' unrealistic or unreasonable requests; a growing independence often expressed by saying no even to reasonable requests; and genuine willfulness, which is unreasonable resistance.

In this respect, too, the child goes through developmental phases: When he is one year old he will usually conform readily when his parents say no. Four or five months later he begins to dislike restrictions upon his newly acquired motor skills. From two to three years, as he grows in ability to "get places," restrictions become still more irksome. Under present conditions, failure to comply with suggestions seems to reach a peak at around three years. By the time the child is five he is usually eager for praise and will conform to adult wishes to get it. Around six he is beginning to transfer his allegiance from the home to the school; he may assert his independence at home by saying, "No, I won't," or become saucy and argumentative.

It is also important to distinguish between a child's desire and his need. A parent may have to thwart a desire but will co-operate with the child in meeting a developmental need.

Parents can win if they are determined to have unconditional obedience. They can get their own way because they are bigger and stronger. But their triumph may be only temporary, or, worse still, it may result in an apathetic child. Surely they do not want to destroy the child's initiative. The solution is for parents and child together to work out a resolution of their conflicting desires on the child's level of understanding. This is constructive discipline; it builds wholesome personalities.

Examples of discipline in the home

Despite the emphasis on the importance of affectionate training, one daily sees serious discipline problems in preschool children. Many parents seem to be caught in a web of circumstances unfavorable for child development. In one case the mother's conviction that the child's will had to be governed or broken resulted in disastrous effects. The irritability and hostility of the members of his family and their apparent lack of genuine affection had aroused feelings of hostility in this child, which he expressed openly in his remarks to his mother, by knocking his playthings around, and by turning his hostility inward against himself.

A very intelligent mother, who had read widely in the field of psychology, described her attempt to apply psychological theory regarding discipline with one of her two children:

I know that books on child psychology are strongly against physical chastisement, but I must admit that in very occasional doses we have found it wonderfully salutary. Two-year-old Sammy has had one taste of spanking. He dearly loves his fun and games, and one monkey-trick is to swing on my arms and refuse to stand up when I take him to the toilet. A couple of weeks ago it went on past a joke and I spoke very sternly a couple of times. When that brought no result, and just before my arms broke off at the elbows, I gave him a smart little slap on the calf of his leg. It was his first taste of punishment and he gave an outraged yelp, but the feet went down. Since then he has continued to play his trick occasionally, with no rancor on either side, but the moment my voice grows stern, the legs go down and he says with a self-reproving air, "Mama pank a leg!"

Shameful confessions! Theoretically I deplore the use of physical strength as a control. Constant slappings and yankings are shocking. But in this harsh world I doubt if it does a well-loved child much harm to discover that even loving patience can be overtaxed.

The kind of discipline which some children experience at home is suggested by their remarks in free play: "The mommy's going to spank him if he doesn't go back to bed. She says, 'You get back in bed or I'll spank you so hard you'll never forget.'" "The little boy called in the night. His daddy doesn't come. His daddy doesn't like to be called in the night. But if he calls five times, his daddy comes." (63, pp. 37-40, 1941) Other children in their play portray extreme punitive situations which they have never experienced, but seem to consider appropriate.

Understanding on the part of both child and adult

Disobedience stems from different ways of looking at things: the child has his way; the parent has his way; they do not agree. Nagging and punishment do not really work. Letting the child do just as he pleases does not work—it retards the child's development. The best way is to work it out together. Parents should look at things from the child's point of view, give in to reasonable behavior but set definite, constant limits beyond which he may not go. The younger the child, the more permissive the parent may be. The older the child, the more he may be expected to conform to reasonable requests. It takes understanding and skill to achieve that balance between permissiveness and firmness that will result in the optimum of self-direction. One child needs firmness; another, all the affection the parent and nursery-school teacher can give him. The teacher needs to understand how much each child should have. When children are too young to understand reasons, the parents' and teachers' attitude of positive expectancy prevents much conflict.

How to build inner controls; self-discipline

There comes a time of readiness for discipline when the child thinks of restrictions and rules as a help to him in developing inner controls. The child's stability in this period will be greater if he has simple rules that do not change, and if he is not expected to take responsibility for making *all* decisions. By holding steady to the necessary controls parents can help the child in his own battle against his aggressive tendencies and his conflict between his needs and desires. When the parents' efforts to influence the child's development are rigid and charged with anxiety, the child often feels a need to resist or to defend himself against being changed.

Analysis of the situation

What can one do when a four-year-old says, "I won't?" Should the father say, "I guess you *will* do what I tell you to," and follow this statement with a spanking? Should the mother say, "Please, darling, do as Mother says"? Should the child's "I won't" simply end the matter?

The response to be made depends on the nature of and reason for the immediate command, on the physical condition, previous experiences of the child and other factors. If the "I won't" places the child or someone else in a position of danger, the adult's action must be prompt and effective. If the request is one that the adult himself would recognize as unreasonable or unjust he should be big enough to acknowledge his mistake. If the child is tired or irritable, due allowance should be made. If the child is greatly fatigued or ill he should be treated as a sick child.

Perhaps the child gets too many orders. If that is the case, a few essential requests should replace the many. Continual orders about every little thing tend to cause a disregard for all rules and regulations.

Perhaps the fault is in the command itself. Is it reasonable? Telling a child to "sit still" or to "keep quiet" for a long time is not reasonable. Is obedience to the command within the child's power? To tell a four-year-old not to touch a plate of freshly baked cookies is to set up a temptation almost too great for his stage of development. The principle of readiness as applied to discipline means postponing certain requests until the child is able to comply or co-operate.

Perhaps the fault is in the way the directions are delivered. Are they spoken simply, slowly, and distinctly? Disobedience may be due to misunderstanding. Many words are still unfamiliar to the preschool child. There would be much "disobedience" among adults who had studied French in an American high school if a Parisian were to give them a series of quick commands in rapid, lilting French. Is the child's attention secured before the directions are given? Sometimes the child is so entirely engrossed in his activity that he does not hear a request.

Is the command made reasonably attractive? Does it fit into the child's scheme of things? Does the child share in the planning which it represents? Better still, does he feel like a partner in the task? When feasible is the child given a reason for obeying; does he see some advantage to be gained? A pleasant manner and enthusiasm in the voice and in the wording of the request helps to put the child in a state of readiness. A warning often helps: "Five minutes more to play."

Little children often forget what parents have previously said. "I've told you that a hundred times" is probably true. The parent just has to accept the necessity for telling the child every time until he remembers to do the right thing himself. It takes time to learn, especially when there are so many things bidding for his attention.

Perhaps the fault is in the way in which disobedience to commands has been treated on previous occasions. Has disobedience to carefully considered requests been firmly associated with dissatisfaction or disapproval? Or have there been parental threats that were never carried out? Have bribes been offered for acquiescence? It is a dull child who will not try continually to drive a better bargain. Have promises been broken? Does the parent "go up in the air," thus entertaining the child with an exciting dramatic performance? Do parents disagree about methods of discipline? Is obedience to certain commands insisted upon consistently, or is the child forced to obey a command one day and allowed to have his own way about it the next? If the child has no way of knowing with certainty how his mother or father will take his actions, he cannot be expected to give consistent obedience.

Perhaps the fault is in the personality of the parent or teacher. If the adult is genuinely disliked, the child tends to take a negative attitude toward everything he or she asks him to do. Attempting to rebuild confidence and good fellowship is the first step toward winning obedience. An adult who is always oppressively right and says, "I told you so," is likely to arouse antagonism of an unreasonable but very human type.

The mother may be irritable because she is busy and worried about many things. Better management of the home might help.

Perhaps the fault is in the environment of the child. Are there interesting things for him to do, things suited to his capacity, safe, and not annoying to anyone else?

> For Satan finds some mischief still,
> For idle hands to do.

Perhaps the child is tired or irritated about something else. There is sometimes a diffusion of discontent that accounts for specific negative reactions. Obviously it is futile to discuss the use of different forms of discipline without analyzing the particular child and the possible causes of his behavior.

Punishment and parent-child relations

Punishment affects parent-child relations and teacher-child relations. A spanking which the child considers unrelated to the situation is likely to make him hostile to the person who administers it. It is better, whenever possible, to let the punishment fit the crime—to let the situation itself punish the child. Then the parent plays a friendly role. He gives warnings. If the child persists in doing the thing, he will get hurt. The parent can be sympathetic, but reminds the child kindly that he said it would hurt. The problem is much more difficult when the forbidden act is rewarding, like running out into the street—an exciting excursion that many times may cause no harm, yet sometimes be fatal. But over a period of time the parent can build a relation based on rewarding experiences in which his advice was needed.

Other effects of punishment

In addition to disrupting personal relations, punishment may have many other effects: on the self-concept of the child, helpless in the face of a punishing world; on his capacity to learn self-direction; on his feelings of hostility and guilt. Punishment often does divert behavior, but in an unpredictable direction.

Parents spank their children for various reasons: to control the child when other means have failed; to release their own feelings of annoyance; to meet the expectations of Grandfather or the neighbors, who do not have the child-development point of view. Spanking seems a quick way of "getting results," but these usually take the shape of temporary conformance, not of growth in self-direction and self-control. Autocratic control usually produces one of two personalities: an oversubmissive child who does what he is told but shows no initiative, or a rebellious child who is constantly waging war against authority. When used, punishment should be administered with the future—not the past—in mind. During preschool years it should be considered from the standpoint of its effect on the child, not from the standpoint of the annoyance or expense he has caused.

Certain other methods of punishment are worse than spanking. Giving the child the feeling, by being constantly cross to him or not speaking to him for hours, that he is a "bad" child or that "Mother doesn't love him any more" is detrimental to the child's best personality development. The effect, as well as the choice of a method of helping the child to build inner controls, can be determined only by considering the specific situation, the parental attitudes, the sanctions of the culture, the personality of the child.

Effect of rewards

If a great part of the child's life comes to revolve around gold stars, special privileges, and other artificial incentives, he tends to become insecure, lacking in spontaneity. It is interesting to compare children who work spontaneously "for the joy of the working" with those who work for an external reward. An individual's natural interest in the task itself is an important incentive all through life.

Even approval can be overdone, as it was with a child who was constantly saying, "I'm a good girl," or "Am I a good girl?" Indiscriminate approval loses its meaning. Moreover, a child may become too dependent upon a parent's approval. He is happy when he is basking in the warmth of his parents' approving smiles. But if this satisfaction is obtained at the expense of his needs for fun and self-assertion, he is failing to live fully as a child. He does not know the pleasures of carefree play because his energy is devoted to pleasing adults. His fear of disapproval may lead to self-effacing conformity; his deprivation of normal childhood activities may pile up unconscious resentment. In this sense a child may be considered "too good." When goodness is accompanied by such negative conditions as overdependence on adult approval and inability to relate oneself to others, then it can be considered a danger signal. But certainly a child who is gentle, industrious, kind, and quiet because this behavior is natural and constructive for him should not be considered abnormal!

WITHDRAWING BEHAVIOR

More serious than the aggressive kind of behavior that most often attracts attention is the extreme withdrawing behavior. Failing to find in his environment the psychological nutrients he needs, the child may withdraw into a world of his own. In pathological cases this world of fantasy becomes more real and more desired than his contacts with reality. The early stages of this tendency to withdraw from reality can be noted during preschool years.

Everything that has already been said about recognizing and accepting the child's feeling, modifying the environment so that it is less threatening, and helping him affectionately step by step to deal with life situations applies here. It is important to distinguish between a normal desire for solitude and a serious withdrawal from the world as it is.

THUMB-SUCKING

Thumb-sucking is one of children's many comforting devices. It is a natural way for infants to dispel loneliness and to learn through hand-to-mouth contacts about the objects in their world (see Chap. 8).

If thumb-sucking persists into the later preschool years, the best ways of treating it seem to be: not to forbid it or focus the child's attention on it by seeming anxious and worried; to avoid mechanical restraints, scolding, and anything that might give him a sense of guilt about it; to provide substitute satisfactions in the form of play materials such as blocks, crayons, finger paints; to recognize and reduce sources of deprivation, strain, and frustration which cause the child to turn to thumb-sucking for solace; and to recognize the child's desire to give up thumb-sucking and help him to stop doing it.

The psychological effects of the wrong treatment of thumb-sucking are more serious than the act itself. The older child who is ashamed of the habit but unable to break it may experience a detrimental loss of self-confidence. If long-continued thumb-sucking is affecting his tooth development and his good looks, it may make him self-conscious in his social relationships.

SIBLING RIVALRY

Each child has his own difficulties in settling into the family group. Some of these difficulties are the result of his own temperament; some arise from conflicts between his desires and the demands made upon him; some from the peculiarities, maladjustment, and the unique relations of members of the group; and some from his parents' inappropriate expectations of him. The parents' own needs and experiences are not constant; they vary with each child in the family.

An older child naturally experiences displacement when another child is born. The advent of the new baby may intensify the parents' demands that the older child grow up quickly. He feels he has to do something special to be loved. If he has been previously overprotected, he feels his displacement more keenly.

Sibling rivalry is common in children, who, previous to the birth of the new baby, have had much of their parents' attention. The younger child may resent the older child's privileges and advantages, while the older child may consider the younger as a usurper. The intensity of sibling rivalry seems to be related to the degree of maternal overprotection and other threats to the older child when the baby is born.

Spock (99, pp. 335-346, 1957) emphasized the possible value of early sibling rivalry in helping the individual to cope with jealousy later in life. He elaborated and illustrated a few practical suggestions for dealing with this problem:

> Prepare the child for the baby's arrival.
> Help the child to feel more grown up at the time a new baby arrived.
> Let him hold the baby and care for him in many ways.
> Don't make a big fuss over the baby in the early weeks.
> Accept the child's mixed feelings of jealousy and affection for the baby.
> Make it perfectly clear that his mother loves him as much as ever.
> Recognize the various ways in which a child may express his jealousy and deal with each sympathetically, firmly, and consistently.

HOW CHILDREN SOLVE PROBLEMS

Some children face their problems and solve them; others retreat in defeat from similar problems. What makes the difference? How does a child work through a serious problem; how does he cope with it? Such understanding is basic to helping children meet tears, disappointment, and conflicts between their desires and their developmental needs. The research method described by Lois Barclay Murphy (81, 1957) may be used by parents and teachers to study how children actually solve problems important to them. For example, two-year-old Molly, who was terrified by the noise of jet planes and thunder, gradually mastered her fear during preschool years. At three years of age, she would seek comfort by getting into bed with her sister and reassure herself by saying, "It's just a noise and it really won't hurt you a bit." When, later in the year a jet plane flew unusually low, she repeated to herself several times, "I'm not scared of planes, just thunder." Shortly after she was four years old, she was awakened from a nap by a thunder storm, and remained quietly in bed. "There was lots of thunder," she said afterward, "but I just snuggled in my bed and didn't cry a bit." When she was four and a half years old, she showed no fear during a storm and reassured her frightened little brother by telling him she used to be scared, too, when she was a little baby.

Parents and teachers may learn much by making similar accurate observations of ways in which children solve their problems and what adults do that help or hinder them in acquiring problem-solving ability.

AN ILLUSTRATIVE CASE OF
COMPLEX CAUSATION OF PROBLEMS

During the preschool years purposeful or passive characters are built in many ways. Self-confidence is built up or torn down (91, 1954); initiative is constructively fostered or harmfully suppressed. It sometimes happens in this way: As an infant, Katherine had not been breast-fed or warmly accepted by her mother. "She was always independent," her mother said, "didn't seem to want to be fondled." During the early preschool years Katherine had spent much of her time with her grandparents, who treated her with understanding and affection. They delighted in her initiative and originality; they were genuinely loving and could set limits without causing antagonism.

Then she went to live with her father and mother. "One thing for sure," her mother said, "I'm not going to have a spoiled child." She curbed every manifestation of what she considered the child's willfulness. When Katherine was working on a problem that she was able to solve herself, her mother would step in and show her just what to do. Thus she deprived the child of the satisfaction of success, the joy of accomplishment. All through the day in various activities the mother's comments would run like this:

Don't do it that way.
I'll show you how to do it.

Why don't you play with dolly instead of with that puzzle?
Let me do it for you.
You can do it better than that.

So many unnecessary restrictions had a marked effect on the child's behavior. She began to dawdle, daydream, talk very little, do nothing on her own initiative. The eager, purposeful three-year-old had changed markedly.

Some of the research on child development helps to explain Katherine's change in behavior. Often hostility or aggression is the result of frustration—frustration from too many don'ts; from too much help in solving problems the child could solve for himself in his own way; from the unnecessary interference with his activities; from trying to change him—to make him the kind of child the parent wants.

The child tries out various ways of coping with his feelings of hostility. He may try resisting authority, being disobedient. Or he may be afraid to be disobedient because of the danger of punishment or loss of love of the person most important in his life. He may try withdrawing into a world of fantasy, thus avoiding, for the time being, facing reality. If he expresses his hostility by hurting people or by destroying property, he adds a burden of guilt to the original problem. If he finds no way to express his hostility it is dammed up inside him, and undermines his initiative, self-confidence, and healthy optimism.

The most seriously spoiled child is one whose will has been broken and his hostility increased, one who has given up trying to be himself. Recognizing this danger, some psychologists and psychiatrists have successfully used methods to encourage the child to express himself, thereby regenerating his ability to strive toward contact with others, toward purposeful activity, and eventually toward the kinds of achievement which restore his trust in himself and in other people. They also recognize the importance of setting certain reasonable limits which the child knows will be held firmly. This procedure is sound. Both healthy and disturbed children become anxious in an environment that is too permissive, feeling uncertain and uncomfortable when there is an absence of outer guide-lines to bolster their tenuous and only partially developed inner controls.

This middle-of-the-road policy is sound. It will avoid unnecessary frustration by unnecessary restrictions and interference with the child's activities. This is hard for the efficient mother who has high standards of how a thing should be done and wants the child to do everything perfectly. But the child needs to learn from his mistakes occasionally, and he needs the satisfaction of having worked out the solution of his everyday problems himself.

It would seem wise therefore to interfere with the child's activities only when the issue is critical. For example, when Katherine was playing a game and began counting the cards she had won, she started to count one that belonged to another player. The mother said rather harshly, "That's not your card. Count this one," and moved Katherine's hand to the next card that belonged to her. The child's first reaction, stemming from resent- ment of similar previous situations, was to stop counting. Whereas before she had counted accurately and confidently, she now faltered—almost as though she did not know how to count. However, her happiness in the game-situation won out over the feelings of resentment, and she finished counting her cards.

In contrast with the mother's abrupt, authoritarian approach, was the father's easygoing attitude. For example, in getting out of the car he asked Katherine to put up the window. Her first reaction seemed to be to persist in her generalized negativistic behavior, but, as he waited patiently with the positive expectancy that she would do as he asked, she complied and they walked happily up to the house.

The arrival of a baby brother came at a time when Katherine was hav- ing this difficulty in handling her feelings of rebellion against the mother's domination. Recognizing the possiblity of Katherine's resenting the atten- tion and affection given to the baby, the mother tried to arouse the child's interest in and affection for the baby brother. Although Katherine held him and played with him, the mother constantly made such remarks as:

Don't push him so hard.
Be careful how you hold him.
Look, you're letting his feet dangle.
Stop throwing your head back; you almost hit him. (This scolding was re- peated twice as Katherine deliberately did it a second time.)

It seemed quite obvious that Katherine wanted to hurt the baby and went as far in that direction as she dared. It would have been helpful if the mother had been able to recognize the positive efforts Katherine was making by saying, "You're holding him very carefully—see, he feels he can trust you; he knows you will take care of him."

When Katherine started to kindergarten at five and a half years, she carried some of her home problems with her. In the first grade she was not learning reading or arithmetic—skills that are easily interfered with by emotional tension—as well as might be expected from earlier indications of her mental ability.

Although she outwardly conforms and, according to her mother, is fond of the baby brother and "loves school and is very sorry not to go if she is sick," the figure drawing that she made when she was almost six years old shows quite a different picture. In response to the request "to draw a person," Katherine drew the following picture:

While drawing, she made these comments:

This is a girl.
I'll make the head first.
Now I'm putting on the hair.
I'll make her arms long.
I'll put in a lot of buttons.
Now I make her chest.
Her legs are close together.
Now I'll "color" her arms.

The drawing was untimed. She worked slowly, took in all about ten minutes. When asked about the sex and age of the figure she had drawn, she said it was a girl, one year old. After completing the first drawing, the examiner said, "Now you can draw a boy." At that Katherine made a face, sticking out her tongue, and then said, "I'll draw a big head." As she drew she made the following comments:

"I'll make a big smile." (Grandmother had commented a few minutes before on the nice big "smile" in the first picture.)

Katherine imitated the smile herself, but in the drawing changed it to a different disagreeable expression.

"I'll make the eyes big." Later: "No, one big and one little, one half-closed."

She then made big teeth, and said, "It's going to be a giant." Just then her mother came by (with the baby brother, seven weeks old) and looked at the drawing. Katherine said, "He's going to get you . . . and Douglas (the baby), too. And I mean *really*" (with emphasis). After making a great deal of hair on the head, Katherine said, "It's going to be an old man."

But instead of finishing it, she drew a frame around the head and said, "It's a window."

WORKER: Is he outside the window?

KATHERINE: No, he's inside.

She also called it a "ghost." Finally she blacked the whole thing out and refused to give it to the examiner.

An expert in projective techniques interpreted the drawings as indicating a functioning mental age of four or five years; a great deal of inattention, aggressiveness, and tension. Without knowing more about actual conditions, he found in the drawings indications of many pressures for doing things correctly, for·conforming; of the mother's concern with minor details rather than development as a whole; and of the child's confusion about the dominant-mother and the passive-father roles. The drawings gave the impression of a seriously disturbed child—a child who is extremely anxious and bewildered; who cannot feel comfortable about having to rely on other people; who tires to shut out stimuli from the outside in order to maintain her *status quo*; who has become afraid to move positively in any direction because she has found no way of being successful.

It seems important for the mother to make a conscious effort to give Katherine as much time and care as she gives the baby. It is even more essential for the teacher, parents, and others who come in contact with her to treat her consistently. Difficult as it may be, it will be most helpful if the mother can treat Katherine consistently—not praise her one time and blame her the next time similar behavior occurs; not speak lovingly to her one minute and harshly a few minutes later. If the mother is consistent in her treatment, Katherine will at least know what to expect. She would rather have restrictions than uncertainty.

The mother should also try to be sensitive to Katherine's feelings of anxiety and try to remember to reassure her casually and naturally that she can do many things well by herself with little or no help. Remarks like: "I *know* you can do it." "You did that so nicely all by yourself." "You didn't need much help this time." When Katherine does something *she* thinks is an achievement, the mother should not put a damper on the child's feeling of having made progress.

In Katherine's present state of bewilderment and struggle to be herself, adults should try to do everything possible to help her develop in her own best way—as a person in her own right. They should welcome any positive expression of self-assertion, let her do many things in her own way and, whenever possible, point out that her way is a good way. By making a special effort to give her many opportunities to do things that she enjoys with mother, father, and friends, they will be meeting her present great need for attention and affection.

CONCLUDING STATEMENT

As parents meet more adequately the changing needs of children in each phase of their development, the special problems described in this chapter will diminish. It is easier for the parent, and much happier for the child, to help a child grow through each of his phases than to try to undo wrong moves or detrimental ways of coping with life situations. Even happy, secure children have problems arising from conflicts between their individual growth needs and the social pattern. Children want to grow up; they want to do the things that are approved; they want to keep their parents' affection. Love is the foundation of discipline. Discipline becomes punishment when the parent, personally very much annoyed by the child's behavior, momentarily loses his love for the child. When problems arise, the role of the parent is, so far as he is able, to ally himself with the child's effort to do the thing he recognizes as right; parent and child work together to this end (118, 1953). Changes may be made in the environment, including parental attitudes. Many problems can be prevented by helping the child to become happy, responsible, and aware of his important place as a useful member of the family or nursery-school group.

Questions and Problems

FOR CLASS DISCUSSION OR STUDY GROUPS

1. Keep a record over a period of time showing how a preschool child solved a particular problem.

2. Observe methods of discipline used by parents of preschool children. Which methods seem to get the best immediate results? The best results from the standpoint of the child's best development?

3. Study some of the references at the end of this section to get a better understanding of the causes of the common problems of preschool children.

4. Apply learning theory to the understanding of children's nagging, temper tantrums, showing off, and disobedience.

5. Recall incidents in your own childhood and how the situation was handled. How would you handle a similar situation now?

6. In the light of your knowledge of child psychology, suggest possible

explanations of the children's behavior in the following situations and how you think they might be handled:

Four-year-old Danny was sitting on the curb watching his six-year-old brother and cousin playing a game of ball. Danny asked them if he could play and they told him he was too little. So Danny went up to them and began to fight. The older boys pushed him away and told him to cut it out, but Danny paid no attention. He went right on punching them. When other children do not let him do something he wants to do, he will pick a fight with them, even though he has no possible chance of winning. He never cries or runs to his mother to be comforted. He just becomes sulky and goes off by himself.

At bedtime six-year-old Jerry, a child adopted at the age of two weeks, often has a temper tantrum. He screams, "I don't want to go to bed." "I don't want to take a bath." "I don't want to brush my teeth." "I want my daddy." "Why don't my daddy come home?" Jerry throws himself on the floor, kicks at the door, and cries as if his heart is broken. His mother says, "Get up, Jerry, and get ready for bed." When he repeats his refusals, the mother says, "I'm going to get my brush [to spank him]." He gets up but still cries, "I want my daddy, I want my daddy." There is conflict between the parents about disciplining their child. If both parents would agree, he would understand that whenever either parent tells him to do something, he is to obey. His temper tantrums seem, on the surface, to be a way of fighting back but may stem from a deep pervasive fear.

At lunchtime Jerry is outside in the yard playing in his sandbox. His mother says, "Jerry, come here, it is time for lunch." Jerry starts crying and says, "I want to eat with my daddy." The mother says, "You will have to take a nap when you have eaten your lunch." He cries as if he is in pain and asks, "Can I sleep in daddy's bed, Mamma?" The mother says, "If you eat your lunch you can sleep in daddy's bed." He sobs, as he plays with his food. The mother keeps saying, "Eat your lunch and drink your milk, Jerry." When she mentions the brush he eats his food in a hurry.

Jerry is happiest when he is in his father's woodworking shop. When his daddy hammers and saws, Jerry hammers and saws, too. While Jerry is sawing a board, he says, "Watch me, Daddy. Watch me saw." His daddy replies, "Don't get in Daddy's way." Jerry keeps repeating his previous remark until his father says he will make him go upstairs to bed. At that Jerry starts his temper tantrum. When his father threatens to whip him, Jerry stops his crying and says, "I can saw like you, can't I?" The father says yes and both of them continue sawing and hammering. Jerry seems to want his daddy to recognize his success in hammering. He wants to feel that what he was doing was important.

Every morning when it is time for school, Jerry starts crying and says, "I don't want to go to school today, Mama. I don't like to go to school." His mother says, "Why don't you like to go to school?" Jerry says, "Sometimes Ken fights me. I just don't want to go to school. I can't read and I can't write." Then his mother says that is the reason she is sending him to school, so he can learn to read and write. He continues to cry and says, "I am sick, my tummy hurts. Please, Mama, don't make me go to school." The mother replies, "You are not sick. You must go to school." Jerry cries loudly, saying again and again, "I don't want to go to school." His daddy threatens to whip him and Jerry gets up from the floor and begins to sob. His mother promises him that he can go to see his little playmate down the street when he comes home from school, but if he does not eat his breakfast he will not be allowed to play with her after school. He eats his breakfast very slowly. His mother urges him to eat quickly or he will be late for school.

What do you think underlies Jerry's behavior? What character traits may be developing in these situations? How might the situations be handled more effectively?

7. Analyze an experimental study of aggressive behavior in preschool children, such as that by Annaliese Korner (60, 1949). Describe the methods of collecting data about (1) children's behavior in play situations, (2) children's attitudes toward home situations, (3) parents' descriptions of children's behavior at home, and (4) parents' attitudes toward and relations with children. What kinds of understanding of children's problems can be gained from studies of this kind?

Chapter 12

UNDERSTANDING AND GUIDANCE

OF PRESCHOOL CHILDREN

To understand an individual child, one should observe the child in his present environment and learn, as Dr. Plant said, to read "the language of behavior." Everything a child does gives clues to the causes of his conduct. Preschool children especially are open and spontaneous in expressing their thoughts and feelings; they reveal themselves in words and actions. Their behavior is easy to observe and record.

Moreover, from intensive, detailed study of individual children, one gains more understanding of the subtle complexities of personality than from "comparisons of many children on a few ill-understood responses to 'standard' stimuli." (63, p. x, 1941) Allport also emphasized the dynamic study of the individual: "The only way to make a certain prediction of effect from cause is to study the life in which the causes operate, and not a thousand other lives." (6, p. 157, 1942) Child study is not an end in itself; it is for the purpose of helping the individual child to make progress toward his growth potentials.

Objective description should be guided by basic concepts (23, 1955):

1. The child is developing and maturing.
2. The child is reacting and adapting to his external environment and his own internal stimuli.
3. The child has his own individual aims and purposes.

From these concepts arise questions for exploration and study:

1. Is the child capable of meeting the demands of the environment?
2. Is the environment meeting the needs of the child; is it making normal demands on the child?
3. How is this particular child meeting his situation?

These questions may be answered on different levels of technical knowledge—from the casual observation of the parent to the detailed analysis of the clinical psychologist or psychiatrist. The latter would include developmental information on physiological maturity, physical handicaps and

233

ill health, intellectual status, emotional maturity, personality variants; primary-habit disturbances of eating, eliminating, and sleeping; secondary-habit and conduct disorders such as speech disturbance, difficulty in personal relations, educational problems; and various fears, anxieties, and psychosomatic, organic, and psychotic symptoms. Records of children's behavior hold up a mirror, as it were, in which parents and teachers can more plainly and objectively view their procedures. Such records also show developmental trends and give clues as to why the child behaves as he does; they are essential in tracing the course of mental disorder.

SOURCES OF UNDERSTANDING

There are three main sources of information about children: (1) their behavior in daily activities, in testing situations, in medical examinations, and in therapy and experimental situations; (2) their products such as letters, stories, essays, drawings, and things they have constructed; and (3) their verbal comments, which indicate their thoughts and feelings, and which aid in the interpretation of their behavior. The childhood memories of adults may also throw light on child development. In the study of infants, reliance must be placed chiefly on the first source, namely, observed and measured behavior.

Research workers have at their command special apparatus and technical knowledge not available to teachers and parents. Stereoscopic pictures, cameras that snap three views of a child simultaneously, sound films, sound recorders, laboratory apparatus that measures physiological reactions, instruments for making anthropometric measurements—these are only a few of the devices now being used by research workers to obtain facts about child growth and behavior. Clinical studies by psychologists, psychiatrists, and play-therapists supply valuable information about the dynamics of the individual case—the sequences of behavior, the meaning of the behavior to the child, and the dynamics of changes in behavior.

Child-study techniques over a twenty-five year period were admirably reviewed by Bayley (17, 1956). Extensive observations have been made of children two to five in nursery schools. Some of the newer studies "were devised to test Gestalt theory and Piaget's studies of the development of concepts. Important new directions in child study were taken around 1935 by Lewin and his students. They placed children in carefully planned situations, observing, recording, and rating such things as frustration, aggression, regression, leadership, and group interactions." (17, p. 280, 1956)

During preschool years development goes on in many directions: skills multiply; dramatic play parallels the child's expanding world.

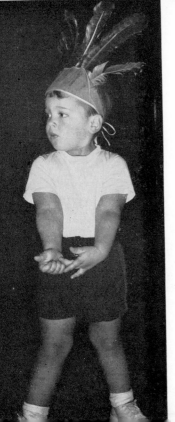

Daddy and Mommy still loom large on the preschool child's broadening horizon.

Longitudinal studies of physical development and behavior were made of certain geographical, racial, and socioeconomic groups from which age norms for mental and physical growth were developed. Early studies of motor development and the possibility of early training in skills were made by McGraw, Shirley and Bayley, and others, but not followed up by similiar studies later. Developmental changes in emotions, personality, and problem behavior in relation to other pertinent variables were studied early in longitudinal samples and continue to be studied.

The influence of psychoanalytic concepts, Bayley also pointed out, has increasingly influenced the methods of studying children. Doll-play and other therapeutic devices, as well as projective techniques, have been adapted as research tools for understanding the emotions and preoccupations of young children.

Dyadic relations—interaction between siblings, mother and child, father and child—is becoming an increasingly significant area of study. In fact, focusing attention on the family or on a segment of the nursery-school situation is much more significant and of much more practical value than observation of the child alone. The still broader dynamic role of social interaction and the impact of cultural differences in child-rearing practices on the development of personality has recently gained much attention. Barker and Wright (16, 1954) studied an entire community, describing the effect of the roles played by different people on children's experiences and modes of adapting.

OBSERVATION: DETAILED, SYSTEMATIC, AND ACCURATELY RECORDED

Child study and guidance involve (1) making accurate observation of a child and (2) trying to infer some significant motives and conditions that are related to his behavior. The observer tries to find out what behavior of children is significantly related to some other behavior. Mothers have opportunities to observe children continuously under varied home and play situations. Through daily systematic observation of these situations, they become aware of sequences of behavior patterns and gain an understanding of what children at a given stage tend to do under certain conditions.

Still more important is the study of the interaction in the family and its influence on the development of the child over a period of time. Among the methods of studying interaction between children and between children and adults are the following:

1. Observation technique which directs the observer's attention in a nursery-school free-play situation to apparent awareness of a common activity or interest; friendly, pleasant, helpful approach or responses; friendly conversation; and expressions of hostility, either verbal or physical.

2. A picture technique for eliciting sociometric choices from preschool-aged children (67, 1957).

The most skillful observer is concerned with the interaction between himself and the child and the effect of his attitudes and behavior on the child. Moreover, the observer looks below the surface and tries to see what the behavior may mean to the child. To do this most effectively, he needs a background of psychological and psychoanalytic insights, which permit more accurate interpretation of hidden forces.

Adults vary in their methods of gaining understanding from observation. One parent or teacher may build an accurate understanding of a child day by day very much as an artist makes an oil painting; it is an evolving *gestalt*. Others, especially teachers of fairly large groups, will collect dated anecdotal records and other sources of information and periodically interpret and synthesize the cumulative recordings. None should be content merely to describe the child's behavior objectively, important as such objective information is; rather, they will use their observation to raise the question why, and try to find and substantiate clues to the meaning of the behavior. For example, when a child persistently goes off by himself, the teacher should try to answer questions such as these: Why is he by himself? What does he do by himself? What satisfactions is he getting? Is this amount of isolation quite desirable for this particular child?

Students of child psychology have made voluminous records, sometimes in code, of every major movement a child makes, every word he speaks, every evidence of emotion he shows. From such records they have constructed timetables of the development of motor, mental, and social abilities under particular environmental conditions. Isolated, fragmentary records have little meaning apart from the setting in which they occur.

One-way vision screens make it possible to observe children without their being aware of an observer. Such observation makes possible, for example, a comparison between the child's social reactions when only one companion is present and when three or four companions are present. His behavior in the nursery school may be compared with his behavior at home; his attitude when his mother is present, with his attitude when she is absent.

Teachers and parents should note a child's exceptional as well as his typical behavior, his positive as well as his negative behavior. Unusual behavior may suggest undeveloped potentialities, or it may represent the first stage in an undesirable trend that can be modified much more easily now than later.

RATINGS OF CHILDREN'S BEHAVIOR

Behavior rating scales may be used to direct attention to positive aspects of child development. Several ratings scales for preschool children have been published. The *Winnetka Scale for Rating School Behavior and Attitudes* (115, 1935) was based on everyday classroom situations. It directed the teacher's attention to the way children behave when they are taking turns with apparatus or materials, are faced with failure, have a social task to complete, and are engaged in other daily activities. The adult's observation was further guided by a series of statements under each heading, which range from the most approved response to the least approved. As a guide to observation and as a summary and evaluation of a child's social adequacy, the *Vineland Social Maturity Scale* (110, 1947) has proved useful. It aims to quantify aspects of social adequacy, most common to all environments, as a part of total development at successive age levels. It records "what the individual habitually *does* rather than what he is capable of doing." The double-scoring device permits an appraisal of the individual (1) in his actual situation and (2) in a more favorable environment. Olson's rating scale (84, p. 290, 1949), while designed for school children, can also be used with younger children. Descriptive paragraphs on the salient characteristics of a child's personality give a still more dynamic picture of the individual.

Ratings and records of observations must be cautiously interpreted for at least four reasons. First, the observed behavior is only a small sample; it may not truly represent the individual. Second, the child changes; his present behavior may be quite different from his actions observed in the past; moreover, his response varies with different people and in different environments. Third, observation reveals the observer as well as the child observed. And fourth, the same observed behavior may have diverse motivation, meaning, and significance for different children.

PHYSICAL EXAMINATION

A thorough physical and medical examination by a physician is essential in understanding the preschool child. Temperature and pulse rate, examination of lungs and heart, an estimate of the nutritional condition, urinalysis, and blood count to detect anemia are well-recognized features of a thorough examination. The throat, nose, teeth, ears, and eyes should be thoroughly examined. Diseased tonsils and adenoids, decayed teeth, and defects of hearing and seeing should immediately be treated according to the physician's direction.

Many of the errors formerly made in testing the hearing of young children have now been eliminated by using an individual test with standardized sounds, words, or symbols familiar to a little child, as well as an easy method of reporting the sounds. One of the simplest tests uses a phonograph record of twelve common words, such as "cat," "dog," and "door." As the child hears the words, he points to the proper picture in the row of cards placed before him. As the testing progresses, the intensity of the sound is usually gradually decreased.

MENTAL TESTS

Tests supplement observation. Mental tests aid the examiner in more quickly gaining an accurate idea of the child's mental abilities in comparison with those of children his own age than can be obtained through observation alone. Tests are valuable to show how a child acts in a standardized situation. Individual tests for preschool children should be given and interpreted by a trained psychologist. When in doubt as to whether the child has worked up to capacity on the test, the psychologist gives an estimate of the child's probable range of mental age, or IQ. Tests for preschool children must be interesting to them, and the examiner must be skillful in calling forth the best response a child is capable of. A skilled tester can usually tell whether a low score indicates a child of low mental ability or a disturbed child of average or superior ability. Nevertheless, his results must be interpreted with caution and in the light of all other information about the child.

PROJECTIVE TECHNIQUES

Various projective techniques have been used with preschool children. By the projective method the child is led to reveal himself without being aware of it. This is accomplished by obtaining his response to unstructured material, i.e., situations to which he has no familiar, ready-made, or adult-influenced response. The Driscoll Play Kit (33a) represents one common type of toys used in play therapy. A projective technique developed to study anxiety reactions in preschool children (33, 1947) consists of two sets of fourteen pictures showing familiar situations. The child completes each picture by adding a happy or a sad face. This technique seems useful in uncovering extremes of anxiety and in showing the specific areas of experience, such as parent-child relations, with which anxiety is associated.

Of all the projective techniques the Rorschach has been the most widely used for many years. It consists of ten inkblots, experimentally selected. The individual freely tells what he sees in each one or what each means to him. The Rorschach test of personality has been used with precocious children as young as two to three years and with average four- to five-year-old children. Its unusual nature attracts children who might respond negatively to less intriguing test material. The use of the Rorschach with children is still in the experimental stage. There are indications that responses signifying pathological tendencies in adults may be normal for children and adolescents; Ford (38, 1946) and others have studied this problem. Sunne (103, 1936) has reported norms for the Rorschach test administered by one method to boys and girls from four and a half to eleven years of age in widely different social-racial groups. Ames and associates (8, 1953) studied development of perception through responses to the Rorschach test blots, and Allen (3, 1955) made a developmental study of Rorschach responses of two children. The administration of the test appears at first glance to be simple, but further study impresses one with the difficulties of recording and interpretation. Reliable results cannot be expected unless the test is given by a highly expert person with clinical experience.

MEASURES OF MOTOR ACHIEVEMENTS

The tests of motor ability included in the batteries of preschool tests have attempted to measure specific motor responses, many of which were not duplicated in the everyday life of the child. To correct this deficiency, Wellman (113, 1937) and her students selected such common motor achievements as ascending steps; climbing a ladder; throwing, catching, and bouncing balls of two sizes; jumping from boxes of different heights; hopping; skipping; walking a one-inch path in a straight line and in a circle. When repeated with the same children these tests showed high consistency and seem to be effective measures of everyday motor skills of preschool children.

STUDYING PRESCHOOL CHILDREN
IN THE NURSERY SCHOOL

A child entering a nursery school is given an examination by a physician and one or more intelligence tests by a psychologist. An interview with the child's parents, preferably in his home, discloses the family background. The teacher makes daily observations of his behavior—his ability in walking, running, and climbing; his response to the children and the objects around him; his response to music; his ability to feed himself at mealtime; the language he uses; and his disposition. These observations are systematically recorded and his progress is noted.

From time to time the detailed nursery-school records of physical and mental growth, habits, and personality should be analyzed and summarized, and recommendations should be made for the child's best development. Experimental nursery schools have used graphs showing time-series of quantitative data, and charts recording the ages when tendencies first appeared, events in the life of the child, and relevant explanatory data. This information synchronizes periods of emotional adjustment and maladjustment with periods of slow and rapid growth and with concomitant events in the child's life, and shows trends in personality development. Another type of chart shows interrelationships between certain personality traits and the influences that may have contributed to their development. In England, Bowley (22, 1942) developed a preschool record form which has proved useful in the study and guidance of children.

It is possible, of course, to waste a great deal of time in keeping records and to emerge with volumes of obvious and insignificant notes. But this is not necessary. The clinical and experimental work that has already been done suggests items that are likely to be most closely related to good development.

Studying the home environment of preschool children is fully as important as studying the children directly. Chapter 6 calls attention to some of the conditions of the physical environment and family relations that should be studied.

UNDERSTANDING CHILDREN THROUGH STORIES

Stories may be used as a stimulus to the child's free expression of feeling. Whenever the adult is able to win the confidence of children, and create an atmosphere in which they feel free to express their true feelings, he may learn much about the dynamics of child behavior. The following procedure was used by Korner (60, 1949) with preschool children:

When a child enters the playroom, doll furniture and dolls representing the members of his own family are lined up in a row on the table. The child is given a few minutes to familiarize himself with the room and the toys. The dolls are then introduced to him in the following manner: "This is the father. This is the mother, and this is the little boy (or girl)." If there are other members of the family, the experimenter adds: "This is the brother; this is sister, etc." As an introductory sample story, the worker then says, "Do you know that you can tell wonderful stories with these? Here is one. Mother gives the little boy some medicine to get his tummy well. The medicine tastes bad and the little boy does not like that one bit. What does he feel like doing, when Mommy gives him the medicine? . . . Now, the little boy could kick his feet and say he won't take it. Or he might swallow it because he thinks Mommy knows what's best for him. What do *you* think he feels like doing?" After the child answers, the worker continues: "I see. Now I will tell you some more stories, and this time you will finish them."

After each story is presented, the worker asks, "What does the little boy feel like doing? What does he do?" When it is not clear whether the response represents evasion, simple noncompliance, or hostility, the worker asks, "*Why* does he do that?" [60, pp. 20-21, 1949]

Any or all of the stories, of which these are samples, may be used:

1. This little boy (girl is to be substituted whenever appropriate) just loves to bathe and splash in the water. Mommy washes him and he loves that, too. There is only one thing which he does not like, and that is to have his ears washed. Today Mommy washes his ears again. He does not like it one bit. What does he feel like doing when Mommy washes his ears? What does the little boy do?

2. Daddy gives the little boy a nickel. The little boy wants to buy some candy with it. Mommy says, "You cannot have any candy before dinner." But the little boy wants to have some candy very badly. What does he feel like doing when Mommy forbids him to have some?

3. The little boy has a fight with his friend. Daddy thinks the friend is right and scolds his little boy for being so mean to his friend. What does the little boy feel like doing when Daddy does that?

4. What is your favorite toy at home? . . . Well, one day the little boy comes home and finds that his favorite teddybear is gone. You know he likes his teddybear as much as you like your (insert subject's favorite toy here). Mommy has given it away because she thinks the little boy is too old to play with it. When Mommy tells him this, what does the little boy feel like doing? . . .

10. One day Mommy tells the little boy a great secret. She tells him that he is going to have a little baby brother. Show me what the little boy feels like when Mommy tells him this.

Reversed roles: "Now let's change. You tell me some stories and I shall finish them."*

UNDERSTANDING CHILDREN THROUGH DOLL-PLAY
OR THE FREE-PLAY INTERVIEW

Instead of asking the child to respond to stories, the psychologist may make available different kinds of play material and merely say, "You may play with these toys in any way you wish." After the child has responded freely in his own unique way the worker may use the play materials to obtain more definite information on certain points. He may finally try to get direct information on behavior that is still obscure—"testing the limits," as it were. In diagnosis through play, the worker carefully records everything the child does and says.

Insofar as the dolls come to represent real persons to the child, he may reveal the way he sees his family or would like to see it and express his feelings about members of his family, his fears and anxieties, his loves and hates, or his needs and motives (77, 1953). Actually, with many children there is little correspondence between real-life behavior and the aggression which they show in imaginative play. Yet valuable insights may be gained from a comparison of the child's behavior at home and in the play sessions (93, 1946). Diagnosis is difficult. Children's play is full of details that call for interpretation. Herein lies a danger—the danger of the observer's projecting his own feelings and theories into the child's responses.

Another source of error, admirably described by Sears (92, 1947), are the variations caused by differences in the therapist's procedures. He urged that the observer be sensitive to the variations that may result from differences in recording and measuring, from the use of different materials, from various interactions between child and worker, and from differences in the length of the play session. The therapist should also note whether the child is willing to play spontaneously, and ascertain whether he has had a recent emotional upset. All these factors should be considered against a background knowledge of the psychology of childhood, play, and mental illness of children in interpreting his play.

The role of the play therapist is to (1) try to understand the child; (2) show him that he is warmly accepted, whatever his feelings may be; (3) reflect some of his most significant feelings; (4) give as much interpre-

* Anneliese Friedsam Korner, op. cit. Quoted with permission of Grune & Stratton.

tation of his feelings and behavior as the child is ready to accept; and (5) maintain a few firm limits, such as the time limit of the session and prohibitions against hurting anyone or destroying the permanent equipment. Unless one has a thorough psychological and psychoanalytic background, it is unwise "to tamper with unconscious conflicts," though one may work helpfully on the "reality level." No untrained person should meddle with the deeper levels of play therapy.

USE OF INFORMATION GATHERED

Nothing is more futile than to collect information about children that is never used either to increase knowledge of the principles of child development or to aid in understanding individual children. The intensive study of a child may be approached in three possible ways:

1. One may look at the child as he appears in the interviews, without using any information collected previously. Those who advocate this approach want to give the child a fresh start; they are afraid of being prejudiced by records.

2. One may begin with a rigid preconceived idea based on a thorough diagnosis of the case.

3. One may study, evaluate, and interpret all the available records as a tentative basis for understanding the child's growth pattern and for obtaining clues as to further work with him.

Of these three approaches, the third seems the soundest; it is also feasible. A teacher or specialist can approach a case with certain tentative hypotheses, that is, with a flexible frame of reference in which to work. The hypotheses change constantly as the worker's understanding of the child grows day by day.

Information from various sources should be synthesized and interpreted. From day-by-day observation of the child in his home, nursery school, and at play, the teacher or parent may acquire a partial picture of his development. Standardized tests supply a check on observation. Through conversations the child may reveal what his behavior means to him. When the child's behavior continues to be baffling, special techniques of diagnosis and therapy are indicated.

METHODS OF STUDYING PARENTAL ATTITUDES

One effective way of studying parental behavior toward preschool children is to observe parents with their children in various situations.

Merrill (75, 1946) kept a running record of her observations of each child's interaction with his mother during a thirty-minute play session. When the mothers were told that their child had not come up to expectation, they increased their tendency to interfere with and direct the child's activity. Individual mothers displayed a persistent form of behavior, but among the mothers, a wide range of behavioral patterns was evident.

To ascertain attitudes and evaluate parental behavior, direct observation should be supplemented by other methods. For these purposes questionnaires and rating scales have been frequently used. The *Fels Parent-Behavior Rating Scales* (26, 1939) were designed for use by home visitors. The thirty items were grouped into eight important areas of parent behavior. The reliability of the scales has been reported as satisfactory, and their validity demonstrated. They have been used as a basic tool in studying patterns of parental behavior.

A self-inventory type of scale—*The University of Southern California Parent Attitude Survey* (97, 1949)—consists of eighty-five items and is divided into four subscales. The scale seems to be a useful instrument in the study of parental attitudes as they relate to children's adjustment.

More recently a *Parental Attitude Research Instrument* called PARI was constructed at the Child Development Section of the Laboratory of Psychology, National Institutes of Mental Health, Bethesda, Maryland. It consists of thirty-two scales of five to ten items each, designed to be used in a variety of situations to ascertain parental attitudes toward child-rearing and family life in relation to parent personality, parent-child relationships, and the personality development of children. The author of the scale thought that these attitudes of parents were more likely to be significantly related to child development than specific child care practices.

The interview method makes possible a study of attitudes expressed and observed. An unstructured approach followed by clarifying questions and even, finally, by direct questions as to parents' attitudes toward their children yields much valuable information. The understanding thus gained may be supplemented by case-study data.

GUIDANCE IN DAILY ACTIVITIES

The first essential of child guidance is to provide experiences suited to the needs of the individual child. For some children the demands of the environment must be reduced. For others, the environmental stimulation needs to be stepped up. Nursery school may be unwise or unnecessary for some children and a wonderful experience for others.

To insure a good start in nursery school, it is desirable (1) for the parent to bring the child in for a preliminary visit and, if possible, plan to remain at the school the first few days; (2) for the teacher to visit the home, if possible; and (3) to introduce only a few new pupils each day. It is also wise to enter a particular child in school several months before a new baby arrives in his family in order to avoid giving the child the impression that he is being pushed out of the home to make way for the newcomer.

The most effective guidance of children takes place in their ongoing activities. By giving the child just enough help to handle the situation himself, he will learn to cope with his problems rather than to resort to nonconstructive or detrimental ways of meeting difficulties. Guidance and living go on simultaneously.

A few examples will show how parents and teachers may hinder or help a child's development: At a party a four-year-old started to push another child away from the swing. His mother said to him, "You take turns. It's Johnny's turn now, your turn next." Both children understood. For the rest of the time they played happily together, making a game of taking turns. Child guidance is often as simple as that.

On the other hand, some children obtain little help from adults in meeting their manifold difficulties. For example, a four-year-old boy whose short life had contained more than a just share of frustration was putting together the tracks of his toy train. He was not succeeding in making one track fit into the other. He closed his eyes and pounded the track on the floor. His stepfather said, "What good did that do you, Billy? The track still isn't put together, and you've bent one piece." Then the boy sat and sucked his thumb. His stepfather could easily have given him just enough help so that he would have learned to put the track together and experienced success and satisfaction.

The following are examples of the guidance of children of different ages as observed in the nursery school.

Three-year-olds:

When a child putting on his wraps was distracted by other things, the teacher said, "What goes on next, Bobby?" She helped him fasten difficult buttons and put on tight rubbers and leggings.

When the children were building a bridge that was too low, the teacher said to them, "Can the dollie go through that bridge?" She entered into their world and saw things from their point of view.

When it was time for them to put their toys away she said, "There's time for you to take one more ride in your train. Then you can put your toys away."

When they had had their extra ride she said, "Now it's time to put your toys away."

Four-year-olds:

When the children were enjoying dramatic play the teacher entered into it and made suggestions from their point of view. "This is a good time for the bears to take their winter's sleep," she said when it was time for them to take their nap.

When the children were telling about their experiences the teacher added information which extended their knowledge.

In the following incident the teacher diverted aggressive behavior rather than trying to suppress it:

The teacher had just brought a plate of crackers to the table. Jane grabbed the plate and said, "I can have two because I'm hungry." There was a chorus of protest, and the others reached for the crackers, but Jane held the plate away. The teacher said, "Jane, there's enough for everyone to have two." Jane took two crackers and passed the plate around, insisting that everyone say please before he took his second cracker. The teacher was relaxed and at ease with the children. She handled any conflicts in a casual, good-natured way, an attitude the children learned to imitate. Frequently she called attention to some specific desirable conduct.

The method of settling conflicts arbitrarily by deciding for or against one of the combatants does not seem to be effective. In fact, in one study, when restraints were removed, the most marked increase in conflicts was found in the group where the teacher interference had been most persistent and deliberate.

INFLUENCE OF THE NURSERY SCHOOL

The nursery school's influence on a child is determined by a number of interrelated factors: the composition and activities of the group in relation to the personality of the child, his previous experience in organized groups, readiness for the group experience, the quality of his home and neighborhood environment, the equipment and space of the nursery school, and the personality and education of the nursery-school teachers. A child of sufficient maturity and ability to relate himself to other children is likely to find nursery school a valuable experience. A child who is resistant to routine is more likely to accept routine in an environment where "everybody's doing it." A child from a rigid home may profit by the greater flexibility of the nursery school, whereas a child from a laissez-faire home may welcome the limits set in the nursery school. The child's age and size are of considerable importance, as are also his stability, physical durability, and sociability. A child who is younger and smaller than the others in his group often has difficulty in making a social adjustment. He should have some companions on his own level of development. Most three-year-olds enjoy being with friends, playing with nursery-school toys, listening to the stories and music. Children often make rapid gains in social adjustment in a short period of time. Rural children, most of whom had never played in a group, seldom heard a story or drawn or painted, soon began to enjoy these activities. They developed imaginative games involving as many as ten children and also dramatized stories and sang in a group.

Nursery school is a natural means of loosening the close emotional ties between mother and child. But a child must be initially secure enough in his mother's love to be willing to part from her. One of the school's most important functions is to provide opportunity for the mother to observe her child's behavior and the methods used by the teacher in handling routine and behavior problems. The teacher should try to understand parents as well as children and to recognize parental strengths and resources. Nursery schools are becoming important centers of guidance and education for the family as a whole. Their main functions are (1) to encourage co-operation between parents and nursery school staff, (2) to emphasize a point of view of dynamic psychology, and (3) to promote child development through group experience (4, 1948).

Co-operative nursery schools are increasing. Their effectiveness depends, first, on employing a teacher-director with adequate training and, second, on effective preparation and continued education of co-operating parents for their responsibilities in the local nursery (105, 1954). The resources within the parents themselves should be recognized. All have had firsthand experience with one or more children; some have had excellent college courses in child study and child psychology; others have read thoughtfully current articles in newpapers and magazines. They can contribute much to teacher-parent planning in establishing standards and developing procedures. Successful training programs have consisted of a combination of observations of children and discussion of the situations observed, gaining understanding of children's behavior, and acquiring skill in using effectively nursery-school materials, such as clay, crayons, finger-painting, easel painting, books, and music, and equipment for large-muscle activity.

The co-operative nursery school has a number of advantages. For the child, the co-operative nursery school involves a less sudden change than the regular nursery school or kindergarten or first grade, because the mother comes to the school part of the time as her share in making the school a success.

Participating in the nursery school helps parents to understand why and how to deal with baffling situations in their own homes. It gives them, too, a more objective attitude toward their children—objective in the sense of not having their communication with the child clouded by their personal emotions. Discussion groups are a rich source of suggestions from other parents' experience. One of the important results of participation is the personal growth of the parents. This growth results from the "fellowship of kindred minds," from the self-confidence arising from competence, and from the feeling of being of service to other children as well as to their own.

TREATMENT OF EMOTIONALLY
DISTURBED CHILDREN

Some children are too much disturbed emotionally to profit by the educational experiences in the nursery school; they need psychotherapy. They may receive special treatment in private practice, in guidance clinics, or in special schools. Allen (2, 1942), Bender (19, 1952), Freud and others (41, 1954), Kanner (54, 1953), and Lippman (66, 1956) have described in detail clinical, psychiatric, and psychoanalytical methods of treatment of emotionally disturbed children. In referring a child in need of psychiatric or psychological treatment, the positive aspect of helping the child develop his potentialities and freeing him from conflicts that are interfering with his best development should be emphasized. Premature, unskillful, unnecessary, or repeated referral may cause a child to become anxious and fear that there must be something seriously wrong with him.

Group therapy is often effective. Placement of emotionally disturbed children in a special group of four or five steady, well-adjusted children has resulted in successful re-education. Individual therapy is often most effective when skillfully interwoven into the group program and parents are actively involved in the therapy. Teamwork among all those who work with and for children is needed.

Some children are so seriously disturbed that they require residential care. The following are some excellent centers that offer this service:

Children's Service Center of Wyoming Valley and Wilkes-Barre, Pennsylvania.

Woods Schools at Langhorne, Pennsylvania.

Southhard School in Topeka, Kansas, a separate part of the Menninger Clinic.

Orthogenic School at the University of Chicago.

Langley-Porter Clinic in San Francisco, located in special quarters in a psychiatric hospital.

These special schools accommodate a very small number of cases. Judged by the cost of treatment of a single child, they are expensive. But the cost of two years in a residential school is very little compared with the cost of lifetime care in a mental hospital.

FAMILY-CENTERED GUIDANCE

Since work with one child or parent affects the whole family constellation, guidance should be family-centered. Treating one child or giving him special privileges may affect other children in the family either favorably or unfavorably. The child lives in an intricate matrix of relations. He needs help in clarifying his relations with other members of his family and with his peers.

The problem is how to make these relations more constructive. Washburn (111, 1944) described clinical procedures for helping parents decrease detrimental conflict. These procedures are on three levels: offering information on child development, helping parents gain new insights into the emotional relations in the family, and furnishing psychiatric treatment for deeper disturbances. Some children need protection from their parents' extreme behavior and intense attitudes. However, teachers and guidance specialists too often identify themselves with the child and blame the parent. This tendency should be nipped in the bud. Parents need as much respect, sympathy, and understanding as their children.

Even though the causes of a parent's present anxieties and problems seem clear to the teacher or social worker, he will not be helped by suggestions or psychological prescriptions unless he is ready for them. He will profit more by thinking it out for himself. As he talks with an understanding, accepting person he clarifies his ideas about himself and increases his capacity for healthy and responsible living. Both child and parents should be active participants in the guidance process.

The child needs his parents' love, their understanding of his assets and liabilities and of his accomplishments and difficulties in growing up, their acceptance of his feelings, their patience in helping him to learn, their skillful guidance, their respect and faith in his ability to realize his best potentialities, and their intelligent help in learning the best way of handling day-by-day situations.

Questions and Problems

1. Observe, if possible, a trained psychologist give the Binet, the Wechsler Intelligence Scale for Children, or other individual test of mental ability to two children, first to a mentally retarded child, then to a gifted child of the same chronological age. Note differences in the children's responses to the same test situations.

2. Try out the two methods of observation suggested in this chapter: (a) build an evolving impression of a given child from your day-by-day observation of him, (b) during the same period of time write dated anecdotal records of what you hope is significant behavior, and interpret and synthesize these snapshots of behavior at the end of the period. Which method seems to give you the most accurate and useful understanding of the child? Does the additional expenditure of time on writing the anecdotal records seem to you to be justified?

3. Collect concrete examples of nursery-school teachers' guidance of children in the group.

4. Visit a child-guidance clinic, if possible.

5. Read Frederick Allen's *Psychotherapy with Children* (2, 1942). What principles underlie his work with children?

6. See how a few preschool children respond to the stories quoted on pages 240-242.

7. After reading more about nursery schools write an answer to a mother who asks, "Shall I send my four-year-old child to nursery school?"

Bibliography*

1. "Aggressiveness in Children," *Child Study*, XXXIV (Fall, 1957), 3-20.

**2. ALLEN, FREDERICK H. *Psychotherapy with Children*. New York: W. W. Norton & Co., 1942. 311 pp. *See also* "The Dilemma of Growth—for Parents and Children," *Child Study*, XXXV (Spring, 1958), 4-7.

3. ALLEN, ROBERT M. "Nine Quarterly Rorschach Records of a Young Girl," *Child Development*, XXVI (March, 1955), 63-69.

4. ALLEN, WINIFRED Y., and DORIS CAMPBELL. *The Creative Nursery Center; a Unified Service to Children and Parents*. New York: Family Service Assoc. of America, 1948. 171 pp.

5. ALLPORT, GORDON W. *Becoming; Basic Considerations for a Psychology of Personality*. New Haven: Yale Univ. Press, 1955. 106 pp.

* All references referred to in the text are included in the bibliography. The single-starred references (*) are specially recommended for their practical suggestions; those double-starred (**) are specially recommended for their technical and research emphasis.

6. ———— The Use of Personal Documents in Psychological Science. ("Bulletin 49.") New York: Social Science Research Council, 1942. 210 pp.

7. Alpert, Augusta. The Solving of Problem-Situations by Preschool Children. ("Contributions to Education," No. 323.) New York: Teachers College, Columbia Univ., 1928. 69 pp.

8. Ames, Louise B., and others. "Development of Perception in the Young Child as Observed in Responses to the Rorschach Test Blots," Journal of Genetic Psychology, LXXXII (June, 1953), 183-204.

9. Ammons, Carol H., and Robert B. Ammons. "Aggression in Doll-Play: Interviews of Two- to Six-Year-Old White Males," Journal of Genetic Psychology, LXXXII (June, 1953), 205-213.

10. Anderson, Harold H., Charles Hanley, and John R. Hurley. "Personality Development in Infancy and Preschool Years," Review of Educational Research, XXV (December, 1955), 453-468.

11. Australian Association for Pre-School Child Development. Play Materials for Young Children. Carlton, Victoria, published for the Australian Association of Pre-School Child Development by Melbourne Univ. Press, 1952. 55 pp.

**12. Ausubel, David P. Ego Development and the Personality Disorders. New York: Grune & Stratton, 1952. 564 pp.

13. ————. Theory and Problems of Adolescent Development. New York: Grune & Stratton, 1954. 580 pp.

14. Baldwin, Alfred L. "The Effect of Home Environment on Nursery School Behavior," Child Development, XX (June, 1949), 49-61.

*15. Barclay, Dorothy. "Safety without Fears for the Active Child," The New York Times Magazine (November 3, 1957), 75.

16. Barker, Roger G., and Herbert F. Wright. Midwest and Its Children; the Psychological Ecology of an American Town. Evanston, Ill.: Row, Peterson & Co., 1954. 532 pp.

17. Bayley, Nancy. "Child Study Technics," in "Twenty-Five Years of Educational Research," Review of Educational Research, XXVI (June, 1956), 280-281.

18. ————. "On the Growth of Intelligence," American Psychologist, X (December, 1955), 805-818.

19. Bender, Lauretta. Child Psychiatric Techniques. Springfield, Ill.: Charles C. Thomas, 1952. 335 pp.

20. Bernhardt, Karl S. "How Permissive Are You?" Bulletin of the Institute of Child Study, Toronto, XVIII (1956), 1-6.

21. Body, Margaret K. "Patterns of Aggression in the Nursery School," Child Development, XXVI (March, 1955), 3-11.

22. Bowley, Agatha H. "A Study of the Factors Influencing the General Development of the Child During the Pre-School Years by Means of Record Forms," British Journal of Psychology, Monograph Supplements, No. XXV. Cambridge: Cambridge Univ. Press, 1942. 104 pp.

23. Cameron, Kenneth. "Diagnostic Categories in Child Psychiatry," *British Journal of Medical Psychology*, XXVIII (March, 1955), 67-71.

**24. Canadian Mental Health Association. *How to Know Your Child*. New York: Human Relations Aids, 1954.

25. Carroll, Lewis. *Alice's Adventures in Wonderland*. New York: The Macmillan Co., 1932. 192 pp.

26. Champney, Horace. *The Fels Parent-Behavior Rating Scales*. Yellow Springs, Ohio: Antioch Press, 1939.

27. Dameron, Laurence E. "Mother-Child Interaction in the Development of Self-Restraint," *Journal of Genetic Psychology*, LXXXVI (June, 1955), 289-308.

28. Davitz, Joel R. "The Effects of Previous Training on Post-Frustration Behavior," *Journal of Abnormal and Social Psychology*, XLVII (April, 1952), 309-315.

29. De Martino, Manfred F. "A Review of Literature on Children's Dreams," *Psychiatric Quarterly Supplement*, XXIX (Part I, 1955), 90-101.

30. Despert, J. Louise, and Helen O. Pierce. "The Relation of Emotional Adjustment to Intellectual Function," *Genetic Psychology Monographs*, XXXIV, No. 1 (First half, 1946), 3-56. Provincetown, Mass.: The Journal Press, 1946. 125 pp.

31. Doll, Edgar A. *The Measurement of Social Competence; a Manual for the Vineland Social Maturity Scale*. Minneapolis: Educational Test Bureau, 1953. 664 pp.

**32. Dollard, John, and Neal E. Miller. *Personality and Psychotherapy; an Analysis in Terms of Learning, Thinking and Culture*. New York: McGraw-Hill Book Co., Inc., 1950. 488 pp.

33. Dorkey, Margaret, and Elizabeth W. Amen. "A Continuation Study of Anxiety Reactions in Young Children by Means of a Projective Technique," *Genetic Psychology Monographs*, XXV (Second half, 1947), 141-247. Provincetown, Mass.: The Journal Press, 1947.

33a. Driscoll, Gertrude. Driscoll Play Kit. New York: The Psychological Corp.

34. Escalona, Sibylle K. *Understanding Hostility in Children*. Chicago: Science Research Associates, 1954. 48 pp.

35. Fahs, Sophia L. "When Should Come a Consciousness of God," *Religious Education*, XXXIV (October-December, 1939), 208-215.

36. Fairbairn, W. R. D. "Is Aggression an Irreducible Factor?" *British Journal of Medical Psychology*, XVIII (Part II, 1939), 163-170.

37. Fingarette, Herbert. "Psychological Perspectives on Moral Guilt and Responsibility," *Philosophy and Phenomenological Research*, XVI (September, 1955), 18-36.

38. Ford, Mary. *The Application of the Rorschach Test with Young Children*. Minneapolis: Univ. of Minnesota Press, 1946. 114 pp.

39. Frank, Lawrence K. *Individual Development*. Garden City, N.Y.: Doubleday, Doran & Company, 1955. 52 pp.

40. Freeman, Frank S. *Theory and Practice of Psychological Testing* (rev. ed.). New York: Henry Holt & Co., Inc., 1955. 609 pp.

41. Freud, Anna, and others. *Psychoanalytical Study of the Child*. New York: International Universities Press, 1954. 380 pp.

42. Goodenough, Florence L. "The Measurement of Mental Growth in Childhood," in Leonard Carmichael (ed.), *Manual of Child Psychology* (2d ed.), pp. 459-491. New York: John Wiley & Sons, Inc., 1954.

43. Haggard, Ernest A. "Social-Status and Intelligence: An Experimental Study of Certain Cultural Determinants of Measured Intelligence," *Genetic Psychology Monographs*, XLIX (May, 1954), 141-186.

44. Hirschberg, J. Cotter. "Some Comments on Religion and Childhood," *Bulletin of the Menninger Clinic*, XIX (November, 1955), 227-228.

45. Horney, Karen. *Our Inner Conflicts; A Constructive Theory of Neurosis*. New York: W. W. Norton & Co., Inc., 1945. 250 pp.

46. Hunter, Edith F. *The Questioning Child and Religion*. Boston: Starr King Press, 1956. 209 pp.

47. Hurlock, Elizabeth B. *Child Development*. New York: McGraw-Hill Book Co., Inc., 1956. 703 pp.

48. Jack, Lois M. "An Experimental Study of Ascendant Behavior in Preschool Children" in Lois M. Jack, and Others, *Behavior of the Preschool Child*, pp. 7-65. ("University of Iowa Studies in Child Welfare," Vol. IX, No. 3.) Iowa City, Iowa: Univ. of Iowa, 1934. 171 pp.

49. Jacobs, Leland B. "What Shall We Read to Our Children?" *National Parent-Teacher*, LI (November, 1956), 34-36.

50. Jersild, Arthur T., and Mary D. Fite. *The Influence of Nursery School Experience on Children's Social Adjustment*. ("Child Development Monographs," No. 25.) New York: Teachers College, Columbia Univ., 1939. 112 pp.

51. Jersild, Arthur T., and Frances B. Holmes. *Children's Fears*. ("Child Development Monographs," No. 25.) New York: Teachers College, Columbia Univ., 1939. 112 pp.

52. Jones, Mary Cover, and Barbara Stoddard Burks. *Personality Development in Childhood: A Survey of Problems, Methods, and Experimental Findings*. ("Monographs of the Society for Research in Child Development," Vol. I, No. 4.) Washington, D.C.: Society for Research in Child Development, National Research Council, 1936. 205 pp.

53. Jones, Vernon. "Character Development in Children—An Objective Approach" in Leonard Carmichael (ed.), *Manual of Child Psychology* (2d ed.), pp 781-832. New York: John Wiley & Sons, Inc., 1954.

*54. KANNER, LEO. *Child Psychiatry* (2d ed.). Springfield, Ill.: Charles C. Thomas, 1953. 778 pp.

*55. ———. "Unwholesome Parental Attitudes and Children's Behavior," *Education*, LXIX (January, 1949), 263-270.

56. KATZ, BARNEY. "The Inferiority Complex: Some Essential Causes," *Education*, LXIX (January, 1949), 293-295.

57. KEISTER, MARY E. "The Behavior of Young Children in Failure," in Roger G. Barker, Jacob S. Kounin, and Herbert F. Wright (eds.), *Child Behavior and Development*, pp. 429-440. New York: McGraw-Hill Book Co., Inc., 1943. 652 pp.

58. KOCH, HELEN LOIS. "The Modification of Unsocialness in Preschool Children," *Psychological Bulletin*, XXXII (November, 1935), 700-701.

59. ———. "The Relation of Certain Family Constellations, Characteristics and Attitudes of Children Toward Adults," *Child Development*, XXVI (March, 1955), 13-40.

60. KORNER, ANNELIESE FRIEDSAM. *Some Aspects of Hostility in Young Children.* New York: Grune & Stratton, 1949. 194 pp.

61. KROGMAN, WILTON M. *The Physical Growth of Children: An Appraisal of Studies, 1950-1955.* Lafayette, Ind.: Child Development Publications, 1956. 91 pp.

62. KUBIE, LAWRENCE S. "The Child's Fifth Freedom," *Child Study*, XXV (Summer, 1948), 67-70.

**63. LERNER, EUGENE, and LOIS BARCLAY MURPHY (eds.). *Methods for the Study of Personality in Young Children.* Washington, D.C.: Society for the Research in Child Development, National Research Council, 1941. 289 pp.

64. LINN, LOUIS. "Some Developmental Aspects of Body Image," *International Journal of Psychoanalysis*, XXXVI (January-February, 1955), 36-42.

65. LINTON, RALPH. *The Cultural Background of Personality.* New York: Appleton-Century-Crofts, Inc., 1945. 157 pp.

66. LIPPMAN, HYMAN S. *Treatment of the Child in Emotional Conflict.* New York: McGraw-Hill Book Co., Inc., 1956. 298 pp.

67. McCANDLESS, BOYD R., and HELEN R. MARSHALL. "A Picture-Sociometric Technique for Preschool Children and Its Relation to Teacher Judgments of Friendship," *Child Development*, XXVIII (June, 1957), 137-147.

68. ———. "Sex Differences in Social Acceptance and Participation of Preschool Children," *Child Development*, XXVIII (December, 1957), 421-425.

69. McCLURE, SUE COOK. "The Effect of Varying Verbal Instruction on the Motor Responses of Preschool Children," *Child Development*, VII (December, 1936), 276-290.

**70. MacFarlane, Jean W., Lucille Allen, and Marjorie P. Honzik. A Developmental Study of the Behavior Problems of Normal Children Between Twenty-one Months and Fourteen Years. Berkeley, Calif.: Univ. of California Press, 1954. 222 pp.

71. Marshall, Helen R., and Boyd R. McCandless. "Relationships between Dependence on Adults and Social Acceptance by Peers," Child Development, XXVIII (December, 1957), 413-419.

72. Marston, Leslie R. The Emotions of Young Children: An Experimental Study in Introversion and Extroversion. ("Studies in Child Welfare," Vol. III.) Iowa City, Iowa: Univ. of Iowa, 1925. 99 pp.

73. Mead, Margaret. "The Comparative Study of Child Rearing: Problems of Simultaneity and Sequence," Human Development Bulletin, Seventh Annual Symposium. Chicago: Human Development Student Organization, Comm. on Human Development, Univ. of Chicago, 1956. 57 pp.

74. Meek, Lois Hayden. A Study of Learning and Retention in Young Children. ("Contributions to Education," No. 164.) New York: Teachers College, Columbia Univ., 1925. 96 pp.

75. Merrill, Barbara. "A Measurement of Mother-Child Interaction," Journal of Abnormal and Social Psychology, XLI (January, 1946), 37-49.

76. Mittleman, Bela. "Motor Patterns and Genital Behavior: Fetishism," Psychoanalytic Study of the Child, X (Annual, 1955), 241-263.

77. Moustakas, Clark E. Children in Play Therapy: A Key to Understanding Normal and Disturbed Emotions. New York: McGraw-Hill Book Co., Inc., 1953. 218 pp.

78. Mowrer, O. H. "Two-Factor Learning Theory Reconsidered, with Special Reference to Secondary Reinforcement and the Concept of Habit," Psychological Review, LXIII (March, 1956), 114-128.

79. Moyer, Kenneth E., and B. Von Haller Gilmer. "Attention Spans of Children for Experimentally Designed Toys," Journal of Genetic Psychology, LXXXVII (December, 1955), 187-201.

80. Mummery, Dorothy V. "An Analytical Study of Ascendant Behavior of Preschool Children," Child Development, XVIII (March-June, 1947), 40-81.

81. Murphy, Lois Barclay. "Learning How Children Cope With Problems," Children, IV (July, 1957), 132-136.

82. ———. Social Behavior and Child Personality; An Exploratory Study of Some Roots of Sympathy. New York: Columbia Univ. Press, 1937. 344 pp.

*83. The New York Committee on Mental Hygiene of the State Charities Aid Association. Some Special Problems of Children Aged 2 to 5 Years (2d ed.). ("Pamphlet Series.") New York: The Committee, 1955. 72 pp.

84. OLSON, WILLARD C. *Child Development.* Boston: D. C. Heath & Co., 1949. 417 pp.

85. OTIS, NANCY BARKER, and BOYD R. McCANDLESS. "Responses to Repeated Frustrations of Young Children Differentiated According to the Need Area," *Journal of Abnormal and Social Psychology,* L (May, 1955), 349-353.

86. PAGE, MARJORIE LOU. *The Modification of Ascendant Behavior in Preschool Children.* ("University of Iowa Studies in Child Welfare," Vol. XII, No. 3.) Iowa City, Iowa: Univ. of Iowa, 1936. 68 pp.

87. PIAGET, JEAN. *The Construction of Reality in the Child.* New York: Basic Books, Inc., 1954. 386 pp.

88. ————. "Perceptual and Cognitive (or Operation) Structures in Development of the Concept of Space in Childhood," *Octapsychologica,* XI (June, 1955), 41-46.

89. RAWN, MOSS L. "Degree of Disturbance in Figure Drawings as Related to Mode of Approach to Problem Solving," *Journal of Genetic Psychology,* XCI (December, 1957), 191-196.

*90. REDL, FRITZ, and DAVID WINEMAN. *The Aggressive Child.* Chicago: The Free Press, 1957. 575 pp.

*91. RIDENOUR, NINA. *Building Self-Confidence in Children.* Chicago: Science Research Associates, 1954. 47 pp.

92. SEARS, ROBERT R. "Influence of Methodological Factors on Doll Play Performance," *Child Development,* XVIII (December, 1947), 190-197.

93. SEARS, ROBERT R., MARGARET H. PINTLER, and PAULINE S. SEARS. "Effect of Father Separation on Preschool Children's Doll Play Aggression," *Child Development,* XVII (December, 1946), 219-243.

94. SEARS, ROBERT R., and others. *Patterns of Child Rearing.* Evanston, Ill.: Row, Peterson & Co., 1957. 549 pp.

95. SEWARD, JOHN P. "Learning Theory and Identification. II. Role of Punishment," *Journal of Genetic Psychology,* LXXXIV (June, 1954), 201-210.

96. SHERMAN, MANDEL, and THOMAS R. HENRY. *Hollow Folk.* New York: Thomas Y. Crowell Co., 1933. 215 pp.

97. SHOBEN, EDWARD J., JR. "The Assessment of Parental Attitudes in Relation to Child Adjustment," *Genetic Psychology Monographs,* XXXIX (February, 1949), 101-148.

98. SKALET, MAGDA. *The Significance of Delayed Reactions in Young Children.* Comparative Psychology Monographs, Vol. VII, No. 34. Baltimore: Johns Hopkins Press, 1931. 82 pp.

99. SPOCK, BENJAMIN. *Baby and Child Care* (Cardinal Giant ed.). New York: Pocket Books, Inc., 1957. 627 pp.

100. STENDLER, CELIA B. "Possible Causes of Overdependency in Young Children," *Child Development,* XXV (June, 1954), 125-146.

101. Stoddard, George D. *The Meaning of Intelligence.* New York: The Macmillan Co., 1943. 504 pp.

102. Stott, Leland H., and Rachel Stutsman Ball. "Consistency and Change in Ascendance-Submission in the Social Interaction of Children," *Child Development,* XXVIII (September, 1957), 259-272.

103. Sunne, Dagny. "Rorschach Test Norms of Young Children," *Child Development,* VII (December, 1936), 304-313.

104. Talbot, Nathan B., Edna H. Sobel, Janet W. McArthur. and John D. Crawford. *Functional Endocrinology from Birth Through Adolescence.* Cambridge, Mass.: Harvard Univ. Press, 1952. 638 pp.

105. Taylor, Katherine Whiteside. *Parent Cooperative Nursery Schools.* New York: Teachers College, Columbia Univ., 1954. 257 pp.

106. Thurstone, L. L., and T. G. Thurstone. *Tests of Primary Mental Abilities for Ages 5 and 6.* (1 form. 60 minutes, in two periods. Manual.) Chicago: Science Research Associates, 1946.

107. Trotter, Virginia Y., and Tessie Agan. "A Room for a Preschool Child," *Journal of Home Economics,* XLI (January, 1949), 8-10.

108. Valentine, Charles W. *Intelligence Tests for Children* (4th ed.). London: Methuen and Co., Ltd., 1950. 80 pp.

*109. ———. *The Normal Child and Some of His Abnormalities.* Baltimore: Penguin Books, Inc., 1957. 279 pp.

110. Vineland Social Maturity Scale, by Edgar A. Doll. (Ages 0-25+ years. Individual test. 1 form. Manual, record blank.) Minneapolis: Educ. Test Bureau, 1947.

111. Washburn, Ruth W. *Re-education in a Nursery Group; A Study in Clinical Psychology.* ("Monograph of the Society for Research in Child Development," Vol. IX, No. 2.) Washington, D.C.: Society for Research in Child Development, 1944. 175 pp.

112. Wechsler, D. *The Measurement of Adult Intelligence* (3d ed.). Baltimore: William & Wilkins, 1944. 258 pp.

113. Wellman, Beth L. "Motor Achievements of Preschool Children," *Childhood Education,* XIII (March, 1937), 311-316.

114. Willsher, E. C. "Discipline in the Nursery Class," *The Scottish Educational Journal,* XL (January, 1957), 6-7.

115. Winnetka Scale for Rating School Behavior and Attitudes, by D. Van Alstyne, L. W. Hattwick, and H. Totten. Winnetka, Illinois: Winnetka Educ. Press, 1935, 1937.

**116. Witmer, Helen L. (ed.). *Psychiatric Interviews with Children.* New York: Commonwealth Fund, Inc., 1946. 443 pp.

117. Wolf, Anna W. M. *Helping Your Child to Understand Death.* New York: Child Study Assoc. of America, 1958. 63 pp.

*118. Wolf, Katherine M. *The Controversial Problem of Discipline.* New York: The Child Study Assoc. of America, 1953. 35 pp.

Films for Child Study

A Long Time To Grow (Part Two), Four- and Five-Year-Olds in School. New York Univ. Film Library. 35 minutes. 1954. Produced by the Dept. of Child Study at Vassar College. Shows children at work and play at Vassar College Nursery and the Poughkeepsie Day School.

Fears of Children. International Film Bureau. 30 minutes. 1951. A parent-child situation is presented in which the mother tends to coddle her five-year-old son while the father advocates sterner discipline. (*See also* other films in the list prepared by the World Federation for Mental Health.)

Frustrating Fours and Fascinating Fives. McGraw-Hill. 22 minutes. 1952. Produced by the National Film Board of Canada. Shows the gradual change from childish helplessness toward cooperation and independence.

He Acts His Age. National Film Board of Canada. Color. 13 minutes. 1949. Shows the development of children at various ages and how parents can help lay the basis for habits which let them grow up emotionally stable and happy.

Preschool Incidents: Studies of Normal Personality Development. McGraw-Hill. 13 minutes. 1951. Produced by the Depart. of Child Study at Vassar College. A series of films showing preschool children in various situations in which grownups must decide on certain courses of action, depending on the situation and their perception of the child's needs.

This Is Robert: A Study of Personality Growth in a Preschool Child. 80 minutes. 1942. Produced by the Dept. of Child Study at Vassar College. "Focuses on the preschool years, but also looks before and after."

Understanding Children's Play. Produced by the Caroline Zachary Inst. of Human Development (now distributed as part of the Vassar Series). 10 minutes. 1950. Understanding children through observing their use of toy and play materials.

Part Four

MIDDLE CHILDHOOD

It is good to have been young in youth, and as years go on to grow older, to travel deliberately through one's ages and to get the heart out of a liberal education.
ROBERT LOUIS STEVENSON

. . . to enjoy what is beautiful and what is good; and to do as one pleases, when the things one wants to do are noble, intelligent, and generous.
ANATOLE FRANCE, *The Crime of Sylvestre Bonnard* (New York: Dodd, Mead & Co., 1918), p. 197.

Chapter 13

DEVELOPMENT DURING
YEARS SIX, SEVEN, AND EIGHT

The preschool child "is father to" the first-grade child. Early developmental trends tend to persist. The child's experiences in the pre-school years determine: What kind of child is sent to school? Is he a self-reliant little chap who meets the mystery and strangeness of his first day at school with good-natured curiosity and co-operation? Or is he a timid child, clinging to his mother or an older sister, crying when she leaves him, afraid of the teacher, afraid of the other children, hiding his face on the desk, and standing alone when the other children are playing games at recess? Does he enjoy taking part in the activities of the group, sometimes as audience and sometimes as performer? Is his conduct occasionally de-termined by goals more remote than the interests and needs of the present? Does he try to get what he wants by working for it in a socially acceptable way? Does he face the fact that there are certain things that he cannot do and certain things that he cannot have? Obviously the best preparation for success in the first grade is to have accomplished the developmental tasks of the preschool years. If, almost from birth, the child has been given responsibilities for which he is ready and if he has been successful in his day-by-day activity, then he will approach the new experiences at school with eagerness and confidence.

A child's behavior, at any age, includes different degrees of maturity. First-graders sometimes act like babies, sometimes like older children. Although they still depend on their home for security, they are moving toward participation in their peer group. At about eight years of age, identi-fication with the parent is often at its peak.

Six-year-olds vary in their readiness for school. Just because they are six years old and in the first grade, it does not follow that they are ready for reading, writing, and arithmetic. If they are forced to acquire certain abilities before they are physically and mentally ready, their progress is slow and painful. Consequently, they may develop negative attitudes toward the learning task and toward themselves that may permanently retard their learning. On the other hand, if a child passes a stage of readiness without having the opportunity to develop the ability, as, for example, reading, his interest may be lost, and regained only with difficulty. Olson has admirably summed up this philosophy of child development in these words:

. . . each child is to be assisted in growing according to his natural design without deprivation or forcing in an environment and by a process which supply a social direction to his achievement. [95, p. 380, 1949]

Child development can be fostered but not forced.

Given a chance to grow at their own rate, most children will make satisfactory progress in the developmental tasks of this period: to increase their physical proficiency, to acquire basic tools of learning including facts with which to think, and to relate themselves to their age-mates. They are curious and eager to achieve and are developing ability to deal with external reality. Successful achievement of these tasks prepares them for later undertakings; failure leads to unhappiness in the individual and a loss to society. Despite fluctuations, the general direction of development should be forward.

OVERVIEW OF THE MIDDLE CHILDHOOD PERIOD

After a relatively quiet, conforming stage, the six-year-old passes through a transition period somewhat similar to teen-age adolescence. As this phase passes, he becomes more stable, less impulsive. His concept of himself becomes clarified; he begins to see more clearly where he stands. The seven- and eight-year-old child is very much concerned with demonstrating his competence. "Watch me," and, "I can do this myself," are characteristic expressions. He shows increasing self-reliance. He wants to do grown-up things. For example, eight-year-old Jerry liked to help his father wash his car. As he worked he said, "We are washing the car good, Daddy. I can wash it good, can't I, Daddy?"

The child of this age is stepping out into a larger world. Each new thing involves him wholeheartedly and intensely. "Wait a minute 'til I finish this" is his frequent response to any interruption of his activity. This is exciting. The wide, wide world is opening out before him and he wants to learn about it as fast as he can, with almost religious fervor. His social distance from his mother is increasing. No longer does he have the constant support of her solicitude. Many more persons are coming into his life. He is more on his own; his success depends more on his own efforts. In the school group he is accepted for what he can do, not just because he is our Tommy. He is moving away from dependence upon adults toward co-operation and friendliness with other children. Entering the kindergarten or first grade makes most children feel important and grown up. They look forward to going to school. For some, however, the experience is ego-deflating, as they see themselves surpassed by other children.

The confident seven- or eight-year-old will verbally assert himself with grownups as well as with children. One seven-year-old asked if he could light the fire in the fireplace. When his aunt said yes, he remarked, "But my mother doesn't let me light the fire." "Then," his aunt said, "you'd better let me do it." "But I know how to light it," he insisted. "Well, go ahead and light it this time," she said wearily. Later he asked, "Why did you let me light the fire when I told you my mother wouldn't let me?" Children of this age will often put the adult on the spot by their persistence in pursuing a point and argue like a lawyer to prove it.

To the verbally gifted child words are playthings. He experiments with language and makes words do what he wants them to do. Eight-year-old Tommy made up innumerable rhymes, invented language games, and substituted his own version for the words of popular songs. He had much scattered knowledge which he had not yet built into a system.

Tommy, like other eight-year-olds, made many kinds of collections, hoarded, and bartered. He also had his share of belief in magic. When two persons came out with the same word, he instituted the proper ceremony of making a wish on that occasion. Superstitions and rituals were interwoven with many of his activities. He was beginning to wonder about himself and the world. One day he said, "God gives us the words we say, but how can He know so many words spoken by so many people?"

Adults too often fail to watch for, cherish, and reinforce children's insights and ideals that flash out occasionally from the midst of their perpetual motion. A child often receives little help and encouragement in his first attempts to communicate his feelings. Adults should warmly appreciate those flashes of affection, insight, and generous impulses that show the quality of the evolving personality.

During the early elementary-school years, other children become increasingly important to a child's development. He sees himself through their frank eyes. He seeks their companionship. His own age group is becoming more important to him than adults. He gains security from being accepted by them. Learning what other persons are like, how they behave, and how one person is related to others expands his self-concept. He himself is growing as an individual in relation to others. His personality is modified by his contact with others. His personal relations expand to include persons in the school and neighborhood.

Children six, seven, and eight are going through a period of relatively calm weather, emotionally. They have lived through the period of wanting the exclusive affection of their parents. They do not yet have to face the developmental tasks of the teen-age. This relative freedom from inner conflicts enables them to give their attention to understanding the world about them and to learning various skills.

Individual differences are always with us. Children in the first three grades vary widely in every aspect of their development and even more in their personality patterns. Their initial differences in maturity and readiness for first-grade experiences are never ironed out. In fact, one of the tasks of effective guidance is to help each child, while acquiring common learning, to develop further those characteristics which make him pleasantly unique.

PHYSICAL DEVELOPMENT AND HEALTH

Children in the primary grades are consolidating gains made during their preschool years. It also seems as though they were gathering knowledge and social competence to handle adolescent changes in body form and functions. Their growth is relatively slower than in the preceding and following periods. Anderson (4, p. 71, 1949) estimated that if infants "continued to grow at the same rate throughout childhood and youth, the adult would be two hundred feet tall and would weigh ten tons."

They are increasing rapidly in strength and in the improvement of motor skills, and have great interest in vigorous bodily activity. The child who is physically weak is usually lacking in motor skills. Consequently he does not have the admiration of his age-mates. If he becomes fatigued easily he fails to get his schoolwork done. Fear, anxiety, and anger may precipitate illness. If he is ill a great deal, he misses many school days; this interferes with his learning to read and write at the time the other children of his age are learning the tool subjects. Such a series of frustrations often results in a concept of himself as inadequate and unacceptable. Poor grades in school may also affect his family relations, especially his relations with ambitious parents.

School achievement may be considered a resultant of the total growth pattern of the child. By knowing the individual growth patterns and providing a suitable curriculum that takes into account these differences, it should be possible for each child to succeed in his schoolwork.

Growth curves

Various aspects of growth tend to go together. By reducing annual measurements to an age standard, Olson and Hughes (98, 1944) made possible simple and easily understood comparisons. From these graphs of different aspects of growth, fundamental growth trends as well as strong and weak points in the growth of individual children can be noted. Wetzel (133, 1943; 134, 1941) developed a grid on which a child's position can be determined in terms of his height, weight, and age. The grid contains seven channels ranging from heavy obesity to extreme thinness. The child's growth normally progresses within a particular channel. Sudden deviations to either extreme warrant investigation as to possible unfavorable changes in a child's social environment or diet; glandular disturbances; or the onset of a disease such as tuberculosis.

Special stimulation of children whose environmental conditions are already optimum may result in a temporary spurt, which, however, is likely to be followed by a return to the fundamental growth trend; the temporary gain tends to iron out. Both body and mind seem to resist special stimulation that is not in line with the child's basic growth pattern. When permanent changes in growth curves do take place, it is probably because the child's real growth potentials had not previously been recognized and given favorable conditions for development.

Hazards to growth

"Injury, deprivation, and mismanagement" (97, 1947) should be avoided as far as possible. Correction of physical defects, prevention of avoidable infection, treatment of illness to avoid complications, and prevention of accidents are of prime importance. Active, adventurous youngsters create many situations of danger to themselves and acute anxiety to adults. For the most part, these dangers are not motivated by mischief, but by exploration and by courage due to ignorance. What a task for the adult to control what is explored, when, and where!

Disturbances in emotional relations often cause physical symptoms. Conversely, malnutrition, bodily illness, organic defects, or generally poor physical condition may give rise to anxiety, depression, apathy, or poor school achievement. Other conditions such as mental retardation, lack of motor skills, and failure in school often make a child feel inferior and rejected. Any of these conditions may deflect the child from his normal development.

Height and weight in relation to body build

By six years of age a child is approximately two-thirds as tall as he will be as an adult. His body as a whole is about two-fifths of his adult size. The average annual gain is about one or two inches in height and three to five pounds in weight. From the sixth through the tenth year the average annual gains in height for both boys and girls tends to decrease. But some six-year-olds are taller than the majority of ten-year-olds or than the shortest fifteen-year-olds. A six-year-old boy may be from 39 to 49 inches in height, and from 39 to 50 pounds in weight, and still be within normal limits. Beyond these limits, he should be studied more closely. Each part of the body grows according to its own rate, in unity with the child's growth as a whole.

The six-year-old girl is about as mature in bone development as the seven-year-old boy. At each age from birth to eleven years boys tend to be slightly heavier than girls and are slightly taller than girls up to eight years. But the curves of height and weight for boys and for girls overlap.

Rhythm of growth is fully as important as rate of growth. Children grow by fits and starts. During the primary period the child's height is likely to be more constant in relation to his classmates than it is in the later elementary-school years. Two boys may remain practically equal in height up to the age of eleven; then one of them may shoot ahead and become much taller than his classmates. The height and weight of children even vary during the day and during the year. Persons weigh a little more at night than in the morning. During the day they lose about a half-inch in height which is restored during sleep. There is a seasonal variation in height and weight, except in those climates where the sun shines brightly the year round.

Height and weight of children seven to nine years old are increasing over the years. For example, in private schools today children are from 2½ to 3½ inches taller and 5 to 7 pounds heavier than children of the same age half a century ago (77, 1950). Too much emphasis on gain in weight may be responsible for some of our overweight youngsters. Their parents' delight in having them eat well may cause them to overvalue their ability to eat more than they really need.

Although the boundaries of a child's growth are determined by heredity, the right amount of sunlight and outdoor play, rest, sleep, and proper diet can account for considerable variation within these limits. Special stimulation or medication, such as gland therapy, seems to produce immediate results, but later, the body begins to resist the special stimulation somewhat in the same way that it resists bacterial infection.

A child is not always big *and* strong, although strength is related to

High
adventure.

Loneliness may mark the transition from home to school.

weight. A combination of size and body build is more accurate in determining strength.

Tooth development

During the sixth year children lose their first teeth. The first of the permanent teeth (the six-year molars) push their way through the gums. In the seventh and eighth years the permanent front teeth (incisors) usually appear, first in the lower jaw. Girls, more physiologically mature, shed their first teeth a little earlier than boys. The engaging toothless grin of seven- and eight-year-olds is the familiar result of this period of dental transition. As in all other aspects of development there are wide individual differences.

Nutritional condition

A child's energy level or "constitutional vitality" may be very important in determining the way he perceives his environment. If he is unable to cope with it because of low vitality and energy, he may interpret it as hostile and unfriendly to him.

Extensive studies have shown much malnutrition and evidence of poor food habits among school children; signs of vitamin deficiency are prevalent, especially in the low-economy city homes; too few children are receiving daily diets adequate in every respect. Rickets and goiter, though practically zero in some areas, are prevalent in others. Children of high economic and educational level frequently present feeding problems, i.e., they refuse milk, meat, eggs, and other important foods; they are fussy about foods, dawdle, or have to be coaxed or bribed to eat properly.

The "basic seven" are a sound and simple guide to healthy growth:

1. Dark green leafy vegetables and deep yellow vegetables.
2. Citrus fruits, tomatoes, raw cabbage, and other good vitamin C sources.
3. Potatoes and other vegetables, and fruits.
4. Milk, cheese, ice cream.
5. Meat, poultry, fish, eggs, dried beans and peas, nuts.
6. Bread and cereals, whole grain or enriched.
7. Butter or other fats rich in vitamins.

The total number of calories a child needs increases with his physical activity and also depends on his size and body build.

During the primary period it is important for a child to build wholesome attitudes toward himself as a growing person and to establish healthful ways of acting, thinking, and feeling. These should grow out of his daily experiences in healthful living. Habits of healthful living are reinforced as the child observes and reads about attractive children doing healthful things and understands the reasons for clearly described health practices.

Physical defects and handicaps

Even easily remediable physical defects are still common among school children. They should be detected early by parents and teachers. The largest number need dental attention. Elementary children have, on the average, three or more cavities. Possible factors in dental decay are:

1. Susceptibility to dental caries; few persons are immune.
2. Presence and activity of acid-forming and acid-tolerating bacteria in the mouth.
3. Presence in the mouth of food—fermentable carbohydrate, usually in the form of sugar—on which the bacteria live.
4. Presence of enzymes necessary to change fermentable sugar to lactic acid, which dissolves tooth tissue.
5. The film on the teeth which prevents the acids from being neutralized by the saliva.

The best way to decrease tooth decay is to provide essential food elements; restricting sugar and encouraging the child to end his meal with an apple or other raw fruit. Parents should also foster the child's habit of rinsing or proper cleaning of the teeth after each meal and having regular dental examination and care.

Second in frequency are defects of vision and hearing. When the child comes to school he is likely to be normally farsighted. The amount of accommodation needed for near vision may be quite fatiguing. By the time he is eight or nine his eyes should have attained adult size and shape, though children reach visual maturity at different rates. From then on nearsightedness is more frequent than farsightedness.

It was estimated "that about 30% of the school population could benefit by eye care." (29, 1955)

The manner in which a handicapped child responds to his handicap is often more important for his adjustment than the nature of the handicap itself. An individual may react to a physical handicap in any of three ways:

1. He may accept the handicap and function as well as possible in other respects, even though being deaf, blind, or crippled limits the range and variety of his experiences.
2. He may resent the handicap and not even try to use the handicapped part, thus increasing his insecurity and affecting his social relations.
3. He may try to compensate for the handicap and make extra effort to

overcome it, as did Beethoven, who was deaf but heard great melodies. A child's handicap may acquire new significance to him when he leaves the accepting atmosphere of his home for a classroom of age-mates who are usually quite critical and frank in expressing their views on abnormality. This influence is intensified by the increasing importance that the child attaches to the opinions and approval of his peers. He needs help in understanding his feelings of frustration and in facing the difficulty frankly and realistically. While he learns to take his place naturally in a group without feelings of inferiority, normal children should learn how to treat handicapped children constructively and with consideration.

Cruickshank (23, 1955) has edited a comprehensive book on the psychology of exceptional children and the National Society for the Study of Education has published an excellent yearbook on exceptional children (87, 1950).

Each handicapped child has certain assets and special problems. For example, although deafness brings a certain amount of physical insecurity, deaf children seem to have fewer fears than normal children. Their most serious problems are educational and social. They lack clearly defined social status and constitute a minority group. In general, they should be encouraged to try to use the tools of communication which other children use and to keep their place in the normal group. For hard-of-hearing children, freedom at any time to move close to the source of sound is recommended. They should be taught lip reading; those more seriously handicapped should also learn to use a carefully selected hearing aid. If the strain becomes too great they may seek relief by associating with other children like themselves. In schools for the deaf, one of the problems is to keep children from resorting to the sign language in communicating with one another instead of using lip reading and other methods that would enable them to participate in normal groups. When deaf and hard-of-hearing children are sent away at an early age for special education, they are cut off from important family relations and may feel rejected.

It is of prime importance that handicapped children be treated as normal children except for their handicap. Too often they are pitied or overprotected. All except the very seriously handicapped can attend the ordinary school and receive outside remedial treatment. By the time they are ready for high school, they should have gained sufficient self-reliance to associate with normal adolscents.

Illness and accidents

The death rate of children from five to nine is relatively low (128, 1955, 1957), even though this is the time when the communicable children's diseases are prevalent. A study of the causes of death between 1947 and 1955 (78, 1956) revealed an encouraging decline in deaths from each of the major causes except cancer and its allied conditions. Deaths from tuberculosis had decreased about 85 per cent during the decade. Almost as rapid has been the decline in deaths from communicable diseases of childhood, and from heart disease, most of which is due to rheumatic fever. At these ages accidents are the leading cause of death, especially of boys. Of these, about seven-eighths were motor-vehicle and traffic accidents; there was, however, a decrease in accident rate during the decade. The chief causes of death in 1954-1955 for years five to nine were as follows (78, 1956):

	Death Rate per 100,000	
	Girls	Boys
Accidents, total	9.8	23.4
Cancer and allied condition	6.5	8.1
Pneumonia	1.5	2.4
Heart diseases, including rheumatic fever	1.0	0.9
Communicable diseases of childhood	0.7	0.5
Acute poliomyelitis	0.9	1.5
Tuberculosis	0.3	0.3

The sickness rate for this age group is high. A relatively few diseases account for most of the absence because of illness in the primary grades. Respiratory diseases are the most common causes of illness among school children, as well as among preschool children and adults (80, 1955). The school has responsibility for helping to prevent the spread of communicable diseases by diminishing the possibility of contagion and increasing the child's resistance.

Equally important is the prevention of complications following a communicable disease. For example, rheumatic fever usually follows a streptococcal infection such as scarlet fever, a bad cold, or tonsilitis. Children are likely to get the first attack when they are about five or six. Early signs and symptoms are poor appetite, no gain in weight, paleness, persistent low fever, pain or soreness in arms or legs, and, especially, inflamed joints. The child is irritable, cries easily, or is nervous. An attack of this disease is likely to leave the heart slightly or even seriously damaged. However, during the quiescent stage the child can return to school and take part in ordinary childhood activities. One attack does not protect him from a recurrence. Therefore, special attention should be given to building up the child's health.

Low frequency and short duration of illness are indications of physical fitness. Though freedom from illness is one sign of a healthy child, this standard fails to take into account the ideal optimum of "vim, vigor, and vitality."

Related factors in positive health

Psychosomatic medicine has emphasized the reciprocal relation between psychological and physical factors. An illness such as influenza may leave a child somewhat weak and depressed, easily discouraged, and dissatisfied with home and school. Physical defects and illness may produce a change in social status. The child may no longer be accepted by his playmates because he cannot contribute to their projects and games, or because he has become physically unattractive. Severe illness, involving pain, turns the child's attention inward toward himself and tends to make him withdraw from others.

It has also been shown that emotional factors enter into accidents. Children who have an excessive number of accidents have been found to be more aggressive and more anxious about their aggression than other children.

MOTOR SKILLS ACQUIRED
IN THE FIRST THREE YEARS OF SCHOOL

Children have an urge to be active. Each child has a unique pattern of motility which has a multiplicity of relationships with his other functions. According to Mittelman (82, 1954), children's play activity is a resultant of this motor urge, fantasies, and striving for mastery. It follows a clear sequence:

Restlessness → Activity → Satisfaction → Relaxation

The motor urge seems to reach a peak at about five to six years, then declines and becomes more goal-directed. If this strong urge to be active is repressed, anger may be aroused or another source of satisfaction such as masturbation may be sought. These facts highlight the need for large-muscle activity in kindergarten and first grade, and the detrimental effect of requiring these little children to sit quietly in their seats most of the school day. One child in the third grade expressed his feeling of frustration this way:

I went out to my aunts and stayed till Sunday. I bagged and bagged to go outside. I sat on a chair and you could see tears in my eyes. I jurst hayt to sit on a chair and talk to big people. It makes me lonely. [126, p. 18, 1947]

The sequences of motor development in the primary grades are more subject to the influence of the child's environment than they were in the early preschool years. He learns to do the things for which he has ability, opportunity, and encouragement. One now asks what children of this age like to do and what improvement they have made in their skills, as well as what they *can* do. One finds much overlapping in activities of six-, seven-, and eight-year-old children.

Nevertheless, there are some common developmental sequences among children of these ages. Reaction time increases rapidly during the first decade of life. Their fervent interest in active play continues throughout this period. At the same time they become better able to co-ordinate eye and hand in craft work, writing, and other small-muscle activities. As they increase in skill, they abandon the tricycle for a two-wheeled bike or roller skates. They begin to be interested in organized games not very competitive in spirit. Spontaneous dramatization appeals to all ages.

Large-muscle activity and play

Children of six, seven, and eight delight in strenuous physical activity —running, climbing, playing ball, running races, playing games of chase, dancing, skating, building houses big enough to play in (51, 1957). Their interest in hide-and-seek and tag—two typical games of chase—increases from six to nine, when it is at its height. Eight-year-olds will probably prefer tag to toys. They climb in higher and more difficult places and balance themselves more skillfully. Some of them learn to ice-skate on single runners. Children in the first and second grades enjoy imaginative rhythms such as:

> Run, run, run, little pony, run.
> Trot, trot, trot, little pony, trot.
> Gallop, gallop, gallop, little pony, gallop.

They run, trot, and gallop in time to music.

Playing ball seems to be the boys' favorite game; its popularity increases with age. The eight-year-old delights in baseball, soccer, and other organized games and is insistent that his fellow players follow the rules of the game. Any activity that uses the large muscles, emphasizes movement more than form, and reflects personal aspects of everyday life will appeal to almost all children of these ages. The main sex difference is in doll-play, which, for girls, decreases slightly from the sixth to the eighth year.

Sex differences in children's play are desirable insofar as they help boys and girls to build a clearer idea of their future masculine and feminine roles.

The play activities of children will vary with such factors as physical maturity, personality, the stimulation of other children, amount of practice, success or failure in performance, environmental opportunities to learn and engage in an activity, current fads, and customs. Physical maturity makes it possible to learn certain skills; on the other hand, the learning of a skill promotes physical development. If a child feels generally insecure, he will lack the self-confidence necessary to learn new motor abilities. If he feels inferior, he will be especially sensitive to the group's attitude and refuse to go through the clumsy, inept stages of learning a new game. Being with a sympathetic group of children also contributes greatly to the development of motor skills: "We need you on our team" is a strong incentive to learn. Seasonal interests, fads that sweep the country, and local interests such as often arise from natural recreational facilities likewise influence the play activities of children and adults.

Each child's rhythm of activity and rest should be observed. Several short periods of complete relaxation during the school day are beneficial both to pupils and teachers. Some children are highly stimulated by school activities and have greater need of rest periods than others. Fatigue may make a child either restless or apathetic.

Play may influence social and emotional development in several ways: through success resulting from skill, through opportunities for the expression and release of repressed feelings, through the positive emotional tone of the situation in which play takes place. If a child is good in one or more games, he will be more likely to weather failure in some of the academic aspects of school life. Success in some corner of one's life is essential to mental health. The importance of skill and its prestige factor are greater for boys than for girls.

Finer eye-hand co-ordination

Active play and large-muscle activity should precede close work with eyes and hands. In the first grade, children are not ready to use their small muscles in fine writing, sewing, or drawing. The Stanford-Binet test of tying a bowknot was passed by 35 per cent of the six-year-olds, 69 per cent of the seven-year-olds, and 94 per cent of the nine-year-olds. Tying shoelaces is difficult for many six-year-old children.

Children in the primary grades like to mold clay into candlesticks, bowls, animals, and other objects useful or ornamental. They use wood in constructing wagons, doll houses, furniture, boats, book ends, and other articles. They use paper in making books, boxes, and toys. They enjoy making cookies, applesauce, cup custard, and stuffed fruits. They use unbleached muslin, gay cretonne, and cambric in making the aprons they wear in school and the costumes they need in plays. With skillful instruction they may do block-printing and tie- and dye-work.

Insight and understanding are the most important outcomes of handwork. One group of first-grade children made a playhouse out of a large wooden box. They laid the floor, painted the walls, wove the rugs on a simple hand loom, furnished the house with useful articles, hung curtains at the windows, and made pottery dishes for the table. Another first-grade group made a village of smaller boxes. Each child made his own doll's house, using originality in planning and furnishing it. Traffic signals were set up on the streets. Electric wiring of a simple kind was installed with the help of an electrician. These activities evoked many questions about life today and in former days, furnished opportunities for reading, for measurement, for writing, and for the application of art principles and health rules. A second-grade group made pottery and Indian costumes in connection with their study of Indian life. A third grade wove cloth and made candles and simple articles of furniture, similar to the products of the colonial period, which they were studying.

Handwriting

In the first grade the child has little use for writing, except to print his name on his drawings and label his other belongings. Even if he felt the need he would not have the eye-muscle co-ordination necessary for legible writing. Legibility is of first importance; speed is secondary. Individuality is acquired after the mechanics of forming the letters have been mastered.

All primary children should not be expected to reach a given quality at a given speed. Many teachers strive too early for perfection and precision. Following the primary period, children's writing, when effectively taught, tends to improve rapidly in speed and quality.

Drawing and painting

Everyone possesses some degree of creative ability. Children's first drawings and paintings are free expressions of their imagination and feeling. But by the time they enter school, custom has already laid a hand on their free, spontaneous expression. So many adults have looked at their drawings and asked, "What is this?" that they have acquired the idea that drawing and painting must be representative. By the time they are nine or ten they are likely to think that they should reproduce what they see, not express what they feel. Adults have told them what to draw and how to draw it. Their own interest, too, is in the world about them.

The majority of six-year-olds have learned to draw a picture of a man which can be recognized as *genus homo*. They can draw a tree or a house which an adult can identify without inside information. They are less likely than they were to draw something resembling a washtub and ask mother to write under it, "This is kitty." But for them drawing is still a silent language, not a form of art. Their drawings at this age usually tell a story, which they want others to understand. They are uncritical and enthusiastic about their works of art. If the picture quickly tells a story or expresses a feeling, or satisfactorily supplements their speech, they are content.

Children draw large the detail that is most interesting to them. If a child is interested less in the house than in the flower by the house, he will draw the flower bigger than the house. Children usualy draw faces large in proportion to trunk and limbs. Boats, airplanes, autos, fire engines, houses, and people are the most popular subjects of children's drawings. Their drawings show not only the extent of their muscle control but also the quality of their observation.

Art activities in school contribute to the child's personal development. Art is a means of deepening self-awareness, pride in achievement, and self-realization. The child feels, "I can create." A child's art may reveal conflicts long before they appear in his overt or observable behavior. Naumburg (90, 1947) found that children and adolescents with behavior problems were at first able only to copy; as they gained confidence they began to experiment and express themselves more freely, using art as a language in which they could reveal what they dared not or could not speak. Creative art provides for the release of impulses that might otherwise be inhibited or lead to socially unacceptable behavior. In their keen interest in the meaning underlying children's drawings and paintings, adults should guard against misinterpretation (46, 1957).

LANGUAGE ABILITY

The development of the child's language ability is indicated by the size and richness of his vocabulary, the length and structure of his sentences, the correctness of his speech, and his general effectiveness in expressing his ideas. Reading ability is built on the foundation of general language development.

All the language arts are related. For example, retardation in speech is related to retardation in reading. In general, children with speech defects are significantly inferior in both oral and silent reading to children with normal speaking ability.

Nature of reading

Reading and other school achievements are part of the total growth of the child; retardation in reading may be one phase of a child's general immaturity. The language that he uses is an important index of his mental maturity and the stimulation which he is receiving from his environment Reading is more than merely saying the words or "barking at print." It involves comprehending the author's thought, evaluating it, and using it in everyday living. From the beginning the child should learn that printed words have meaning for him.

Reading is built on firsthand experiences, described, compared, and discussed. When a child says, "Meow," on seeing a picture of a cat, he is associating the picture with his previous experiences with cats. Later he associates the printed word with the spoken symbol for "cat."

Individual differences in ability
and readiness to read

Each child comes to the first grade with widely different reading potentialities and readiness for reading. A bright child who talks a great deal and enjoys listening to stories and rhymes, and in whose home reading is a necessity, often learns to read with little instruction before he comes to school. A bright child from a home that provides little incentive to read usually learns quickly in a stimulating school environment. A child with low mental ability from a cultured home feels a strong need to read but will take longer to learn. The mentally retarded child, who lacks the ability to distinguish similarities and differences in the form and sounds of words, can make little progress in reading in the first grade. He becomes a "reading problem" when he is forced to begin reading before he has reached the mental age at which he is able to associate printed symbols with their meanings. If a slow child is constantly prodded and urged to hurry, he will usually develop either anxiety or negativistic attitudes toward reading.

Since girls, in general, mature faster than boys and are apparently more interested in language, in the United States, they tend to have larger vocabularies. However, a study of the vocabulary of 2,000 British children

(34, 1955) showed a superiority on the part of boys at every age from five to fifteen.

In many situations, a larger proportion of boys are referred to reading clinics and placed in remedial reading classes. Several explanations of this sex difference in reading ability have been suggested. One is that though boys are introduced to reading at the same chronological age as girls, they are less mature in mental ability and linguistic development and consequently have more difficulty in learning to read. Thus they are early labeled as failures in reading, and acquire a concept of themselves as boys who cannot read. Other explanations are that boys, eager to establish their masculine identification, think of reading as "sissy stuff." There is also some evidence that more boys fail in reading than girls because of their poorer auditory discrimination.

Signs of readiness to read are easily recognized. When a child asks the meaning of printed signs, wants to know what the words in the picture book say, pretends he is reading, listens attentively, can repeat simple sentences that he hears, he is showing a readiness to read. The child's response to good instruction in reading will quickly show whether or not he is ready. Children from foreign-speaking homes are likely to be slow in achievement during their first years of school. They need many opportunities to talk and work and play with children who speak English.

Experience with words and books

It is an advantage to children in learning to read to have had experience with words and books:

To recognize signs and follow simple printed directions like "Go" and "Stop."

To be familiar with the phraseology of stories; this helps children anticipate meaning more readily when they begin to read.

To look at the book while someone reads to them; thus they will get the feeling of correct eye movement from left to right and from one line to the next and may begin to recognize words that frequently recur.

Growth in vocabulary

By the age of six a child's rate of vocabulary development begins to slow down from its very high preschool level, especially if his school gives children little opportunity or incentive to talk. Under such conditions he will pick up most of his new words outside of school. Various estimates have been made of the vocabulary of six-year-old children. One estimate gives 2,500 words; another, six times as many; a great deal depends on the methods of study used.

Several methods of studying children's vocabulary have been suggested. A simple method second- and third-grade teachers can use is to ask the child to write as many different words as he can in fifteen minutes. However, the response thus obtained is influenced not only by the size of his vocabulary, but also by his application to the task in hand, writing ability, and interest. The average number of words per pupil written in fifteen minutes by more than two thousand children in the second grade was seventy-three. In the third grade the average number was ninety. This method, of course, does not measure a child's true vocabulary capacity. The method of having children check the words they know is likewise unsatisfactory. Actually pupils are unable to define more than half the words they check. Moreover, a child does not use many of the words he recognizes. Recording the words a child uses is also unsatisfactory since he will know many words which he does not have occasion to use in the situations observed.

The usual method is to estimate a child's total vocabulary on the basis of his definitions of a sampling of words. In the vocabulary test of the Revised Stanford-Binet Scale a six-year-old child is expected to know at least five of the forty-five words on the list; and at eight years, at least eight words (122, pp. 94, 100, 1937). A fairly correct idea of their meaning is expected. For example, the following are considered adequate definitions for the words given: an orange, "a fruit"; an envelope, "is to mail"; tap, "you make a little noise"; roar, "a lion roars." Growth in vocabulary is

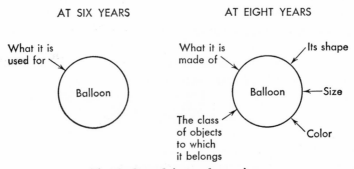

Fig. 4. Growth in word meanings.

shown not only in the increased number of words but also in "their ever-widening range and precision." A six-year-old is likely to define a balloon as "what you go up in," or, "to play with." An eight-year-old can describe the balloon as "a great big thing that goes up in the air with people in it." A six-year-old is likely to say that a tiger is "to eat you up." When he is eight years old he is able to give this definition: "It's an animal like a big old cat that I saw in the circus." The child's vocabulary grows in vividness and richness of associations as his experiences broaden and deepen.

In limiting the number of different words in basal readers, it is easy to forget the modern child's extensive acquaintance with words. On radio and television and in conversations outside the classroom, as well as through a broad expanse of subject matter, he becomes able to identify a large number of words by ear at least.

The sequence in the development of word knowledge is somewhat as follows: At first children learn the names of things they can see and define them in terms of use. Later they put objects into classes—carrots and potatoes are "vegetables"; roses and daisies are "flowers." The next stage is to classify according to less obvious qualities. As children grow older they learn to see relations and organize their ideas in more comprehensive patterns.

Oral reading

No longer merely a tedious drill, oral reading now takes its place as one of the social activities of the school. Children read orally to give pleasure and entertainment to others. They choose selections that are new and entertaining to their listeners.

Oral reading has many values. The child who reads effectively out loud has learned to pronounce the words correctly, articulate clearly and correctly, and speak loudly enough to be heard by everyone in the audience. He has learned to read in meaningful thought groups, pausing between ideas long enough to be understood. He speaks in a pleasing, natural voice that is alive and expressive, not monotonous, and not pitched too high or too low. He uses emphasis to make the meaning clear. Oral reading has value in teaching children to listen as well as to read. Properly taught, both oral and silent reading are desirable (88, pp. 254-265, 1949).

At some point between the second and fourth grades, children begin to read faster silently than orally. They begin to comprehend content faster than they can speak. Continuing extensively to read out loud after this point may retard their speed in silent reading.

Sentence development

Children's ability to carry on a conversation and to give a connected account of some experience develops in response to their need to express themselves clearly and forcefully. It is difficult to say when a child has learned to use the complex sentence form. The occasional use of a complex sentence does not mean he has acquired this ability; he may be merely repeating a formula or imitating an adult's sentence. By six and a half, gifted children use complex sentences such as, "I'll come when you call," "I don't know how he does it," or "See where it went." Complex sentences introduced by "if" may not be used until a year later.

Physical factors in reading

Ability to see printed words is obviously a prerequisite to reading, especially when children are taught by the "look-and-say" method. Auditory defects influence learning more seriously when the phonetic method is used. Even a small degree of farsightedness, astigmatism, or aniseikonia (a difference in size or shape between the images formed by the two eyes) may cause discomfort and increased difficulty in reading; these conditions may cause a child who is not highly motivated to withdraw from the reading situation.

Personality factors in language development

Word fluency may be related to temperamental as well as to intellectual traits. According to Robinson (108, pp. 114-122, 1946), the seriously retarded readers tended to be aggressive or to withdraw, to feel insecure and apprehensive. They were also subject to a higher-than-average incidence of irritability, negativism, extreme shyness, short attention span, and reluctance to attack new problems. According to a psychoanalytical point of view (108, pp. 133-140, 1946), failure to read may be a neurotic symptom, a dynamically active unconscious suppression of the desire to learn through books.

It is easy to see how a child becomes emotionally upset by failure to read. If the child is given instruction in reading before he is able to succeed, he experiences the stigma of failure. Because reading is a culturally prized accomplishment, his failure may affect his relations with his parents and even with other children. On the other hand, success in reading may have an integrating effect. Extremely high reading achievement, however, is sometimes the result of the child's compensatory effort to meet his parents' expectation.

Children's questions

Children six, seven, and eight often ask why, when their observation runs counter to some general rule which they have begun to formulate for themselves. By thoughtfully answering the child's questions, parents and teachers can help him gain a sense of security in the physical world and at the same time open avenues for further exploration. Interests are built by engaging in activities that lead to further activities.

An observant mother recognized that a parent can go too far in giving verbal explanations. She wrote:

> The effect of too much explanation was to deprive the child of practice in making generalizations for himself. It is difficult to draw the line between too much explanation and too little, but I think it is very important to realize that there *is* a line.

Some questions are basically appeals for reassurance or for a statement of the adult's conviction. Unless the adult knows what he believes, he will find it difficult to give children anything but a "dusty answer." The parent or teacher should encourage the child's quest for truth (58, 1954).

Written compositions

Children begin to write in response to some need to communicate, such as to send a letter to a sick classmate, to write or accept an invitation to a party, or to compose a valentine or some other holiday greeting. Some classes record their group or individual activities daily. Other classes publish a weekly newspaper containing editorials, stories, poems, news, and pictures, which children in other rooms also enjoy reading. One group was interested in writing book reviews, some of which were published in the literary section of the city paper. A third-grade group in New York City received a letter from some children in North Carolina, telling about the raising of cotton. They replied with a letter telling the southern children about New York City.

With skillful teaching, children often express their feelings imaginatively and sometimes poetically. The following verse was written by a third-grade child in the Horace Mann School:

THE DEEP WOOD

It's fun to walk in the big deep woods
And see the trees way above my head.
It's fun to get a glimpse of a small squirrel
In a brownish coat of red.

It's fun to hear the birds singing
Way up in the trees,
And sway and rock so gently
At every passing breeze.

A favorable environment

The most favorable environment for language development has the following characteristics:

A sympathetic pupil-teacher relation and attitude of acceptance in which the child can build self-confidence and security.

Provision of prereading experiences and reading materials simple enough and varied enough to meet all the children's different developmental needs.

A partial "self-selection" policy which grants the child freedom to choose the experiences he wants and needs, plus instruction in the best methods of word recognition and other basic reading skills.

Avoidance of a competitive atmosphere where poor readers feel humiliated.

Small groups in which there is stimulating interaction among pupils and an attitude of encouragement and acceptance by one another.

Opportunity for each child to achieve excellence in some activity, even though he is not able to make much progress in reading or any other phase of the academic work.

Practice in enjoyable oral and silent reading as the child is ready for it.

NUMBERS

Readiness for arithmetic

Before they come to school, children gain some incidental understanding of numbers as they mature mentally. "Size language"—*bigger* or *smaller, heavier* or *lighter, taller* or *shorter, few* or *many*—should be introduced before counting. For young children, *few* means seven or eight objects, while for older children it means four or five (104, 1954). By the time children enter school they can recognize groups of four or five objects. Counting makes possible the recognition of larger groups.

By eleven, according to Piaget, the child has constructed "a natural system of reference, including an understanding of horizontal and vertical lines." Perceptual estimates of apparent size (and not true size) are best at six to seven years; understanding of perspective begins at seven or eight, but does not influence drawings of a child until nine or ten years (102, 1955).

As in the language arts, children bring different degrees of readiness to their first arithmetic lesson. Knowing that readiness can be developed, the teacher will not sit back and wait for it; he will stimulate readiness for reading, arithmetic, and other kinds of learning by providing suitable experiences. The newly revised Achievement Tests for Elementary and High Schools include an arithmetic readiness test that measures ability to recognize quantitative matters (7, 1955). Torgerson and Christiansen have prepared a workbook to develop arithmetic readiness (125, 1950).

Achievement in arithmetic

Hildreth (53, pp. 843-890, 1947) suggested an initial check on the accomplishments of individual children in arithmetic at each grade, beginning with the second grade. The learnings of the second grade should merge into accomplishments at the third-grade level. The class activities still provide experiences and problems in number. Children should be expected to make progress toward a clearer concept of number. They should increase in ability to estimate the approximate answer to a problem and to read material that involves numbers. Greater speed and accuracy in simple computation and problem solving may also be expected.

OTHER ASPECTS OF MENTAL DEVELOPMENT

During the primary period children continue to grow in mental abil ity. Primary children are becoming increasingly capable in distinguishing similarities and differences, as illustrated by the followng comment:

"Many hands make light work," said Phebe's aunt to the children who were helping her shell peas.
"Yes," said seven-year-old Phebe, "but too many cooks spoil the broth."

The revision of the Stanford-Binet scale contains many tests which involve reasoning. At the six-year level it includes a test which involves distinguishing pictorial likenesses and differences, and another which presents the practical problem of finding the shortest path to a given goal. In the scale for the seven-year-old are tests of distinguishing similarities between two things, such as wood and coal or a ship and an automobile (122, pp. 98-99, 1937). Thinking and reasoning are further tested by questions concerning the best thing to do in certain common problem situations. Children eight years of age may be expected to detect simple absurdities and to solve simple everyday problems of living.

By finding and testing solutions to everyday difficulties, children gain practice in thinking. With thoughtful guidance and good examples of logical thinking, children who have a wealth of concrete experience will learn to organize their knowledge and to state their simple, tentative conclusions. These will gradually crystallize into more and more adequate generalizations.

Memory span increases with age. Memory span for words varies greatly with their familiarity, interest, and meaning for the child, and with the context in which they are used. The majority of eight-year-olds can answer five out of six simple questions on a story one paragraph in length and can repeat without errors a sentence of about sixteen syllables after hearing it once.

Memory for movies is high. Eight- and nine-year-old children, tested on their knowledge of movies they had seen, recalled 60 per cent of the content as tested; eleven- and twelve-year-olds recalled 75 per cent; and children fifteen and sixteen years old, 91 per cent. Memory is related to attention span. When engaged in an interesting occupation such as building, six-year-old children were observed to keep at it voluntarily for three-quarters of an hour. More common at this age are attention spans of two to ten minutes. Normal children remember goal-directed, unfinished tasks better than feebleminded children and tend to persist in their activity even when interrupted.

Mental ability and socioeconomic status

Education of parents is positively related to the mental ability of the children, either because of a more stimulating environment or the maturing of hereditary potentialities. In general, children of higher-family social status score significantly superior on both verbal and nonverbal tests of intelligence. Children from poor socioeconomic environments showed relative superiority on tests of counting, handling of money, and sensory discrimination. There is, however, much overlapping in intelligence between different occupational groups; occupational success and selection are only in part determined by intelligence (60, p. 649, 1954). It is also significant that, after three more years of schooling, differences initially found in IQ between upper and lower socioeconomic groups in the second grade no longer existed (38, 1955).

The possibility that intelligence tests now most widely used may not measure the real learning ability of children from the lower socioeconomic groups was examined by Davis in his Inglis Lecture for 1948 (26, 1948). He contended that the present tests are unfair to the economically disadvantaged, whose potential ability is neither recognized nor developed. Insofar as the tests include tasks which require certain educational opportunity or involve words, experiences, and problems that are more familiar to some groups than to others, certain children are bound to be at a disadvantage. Davis and Havighurst (27, 1948) therefore recommended tests constructed on the basis of experiences common to all socioeconomic groups, equally motivating, and phrased in language common in the environment of all groups. On the Davis-Hess Individual Test of Intelligence, for children six to nine, the IQ score advantage of the high-occupational white group was reduced by more than ten points (28, 1949). According to Davis and Hess, this type of test seems to discover individual "children from the lower economic group whose real intellectual potential is not revealed by standard intelligence tests." (28, p. 605, 1949)

In a more extensive study of approximately five thousand children, ages nine and ten, and thirteen and fourteen, Eells, Davis, and others, found test items showing differences in socioeconomic status which could not be accounted for by the cultural bias of their content (36, 1951).

Other factors related to mental ability and development

Social and educational factors may also account for some of the differences in intelligence found between rural and urban groups of children. According to a number of studies, schooling makes a difference. Less clear is the relation between mental performance and health, physical defects and nutrition. Though physical and mental handicaps tend to go together, correction of physical defects or improved nutrition cannot be counted on to raise the IQ. The fond hope that a child will become brighter if his infected tonsils are removed is often not realized. Effects of improved physical conditions are more likely to show up in school achievement than in intelligence test scores. Evidence is lacking on the consistent relation of specific personality factors to intelligence.

The difficulties involved in attempting to control and manipulate all the significant variables in these studies makes it impossible to identify causal relationships. Although studies show that certain qualities tend to go together, it is impossible to be certain (1) which is the cause of the other, (2) whether there is a circular relation between both, or (3) whether both are caused by a third factor. This situation often makes it difficult to know which factors one should change to help an individual child most effectively.

Mental growth may be modified by personality disturbances. It has been reported that children with behavior problems, tested during the latter part of the primary period, tend to lose in intelligence rating after an interval of from five to twelve years. There is some evidence that a gain in intelligence quotient may be associated with improved emotional control and with a more favorable parental attitude.

The intelligence tests tell us little or nothing about the process by which the answers to the questions asked were obtained. To gain this kind of understanding, Piaget analyzed the replies of children in the interview situation to an absurd sentence—"I have three brothers, Paul, Ernest, and myself."

Constancy of the IQ

A child tested at six years of age, under fairly constant environmental conditions, will likely be in the same broad category of intelligence—dull normal, average, or superior—when tested three years later; a school child initially classified as gifted rarely falls to the average or inferior level during adolescence. It is even more improbable that a child accurately classified as dull normal or borderline will rise to a superior classification. This is especially true of classifications based on the Stanford-Binet test. In other words, very low IQ's are more stable or reliable than very high IQ's. This is due to the nature of the intelligence tests themselves, not the abilities involved. Changes that do occur tend to be away from the extremes and toward the intelligence of the parents.

Many factors other than error in the administration of the test may account for differences between several intelligence quotients. The first test may have required no reading ability; the second, high reading proficiency. The first test may have emphasized speed; the second may have allowed unlimited time. Intelligence quotients from two different kinds of tests are not comparable. The child may have been emotionally disturbed in taking one of the tests.

Exceptional mental development

Through observation, teachers can get clues of children's exceptional mental ability or limitations. However, true mental retardation and feeblemindedness are difficult to diagnose. These conditions have sometimes been confused with lack of knowledge, delayed speech, retardation caused by severe illness, brain injury, or other conditions that have prevented learning (8, 1947; 23, Chap. 9, 1955). Psychologists also increasingly recognize the importance of developmental factors, the life situation of the individual, and emotional causation in cases that seem to be mentally deficient.

Owing to the quality of his nervous system, a bright child is able to profit more fully from past experience and to see relationships in a new situation more quickly than a slow-learning child of the same chronological age. For example, some gifted children in a nutrition class gained in one period an understanding of the relation of food to health and growth that was only acquired by the slow-learning group in a semester. As bright children mature, they gain insight more and more rapidly into increasingly difficult situations and reach their goals more rapidly.

Many fallacies regarding the gifted child persist. It is false that children with high IQ's are generally queer, eccentric, or unsocial. It is true that they are sometimes impatient with the immaturity of their age-mates and are often impatient with classwork that is lacking in information or interest for them. Said one first-grader who had learned to read before he entered school: "Take that pusillanimous primer away." Another youngster of the same age remarked, "I find phonics intolerable."

IMAGINATION AND FANTASY

The primary period is generally said to be a time in which fanciful imagination flourishes, and in which fairy tales and myths satisfy a need. However, some studies of children's interests in reading show a preference for stories about children like themselves, animals, adventure, and familiar experiences. Children of these ages are becoming increasingly able to distinguish between reality and fantasy, the while they still enjoy the magical. For the majority of children the most useful kind of imagination is that which helps them to work out plans in their heads, to put themselves in the other fellow's place, and to picture objects not present to the senses. Some of their descriptions are highly imaginative, as the following written by a third-grade child: "This morning when I was pracktishing home sweet home on the piano and when I looked inside it looked like hundreds of little ducks bobbing for fish." (126, p. 19, 1947) Many children spend considerable time in fantasy.

Children's daydreams, reveries, and fantasies appear to fit into their total pattern of thought and action; they are part of the average child's growing up and often give adults leads as to what goes on below the surface. Some fantasies are useful and creative in their influence. For example, children between five and eight may gain a sense of having grown up when they make the transition from Santa as a reality to Santa as a symbol of the loving spirit. For some children daydreams are a path of least resistance, since these require less energy and effort than action. They may become a substitute for reality and a means of easy wish fulfillment. Fantasy may be a safety valve for some children when their desires are blocked in real life. It is therefore important for parents to help children achieve a balance between fantasy and reality.

DREAMS

Age, personality, socioeconomic status, intelligence, health, and the day's experience affect the frequency and content of children's dreams. A review of the literature on children's dreams (31, 1954) showed that (1) children who sleep in bed alone have fewer unpleasant dreams than those who share a bed; (2) children from poorer environments dream more than children from superior environments; (3) the difficulties encountered during the day are frequently overcome and removed in children's dreams; (4) reading exciting books before bedtime affects dreams; (5) the better the health, the more pleasant the dreams; (6) children with IQ's higher than 120 have fewer and less unpleasant dreams than children below 120 IQ. Children five to seven have many fear dreams which seem to be governed by *fear belief*, rather than by *fear experiences*. Aggressiveness in dreams seems to be related to aggressiveness in life; frequent dreamers are usually anxious. Neurotic children have more dreams about death than normal children. Children in industrial and orphan schools often had vivid dreams of home life, visits of parents to the school, presents from home, changes in fortune, deeds of valor, promotion to positions of responsibility.

Not many significant sex differences were reported. Girls had slightly more dreams than boys. They had more dreams of being chased or threatened, more wish-fulfillment dreams of receiving presents, eating, traveling, entertainment, and visits to the country. Boys much more frequently than girls had dreams of bravery and adventure; more fear dreams of animals, burglars, and robbers; more dreams about accidents, falling, bodily injury.

These generalizations are based on limited samplings of children's reports of their dreams, which may be quite inaccurate due to faulty memory, confusion of dreams with reality, or a tendency to repress certain aspects of their dreams.

MORAL AND SPIRITUAL DEVELOPMENT

Moral development

The following stages, not, however, in fixed sequences, have been observed in moral development, beginning with egocentrism, in which the only thought is of oneself:

Sociocentrism—obedience and respect for moral rules and customs.

Social awareness in the form of fear of social disapproval.

Negative reciprocity stemming from fear of disapproval or from a feeling of guilt.

Positive reciprocity stemming from a desire to maintain a good relation with one's friends.

Sense of justice.

Satisfaction in subordinating one's own interests to make others happy.

Moral values of the child

On the basis of their experience and background, children six, seven, and eight years old are developing a conscience, a sense of fair play and honesty, and a sense of values. Values are the organizing core. They largely determine the way in which children use their experiences.

What is naughty to a grownup may not seem at all naughty to the child. The child should be shown that the *act* is undesirable, unkind, or simply not permissible. He can find a more acceptable response. This can be done without instilling feelings of guilt, fear, or anxiety.

Piaget (101, 1948) observed a gradual development of moral ideas in the groups of French children whom he studied. Up to the age of seven or eight they tended to judge an act by its material results. For example, they considered a child who accidentally broke fifteen plates naughtier than one who broke a cup while he was stealing jam. To the younger child any act that runs counter to adult rules is wrong. Later he weighs the practicality of the act before concluding that it is wrong; and still later he calls an act wrong that is unfair to anyone. Although American investigators do not wholly agree with all of Piaget's early conclusions, his method of studying children's responses in an interview situation has produced valuable insights into their thinking and moral judgments.

The child's moral judgments seem to be influenced by his suggestibility and by his egocentricity. Suggestibility, which appears to reach a peak at about seven years, increases the child's tendency to conform to adult rules and wishes. Egocentricity prevents him from feeling with others and seeing things from their point of view. Sensitivity to others' opinions is basic to the development of self-criticism, conscience, or the superego. A child will do the right thing at first because someone whom he wants to please believes in him, or, conversely, depending on the manner in which he has been disciplined, because he fears someone will be displeased with him. As he grows older he wants to know why certain demands are made upon him; then he can internalize the rules that he has previously accepted as outside himself. He will do the right thing because he thinks of himself as a person who does the right thing.

Children observe their parents and teachers. They note the choices they make and absorb the values that lie in back of their choices. On the basis of these values they then make choices of their own. In addition to setting a good example of responsibility, perseverance, self-reliance, co-operation, friendliness, respect for others, honesty, and courage, parents and teachers can take a more active part in this important phase of children's development. When the child is confused by situations in which his willingness to take responsibility is imposed upon or when being generous prevents him from being first, the parent or teacher may help by reinforcing the values he considers important. Whether he wants to or not, the adult conveys in many subtle ways his own values to children.

Moral valuations do not necessarily insure moral behavior. A child may give lip service to the idea of brotherly love but promptly hit a child who is annoying him. As measured by tests of moral knowledge, children do not seem to become less deceitful or selfish as they grow older unless their environment becomes more conducive to honesty and unselfishness.

Spiritual values and ideas

The child's spiritual values likewise develop with experience and with his readiness to sense the unseen world. One group of six- and seven-year-olds in a church school, not yet ready for scientific or theological explanations of the universe, expressed their feeling in the refrain to an original song: "We can but watch and wonder." They drew pictures of natural phenomena that seemed marvelous to them, such as the night sky with its myriads of stars, appleseeds that could produce trees, the coloring of a butterfly's wings. These children preserved the sense of wonder that is often destroyed by premature attempts at explanation.

Children of eight and nine are intensely practical and matter of fact. They want yes and no answers to their questions. They are escaping from childish misunderstandings. They are ceasing to accept the supernatural implicity, and are beginning to question statements about God; they wonder how He can see everything, be everywhere, do everything. Although there may be confusion in the child's mind about the extent of God's power, religious doubts do not usually disturb him. He may, however, have some difficulty in reconciling his earlier ideals with his expanding experience. These children need to realize that there are things that no man knoweth, that there are different ways of being right, and that people may think and feel differently. Each child can be helped to see God in his own way.

Any aspect of life may be a religious experience. The wise teacher listens and enjoys the children's conversation, occasionally highlights a satisfying experience, and goes beyond the child's own interpretation only when the group is ready for it. Children catch ways of thinking and feeling from their daily associates. Every group experience changes to some extent their value system and their social orientation.

During school years the child's religious ideas, based on his early experiences in the family, broaden. He learns about the faithfulness of God and dependability of people by experiencing dependability in his relations and in his daily life. He identifies with persons other than parents. According to Hirschberg (54, 1955), the school child's religious attitudes, although still realistic and concrete, are not so entirely self-centered and egocentric; he becomes more concerned with giving. His religious experience becomes less unique, more impersonal.

To the school child, God is viewed as a Person who can do things for him—as "a very present help in time of trouble." His religion is more practical, more pragmatic; it is a means to an end. His belief in God gives him a sense of belongingness, of security, of close, intimate companionship that can dispel loneliness. A healthy religious development also includes the concept of God as omnipotent and just. A person's religion sets impersonal limits to his behavior and contributes to self-discipline. It helps him to control his impulses, giving reinforcement to his sense of responsibility and helping him to face some difficulties.

Religious education

Modern religious education includes stories in which the child can see himself and gain understanding of some of the doubts and fears he feels but cannot talk about. Many of the activities of today's Sunday school, such as arts and crafts, dramatization, discussion of many topics, deepens the child's understanding of his world, gives him experience of living and learning with other children, makes him more sensitive to others' feelings, and gives him more joy in living. By thinking about their everyday experiences, children may gain insights and feelings that have a religious quality (39, 1954).

SOCIAL DEVELOPMENT

Many changes in a child's personal relations occur in his sixth to ninth years—changes in his relation to parents, to other adults, and to children of his own age. This is "a self-correcting phase of development" of great importance for the child's future social life.

The school is a laboratory for social relations. Participating in co-operative construction and taking turns is learned around seven years of age. Engaging in creative activities together tends to further friendships, emotional adjustment, and, to some extent, academic achievement. The active child in small groups learns to take the initiative. Lasting co-operation often results from pressure outside the group. Home habits of courtesy, helpfulness, co-operation, and personal cleanliness will not automatically carry over into the school situation, although the children best adjusted socially tend to come from a stable home background. "New occasions teach new duties." For many children, school is the first experience in group life outside the home. They now have to learn to live in two worlds.

Social behavior in school situations involves being fairly courteous in everyday school associations, keeping quiet at certain times, taking turns, not laughing or making fun of the mistakes of other children, paying attention when someone else is talking, not getting angry when the good of the group demands an interruption of one's activity, and not taking more than one's share of time and attention. Co-operation in school means obeying the reasonable rules of the school, sharing work with other children on a group project, taking the lead or doing the particular job assigned to one, being in the right place at the right time, and playing fair. Helpfulness in school means doing one's share to keep the school building and grounds clean, and performing faithfully the duties to which one is elected or assigned. Underlying this specific social behavior is an increased social insight or empathy from seven years of age and ability to communicate it verbally.

Stages in social development

Piaget distinguished three stages of social development in the children he studied. In the first stage, which he designates as egocentrism, the individual is impervious to social stimulation from without. In the second stage the child makes an effort to enter into real social communication. In the third stage there is reciprocity and mutual respect between persons. The age sequence of these stages of social development probably varies with different socioeconomic groups and different cultures. There is already a little evidence that children from more privileged homes pass through the earlier stages more quickly than do children from underprivileged homes.

From infancy boys seem to be more restless than girls; they get more enjoyment from playing at being fierce; they court danger more than girls. After the age of six some of this combativeness in boys seems to be converted into building activities. Girls tend to admit their dependence more than boys.

Relations with adults

Six-year-olds desire to get close to adults; they want adult approval of their undertakings; they thrive on genuine, specific praise. Although they are willing to take orders, they have not learned to take criticism, unless they see it as the adult's way of helping them to make progress in something they want to do. Up to seven years, children are likely to mention members of their family as the persons they admire most. Then parents tend to lose prestige. From the age of seven to adolescence a decreasing percentage find their heroes in their own family. The childish faith in the infallibility of parents and other adults suffers a decline. When the father holds a position of low prestige, it may make the child feel insecure and inferior. However, in our culture, eight-year-olds are still dependent on their mothers and express a preference for them. They appeared to like best the parent who satisfies their material wants, plays with them most, and punishes them least. In general, gifts do not make a parent popular.

Some intellectual, brilliant parents are not appreciated by their children until the latter have reached a certain stage of maturity. The genuine goodness and kindliness of other parents are frequently not fully appreciated until after their death or until their children have themselves had experience in parenthood.

Concern about family relations is especially strong in foster or adopted children. If their foster parents do not tell them they are adopted, other persons may hint at it, as in the case of Charles:

One day six-year-old Charles, an adopted child, was down the street playing with his little friend Elaine. He came running to his mother who was on the porch, crying as if someone had hurt him terribly. He said to his mother, "Are you my real mama? My real mama is bad. Are you my real mama?" He kept asking this question over and over. His mother responded by saying, "I am the only mama you know." He said, "Is my daddy my real daddy?" His mother replied, "We are your real mama and daddy." Then he said, "Elaine says you are not my real mama and daddy." The mother replied, "You are always to believe your mama and daddy, do you hear?" He stopped crying and said, "O. K., Mama."

The little boy did not know whom to believe. He kept repeating his question, "Are you my real mama?" for reassurance. The mother did not know how or when to tell him he was an adopted child.

Relations with other children

As children move away from dependence upon adults they enter more fully into the world of children. In young groups there is at first much bossing and domineering, name-calling, even cruelty to the weak or incompetent. Everyone wants to be first. The most enjoyable parties are, according to adult standards, somewhat rowdy—no little ladies and gentlemen are present. Parents are frequently disconcerted by their children's party behavior; they apologize to the hostess.

Children also tend to go through a period of blaming others, giving excuses—"I was going to do it"—sometimes lying and appropriating the property of others. Children six and seven years old are likely to say, "I don't know," to questions about the reasons for their behavior. Through their daily experiences they see for themselves what kinds of behavior bring the most satisfaction. They gradually become more critical of themselves and less critical of others. To avoid being rejected or hurt, or to win recognition, they do the acceptable thing.

As they become more expert in handling their own affairs, they want less adult supervision in their play. With proper guidance they learn to handle their own disputes and make their own rules. They prefer suggestions to authoritarian direction. By the end of the primary period they have gained considerable ability to plan together and carry out their plan of action co-operatively.

Toward the end of the period they acquire best friends. Each child seeks someone whom he especially likes to work or play with; preferences begin early and change from time to time. Even in the kindergarten, sociometric first choices were found to correspond to the children's actual choices in their play groups. Having close friends is a valuable experience which helps children learn to relate themselves to others. There are many varieties of friendship. In many situations children of these ages tend to be cosmopolitan and show very little prejudice toward children of other nationalities, races, and creeds.

The general impression is that bright children are unpopular. However, in heterogeneous classes of children in grades four to seven, Barbe (10, 1954) found that bright children were chosen by the average child in the class far more frequently than were the slow learners. Although the bright children tended to select friends from those above average in intelligence, they chose only 30 per cent from their own IQ group. Some of their friends came from each mental ability level. The slow learners chose friends from the 120-IQ level downward; the below-average tended to select their friends from among children in the high average range—100 to 110.

Stronger differentiation between boys and girls develops during the latter part of this period. In drawing a human figure, children six to eight years old showed a differential treatment of the male and the female (65, 1952). Through vigorous games and sports boys usually have more opportunity than girls to work off their feelings of hostility in socially acceptable ways. More information about the distinctive roles of father and mother helps them to clarify their own appropriate sex role.

Imaginary companions, which seem to be a developmental phenomenon characteristic of children two and a half to four and a half years old, may persist into the school years (118, 1954). About one fifth of the 210 school-age children seen at a guidance service and nursery (3, 1946) were found to have imaginary companions or related imaginative phenomena. Although the adult should not be disturbed by this common experience, it is best not to encourage it too actively and too long.

Children differ greatly in the social perception which is basic to social responsiveness, namely, the ability to respond appropriately to individuals and social situations. Aggressive, nonconforming, excitable children tend to center their attention chiefly on themselves and to show little social responsiveness to other children. Harris (50, 1946) studied this quality in a limited sense by means of a pictorial "guess-who" technique, which was useful in revealing "responsiveness to aspects of behavior which the child could not put into words," and by verbal descriptions, which supplemented the picture test. This study revealed individual differences among kindergarten children in degree and breadth of social responsiveness.

Developing social behavior

Of major importance to the child at this age are group experiences which help him to develop a sense of responsibility for others and to find satisfaction in their success. Practice in learning to relate oneself to others is provided in a school in which the child is free to move about, to consult and assist other children, to solve group problems, and to play a variety of active games—all with the guidance of a teacher who frequently gives his approval to the desirable social behavior she notices and occasionally suggests better ways of acting. Such a school furnishes children the best environment for learning to live happily with others. A classroom atmosphere of security and belongingness built on pupil-teacher and pupil-pupil relationships aids the development of social acceptability. Such development in turn helps to create a favorable climate (116, 1953).

The influence of the teacher in the first three grades is unobtrusive but very great. It has been noted that certain teachers seem to inspire courtesy and friendliness, while other teachers evoke discourtesy and quarrelsomeness. The truth of the old saying, "Pay out a smile and get a smile," is supported by observation in schools here and abroad. Daily association with persons of genuine social sensitivity and skill contributes a great deal to a child's social development. An interesting analogy of the effect of association in the animal world was described by Murphy, Murphy and Newcomb in their *Experimental Social Psychology* (86, 1937). A sparrow, growing up with canaries, modified his hoarse chirp; his voice became soft and musical; he eventually gave a genuine musical trill. When placed among sparrows, the fledgling resumed the sparrow voice. When placed with canaries again, it quickly regained the canary song.

PERSONALITY DEVELOPMENT

A recent study of factors in personality development was based on rating schedules sent to parents of first- and second-grade children. From these ratings Cattell and Coan (22, 1957) analyzed sixteen factors. Among these are intelligence, the lack of which increases the school child's need for affection and security and may drive him to self-assertion or fantasy. On the positive side, the intelligence factor is associated with poise, conscientiousness, and wider interests. Another major factor might be called social responsiveness—or its opposite—and is shown in the outgoing, sociable, frank, self-sufficient behavior of an active child. Closely allied to this factor is the happy, fearless, outgoing disposition and the co-operative, adaptable, complaisant type of disposition, or the opposite. Two other closely related factors Cattell has designated "ego and superego strength." These involve persistence, responsibility, quiet and generally good behavior. Another factor, more self-explanatory, is dominance-vs.-submissiveness. Others involve a continuum of spontaneity, imaginativeness, daydreaming; co-operativeness toward conventional learning; feminine sensitivity at one extreme to masculine toughness at the other; plaintiveness and demandingness; tension; and insecurity from physical handicap. Some of these factors seem to be related to the child's ordinal position in the family, which, in turn, is conditioned by the time elapsing between births, the child-parent relations, and other aspects of the situation (68, 1956).

Although a child's personality is still in the making, its central core and pattern becomes more or less clearly defined. A child is influenced by the labels adults and other children give him—*lazy, dumb, mean, helpful, bright, friendly*. As the child weaves back and forth from dependence to independence, from rebellion to docility, from questioning to credulity, every personal contact to some degree modifies his response potentialities. As his self-concept becomes more mature and stable, the child tends to reject those things that are not in line with this concept of himself.

It is very important for a child to feel that he is an independent, competent person. But the teacher or parent cannot expect him always to be independent; he has lapses. In striving for independence, he may experience loneliness. If he is forced to shoulder too much responsibility too rapidly, as often happens with the oldest child, he may avoid independence. The goal is to foster a realistic balance between independence and dependence. The more secure he feels in his own ability, the better he can meet difficulty, failure, and criticism; the better able he is to focus his attention on his school tasks and his own developmental tasks.

Effect of adults' behavior

The way in which adults act toward the child profoundly affects his personality. Complete or partial rejection by adults frequently evokes these reactions: compulsive dependency, power strivings, detachment, aggression, emotional immaturity, an inordinate preoccupation with sex. Children who were babied or pushed by their parents in the first six grades had many more social difficulties than children who were encouraged to act according to their age and ability. Children from disturbed homes who are constantly working out emotional conflicts with themselves have little energy left for school tasks; they are too preoccupied with problems within themselves. Emotional readiness for school is the most difficult kind of readiness to achieve.

Parents exert a great influence on their children's level of aspiration. Some children aim far too high; they are way up in the clouds; they cannot possibly attain their goals. Other children set their level of aspiration too low; they want to be sure not to fail; they lack incentive to achieve to their capacity. The children whose goals are too high increase their feeling of inferiority with each new failure. The children whose level of aspiration is too low may avoid conflict, but they do not realize their best potentialities.

A CHILD AS THE TEACHER SEES HER

It is difficult to get into a child's world. Even the teacher who lived very closely with eight-year-old Alice in an informal school situation knew little of her inner world, of which the child gave occasional glimpses such as the following:

On one occasion Alice made a picture which showed, at the left, one girl who resembled Alice and two other girls, at the right, whispering to each other. Alice brought this drawing to the teacher and asked anxiously, "What do you think they're doing?: The teacher said, "Are they at a birthday party?" Alice said sadly in a heavy voice, "Can't you see? They're making fun of her."

One day in the baseball game, when she came up to bat, she blinked as the ball was pitched, shied away a little, and struck at the ball weakly. After striking out, she looked around at her teammates anxiously. One said kindly, "That's tough," and she smiled her halfway smile. Another day when she managed to hit the ball, she went to the teacher, eyes shining, and said in an exultant voice, "I hit it, I hit it!"

She had one ability that gave her prestige in the group—her art of telling stories with pictures. She was able to keep the other children enthralled as she unfolded a story cartoon about a party attended by a puppy, a mischievous mouse, a shy little lamb, and a bear who was a teacher. The class declared Alice the best "drawer" and chose her picture illustrating a scene from the class play to appear in the school paper. When her pictures were hung up in the room she smiled in an embarrassed way and shrugged off the praise, so uncertain was she of her ability.

At first she was devoted to one other child—the most popular girl in the room. Alice shyly sought her suggestions, and tried to win her for a friend. Later Alice made tentative friendships with two other girls.

Some of her remarks and the brief observations of mother and child together indicated that she might feel unloved. On the day of the picnic when the children came back late, Alice said, "Oh, goody, if we're late maybe then they [her parents] will worry about me."

Here was a child whose sensitivity and imagination found outlets in her creative work. But underneath she seemed to have a feeling of insecurity, of not being loved or appreciated. In this case the school seemed to be correcting deficiencies in the home and, by giving the child many opportunities to contribute to the group, helped her to attain self-confidence and a sense of belonging.

A DAY WITH SIX-YEAR-OLDS*

The teacher had everything in readiness before the children came into her room. She greeted each child by name and added a personal remark in some cases.

During the free period the children chatted with one another, looked at books on the table, watched the fish in the aquarium, and did room chores.

They came together when the bell rang to tell them it was time to read the Bible and sing the songs they wanted to sing. Then they made their plans for the day and wrote them on the board:

Our Plans for Monday
We want a work time.
We need a clean-up time.
We want to sing.
We must plan our trip to the firehouse.
We want to dance a little.
We must write invitations to the kindergarten.
We want a reading time.
We want to work with our number boxes.

The teacher then helped each individual and each group to get started. In one corner of the room two boys were building a dock for the boats several others were painting. Two were painting scenery for the play which they were going to give for the kindergarten. Others were playing house in the doll corner, and still others were experimenting with a magnet in the science corner. The teacher walked among the children, guiding their learning. When the work period was nearly over the teacher said, "We'll have to stop work in five minutes." When they stopped, they talked over the things they had been doing.

During recess, which was a free-play period, the teacher observed individual children and their social relations. She occasionally made suggestions to bring shy children into a group or to help others develop skills and better methods of getting along with individuals and in groups.

After recess they had their midmorning lunch. When they had finished the teacher held up cards with the children's names on them. As each recognized his name he took his milk bottle to the clean-up committee.

Reading time came next. The teacher had provided suitable experiences for the children in each group—those who were building readiness for reading, those who were reading charts which they had dictated about their experiences, those who were reading preprimers, and those who were matching words to pictures, looking at picture books, making scrapbooks, or putting puzzles together.

After the reading period they went to the playroom and skipped and danced to the rhythms of well-chosen records.

* Adapted from *The Elementary School in Action* (100, pp. 11-16, 1948), Curriculum Office, Philadelphia Public Schools. With permission.

They spent the few minutes remaining before lunch in discussing good eating habits and safety rules.

After lunch they had practical experiences with numbers: telling the time, counting the unused bottles of milk, and so on.

Then they had their singing period, which they enjoyed very much. The afternoon recess out of doors allowed them to have large-muscle activity and a half-hour of fresh air and sunshine.

The rest of the day they spent in planning the play for the kindergarten children. This involved learning to write the invitations. At the end of the day they discussed their accomplishments, contributing their own childish evaluations, and made plans for the next day, taking account of suggestions for improvement.

The modern trend in early childhood education is toward a combination of group experiences and individual work. Rather than having all the children do the same thing at the same time for a considerable part of the day, the modern teacher works more with small groups and guides individuals engaged in different activities.

Questions and Problems

FOR CLASS DISCUSSION OR STUDY GROUPS

1. Observe six- to nine-year-old children engaged in unsupervised play at school, in a public park, or in a play space in the neighborhood. Record the kinds of games and other play activities that take place, the length of time they spend on each, the ones they appear to enjoy most, and the interpersonal relations and interactions in the group. Note also any evidences of sympathetic behavior or of moral judgment, as, for example, in connection with disputes that may arise.

2. In order to study the effect of teachers on children's behavior and attitudes, observe sequences of pupil-teacher behavior—the pupil's act, the teacher's response, the pupil's subsequent reactions.

3. Which physical defects are most common among children in the first three grades of your school? What environmental changes can be made to help prevent, correct, or minimize these defects?

4. Describe experiences which prepare children for reading and arithmetic.

5. Describe the divergent personality trends of several children of the same age whom you know intimately. How do you account for these differences? Test your hypotheses by reading Part Four of Mussen and Conger's *Child Development and Personality*.

6. Work out a method by which a teacher could assess a child's growth in self-understanding.

7. Read Moustakas and Berson's *The Young Child in School* (85, 1956) and analyze the interaction of some of the classroom situations they report. Study Harold E. Jones' review of research on "The Environment and Mental Development" (60, 1954) to arrive at his main conclusions on this still controversial question.

Chapter 14

HOW PRIMARY

CHILDREN LEARN*

If the child's world has been friendly and stimulating he will reach out to new experiences. His earliest attitudes toward learning go to school with him. One is likely to find a preponderance of poor work habits in homes where children have been babied or pressured by parents. School experiences may reinforce or distort happy and successful home experiences or help to neutralize or intensify the effect of unfavorable home conditions. Fortunately at every stage of development there is possibility of correcting earlier warps.

Children like to learn. Normally they come willingly to school. They are happy when they are successful doing worthwhile things suited to their ability and temperament. Too often precious school days are wasted in learning things no one needs to know. In many schools the curriculum is still full of deadwood. Much time is also wasted on explanations and drills that bright children do not need, and on drilling slow-learning children on subject matter and skills that would be more meaningful and easier to learn later on. Boredom often breeds fatigue and dislike of school.

According to Chapter 10, to learn, an individual must want something (be motivated), notice something (receive stimuli from within or without), do something (respond to these stimuli), and get something (satisfaction of some kind).

MOTIVATION OF LEARNING

Motivation is the spark plug of learning. Although, in a sense, all children are motivated, the kinds of motivation involved in school learn-

* Those who want to delve more deeply into the theory of learning should read Ernest R. Hilgard, *Theories of Learning* (2d ed.; New York: Appleton-Century-Crofts, Inc., 1956), 563 pp.; Fred S. Keller, *Learning Reinforcement Theory* (Garden City, N.Y.: Doubleday and Co., 1954), 37 pp.; or other recent references on learning.

302

ing are themselves learned. A motive is identified by the specific kinds of action or goals which it involves. The absence of any apparent motivation to learn certain things has most often brought parents and teachers to their wits' end. As one mother described it:

> Teddy has never suffered from lack of ability to learn, but when he has no desire to learn he is the world's prize exponent of passive resistance. No approach (and I think we have tried all of them at one time or another) arouses a flicker in him, and obviously there are many things which a child must learn whether he wants to or not. . . .
>
> When he wants to learn, he learns quickly and with great determination, but what conditions his wanting to learn is anybody's guess. Letter writing is a good enough example. He has always had a lot of it to do, and judging from the recipients' enthusiasm as well as my own standards, I think he does it very nicely. He has never shown any spontaneous interest in writing, and his marks for composition in school are deplorable. Any achievement on his part is the result of persistence on mine, because I have a bee in my bonnet that good self-expression in writing is an acquirable skill rather than a talent. For years we had some very sorry sessions over the subject. At first he rather enjoyed writing letters, but he was so slap-dash about penmanship and punctuation and orderly sequence of thought, and so completely satisfied with his own efforts, that reluctant as I was to dampen his enthusiasm I couldn't get any improvement without slave-driving. Never at any time did I demand a higher standard than he was capable of attaining with reasonable care, but many were the tears he shed over my inflexibility, and many the times that I lost patience with his carelessness and inattention. But I consistently praised him for effort, pointed out the merits of every letter that was finally sent, and passed on to him any compliments that were made to me on his letters.
>
> The tide suddenly turned two Christmases ago when he was 11, and without the slightest urging he wrote, I think, 17 letters before the New Year, and self-righteously refused my offer to relieve him of the last two or three. He now takes some real pride and satisfaction in his letters. He may need to be reminded that he owes a letter, but he willingly writes it, brings it to me to be corrected, and retires again to copy it out with the necessary improvements. In fact, my reading of them has become almost unnecessary.
>
> So we came out all right in the end, as we usually do with Teddy, but I always have the nagging feeling that we ought to be able to achieve the same results with less turmoil. I don't for a moment imagine that his younger brother will grow up without presenting any problems or difficulties, but I will be very surprised if he ever puzzles us to the extent that Teddy has sometimes done.
>
> At the other end of the scale, Teddy's determination is quite capable of carrying him through some project which appears to me far too difficult for him. For the past four years he has done quite a lot of camping out in the garden, sleeping out and cooking his breakfast over a campfire, and improving his technique all the time. Last year, when he was 11, he decided that he needed a store tent as well as a sleeping tent. Prices being high, we flatly refused to allow him to buy one. Well then, he would make one; could he

have the old canvas cover for the garden swing? It was so derelict that I didn't care if he wasted it or not, so I handed it over, not really believing that anything would come of it. But without either advice or assistance he made paper patterns of his old tent, cut out the new one which required considerable piecing to avoid the holes, and sewed it up by hand, whipping over all the seams to make them strong. He completed it with all the necessary loops and ties and flaps, and then hurtled into town for waterproof paint, and I would have been proud to claim it as my own work. When I saw that the tent wasn't going to prove just another of his grandiose notions, I offered to sew it on the machine, but he would have none of it. He wanted to do it all by himself, and he did. His attitude seems to be, "I'm all *right* if you just let me have my own way."

The ego-drive—the desire to maintain self-esteem—is a strong motive for learning.

A child perceives and responds to a situation in accord with his self-structure, consciously or subconsciously. A healthy person makes the kind of response that gives him the greatest satisfaction in accord with his self-structure at the moment of action. If he perceives a teacher as mean, unfair, or rejecting, he will respond accordingly, even though to others the same teacher may seem kind, just, and understanding. Words, previous reactions, and values, associated with elements in the situation, are cues that condition an individual's responses. Teachers should more often point out to children what to look for (127, p. 19, 1954). Nonreinforcement of incorrect or undesirable responses as well as reinforcement of approved behavior leads to learning.

Individual differences in learning skills, acquiring knowledge, and solving problems result from variation in (1) interest and drive; (2) general and specific mental abilities; (3) methods of learning already acquired; (4) personal relations involved; (5) the trace left by previous experience; and (6) the nature of the task and probable success in it. Consequently, there are marked differences both within a given group, in the rate of learning a given task, and in a particular individual in the learning of different kinds of tasks. The course of learning does not run smooth.

LEARNING ON ALL FRONTS

School-learning is no longer limited to academic achievement. Growth in interests and in attitudes toward learning are as important as growth in knowledge. Learning methods of solving problems is fully as valuable as the facts gained or improvements made in school or community in the process. Children learn words, skills, attitudes, and conduct (127,

1954). The goal of education is desirable ways of acting, thinking, and feeling.

Learning proceeds on all fronts at once. During the stage in which a child is learning to read or do arithmetic he is also learning to play softball and to function successully in the social world of both his peers and adults. Lack of success and consequent recognition in one area may bring about increased effort in another where rewards are more readily obtainable. Parents and teachers should not demand the same rate of learning in all areas at any one time. Yet they should not allow the child to neglect learning certain skills which he will need in later learning. Difficult as it is, the teacher should be aware of the concomitant learnings.

CONDITIONS CONDUCIVE TO LEARNING

There are various conditions under which certain kinds of learning take place most efficiently. Children learn best when they are mature enough and ready to learn; when they feel confident that they can learn; when what they are learning is meaningful to them, i.e., has functional significance to them. Also essential to learning are suitable equipment, materials, and companions, freedom to select and use them, and skillful guidance in learning.

Readiness for learning

The concept of readiness for learning applies to all kinds of learning. The psychological moment for learning, different for each child, depends upon his physical condition, emotional adjustment, interest, and purposes. In some instances it is sound procedure to wait for readiness when skill depends on structure—on whether the mind and body have grown enough to make the learning possible. On the other hand, certain desirable modifications or refinements of structure can be accelerated by practice on more elementary, basic skills. The teacher's task is to develop enough initial readiness so that the child can take the first step successfully.

Self-confidence and self-esteem

A child's learning is influenced by his concept of himself. If he puts no value on himself or thinks of himself as a failure, he meets each learning situation limply; he has no zest for learning. A school child's self-confidence grows with the realization that the group needs him and that he has a place there whether he is good or bad, bright or dull, large or small. A child's sense of adequacy as a person grows as he experiences success in human relations and in suitable tasks. He begins to value himself as teachers call attention to his strong points and as he senses that he is liked and respected by persons important in his life. The teacher who asked a poor reader to help a group with their arithmetic—which he did well—was building the child's self-esteem and increasing his general feeling of adequacy. Success is possible for all when children strive to reach attainable goals that they have set for themselves, and teachers have the know-how to guide learning skillfully.

If a child senses that he has not met his family's expectations or if he fails every day in school, he will soon come to think of himself as a failure. Such a self-concept undermines productive work and play. To a retarded child a remedial teacher may seem just another person who expects him to do better than he can. With the best intentions, parents and teachers often put so much pressure on a child that he feels they are threatening his security. Consequently he resists their efforts. Though a classroom in which competition is rife may stimulate some children to greater effort, it intensifies others' feelings of inferiority. They feel, "What's the use anyway!" Experiments have shown that "threat and anxiety reduced a person's ability to learn, remember, and even to perceive accurately." (112, p. 383, 1949) Reduction in anxiety and better emotional adjustment may result in increased mental efficiency.

Learning how to meet failure when it occurs is also important. Many persons fail despite intelligence, courage, and good intentions. Sooner or later children have to realize that difficulty is a part of life. Sometimes it is necessary to set a more realistic level of aspiration and accept limitations. If a child's parents accept him as he is and as he can become, his ideal self is realizable. There is no need for anxiety evoked by a discrepancy between his level of aspiration and his performance. He does not fear exposure of weakness. Even failure can be used as an opportunity to learn. With increasing experience the child acquires a general expectancy level of probable success or failure and becomes less dependent, and less influenced by the immediate evaluation of others.

Competition creates anxiety through arousing repressed hostility and aggression (25, 1955). "Loss of face" occurs in a competitive situation where success means triumph over another person. The sensitive, less-able learner is harmed most in a competitive climate. To help a child gain satisfaction from the feeling of having done a job well or having solved a problem himself is difficult, but a teacher should be "capable of developing a technique for the non-competitive motivation of pupils." (25, p. 166, 1955)

The ungraded primary school, in which children beyond kindergarten age and below the fourth grade are grouped together in classes where the labels "first grade," "second grade," and "third grade" are eliminated, eliminates points of crisis during the first three years of school. For the less mature child, this form of organization avoids the frustration of failure or the false security of promotion at the end of the year. Instead, the child's progress is continuously measured, and suitable learning experiences are provided for both the slow and the able learners as well as those in between. Pupils who are physically, socially, and emotionally, as well as mentally, mature are permitted to move rapidly through the ungraded primary program; other bright children are given enriched programs.

Meaningful learning

Children learn most efficiently what is meaningful to them. Meaningful learning implies that the children themselves see the sense or purpose for learning a task. Further, it means that what is to be learned fits in with or is closely related to what is already known. It is through previous experience with a certain kind of skill or activity and the reward derived therefrom that the child acquires a motive or drive to further his experience in that area. Hence the idea of motivation has become associated with meaningfulness. Lastly, since primary-school children live in a here-and-now world, their motives tend to be immediate and related to themselves. Consequently, meaningfulness tends to lead to action.

According to this concept of meaningfulness, learning can be aided by helping the child to organize his material and to relate it to what he already knows, and by helping the child to see the immediate usefulness of the task to him. The influence on learning of an organizing principle was demonstrated by a Gestalt psychologist who presented a match trick to several subjects, all of whom fumbled for some time before solving it. As soon as they discovered for themselves or were shown the organizing principle of the puzzle they solved it at once. Moreover, when puzzles involving the same principle were later presented, the subjects solved them quickly and without difficulty.

Sustained attention

Ability to pay attention is, of course, basic to learning. Children learn the habit of sustained attention by persisting at things that interest them greatly. If the schedule is flexible, each child will be able to build, or read, or write as long as the task holds his attention. Thus they become accustomed to longer periods of sustained activity. If a child quickly becomes restless, listless, or apparently fatigued, the teacher will check on his health, home duties, and sleep habits, and on the appropriateness of the school work to his ability and maturity. A child's attention cannot be demanded. It is a by-product of interest and maturity. It acts as a reward, strengthening many kinds of activity.

Varied experiences in learning

Children's experiences should be as broad as their many-sided aspects of development. Nature study contributes to the mental health of the child. Many experiences may be provided out of school, as, for example, bird-watching which is often an April program of Cub Scouts. An awareness of differences in shape, color, songs, and activities of different birds is a good beginning. This quiet observation may lead to other activities— planting sunflowers for the seeds birds like best, setting up a bird bath, or providing ravelings from an old sweater or mitten for nest building. Parents should respond to the child's eager interests in such activities, which may develop into permanent hobbies.

Similarly, the stars of a summer night or the Christmas sky give delight to many children. They love the vast distances in the solar system, the colors and configurations of the stars, the legends about them, the movement of the earth, which is traveling at the rate of some 1,100 miles a minute. In this changing world they gain a sense of security from the steadfastness of the stars.

Nature plays an important part in the life of a small child. Probably the child associates beauty first with nature and natural objects. To little children the out-of-doors is sheer joy. The sun is like enchantment on their faces and bare arms and legs. The rustle of the wind in the trees and the tinkle of a brook delight them. Like Shelley they are comrades of the wind in its "wanderings over heaven." The freedom to run and jump satisfies their natural desire for large-muscle activity. Surely it is good for children to experience these joys and to recollect them later in tranquility. It is more often the teacher than the children who fails to respond to nature and to "miss the many-splendored thing."

In the primary grades, children learn a great deal about the physical world. They can draw a map showing the location of their house or the route to school. They can learn the correct explanation of many natural phenomena and are eager to do so. They are able to formulate simple generalizations and conclusions. They begin to learn about the world of work, and their helpers. In one school, children in the kindergarten not only studied how the milkman, garbage man, mailman, and other workers contributed to their welfare, but also investigated how they could help the garbage man, for example, to do his work more easily. Excursions stimulate quiet children to talk; shy children begin to share in the songs, stories, and projects that often grow out of an excursion. Parents can help children satisfy their scientific curiosity by giving them time and freedom to observe and simple equipment such as a good magnifying glass, a prism, an inexpensive gyroscope, and magnets.

Children find success and security through the arts. Parents can encourage art interest in children by trying it themselves. Holidays offer opportunities for the family to combine love of nature with creative art work. Absorption in a creative activity reduces restlessness and gives children the happiness of actively using their mind and imagination (73, 1954). In the dance they may interpret stories they have read or listened to, ideas gained in social studies or science. Music and drama likewise offer opportunities for individual creativity and a feeling of unity as youngsters participate together.

Practical activities—real jobs that have to be done, routine jobs, or jobs requiring initiative—are another kind of experience children need. Primary children take responsibility for the midmorning milk, for plants and pets in their classroom or at home, for making jelly or jam from fruit they have picked.

School should be a place where children do things that count for something, not a place where they merely follow every whim or conform to imposed requirements which they had no share in making. Children working in a well-conducted activity program can gain as much measurable information as do children working under a more formal, prescribed curriculum and, in addition, tend to show superiority in social and emotional development. In such an environment enough routine is provided and suitable limits are set for children who need them.

Guiding children's learning*

Providing a favorable environment is only the first step. By guiding the child in the use of appropriate experiences and materials, the teacher helps him to discover what he can and cannot do, what he likes and dislikes. Some children do not respond to a rich environment—the opportunities are there but the individual, for some reason, does not use them.

* (19, 1952)

Something seems to be blocking him. Only to the extent that this block is located and removed can he realize his capabilities. This is the task of the astute teacher and skilled guidance specialist.

Guidance in learning involves knowing the individual child, providing suitable materials of instruction as soon as he is ready for them, helping him to see meaning in the work to be done, and giving him just enough help so that he can accomplish his objective in good form. Children's mistakes show how their minds are working. Errors have causes; Laycock (71, 1956) has analyzed and illustrated some of these causes:

1. The child lacks facts and experiences; his thinking goes astray because he lacks the necessary facts with which to think.

2. His facts are embedded in misleading or erroneous associations.

3. He interprets the unfamiliar in the light of the familiar—a gauntlet as "a thin, little person," the President's Cabinet as the place where he kept his collars and ties, or a little black and white animal with a bushy tail as a "nice kitty." [127, p. 20, 1954]

4. He interprets the unfamiliar against a familiar but inappropriate background.

5. He uses facts only in the limited setting in which they were learned, as the child who thinks that the meaning of a passage depends on its position on the page.

The skillful teacher uses errors as a chance to understand and clear up difficulties.

There is no point in letting a child learn everything by trial and error. A little guidance in the learning process helps the child to discover and use the best way out of a frustrating situation. For example, a first-grade child wanted a wagon with which another child was playing. He was about to grab it. But before he did so the teacher said, "You can have more fun playing with the wagon together." In this instance the teacher anticipated the conflict and removed its cause by suggesting a new motivation. Some of the techniques for managing conflicting forces a child will discover for himself; some may be suggested by parent or teacher. By using these techniques of living, the child will discover that he is able to handle everyday situations successfully.

In spite of obstacles, teachers should make a still greater effort to translate three major principles into their daily classroom procedures: look for children's assets and start to build on them, provide for individual needs, and focus attention on what is happening to the children—on *how they* are growing.

MATERIALS AND EQUIPMENT

The school environment should provide enough floor space to allow freedom of movement without interference with others' activity. The desks or chairs should be movable so that they may be arranged in small groups or put to one side in order to give space for dramatization or games. It is essential to have a cupboard, or at least a box or folder for each child's work. "A place for everything" helps to build habits of neatness and orderliness. A workbench in one corner equipped with small-sized standard tools and a supply of boards and nails gives opportunity for woodworking.

Ferns and other growing plants encourage the development of aesthetic appreciation. One teacher kept her two window sills banked with potted plants which blossomed in their season. In the fall chrysanthemums held sway. In the early spring, tulip buds opened and bloomed until Easter vacation.

Tables with attractive books on different subjects and of different degrees of difficulty invite browsing. An aquarium is a source of pleasure to primary children. A few pictures should be hung low on the walls and changed from time to time. Bulletin boards are indispensable. Suitable materials of instruction make effective teaching possible.

A swing, ladders, and ropes comprise the apparatus needed for climbing, swinging, and jumping. A country school may have attractive grounds with trees, flowers, shady places, a brook, and a pond. A playground with strong, simple apparatus, jungle gyms and slides, large blocks, bricks, wheelbarrows, shovels, a big sand pile, individual garden plots, a yard for pets, and a birdbath can be cared for by the children. Where the school equipment is inadequate the home should make a special effort to supplement it. Where the home environment is meager the school should try to supply the deficiencies.

ACQUIRING GRACE AND SKILL IN MOVEMENT

Anyone engaged for the first time in a manual or physical skill is clumsy. He makes unnecessary and awkward movements. "His fingers are all thumbs." With practice he simplifies the pattern of performance. A teacher may help a child by showing him how to assume a correct starting position and by demonstrating successful movements, such as, "Look, this is the way to move the saw," or, "This is the way to get the cut started."

Improvement in motor control, skill, and poise is only one of the values of physical activity. Social, moral, and personal habits—learning to play with others, to take turns, to play fair, to plan a piece of work, to face difficulties, and to stick to a job until it is finished—these and similar habits may be learned through play and constructive activities. In lower-class groups, children's play is more aggressive than in the middle- or upper-class groups. Fighting wins approval in their neighborhood, but not in the school. Through the school games they may learn a different pattern of behavior.

LEARNING TO WRITE

Writing is a complicated skill that must be learned (53, pp. 581-704, 1947). It involves more than muscular co-ordination. The child has to perceive the copy clearly; he must have sufficient motor co-ordination to make the strokes necessary for forming the letters; he must be able to compare his attempt critically with the copy, and to note and correct errors. His writing must, first of all, be legible, and, second, rapid enough to meet life's demands.

Readiness for writing

In teaching primary children to write the teacher should recognize the fact that the children have had widely varying amounts of prewriting experience. Some have scribbled to their hearts' content and, through keen self-criticism and a little help from their parents, have taught themselves to write their names with ease, accuracy, and speed. Others have been shown how to write their names, but have been given little practice in doing so. Still others may already have acquired a dislike or sense of failure in regard to writing as a result of criticism of their early efforts. For the left-handed child writing is more difficult. Accordingly, the teacher should first ascertain a child's present stage of interest and proficiency in writing and begin instruction at that point.

What can the teacher do to help a child learn to write?

When the child has attained sufficient motor co-ordination and intelligence to succeed, the teacher should watch for and encourage any evidences of a desire to write, and take advantage of opportunities for writing as they occur. Natural situations such as the following provide motives for learning to write:

(1) A first-grade child has difficulty in identifying some of his belongings. If he knew how to write his name he could label his things and would always know which are his.

(2) Some third-grade children want to make valentines for their friends. They practice writing the little verse which they have composed and, when they have learned to write it well, copy it on their valentines.

(3) A third-grade class invites a second-grade group to their play, and the second-grade children are eager to reply to this invitation. In such situations the strong incentive results in easier and quicker learning and willingness to practice to improve the writing of certain words and even letters.

The teacher will let the children use the blackboard space freely and provide crayons or pencils large enough to prevent the strain attendant on muscular adjustment to small letters. In one third grade, pen and ink were introduced as a special privilege for the children who had attained a certain standard in writing with pencil. The teacher can also help the child by showing him a natural, comfortable way of sitting and holding the pencil. For right-handed pupils doing the slanted cursive writing, the most natural position is with both forearms resting on the table and the paper placed directly in front at a slant of about 30 degrees to the left. The hand rests on the third and fourth fingers, not on the side, and slides across the page as the letters are being formed. Both hand and arm contribute to the forming of the letters. The pen is held lightly (42, p. 16, 1954). As the child works, the teacher may help him repeat the movements that are bringing success. Experiments have shown that it is of little value to guide the child's hand through the movements. Verbal instruction is usually less effective than a demonstration.

Many schools begin with the printed form of writing, called manuscript writing, which seems easier for beginners and may aid them in learning to read and spell. Freeman (42, 1954) recommended that children change from manuscript to cursive writing in the latter half of the second grade or the first half of the third grade. After it has been learned, cursive writing is more efficient.

Handwriting scales such as the widely used Ayres scale (9, 1917) are useful in helping the child to evaluate his writing. He may compare his own attempts with the models and thus see his progress more clearly. Knowledge of the results of one's efforts is an aid in learning. If he dates samples of his writing and files them away, they will later serve as objective evidence of improvement. Each evidence of progress in the right direction should be reinforced.

What can the parent do to help a child learn to write?

The parent, too, can support the child's desire to learn and give him needed practice by encouraging his spontaneous attempts to communicate in writing. For example: "Mother is writing to Daddy. Jimmie wants to send a message, too." "Mother is very busy. The laundry man will be here any minute. Will Mary please copy the laundry list for her?" Or, "Aunt Susan enjoyed the nut bread Mother served for dinner. She wants the recipe for it. Will Mary copy it for Aunt Susan?" Such real and vital opportunities for writing arise daily in the home.

To have the skill to write something in which he is intensely interested, to see the progress he is making, and to receive praise for it are strong incentives for the improvement of writing ability.

LEARNING TO DRAW

The teacher's part

As in writing, the teacher's part is to encourage the child's interest, provide the needed materials, show how to use them, and call attention to the good points in his method and in his products. One teacher encouraged children to take plenty of time to observe things about them before they began to express with paints and charcoal what they saw. Ideals of art—organization, sincerity, movement, proportion, significant form, and avoidance of trivial details—may gradually grow out of discussions of a variety of pictures: "Why do we like these pictures?" Instruction should come as a supplement to the children's free expression. Using their own work as a starting point, the teacher may help them learn certain techniques and discover certain principles.

A teacher may hold up each child's drawings and make some specific positive comment such as, "James has chosen such lovely colors, hasn't he?" or, "I like this because Jack has said so much in a few simple lines," or, "By repeating the same flower Betty has made a lovely picture," or, "See how the lines in this picture run out from the big bird in the center," or, "This picture has an interesting rhythm of light and dark forms." In this way, by pointing out with approval some specific qualities which every child shows, the teacher can help them all to grow in discrimination and eagerness to improve without discouraging any of them. Children eight or nine who have become discouraged because they cannot represent people and things realistically may be stimulated by the suggestion to draw a happy line, a lazy one, or to express their feelings on a cold winter day.

Art materials

Art work in the primary grades requires crayons, a covered jar for clay, individual boards for modeling, and several wooden easels, about 43 inches high for the kindergarten, 47 inches for the first grade, and 50 inches for the second grade. Large sheets of wrapping paper, newsprint, or bogus paper are thumbtacked on the easels, and tempera watercolors and large paint brushes such as the Japanese watercolor brush are used. If showcard paint (tempera) is too expensive, wall paint in powdered form may be purchased, mixed with water, and kept in little jars with covers. These paints and brushes are excellent for painting scenery for plays. The easels in a primary room are almost always in use.

Considerable interest has been shown in finger painting (14, 1956; 37, 1954; 93, 1954; 114, 1934). The paints are of the consistency of mud and are smeared on the dampened paper with the fingers, palms, or forearms. They do not stain the children's skin or clothing. This kind of painting encourages children to express their feelings, relieves tensions, and has possible diagnostic and therapeutic value in the hands of trained persons.

LEARNING TO READ*

Why children learn to read

It requires effort to associate printed symbols with spoken words that have already gathered meaning. Why bother to put forth this effort? Agnes Repplier did not make the effort until she was ten years old. Before that time she had enjoyed the adventure, information, and fun contained in books by having someone read to her. Consequently, she did not learn to read until her mother perceived what was happening. Then came the edict, harsh and menacing: no one was to read to her. All "the delight that lay between the covers of books" was closed to her. So she went to work, and "not without difficulty" learned to read.

There are a number of reasons why children *do* make this effort:

1. "Everybody's doing it," and children do not like to be different. They have the idea that, when one goes to school, learning to read is the thing to do.
2. It is satisfying to use one's abilities, to attain one's growth potentials. A

---

* For more thorough treatment of reading see Blair, *Diagnostic and Remedial Teaching* (12, 1956); Bond and Tinker, *Reading Difficulties* (13, 1957); Gray, *On Their Own in Reading* (44, 1948); McKim, *Guiding Growth in Reading* (75, 1955); Monroe, *Growing Into Reading* (83, 1951); Strang and Bracken, *Making Better Readers* (120, 1957); and Vernon, *Backwardness in Reading* (130, 1957).

first-grade class had a hilarious time learning a few basic vocabulary words: their names, "run," "hop," "jump," "clap." The teacher printed the name of each child on the board, saying, "This is the way the chalk says 'Billy.' " Working with five children at a time, she wrote the names rapidly on the board and the children, each armed with an eraser, had a merry scramble, each keeping his own name off the blackboard.

  3. Learning to read brings approval and praise.

  4. The need for reading permeates the school program. When a child first comes to school he may be expected to find his locker by recognizing his name above it. On the blackboard the teacher writes the activities the children have planned for the day and the special duties of individuals. On the bulletin board they find notices of importance to them. One third-grade teacher put the following notice on the bulletin board: "Mary's mother has some pictures of the children. If you want one sign your name here." Those children who read the notice and signed their names were given the pictures. Before going to the park to give the squirrels a Thanksgiving party some first-grade children read the following directions:

> Stop. Look. Listen.
> Cross the street at the crossings.
> Walk across the street.
> Do not run across the street.

In an activity program the storekeepers, the editors, and the printers of the class newspaper, the secretaries of clubs and class groups all find that they need to know how to read and write.

These experiences convince children that reading has meaning, use, and purpose for them. They will not merely learn to pronounce printed words without understanding or caring to understand their meaning; they will be more receptive to instruction in reading.

How children learn to read

In beginning reading, children associate printed symbols with familiar spoken words. The relation of oral language to reading may be represented schematically:

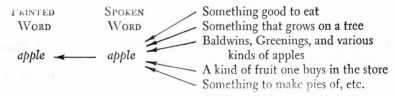

PRINTED   SPOKEN   Something good to eat
 WORD   WORD   Something that grows on a tree
                        Baldwins, Greenings, and various
apple ←——— apple   kinds of apples
                        A kind of fruit one buys in the store
                        Something to make pies of, etc.

If someone shows a child the unfamiliar printed word "apple" and pronounces it, the child's previous experiences with apples become attached to the printed symbol. Thus the printed word acquires meaning for the child. Reading is rooted in many firsthand experiences with things and people, and in practice in telling about these experiences.

The reading process involves seeing and recognizing shapes of letters and their relationships in words, hearing and pronouncing letter sounds correctly, associating the printed letters with the right sound patterns and thus getting the meaning of words through pronouncing them. At first children recognize words by their form—length, general appearance, and distinguishing characteristics. For example, the two tall letters in "ball," the double o in "book," the tail on the first letter of "yet" help the beginner to identify these words. This means that children need practice in seeing similarities and differences. The association between the printed symbol and the sound and meaning of the word is most easily established by showing the child the printed word as it is spoken in meaningful context. He should be taught to check the accuracy of his perception of a new word by asking himself whether it makes sense in the sentence.

By making scrapbooks containing different pictorial illustrations of the same word—as, for example, many kinds of rabbits engaged in various activities—children get the idea that a word is a symbol for a variety of objects and actions. As they encounter new meanings of a familiar word form, the teacher should help them to associate these additional meanings with the already familiar symbol. The older child may keep a record of sentences in which he has found the same word form used with different meanings:

Home, sweet home.
Go *home,* Fido.
He reached the *home* plate just in time.

Methods of teaching reading

In schools where reading is not systematically stimulated and taught in the primary grades, children are often embarrassed by the superior accomplishment of their friends in other schools. Children who have not chosen to learn to read by the end of the third grade begin to feel peculiar or dumb. Or if a child does not read in the second grade, someone says, "What! You can't read yet? What kind of school is that!"

The skillful teacher, as Olson has said, will pace his expectancy of each child in accordance with the child's growth potentials. By watching how the good readers learn—observing both the naturally fast and the naturally slow learners—the teacher gains valuable suggestions for the teaching of reading.

There is no one best method of teaching reading. The method must be appropriate to the child who is taught. Some children need more phonic drill than others. A few seem to learn best by tracing the word with their finger, looking at it and pronouncing it as they do so, and then writing it without looking at the model. This kinesthetic method may be employed when a child has failed to learn by other methods (40, 1943).

In general, a combination of approved methods should give the best results. For example, one group of children were first told a story in such a way as to arouse interest in it. Next the teacher wrote the new words on the board and gave the children a phonetic drill on each one. After they had studied all the new words the children read the selection orally and were drilled on following the lines of print. A similar group of children were allowed to attempt to read very interesting material in order to get meaning and enjoyment from it. Lines, phrases, and finally words were studied individually as the need arose. The first group was able to follow the printed lines better and to pronounce all the words, but was not much interested in what the story was about. The second group was keenly concerned with the content of the reading material, but did not recognize words or follow the lines as well as the first group. Both groups learned specifically what they had been taught.

The look-and-say, or word, method is best for learning words that are irregular or unphonetic. It needs to be complemented by knowledge of the alphabet and of the sounds that make up words. The sentence method is interesting and enjoyable to the child, and convinces him that printed words have meaning. It makes reading a thought-getting process from the beginning.

The so-called "experience reading" method is the most comfortable, happy, and natural way for children to begin to learn to read. The teacher notes some experience which the children have enjoyed—a trip to a flower store, a walk in the autumn woods, a stray kitten that has wandered into the classroom, a pet turtle. He gathers the children around him as in a family group. One tells what has interested him. Others add their ideas. The teacher carefully prints their exact words on the board or on a large chart. Later the children read the story as a whole, and also by phrases and words, to test their comprehension. Almost everyone agrees that experience reading is a good place to begin. In this way children acquire a basic vocabulary and learn to use many clues to word recognition.

After one or two hundred words are learned in this way, the need for phonic instruction becomes evident. The teacher points out the relation of letters and sounds in the words the children have already learned. They note that "chair" and "child" begin with the same initial sound and with the same letters. Later they learn to recognize short vowels and the part they play in words of one syllable, then to recognize long vowels, and finally to study how longer words are built up of (syllables) Along with this instruction in phonics the teacher continues to help them develop other word-recognition skills (44, 1948). The three main methods of learning new words are by context clues, by word-form clues, and by word analysis. Word analysis may be either phonetic or structural—i.e., analysis of roots, prefixes, suffixes, inflectional endings; or of syllables.

In the primary grades the children should begin by reading only words whose meaning they know when they hear them spoken. According to Gray (44, p. 42, 1948), it is too much to expect them to handle three unknowns—the unknown printed symbol, the unknown sound, and the unknown meaning of the word. If they can recognize the spoken word, then they have a check on the accuracy of their attempt to get its meaning.

When, through a combination of methods, children have learned enough words to read in preprimers and primers, they embark on a wide reading program. Their fluency increases as they read all the available material beginning with their present level of reading ability. A table or shelf of interesting, easy books and children's magazines invites children to browse in their leisure time. Other aids in developing reading ability in the first three grades include oral reading in an audience situation, other social situations requiring reading, bulletin boards and posters, and a graphic record kept by each child to show the progress he is making in reaching the reading goals he has set for himself.

The developmental approach brings better results than the pressure method. In fact, attempts to force growth in reading may defeat their own purpose by causing the child to feel inadequate and insecure. At home the child has pressing need of a quiet place to read, out of the range of radio and television sets. *Very Important!*

Testing comprehension

One may test a child's comprehension of vocabulary by asking him to tell the meaning of words in a story or to indicate their meaning by pointing to the corresponding picture. To test his comprehension of what he has read, he may be asked to answer questions about the passage he has read, to follow the directions it contains, to use the information it presents in solving simple problems, or, in other natural ways, to demonstrate his ability to use what he has gained from his reading.

These practical informal ways of appraising children's reading progress through the primary grades may be supplemented by standardized tests. The Pintner-Durost Elementary Test, Scale J, and the Durrell-Sullivan Reading Capacity Test, Primary, Form A, are especially suitable for poor readers in the second grade. Gray's Standardized Oral Reading Paragraphs Test measures oral reading ability. The Gates Primary Reading Tests and the Durrell-Sullivan Reading Achievement Test, Primary, Form A, Test I, Word Meaning, are useful in measuring silent reading in the primary grades.

Reading materials

Beginning reading material should be so interesting that the child will want some more. It should be so simple that he can read a great deal. It should deal with familiar experiences so that he will have many associations with the printed symbol as soon as he has identified it with the spoken word. Beginning reading material should be natural, logical, conversational, and familiar enough in its language pattern so that he will anticipate meanings.

Reading charts, games, picture books, and preprimers lead up to simple stories that children like to read and books giving information that children want. Olson (96, 1947) gave an example of a second-grade teacher who developed a room library of 115 titles, ranging in difficulty from preprimer to fourth grade. She continued with the instruction in reading but gave no assignments. She guided children in their choice of books and played the role of an appreciative audience. The children browsed and sampled. One boy read thirteen books and gained twelve months in reading (the average gain); another read twenty-one books and gained nineteen months; the third, who was generally immature, read four books and made no measurable gain, even in this inviting reading environment. All received commendation for reading up to their capacity.

One of the chief problems in the teaching of reading is to provide a wealth of varied, interesting, graduated reading material. Any experience, such as a blustery day or delight in the first signs of spring, may create a specific readiness for books related to it. When children are still identifying themselves with inanimate objects and animals, they especially enjoy books in which animals talk and act like people. At this stage the *Jungle Books, The Wind in the Willows,* and similar stories make a strong appeal. Later, when their strongest interest is in the practical world about them, they read eagerly books of information and realistic stories about animals, nature, and everyday phenomena. Individual children extract different meanings from the same book; each takes from the book what he needs at the time.

Eaton's booklist for boys and girls (35, 1957) is indeed a treasure house of suggestions. The entire range of children's reading interests is represented—from picture books and easy reading; through animal stories, myths, and folk tales, and narratives of far-off times; to stories about careers, occupations, and heroes of today. Arbuthnot (6, 1957) included in her list of books selections from some of the finest children's books and suggestions for developing reading tastes. At a certain stage in his development a child may show great interest in some one story. Analysis of such a story often shows that it expresses or aids the child in overcoming some conflict.

Why children fail in reading

Even under favorable conditions some children do not realize their reading potentialities. Some bright children fail to make the expected progress in reading and other basic subjects because of physical, emotional, or social difficulties. There are multiple causes of reading difficulty; no one factor appears in all cases. But in almost every case the child is confused and uncertain as to the relationship between the form of printed words, their sounds, and their meanings. He may not recognize the order of letters within the word or connect the visual impression with the sound of the letters or phonetic units. This failure to learn these essential processes may be due to absence from school when the first steps in reading were being taught; to an antagonism between child and teacher; to restlessness and lapses in interest and attention. Visual factors and lack of mental ability should always be considered as possible causes.

Failure in learning to read often causes secondary emotional difficulties harder to overcome than the initial difficulty in the reading process itself. Parents tend to put pressure on the child who is failing; that makes him tense and anxious. The harder he tries, the less successful he is. In some cases, failure to learn to read is an expression of hostility toward parents, teachers, or school in general.

Summary

The modern emphases in beginning reading are on:

1. Providing firsthand prereading experiences.
2. Giving attention to the child's total development and to the correction of physical defects.

3. Providing a wide variety of reading material to meet the needs of every child.

4. Guiding the individual in his choice and use of reading material, in accordance with his own developmental pattern, so that each child will succeed; not keeping him on work he cannot do or on drills he does not need.

5. Giving systematic instruction in reading, using different approaches with different children, and being sensitive to their response to the methods used.

6. Encouraging discussion of experiences and books read.

7. Making reading part of the total language-arts program of experiences in listening, speaking, writing, and reading.

Reading development and personal development through reading go hand in hand from kindergarten through college. And Life.

LEARNING TO SPEAK AND LISTEN

Study of twins has shown considerable retardation of language attributable to the absence of a need for verbal communication. Similar retardation has been noted in children brought up in institutions where the youngsters received little personal attention. Children in the primary grades should have as much opportunity as possible to talk spontaneously. Recordings of the spontaneous conversation (32, 1955) of four children, four, eight, and nine years of age, show the following topics: clubs, club rules, fighting, storytelling, baiting a younger child, sex, and sex organs. In school primary children should have many opportunities to discuss, clarify, and classify their ideas. Accurate, fluent, and correct speech stems from clear thinking.

Choral speaking is a more formal way of developing good habits of speech. Abney and Row (1, 1937) have prepared some choral-speaking arrangements for the lower grades. Rasmussen (107, 1939) and Van Riper and Butler (129, 1955) have given a background and many practical suggestions for teaching speech in the elementary school.

Dramatization of various kinds stimulates language development. Children like to take parts and read the conversation in stories. Role-playing, or the sociodrama, in which children speak as they think the characters they are representing would speak, has value for language development as well as for mental hygiene.

Effective speech is encouraged by an audience situation. A child can readily see the class lose interest when he fails to make his ideas clear. To talk in order to cause other people to like something, do something, or learn something is the strongest motive for effective speaking.

Too little attention has been given to helping children learn to look and listen. With the widespread use of radio, television, and motion pictures, these avenues of learning have become increasingly important. Listening experiences may be set up in the classroom. The children should be helped to state their specific purpose in listening to a record or seeing a film. They may raise questions to which they would like to find answers. After the film has been shown or the record played, they can check on their success in accomplishing their purpose.

Children's records by gifted readers and storytellers are now available to children in the most remote places, as, for example, Mrs. Gudrum Thorne-Thomsen's telling of "The Billy Goats Gruff," Paul Wing's "The Little Engine That Could," Ruth Sawyer's "The Frog," and "Schnitzle, Schnotzle, and Schnootzle," and Mrs. Frances C. Sayers' "Br'er Mud Turtle's Trickery." * In addition to gaining sheer enjoyment from listening to these classic stories, children also grow familiar, unconsciously, with good speech patterns and with the language of books. Shaw (113, 1955) has brought together much useful information on recordings for the elementary school.

The part of the parent or teacher in developing primary children's language ability may be summed up as follows:

1. To increase and enrich the child's vocabulary:
   a. Provide new experiences and talk about them afterwards.
   b. Provide pictures and talk about them informally.
   c. Introduce several new words each week in your own speech, using them frequently and casually in talking with the children.
   d. Use vivid and correct language in talking to children. Do not "talk down" to them.
   e. Enunciate clearly and speak slowly and directly to the child.
   f. Tell stories, rhymes, and jingles, often repeating favorites.
   g. Encourage the child's own reading.
2. To increase the child's ability to speak in an interesting, direct, and forceful way:
   a. Provide opportunities for each child to tell a group something that the group is eager to hear.
   b. Provide opportunities for one child to make explanations to another child.
3. To correct language errors resulting from poor environment or poor teaching:
   a. In certain audience situations tell the child to make believe he is the teacher and to speak as correctly as possible.
   b. Find out which grammatical errors occur most frequently. Provide frequent situations which call for the correct form. Sometimes a child is helped by an explanation of why one form is right and the other wrong:

* American Library Assoc., 50 East Huron Street, Chicago 11, Illinois.

"He ain't" means "He am not." We say "He is," not "He am." "He isn't" would therefore be correct.

4. To correct speech defects in individual cases. The most common of these are lisping or some form of baby talk, and stuttering. Defective speech should not be neglected, for it may grow worse. Its cause may lie in a defect of the speech organs, defective hearing, imitation of speech defects, emotional difficulties, lack of motor control, or a combination of factors. The treatment depends upon the cause, and expert help in diagnosis and therapy should be obtained if possible.

LEARNING TO COMMUNICATE IN WRITING

Any teacher can develop creative writing by children in his class. The method used by one teacher (137, 1947) was as follows: She started by asking the children if they would like to tell a story or write a poem about a little white kitten that had come into the room. This they enjoyed doing. The teacher transcribed what they said, and all the children were interested when their stories and poems were reread to them. Sondra's was perhaps the most poetic:

> From out of the rain and into our room
> Came a little white kitten
> With fur soft as a mitten.

Others were simple narratives.

After a field trip on a beautiful autumn day, the children were encouraged to write about the most interesting thing they had seen. They made a "group poem" from the ideas they had written separately. Then some of the children wanted to write poems of their own. The teacher never read a child's writing to the class unless the child gave his consent.

Later in the year the children came in talking about the circus. The teacher suggested they write their thoughts down. Many of these efforts seemed more alive and had more feeling and rhythm than most of their earlier attempts. Their reading and conversation also helped build their ability to write. More and more children were having fun expressing their ideas in writing. Many wrote Halloween poems and stories. A windy winter day, an ice-covered world, the coming of springtime elicited more imaginative poems. By the end of the school year every child had gained some skill in writing his thoughts with genuine interest and enthusiasm. Language teaching in the primary grades can be an exciting experience for teacher and pupils.

LEARNING ARITHMETIC*

Experience with numbers begins early and comes before computation. School affords numerous opportunities for number experiences. Counting precedes the development of numerical concepts. Taught by traditional methods it does not involve discrimination and generalization. However, there are many real things which children are interested in counting: the number of children who order milk for lunch, the number in different groups, the number of napkins needed for a party, and the like. There are many opportunities for children to comprehend quantities by seeing collections of definite numbers of things: 50 books, 100 pencils, 75 children on the platform, 90 tickets, a pile of 150 apples brought by the children as a Thanksgiving gift, and similar groups of known number. They get concrete experience with fractions when they divide various things into halves, thirds, and fourths, and sometimes into sixths, eighths, tenths, and twelfths. Through buying crackers and milk for a midmorning lunch or a regular noon lunch, counting money contributed for some special purpose, or buying stamps to put on letters written to absent classmates, children get practice in the accurate and meaningful use of money and, incidentally, in number combinations. A child's birthday and special events and holidays furnish opportunities for writing dates and ages. Watching the clock in order to follow the daily program written on the board gives practice in telling time. When cooking, building a playhouse, or being weighed and measured, children learn to use pints, pounds, ounces, inches, and feet. They need practice in constructing numbers in order to gain an understanding of 1's, 10's, 100's, and 1,000's. They need many experiences with two-place numbers. Understanding gained through firsthand experience with numbers pays large dividends later on. It helps children to understand the rational principles underlying computation.

The following quotation taken from Maxim's *A Genius in the Family* (76, pp. 113-121, 1936) illustrates the importance of concrete experience with numbers:

When Florence had been at school long enough to begin arithmetic, something happened and she could not go on. The child appeared unable to

* For more detailed treatment of elementary arithmetic see Brownell and Moser, *Meaningful vs. Mechanical Learning* (16, 1949); Buckingham, *Elementary Arithmetic* (18, 1947); Morton, *Teaching Arithmetic* (84, 1953); National Society for the Study of Education, *The Teaching of Arithmetic* (89, 1951); and Spencer and Brydegaard, *Building Mathematical Concepts in the Elementary School* (117, 1952).

grasp what it was the teacher wanted her to do. Possibly it was the combination of a stupid and unimaginative teacher and an intensely imaginative and high-strung child. . . .

The teacher informed my mother that Florence had exhibited a total inability to understand arithmetic. Manifestly the child was defective mentally.

There was a long conference during which my mother got it across to my indignant father that the trouble had been arithmetic, and if he would take a hand in the matter Florence might be brought out of her difficulty. . . .

After supper he inveigled Florence into some sort of conversation about games and puzzles. . . . Finally he said:

"I say, Florence, you ought to be the kind that enjoys arithmetic. You have such a clear mind that you would be good at it. It's lots of fun when you play it the right way. Do you have arithmetic at your school?"

Florence was not enthusiastic. She indicated that they had arithmetic at her school but she did not like it.

"Oh well, if you don't like it then they are not playing it right. Let me show you how we used to play it when I was a boy down in Maine. Percy, go down to the kitchen and fetch me a handful of beans. . . .

"Now, Florence, I'm going to play arithmetic with Percy first. After you see how we play it I shall play it with you, because I know you would play it better than most people. You are much smarter than most children of your age." . . .

In a short time Florence was insisting upon adding the groups of beans that her father laid out, and the two children were soon shouting out the answers with the greatest enthusiasm.

He led little Florence into adding all sorts of combinations, gradually shifting into subtraction without her realizing it. We played the game all the evening, he being clever enough to keep changing it so that our interest was not allowed to flag. . . .

From that day Florence stood first in her class.

None of us ever found out what happened in Florence's mind to cause this remarkable shift. I think I knew her better than did any one and I have always believed that the clever manipulation by my father straightened out some sort of preconceived notion which had been holding her back.*

It has also been suggested that after six the child tries to shift from very personal attachments to more abstract subjects such as mathematics and science. Boys seem to feel this need for something impersonal more than girls. Consequently they show more enthusiasm for abstractions.

Arithmetic must be taught as a meaningful subject (15, 1945) if it is to function in intelligent living and if it is to be learned most easily. Three groups of meanings are important:

* Hiram Percy Maxim, *A Genius in the Family, Sir Hiram Stevens Maxim Through a Small Son's Eyes* (New York: Harper & Bros., 1936). Page Ref. 113-121. Quoted with the permission of Harper & Bros. and Michael Joseph Ltd.

1. Meanings of whole numbers, common fractions, and other quantitative terms as well as of the number system as a whole.
2. Meanings of the fundamental operations.
3. Meanings of the rationale of computation.

The child who merely follows a mechanical rule of thumb, gets lost easily when the going becomes at all rough. It is much better for him to understand addition, for example, "as a mathematical way of treating numbers when we want an answer to a particular question: 'How many (much) in all?' or 'What is the total?'" He should know that the sum is always larger than the separate numbers, except when zero is added—and understand why this is so. A meaningful method of learning arithmetic is based on insight into the structural relations of numbers.

One of the most significant experiments in learning was reported by Brownell and Moser (16, 1949). The experiment was carried on with approximately 1,400 third-grade children who had not yet had any experience in borrowing in subtraction, but had learned to carry in addition. Specific instructions for teaching were given to all teachers before the experiment began. The effectiveness of the particular meaningful method of teaching borrowing, developed in this experiment, varied with the previous experience of the children and the particular learnings the teacher had in mind as outcomes of his instruction. It was more effective with children who had been taught arithmetic rationally than with children who had been taught mechanically. It seems clear that "systematic attention to understanding pays dividends." (16, p. 158, 1949) In correcting papers it is important for teachers to examine the procedure by which the child arrives at the wrong answer, rather than merely checking the correctness of the answers.

The following are some specific suggestions for teaching arithmetic in the primary grades:

1. First of all, learn about the experiences which each child brings to the grade and begin instruction at that point. If arithmetic problems and processes are introduced before the child has attained sufficient mental maturity and experience, he will perceive arithmetic as a difficult subject with which he feels unable to cope.

2. Teach the fundamental arithmetical concepts and processes in connection with the number situations of everyday life, with problems and purposes of real significance to the child.

3. Introduce new number facts and processes slowly enough so that essential facts will be learned before the next step is taken. Introducing new material too rapidly is also likely to cause children to practice errors and resort to

indirect methods of computation such as counting on the fingers. "Haste makes waste" in learning.

4. When using a new concept, stop for a moment to allow the children to grasp it clearly. Since arithmetic concepts are understood in terms of the operations involved, pause a little longer for the more complicated concepts.

5. Adapt goals, materials, and methods of instruction to individual differences in ability, maturity, and previous experience.

6. Give instruction in what appear to be the most efficient methods of performing specific operations.

7. When difficulties are encountered, help the pupil to locate the causes and to correct them before going ahead. Difficulty in arithmetic is cumulative. The burden of unsolved problems increases as the child goes from grade to grade. An adequate diagnosis (53, pp. 610-647, 1947) would show the specific arithmetical abilities in which the child is weak, the arithmetical processes by which he arrives at a given result, his attitude toward arithmetic, and any physical or emotional factors that may be interfering with his success.

LEARNING TO LIVE WITH OTHERS

The self-concept has social aspects. It develops through social experience and in accordance with the evaluations and expectations of persons around the child and with environmental pressures interacting with the child's personality and temperament. As children come to understand others better, their understanding of themselves increases. They come into conflict because they know little about others' feelings and are not able to perceive what impression they are making. As in other kinds of learning, experience is basic. Only by experiencing the give-and-take of living with other children can an individual learn to relate himself to others. Ojemann (94, 1950) proposed a dynamic approach to human relations which might be introduced into all the subjects that the child studies. Children today are living in a baffling culture, and are moving out into an ever-changing world. They need, especially, understanding of human relations. The public school is a social laboratory for learning to live constructively with others.

Responsibility and concern for others—to understand how others are feeling and to look for and value abilities in other children—has to be learned. The child's desire to be independent is an ally in teaching responsibility; his interests create opportunities for the exercise of responsibility. If his experiences in fulfilling the group obligations he accepts bring satisfaction, he will learn to work co-operatively. However, parents and teachers should not expect the impossible of him (41, 1953). Stories that involve social and moral issues have been used successfully to bring out, through group discussion, various solutions. Having arrived at the best solution themselves, they are more ready to translate it into conduct than if it had been superimposed upon them by adults. One of the teacher's most important tasks is to facilitate favorable interaction in the classroom, through which social learnings take place.

Questions and Problems

1. Help a group of children dramatize a favorite story. Notice how a little costuming and a slight rearrangement of furniture help them to act. How may the giving of a play be used to improve children's reading and writing ability, as well as their conversation?

2. Find concrete examples of how home conditions and relations have affected children's learning in school.

3. Observe teachers who are most successful in helping children to learn. Describe concretely the methods they use and the pupil-teacher relationship. Ask the children how the teacher has helped them learn and why they like him or her.

4. Show how the general principles and conditions conducive to learning can be applied to learning to read, to learning arithmetic, to learning to be friendly.

5. What makes books interesting to children of these ages?

6. Give an illustration of the effect of success or failure in reading on a child's concept of himself. On his relations with his parents, teacher, and classmates.

7. Describe concretely how children in these three grades have solved some of their problems and gained a sense of accomplishment.

8. Compare the research method of studying personality employed by Cattell (21, 1957) with the major experimental studies described in Part Four of Mussen and Conger's *Child Development and Personality*.

Chapter 15

DEVELOPMENTAL PROBLEMS

OF MIDDLE CHILDHOOD

A problem is ordinarily defined as the kind of behavior that fails to meet a minimum standard of social acceptability. From a developmental viewpoint, a problem may be defined as an individual's failure to achieve his best potentialities—potentialities that are also important in a given society.

Teachers and mental hygienists do not agree regarding the relative seriousness of children's problems (119, 1952). In 1950, teachers still regarded problems related to honesty, sex, truancy, and classroom order much the same as teachers did in Wickman's pioneer study in 1926. And, indeed, from the standpoint of classroom management, these are serious problems. But in the more recent study, teachers also recognized more fully the seriousness of unhappiness, depression, unsociability, and withdrawing behavior. This change in attitude is more prevalent in certain parts of the country than in others (56, 1957). Number of years of experience seem to have little relation to teachers' attitudes toward behavior problems, but teachers with more education tend to be closer to the clinicians in their ratings.

THE NATURE OF PROBLEM BEHAVIOR

A "problem child" as seen in school is a frustrated, unhappy child. He may be troubled about many things at home. Some of his worries will spill over into school. For example, one second-grade child who could not concentrate on his reading said he was always thinking of his mother and his little sister, of whom he was very jealous, being together at home. A child often tries to relieve his inner tension by fidgeting, daydreaming, or aggressive behavior. These are the only ways he knows to cope with the situation. Unfortunately such negative behavior evokes punishing responses from others that reinforce the child's maladjustment.

A child's problem behavior should be viewed steadily as part of his development. Problems are inherent in the process of continuous adjustment and readjustment as the child moves from the security of his home to the more impersonal school situation. At school the child's inadequacies become more obvious; his behavior is more subject to social control. Friends become important to him. New standards of conduct are set by the school. These adjustments are not easy. In the trial-and-error stage, efforts to learn may be mistaken for problem behavior. Before worrying about any specific problem it is wise to look at the child's life pattern.

The teacher should not take a child's rudeness personally. He should try to understand the meaning of the behavior to the child. To label a child's behavior is not to understand it. In fact, merely labeling a child as aggressive, lazy, or stubborn, often obscures rather than clarifies his real difficulty. A friendly teacher can help disturbed children to understand their feelings, and to find more acceptable outlets for them. In private conferences, in drawing and painting, or in free-play sessions, children often reveal their emotional disturbances.

When immature behavior continues or reappears in later years, it represents not just a habit but a need. Behavior that might thoughtlessly be classed as a bad habit may represent either the child's essential efforts to grow up or his need to retain or recapture attention and affection which he has lost or fears to lose. If it is the first, it will drop out of the picture when he has achieved his developmental tasks. If it is the second, it will continue until the need is met in some more constructive way.

Problems do not occur singly. For example, Georgie, eight years old and the younger of two brothers, was a persistent feeding problem. His mother continually tried to force him to eat when his desire for food was low. As a result, eating became an emotional situation. He was retarded in speech and reading, and appeared to enjoy the power over adults that he gained from his failure to talk and read like other children. He may also have sensed his older brother's hostility and have been afraid to succeed in school, lest he increase his brother's hostility toward him. He was restless and nervous. He was disobedient. His resistance to authority seemed to stem from a normal desire to be independent, in the face of his mother's attempts to keep him her baby. He was entering a boys' world and needed to play a boy's role, not the quasi-feminine role his mother preferred. This indecision about his role left him unsure of what was right for him to do. At home he resented his mother's attempts to invade his private world. In the testing situation he gave the impression of being an emotionally tense child who did not want to give his private world away. The father was aware of the difference between his two children and said, "Georgie is a conscientious child; he tries to please." His relation with the child seemed to be the most constructive element in the situation. This is only one illustration of the muliple manifestations and multiple causes of problem behavior.

Behavior is caused. This oft-reiterated statement is true, even though, as a father facetiously remarked, it makes no allowance for original sin. A child's behavior at any moment is the result of interrelated factors— physical make-up, physiological state, and environmental conditions, including personal relations.

CONDITIONS GIVING RISE TO PROBLEMS

Many normal problems arise in connection with details of daily routine. Adventurous eight- and nine-year-olds find home and school restrictions irksome. One youngster, brought up according to an inflexible schedule, complained one day, "Well, now I eat, and then I sleep, then I go outdoors, then I eat, then I sleep, then I go outdoors. That's all I do." Adults always seem to be wanting to have *their* way. Many youngsters think of running away. Some do. One mother matter-of-factly told her child that she loved him and wanted him to stay, but that if he wanted to leave she would not interfere. When he decided to unpack his suitcase she resolved to change some of the conditions that were making him unhappy—not to demand her way unless it were necessary, to give him every day some time with her that was all his own, and to let him take responsibilities for which he was ready. A child's life need not be so patterned, so sheltered, that adventures are impossible. Life must first of all be worth living.

A child's behavior is related to his physical condition. This principle is cardinal to the psychosomatic emphasis—the interrelation of mind and body—already mentioned. If the child's physical condition is poor he may become emotionally disturbed; if he is emotionally disturbed, problem behavior increases; even his growth may be retarded. Nutrition studies show that when children are emotionally disturbed, the food they eat goes through the body faster than normally and less of its mineral content is retained for body-building. It is well known that a child's reserves of energy may be depleted by emotional disturbance, and that a nervous breakdown may result from prolonged stress.

More pervasive are the difficulties arising from personal relations in the home. An insecure child may simulate stupidity; then he is not even expected to try. The psychological instability of the parent may be reflected in the child. When home conditions have aroused feelings of anxiety, guilt, or inferiority, the child may try to find relief by withdrawing from the situation, getting angry, or blaming someone else. Or he may suppress the anxiety—try not to think about it at all. Such repression is seldom if ever complete, and the feeling returns to disturb the child. Punishment may only add to the original anxiety. Good adjustment is attained only when the anxiety is faced and understood, and improvement is made either in the conditions which produce the anxiety or in the individual's attitude toward these conditions. Children should gradually learn to adjust to necessary external demands.

Some of the home conditions that may be related to school children's problems were brought out in an extensive study by Rouman (109, 1955). Although there is no one-to-one relation between a certain kind of home condition and a specific behavior, certain problems seem to be associated with three parental factors. The children, especially the youngest, from homes where mothers were employed seemed to lack a cordial relationship with people in general and had a tendency to substitute fantasy for success in real life. Those having stepparents or guardians seemed under the greatest emotional strain and lacked social skills and a sense of personal freedom. The younger children seemed to make the adjustment to stepparents easier than the older children. Those who had no adult male in the family seemed more lacking than the average child in a sense of personal worth, motivation, and standards.

Some children may find in school a stability and consistency which is lacking in their own homes. The good relationship with the teacher and other pupils may have a stabilizing effect on a child who shows evidence of emotional disturbance at home. By gaining strength from his school environment he may be able to exert sufficient control to adapt to the school situation, to overcome personality faults, and to make academic progress (103, 1952).

Certain school conditions create problems. In many schools, standards of achievement are one or two years higher than the learning ability of the majority of the children. This leads to failure. Failure in schoolwork frequently leads to truancy, hostility, aggressive behavior, daydreaming, inattention, apathy, and other problems. If the child cannot achieve success in socially approved ways, he seeks a false kind of superiority in misbehavior. When maladjusted children were transferred from a rigid classroom to one in which the teacher adapted instruction to individual needs, provided realistic projects, and gave little formal instruction, they made large gains in achievement and were less frequently absent and ill.

To many children their teachers are a problem. Teachers often come from home backgrounds quite different from those of their pupils. This difference in values, standards, and interests makes it difficult for them to understand their pupils. It also makes it difficult for their pupils to act in socially approved ways—behavior that is approved at home may be criticized at school by the teacher and by other children.

Conditions of modern life also make children's adjustment difficult. In cities the rapid tempo of life, difficult enough for adults, is still more difficult for children, who should not be hurried in their growing. The conflict between property rights and the child's needs is often acute. Neighbors complain that children play noisily, roller-skate on the sidewalks, and cry at night. Older children are expected to meet high standards of achievement and social competence, and to be continuously on the go, regardless of their individual temperament. To change some of the unfavorable conditions outside the home is a task requiring action by groups of parents in a city block or school district.

War breeds behavior problems in children, even in countries remote from actual fighting. War creates many conditions detrimental to child development. These conditions affect children differently. The same conditions may arouse anxiety in a six-year-old or stimulate an adolescent to become more mature and responsible. Boys are affected differently than girls by war conditions.

The culture itself may create or bring to the surface certain kinds of behavior problems in children. Adult ways are early reflected in children's behavior. Adults often reward or punish children's behavior according to whether it is acceptable in the social environment in which they grew up. Individuals who deviate from the cultural norms are viewed as unfortunates who cannot conform, victims of a sick society, or rebels resisting the voice of experience. In the United States there is no unitary culture. Many different folkways and mores prevail. Children are often caught in the clashes of cultures. They struggle to conform to the divergent, rapidly changing culture of their parents, their peers, their gangs, and their teachers.

Lack of suitable play outlets is another condition related to the prevalence of behavior problems. Channeling destructive aggression in constructive ways is an important developmental task of school children. Much of their aggressive impulse comes out in play. But aggression can go too far. When children begin to realize this they are concerned with its control. A reasonable degree of self-control gives them a sense of security. Under various conditions children may handle aggressive impulses in several ways: (1) they may repress their feelings of affection toward everyone—they are afraid to become intimate with anyone; (2) they may work off their aggressive impulses in physical activity and constructive or creative work or play instead of hurting people or destroying property; (3) they may express their aggression in an interview or in play therapy instead of directing it inwardly against themselves.

TRANSFORMING PROBLEM BEHAVIOR
INTO DESIRABLE DEVELOPMENTAL SEQUENCES

Changes in interpersonal relations are often necessary to help the child move ahead on the path of his best development. Giving him a daily fifteen minutes that are all his own with an adult who means much in his life may start a cycle of beneficial responses. His anxieties and fears will be relieved by the opportunity to talk about them freely in an accepting atmosphere. If his problem is a symptom of his underlying feeling of inadequacy in an environment which has more strain and pressure than he can handle, the obvious thing to do is to modify the sources of stress. As he gains confidence, he should be encouraged to set realistic goals for himself and to work out the steps by which they may be reached. To merely treat symptoms is likely to result in a shift to another kind of problem or, at best, a *temporary* change in behavior.

In the treatment of emotionally disturbed children the whole family is involved. Ideally they should move forward together toward a better adjustment. The case of the Smith family illustrates this family-centered approach:

The father wanted his seven-year-old boy to compare favorably with other children—to be a credit to him. He was much more concerned about the child's achievement than about the child as a person. Despite evidence to the contrary, the father believed that the child was of normal intelligence and that his abilities had not been developed. It was clear that the father had a strong need to have a child of whom he could be proud. He could not accept the fact that his child was below average.

The mother was a beautiful woman whose whole existence centered in her children; she was apathic until they were mentioned. She had had many difficult adjustments to make. When she married she had to accept a complete change in status and social relations. As a young girl she had had many friends and social activities. After marriage her husband forced her to move in a restricted social world. One by one she lost her friends. Her feeling of inadequacy and unworthiness mounted. Her husband dominated her much as she had been dominated by her mother as a child; she had no part in making decisions—for example, about the religious education of her children. She was embarrassed by having a child who was so inferior in behavior and appearance, and, like many parents of subnormal children, felt that she was in some way to blame.

The child had little power of attention; his diffuse behavior was observed in the play interviews. He showed facial tics when he was in situations that evoked uncertainty or fear. A thorough neurological examination was inconclusive.

All three members of the family were treated at a guidance clinic; each had a different worker. Little progress was made with the father, although in the two interviews he seemed to comprehend that his pressure on the child was defeating its purpose. The mother, in a series of interviews, began to talk about things she could do. The worker's warmth of feeling, his attitude of sympathetic understanding, and his recognition of the mother's inner resources did much to rebuild her self-esteem and confidence. She also clarified her role as a woman and as a mother, and gained some understanding of her husband's need to dominate and have children who would be a credit to him. As time went on the mother began to feel less guilty about the child and to avoid out-and-out quarrels with her husband.

With the child, the worker used play techniques, responding to the feelings the child expressed in his play activities. For example, when the child expressed a positive feeling about something he could do, the worker said, "Yes, there's lots of things you can do." The worker also helped him to face reality. The child's successful adjustment depended a great deal on the changed attitude of his parents toward him and on their acceptance of him as he *could* become.

The strong features of this case were the closely synchronized work with three members of the family; the genuine warm relation of the workers with the clients; and the understanding which the parents gained of the interaction in the family, of their difficulty in accepting their child's subnormal behavior, and of the detrimental effect of their initial attitudes toward the child.

By early treatment we may be able to minimize emotional difficulties in later life. Children who are likely to develop mental disorders give early indications of their need for a less demanding environment, less strain and stress. If they receive special consideration and understanding, they may not become seriously maladjusted. It is often possible to give a child the feeling that he is liked and accepted as a person, and at the same time to suggest more acceptable action on his part.

There are problems about which teachers can do little: disturbances caused by organic diseases, by constitutional differences that result in behavior problems, by severe parental rejection, and by deprivation in the opportunity to grow up, as well as psychoses and severe neuroses.

When a teacher is unsuccessful in working with a child, he should not become bitter or discouraged, but focus his attention on the positive growth aspects rather than on the persisting problems.

ABSENCE AND TARDINESS

Absence and tardiness are usually signs of maladjustment; they are essentially guidance problems. The whole school program may be involved. Children go willingly to school if its curriculum and methods of instruction are suited to their abilities, interests, and needs. They want to stay away from school if their needs are not being met and they are unable to succeed. In one school in which children had pleasant and successful experiences, even those with IQ's below 90—who are usually frequently truant —came regularly to school.

Causes of absence

Absences from school often reflect the condition of the child's health. The causes for children's absences were reported in one study (79, 1950) as follows:

	Per Cent
Respiratory disease	46
Other communicable diseases	13
Digestive disturbances	6
Skin conditions	5
Injuries	3
Other medical causes	14
Nonmedical causes	13

The highest rate of absence is among five- and six-year-olds, who are absent, on the average, more than one in every ten days (79, 1950).

Parents can reduce absence because of communicable diseases by detecting the first signs—sore throat, sneezing, running eyes and nose, flushed face, cough—and keeping the child home from school. If he does come to school, the teacher should either send him home or, if the parents are at work, to a neighbor's house, or to an isolation room in school—or at least keep him six feet away from other children. Absence has been reduced when both children and teachers with colds stay at home.

Health-teaching improves attendance by reducing illness. There are many occasions for teaching healthful living: a child returns after being quarantined with a communicable disease; another has had to have a tooth pulled; still another has brought an outstandingly good lunch. If their own experiences are thus pointed up, children learn, for example, how highly contagious colds are during their early stages and that a cold "which puts one person slightly under the weather can make another very ill." (79, p. 12, 1950)

Absence is also the result of other causes. Some parents keep children out of school to work in factories, on farms, or in the home. On another social level, children are over-coddled and not permitted to leave their homes because the weather is cold or rainy. A strong emotional attachment to his mother or severe anxiety about home conditions sometimes makes a child unwilling to go to school. Occasionally absence is due to forces which neither child nor parent can control, such as a railroad tie-up, impassable roads, and quarantine.

Causes and remedies of tardiness

The most frequent causes of tardiness among primary children are an undeveloped sense of time, other interests greater than interest in school, late hours the night before, poorly planned morning schedule, home duties, failure of parents to co-operate in helping the little child get to school on time, forgetting something and having to go back for it, dislike of school, and satisfaction in the attention attracted by late entrance.

Following are some specific ways in which the above conditions can be changed:

1. Develop the child's time sense by asking him, for example, to "See how much you can read in five minutes."
2. Make school more interesting than the things that cause delay. One teacher of retarded children noticed that they were always on time on the morning when they went to assembly with the other children, while they were frequently tardy on mornings which began with their regular class periods. Scheduling a story, a game, a class program, or a favorite subject for the first period in the morning will furnish a stimulus to come early.
3. One requisite for getting up early in the morning is to go to bed early the night before. This is the first step in starting the new day right.
4. Even first-grade children can participate in a well-planned morning schedule which allows time enough for everything. The teacher may help by having them dramatize "what to do in the morning before school." A cardboard clock may be used to point out the hours, and the details of bathing, dressing, eating, collecting books and wraps, starting for school, walking or riding to school, and entering the classroom at the appointed time may be worked out and made vivid by dramatization.
5. If the child has chores to do at home which make him late, some arrangement should be made with the parent. In exceptional cases some adjustment may be made by the school.

Teacher, parent, and child should all work together on these problems.

Attendance and promptness have sometimes been emphasized out of proportion to their significance in the child's development. They are causes of much irritation and, in some school systems, loss of financial support. As indications of underlying problems of adjustment, however, they have guidance value.

PROBLEMS OF EXCEPTIONAL CHILDREN

The physically and mentally handicapped

Children who are physically or mentally limited are greatly in need of being understood and often have special problems of adjustment. They are often subjected to situations too difficult for them. The special leniency and attention they receive because of their handicap is often diminished as they grow older, and sometimes discontinued altogether when a baby arrives. They may interpret this decrease in consideration as a sign of rejection. The great need is to break the pattern of rejection→misbehavior→more rejection→a vicious cycle.

Children are strongly affected by people's attitudes toward them. Whether physically perfect or deformed, healthy or sickly, well-spoken or incoherent, whether their IQ is 50 or 70 or 150, exceptional children have the same basic needs for affection, acceptance, and approval as do other children. They can be comfortable and secure only when they know they are wanted and loved; they are uneasy and crushed when they experience, or think they experience, rejecting coldness. This lack of social acceptance resulting from their physical, intellectual, or emotional limitations is often more difficult to cope with than the original handicap (59, 1950).

Parents take various attitudes toward their handicapped children. Some parents are able to accept their handicapped child as he is. They do not blame themselves or him for his disability (111, 1950). They expect only the best of which he is capable. They get satisfaction from the progress he has made, directing their attention to his abilities and gains rather than to his disabilities and the slowness of his development. Moreover, they do not neglect their other children in order to spend a disproportionate amount of time and money on the handicapped child.

Other parents recognize, but refuse to accept, the handicap. They ascribe the child's slowness or defectiveness to stubbornness or laziness, or to some physical condition that can be remedied by operation, thyroid extract, or other medical means. They employ tutors and remedial teachers to speed up his development instead of permitting the child to develop at his own best rate. Even the parent who does all the acceptable things for his child without really loving him usually has a severe problem with the child. Such a parent may subconsciously reject the child, feel guilty, and attempt to reduce the guilt by smothering the child with affection.

Still other parents are unable to face the fact that they have a handicapped child. They insist that nothing is wrong with him. They seize upon every slight indication of progress as evidence that the child is normal.

These attitudes are so deeply rooted in the personality of the parents that one can do little for the child without, at the same time, working with the parents. In the presence of an experienced and sympathetic listener, parents feel free to reveal and discuss their real feelings. Gradually they gain a new orientation toward family relations and appreciate the place of the exceptional child in the family structure. Kirk, Karnes, and Kirk (64, 1955) have written a sound, practical guide for the parents of a retarded child.

Slow-learning pupils, and all children in fact, use their mental abilities to best advantage when:

Their limitations have been recognized and their needs met early in life to prevent their having a thoroughly unsatisfactory elementary-school educational experience.

The schoolwork is concrete, closely related to their experience, and organized around life problems. A core curriculum of common learnings can be adapted to different levels of ability.

Classes are small enough so that the teacher can give the children individual attention and guidance and the work is adjusted to realistic educational expectancies.

All avenues of learning are used—visual aids, field trips, records that can be played over and over, and appropriate printed material.

The children have an opportunity to work with their hands.

They have an opportunity to work together co-operatively.

Marks and other artificial rewards are not emphasized, but each task is useful and interesting in itself.

Special education includes much more than education in special classes. According to Newland (92, 1956), about 85 per cent of our exceptional children are in regular classes. Specialists, if available, will help teachers to identify the exceptional children, to understand their special needs, to provide experiences they need, and to participate in case conferences on individual children. Teachers of these handicapped children in the regular classroom try to acquire an attitude of acceptance rather than of rejection or overprotection, to adjust their expectations and standards to the child's capacity, and to recognize the special abilities that these children often possess.

For the partially-sighted children in the regular classroom the teacher should be acquainted with the many kinds of materials, equipment, and mechanical aids now available: large-type text and reference material, the large-type typewriter, sound recordings, and special magnification and lighting equipment. Administrators and school boards should provide adequate facilities. Even the blind child may be educated in the public school with sighted children. Being with normally-sighted children he learns to adjust to the situation he will have to face later in life. Moreover, the regular class may furnish a more varied, meaningful, and stimulating environment than a group in which the blind are segregated.

Children with hearing loss are about six times as numerous as the visually handicapped. Fortunately, great advances have been made in developing and improving hearing aids (92, pp. 73-74, 1956). The teacher makes an important contribution in the identification of children with hearing loss and in making adjustments for them in the classroom situations.

Concerted action is necessary. In the case of Carl, a seriously handicapped boy in the third grade—diagnosed at the Mental Health Center as "chronic brain syndrome associated with circulatory disturbances; cerebral palsy; conduct disturbance"—marked improvement was noted in his behavior following a case conference with the principal, Carl's teacher, and the school nurse, who had been working closely with the clinic and with Carl. The teacher found ways of giving Carl recognition, broke up the activities into smaller units, allowed him to eat part of his lunch at recess time when he was hungry, and was quick to praise improvement in his behavior. She also talked with Carl's sister, who was taking care of him, and made arrangements for the correction of a visual defect and for surgery during the summer which would make it possible for him to use his right leg like other boys. One of the children in the class invited him to her birthday party and others became friendly and accepting as his disruptive behavior decreased.

Although recognizable differences have been found between certain groups of handicapped children, as, for example, between brain-injured mentally retarded children and those showing no evidence of organic damage (43, 1957), no type of handicapped children can be treated as a homogeneous group, because of great individual differences in problems and in other respects.

Gifted children

Behavior problems among gifted children in the elementary school are surprisingly numerous. Some of them arise from the schools' failure or unwillingness to recognize these children's readiness for achievement beyond the typical grade standards and offer suitable outlets for their energy and initiative. In other cases, home and family relations are the primary cause of maladjustment. Some parents exploit their children's cleverness; they put undue pressure on their gifted children. Others are possessive and overprotective; still others repress the child because he makes them feel inferior.

Dorothy, for example, a little second-grader aged seven, was becoming restless, irritable, and difficult to get along with at home. This behavior had begun when she entered school. Her IQ was reported to be 150. A retest revealed an unevenness of response and a poor performance on memory items, which suggested that she may have been coached on the test. Her parents proudly related examples of her precocity. Perhaps she sensed she was not receiving warm and genuine affection from her parents and sought to win their admiration and approval through her intellectual feats. Her underlying resentment of her parents' exploitation was manifested in her behavior toward her mother, whom she exasperated and humiliated in many ways. The parents felt that the fault was entirely in the school, which had refused to let her skip a grade. So firmly established were their attitudes that it was extremely difficult for them to see that their behavior and feelings about the child had anything to do with her behavior.

Gifted children seem to be able to solve their personality problems more easily than children of lower intelligence (123, 1945). The disciplinary problems referred to one clinic were, with some guidance, resolved largely through the energy and initiative of the children themselves. Helping gifted children to develop their potentialities is the best way of preventing problem behavior.

The gifted child should have the opportunity to learn as fast and as much as he wants to, at any stage of his development. Experiments have shown that gifted children placed in a special class for part of the day seemed to show initiative, leadership qualities, and a many-sided approach to problems more often than equally gifted children who remained in the usual classroom situation. Their enthusiasm is in marked contrast to the boredom and daydreaming of children in the usual classroom. Gifted children in ordinary schools usually achieve less in relation to their ability than do less gifted children. This is because the school environment fails to provide them with the opportunity and challenge to use their potentialities.

Three types of special program have been tried: enrichment, acceleration, and grouping. Acceleration enables the gifted child to complete his basic education in fewer years. The time saved can be devoted to his long university education and consequently makes more of his productive years available to society. However, unless he is physically and emotionally mature, he may not attain his optimum social and emotional development. Grouping has been beneficial when the teacher recognizes individual differences and provides the experiences which these children need for their all-round development. On the other hand, if the children are in a special school or a special class for the entire school day, they do not have contacts with a wide range of abilities and interests such as they will have to deal with later in life. Enrichment provides special opportunities for intellectual and social experiences within the framework of a group having a wide range of interests, abilities, and backgrounds. It has the advantage of meeting individual needs for depth and breadth of knowledge, for social relations through field trips and committee work, and for emotional satisfactions such as contributing to the welfare of the group. Its chief limitation lies in the difficulty of providing sufficiently varied instructional facilities and teachers who are versatile, brilliant, and energetic enough to meet such diverse individual needs and interests.

A variation of the enrichment-type of program provides for a home-room in which all the pupils meet for music, art, shop, physical education, and varied projects requiring a wide range of abilities. In addition, special classes are provided for the gifted and the retarded. For example, there would be an advanced class in writing or a special science laboratory for the gifted. A consultant is employed who teaches some of these classes and works with teachers of gifted children in regular classes. This modified enrichment-type with adequate provision for meeting the needs of individual children seems to be the most effective kind of program. Acceleration of one year in the elementary school is also recommended on an individual basis for certain children. The most serious problem of the gifted is underachievement in whatever line of socially useful endeavor they have exceptional ability.

DISCIPLINE

Effective living requires "discipline in behavior, discipline in listening, discipline in working." (135, p. 19, 1953) Discipline refers to the process whereby socially approved controls for behavior are learned and become self-imposed.

Primary children are not naturally naughty. Probably in no other age period do children co-operate so willingly with adults if conditions are favorable—if the basic needs of childhood are satisfied in legitimate ways. They should have freedom of choice whenever possible. They should have a part in making the few sensible and reasonable rules of the home and classroom. If they understand why these rules are necessary, they will usually obey them willingly.

Discipline in the home and classroom should "accentuate the positive." A search through more than a thousand biographies (124, p. 140, 1935) revealed that rewards, in retrospect at least, were considered to be almost universally beneficial, whereas punishment appeared to do harm twice as often as good. In certain homes and schools the ratio of sincere and individualized approval to blame has been increased with excellent results; it might advantageously be as high as fifty to one. Children who have a high ratio of positive to negative experiences tend to be co-operative, pleasant, enthusiastic. Children who have a low ratio of positive to negative experiences tend to be mean, disturbing, and to show other behavior problems.

Discipline need not be punishment. In its best sense, discipline directs the child's energies and impulses into constructive channels and helps him to become self-directing. It may be used to protect the child from harm, to help him correct personality faults, and to sustain a love relationship. It can be a positive part of a child's life (135, p. 30, 1953).

Parents and teachers use a variety of good and bad ways of helping children to learn the give-and-take of group life and to gain inner control appropriate to their age. The completely uninhibited child is a socially handicapped child. If an adult says to a child, "Aren't you ashamed to feel that way?" the child will then not dare to express his real feelings. If, however, the adult gives the child opportunity to talk out his feelings, he will understand them better and have less need to express them in destructive behavior.

Too frequently adults consider the punishment successful only if the child stops doing the thing for which he was punished. They say that their method of discipline "gets results." But a deeper understanding of the dynamics of child behavior shows the failure of a punitive attitude. The "results" may be a shifting to a still more undesirable kind of behavior. In addition, the child's self-confidence and self-concept may be damaged; he may feel a pervasive sense of helplessness in a hostile world. The relation of mutual confidence and trust between child and adult may be distorted or destroyed; feelings of guilt or anxiety aroused; and resentment or anger directed at the person who punished and even at the school or society as a whole. If the child feels that the punishment was unjust because he is innocent of the wrongdoing, or could not help it, or did not mean to do it, his sense of justice may be distorted. Severe punishment tends to produce apathetic children who stand around doing nothing, or aggressive children who damage things and hurt people.

The ineffectiveness of corporal punishment has been repeatedly demonstrated. The punishing parent or teacher "frequently forgets that he loves his child; he forgets it because something in the child's behavior has made him forget that the child loves him." (135, p. 31, 1953) Of the problem cases described by one hundred teachers, not one was improved by whipping. School social workers frequently report that a child's emotional difficulties are aggravated by beatings at home. Delinquents have been spanked more often than nondelinquents. Many parents have said, "The more I whip him the worse he gets." Punishment may be used to check or inhibit certain responses or to instigate behavior. It is difficult to know what kind of behavior is being reinforced by punishment. Sometimes punishment motivates through fear and anxiety. In a few cases a seriously disturbed child may have a neurotic need to be punished; then he persists in the disapproved behavior in order to be punished.

The *kind* of punishment, however, is not so important as the child's total attitude and relations. For example, deprivation of some privilege may serve as a spur to a secure child, but with an unloved child it may only intensify the need that gave rise to the disapproved behavior. A child may interpret the ignoring of his behavior in various ways: He may consider it as punishment, as failure to reward him, as approval, as indifference, or as lack of affection.

The psychology and philosophy of punishment are far in advance of practice. Schools still make extensive use of such artificial and extrinsic rewards as prizes and honor rolls and of such punishments as detention, extra work, threats, restitution, isolation, and sarcasm. Teachers still focus their attention too often on deviations rather than on development and on remedial rather than on preventive work.

There is no quick and easy way of helping children correct personality warps. To sustain motivation toward distant goals, the environment should offer some present satisfactions. The wholesome personality grows slowly but surely in an understanding and loving environment. Bad habits may persist even after a good relation has been established. But in time the child learns that he can find outlets that are acceptable to himself and to others.

EMOTIONALLY DISTURBED CHILDREN

Some persons are nervous when they have to speak before an audience. They feel inadequate to the situation. Some persons are nervous about undertaking a new piece of work. They fear they may not be able to succeed in it. Nervousness usually accompanies a feeling that one is unable to meet the situations life offers.

Behavior of emotionally disturbed children

Emotionally disturbed children often overreact to failure and difficulty; they take things hard. If they have suffered from failure, they approach new problems with anxiety. They are afraid they will not pass the test or win the approval of the group. This often leads them to do the thing that is easiest regardless of whether it is best. Speech and reading difficulties may appear. They may become irritable, extremely sensitive to criticism, laugh or cry over nothing, or lose their temper easily. They lack the equanimity which is needed to bear any thwarting of desire; they respond to difficult situations as a very young child might. They withdraw from social contacts.

They may show various physical, or somatic, manifestations: vomiting at times of stress, lack of appetite, headaches, colds and allergies, disturbed sleep. They may show jerky, involuntary movements, called tics, or motor habits, partly voluntary and partly involuntary. They may manifest nervous habits such as picking the nose, nail-biting, and handling the genitals, and are often inattentive and fidgety. For example, nail-biting, according to one estimate, occurs in more than one fourth of elementary school children. It is especially frequent among children showing other disturbances. Nail-biting is one way in which many children show that they are under strains and pressures.

Any combination of these characteristics may be observed in emotionally unstable children in a more intense and persistent form than in well-adjusted children. The most serious problems are those which are long-standing and intense, affect many aspects of the child's life, and are constantly reinforced by deep-seated parental attitudes and by other environmental conditions that are difficult or impossible to change. By means of these characteristics—persistence, intensity, and pervasiveness—the teacher or parent is helped to distinguish pathological or neurotic behavior from problems that are a normal and necessary part of growing up.

Severe emotional disorders, such as functional psychoses, are relatively rare in early childhood. Of one thousand children with behavior problems in the age range from five to seventeen, 2 per cent were diagnosed as psychotic. All cases were characterized by abnormal social, emotional, and intellectual development (74, 1936). These kinds of difficulties indicate the need for expert diagnosis and therapy. Inexpert tinkering with a deep-seated problem may make a child's last state worse than his first.

Conditions giving rise to emotional disturbance

Maladjustment results when a susceptible child, in poor physical condition, is subject to home, school, and social conditions with which he is unable to cope. The way he responds to this environment affects, in turn, the way others respond to him. For example, a child who behaves in ways that irritate and annoy others loses the love that he needs so much. It is not only the child who must change himself; the situation, too, must be altered. To send a child back into the same conditions that originally caused the difficulty is to invite failure in adjustment. The resulting failure may intensify a child's lack of self-confidence.

The following are some of the environmental conditions that contribute to children's emotional disturbance and feelings of personal inadequacy:

1. Too great expectations. The work given him is too hard for *him*. The same level of achievement cannot be set for all children in a family.

2. Inability to adjust to a home situation in which the child never knows what will be expected of him. The parents squabble over policies and methods of treating him. Moreover, a bright child notices a discrepancy between the standards that parents set for themselves and those that they set up for the children.

3. Emotional conflicts on the part of parents. The child is disturbed by family dissension. Parents who quarrel with each other, who are tense, gloomy, worried, anxious, and fearful may transfer some of their emotional disturbance to the child. Constant reminders of the parents' conscious sacrifice for the child may likewise make him feel unwanted and insecure.

4. Teacher personality. A teacher weak in instructional skills and classroom management and insensitive to pupils' needs can lower health values and contribute to nervous disorders and emotional difficulties.

5. A school program that is too confining, that provides little opportunity for physical activity and for working uninterruptedly on absorbing tasks. Such a program increases restlessness and irritation.

6. Lack of opportunities to take initiative and suitable responsibility. Parents and teachers should not assume responsibility for a child's acts long after he is able to take the responsibility himself.

Treatment of seriously disturbed children

The first step is to modify the environment so that the child can handle it (11, 1948). Then he will experience success in coming to grips with reality, whereas he previously met nothing but defeat. For example, one child who feared competition was taught individually until he had gained enough knowledge, skill, and confidence to meet the classroom situation successfully. To avoid academic failure the teacher can let each child begin his reading or other schoolwork at a level below his present achievement and at his own speed. The child's own experiences will demonstrate to him that the world is not so hostile and defeating as he had thought. As he gains in proficiency, his work can gradually be made more difficult.

The second step is to help the child gain inner control. One prerequisite for this process is a strong positive relation between the child and the adult—the quality that we have earlier called "unconditional love." The child's desire to maintain the desired relation, plus the conviction that he *can* do so by acting in socially acceptable ways, will lead to the building of inner controls. Parents and teachers show their love for the child by the very fact that they are ready to discriminate in their affection between his more acceptable self and his less acceptable self in order to help him develop inner controls, which will make him a happier, more successful person.

Special groups of five or six children may be formed—one or two destructive and disorganized, one or two withdrawn, one or two superior in maturity but needing more opportunity to talk and do creative work. These children are taken into a separate room for free-play, discussion of their experiences, dramatization, and stories. Sometimes they are asked to respond to pictures selected to evoke their feelings about life situations. These activities, under the supervision of a trained therapist, have helped children to relieve tension, gain insights and skills, and relate themselves to other children and to the adult (2, 1947). The special play-therapy group presents a problem when it leads the children to expect the same degree of permissiveness and freedom in their regular classes.

EMOTIONS IN THE PRIMARY PERIOD

Emotions are a natural part of children's behavior (105, pp. 394-416, 1957). Mild emotions have a tonic effect; strong active emotions mobilize the body for action; strong depressive emotions reduce action to a minimum; disorganizing emotions make it impossible for the individual to handle the situation. Under diverse situations, a child's needs find expression in fear, anger, or overdependence. To understand the meaning of the behavior to the child is a most important ability for all parents and teachers.

Fear

"Fear is in one's bones." It is a basic part of the drive toward self-preservation. It interferes with development when it is persistent, intense, and irrational. Reasonable fears are a normal part of life. Adults should try to understand the background of a child's fears, their meaning to him, and ways in which they may find expression.

Fears may arise from experiences in which the child has been hurt or otherwise harmed. Naturally the child is afraid of similar situations. Fears may arise out of a general feeling of inadequacy, anxiety, or insecurity; life itself is fear-provoking if the child feels unable to cope with it. Fears may be associated with guilty feelings about thoughts or actions, or may stem from unsolved conflicts. To a child who has had to move from one foster home to another, any sign of rejection may arouse a deep-seated fear.

The first days of school frequently call forth this reaction in shy or too-dependent children. The strangeness of the room, the teacher, the other children, and the absence of the mother combine to make such a child afraid. Some children acquire wrong associations with the ideas of school and teacher: school—a place where children do not like to go; teacher—someone who will whip you if you are naughty and do not learn your lessons; school children—children who will tease you or hurt you. Instead, pleasant associations should be built of school as a place where you learn to read stories, play games with other children, and see and hear new and interesting things.

Providing the timid child with work that he enjoys and can do successfully is one of the best ways of changing his attitude toward school and of driving out fear. Gaining knowledge and skill in handling the specific fear-arousing situation successfully is particularly effective. Since excessive and persistent timidity may often be traced to poor physical condition, attention should be given to providing a healthful school program and to co-operating with the parents with respect to food, sleep, and other health habits. In cases in which the child's timidity is the result of brutal treatment at home, the school must co-operate with social agencies.

Fears not only have different meanings to the child; they may find widely different forms of expression. Aggressive acts may be a mask for fear. Apparent snobbishness or withdrawal from social activities may be caused by fear of not being able to handle social situations. Docile obedience and overdependence may really represent a fear of losing love or approval.

Love

A fine positive view of love is presented by Prescott (106, 1958). Love involves feeling with the loved one, acceptance of his uniqueness, active concern for his welfare, sharing resources with him, but not dominating or trying to change him. Love is mutually beneficial. Love, in this sense, "is not rooted primarily in sexual dynamics or hormonal drives. It is rooted in the individual's value dynamics." (105, p. 358, 1957) The child who has learned to love in his preschool years is able to relate himself to his new school associates. It is the unloved child who is likely to be overdependent, dominating, withdrawn, or overaggressive.

Should a child love his teacher? Yes, if "love" is taken to mean a warm, constructive relation in which the child is truly valued and helped to develop his best potentialities. No, if it means a relationship that is intense and meets the emotional needs of the teacher at the expense of the child. A teacher's strong personal affection for one child may lead to favoritism, which children keenly resent. Or it may make the child oversensitive to the teacher's opinion. Consequently, he feels hurt when he is not given the expected attention or praise. The child tends to take a negative attitude toward persons whom he dislikes but will co-operate with persons whom he genuinely likes. Although the motive of pleasing the teacher is not the best reason for doing the right thing, it helps the young child to build inner controls.

The effective teacher is sensitive to the diverse emotional needs of each child. Some children need affection more than anything else; others need to acquire a less antagonistic attitude toward authority; still others should be helped to become more independent. Too often teachers unwittingly reinforce parents' detrimental behavior. Teacher and pupils are likely to reject the child who has been rejected at home and to baby the child who has been treated as a cute little fellow at home.

Sex problems should always be considered as part of the child's total life adjustment. Psychologists have reported instances of sex satisfaction in very young infants. But there has been little research on the relation of sexuality in early childhood to the sex drive in later childhood, adolescence, and adulthood. Questions about sex should be treated with acceptance, frankness, and lack of tension. Pets at school and at home frequently give children an understanding of the way life begins. One cannot assume, however, that a child who has had this experience with pets necessarily understands about humans. The facts of sex behavior in humans should be clearly explained when he has expressed an honest curiosity about them.

Hate and anger

The earlier discussion of the psychology of "love against hate" is applicable to primary children who have not yet outgrown their primitive reactions to frustration. Temper tantrums may still occur in the primary grades. Parents frequently give in to temper tantrums because they just can't stand the noise and contention, because the child disturbs the neighbors, or because they fear the child will harm himself.

A group of primary teachers listed the following situations which, in their experience, had made primary children angry:

1. Stimuli to anger which should be avoided by the teacher:
   a. Making a promise to a child and not keeping it.
   b. Taking hold of a child.
   c. Withdrawing love because of the child's behavior.
   d. Having no regular schedule through which the child may know when to expect a change in activity.
   e. Interfering unnecessarily with a child's activity when he is interested and able to carry it on by himself.
   f. Giving a child work that is beyond his capacity, with the result that he is constantly failing in it.
2. Stimuli to anger which cannot be avoided entirely by the teacher (the child's attitude toward the situation, however, may be changed, and his ability to deal with the situation constructively can be increased):
   a. One child does better work than another child.
   b. One child is chosen to be "it" in a game, and another child becomes angry.
   c. A child who interrupts the classwork is reprimanded.
   d. A child loses in a game.
   e. A child wants to play a game which the majority of the children do not want to play.
   f. A child wants something that belongs to someone else.

g. A child is not permitted to read because there is not time enough for everyone to take part.

h. One child teases another child.

3. Some stimuli to anger which occur outside the school:

a. Parents reject the child or overprotect him to the extent of depriving him of needed experiences and relationships with other children or adults.

b. The child's environment is characterized by constant thwartings and irritation such as nagging or unreasonably severe discipline.

c. The child has found that he can get what he wants by flying into a rage.

d. The child is suffering from some physical irritation or from malnutrition or fatigue which makes him easily provoked.

e. The child seems to be constitutionally unstable; consequently disappointments and annoyances which others would hardly notice result in violent outbursts of temper.

f. An attitude of suspicion has been built which causes the child to go about with a "chip on his shoulder."

g. The child is deprived of affection and is contrasted unfavorably with his siblings; he feels anxious and insecure in his personal relations.

Any of these situations may give rise to a variety of emotional reactions.

Children find a variety of ways—desirable and undesirable—of coping with emotional tension. There are many constructive ways of dealing with emotional tension. Attention to the child's physical condition —nutrition, sleep, activities—is a wise first step. A child eight or nine years old can be helped to learn how to direct emotional energy into other channels. Creative activity and active exercise in the form of an enjoyable game, a race upstairs, carpentry work, or other activity keeps him from brooding and picturing himself as a suffering hero, uses some of the energy released by the emotion, and shows him a method of gaining self-control. Helping the child to see a funny side to the matter is also a constructive method of dealing with a tense situation. After the anger has subsided the child may be reasoned with to some extent, helped to face facts, see the other fellow's point of view, and find more acceptable outlets for his feelings.

Some education of the emotions may be achieved through dramatizations and role-playing. It may begin with the acting out of familiar jingles and move into dramatization of simple everyday situations. These experiences may help all the children in a class to understand, to some extent, why they behave as they do and how a six-, seven-, or eight-year-old can handle situations more satisfactorily.

PROBLEMS OF PERSONAL RELATIONS*

The child's relationship with his parents changes when he goes to school. He compares them with the teacher, the policeman, and other authority figures. This re-evaluation, and often devaluation, of the parents' role is a normal part of growing up.

The child's relationship with his teacher reflects the home situation. If he has always been given what he wants when he wants it, if he has been completely oblivious to his parents' feelings, or if he has been overdocile and subservient to their wishes, he will have major adaptations to make to the school situation. The skillful teacher will distinguish between a child's *wants* and *needs* and meet as many of his needs as the classroom situation allows. If a child is constantly required to conform to outer demands, the unsatisfied needs may crop up in daydreams or disturbed sleep.

The school child has many opportunities to learn how his behavior affects others, when he must subordinate his own desires, and when it is best to accommodate his ways to those of teacher and classmates. This task is made rather obvious because children of these ages often treat one another with undisguised crudeness. Their personal relations are also greatly influenced by the classroom atmosphere. Although they are naturally somewhat competitive, a classroom atmosphere in which the aim is to get ahead of someone else will have a bad effect on their relationships. Especially if a child is handicapped and does poorly on competitive performances, he is likely to feel that something is seriously wrong with him. Being ostracized or not accepted by the popular children affects a child's self-esteem, even though he associates with other children who are similarly unfortunate. Children whose parents have a bad reputation, who have moved from place to place during the primary years, who have tried to build up their self-esteem by disparaging other people, have special problems of establishing vital personal relations.

HEALTH PROBLEMS

Eating problems

"Nancy is so excited about school she has no appetite at all. In the morning she is so anxious to get to school early that she runs off without her breakfast. At noon she won't take time to eat for fear she will be late getting back." What should the mother do? Nancy may be

*(121, pp. 227-244, 1953)

helped to work out a schedule that suits her. She may make this schedule in picture form—a picture of her main activities on a clock face with hands pointing to the time at which each activity begins. She will need reminders and approval at first, but before long the early morning routine should become a habit, especially if breakfast is something to look forward to. Often, however, breakfast problems stem from deeper personal relations.

Lack of appetite may arise from many different conditions. It may be caused merely by eating between meals. Children of this age have opportunity for the first time to patronize the candy stores and pushcarts so often located near the school. Being indoors during a large part of the day may account for a slump in appetite. Walking at least part of the way to and from school, being outdoors in the sunny afternoon, keeping the temperature of heated rooms down to 68 degrees and at the optimum humidity, and having fresh air night and day help to keep the appetite normal. Lack of vitamin-B complex may also affect a child's appetite.

Actually a child whose mother considers him an "eating problem" may be eating as much as he needs under the circumstances. A child's preferences for certain foods and for certain times, places, and modes of eating may be right for the particular child. The parents' attention should usually be directed toward the other poor habits of which lack of appetite is a symptom.

The following account of an eating episode illustrates the complex personal relations that may be involved in an eating problem, as well as demonstrating several poor practices that are still common: urging a child to eat a disliked food, withdrawing privileges if he does not eat it, and arguing in the child's presence about the best way of handling the situation.

Six-year-old Hilda sat with elbow on the table and chin in hand. Then she raised her head and said, "I don't want pea soup, Mummy. I want something else to eat."

"But, Hilda, I have nothing else now. Take just a little of this nice warm pea soup, your apple, milk and cake. After school you will have your chocolate malted milk."

"I won't. I don't want that green stuff. I won't eat it. I won't have no lunch."

"But, darling, just two or three spoonfuls. I will give them to you myself and you will finish quickly. Try it, it tastes good."

"No, I won't," she said, angrily moving her head from left to right. She pushed the plate aside stubbornly, and looked at her mother.

"O.K., don't have pea soup, but don't ask for the chocolate malted milk this afternoon. You should eat now because otherwise you won't have anything to eat till six o'clock when your father gets home." In answer the child moved away and started off to school.

After school, on their way home the child asked timidly, "Mother, chocolate malted?" and looked up at her mother beseechingly.

"No pea soup, no chocolate malted," her mother answered firmly.

At home the mother began to prepare dinner. The child stayed around, asked for water and got it. Seeing that she was going to get nothing else, she went to play quietly with her blocks. Sitting on the floor she put the blocks one on top of another forming a tower and then suddenly she smashed them down on the floor. She did the same thing five times, perhaps as an expression of aggression that she dared not even feel toward her mother.

When the father came the mother told him about Hilda's not wanting the pea soup and he answered sternly, "Let her have it for dinner; she will learn."

At dinner time the mother got the pea soup out of the refrigerator to give to Hilda, but then she changed her mind. She gave the child, instead, fresh vegetables and other things, and heated the pea soup for herself. The father was angry and said, "You always let her have her way, you spoil her." The mother answered, "She had nothing for lunch. I will let her enjoy her dinner now. She needs it." He was silent and went on eating. The child sat down and ate very well without any urging from her parents.

The next day at lunch the mother told Hilda that there was only pea soup. She looked at her mother and said, "O.K., Mummy, I'll have some pea soup." She ate all of it while she babbled happily about school.

In the afternoon she had her chocolate malted milk as usual. And just when her mother was getting her down from the stool at the drugstore, she hugged her and said, "I love you, Mummy. I will eat my soup every day and be a good girl."

Although the eating problem seems to have been solved, the situation as a whole has unhealthy features. There is a split between the parents over the child, and she may feel that she has gained a victory over the one with the help of the other. Hilda's behavior must be seen in the total context of the family relation.

There is growing evidence that some of the serious mental disorders are in part biochemical, not illnesses of the mind as such. Watson (131, 1956) stated that the nutritional displacement caused by psychological stress is itself a contribution to the biochemical aspects of mental illness.

Fatigue

City children are often overstimulated. Noise, speed, manifold distractions and attractions, ambitious parents, a competitive school atmosphere often stimulate the child to be more active than he would naturally choose to be. Country children, on the other hand, may come to school physically tired by early morning chores. The self-selection principle operates with respect to sleep only when there are no competing bids for the child's attention. In a world of movies, radio, and television, fatigue is often ignored in favor of these other exciting experiences.

Accidents and illness

Some accidents have psychological causes associated with feelings of guilt and worthlessness. An accident may represent the child's attempt to punish himself, to demonstrate helplessness, or to arouse sympathy. During the child's recovery the parents should steer a middle course between oversolicitude and severity. The first of these attitudes gives the child too much satisfaction from being hurt, while the second may intensify the feelings of guilt or inadequacy that gave rise to the accident.

An adequate school health program does much to promote the health of children. One elementary-school program has the following features:

1. Each child is periodically given a complete health examination with the parent present. The results of the examination are recorded on the child's cumulative record, and significant information is passed on to persons who need it in order to make the necessary adjustments—a lightened program of work, modified physical education, a midmorning lunch, sight-saving measures, more favorable seating, referral for psychological service, or other adjustments.

2. Parents can help to co-operate in preventing communicable diseases. If a child comes down with the mumps or some other communicable disease, letters are sent to the parents of all the children in the class, telling them what to do if the child is susceptible or if he has had the disease. They receive a printed postcard about the disease, stating the length of the incubation period and of the quarantine, and other information.

3. First aid is available. Children who are in need of first aid go to the nurse willingly, the children have a friendly attitude toward the medical office. A child is never sent home without first notifying the parent.

4. An atmosphere of children learning happily and successfully prevails in the school.

Eyestrain

A few simple measures will do much to decrease eyestrain in the primary grades.

1. Avoid glare from lights in the direct line of vision and from the reflection of glossy surfaces.

2. Adjust seats and tables so that the child may comfortably hold his work up—not leave it flat on the desk—at a distance of twelve to fourteen inches from the eyes. Teach him to place his chair so that the light shines on his work, not in his eyes.

3. Encourage the child to change from reading or similar activities to work requiring less close application whenever he becomes tired.

4. Note any signs of eyestrain or infection such as headache, nausea, or redness of the lids, and refer the child to an eye specialist.

5. See that children who have eye defects obtain carefully prescribed glasses and wear and care for them properly.

STUTTERING

Why does stuttering occur in approximately ten out of every thousand children? Probably there is no single cause. With little children it may be merely a stage in speech development, occurring when the child has not yet attained fluency. The condition may be acquired by imitation. Under conditions of general tension one stuttering child in a class may start a mild epidemic of stuttering. Sometimes a child may be shocked or alarmed into stuttering. He catches his breath in fear or excitement. Words and sentences are normally spoken on the outgoing breath, but in stuttering, speech is attempted during inspiration. Frequently, a stutterer can speak freely under certain circumstances, whereas under conditions of fear or anxiety or in the presence of certain persons his speech difficulty becomes marked. One mother took her eight-year-old boy to a speech specialist. The boy talked to the doctor without hesitancy, whereas in the classroom he stuttered badly. Curiously enough, stutterers have been found, in an individual testing situation, to be actually more talkative than nonstuttering children. It is probable that stuttering is partly related to a disturbance of normal cerebral dominance and partly a learned behavior influenced by an unfavorable home environment.

The child's feeling about his stuttering is important. If he thinks of himself as abnormal, the symptoms are aggravated and accentuated. Any method that relieves the individual's tension about stuttering and gives him greater emotional security may result in more effective control of speech.

Different methods will be effective with different children. There is no *one* best method. When dealing with a tense, anxious child the teacher or parent should speak slowly with no appearance of haste, impatience, anxiety, or annoyance. The child should be encouraged to take plenty of time, prolonging the vowels in the same speech pattern that the teacher uses in speaking to him. When a child begins to stutter the teacher should ignore the stuttering and wait patiently for the child to finish. If he repeats the troublesome sentence easily, he will gain confidence. It has sometimes been found helpful to have the child make slow rhythmical movements with his hands while prolonging the vowels. Under favorable conditions of instruction and classroom relationships, the child should be given more opportunity to speak in natural situations. Treatment of persistent stuttering should be carried out by a skilled person who can help the parent accept the situation with patience.

Questions and Problems

1. In co-operation with a school or a child-guidance clinic, study a child whose behavior is causing much concern to his teacher. Ask him to do some interesting thing with you such as going to a zoo or making a gift for someone he likes. Write a description of his co-operation with you, adding some suggestions by which other adults who deal with him might profit.

2. Visit several classrooms and observe the teacher's behavior and attitude toward the children, and the children's responses. Try to classify these different types of classroom: (a) Teacher directs, children follow specific directions. (b) Unplanned or laissez-faire attitude; children do as they please for the most part. (c) Teacher directs activity of the group but also works with individuals. (d) Teacher has made general plan but children work out details of how to carry it out co-operatively. (e) Teacher uses a combination of methods, each appropriate at the time.

3. Plan a meal for a seven-year-old child which is satisfactory in every respect—the kind and amount of food, the child's opportunity for choice, the way it is cooked and served, the appearance of the dining room, the attitudes of the other members of the family toward the food and toward the child, the activity of the child before, during, and after the meal; and the time allowed.

4. In the following incident, what opportunities were offered for learning to get along with others? Might an adult have helped or hindered in this situation?

Carol, aged seven, and two other little girls, aged five and eight, were playing in front of Carol's house. The oldest child, Jane, went home to get her bicycle. When she returned Carol asked to ride.

CAROL: Let me ride your bike, please?

JANE: I want to ride first.

CAROL: I let you sit on my steps.

JANE: I don't care, it's my bike.

CAROL: Take your old ugly bike. I don't want to ride it anyway. (She went back to her steps and sat down, her lips pouted. The other child stayed on her bicycle but didn't ride away.)

CAROL: Why don't you go 'head and ride your old bike? We don't want to play with you anyway.

JANE: It's my bike. I don't have to go until I want to.

Carol did not say anything else. She rang her doorbell, took the five-year-old's hand and, when her mother pushed the buzzer, went inside. The other little girl rode away on her bicycle.

Read the following incident, trying to understand what the child's behavior meant to him:

Father and nine-year-old David were out in the backyard; father was working on the rosebushes.

David, close by, picked up some of his father's tools.

Father said politely, but firmly, "David, I don't need your help. Move off."

David slowly put down the tools and walked over to his golf clubs, picked one up and swung vigorously in the air. Father ignored the act. Moments later David, brightened up, asked, "Daddy, could we go golfing after lunch?"

"No, children do not play on adult golf courses."

"Then could you golf with me, Daddy?"

"Well, maybe sometime, but not today."

Later the father called to David, "David, get me the extension cord to the power mower, please."

David jumped up eagerly and ran into the house calling, "Okay," as he went. It was not long before David was eagerly cutting the lawn with father guiding closely to protect the flowers. David's expression seemed to indicate pride in his relationship and abilities and he did not seem to mind the close parental supervision. He was happy in being given an opportunity to work with his father and was thrilled to do something adult.

5. Clip from current newspapers and magazines references to child psychology and child care. Evaluate these references, bringing the best to class.

6. How can you distinguish between problems that are an essential part of growing up and serious emotional problems that should be referred to a psychologist or psychiatrist?

7. Give illustrations of how a teacher can counteract unfavorable home influences in the case of individual children. Show how goal-directed activity and setting certain limits to a child's behavior help him to gain self-control.

8. As an example of an excellent experiment in the field of beginning reading, analyze Goin's *Visual Perception as Related to Reading*, published by The University of Chicago Press, 1958. What practical suggestions for teachers of beginning reading came out of this research?

Bibliography[*]

1. ABNEY, LOUISE, and GRACE ROWE. *Choral-Speaking Arrangements for the Lower Grades*. Boston: Expression Co., 1937. 80 pp.
2. ADLERBLUM, EVELYN D. "Mental Hygiene Begins in School," *Mental Hygiene*, XXXI (October, 1947), 541-555.

[*] All references referred to in the text are included in the bibliography. The single-starred references (*) are specially recommended for their practical suggestions; those double-starred (**) are specially recommended for their technical and research emphasis.

3. AMES, LOUISE BATES, and JANET LEARNED. "Imaginary Companions and Related Phenomena," *Journal of Genetic Psychology*, LXIX (December, 1946), 147-167.

4. ANDERSON, JOHN E. *The Psychology of Development and Personal Adjustment*. New York: Henry Holt & Co., Inc., 1949. 720 pp.

5. ANDERSON, ROBERT H. "Ungraded Primary Classes—An Administrative Contribution to Mental Health," *Understanding the Child*, XXIV (June, 1955), 66-72.

*6. ARBUTHNOT, MAY H. *Children and Books*. Chicago: Scott, Foresman & Co., 1957. 626 pp.

7. ARITHMETIC READINESS TEST. (Adapted in 1955 from the Numbers Section of the Primary American School Achievement Test. Measures ability to recognize quantitative matters. Kindergarten-Grade 1.) Cincinnati: Public School Publishing Co.

8. ARTHUR, GRACE. "Pseudo-Feeblemindedness," *American Journal of Mental Deficiency*, LII (October, 1947), 137-142.

9. AYRES, LEONARD P. *Measuring Scale for Handwriting*. (Gettysburg ed. Grades 2-8. Based on legibility.) Princeton, N.J.: Cooperative Test Division of the Educ. Testing Service, 1917.

10. BARBE, WALTER B. "Peer Relationships of Children of Different Intelligence Levels," *School and Society*, LXXX (August 21, 1954), 60-62.

11. BETTELHEIM, BRUNO. "The Special School for Emotionally Disturbed Children," in *Juvenile Delinquency and the Schools*, pp. 145-171. ("Forty-seventh Yearbook of the National Society for the Study of Education," Part I.) Chicago: Univ. of Chicago Press, 1948. 280 pp.

12. BLAIR, GLENN MYERS. *Diagnostic and Remedial Teaching* (rev. ed.). New York: The Macmillan Co., 1956. 409 pp.

13. BOND, GUY L., and MILES A. TINKER. *Reading Difficulties; Their Diagnosis and Correction*. New York: Appleton-Century-Crofts, Inc., 1957. 486 pp.

14. BREEN, L. C. "Diagnosis of Behavior by Finger Painting," *Elementary School Journal*, LVI (March, 1956), 321-324.

15. BROWNELL, WILLIAM H. "When Is Arithmetic Meaningful?" *Journal of Educational Research*, XXXVIII (March, 1945), 481-498.

16. BROWNELL, WILLIAM H., and HAROLD E. MOSER. *Meaningful vs. Mechanical Learning: A Study in Grade II Subtraction*. ("Duke Univ. Research Studies in Education," No. 8.) Durham, N.C.: Duke Univ. Press, 1949. 207 pp.

17. BRUECKNER, LEO J. "The Development and Validation of an Arithmetic Readiness Test," *Journal of Educational Research*, XL (March, 1947), 496-502.

18. BUCKINGHAM, BURDETTE R. *Elementary Arithmetic; Its Meaning and Practice*. Boston: Ginn & Company, 1947. 744 pp.

*19. Burton, William H. *The Guidance of Learning Activities; A Summary of the Principles of Teaching Based on the Principles of Learning.* New York: Appleton-Century-Crofts, Inc., 1952. 737 pp.

20. Buswell, Guy T., and Maurice L. Harting (eds.). *Arithmetic 1949; Papers Presented at the Fourth Annual Conference on Arithmetic.* ("Supplementary Educational Monographs," No. 70.) Chicago: Univ. of Chicago Press, 1949. 100 pp.

21. Cattell, Raymond B. *Personality and Motivation, Structure and Measurement.* Yonkers-on-Hudson, N.Y.: World Book Co., 1957. 950 pp.

22. ———. and Richard W. Coan. "Personality Factors in Middle Childhood as Revealed in Parents' Ratings," *Child Development,* XXVIII (December, 1957), 439-458.

**23. Cruickshank, William M. (ed.). *Psychology of Exceptional Children and Youth.* Englewood Cliffs, N.J.: Prentice-Hall, Inc., 1955. 594 pp.

24. Danziger, K. "The Child's Understanding of Kinship Terms: A Study in the Development of Relational Concepts," *Journal of Genetic Psychology,* XCI (December, 1957), 213-232.

25. Davidson, Henry A. "Competition, the Cradle of Anxiety," *Education,* LXXVI (November, 1955), 162-166.

26. Davis, Allison. *Social-Class Influences Upon Learning.* Cambridge, Mass.: Harvard Univ. Press, 1948. 100 pp.

27. Davis, Allison, and Robert J. Havighurst. "The Measurement of Mental Systems (Can Intelligence Be Measured?)," *Scientific Monthly,* LXVI (April, 1948), 301-316.

28. Davis, Allison, and Robert D. Hess. "What about IQ's?," *NEA Journal,* XXXVIII (November, 1949), 604-605.

29. Davis, C. Jane, and Frederick W. Jobe. "The Variation of Visual Characteristics in School Children as Measured by the Ortho-Rater," *American Journal of Optometry,* XXXII (May, 1955), 251-258.

30. De Hirsch, Katrina. "Tests Designed to Discover Potential Reading Difficulties at the Six-Year-Old Level," *American Journal of Orthopsychiatry,* XXVII (July, 1957), 475-483.

31. De Martino, Manfred F. "A Review of the Literature on Children's Dreams," *Psychiatric Quarterly Supplement,* XXVII (Part I, 1954), 90-101.

32. Dreger, Ralph Mason. "Spontaneous Conversation and Story-Telling of Children in a Naturalistic Setting," *Journal of Psychology,* XL (July, 1955), 163-180.

33. Dunfee, Maxine, and Julian Greenlee (eds.). *Elementary School Science: Research, Theory and Practice.* Washington, D.C.: National Education Assoc., 1957. 67 pp.

34. Dunsdon, M. I., and J. A. Fraser-Roberts. "A Study of the Performance of 2,000 Children on Four Vocabulary Tests," *British Journal of Statistical Psychology,* VIII (May, 1955), 3-15.

35. Eaton, Anne Thaxter. *Treasure for the Taking* (rev. ed.). New York: The Viking Press, 1957. 322 pp.

36. Eells, Kenneth, Allison Davis, and others. *Intelligence and Cultural Differences.* Chicago: Univ. of Chicago Press, 1951. 388 pp.

37. Eng, Helga K. *The Psychology of Children's Drawings* (2d ed.). New York: Humanities Press, 1954. 224 pp.

38. Estes, Betsy Worth. "Influence of Socioeconomic Status on Wechsler Intelligence Scale for Children: Addendum," *Journal of Consulting Psychology,* XIX (June, 1955), 225-226.

39. Fahs, Sophia Lyon. *Today's Children and Yesterday's Heritage. A Philosophy of Creative Religious Development.* Boston: The Beacon Press, 1954. 224 pp.

40. Fernald, Grace M. *Remedial Techniques in Basic School Subjects.* New York: McGraw-Hill Book Co., Inc., 1943. 349 pp.

*41. Foster, Constance J. *Developing Responsibility in Children.* Chicago: Science Research Associates, 1953. 48 pp.

*42. Freeman, Frank N. *Teaching Handwriting.* ("What Research Says to the Teacher," No. 4.) Washington, D.C.: Dept. of Classroom Teachers, American Educ. Research Assoc. of the National Education Assoc., 1954. 33 pp.

43. Gallagher, James J. *A Comparison of Brain-Injured and Non-Brain-Injured Mentally Retarded Children on Several Psychological Variables.* Lafayette, Ind.: Child Development Publications, 1957. 79 pp.

*44. Gray, William S. *On Their Own in Reading.* Chicago: Scott, Foresman & Co., 1948. 268 pp.

*45. Gritzner, Florence A. "Why Parents Annoy Us," *National Parent-Teacher,* LI (May, 1957), 29-31.

46. Harms, Ernest. "Genesis of Esthetic Creativity in Children," *Progressive Education,* XXXIV (May, 1957), 84-90.

47. Harrell, Lester E., Jr. *A Comparison of the Development of Oral and Written Language in School-Age Children.* ("Monographs of the Society for Research in Child Development," Serial No. 66, No. 3, Vol. XXII.) Lafayette, Ind.: Purdue Univ., 1957. 77 pp.

48. Harris, Albert J. *How to Increase Reading Ability* (3d ed.). New York: Longmans, Green & Company, 1956. 633 pp.

49. Harris, Dale B., and others. "Personality Differences between Responsible and Irresponsible Children," *Journal of Genetic Psychology,* LXXXVII (September, 1955), 103-109.

50. Harris, Esther K. *The Responsiveness of Kindergarten Children to the Behavior of Their Fellows.* ("Monographs of the Society for Research in Child Development," Vol. XI, No. 2, Serial No. 43, 1946). Washington, D.C.: National Research Council, 1948. 184 pp.

*51. Hartley, Ruth E., and Goldenson, Robert M. *The Complete Book of Children's Play.* New York: Thomas Y. Crowell Co., 1957. 462 pp.

52. HEIDER, GRACE M. "Adjustment Problems of the Deaf Child," *Nervous Child*, VII (January, 1948), 38-44.

*53. HILDRETH, GERTRUDE. *Learning the Three R's* (2d ed.). Minneapolis: Educational Publishers, Inc., 1947. 897 pp.

54. HIRSCHBERG, J. COTTER. "Some Comments on Religion and Childhood," *Bulletin of the Menninger Clinic*, XIX (November, 1955), 227-228.

55. HONZIK, M. P., JEAN W. MACFARLANE, and L. ALLEN. "The Stability of Mental Test Performance between Two and Eighteen Years," *Journal of Experimental Education*, XVII (December, 1949), 309-324.

56. HUNTER, E. C. "Changes in Teachers' Attitudes Toward Children's Behavior over the Last Thirty Years," *Mental Hygiene*, XLI (January, 1957), 3-11.

*57. HUNTER, EDITH F. *The Questioning Child and Religion*. Boston: Starr King Press, 1956. 209 pp.

*58. ISHERWOOD, MARGARET. *The Root of the Matter*. New York: Harper & Bros., 1954. 238 pp.

59. JOHNSON, GEORGE ORVILLE. "Guidance for the Mentally Handicapped," *Journal of Exceptional Children*, XVI (January, 1950), 102-108.

**60. JONES, HAROLD E. "The Environment and Mental Development," in Leonard Carmichael (ed.), *Manual of Child Psychology* (2d ed.), pp. 631-696. New York: John Wiley & Sons, Inc., 1954.

*61. KAWIN, ETHEL. *Parenthood in a Free Nation*. ("Basic Course; 2d experimental ed."). Chicago: Univ. of Chicago, 1956. 133 pp.

62. KEPPIE, ELIZABETH E., CONRAD WEDBERG, and MIRIAM KESLAR. *Speech Improvmeent Through Choral Speaking, a Textbook for Teachers of Primary Grades*. Boston: Expression Co., 1942. 279 pp.

63. KERR, JEAN. *Please Don't Eat the Daisies*. New York: Doubleday & Co., Inc., 1957. 192 pp.

*64. KIRK, SAMUEL A., MERLE B. KARNES, and WINIFRED D. KIRK. *You and Your Retarded Child*. New York: The Macmillan Co., 1955. 184 pp.

65. KNOPF, IRWIN J., and T. W. RICHARDS. "The Child's Differentiation of Sex as Reflected in Drawings of the Human Figure," *Journal of Genetic Psychology*, LXXXI (September, 1952), 99-112.

66. KOCH, HELEN L. "Children's Work Attitudes and Sibling Characteristics," *Child Development*, XXVII (September, 1956), 289-310.

67. ———. "The Relation of 'Primary Mental Abilities' in Five- and Six-Year-Olds to Sex of Child and Characteristics of His Sibling," *Child Development*, XXV (September, 1954), 209-223.

68. ———. "Some Emotional Attitudes of the Young Child in Relation to Characteristics of His Sibling," *Child Development*, XXVII (December, 1956), 393-426.

69. KROGMAN, WILTON MARION. "Biological Growth as It May Affect Pupils' Success," *Merrill-Palmer Quarterly*, I (Spring, 1955), 90-98.

70. KUHLEN, R. G., and G. G. THOMPSON. *Psychological Studies of Human Development.* New York: Appleton-Century-Crofts, Inc., 1952. 533 pp.

71. LAYCOCK, SAMUEL R. *Brief Chats with Parents; How to Help Your Child Grow Up.* Toronto: Copp Clark Company, 1956. 185 pp.

72. LEAVITT, HELEN S., and WARREN S. FREEMAN. *Recordings for the Elementary School.* New York: Oliver Durrell, 1949. 127 pp.

73. LOWENFELD, VIKTOR. *Your Child and His Art.* New York: The Macmillan Co., 1954. 186 pp.

74. LURIE, LOUIS A., ESTHER B. TIETZ, and JACK HERTZMAN. "Functional Psychoses in Children," *American Journal of Psychiatry*, XCII (March, 1936), 1169-1184.

75. McKIM, MARGARET G. *Guiding Growth in Reading; in the Modern Elementary School.* New York: The Macmillan Co., 1955. 528 pp.

76. MAXIM, HIRAM PERCY. *A Genius in the Family, Sir Hiram Stephens Maxim Through a Small Son's Eyes.* New York: Harper & Bros., 1936. 193 pp.

77. MEREDITH, HOWARD V., and E. MATILDA MEREDITH. "Annual Increment Norms for Ten Measures of Physical Growth in Children Four to Eight Years of Age," *Child Development*, XXI (September, 1950), 141-147.

78. METROPOLITAN LIFE INSURANCE COMPANY. *America's Children; the Health of School Children and Youth*, 1956, pp. 1-7.

79. ———. *Absent from School Today*, 1950. 14 pp.

80. ———. *Respiratory Diseases*, 1955. 11 pp.

81. METROPOLITAN READINESS TESTS, by Gertrude H. Hildreth and Nellie L. Griffiths. Forms R and S. Yonkers-on-Hudson, N.Y.: World Book Co., 1949, 1950.

82. MITTELMAN, BELA. "Motility in Infants, Children, and Adults: Patterning and Psychodynamics," *Psychoanalytical Study of the Child*, IX (1954), 142-177.

83. MONROE, MARION. *Growing into Reading.* Chicago: Scott, Foresman & Co., 1951. 274 pp.

*84. MORTON, R. L. *Teaching Arithmetic.* Washington, D.C.: National Education Assoc., 1953. 33 pp.

*85. MOUSTAKAS, CLARKE E., and MINNIE P. BERSON. *The Young Child in School.* New York: Whiteside, Inc., 1956. 256 pp.

86. MURPHY, GARDNER, LOIS MURPHY, and THEODORE M. NEWCOMB. *Experimental Social Psychology.* New York: Harper & Bros., 1937. 1121 pp.

87. NATIONAL SOCIETY FOR THE STUDY OF EDUCATION. *The Education of Exceptional Children.* ("Forty-Ninth Yearbook of the National Society for the Study of Education," Part II.) Chicago: Univ. of Chicago Press, 1950. 350 pp.

88. ———. *Reading in the Elementary School.* ("Forty-Eighth Yearbook of the National Society for the Study of Education," Part II.) Chicago: Univ. of Chicago Press, 1949. 343 pp.

89. ———. *The Teaching of Arithmetic.* ("Fiftieth Yearbook," Part II.) Chicago: Univ. of Chicago Press, 1951. 302 pp.

90. NAUMBURG, MARGARET. *Studies of the "Free" Art Expression of Behavior Problem Children and Adolescents as a Means of Diagnosis and Therapy.* ("Nervous and Mental Disease Monographs," No. 71.) New York: Nervous and Mental Disease Monographs, 1947. 225 pp.

*91. NEISSER, EDITH G. *The Eldest Child.* New York: Harper & Bros., 1957. 174 pp.

92. NEWLAND, T. ERNEST. "Helping the Exceptional Child in the Regular Classroom," *Understanding the Child,* XXV (June, 1956), 66-79.

93. O'GRADY, R. M. "Study of Selected Aspects of Finger Painting by Special Class Children," *Journal of Genetic Psychology,* LXXXIV (March, 1954), 27-38.

94. OJEMANN, RALPH H. "An Integrated Plan for Education in Human Relations and Mental Health," *Journal of School Health,* XX (April, 1950), 101-106.

95. OLSON, WILLARD C. *Child Development.* Boston: D. C. Heath & Co., 1949. 417 pp.

96. ———. "Experiences for Growing," *National Education Association Journal,* XXXVI (October, 1947), 502-503.

97. ———. "Hazards to Growth," *National Education Association Journal,* XXXVI (November, 1947), 580-581.

*98. ———. and HUGHES, BRYON O. "Concepts of Growth—Their Significance to Teachers," *Childhood Education,* XXI (October, 1944), 53-63.

**99. PAULSEN, ALMA A. "Personality Development in the Middle Years of Childhood: A Ten-Year Longitudinal Study of Thirty Public School Children by Means of Rorschach Test and Social Histories," *American Journal of Orthopsychiatry,* XXIV (April, 1954), 336-350.

100. PHILADELPHIA PUBLIC SCHOOLS. *The Elementary School in Action.* Philadelphia: Curriculum Office, 1948. 77 pp.

**101. PIAGET, JEAN. *The Moral Judgment of the Child.* Glencoe, Ill.: The Free Press, 1948. 418 pp.

102. ———. "Perceptual and Cognitive (or Operational) Structures in the Development of the Concept of Space in the Child," *Acta Psychologica,* XI (June, 1955), 41-46.

103. PILZER, ELIZABETH. "Disturbed Children Who Make a Good School Adjustment," *Smith College School for Social Work,* XXII (June, 1952), 193-210.

104. PRATT, KARL C., WALTER E. HARTMAN, and J. L. MEAD. "Indetermi-

nate Number Concepts: III. Representation by Children through Selection of Appropriate Aggregations," *Journal of Genetic Psychology*, LXXXIV (March, 1954), 39-63.

*105. PRESCOTT, DANIEL A. *The Child in the Educative Process*. New York: McGraw-Hill Book Co., Inc., 1957. 502 pp.

*106. ———. "Without Love, What Luster?" *National Parent-Teacher*, LII (January, 1958), 18-20.

107. RASMUSSEN, CARRIE. *Choral Speaking for Speech Improvement (Elementary School)*. Boston: Expression Co., 1939. 93 pp.

108. ROBINSON, HELEN M. *Why Pupils Fail in Reading*. Chicago: Univ. of Chicago Press, 1946. 257 pp.

109. ROUMAN, JACK. "School Children's Problems as Related to Parental Factors," *Understanding the Child*, XXIV (April, 1955), 50-55.

110. SARASON, SEYMOUR B. "Mentally Retarded and Mentally Defective Children: Major Psycho-Social Problems," in William Cruickshank (ed.), *The Psychology of Exceptional Children and Youth*, pp. 438-474. Englewood Cliffs, N.J.: Prentice-Hall, Inc., 1955. 594 pp.

111. SEIDENFELD, MORTON A. "Care and Treatment of Language Deficiencies," in Douglas H. Fryer and Edwin R. Henry, *Handbook of Applied Psychology* (Vol. II), pp. 400-404. New York: Rinehart & Co., Inc., 1950.

112. SHAFFER, LAURENCE F. "Experimental Contributions to Mental Hygiene," *Review of Educational Research*, XIX (December, 1949), 379-385.

113. SHAW, S. G. "Children's Records; An Evaluative Appraisal," *Library Journal*, LXXX (October 15, 1955), 2316-2323.

114. SHAW, RUTH F. *Finger Painting; A Perfect Medium for Self-Expression*. Boston: Little, Brown & Co., 1934. 232 pp. (*See also Finger Painting and How I Do It*. New York: Leland Brent Publishing Co., 1947. 47 pp.

115. SHEPARD, WINIFRED O., and MAURICE S. SCHAEFFER. "The Effect of Concept Knowledge on Discrimination Learning," *Child Development*, XXVII (June, 1956), 173-178.

116. SPECTOR, SAMUEL I. "Climate and Social Acceptability," *Journal of Educational Sociology*, XXVII (November, 1953), 108-114.

117. SPENCER, PETER L., and BRYDEGAARD, MARGUERITE. *Building Mathematical Concepts in the Elementary School*. New York: Henry Holt & Co., Inc., 1952. 372 pp.

118. SPERLING, OTTO. "An Imaginary Companion, Representing a Presage of the Superego," in *The Psychoanalytic Study of the Child*, Vol. IX, pp. 252-258. New York: International Universities Press, 1954. 369 pp.

119. STOUFFER, GEORGE A. W., JR. "Behavior Problems of Children as Viewed by Teachers and Mental Hygienists. A Study of Present

Attitudes as Compared with Those Reported by E. K. Wickman," *Mental Hygiene*, XXXVI (April, 1952), 271-285.

120. STRANG, RUTH, and DOROTHY K. BRACKEN. *Making Better Readers.* Boston: D. C. Heath & Co., 1957. 367 pp.

**121. SULLIVAN, HARRY STACK. *The Interpersonal Theory of Psychiatry.* New York: W. W. Norton & Co., Inc., 1953. 393 pp.

122. TERMAN, LEWIS M., and MAUD A. MERRILL. *Measuring Intelligence: A Guide to the Administration of the New Revised Stanford-Binet Tests of Intelligence.* Boston: Houghton Mifflin Co., 1937. 460 pp.

123. THOM, DOUGLAS A., and NANCY L. NEWELL. "Hazards of the High I.Q.," *Mental Hygiene*, XXIX (January, 1945), 61-77.

124. THORNDIKE, EDWARD L., and others. *Psychology of Wants, Interests and Attitudes.* New York: Appleton-Century-Crofts, Inc., 1935. 301 pp.

125. TORGERSON, T. L., and GRACE CHRISTIANSEN. *Getting Ready for Numbers.* Eau Claire, Wisc.: E. M. Hale & Co., 1950. 96 pp.

126. TRIMBLE, HANNAH. "Out of the Mouths of—the Third Grade," *New York Times Magazine* (June 22, 1947), 18-19.

**127. TROW, WILLIAM CLARK. *The Learning Process.* Washington, D.C.: National Education Assoc., 1954. 33 pp.

128. U. S. NATIONAL OFFICE OF VITAL STATISTICS. *Vital Statistics of the United States, 1955; Part 2, 1957*, pp. 52-102.

129. VAN RIPER, CHARLES, and KATHERINE G. BUTLER. *Speech in the Elementary School.* New York: Harper & Bros., 1955. 182 pp.

130. VERNON, M. D. *Backwardness in Reading: A Study of Its Nature and Origin.* London: Cambridge University Press, 1957. 228 pp.

131. WATSON, GEORGE. "Is Mental Illness Mental?" *Journal of Psychology*, XLI (April, 1956), 323-334.

132. WATTS, ALBERT F. *The Language and Mental Development of Children: An Essay in Educational Psychology.* London: George G. Harrap, 1944. 354 pp.

133. WETZEL, N. C. "Assessing the Physical Condition of Children," *Journal of Pediatrics*, XX (1943), 82-110 ff.

134. ———. "Physical Fitness in Terms of Physique, Development and Basal Metabolism," *Journal of the American Medical Association*, CXVI (1941), 1187-1195.

*135. WOLF, KATHERINE. *The Controversial Problem of Discipline.* New York: Child Study Assoc. of America, 1953. 35 pp.

136. WOLFENSTEIN, MARTHA. "Children's Understanding of Jokes," *Psychoanalytical Study of the Child*, VIII (1953), 162-173.

137. WYLIE, JULIA ELEANOR. "Group Creative Writing by Children." *Understanding the Child*, XVI (October, 1947), 102-106.

Films for Child Study

A Long Time to Grow (Part III), Six-Seven-and-Eight-Year-Olds-Society of
    Children. 30 minutes. 1957. Produced by The Dept. of Child Study at
    Vassar College. Shows typical group behavior of children of middle child-
    hood years.

Family Circles. National Film Board of Canada. 31 minutes. 1949. Parental
    indifference and conflict at home destroy a child's self-confidence at school.

From Sociable Six to Noisy Nine. McGraw-Hill. 22 minutes. 1954. Produced
    by the National Film Board of Canada. Shows the typical behavior and
    sensible parental guidance of several children from six to nine years of age.

Meeting Emotional Needs in Childhood: The Groundwork of Democracy. New
    York Univ. 33 minutes. 1947. Produced by the Dept. of Child Study at
    Vassar College. Children's need for security and acceptance for develop-
    ment into emotional maturity.

Maintaining Classroom Discipline. McGraw-Hill Series on Teacher Education.
    14 minutes. Illustrates the effect of the attitude of the teacher upon the
    children in the classroom.

Part Five

FROM

THE PRIMARY PERIOD

TO ADOLESCENCE

At first I hated the school, but by and by I got so I could stand it. Whenever I got uncommon tired I played hookey, and the hiding I got next day done me good and cheered me up. So the longer I went to school the easier it got to be. . . . I liked the old ways best, but I was getting so I liked the new ones, too, a little bit. The widow said I was coming along slow but sure, and doing very satisfactory. She said she warn't ashamed of me.

Huckleberry Finn by MARK TWAIN

Chapter 16

DEVELOPMENT IN

THE LATER CHILDHOOD

AND PREADOLESCENT YEARS

Children in the fourth, fifth, and sixth grades, as well as some in the seventh and eighth, are included in this period. In age they range from about nine to twelve or thirteen years. The boundary lines of this period are even more flexible than those of the earlier periods because the time at which physiological maturity is attained varies so widely with individual children.

The behavior of any child in this age group is influenced by many factors: his stage of physiological maturity, his previous experiences, his present attitudes and bodily condition, the pulls and pushes in his immediate environment, his unique personality as it has already developed, his individual growth pattern, and his self-concept, including his feelings about himself. Interwoven with these individual characteristics are certain common developmental trends and pervasive cultural influences. His strong tendency to identify with his peer group is not only a withdrawal from and sometimes a turning against his parents, but also a positive moving toward his peers.

There is an inherent positive value in childhood itself. This attitude, according to Margaret Lowenfeld, is more characteristic of English culture than of the United States. English children depend less on adults; they live more in a world of children of different ages. Adults do not generally enter this world except when something happens and the children do not know what to do. Children and parents are absorbed, each in their own concerns. Consequently, parents do not discuss before children adult problems which they consider outside the understanding of children.

371

OVERVIEW OF THE PERIOD

Two epochs really are represented in this period. First there is the slow, steady growth of children around nine, ten, and eleven years; then the period of rapid growth culminating in early adolescence.

Children around ten years of age are often in "a happy stage of equilibrium." They still accept their parents, like to learn, enjoy their friends. Their optimistic, practical point of view about growing up is expressed in the following composition written by a ten-year-old girl in grade five:

GROWING UP

Now that I am growing up I feel differently. I don't feel so small any more.

It is very nice to be growing up. It has many good points. As I get older I can stay up later. My parents give me more responsibility. People trust me to baby sit for them. I am allowed to go places by myself. I am permitted to choose my own clothes.

Just the same as everything else, growing up has its bad points also. People expect more from me now. I get harder work at school. My parents give me more chores to do. I am expected to give up things for my younger sister. If I stop and think how many good points it has, I know growing up isn't so bad after all.

Nine- and ten-year-olds take themselves seriously. Since leaving the primary grades they have become more mature and still more eager to take initiative and work things out for themselves. They are becoming more critical of adults. Their resistance to keeping clean, to coming in from play at a stated time, to going to bed, and to other virtues approved by adults is a sign of emerging independence. By the end of this period many children have made rapid progress toward achieving a balance between adolescent independence and mature dependency. They have an inherent drive toward growth and independence and want to be respected and treated as grown-up, yet unconsciously they want to retain the advantages of childhood. Consequently they fluctuate between adult and childish behavior. Preadolescence is a prelude to instability or reorganization, out of which a more adult pattern of life should emerge. Despite the primary importance of the peer group, these youngsters still need parents who have standards and values, maintain firm limits, stick by their children through thick and thin.

A spurt of activity is characteristic of both boys and girls. It represents an attempt to gain mastery of the environment. Nine- and ten-year-olds set standards of achievement for themselves and practice skills that they want to learn. Though they are less dependent on praise than formerly, they still benefit from it. They have a need for definiteness and clarity.

Kirkpatrick has described these years of later childhood as the period of "competitive socialization." This term calls attention both to the competitive spirit that develops in this period, and to the co-operative group spirit that begins to emerge. They hate anything that seems to them unfair. The term "Big Injun age" calls attention to the delight which many preadolescents show in campfires, scouting, hunting, and other primitive activities. Play interests, especially of boys, are predominantly engaged in with the same sex.

According to Sullivan (148, pp. 245-249, 1953), the most important phase of personality development during preadolescence is the experience of intimacy. A playmate may become a chum or close friend. These friends want to contribute to the happiness and self-esteem of each other. They help each other to gain a realistic idea of their most acceptable self. Having had this experience of intimacy, which can "consist of a great many things without genital contact" (148, p. 246, 1953), individuals are likely to feel more at ease with their own sex all through life.

These two-group chums may expand or interlock to form groups of three or four. Usually these larger patterns of relationship are held together by natural leaders, who may exert influence in inconspicuous ways. Thus close friendships may be incorporated as members of a gang or club. Through interaction in all these groups the individual may discover his own worth—what he is really good for.

INDIVIDUAL DIFFERENCES
IN RATE AND PATTERNS OF GROWTH

Although stages of development show characteristic patterns, one pattern merges into the next stage, more like a panorama than a kaleiodoscope. These patterns of development follow an orderly succession but the age at which each pattern appears is partially determined by the environment, which can either accelerate or retard their appearance (150, pp. 84-86, 1957).

It is important to distinguish between the child who is constitutionally slow in all aspects of maturing and the child who is retarded in a certain aspect (such as reading) by some physical or psychological hindrance or environmental lack. An example of the first pattern was a boy whose teachers said, "We can't do a thing with him." He was slow-moving, very low in reading age, and retarded in physiological processes. Though his parents were employing tutors to bring him up to grade, he did not respond to special stimulation but continued to grow at his own slow rate. In the case of a girl who was retarded three years in physical growth and equally retarded socially, thyroid treatment was ineffective. Special stimulation seemed merely to cause confusion in growth. When she was thirteen, however, she began to grow faster as part of the normal cycle of puberty. Another girl was well developed in height, weight, and strength but retarded in mental development. She was the best ball player and the fastest runner in the class, and also showed special talent in music. Her teacher used these abilities to build up her ego. In high school she obtained A's and B's in art, music, and physical education. Passing marks in the other subjects were an unearned increment.

Many cases of this kind have been presented by Millard and Rothney (106, 1957) to show differences in the growth patterns of various children and in the strands of development within an individual child. Some children grow steadily, others by fits and starts. For example, one of two children made steady progress in reading; the other showed little progress until the age of nine. After that point the second child gained as much in the next year and a half as the other child had gained in five years of steady progress. A deficiency at any point is not necessarily an indication of permanent retardation. However, fast-growing children have one advantage: they often skip lightly over a disturbance, just as a fast plane shoots across an air pocket. Slow-growing children are likely to be more seriously influenced by the same disturbance.

PHYSICAL DEVELOPMENT

Developmental sequences

The developmental sequences in height and weight are as follows:

1. A year or more of relatively slow growth, beginning around the ninth year, in which children seem to stabilize their previous growth gains; their pattern of change is more gradual than it was previously. Nevertheless, from the time they enter school to their growth spurt, they often gain one and a half feet in height and double their weight.

2. A growth spurt lasting one to two years, reaching a peak for boys around thirteen and for girls from one to two years earlier. At twelve or thirteen years of age girls are about a year ahead of boys in the development of the bones of the wrist, which is one of the best single measures of physical maturity. During this accelerated phase the taller children seem to grow more

rapidly. There is marked individual variation. Two friends who have been about the same size for several years may now part company because one has suddenly grown up so much more quickly than the other (87, 1950).

Relation of physical development
to physiological maturity, sex, and mental ability

The child's sex and physiological maturity determine how early or how late this sequence occurs. Early-maturing children enter the cycle sooner than late-maturing children and tend to be taller and heavier at each age prior to adolescence. When a child reaches a peak in rate of increase in height and weight, he will probably show the other signs of physiological maturity within one to one and one-half years (7, 1955). Many girls have their first menses while still in elementary school. Some children take as much as eight years longer than others to grow from birth to puberty (the point of development at which indications of sexual maturity appear).

The teacher of any class may expect preadolescent girls to be taller and heavier than boys of the same age. Should not this difference in maturity be considered in the school classification of pupils? What is the effect on boys of being in the same grade-group with girls who are advanced in every respect? Is it because these immature boys feel unequal pressure that they show a larger percentage of speech and reading difficulties and behavior problems? (82, 1950)

Mental deficiency is also associated with physical growth. The rate of physical growth of mentally deficient boys is slower than that of normal boys, depending upon the degree of the deficiency (45, 1936). Although subnormal boys continue to grow over a longer time than do normal and superior boys, their ultimate size, on the average, is below that of the private-school boys studied. They show retardation not only in height and weight but also in other developmental factors such as learning to walk, teething, and the onset of pubescence. Their mortality rate is nearly twice as high as that of the general population. The evidence brought to light in Flory's investigation (45, p. 95, 1936) points to the general conclusion that mentally deficient boys at the extreme end of the distribution of intelligence tend to be physically inferior.

Mass investigations on the basis of age norms, however, have indicated only a slight relation between the mental and physical status of children. A spurt in mental growth does not appear to parallel the preadolescent spurt in physical growth. The pattern of mental development is similar in boys and girls, despite the difference in their rates of physical maturing. Abernethy (1, 1936) called attention to the rather low correlations between mental and physical measures, becoming still smaller after age fourteen or fifteen. Of the various measures studied, standing height was most closely related to intelligence. However, individual case studies reported by Millard and Rothney (106, 1957) show rather similar spurts in height, weight, mental age, and achievement patterns. Exceptions occur, of course, but more synchronization of different aspects of growth is evident in the case studies than in the mass investigations.

Prediction of adult stature

Adult stature can be predicted more accurately from a series of measures taken at nine, ten, and eleven years than from a series taken at eleven, twelve, and thirteen when the child is in the puberty cycle. It is also important to know whether the child is at the beginning, the peak, or the tapering off of the growth spurt. Gray (51, 1948) worked out a technical procedure for height prediction, based on the best features of methods already developed. Bayley (15, 1956) has shown that children of these ages have definite patterns of development which allow fairly accurate predictions of adult-growth status.

Effect of deviations in physical development

Extreme disturbances and deviations in physical maturity affect the child's adjustment. Among these deviations may be mentioned oversize, undersize, extreme acceleration or retardation in rate of growth, disproportionate growth of certain parts of the body, and inappropriate growth. Very tall girls feel especially self-conscious; during adolescence they may find heterosexual adjustment exceedingly difficult. Boys, on the other hand, are usually more disturbed at being undersized. One undersized boy felt much better when the school physician explained that the X-ray pictures of his wrist bones showed that he had not yet reached his physical maturity and that he would undoubtedly grow taller. Rapid acceleration in the rate of growth puts an additional strain on the vital organs and requires protection against overexertion. Uneven growth may create problems of awkwardness and self-consciousness. Inappropriate growth, as in the case of the boy who develops feminine contours, presents still more serious problems of adjustment. Personality difficulties and emotional conflicts often arise out of fears of physical inadequacy. On the other hand, physical acceleration, among boys, may contribute to better social and psychological adjustment.

Physical acceleration coupled with mental retardation is an especially disturbing form of development. In the traditional school such an individual's mental status places him with children much smaller. Owing to his apparent maturity, he is constantly prodded to achieve beyond his real ability, often with resulting apathy or antisocial conduct.

Development of strength

Children vary more in muscular strength than in any other physical characteristic except weight. Most boys double in strength between six and eleven years of age, more so than girls. Jones (81, 1949) made a developmental study of four aspects of strength—strength of grip of right hand and of left hand, strength of pull with dynamometer held against the chest, and strength of thrust or push also with dynamometer held against the chest. He studied these aspects of strength in 183 children ranging from the fifth grade to the senior year of high school. Boys showed marked increases in strength during the growth spurt of preadolescent years.

Nutritional status

Various measures of nutritional status have been devised by Pryor and Stolz, Franzen and Palmer, McCloy, Dearborn and Rothney, Wetzel, Pyle, Massler and Suher, and others (156, pp. 313-315, 1954). Of the various physical measurements, weight is the most indicative of nutritional status, but it varies with individual factors such as age, stature, and body build. The best method of appraisal is a thorough medical examination. During these years total energy expenditure is high, largely because of the spurt of activity. Energy requirements are about twice as high when children are engaged in an activity such as bicycling as when they are playing quietly.

Tooth development

Children of this age are still getting their permanent teeth—cuspids, bicuspids, and second molars. Tooth decay is still the most prevalent physical defect in the country as a whole. Surveys have shown that more than 95 per cent of children have had some decay in their permanent teeth by the age of fifteen.

OTHER ASPECTS OF HEALTH

The years from eight to twelve tend to be the most healthy years of a child's life. There are a number of reasons for this. In the close contacts of classroom and street the children have already been exposed to the communicable diseases of childhood. Many have gained specific immunity by having caught the "children's diseases." Their interest in active games encourages sufficient outdoor exercise. As a rule, evening parties do not yet tempt these youngsters to keep late hours, although movies, radio, and television often do reduce their sleeping time.

The healthy child

A healthy child gives the impression of physical fitness, vigor, vitality, and alertness. He grows in height, weight, and other body measurements, showing gains over several months. His appetite is good and he does not eat too large a volume at one time. He sits, stands, works, and plays in good functional posture and has the strength and energy he needs. He sleeps well, and readily recovers from fatigue. He has no remediable defects of teeth, nose, throat, ears, skin, or other parts of the body. He does not think too much about his health; he does not worry about it at all.

A healthy child is also more likely to show the following characteristics: He is interested in many suitable activities and appears happy and emotionally stable. He adapts to new conditions. He concentrates on what he is doing and lives fully in the present. He is self-confident but not over-confident, and meets difficulty, failure, and criticism constructively; he is not given to making excuses, withdrawing, blaming someone else, saying that he does not care, or using other escape mechanisms. He shows concern for the welfare of others and is able to relate himself successfully to other boys and girls, as well as to older and younger persons. He progresses toward goals he has chosen, and makes wise decisions.

Disease and accidents

Among children from ten to fourteen the leading causes of death reported by the Metropolitan Life Insurance Company for 1954-1955 (104, p. 6, 1956) are quite similar to those in the primary grades, accidents leading by a very large percentage (23.7 per cent for boys, but only 7.4 per cent for girls). Although death rates for this age group are relatively low, illness rates from communicable and respiratory diseases are still high.

Viewed in the perspective of a half-century, however, great progress has been made in improving the health and in reducing the mortality of children of school ages. In 1955 the death rate for ages five to nineteen years was about 40 per cent less than in 1946. The decline has been relatively more rapid for girls than for boys (104, p. 5, 1956). The present low death rate can be further reduced. Though effective methods for treating the major causes of children's deaths are available, treatment is still often delayed until it is too late.

Much more progress needs to be made in accident prevention. However, some encouragement may be derived from recent statistics, which show a decrease in total accidents in the ten- to fourteen-year-old group from a rate of 34.4 per 100,000 in 1946-1947 to 23.7 in 1954-1955. Girls showed a slight increase from 7.4 to 8.4 (104, p. 6, 1956). Some cities with sound safety programs have been able to reduce child accidents by as much as 20 to 30 per cent.

Illness and accidents often affect social adjustment. For example, the child with a heart condition that prevents him from engaging in athletics is doubly handicapped, especially during his preadolescent and adolescent years. Proficiency in sports gives a boy of this age self-esteem and confirms his sense of masculinity. Boys who do not take part in competitive games are often called "sissies."

Although illness and death are no respectors of persons, some groups seem to suffer more than their share. Between the ages of ten to fourteen the death rate of boys exceeded that of girls by 70 per cent (137, p. 22, 1958). One survey showed that lower socioeconomic groups had more illnesses and physical defects than professional, clerical, and business groups.

MOTOR SKILLS, GAMES, AND HOBBIES

In general, preadolescent children are eager, active, and alert. They have good control of their bodies. They are able to run fast and to get their wind again quickly. They readily acquire skill in sports. For example, during one summer at camp a twelve-year-old boy who had had no experience in water sports learned to swim one hundred yards in excellent form and to handle a canoe and rowboat expertly. Motor control is important for a child's general adjustment. Both sexual and aggressive impulses may be channeled through games and sports.

Motor ability

Growth in motor ability is shown by tests as well as by continuous systematic observation. The Oseretsky scale of motor proficiency (26, 1949; 91, 1948), suitable for children aged four through sixteen, is comparable in structure to the Binet-Simon scale for measuring intelligence and the Vineland Social Maturity Scale for measuring social competence. It can be applied either to groups or individuals. Development of the large muscles of shoulder, arm, and wrist appears to approach adult levels more rapidly than does speed of finger movements. Children who are taller, heavier, and older tend to be the ones who are superior in motor and physical efficiency.

Play interests

Children of these ages are normally energetic and reach out for information and new experiences. Their play is varied and includes arts and crafts as well as sports and games (64, 1957).

A number of reasonable theories have been devised to account for children's interest in play: it has been said to represent a release of surplus energy, preparation for adult life, escape from conflict or boredom, spontaneous activity engaged in for its own sake, a biological need, and a psychological need. Although there is some relation between the kind of play and the child's strength and physical fitness, the play life of a child is an index of his social maturity and reveals his personality more clearly than any other activity. Increased emphasis is being placed upon diagnosis and therapy through play activities.

Although the nature of children's play varies with the environment, surveys of children's play interests have been sufficiently extensive to warrant certain generalizations. Some of their games such as hide-and-seek, blindman's bluff, hopscotch, Red Rover, dodge ball, have existed for centuries. The peak of variety in play activities appears to be in the ninth year. After the tenth year there is a decrease in the number of different play activities reported. Freedom to engage in a wider range of activities takes children out of their homes to the hillsides to build caves; to the woods to climb trees, gather nuts, construct cabins, make campfires; to the town to buy parts for radio sets and model planes and to watch the big machines at work erecting new buildings; to the pond for skating and swimming; and all over the surrounding country or city streets on foot or on bicycles and roller skates. There is scarcely a play activity that some ten-year-olds do not check. However, it is evident that there are individual differences in variety of play interests. Some children engage in fewer than ten activities while others engage in almost one hundred kinds of recreation during a single week.

The present-day play patterns of preadolescent children reflect the recreational emphases of our times. Children's play seems to be increasingly patterned after the interests of our mechanized, effort-reducing civilization. The spontaneous, adventurous, resourceful play of a generation ago is being replaced by the planned, expensive, supervised, spectator-type activities of many children today. This trend may be deflected by provision of more creative play facilities and freedom to use the natural play resources in the environment. When necessary, skillful supervision will encourage the children to plan their own activities and guide them just enough so that they will have the satisfaction of reaching the group goal by working together. Adults have probably been intruding too much in the closed circle of the society of children. In these societies are natural leaders who may be both admired and feared; their influence may be either constructive or unwholesome. The gang often has a language of its own. It is difficult for adults to know what is going on in these preadolescent groups.

At no age is play exclusively individualistic or entirely social. Under favorable conditions, ten-year-old boys become interested in teamwork, show loyalty to their team, and play a larger number of organized games such as baseball. This growing interest in the team partly accounts for the increasing popularity, between the ages of nine and sixteen, of ball games which require skill in throwing and catching and participation in more complicated group organization.

During these years playing ball takes precedence over games of chase and playing with toys. Imaginative play decreases during this age period. For girls there is a rapid decline in doll-play toward the end of this period. Boys would probably show a similar decline in their interest in playing space cadets, pilots, G-men, and cowboys. At thirteen or fourteen there is a marked falling off of interest in childhood games. No abrupt cessation of any specific play activity, however, occurs for all children at any age level. Changes in play interests are gradual. Differences in play activities between age groups are smaller than those among children of the same age; play interests overlap from age to age.

Boys and girls seem to differ more widely in play interests between the ages of eight and ten than at any other age period. This tendency is probably part of a general social divergence of the two sexes that occurs at this time. Eleven-year-old boys and girls in a semirural, semi-industrial midwestern city did not differ greatly in their outdoor living, although the boys were somewhat more active and adventurous (163, 1948). Constructions made with blocks and toys by boys are quite different from those made by girls. When preadolescents were given different types of play materials and told to construct an imaginary scene, boys used more blocks and vehicles; girls more furniture and family figures (69, 1951). Boys usually build outdoor scenes and girls house interiors (39, 1951). During adolescence boys and girls are in closer agreement as to preferred forms of play. At all ages, however, girls' activities are usually more restricted by customs and mores than are boys', but the play interests of both vary, to some extent, with the surrounding culture.

Boys nine to twelve tend to engage in vigorous play stunts, timed races, and other activities involving competition, dexterity, and skill. They are willing to practice in order to acquire the desired proficiency. They also like to make radio sets and tinker with bicycles, electric bells, and other kinds of mechanical devices. Woodworking and general science are favorite subjects.

Although bright children include in their repertory of activities games enjoyed by mentally retarded children, they prefer more mature games and spend much more time in reading. They tend to be less interested in competitive games. Davidson (30, 1943) reported that gifted children aged nine to thirteen, from both high- and low-income levels, showed play interests and activities different from those of other children; games such as baseball and sports such as ice skating were popular at all economic levels.

The best play activities for children help them to find themselves and learn to get along with their age-mates. Some carry over into adult life, for example, baseball, skating, swimming, cooking, assuming full responsibility for pets, doing useful odd jobs in the house and out of doors, hiking, camping, nature study, and music. Through group games, children in this period develop courage, resourcefulness, concentration, co-operation, understanding of and obedience to rules, and willingness to endure drudgery to gain skill.

During this age period children interested in music may develop skill in playing the piano, the violin, or some other musical instrument. Their sense of rhythm, discrimination of sound, associative memory, and muscular control are almost as good as they will ever be. Moreover, they have more time to practice than they will have later when they enter upon the wider relationships and duties of adolescence. But parents should avoid overscheduling the child's day. In the growing-up process children need a combination of rough and tumble out-of-door play, other group activities in which they learn human relations, and time for solitary reading or doing nothing in particular.

There is a point, usually between the fourth and seventh grades, when the family-group atmosphere of the classroom changes to an age-group feeling. The lines of attraction or association now extend from child to child, rather than from child to teacher. Children may even gang up against a teacher who misunderstands them. Having relinquished much of their dependence on their parents, they may become too subservient to their peer group—in a world apart.

Children's collections

Of all the hobbies of this age, making collections is the most prevalent. Probably more than half of the children between nine and fourteen have collections. Many are interested in the collecting process itself. Often the items themselves, however worthless they appear to adults, are cherished by the children. What they collect depends upon their environment and age and is determined more or less accidentally. From a mere jumble of things of slight educational value, they may move toward collections that vivify facts and give experience in organization and classification. One fifth grade became interested in making geography scrapbooks; their collections were not only large, but also well selected and organized. Though many items are common to the collections of both boys and girls, marbles, stamps, guns, bits of machinery, and rocks are generally more characteristic of boys, and dolls, pieces of cloth, pictures of movie stars, letters, photos, and four-leaf clovers are more likely to be found in girls' collections. Stamp collecting has potential educational value and may become a financially profitable hobby. Even though the collected objects may be unimportant, the process of collecting serves a need of the child. Collecting may contribute to systematic and discriminating habits of mind. It "is a godsend to an untidy world"; it is one way in which the child feels that he can control the world.

HANDWRITING

Handwriting is no longer revered as an art; nowadays it is primarily regarded as a means of communication. Its place is being increasingly usurped by the typewriter, which even elementary children enjoy using. Handwriting, however, is still far from being obsolete; most people still have need of legible and fairly rapid handwriting.

For practical purposes a quality of fifty to sixty on the Ayres scale written at the rate of sixty to seventy words per minute (see page 384) for ordinary handwriting is adequate, with special attention given to the writing of names and numbers. Speed and quality of handwriting normally increase rapidly between the ages of eight and twelve (48, 1954). Modern standards do not demand the copybook perfection formerly aimed at; they emphasize neatness, ease, and rapid and legible writing for everyday use.

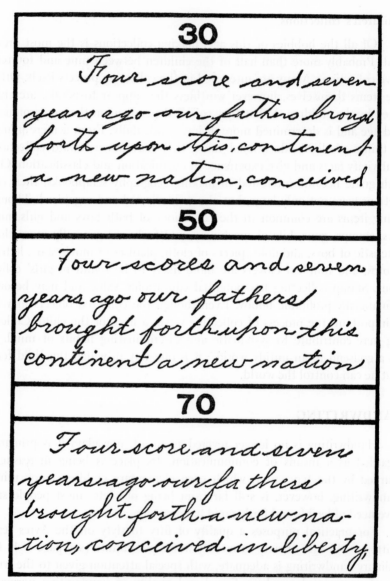

Fig. 5. Three qualities from the Ayres handwriting scale.

ART AND MUSIC

As the child proceeds through the grades, his art work generally becomes less spontaneous and original. This is partly because he becomes increasingly concerned with skills and more willing to conform, and partly because many schools discourage originality and initiative and do not stimulate each child to work up to his capacity. Schools have a real problem in helping the child acquire the necessary technique to express his creative ideas.

Children grow more critical of and less satisfied with their drawings and paintings during this period. They are conscious of the defects in their attempts to capture, on paper or canvas, with clay, or with other media, their glimpses of beauty. Hence many children's artistic careers end in this period. Since such slight emphasis is put on ability to draw, children tend to stop trying if their results are unsatisfactory to themselves or are criticized by others.

The talented pupil who will produce the art of the future should be discovered through submitting samples of children's art work to a committee of experts. Talented children should then be given experiences which will lay a good foundation for their future work. Their vocational aptitude in this field should be developed in an environment in which they will have inspiration, freedom, instruction, and recognition.

Artistic effort may be directed into many avenues such as lettering, making posters, decorating articles of furniture or clothing, designing costumes, and drawing maps and diagrams. Art work in the schools should give the pupils not only pleasure in creating pictures and designs, and in finding new forms of expression, but also an understanding of their physical and human environment and appreciation of significant form in everyday surroundings. One major objective of art education for every pupil is to build a more beautiful America. As a consumer of art he should be able to buy art products with good taste and judgment.

Similar principles and procedures apply to the development of appreciation and proficiency in music (89, 1958). Exceptional achievement in any line is usually associated with high general ability. In any kind of musical performance many physical and psychological functions are involved. During these years an inventory of certain elements in musical ability may be made by means of the Seashore tests of pitch, intensity, time, consonance, rhythms, and tonal memory. The results of the tests or auditions should be considered in connection with teachers' observations of the child's proficiency in and attitudes toward music.

LANGUAGE

Interest in language is still strong in this period. Vocabulary increases and sentences improve in grammatical correctness, in terseness, and in fluency. By the time the child enters the fourth grade, he should have acquired fundamental word-recognition skills, accurate return sweep from one line to the next, a basic vocabulary rich in meanings, ability to comprehend thought units and to enjoy or apply what he reads. Without doubt this age period is a crucial time for perfecting the skills already acquired and for developing higher levels of reading comprehension. It is also a time when voluntary reading reaches a peak. Through reading, children of these ages should gain a broader view of a world beyond their own and a deeper understanding of themselves and family relations.

Language is basic to thought and to communication. Linguistic development is part of mental development as a whole.

It is not merely the ability to memorize words and phrases with a view to being able to reproduce them more or less mechanically upon the receipt of a given cue; it is the ability to make intelligent use of words for the purpose of defining our thoughts and feelings as clearly as possible to ourselves, and of expressing them, when necessary, as clearly as possible to others, in order to share our experiences with them, to bring about their intellectual enlightenment or to influence their behaviour. And this being so, no genuine enlargement of vocabulary can be secured except through an enlargement of the understanding, and equally no development of sensitivity in the use of language except through a general quickening, maturing, illuminating, and energizing of the mind in all its functions.*

The study of a child's language throws light on his whole personality and the nature of his thinking. The purpose for which he uses language is significant—whether to attain social ends, to communicate his feelings, to gain personal power or mastery of language itself, or to display his knowledge or self-importance. The scope and precision of his verbal expression indicate his habits of thought. His spontaneous remarks and the answers he makes to questions give adults an idea of the way the world appears to him. His growth in ability to see relationships is reflected in his

---

* A. F. Watts, *The Language and Mental Development of Children* (London: George G. Harrap & Co., 1944), p. 30. Quoted with the permission of George G. Harrap & Co. and D. C. Heath & Co.

sentence structure—in his use of subordinate clauses, prepositional phrases, and verb forms.

The following poem was written by a twelve-year-old boy (111, p. 51, 1928):

SWALLOWS

The air is thick with swarms of swallows
    High among the clouds,
    Flying all in crowds;
Up the hills and down the hollows
Swarms of swooping, swerving swallows,

Burnished, dark blue, darting swallows,
    Sailing o'er the sea,
    Flying blithe and free;
Every bird the next one follows,
Swarms of flying, floating swallows.

        GEORGE R. (age 12).
        The Perse School,
        Cambridge, England

During these preadolescent years the child's vocabulary should grow in size, vividness, and precision. The number of words recognized and the number of words used increase as the child grows toward maturity. The vocabulary estimated from the Binet test is 5,400 words for ten-year-old and 7,200 for twelve-year-old children.

The cultural background may make a difference of as much as eight months in the linguistic development of children of the upper and the lower social classes. A ten-year-old child who has acquired incorrect, inappropriate habits of speech is definitely handicapped; firmly established habits of incorrect grammar and articulation are difficult to eradicate. Many youngsters develop two languages, one for use in school and the other for use at home and on the street. In school one boy was marked A in oral English; at the same time he was using such expressions as, "I ain't got nothin'," outside of school.

The age of a child's associates is related to his language development. In this respect the younger children in a family have an advantage. They gain a great deal from their conversations with older brothers and sisters whose language is somewhat in advance of theirs. Children closely associated with cultured adults have an advantage in language development.

Under typical school conditions, children make a noticeable degree of progress from grade four to grade six in correcting grammatical errors such as, "He is badder than I," "She dresses nice," "I ain't got any," "I don't want no more," "We was on time," "We laid down last night." The correct use of pronouns also increases. There is some evidence that children from lower socioeconomic groups tend to make the greatest improvement in the elimination of errors during the early school years.

From the first grade on there is an increase in the complexity of the sentences and in the length of written compositions. This increase is associated with maturity and experience as well as with mental age. The complexity of sentences children use in oral and written language expression was thoroughly studied by Harrell (58, 1957). Children nine, eleven, thirteen, and fifteen years were asked to write, and later to tell into a microphone, their response to two equally interesting films. Thus their oral and written expression could be compared. The results were then analyzed. The following are some of Harrell's findings: Girls wrote longer stories than boys, especially at the lower age levels; but other than this, there were no significant sex differences. Nearly every aspect of language studied increased with age, even beyond fifteen years. The older children "wrote and told longer stories, used more words per clause, and used a greater percentage of each type of subordinate clause." (58, p. 70, 1957) These increases with age were greater for written than for oral stories. The children used more subordinate clauses in writing than in speaking, especially more adverb and adjective clauses. About two-thirds of all adverb clauses were time clauses. The percentage of subordination was positively related to chronological age, mental age, intelligence quotient, and occupational status.

Secret languages such as "pig Latin" appear in this period. This interest in secret language may be sublimated into an interest in the study of a foreign language in these grades if it is introduced in such a way as to fit the children's level of maturity.

Slang begins to appear in this period. That "the rest of the gang uses slang" is to a ten-year-old sufficient reason for adopting it. Forceful, vivid slang should be retained in the particular situations to which it is appropriate. It is a contribution to our contemporary language. For example, the phrase "up against it" expresses tersely the idea of being face to face with an insurmountable difficulty. Adults must admit the vividness of some of the expressions current in 1958: "I'm bugging out," (leaving the place in a hurry); "I don't dig that," (understand it); "That's neat," (all right in every way); "What a drip," (odd person); "He's a square—not hep to the jive," (behind the times); "That's a real bomb," (fast car); "Digit dazzle," (fingernail polish). By finding other expressive words to substitute for the overuse of slang, children will make a good start in progressing beyond "the moron level of conversation." The kind of slang which should be prevented from gaining headway in this period is that which is ungrammatical, vulgar, or applied inappropriately and indiscriminately to all occasions.

Swearing is another language response which may make its appearance in the preschool period. Young children use such words imitatively at first, probably without half understanding their meaning. If the words produce a startling, exciting effect on some adult, children tend to repeat the experiment. If the words are ignored a child may drop them of his own accord. One day a preschool child walked into his father's room and called joyfully, "Well, Godandamn." His father was somewhat amazed, but he merely said, "What does that mean?" "Jackie says it means, 'Well, isn't this grand!'" At his father's suggestion the small boy willingly substituted the latter expression for the objectionable one that had little meaning for him. Older boys can realize the deep religious significance of taking the name of God in vain.

Older children are likely to stop using socially objectional words if they learn a better vocabulary early and if they realize that some people do not like certain words and that it is inconsiderate and somewhat immature to use them in certain situations. The boy should think of swearing not as something that distinguishes him as a man of the world, but as something out of place and inappropriate in most situations. Children's use of words in an objectional way is usually transient.

Magic and ritual play a part in the speech of children during these years. The counting-out rhymes, magical incantations and wishing ceremonies, coded talk and writing—all apply the touch of magic to language.

SPELLING

More children spell a given word correctly in each succeeding grade. The largest improvement, according to Swenson and Caldwell's investigation (149, 1948), occurred between grades five and six. This improvement seems to be associated with maturation, improved reading, and increased incentive to spell, rather than with the amount of time spent in teaching spelling. Less than fifty words, only 4 per cent of all the words misspelled in children's letters, made up 28 per cent of all errors. Horn (70, 1954) has made a useful summary of research in teaching spelling, which students should read carefully.

The successful speller tends to be systematic in his attack on words, to look at them discriminately, to reinforce his first impression by visualizing and vocalizing them, and to check the accuracy of his spelling. He has acquired "a spelling conscience." He is eager to learn, concentrates well, shows initiative and good motor control, makes his own lists of words to be learned, and is good at writing. The poor speller, on the contrary, lacks self-direction, initiative, and a systematic method of attack. He tends to be careless and indifferent, and habitually mispronounces words. Retarded spellers also tend to be poor in handwriting and in reading (134, 1955).

READING

Many persons have the impression that the schools today are raising a generation of poor readers. Actually today's children have scored as high or higher, on the average, in silent reading than those of twenty-five years ago. But now there are more extremely poor readers as well as more extremely good readers than earlier. This variability might account for the impression that there are more poor readers now than "in the good old days."

In many schools the intensive attention given to reading decreases after the third grade and gradually dies out. This should not be. There is need of a systematic development of reading skills appropriate to each rung of the educational ladder from kindergarten to graduate school. San Diego (135, 1956) has emphasized this developmental aspect of reading by preparing a guide listing the reading skills to be introduced and developed at each grade level.

Individual and sex differences in reading achievement

Any reading test administered in any typical class reveals a wide range of ability. In the sixth grade, for example, one sometimes finds a range of ten years in reading ability; a range of seven years is common. One pupil may take two minutes to read a passage which another pupil can read and comprehend in ten seconds. Consequently, the latter is able to complete in five minutes an assignment over which his classmate may need to puzzle for an hour.

In general, more boys than girls come to reading clinics. This may be a reflection of a fundamental difference in maturity between the sexes. Failing to recognize this difference in maturity, teachers expect the same reading achievement of both boys and girls. The larger proportion of poor readers among boys has also been attributed to poor auditory discrimination, greater interest in outdoor activities, and poor relationship with the teachers. The boys' initial sense of failure and inadequacy may persistently influence their approach to reading.

Oral reading

At about the fourth grade the silent-reading rate begins to forge ahead of the oral-reading rate. When this fact was discovered, it became apparent that pupils' reading progress might be retarded if they continued to read aloud. Thereupon the pendulum swung to the opposite extreme of giving practically no attention to oral reading. At present, oral reading is beginning to occupy its rightful place in the reading program. It has social value as a means of sharing one's enjoyment of a book or article, and diagnostic value as a check on the mechanics of reading and on accuracy of reading comprehension.

Silent reading

The norms on standardized reading tests for a given type of reading material are much more meaningful than any average figures of rate and comprehension at different ages, since the rate of silent reading varies greatly with the kind of material and print, the child's interest in the material, the purpose for which he reads it, and his familiarity with the field. Simple stories can be read more quickly than science, and general science more quickly than problems in arithmetic. Effective methods of comprehending the thought of a passage should be stressed, not speed per se. The good reader is versatile in his attack on unfamiliar words; he uses phonetic analysis when it is useful to him, divides and combines syllables, or studies the way the words are built.

Favorite books

Many studies have been made of children's reading interests. Children's choice of books is influenced by the physical make-up of the book, the vocabulary burden, the type of content, and the literary character. Other things being equal, children of these ages prefer a reasonably small book, in good clear print, set in short paragraphs and illustrated by action pictures. The vocabulary burden is least when new and difficult words are introduced gradually in a familiar context. The most interesting content appears to include surprise, action, animals, conversation, children's humor, and plot. Pupils in grades four to eight, especially boys, are most interested in dramatic action, adventure, and heroic qualities. Fairy and supernatural elements have less appeal in the latter part of this period.

During the preadolescent years, interest in comic books comes in as a veritable tidal wave. Comics are ubiquitous; children of all levels of intelligence and socioeconomic status read them—rich and poor, bright and dull, urban and rural. Their sale is enormous: fifty million comic magazines were sold in one month.

Though the comics deal with the same themes as children's books, they put more emphasis on crime, horror, and sex. They vary enormously in their quality. Some are suitable for children; others are not. Some are very well drawn; others are hideous in line and color. Some are comical, imaginative, informative, and amusing; others picture cruelty and violence. Some are carefully censored and checked by advisory boards of educators and psychiatrists; others "get away with murder."

Children like comics because the action is sustained from start to finish and is easy to comprehend. Many children "read" the pictures and skip most of the captions. Comics give the same kind of pleasure as reading but require much less effort. The comics, like the old melodramas, never leave one in doubt as to the identity of the hero and the villain, or as to which will triumph. According to Frank (47, 1955), children from nine years on tend to turn to more realistic stories.

For some children the comics provide release of aggressive impulses. Children seven to nine seem to prefer the more fantastic and magical comics, which, like folktales, offer an escape into fantasy. By identifying themselves with the characters, children can break through the routines and restrictions imposed by civilization. Although children and young people may blame the comics or the movies for crimes they have committed, this is not proof of causation. Children tend to take in what is of value to them at the time and to bypass much of the content that seems to be unsuitable for them.

However, on the basis of confessions made by delinquents, Healy and Bronner believe that magazines and comic books dealing with bandits and underworld life have a pernicious influence upon the development of young people and create an addiction to this type of reading. Comics, although they sometimes meet the needs of an individual child for release of aggression or understanding of his own impulses and the attitudes of others toward him, often counteract the teaching of home and school and decrease the child's initial revulsion to cruelty and crime. Different comic books have different effects on different children: A few may be beneficial; many may have a neutral effect on most children; a few may be harmful to all or to most children (83, 1954). Therefore, the actual effect of comics cannot be stated in general. The comics may only play upon a need that is already there, a fear or anxiety that has previously lain dormant. The important thing is to know the individual child and his responses to the particular book. If moderate reading of the comics makes a child preoccupied with crime and horror, special study of the child is indicated. Children's choice of comics often reveals their needs. The main problem is to put comics in their place. They should not crowd out a child's outdoor play, group activities, home duties, other reading, or more serious work to be done in school.

Of their own accord most children outgrow their intense interest in the comics. Parents and teachers can further this process by (1) providing other reading material and facilities for broadening children's interests, (2) helping them to evaluate the comics and select the best, and (3) understanding and respecting their opinions when they talk about the comics.

CHILDREN'S HUMOR

Relatively little is known about the sense of humor in general and still less about the objects or situations that children find amusing. The humor of ten-year-olds seems to center around nonsense rhymes, comics, and caricatures. School children laugh about comical situations within their own experience, especially those having elements of incongruity, discomfiture of others, and grotesqueness such as clowns, minstrels, and performing animals. Novelty is also amusing. One child wrote, "It was the first time I saw an elephant, so I laughed." They like to play with word meanings, as in punning in which the same word is used in two different senses. Making wisecracks often is a form of defense, and other jokes about things that worry them help to decrease their anxiety. They tend to take themselves too seriously to make jokes about themselves and are vulnerable to being made the butt of jokes. It seems quite clear that children's sense of humor parallels their intellectual and emotional development (79, pp. 902-904, 1954). One metaphysically minded eleven-year-old girl wrote, "I think the funniest thing was that I was taught that God is everywhere, for if He is everywhere, He would be fat and thin and long and wide."

Teachers and parents who are able to enter into the child's world of amusing happenings have established a real bond of sympathy and understanding.

ARITHMETIC

When the child enters the fourth grade his knowledge of the fundamental computations, the language of arithmetic, and also his ability to apply thinking in situations involving number should be inventoried. No new structure can be erected save on a firm foundation, and, if this foundation is lacking, the first task is to supply it. Having ascertained the individual needs and abilities of his pupils, the teacher should begin instruction at the level of their readiness and proficiency, and should provide practice for each new step.

Among the factors associated with successful achievement in problem-solving in sixth-grade arithmetic are (1) arithmetic factors such as skill in fundamental operations; (2) ability to think abstractly with numbers and to estimate the answers to problems; (3) general reasoning ability; ability to note differences, likenesses, and spatial relations; memory; and ability to draw inferences; (4) general language ability; and (5) skill in the reading of graphs, charts, and tables. In correcting errors, the better students may be expected to show greater insight, be more concerned about their errors, reason more effectively in attempting to locate errors, and show greater ingenuity in eliminating errors by proving their results.

SCIENCE AND SOCIAL STUDIES

Nine- to twelve-year-old children generally have an avid interest in facts. They are keenly interested in ancient plants and animals, astronomy, magnetism, the earth and its surface. Their accurate knowledge about airplanes, automobiles, and practical science puts many an adult to shame. Junior-high-school students have a lively interest in biological sciences, animal life, health, growth and reproduction if they are taught in a vital way. This increase in geographical, historical, and scientific facts should be accompanied by an advance in solving problems, seeing relations, and making application to real-life problems. These abilities are ends to which the acquisition of facts is only a means. The building of permanent interests and the recognition of causal relations are important objectives.

Reports concerned with the teaching of social sciences emphasize the basic importance of studying the local community, beginning with an understanding of human relations in the class group and reaching out to wider relations. Gradually, through the social studies in grades four to eight, pupils should achieve a growing understanding of their role in the world today.

Research in these subjects, as in spelling and arithmetic, indicates the need for a map of values, uncluttered by insignificant detail. Parallel with this elimination of deadwood, several trends are noticeable: to devote more time to science in grades four to six, to provide more opportunity for experimentation and discovery, to use informal school activities as opportunities for teaching the ways of democracy, to use community resources and improve the local community, to apply the problem approach in these fields, and to integrate each study with other subject areas.

INTELLIGENCE

Manifestations of intelligence

Children nine to twelve years old reveal their intelligence by the way they respond to problem situations, by their ability to detect absurdities and to see significant elements in a situation. Their awareness of social problems is related to intelligence, as well as to social status and sex, and to what is psychologically near for them (41, 1952). Their mental ability is also indicated by their sensible answers to questions, by their success in understanding the precise meaning of words and in defining abstract words, by their power to detect verbal and mathematical relationships and to make generalizations, by their use of language, and by the possession of such information as might be acquired by an alert mind in daily contact with things and persons. These are attributes of educability. They constitute what is commonly called intelligent behavior.

One of the notable advances made between the ninth and the twelfth years is the ability to define abstract words. Average ten-year-old children cannot give a satisfactory definition of "revenge," "justice," "pity," or "charity." But twelve-year-old children will tell you that revenge means "to get even with someone," that justice means "to give people what they deserve," that to pity means "to be sorry for someone," and that charity consists in helping "those who are needy."

During this period, children grow in ability to see relationships. At least half of eleven-year-old children recognize that a snake, cow, and sparrow are alike in that they "all are animals" or "all move." (152, pp. 265-266, 1937) The younger child classifies objects according to relatively superficial, concrete, specific, or vague characteristics; the older child according to more fundamental and less obvious common characteristics.

Interest in puzzles and riddles is said to culminate in this period. Since many are problems in interpreting word meanings and in reasoning, this absorbing activity should be encouraged.

Memory is a major factor in intelligent behavior. At least half of the ten-year-old children tested are able to repeat six digits that have just been pronounced distinctly and with uniform emphasis. At eleven years of age the majority of children repeat without errors sentences of approximately twenty syllables (152, p. 109, 1937). On certain memory tests there is a decline in rate of growth of children after age twelve. Memory is not mere mechanical recall; it involves an active translation of the new facts into one's own preconceived scheme of things. Children from different social groups draw on their respective backgrounds; they tend to change unfamiliar names and idioms in a story to more familiar ones. Usually they recast the story around a general scheme or some detail which is highly meaningful to them. Most difficult for a child to remember is something foreign to his psychological field. Certainly rote memory should not be emphasized at the expense of practice in reasoning and the organization of knowledge.

Growth in intelligence

Individual curves differ markedly in form, and comparatively few conform closely to the average; each is unique (15, 1956). In an analysis of data from the Harvard Growth Study, Armstrong (7, 1955) found that among three-fourths of the boys and one-half of the girls, there was a two- to three-year period in which they showed almost no mental growth. This plateau is followed by a sudden jump in IQ, after which the child proceeds according to his previously expected pattern. Individual differences in development may therefore cause a child who is at one age doing average work, compared to his peers, to drop behind during the period of little or no growth. Extra pressure at this time tends to aggravate the problem. Later he should revert to his normal pattern of development. Armstrong's study casts serious doubts on the reliability of intelligence scores obtained immediately prior to puberty, especially after the onset of the spurt in physical growth.

Conditions influencing growth in intelligence

Education influences mental growth. Within the limits set by heredity, intellectual functioning can be improved by education. From about twelve years on, education appears to play an increasingly important part. The teacher, in appraising a child's ability, should take into consideration his background and previous experiences.

Though, for example, it has been commonly accepted that a verbal intelligence test is the best test available for selecting children for academic education at around the age of eleven, we cannot always be sure that justice is being done to children from homes where linguistic standards are low. In Birmingham, England, some years ago, several thousand children who took Watts's vocabulary tests were divided into two groups representing poor and comparatively well-to-do districts respectively. The results showed that at ten years of age the children from the higher socioeconomic levels were able to score an average of fifty per cent better than their less fortunately placed fellows. As the age rose this advantage gradually slipped away and at the age of fourteen there was little difference in scores between children from the two types of home background. Judgments, therefore, as to the relative amounts of intelligence possessed by those who have been subjected to linguistic tests may be dangerous, unless we can be sure that the tested persons have been brought up in similar environments and had the same kind of schooling.

Other things being equal, however, a person's mastery of language for general purposes is a reliable index to his intellectual powers (170, pp. 25-26, 1944). In fact, it has been demonstrated that verbal comprehension and word fluency is influenced by inheritance to a larger extent than any of the other primary mental abilities that have so far been isolated. Number ability seems to be more readily educable than either verbal or reasoning abilities (18, pp. 922-933, 1954).

Nonacademic children

Children are not equally educable. It has been estimated that approximately 15 to 18 per cent of elementary children fall in the dull normal group, having intelligence quotients between 70 or 75 and 90. These are not morons. A moron is a feeble-minded person who, through the imperfect development of intelligence, is so lacking in "practical judgment as to be in need of social assistance or supervision." (37, 1948)

Teachers can recognize marked mental retardation. Among 592 children whom teachers referred to a psychological bureau because of suspected feeble-mindedness, 51 per cent were classified by the Binet test as feeble-minded, 46 per cent as borderline, and only 3 per cent as above the borderline level.

Mental defect appears to be associated with a constellation of factors: retardation in traditional school systems, mentally defective brothers and sisters, oversuggestibility, preference for younger children as playmates, and a slow or dull manner. The vocabulary of mental defectives is markedly below normal. Even in practical, nonabstract types of work mentally deficient children are characterized by limited attention, limited use of experience, and a poor understanding of interrelations. They find concentration increasingly hard as the work becomes more difficult. On the other hand, because they work less intensely than normal children, they may not be so easily fatigued. Their rate of mental growth in later adolescence is relatively rapid; they can profit by continued education. These characteristics should be recognized and taken into account in their instruction.

Fay and Doll (42, 1949) reported a striking instance of a seven-year-old boy whose case the psychologist and pediatrician had diagnosed as one of "essential idiocy." The mother was advised to "place the child in an institution and forget that he had been born." Further diagnosis showed normal social behavior. The retardation in language development appeared to be the result of impairment of a portion of the brain. During treatment his behavior improved markedly; his progress at the clinic school was slow but positive. Parents of mentally retarded children are greatly concerned with this question: "Is my child genuinely feeble-minded, i.e., essentially incurable, or does the mental deficiency arise from causes which will yield to treatment?" Only a comprehensive diagnosis and an ample period of observation can answer this question.

Follow-up studies have shown that nonacademic boys who have had training in special schools hold a variety of useful positions and become worthy citizens (98, 1949).

Gifted children

Children recognized as gifted may be superior in abstract verbal ability or may possess special talents or abilities. It has been estimated that in the United States there are about one hundred thousand children with IQ's of 130 and above. A large proportion of these gifted children are not identified, especially in the lower socioeconomic groups. In the absence of psychological services, many gifted children can be recognized by the characteristics already described (see Chap. 15). They show these characteristics at an earlier age than the majority of children; they are "old for their years."

Gifted children as a group show a wide variation in characteristics. Those above 170 IQ sometimes have special difficulty in social adjustment. Children with Binet IQ's above 150 have many problems of adjustment which tax even their high degree of insight and adaptability. Not the least of these is the problem of getting along with their peers and with inefficient and unreasonable persons in authority. Like other children, those with high mental ability must be given individual attention for optimum development (31, 1957).

Having identified the gifted children, the teacher should be sure to (1) give them room to grow and not restrict their natural urge to learn; (2) provide opportunities for them to select experiences appropriate for them, including typing, handicraft, experimentation, recreation, and creative work; and (3) offer incentives for them to use their special abilities. Since they are capable of learning quickly, they should be helped to acquire suitable study and reading methods.

Gifted preadolescent children should have a large measure of individual freedom to suggest special projects, set goals for themselves, work out problems on their own initiative, and engage in work more or less akin to research. They should be excused from unnecessary drill. In the classroom and at home a wide variety of books should be available to them; excursions and visits to museums should be part of their curriculum. Their tendencies to work below capacity, to daydream for want of something more interesting to do, and to "get by" on superficial quickness and clever guesses should be nipped in the bud. Gifted children should feel a sense of responsibility in return for their fortunate combination of heredity and early childhood and school experiences.

Some gifted children fail in school and become behavior problems. What makes the difference between success and failure for bright children? The successful children tend to be sociable and outgoing. They like school. In contrast, the bright children who fail in school tend to be unsociable and withdrawn, immature, and overprotected. Emotional relations in their homes are likely to be poor. Those from higher socioeconomic levels have less monetary motivation to succeed than gifted children from poor homes.

The learning of gifted children has been seriously neglected in many schools. At ten years of age some of Terman's group of gifted children had learned in spite of unsuitable curriculum and instruction,

Terman and Oden have stated that a considerable proportion of those in their gifted group "languished in idleness" throughout elementary and high school and failed to develop the ambition or habits of work necessary to succeed in college (153, 1947). Subjected to an unsuitable school program, they gradually forgot how to study or lost their interest and their drive to accomplish.

SPIRITUAL AND MORAL VALUES

Spiritual values become real in acts of co-operation, sharing responsibility, courage, kindness, fair play, sensitivity to other persons, appreciation of beauty, and creative thinking. All these stem from a deep respect or even reverence for human beings. Persons, not material things, are the deepest concern of society; love, not force, is the path toward human betterment. These are basic principles that must somehow be translated into the daily conduct of children. Children need parents and teachers who speak of human values concretely—"not being mean to a new pupil, but thinking about how he feels." Something the adult says casually may simmer in the child's mind and emerge later as his own value.

The broad point of view about spiritual values has been presented in a practical way in a year book of the National Education Association, Department of Elementary School Principals (118, 1947). There examples are given of creative work and the ways in which it developed—clubs initiated through student interest, co-operative planning by students and teachers, a church program planned and carried out by the children themselves.

Sixth-grade children have a strong sense of justice. If they think adults have been unfair, they are quick to say so. Boys listed the following as things that annoyed and irritated them most: injustice, war, sarcasm, bullying, and "laughing when others get hurt." (176, 1945) They are sensitive to questions of right and wrong and to moral inconsistencies. It is important for children to feel strongly and to be concerned with principles of justice.

In the intermediate grades children's judgments become more finely drawn, and they take into consideration a larger moral field. Wide individual differences in the development of moral judgment result from differences in intellectual development, experience, social environment, and the habits and attitudes that grow out of these varied conditions.

During this period children develop increasing self-control. According to Sanford and associates (136, pp. 639 ff, 1943), they learn to internalize social prohibitions and sanctions—in other words, to integrate them with the ego, thus making the socially acceptable behavior the thing they want to do. Instead of being controlled by environmental pressures, the child becomes able to control himself.

When a child is beginning to gain self-control, to internalize the social pressures that have been previously imposed upon him from without, he has normal feelings of guilt and anxiety. He will blame or criticize himself even when others do not disapprove. However, unsocial impulses seem to be either redirected or submerged, not eliminated. To outward appearances at least, the child becomes increasingly socialized as he grows older. He moves from self-centeredness to a gradual development of capacity to feel for others (139, 1956).

Can we expect a child to be responsible for his behavior? If he is driven by his innate predispositions and influenced by the culture, can he be held accountable for his acts? To explain behavior does not in itself excuse one from accepting responsibility for it. The acceptance of responsibility implies orientation to the future inasmuch as consideration of the consequences of one's acts to oneself and others, as judged according to one's own value system, are part of the complex causal factors that determine his behavior. The process of socialization demands that children learn to consider and allow for the future consequences of their behavior. They can acquire this ability to a reasonable degree during middle childhood and preadolescence.

The socially responsible child has been described as one who is dependable in carrying out a task and whose values and attitude toward others conform to expectations of the larger society. Such responsibility was found to be more closely associated with the quality of emotional and personal relationships between parent and child than with the number of home chores (61, 1955). Through personal relations at home and also at school, the child develops an attitude toward life. Realizing that life is not easy, that it is real and earnest, he will develop tolerance of frustration and persistence in the face of difficulty. This is an old-fashioned idea quite contrary to the modern emphasis in songs and slogans. It is basic to good character development.

Children's ideals help to guide their conduct. Their heroes and ideal persons change as their experience widens. As childhood ties loosen, they seek persons outside their family with whom to identify. From essays on the subject "The person I would like to be like," Havighurst and others (66, 1946) found that as children grew older they tended to choose glamorous adults outside the family circle and, later, composite or imaginary characters. Their ideals are influenced by their social environment and socioeconomic status, and by the presence and behavior of leaders in schools, churches, and other agencies. Children need good examples. This, too, is an old-fashioned idea, whose modern phrasing is that they need to identify themselves with others—not so completely, however, that they lose confidence in themselves.

Children nine to twelve want "yes and no" answers to questions about moral issues. This is a chance to help them accept the idea that there are different ways of being right—that it is not "bad" to think and feel differently from other people. For example, the child of immigrant background is likely to assume that his parents' ideas are wrong because they do not accord with those of his schoolmates. Since his security comes partly from being liked by his companions, he tries to be like them and to conform to their ways, instead of finding "plus values" in both ways of life.

ATTITUDES AND INTERESTS

Attitudes and interests are dynamic factors in learning, influential in determining children's behavior.

Trends in interests from age to age have been studied. In an extensive questionnaire-study of children's interests, Jersild and Tasch (80, 1949) reported that children find satisfaction in definite tasks like arithmetic in which they can see results. They are most interested in activities that have meaning and use for them. They prefer activities in which they participate. Their interests in arts and crafts flourish more often in school than out of school, unless they belong to the Scouts or some other organization in which arts and crafts are taught. About the fifth grade, boys and girls differ widely in their interests.

Can attitudes be taught?

The few investigations prompted by the question, "Can attitudes be taught?" have yielded inconclusive results. Lichtenstein (93, 1934), in addition to reviewing the literature, reported an original research in grades four to six. He studied two attitudes—appreciation of the outdoors and the so-called scientific attitude. Although instruction tended significantly to reduce superstitions, it did not affect social attitudes, scientific attitudes, or preference for movies rather than the out of doors. All that can be said is that under certain conditions certain attitudes can be changed. Motion pictures appear to be a particularly successful means of relaxing overrigid attitudes and imparting more desirable standards. *The Birth of a Nation*, for example, was found to improve children's attitudes toward the Negro. In some, the new attitude persisted for ten weeks or longer before it was replaced by old ways of thinking and feeling (123, 1933).

DEVELOPMENT OF SELF-AWARENESS

A twelve-year-old boy said, "I like being myself. I wouldn't want to be anything else." Children seem to reach a peak of self-acceptance around eleven or twelve years. They admit their strengths and weaknesses as in the following quotations from two eleven-year-old boys. The first wrote:

I enjoy reading and I think I am fairly smart. I have several hobbies and favorite sports, all dealing with the water, fishing, swimming, sailing, and fly-tying. I love animals and have several pets. I have a hot temper and blow my top often. Other people think I am a queer and always tease me about my temper, so I blow my top; they tease me some more and my lid goes higer. I have a few friends who don't taunt me, thank goodness.*

The second boy, much less intellectually able than the first, took a realistic but not a discouraged view of himself:

I am a slow worker and the things I do are mostly always right. I get pretty good grades in my report card. In school I try to do my best but sometimes I have trouble.

In one study, children nine through thirteen, in the midwest, tended to rate themselves lower on most personality traits as they grew older. The one notable exception to this tendency was their rating on energy and pep (2, 1957).

The frank appraisal of their peers and the labels which the gang gives them, as well as their own sense of adequacy and competence based on the things they know they can do, result in increased self-awareness during these years. It is a circular response: the individual's physical and social characteristics affect others' response to him, and this in turn influences his concept of himself. Several investigations have supported the hypothesis that awareness of self comes about through awareness of others and that a positive relation exists between acceptance of self and acceptance of others (54, 1955).

An important developmental task of this period is to establish masculine and feminine identity. The feminine sex role is learned

* Spelling and punctuation have not been changed in these quotations.

relatively easily if the girl is given continuous experiences in doing "woman's work" about the house. Unlike his sister, a boy has no tangible model to emulate. Furthermore, many of the masculine functions are less obvious to the child (122, 1953). Moreover, when boys and girls dress alike, play the same kinds of games, observe the similarities in the home activities and occupations of their fathers and mothers, and the cultural drift toward he-women and she-men, it becomes difficult for a boy to learn what it means to be a man and a girl to learn what it means to be a woman. A boy may try to assert his masculinity through interest in machines, science, strenuous outdoor activities, and daring adventures. But his distinctive masculine role becomes dimmed when he finds girls also tinkering with cars, getting as high marks as he does in algebra and science, playing most of his games except football and boxing. Girl gangs as vicious as those of the opposite sex have made their appearance.

How can this problem of masculine identity be solved? One suggested way is to emphasize the development of individual potentialities, regardless of sex. Another is to make clear the distinctive qualities and contributions of men and women respectively. Of these, the child-bearing, homemaking function is primary. Secondary is a certain creativity and social concern and sensitivity that seem to be more readily developed by women than by men.

SOCIAL DEVELOPMENT

Family relationships

The tendency to move away from parents, and the adult world in general, or even to be antagonistic to them is frequently mentioned as a characteristic of this stage of development. It is important to know how a child perceives the interpersonal relations in the family and the guides and restrictions that are placed upon him. Dales (29, 1955) devised scales for measuring the developmental status of children with respect to affection, social relations, and their sex role. Using a variety of methods —incomplete sentences, picture-story method, and direct questions about the child's preference for mother or father—investigators have reported more favorable than unfavorable attitudes toward both mother and father (60, 1957). There was a decreasing preference for fathers between ages five and nine with an accompanying slight increase in positive attitude toward mothers. During the intermediate grades both boys and girls took a more neutral attitude toward parents or stated that they prefer both. Later, boys showed slightly more positive attitudes toward each parent whereas, during high-school years, girls showed a more positive attitude toward father than toward mother.

To measure preadolescents' views of family control of behavior, Hawkes and his associates (67, 1957) have constructed two forms of a questionnaire type of scale, one consisting of items based on children's typical responses and the other based on competent judges' ranking of the responses from the most healthful to the least healthful means of controlling children's behavior. According to these scales, groups of rural and small town children in the fifth grade seemed to perceive control of their behavior as not unduly restrictive; they were reasonably satisfied with their home conditions and relationships. Boys, however, tended to be "more critical and less satisfied with their home conditions and their relations with their parents than girls." Both boys and girls tended to rate their relationships with their mothers more favorably than similar relationships with their fathers (67, 1957). Studies of urban children and young adults have shown similar results.

Peer relations

The peer relations of children and adolescents have been studied in various ways—by direct observation in informal coeducational groups, by sociometric or other preference techniques, and by sentence completions. The results of these diverse methods are quite similar. In general, at every age boys and girls are inclined to prefer their own sex. This tendency is most marked during the four or five years preceding adolescence. Children tend to choose the opposite sex less and less frequently from the first to the sixth grades. Between the ages of eight and ten, boys and girls tend to play together less and to manifest divergent interests. There may be open teasing and antagonism. At these ages mixed children's parties are frequently a howling failure. But even during this stage both boys and girls are aware of their popularity or unpopularity with the opposite sex. About the fifth and sixth grades interest in love stories is at its lowest ebb. From the sixth to the twelfth grades, according to a recent study using the incomplete-sentence technique (60, 1957), the favorable attitude toward or preference of girls for girls tends to decrease markedly, while the favorable attitude of girls toward boys shows a sharp increase from the sixth to the ninth grades. From the tenth to the twelfth grades, boys tend to prefer boys to girls. These trends, substantially supported by other studies, are shown in several graphs (see Fig. 6).

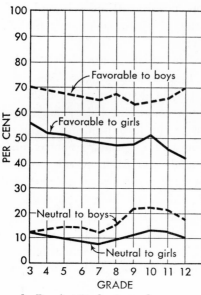

1. Boys' attitudes toward peers.

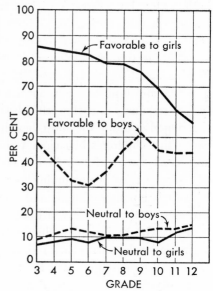

2. Girls' attitudes toward peers.

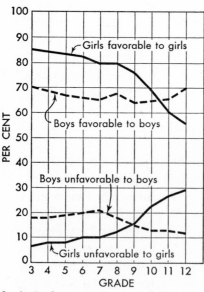

3. Attitudes toward peers of like sex.

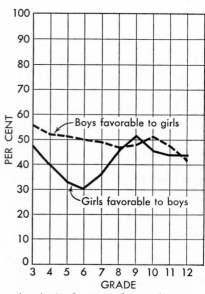

4a. Attitudes toward opposite sex.

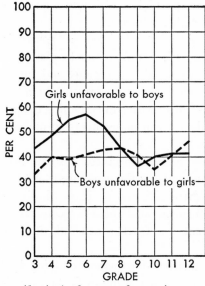

Fig. 6. Children's attitudes toward peers.

(Dale B. Harris and Sing Chu Tseng, "Children's Attitudes Toward Peers and Parents as Revealed by Sentence Completions," *Child Development*, XXVIII (December, 1957), 403-405.)

4*b*. Attitudes toward opposite sex.

Preadolescents tend to be somewhat flexible in their friendships. In one investigation (9, 1948), sixth-grade pupils were asked to write the names of their three best friends and their reasons for choosing them. Two weeks later they were again asked to name their best friends and to give reasons for any changes. One-fifth made no changes, and almost the same number made one change. The rest—about three-fifths—made two or more changes. Children's choices of friends appear to be more democractic when restricted to the classroom, and more along class lines when out-of-school choices are given.

Group experience

Success in establishing himself in a group is of utmost importance to a nine- or a ten-year-old. During preadolescent years team spirit, class spirit, and group loyalties develop. From the fourth grade on, groups show an increase in the proportion of pairs of mutual friends, in unattached or unchosen children, and in the complexity of interrelations.

The word "gang" has an unsavory connotation which appears to be justified (172, 1955). Thrasher (158, 1936) pointed out that the gang appeals to boys as an escape from humdrum existence and that the experience it affords may hinder adjustment to adult routine. For this reason it may have a demoralizing rather than a constructive, socializing effect.

Boys' clubs, on the other hand, may meet preadolescents' need for adventure and, at the same time, exert a constructive influence.

Children of this age are likely to resist adult interference: "You can't play with so-and-so," or "Why don't you ask so-and-so over to play with you?" They are frequently indifferent to social conventions and impatient with the little acts of politeness for which they see no reason. In polite society this attitude is a major source of conflict with adults. During the period when boys and girls are making their social adjustments to one another, they tend to avoid adult supervision.

The teacher sometimes encounters group resistance. He can best handle this by letting them go ahead and helping them to thresh out the issue. Through concrete experience children learn how to deal with dilemmas. They need to test limits. But in their moments of outrageous rebellion children need to feel that their parents and teachers can "take it" and will not disown them.

Children like to make rules and regulations for themselves. They like to vote—an expression of collective feeling. They want to be taken seriously in their attempts to function as a group. They want to work out their social relationships for themselves and to be accepted by the group on their own merits. A solicitous teacher or parent cannot bestow the gift of popularity on any boy or girl; it must be achieved.

The "social atom" (108, 1947) is a useful concept. It includes a "nucleus of persons emotionally related to an individual"—a center comprising persons with whom relations actually exist and an outer part consisting of persons with whom relations are desired. Outside this nucleus is an area of acquaintances who lack emotional meaning for the individual. Associated with persons are preferences for certain objects, values, and objectives, which may also be measured sociometrically.

Social characteristics

Children seem to go through stages in their understanding of people. According to Watts (170, 1944), the first is the black-and-white stage: persons are either *good* or *bad, kind* or *unkind.* Each is characterized or labeled by his dominant trait. At this stage children enjoy Aesop's Fables, which focus attention on the central quality in each character. The second stage is the pattern-of-traits description of persons. Many personalities seem to be organized in this way. Most of the great characters in history comprised a constellation of characteristics operating harmoniously. Children later recognize the existence of flaws or defects of character in otherwise admirable persons. When children realize that good and bad qualities can exist side by side in the same persons, they have progressed far toward an understanding of human nature. A still more mature stage of development is represented by the "individualized portrait." Here one recognizes the subtleties of personality and the infinite complexity of an individual's motives in interaction with his environment. Each stage of development has value to the child, and premature attempts to bring him to a mature stage of understanding and tolerance are likely to be not only unsuccessful but detrimental. Prejudice tends to be reinforced or overcome by direct personal relations more than by formal education. Preadolescents, in general, are not good judges of the way others feel toward them. Hartley (63, 1946) reported that 140 ten- to twelve-year-old boys were not able to judge accurately how well they were accepted by others of their own age and sex; they were often not aware of how well they were liked by classmates. Nor was there a relation between their popularity and the intensity of their desire for social contacts.

The gregariousness of preadolescents has a practical slant: being a member of a group increases their sense of security and worth at a time when they are trying to become independent of adults. Their peers' frank appraisal helps them find themselves. They derive support from the group and change their standards to conform to those of their peers. It is rare for a child at this stage of development to have and maintain a conviction regardless of the prevailing attitudes of the group (136, p. 647, 1943).

Factors related to social acceptance

According to sociometric analysis, the child who is able to relate himself to at least one other child is better able to establish friendly relations in a group. The child who does not have a friend is not so well accepted by his peer group. Those who have received social recognition develop a positive self-concept. As a child gains inner security, he becomes better able to relate himself to others and more spontaneous and flexible in working in a group.

The relation between intelligence and selection-rejection is not clear. Jennings found little difference between the IQ's of the most chosen and the least chosen of the four hundred girls whom she studied at the New York Training School for Girls (75, 1950). Grossmann and Wrighter (55, 1948) obtained from questionnaires answered by 117 sixth-grade children the names of the children they liked and did not like to sit near, walk home from school with, play with, have as a best friend, and elect as a class officer. The correlation between intelligence and selection-rejection was low, but the coefficient of correlation did not tell the whole story. "Intelli-

gence did make a difference up to a certain point—normal intelligence,"
but superior intelligence made no appreciable further increase in a child's
chances of being chosen. A similar relation was reported between reading
ability and selection-rejection. High academic success and intelligence
quotient, as measured by available tests, do not seem to be determinants of
social acceptance.

Social acceptance appears to have the same sort of relation to socioeconomic status. The most-chosen children came from middle-class homes
or homes of higher standing on the Barr scale, but status higher than middle class did not raise the selection-rejection score. An unskilled-labor background seemed to be a handicap, but children from a professional background seemed to have no advantage over those whose parents were
skilled workers or engaged in business (55, 1948). Boys and girls of higher
socioeconomic status put a higher value on conformity to adult standards
and rules, whereas those of lower status valued self-assertion and aggression (124, 1953). The amount of social participation is greater among
children from upper-class families.

The reasons preadolescents give for choosing friends are primarily
personal: they choose friends who are cheerful, kind, co-operative, generous, honest, even-tempered, polite, loyal, agreeable. Children eight to
eleven usually put a high value on courage and loyalty. They break off
friendships with children who are incompatible, conceited or bossy, dis-
loyal or underhanded, bullying or quarrelsome, dishonest or untruthful,
unco-operative, noisy, or silly. As children grow older they show an increasing preference for responsibility and cleanliness in their friends.

Other reasons for choosing friends vary with the situation. Propin-
quity and similarity of interests seem to be important factors in choosing
and changing friends. Two factors found to be associated with the preadolescent's social relations were his school achievement and his father's
income. The child's social relations were apparently unaffected by place
of residence, length of residence in the community, the section of the
country and the size of the town from which he came, and his religious
affiliations.

Many other factors enter into the complex network of acceptance and
rejection. Individuals whom other children esteem highly are slightly superior in many respects: general health and vigor, conformity, poise, initiative, courage, adaptability, dependability, emotional warmth, consideration for others, and originality (20, 1947). Children who are gentle,
friendly, and charming frequently become centers of attraction although
they are not likely to be elected to positions of leadership. Little is known

about the deeper relationships of intimacy between close friends, such as Sullivan describes (148, 1953). Social maturity depends largely on the life experience of the individual. Consequently it varies with the environment in which the child has grown up (43, 1955).

Research shows a moderate positive relationship between adjustment and sociometric status among children and adults. In these studies, various measures of adjustment have been used: a scale of "neuroticism" developed by Eysenck, the California Test of Personality, the Mental Health Analysis, the Rorschach test, human figure drawings (159, 1955), as well as teachers' or other observers' ratings, interviews, case histories, and problem checklists. McCandless and his associates (96, 1956) have used the children's form of the manifest anxiety scale (CMAS) with children in grades four, five, six to study its relationship to two teacher-administered sociometric techniques. Both the CMAS and the sociometric scales were administered by classroom teachers. The results for the three grades showed the more anxious children to be less popular—a statistically significant r of —.32. This was true for both boys and girls. But the relationship varied with the grade: it was high for children in the fifth grade, moderate for those in the fourth grade, and approximately zero for boys and girls in the sixth grade. Such difference may possibly be related to the teachers' influence. Similarly, in a study of sixth-grade children (16, 1953), the pupils who possessed superior sociometric status gave evidence of better mental health than those who were ignored, unwanted, and disliked by their peers.

It is significant that a child often chooses as friends those whom he perceives as somewhat similar to him. Moreover, he tends to see best friends as more like his ideal self-image than his present concept of himself (99, 1956). Apparently love has an element of wanting to be like one's preferred friends.

Conditions favorable for social development

Favorable social attitudes and social sensitivity tend to develop when these conditions prevail:

A classroom atmosphere of confidence and trust.

Recognition for considerate attitudes shown by children. (Too often success is obtained by defeating others.)

Acceptance of the quiet child's tendency to make few friends.

Freedom for children to work out their relations in their peer culture without domination by adults. At times they may discuss both altruistic and aggressive behavior which they have observed, and arrive at sound principles and generalizations that will guide their future conduct.

Children's sense of personal worth increases as they contribute to the welfare of the group. They develop a social imagination which helps them to put themselves in the other person's place. Being ignored or shut out from the group has the opposite effect. The following statement shows how a ten-year-old girl in the fifth grade felt:

The girls in my class don't like me. They don't want me on their teams. They will fight over who's team I should be on, because I'm not good, and they don't like me. . . . I try to keep up my courage but I just can't.

The network of relations in a group at any one time may be quickly ascertained by the sociometric technique. The following configurations showed up in response to the question, "Who would you like for your best friend?" The same question, asked three months later, showed a similar configuration. Gerry was still the center of attraction; David was chosen by Paul as well as Diane, and the unconnected threesome of Tom C., Tom H., and Malcolm remained unchanged.

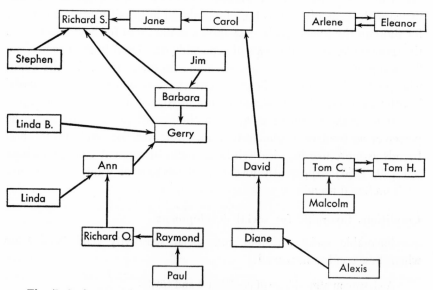

Fig. 7. Sociogram of a sixth-grade class as first obtained. (Arrows indicate direction of choice.)

Teachers should be aware of the network of feelings of attraction and repulsion that exists in the group, should know how these feelings originate, and how they affect pupils' behavior and learning (46, 1954). They need to know why two children of equal intelligence and similar home backgrounds appeal so differently to their classmates, and why one is sought by many and the other is disliked. There are individual differences in social potential; a child cannot expect to be liked by everyone. And adults' attempts to maneuver peer relations are seldom successful. The fact of preferences must be accepted.

Many persons ask: "What happens to socially minded children brought up in a reasonably permissive, friendly home and school environment when they go out into a competitive world?" The answer is that the self-esteem and self-confidence which they have built usually helps them to meet new tasks and difficulties.

EMOTIONAL DEVELOPMENT

Children nine to twelve should be helped to achieve satisfying, socially acceptable channeling of, rather than the repression of, their emotions, for emotional feeling and expression underlie and color all of life. Childish fears should decrease; caution increase. Children of this age perform daring stunts, but have more skill and better co-ordination to prevent serious injury. Nevertheless, the spirit of adventure and certain recklessness make the accident rate for these years very high. Fear of certain dangers have been reported as more frequent than actual incidence of these dangers. Failure, ridicule, or being called a "sissy" is more often reported as a misfortune than a fear (79, 1954).

Some children worry most about the health of members of their family, about their mothers working too hard or getting sick, about their fathers losing their jobs, about school marks and failure on tests, about their own personal adequacy and the possibility of war.

Certain rural school children mentioned fear of animals most frequently (125, 1945). This fear decreases with age. Next in frequency were fears of natural phenomena—fire, storms, darkness. Girls expressed more fears than boys, except with respect to school work. There are many weaknesses in the investigations of children's fears; e.g., only certain fears may be reported, others may be repressed; the degree of emotion attached to the alleged source of fear is not indicated.

Outbursts of anger decrease as children acquire more subtle or effective ways of getting what they want, or learning more socially acceptable ways of meeting frustration and difficulty. However, fights are still frequent among eight-, nine-, and ten-year-old boys.

Some tensions caused by disturbed social relations in the home may disappear with widening school relations. More often these tensions are merely concealed. Under a mask of indifference a child may be very sensitive to his teacher's attitude toward him. He may be deeply hurt by criticism or by being unfavorably compared with another child. A child who is rejected both at home and at school may suffer in silence or become rebellious and defiant.

However, the child's personality has capacity for self-repair and readjustment and an amazing ability to resist detrimental influences. Personal adjustment has been described by Lowrey as having these positive aspects: "inner emotional security," "feelings of personal adequacy" and of being successful, happiness in personal relations, "a realistic evaluation of the self," adaptability and acceptance of one's limitations (95, p. 15, 1947). Certain personality traits seem to go together and form patterns that are persistent, pervasive, and predictable. For example, the conscientious child is characterized by persistent effort, effective study habits, diligence in school, and creativity. His anxiety to measure up to standards may stem from a desire to avoid blame or feelings of guilt or to maintain his self-concept.

Questions and Problems

FOR CLASS DISCUSSION OR STUDY GROUPS

1. Study one child's development during the preadolescent years in writing, drawing, written and spoken language, and arithmetic. Compare your records with the development described in this chapter.

2. Study any outbursts of anger or fear that have come to your attention. Describe the situation in which each one occurred. Who was present? What was the child's relation to these persons? What did they do? What did the child do? What explanation did he give afterward?

3. Make a "social atom" diagram of yourself or of some child you know very well, showing personal relations from birth to the present time.

4. Observe a group of eight-, nine-, or ten-year-old children. What interaction takes place; what forces are operating; how do the adult leader's words and acts influence the interaction? Why is group experience so important for children of this age?

5. What kinds of games are preferred by the preadolescent boys and girls whom you have observed? What motor skills do they develop?

6. How many children whom you know have been interested in making collections? What kind of things did they collect?

7. Give examples of reasoning in children of these ages. What was the stimulus to reasoning? What facts were used in the process? What factors may have caused errors in the conclusions?

8. The case study approach to research in child development may be represented by Millard and Rothney's book of cases of elementary school children (106, 1957). Read carefully the description of method, some of the cases, and the conclusions. What does this approach contribute that is lacking in statistical studies?

Chapter 17

LEARNING IN LATER CHILDHOOD

AND PREADOLESCENCE

Children in the intermediate grades learn better than infants because of their greater neuromuscular maturity, retentiveness, and problem-solving ability; their conscious motives for learning; and background of experience that can be applied to new situations (115, 1954). Counteracting these favorable aspects is a certain resistance to learning, a decrease in docility. Accordingly, incentives to learning become increasingly important. In the child's psychological field are forces that attract or repell him with reference to a learning task. It is therefore most essential to discover what motivates children of these ages and what procedures are most effective for different kinds of learning. Children learn by many methods in many different ways. They select what they will see, what they will listen to, what is important and meaningful to them. They find ways of doing the things they are good at and have some need for.

Certain rewards or reinforcements are probably of major importance in the socialization of the child. Children, in general, are most frequently praised for academic performance—lessons well done, good grades, improvement; assistance to mother or other member of the family, to unfortunates; being quiet, polite, obedient; performance in sports and games; giving or sharing; doing creative work. However, in a progressive American school relatively little praise was given for academic performance and for being quiet, polite, and obedient. These children received a larger portion of their praise for giving and sharing, being creative and good in games and sports. In Near Eastern groups most praise was given for academic achievement, assisting people, especially the unfortunate, and being quiet, polite, and obedient (32, 1957). The behavior of these groups was, to some extent, shaped by the kind of praise they received. Thus knowing what children are being praised for helps to predict their future behavior, since the strength of a response can be increased by reward.

416

LEARNING THEORY*

As a result of reinforcement, cues that previously had no significance to the child can come to function in the same manner as primary drives. With his increased experience, vocabulary, and reasoning ability, the preadolescent is able verbally to carry out long chains of cue-producing responses, i.e., one cue elicits a response, which in turn elicits a further response, etc. This process enables the child to be aware of the future consequences of his actions and to anticipate long-distant goals. It is for this reason that he is able to persist in the face of repeated difficulty. Parents and teachers should help the child to become responsible for the consequences of his actions and to set realistic, long-term goals for himself (i.e., to anticipate future needs). The child's perception of a particular learning situation is largely determined by his previous responses and the context or field in which the learning occurs. His curiosity about the world and the sheer delight in being physically and mentally active still persists from early childhood. In addition, the child's expectation of himself and others' expectations of him have become more definite. All these operate in a complex matrix of past, present, and future which influences any particular learning situation.

The child usually resists learning anything that is not in accord with his concept of himself. As experiences occur in his life, he tends to perceive and organize them in relation to his self-concept. If the experience is a threat to his self-esteem, he may deny or distort it. Interest in an activity thus depends on his recognition of the suitability of the activity to his idea of himself and his capacity to succeed in it. When a child resists learning something that he should learn, he may be protecting his concept of himself from being changed. If he submits to a stronger will, while resenting such submission, psychological stress will be induced, with the possibility of undesirable physical symptoms. Learning takes place best when the uniqueness of the individual is respected and the threat to his concept of himself is at a minimum.

Children work hard on their tasks of growing up—learning to respond affectionately to people, learning to get along with age-mates, to plan their work and evaluate what they have learned, achieving independence and a realistic self-concept. These efforts on the part of children should be viewed positively. Teachers and pupils are partners in this

* (40, 1956; 102, 1956; 165, 1957)

shared responsibility; the child should therefore view the teacher as his ally and have no need to resist learning in school.

Even when a child is failing in his subjects, it is usually more helpful to assume he is doing the best he can at present and to discover conditions that are interfering with his best performance. By asking each pupil to solve a problem by explaining audibly each step in his procedure and recording his comments, hesitations, silences, and tone of voice, De Moraes (33, 1954) gained an understanding of the child's difficulties, uncertainties, and blockings. The focus of research on children's learning seems to be slowly shifting from the subject matter to the learner. More studies are needed of the functioning of the child's mind as he studies, reads, or solves problems. Future work on learning will attempt to explore the personality dynamics of the learner and the deeper motivations that determine children's learning.

THE SCHOOL AS A LABORATORY FOR LEARNING

The school should be a laboratory for learning in which the teacher serves as guide, instructor, and consultant in an environment that offers suitable experiences for all the children. To guide children's learning the teacher should ideally know the abilities, interests, and desires or motives of each child. As instructor he should know how children learn reading, arithmetic, and other fundamental processes (117, 1950). One child said when asked why the class liked their teacher so much, "She learns us good." This teacher had analyzed the steps in children's learning and could help them go forward without unnecessary failure. As consultant, the teacher should know the nature of the children's specific difficulties, why they encounter these difficulties, and how they can avoid them.

In providing a favorable environment for learning, the teacher is concerned not only with appropriate materials and methods of instruction but also with his relation to the children and their relation to one another. A favorable emotional climate will accelerate learning; it will make learning a vital, happy experience for both teacher and child. The main problem is to discover the conditions and develop the procedures that will best facilitate the learning process with children of different ages engaged in different kinds of learning.

In school, children should learn the things they need to know and which are not offered elsewhere. For example, in a rural community they should learn how to use their land resources to best advantage and to maintain its fertility; how to obtain better food by raising chickens, rabbits, or other animals more efficiently; how to improve community and personal health; how to bring up children; how to be good citizens; how to prepare for the socially useful work which one can do best; and how to read to keep up to date. Reading aloud books and poetry about persons and events that have made our country great, and visits to historic places with discussion of the meaning of the past and of our responsibility for the future are practical ways parents and teachers can help children gain appreciation of our American heritage.

A DAY WITH TEN-YEAR-OLDS*

When the children came in before school, they busied themselves by bringing the bulletin board up to date, experimenting in the science corner, working on committees, writing, drawing, or reading at their desks.

After the bell rang and after the reading of the Bible, they planned the days' work. The day was blocked out in large units. Within each block of time pupil-teacher planning was necessary: How much time would Jane's social studies group need for their report? Frank's group needed some class discussion on their project. The trip to the sugar refinery, which Ted's father had arranged, must be discussed. And so on.

After the planning session the teacher went from group to group, guiding their learning as they worked on their respective projects. The social studies period included numerous activities appealing to a variety of interests and appropriate to a wide range of abilities: Jim's committee was getting information from a book on individual contributions to science, industry, agriculture, and human welfare. Nancy's committee was preparing a report on the work songs of the South. Dan was making an illustration for his committee. Donald's group was writing a report on the cotton gin, using the dictionary as needed. Most of the children were working with interest; concentration was intense, and the room was quiet except for the hum of discussion here and there.

After social studies came recess with its opportunity for fun and good sportsmanship.

Following recess the group worked on original stories, first writing spontaneously and then checking on grammar, spelling, and improvement in style. As each pupil finished his composition, he put it in a folder on the teacher's desk and returned to work on individual tasks. The teacher checked their progress and helped them to do still more effective work.

* Adapted from *The Elementary School in Action* (Curriculum Office, Philadelphia Public Schools), pp. 17-22. With permission.

After lunch an arithmetic lesson with the entire group began with some large numbers and graphs that Jane's committee had found in their reading. They decided to bring in other graphs and charts they had found. Later some children who were having difficulty with fractions came to the teacher for special instruction. Others were practicing arithmetical processes in which they were weak.

The music period provided release for mind and body; some sang while others danced to the music.

The last period was used for reading and library experiences. The class was divided into three groups, each guided in selecting suitable reading material. The teacher spent her time in several ways: working with a small group of retarded readers, conferring with individual children about their choice of books, leading a discussion on books they had enjoyed, and reading aloud to the entire class.

Several times during the day attention was given to the available health services and to other all-school matters.

They stopped work in time to evaluate their day's accomplishments and to suggest activities for the next day.

A number of factors favorable to learning were present in this class:

The teacher's personal contact with the children as they came into the classroom.

Free activity before school officially began.

Pupil-teacher planning.

Work periods in which individuals and small groups concentrated on work they had chosen and planned. In these periods the children lived together, co-operating and contributing to their common goals.

Learning of skills in connection with projects and in special periods assigned to skill subjects.

Pupil participation in creative activities of their own choice on their present level of development. This is the "self-selection" idea applied to the school-age child. From a variety of experiences he chooses those which he needs.

The program was flexible and balanced. This kind of program cannot be suddenly introduced. Children have "to learn to learn that way." Though it is never 100 per cent successful, it is a growing, vital experience for pupils and teacher.

INCIDENTAL LEARNING OUTSIDE OF SCHOOL

A great deal of learning goes on outside of school. Every experience is a learning experience. Modern media of communication exert increasing influence on children's linguistic development. Much of children's education takes place in the home, on the playground, at movies, and when they are listening to radio programs, viewing television, or reading comics. The time spent on radio and television, the various programs available, the favorite programs of children and youth, parents and teachers, the possible values, and the effect of television upon pupils' academic success have been studied and reviewed by Witty (174, 1958). During a week some children spend as much time viewing television as they spend in school. They spend more time in viewing TV than in any other single activity except sleeping. Obviously this use of time crowds out voluntary reading for some children.

Many programs feature crime, violence, sex, horror, and murder. They are overemotionalized, unrealistic, untrue to life, antisocial in their effects. Although a few programs of this kind may serve as an outlet for pent-up emotions, continued viewing and listening may condition children to low levels of values and attitudes. For example, one little boy who had been listening to a particularly lurid crime drama, when asked what it was about, replied casually, "Oh, just murder." Thus adults and children become accustomed to values and ideas that were initially shocking to them. Results have shown much identification and projection on the part of the young spectators in the situations presented by the film.

These programs, like comic books (see Chap. 15), affect different children in different ways. If radio or television programs increase a child's tensions, fears, and anxieties, other conditions in his life should be examined. Prohibiting him from listening to the radio or viewing television will not remove the underlying cause of the emotional disturbance, though it may protect him from too exciting experiences.

Although results of research are conflicting (12, 1955), partly due to variation in the quality of the media studied and individual differences in the children, the possible detrimental effects deserve attention. Radio and television may promote a harmful passivity in children unless combined with group participation in singing and discussion.

According to Joy Elmer Morgan, these modern media of widespread communication

can become deadly instruments for the prevention of thought. They can keep attention on the trivial and the transient. They can habituate people to passivity in the face of great needs and great issues. They can destroy the leisure and peace and freedom from distraction out of which the exceptional mind is born. They can debase the mind stuff of the people—which is the soil of greatness and achievement. Our generation is the first that has ever allowed the child's mind, even the preschool child's mind, to be commercialized as it is now through radio and TV, which reach into the home. [109, p. 25, 1956]

This generation of children is also unique in trying to study while listening to radio or viewing television. The effect on children's reading comprehension while listening to a radio program was studied by Mitchell (107, 1949). Children in the sixth grade listened to transcriptions of two variety programs and to two musical programs. Reading achievement, as measured by the Iowa Silent Reading Test, of children below 100 IQ was adversely affected by the variety programs; pupils with IQ's above 100 made a gain in reading achievement while listening to the musical programs. Those who habitually listened to the radio while studying were more adversely affected than those who did not do this habitually.

Radio and television programs have potential values. Some of the best daytime dramas of family life may give insight into emotional relations. When the family listen together, this type of program may serve as a springboard for some excellent discussions. The very variety of programs offers opportunity to develop standards. Children should learn to discriminate the humorous from the inane, the true-to-life from the fictitious, the important from the trivial. Desire to listen to favorite programs may stimulate some children to work more efficiently and to budget time more wisely. Educational radio and closed circuit television programs can be used constructively in elementary education.

Motion pictures likewise vary greatly in quality from excellent dramas, historical pageants, and clever cartoons to confusing and distorted portrayals of life. Ratings of films suitable for children are available in the Children's Film Library organized by the Motion Picture Association of America. Various community agencies and Parent-Teacher Associations also supply selected lists of movies.

Eight years has been suggested as a minimum age for attendance at motion pictures. The long period of sitting still, the danger of infection, especially when colds and other communicable diseases are prevalent, the loss of sunlight and outdoor play, or, if at night, the late hours and excitement just before going to bed—all are reasons for not taking young children to the movies.

Parents and teachers can help children to incorporate these modern means of communication into a total well-balanced pattern of experience. They should know what children are reading, seeing, and listening to, and discuss these programs with them. Out of the discussion should come evaluation and the development of standards.

LEARNING IN ORGANIZED
OUT-OF-SCHOOL GROUPS

The Scouts, 4-H Clubs, Future Farmers of America, and other youth-serving agencies have helped millions of children and young people to grow physically, socially, and emotionally. For example some of the ways in which girl-scouting helps a girl to grow are by:

Giving opportunities to choose activities, express ideas, listen to others, take part in making plans, accept choices of other members.

Helping her to learn how to do and make things of value to her and the group.

Encouraging her to accept as much responsibility as she is able to carry without strain.

Helping her to learn to do home duties, to appreciate the beauty in her environment, and to understand family relations.

Planning the participation of troop members in community services and in world friendship projects.

Girls' Clubs of America encourage homemaking activities, as well as providing facilities for fun and friendship. The clubhouses are open every school day after three o'clock and again in the early evening and on Saturdays until midafternoon. At least one professionally trained, paid woman worker is on hand to serve as counselor, guide, and friend. Girls from first grade through high-school age may belong.

Play schools for children from five to twelve years old supplement home and school experiences. The play school at its best has both a therapeutic group to help the disturbed child adjust to other people and learn to handle his aggressive impulses, and play groups for normal children at each stage of development. One important feature of the play school is dramatic play in which children can re-create their experiences and express their emotions. Leaders should, on one hand, guard against being overpermissive or, on the other hand, unwilling to accept a flexible program. Parent participation should be encouraged.

The summer camp also supplements the learning experiences offered in the school. Summer camps have done wonders for some children. In camp, children have a strong need to learn to adjust to others; they also have the chance to see themselves objectively.

CONDITIONS AFFECTING SCHOOL LEARNING

Teacher's understanding of individual pupils

To teach effectively, the teacher needs to understand his pupils. He takes his clues from the child as he responds to instruction. He recognizes individual differences in the child's physical condition, physiological maturity, intellectual interests and abilities, emotional development, and home background. Energy level may make a difference in school achievement. For example, one boy suffered from an initially low energy level, which interfered with his achievement in school subjects. He used up more calories in walking home to lunch than his lunch supplied. Since he needed rest and adequate food more than anything else, the teacher arranged for him to have a substantial hot lunch in school and rest periods during the school day. Good mental ability enables a child to do the verbal tasks and abstract thinking that the traditional school requires. Perception, memory, and ability to see relations are all basic to learning. Some pupils are able to understand simple facts but are unable to draw conclusions from them. Emotional conditions may facilitate or block learning. During these years there is usually a strong emotional readiness to learn. Success in schoolwork, stimulated in the beginning by the approval of others, builds self-confidence in the child. This self-confidence, in turn, makes him more independent and able to weather a certain amount of criticism. A sense of security and self-esteem acquired during these years helps the child to make the best use of his abilities.

Disorganizing anxiety may be induced by too much stress on grades. Low marks on report cards often lead to dissatisfaction with school, and dissatisfaction leads to dropping out of school. As several youngsters said, "I fell behind and lost interest," "Poor grades got on my nerves," "I failed seventh grade and didn't want to repeat." Nonpromotion seems to intensify children's feelings of inadequacy; but promotion by age, without reference to the child's achievement, also presents problems when grade standards are maintained and teachers do not have time to give the individual remedial instruction needed.

The parents' own education and their attitude toward schooling, their occupational and socioeconomic status, their expectations and ambitions for the child, the degree of intellectual stimulation in the home and neighborhood, the pressure of home duties and remunerative work, all are conditions that influence learning. In general, a combination of favorable factors in the child's home environment are associated with school achievement.

Only daily observation of the child, supplemented by test results and other sources of information, can furnish the understanding a teacher needs for guiding individual pupils' learning.

Self-appraisal

Pupils' evaluation of their activities, individually and in groups, is part of instruction; it makes children more aware of the learning process. Hildreth (68, 1948) suggested the following form of pupil self-appraisal:

> I have improved in _____.
> I need to improve in _____.
> I have done the best I can in _____.

Before going ahead with a new activity they may gain suggestions from their previous experience. At the end of a work period they can appraise what they have done and discuss how to improve their methods next time. If the project was unsuccessful they may discuss "what was wrong with our planning." In the midst of an activity or game they may stop to settle some serious dispute about rules or the behavior of individuals. Both children and parents should be more aware of the learning that has actually taken place.

PROVIDING SUITABLE EXPERIENCES

Firsthand experiences

Firsthand experiences in daily situations are still the foundation of word meanings. As children begin to use more abstract words such as "goodness," "beauty," "justice," these concepts acquire varied meanings according to each child's experience. A child's idea of "good" is formed by his experience with good people. His concept of beauty is built through experience with the beautiful in nature, art, music, and other aspects of life. Without direct experience, verbal symbols are weak and empty.

Field trips have many learning values. Usually it is best to have one or two definite purposes in making each trip. One fifth grade took a trip to the old Van Cortlandt Mansion to study colonial life and industries. They went to a bakery, to neighboring stores, and to a food exhibition to supplement their practical work in home economics. In order to derive the most benefit from field trips, the class should discuss beforehand what to look for and should summarize their findings after the trip.

During these years children may learn much about the workers in their community and the work they do, about the plants and animals and soil of the region, about the history and folklore and folk songs of their part of the country. One class selected as a project the study of their community. This study took them to the library to look up the history, to their parents and grandparents for firsthand information, to farms and industries, to businessmen and workers. They summarized their knowledge in charts, pictures, and other visual aids, and invited the citizens of the town to an exhibit of their work. In experiences of this kind, social learnings; increased size and vividness of vocabulary; practice in taking initiative and responsibility, in reading and study skills, effective writing, and the problem-solving method; and improvement in communication skills are important outcomes. An environment that creates a real need and use for reading, writing, and oral communication is conducive to improvement in the language arts.

Instructional materials

A classroom library covering a wide range of interests and levels of ability offers children an opportunity to select the reading material they need. To prevent retarded readers from feeling embarrassed, books should not be labeled by grade. Differentiated assignments are impossible without a wide range of suitable books and other materials. Dramas, short stories, and films that help children to gain insight into human relations should have a prominent place.

Using the class library is good preparation for using the school library. Using the school library is good preparation for using the public library; the school library is a "junior partner" of the public library. Children may be permitted to take books out of the public library when they reach the third grade. Before that, of course, children can enjoy the story hour and the wide variety of picture books and easy-to-read materials available in public libraries.

Parents who have had some experience in library work or are willing to learn may volunteer to help in the school library. They can work at the desk while the teacher guides children in their choice of books and in their reading and study methods.

Community resources can usually be found to supplement a meager school supply of books. Individuals may donate suitable books and magazines. Social and civic organizations can influence the schoolboard to buy needed reading materials and visual aids; sometimes such organizations meet an immediate emergency by raising funds themselves. It is of the ut-

Preadolescents live in a society of their peers and actively shut out adults from much of their world.

Preadolescents are partial to pets, which meet an emotional need of childhood.

most importance to meet every child's interests and needs with a wide variety of instructional materials.

Extensive reading of interesting material is effective in increasing vocabulary and fluency of reading. During the preadolescent years children generally do more voluntary reading than at any other age. This interest in wide reading should be encouraged and stimulated. Well-selected books bring their own sufficient reward (131, 1955).

Special book lists have been compiled on all sorts of topics. For example, a bibliography, *Books Are Bridges* (A.F.S.C.), prepared and edited by the staff of the American Friends Service Committee in co-operation with representatives of the Anti-Defamation League of B'nai B'rith, includes books representing people of many religious, racial, and national groups as individuals worthy of respect. Other lists emphasizes the personal value of reading. Skillfully led discussion of books of this kind is particularly useful. It corrects wrong impressions, clarifies their meaning, increases the children's pleasure, and helps them relate reading to their lives. Reading may also be stimulated by attractive displays of books, excerpts read by teacher or librarian, book reviews written by pupils, and discussions of books and articles read.

Many other kinds of instructional materials are useful for specific purposes. Quiz games may teach children to ask intelligent questions and to give definite, precise, relevant answers. Listening to effective speech and oral reading gives pleasure, aids children in their linguistic development, and increases knowledge and appreciation of literature. Some excellent recordings are available for older children: Basil Rathbone's Dickens' "Christmas Carol," Helen Hayes's introduction to patriotic selections in "Mine Eyes Have Seen the Glory," Jack Lester's telling of "A Yarn from Paul Bunyan" and "A Tale from Pecos Bill." Children may develop special reading skills through many kinds of practice: through games (145, 1957) as, for example, matching the title of a news item with the article from which it was cut; asking "What word could be used in place of_____?"; practicing the correct use in sentences of words that have more than one meaning; giving the category to which several objects belong; telling in one sentence the main idea of a fable; rearranging jumbled sentences as the first step in learning to outline and to construct logical paragraphs. To test comprehension of descriptive passages the teacher may ask children to draw what is described. This last device often reveals amazing misconceptions, as, for example, when children were asked to illustrate the story of God driving Adam and Eve out of the Garden of Eden: most of the children drew God at the wheel of a Ford car with Adam and Eve in the back seat! Exercises of this kind are an interesting supplement to the teaching of word meanings in context.

Books may also be preceded or supplemented by related pictures, film strips, motion pictures, radio broadcasts, exhibits, and talks or demonstrations by members of the community who have traveled or who possess special skills. For example, one old fellow in a rural community was asked to come to school to show the children how he made his fine, strong hickory baskets. Other members of the community were invited to demonstrate their weaving methods; still others to teach the children unpublished folk songs.

With a wealth of suitable materials, it is possible for every child to go ahead at his own rate. If he needs instruction in some specific skill, he can join a small group of children who need similar help from the teacher. Taking part in group activities provides practice in communication and stimulation to further learning.

Group experiences

Group experiences are learning experiences. Many studies of the emotional climate of groups have shown how the leader's attitude and methods affect what children learn and the ways in which they learn (142, 1958). Under certain conditions children learn more efficiently through pupil-teacher planning. When they share in the management of the classroom, they feel that they are an important part of a going concern. Because they have had a part in determining their daily activities, they understand better what they are to do and co-operate more effectively.

One of the most effective ways of meeting the needs of individual children is the small group or subgroup technique (155, 1949). Each committee or subgroup takes responsibility for studying one phase of a problem and reporting it clearly, correctly, and vividly to the class. This method improves comprehension because the pupils have a social motive for understanding what they read and hear. Successful subgroups do not "just happen"; considerable skill and knowledge of the science of group dynamics is involved in making them successful. Knowing his pupils, the teacher tries to group children of different abilities, each of whom will feel responsible for contributing his special knowledge or skill to the group. The teacher will also help them to state their goal definitely and learn to work together toward it. Any group experience that increases a child's self-esteem and sense of worth has a tonic effect on his learning.

The role of instruction in learning

It is not enough simply to provide group experiences, an emotional climate favorable to learning, or a wealth of instructional materials. Neither does adequate motivation alone ensure the most effective learning, although the intensity of the need which drives an individual to action probably determines the amount he learns and the speed with which he learns. Nor is learning guaranteed by mere repetition of the task, although practice is one of its basic conditions. Instruction in effective ways of learning is necessary. For example, children acquired skill in ring-toss most efficiently when they used correct form in holding and throwing the ring, and were given knowledge of results in a positive form: "Throw a little lower next time." Good learners continued to use the procedures that brought success, whereas poor learners seldom took time to observe the process. In another experiment in learning to throw darts at a target children in one group were encouraged to do their best but received no specific instruction. As a result of practice alone, their skill was no better than that of another group who had had no practice. Obviously they needed to understand concretely how to improve their performance. In the absence of analysis and critical evaluation of their work, errors tend to persist. One can practice errors as well as effective methods of work. This is the "tragedy of errors."

Pupils frequently fall into inefficient ways of learning because they have not had expert guidance in the initial stages of the process. Somehow the pupil must learn to find the principle, to discover the structure and inner connections of a learning situation. This means, first of all, selecting learning material which contains form and structure, and, second, teaching pupils how to discover such inner relationships for themselves. For example, by preliminary skimming of a reading passage children can learn to find the author's pattern of thought. Individuals of every age are in a better position to solve a problem as soon as they find an organizing principle. Instead of telling the child the principles underlying the solution of a problem, it is better to help him discover them for himself. Sometimes a question will call the child's attention to the principle. Sometimes situations can be modified so as to reveal new elements that make the solution evident to the child.

More school learning should be goal directed. A definite goal, plus a knowledge of the results he is achieving, evokes the child's optimum interest and effort. Extrinsic rewards and punishments are not substitutes for a task which the child considers worthwhile and important. Moreover, what constitutes satisfaction varies with the particular child and the particular circumstances. A parent's or teacher's approval, especially if manifested in the presence of his gang, may annoy or embarrass a twelve-year-old. Some children actually find it exciting to be scolded. Only when parents and teachers enter a child's world can they really know what gives him satisfaction or annoyance.

Every pupil has his own preferred method of learning, which the teacher should recognize and respect. However, a most important function of the school is to help pupils develop their most efficient methods in each subject. A laissez-faire attitude is not the answer. Respect for work itself, recognition of the importance of good scholastic achievement, psychologically sound study skills—these can and should be taught.

Giving instruction in art involves (1) encouraging a pupil first to observe form, color, and rhythm in his environment, (2) acquainting him with some productions that are only a little better than his own, (3) helping him to express in his art the principles of design and color, (4) encouraging his successful attempts, and (5) most important of all, accepting whatever he creates if it is a valid effort for him. This is not to advocate abandonment of self-criticism but to stress constructive self-criticism: "How can I say what I want to say more effectively?"

Improvement in writing may be made through instruction in form and wording, in the use of metaphors and similes, and in variety of sentence structure, as pupils feel the need for it. Specific recognition and approval should be given of the pupil's own efforts to write well—for example, to use simple, forceful words in place of high-sounding phrases. The child should be encouraged to write in the same spontaneous way in which he speaks about subjects that interest him. Children tend to write "plain talk." When the child is ten or eleven years old the teacher can help him to organize his thoughts in outline form before he writes a factual type of composition.

Children in grades four to eight have written exceptionally vivid poetry and prose. With a little encouragement one fourth-grade class (22, p. 211, 1948) first wrote lists of sounds they enjoyed:

I Like to Hear:
The wind tearing paper,
Water falling,
Soft music,
Horses running over the ground,
A car flashing by,
The wind blowing trees,
People walking in the snow.

Later they wrote imaginative poems and stories. After listening to the wind in the trees, Jenine wrote:

> The wind is an ocean
> Swishing thru trees.
> It sounds like a wave coming in fast;
> Then it hits the shore and runs
> back into the ocean.

Children's imaginations are stimulated by poems such as Robert Louis Stevenson's "Windy Nights," Ethel Fuller's "Wind Is a Cat," or William Sargent's "Wind-Wolves." From poems like these and from sensitivity to their own experiences children "catch the spirit of the wind."

Instruction in spelling along the following lines is recommended (70, 1954):

1. Select words which the children need to use at present. These words constitute the best kind of spelling list—one that is appropriate to each pupil. This list may be supplemented and checked by lists derived from scientific studies of the words most frequently used in writing and of those most frequently misspelled. Spelling demons, i.e., words which have nothing to recommend them but their difficulty, are no longer taught.

2. Be sure that the children comprehend the meaning of each word. Firsthand experience with the word and practice in using it in sentences and in conversation make its meaning clear.

3. Plan the daily school activities to provide many opportunities for pupils to see, hear, pronounce, and write the commonly used words which they should learn to spell. Teachers can help children reinforce the perception of a difficult word by pronouncing it accurately and clearly, noting its parts—phonic elements, syllables, prefixes, suffixes—and calling attention to any peculiarities that may cause difficulty. It helps some children to trace the word, written large; this reinforces the auditory and visual stimuli. Children's attention should be directed toward the correct spelling of the word, not toward the errors they have made. For this reason it is better for the teacher to make a list of the words the child has misspelled rather than to underline the misspelled words in his composition before returning it to him. Since spelling achievement in the upper grades is largely the by-product of reading and writing, it is essential to develop habits of clear word perception.

4. Encourage the child to plan his own spelling lessons, set his own goals, and make progress toward them.

5. Provide special drill on difficult words and difficult parts of words as the need is indicated. It has been found that *ie* and *ei, al* and *le, ence* and *ance, ent* and *ant, able* and *ible* are frequently confused, and that misspellings occur more often in the middle of the word than at the beginning or end.

6. Encourage the habit of using the dictionary in case of doubt.

7. Develop a desire to spell accurately.

Three essentials of instruction in problem solving are a clearly recognized goal, some interference in reaching the goal, and a desire to attain the goal. Sometimes a child's failure to reach the goal is blocked by emotion, sometimes by inability, sometimes by lack of knowledge of the steps to take. Problem-solving behavior varies with the task and with the experience and motivation of the individual and the social factors in the situation (132, p. 261, 1956).

The following steps in problem solving may not all be used in a given situation or may be combined in various ways:

1. Identifying the problem and feeling a need to solve it.
2. Seeking to clarify the problem by understanding its nature, scope, and sub-problems.
3. Collecting facts and points of view related to the problem.
4. Selecting and organizing the data collected.
5. Determining and evaluating the possible solutions.
6. Putting the chosen solution into action.
7. Appraising the methods of problem solving used.

Instruction in arithmetic involves making the process meaningful to the pupil. For example, if the pupil understands that subtracting 57 from 92 really means writing the problem like this:

"8 tens and 12 ones
take away   5 tens and 7 ones" (38, 1956),

he will not be dependent on a rule of thumb. He will understand the why as well as the how of a process and see the pattern, meaning, and organization of the task. He will discover rules himself (112, 1953). This will enable him to deal with similar problems in the future. Mathematics will make sense to him. Teachers should give practice and instruction in seeing how the parts of a problem are related to its solution; otherwise, the pupils become skillful only in numerical manipulation. It pays to develop meanings.

It is also important to arrange the arithmetic problems in a sequence, one task leading to the next in easy stages. There should be a gradation from easy to difficult, from concrete to abstract processes. When one combination is mastered, it should be easy to make the correct response to the next. If sequences are carefully worked out and the pupil starts at his present level of accomplishment, the number of failures, with their attendant discouragement, anxiety, and dislike for mathematics, will be reduced (38, p. 10, 1956). Time should not be wasted, nor failure invited, by attempts to bring all the children of a grade up to a common level of accomplishment. There are some pupils who cannot grasp the abstract aspects of arithmetic; they should not be forced to attempt the impossible. Work in arithmetic should be made socially significant as well as mathematically meaningful (68, pp. 102-104, 1948; 146, pp. 148-160, 1957). Children like to learn.

Previous research on the teaching of mathematics has been scattered and inconclusive. Much more should be learned about the process by which children of different ages cope with mathematical concepts, what motivates them to learn, how the subject matter may be organized in developmental sequences, what makes an effective mathematics teacher (38, pp. 26-30, 1956).

LEARNING TO UNDERSTAND OTHER PEOPLE

Through association with others in a large family, in school, and in play groups, the child learns how his words or acts affect them. He learns that insistence upon having his own way ostracizes him from the group, while a generous act wins friends. By observing persons who are successful in social situations, an intelligent child can learn to recognize the kind of behavior that is socially desirable. A child who has less social sensitivity may need specific help in learning to understand others as part of a gradually enlarging social experience.

The sociodrama is effective in helping children to think and feel with other persons, to put themselves temporarily in someone else's place. Dramatization and role-playing are forms of imaginative experiment. Children learn about people by trying to act as they do, just as they learn about material things from handling and using them. Role-playing gives children a chance to try on a variety of personality patterns.

The reading of autobiographies and true-to-life fiction gives insight into people's behavior and motives. The writing of dramas and stories gives practice in seeing things through others' eyes. In history one tries to discern the motives and intentions of the men and women who have influenced national and world events. The value of movies, television, and radio for the understanding of personality depends upon whether they portray character accurately or falsely.

Children need to know more than half-truths about the people of other lands. They can come closer to children in other countries by means of truthful motion pictures and stories that tell what other children talk about, what they think about, the games they play, and the way they spend their time. When they give money for food, seeds, or other things needed by underprivileged people in any part of the world, they should see pictures of these people and hear or read true stories of how their money was used. A rewarding type of project is the exchange of drawings, pictures, letters, and gifts with individual children or classes in other parts of the world.

DEVELOPING MORAL AND SPIRITUAL VALUES

Moral and spiritual values are developed basically in the home and the church. "Where love is, there God is"—wherever there is kindness, considerateness, friendliness, spiritual values flourish. Children catch the spirit. Soon they begin to be and to feel kind and good. Nothing contributes so much to the development of moral and spiritual values as the opportunity to live them.

The church school may make a special contribution to growth in the spiritual aspects of life through the atmosphere during periods of worship. The physical setting helps. One junior department during their period of worship faced a beautiful stained glass window. The music was carefully selected to create the mood of worship—selections from Bach, Mendelssohn, Sibelius, which were played often enough so that the children became familiar with them. The children shared in the planning of their periods of worship and the prayers and discussions were in the children's language. The period was short—appropriate to their attention span; it was over before the children became restless. This atmosphere was in marked contrast to the inattentive restlessness one sometimes sees in children's services of worship. The right atmosphere is important because children learn what they experience, what they respond to, what they do.

"TOWARD BETTER TEACHING"

According to the 1949 Yearbook of the Association for Supervision and Curriculum Development (8, 1949), good teaching has seven characteristics:

1. It creates an environment in which every child can succeed because the school experiences offered are appropriate to his ability and needs.
2. Teacher and pupils learn together; the class is a group working together to achieve goals which all accept as worthwhile.
3. The teacher's most important work is to guide pupils' learning and behavior so that they develop self-direction and self-reliance.
4. Teachers encourage pupils to discover, to create, and to gain new insights in the fields of their choice.

5. Teachers help pupils to develop values through example, individual and group guidance, and social living; to translate their values into community-betterment projects suited to their age and ability.

6. Teachers show pupils how to evaluate their learning—how to determine whether they are reaching the specific goals.

7. If teachers expect the best of each pupil, he will want to live up to their expectation.

To translate these generalizations into psychologically sound day-by-day procedures is indeed a challenging task.

Questions and Problems

FOR CLASS DISCUSSION OR STUDY GROUPS

1. Observe the study habits of a small number of pupils who are doing exceptionally good work. Watch them at work; analyze with them their written and oral work. Obtain diary-records of their twenty-four hour activities, and discuss their study habits with them. Study in the same way a number of pupils doing the poorest academic work. Compare the results for the two groups.

2. Sit beside a child while he is doing an arithmetic problem and ask him to think aloud as he works. What are his mental processes?

3. How can a teacher help a child acquire some specific skill, e.g., playing ball, writing, etc.?

4. How can a teacher or parent encourage a child to read more suitable books and magazines?

5. Outline a procedure for teaching spelling to children who have special spelling difficulties.

6. Show how learning theory can be applied to specific learning tasks of this age group. Read David Russell's *Children's Thinking* (132, 1956) with special attention to methods used for studying how children learn to think.

7. Show how important factors influencing learning can be taken into consideration in a specific home or school situation.

Chapter 18

DEVELOPMENTAL PROBLEMS

OF LATER CHILDHOOD

The developmental tasks of children nine to fourteen, described in the previous chapter, concern personal relations and the gaining of knowledge. The two are related: if the child feels secure in his family relations and successful in relating himself to his age-mates, he is free to learn. Problems arise in connection with these developmental tasks.

KINDS OF PROBLEMS

Some problems are manifestations of desires and drives that lack adequate outlets. There are times when disobedience is a healthy sign of growing independence and when a flare-up against injustice is commendable. However, it is important to distinguish between momentary or transitory behavior and that which is persistent, intense, inappropriate to the age of the child, an indication of habitual unhappiness, and symptomatic of serious emotional disturbance (171, 1954). These and other kinds of behavior are expensive to the individual and to society (116, p. 23, 1950).

From some adults' point of view, problem behavior represents "a discrepancy between the way a child behaves and the way someone wants him to behave." If a teacher encourages children to talk freely in his classroom, then talking is no problem. If a teacher forbids conversation, then talking becomes a problem. According to this view, one way to create problems is to make many rules and restrictions. Pushing a child too hard and too fast toward achieving grade standards or toward changing his cultural standards may result in confusion, emotional turmoil, lying, or feelings of guilt. Discrepancy between school and home standards may produce feelings of disloyalty, humiliation, or guilt in the child. When the school offers these youngsters more suitable programs, they show an improvement in adjustment.

Problem behavior is often the child's way out of difficult situations—

the way he has learned to respond to the unreasonable demands of his environment. Individuals find many ways of coming to grips with a reality that is threatening and blighting. By their disturbed behavior children tell us that something is wrong with their home, school, or neighborhood (116, pp. 14-29, 1950). Sometimes, as Dr. Plant said, their voices are too soft for us to hear.

Some problem behavior stems from deeply disturbing experiences of early childhood. Such problems tend to persist. Their manifestation in elementary school is related to later delinquency or mental disorder. Children differ in their susceptibility to psychic disturbances; some are highly resistant and "some highly vulnerable." A very few children of this age are so seriously disturbed that they require treatment in a mental hospital.

Surveys have shown some evidence of poor mental health among preadolescents. Boys appear to be more maladjusted than girls; children of low mental ability, more maladjusted than average or superior children. A combination of conditions at present seems to result in behavior problems, recognized by teachers, reaching a peak at about thirteen or fourteen years for boys and at fifteen or sixteen for girls.

Cases observed in child guidance clinics seem to show three main types of personality structure (74, 1944):

1. The excessively inhibited child. He is likely to have rather cold, critical parents whose approval can be won only by "very good, very conforming, very inhibited behavior." To meet his parents' demands this child has strongly repressed his primitive impulses. The consequent inner tension mounts to the point where it is relieved by neurotic behavior.

2. The excessively uninhibited child. He is likely to have suffered from severe deprivation of affection and constructive education and support. As a result, he is unsocialized, destructively aggressive, and continually in conflict with others.

3. The child who is an acceptable and loyal member of his own group but moves against outsiders. He will rob, fight, deceive, and injure persons outside his gang, "will not accept blame, feels little guilt over misconduct." He is likely to have experienced disharmony in the home, a poor example set by his father, laxness in constructive discipline, and parental indifference. Consequently he has yielded to delinquent influences in his neighborhood.

There are, of course, no pure types. Each child may show some of each kind of behavior in different proportions under different conditions.

BEHAVIOR IS CAUSED

In child-study groups, teachers and parents spend most of their time trying to understand the causes of behavior that they have observed. What are some of these causes? Physical discomfort and impairments, inability to keep pace with schoolwork, family relationships, social relations and social status, and demoralizing influences in the neighborhood may all enter into the complex causation of behavior problems in the preadolescent years.

Physical causes

Vitamin deficiency, disturbances in blood chemistry, and the psychological effects of illness influence the mental health of children. Long-continued pain may cause irritability or a tendency to withdraw from social contacts. A defect of hearing or vision may be the starting point of a chain of failures. Uneven or unusual growth may result in anxiety and awkwardness. The fat boy or the overweight girl, sensitive to teasing, may turn against others or assume a clowning role that at least wins laughter. The undernourished child may lack energy to cope with his school tasks and to maintain satisfying social relations. Health is basic to good adjustment, and peace of mind is basic to good health.

Failure in school

An unsuitable curriculum is at the root of many behavior problems. The cause of failure is not the intelligence level per se, but rather the relation between the child's mental ability and unrealistic expectations—too high or too low—which the home and the school have for him. The school curriculum may be unsuited to the particular pupils. For example, the grade placement of boys ten to seventeen years old in a corrective school was, on the average, two years above their achievement. This meant that these boys, day in and day out, were expected to do work beyond their ability; they were constantly experiencing failure. Laycock described the "problem child" as "trailing clouds of failure." Indeed, problem children often think of themselves as physically inadequate; as rejected by parents, teachers, and pupils; as intellectual or social failures. A large proportion of them needs remedial work. Failing to get help, they tend to withdraw from a situation that is thoroughly unsatisfactory to them. Truancy is an "indication of impending delinquency."

Gifted children, on the other hand, may react to a school situation that is frustrating and blighting by doing poor work in their subjects, causing disturbance by talking back to the teachers, and acting smart. When put in a class with an understanding teacher who provides suitable reading materials and gives them instruction in any fundamentals in which they are weak, they usually make rapid progress academically and socially.

Influence of parental attitude

Much conflict between parents and children aged nine to twelve seems to be caused by parents' interrupting or interfering with the child's activities. According to the children (53, 1957), "Parents don't want you to interrupt them but they will interrupt you." They also "take it out on us kids" when they are nervous. Sometimes, the children say, parents abruptly shut off a television program they want to see or turn it on "when they are practicing or want to sleep." "When they want us to ride, we want to walk." "When they want us to work, we want to play," and vice versa. It would seem as though many annoyances of this kind could be prevented by getting together and agreeing on a reasonable daily schedule.

It is more difficult to do something about the annoyance caused by parents' watching over their children too closely. This is distasteful to preadolescents because it means "being kept too young" or "made to feel so young." Other causes for children's complaints are parents' lack of time to listen, to talk, or to play with their children; they are always too busy. Even more serious is the child's sensing that the parents lack faith in them. "They will never let us tell them what they do that is wrong." (53, p. 31, 1957) The degree of parent-child conflict depends upon the parents' sensitivity to the child's feelings, as well as upon the parents' genuine affection for the child and their skill in helping him to learn appropriate behavior. Fathers seem to have the greatest awareness of their son's feelings; and mothers, of their daughter's feelings (90, 1954).

It is the way children perceive their parents' attitude toward them that is most likely to affect their behavior. Dr. Plant's concept of "whoness" and "whatness" corresponds to Ausubel's "intrinsic-extrinsic valuation" by parents. By giving a variety of projective tests to forty fourth- and fifth-grade children, Ausubel and others (10, 1954) obtained evidence of a high correlation between children's perceptions of acceptance and their intrinsic valuation by their parents. Girls perceived themselves as being more accepted and intrinsically valuated than did boys. As the authors pointed out, the meaningfulness of the results are limited by the unreliability and transparency of the measures and the lack of knowledge of responses common to ten-year-olds.

Parents' attitudes toward behavior problems and emotionally disturbed children are significantly different from their attitudes toward normal children. Toward their emotionally disturbed children, parents have shown a variety of unfavorable attitudes: undisguised hostility, rejection, antagonism, demanding, restrictiveness, indifference, laxity, cool detachment, overprotectiveness, excessive solicitude, overindulgence, or ambivalence. They often show a marked preference for the child's brothers or sisters. Some mothers do their duty, but without love. When a child is ignored, rejected, or harshly treated, he early learns to be wary, suspicious, or hostile. Rejection by others may result in attitudes of self-rejection. In self-protection the child resorts to various mental mechanisms—ways of adjusting that are not socially acceptable or constructive.

Although some behavior problems and emotional disturbances arise from parents' initial attitude, the child's disturbed behavior is likely to intensify the parents' unfavorable attitude and response to the child. It may be a cause of friction between husband and wife. As one mother said, "My husband and I would get along fine if it weren't for our eleven-year-old child. We fight every night on her account and half the time she starts us going in the morning, too." (24, p. 60, 1956)

The emotionally disturbed child is often punished for behavior which should be regarded as normal for his age and maturity. His parents too often punish the child to relieve their own feelings, rather than to promote his self-discipline. Such treatment tends to suppress positive growth factors in the child. Truly loving and understanding parents respect the exceptional child's individuality and needs. Their response to him is fairly consistent and predictable. They give him freedom, yet protect him from the hazards with which he is unable to cope.

Social relations and social status

A child's social relations have much to do with his satisfactions in school. Failure to make and keep friends may cast a shadow over other aspects of school life. Lack of skill in games or in handwork may prevent a child from finding his place in the group.

Animosities against certain teachers may distort a child's entire school life. On the other hand, a friendly, constructive relation may make the difference between juvenile delinquency and good citizenship. Children of these ages say that the teacher who has helped them most is kind and considerate of individuals, co-operative and democratic, and has wide interests and great patience (173, 1947). The effect of the teacher's personality on pupils' behavior was demonstrated by Anderson, Brewer, and Reed (5, 1946). A teacher who was "flexible, adaptive, noncoercive, co-operative, and understanding" encouraged similar behavior in the pupils. A teacher who was "rigid, quarrelsome, commanding, and coercive" tended to increase conflicts and misunderstanding and to "stifle spontaneity and social development."

The relation of socioeconomic status to adjustment is not clear. According to some studies, juvenile delinquency tends to increase in periods of prosperity and to decrease during economic depressions. Although more maladjustment and undesirable personal characteristics are reported among children of low socioeconomic groups than among middle-class children, factors other than the socioeconomic level may account for the difference. The attitude of parents and other aspects of family relationships appear to be the most crucial factor in the social behavior of children.

Out-of-school influences*

Preadolescents are at the crossroads, ready to take either of two paths. They are particularly susceptible to demoralizing influences in the community. It is very important that they get started on the path of wholesome recreation before they have experimented with demoralizing roadhouses and commercial amusement places. Modern spectator-type entertainment may contribute to delinquent behavior in three ways: (1) by gradually shaping the child's attitude over a long period of time, (2) by teaching techniques of crime, and (3) by stimulating individuals and groups just enough to set off, by "trigger action," already "strong antisocial inclinations or pent-up resentments." (83, p. 808, 1954) Motion pictures, television, radio, comics, and paper-back books may be used by children, wisely or unwisely. They become harmful when they divert children from their goals and when they deprive them of the satisfaction that comes from genuine personal achievement.

Multiple causes of behavior problems

Search for specific causes of behavior is being replaced by study of the complex situations out of which certain kinds of behavior arise. In the yearbook on *Juvenile Delinquency and the Schools* (116, 1950), Plant, in the first chapter, and Healy and Bronner, in the second, have shown how complex the causation of behavior problems is.

The following is an example of how parents in a child-study group tried to recognize multiple causes in analyzing the problem of daydreaming presented by one of the mothers. She described her boy as "just sitting and dreaming at school, going into flights of fancy, usually happy but reticent." The group recognized daydreaming as a symptom and suggested a number of possible causes. They said he might:

Be distracted by a large group of classmates.
Be using his imagination to escape from an unpleasant reality.

* See Chap. 17.

Be bored with academic subjects because his main interest was in art; the daydreaming might be merely a release from boredom.

Want to do everything perfectly and lose interest if he could not reach his level of aspiration.

Be a bright child for whom schoolwork had no challenge; he would change only when school became more interesting than his imaginative musings.

Feel rejected by his classmates; a child may daydream his way through a school in which he feels himself to be a social misfit.

Have an eye defect that made reading and writing fatiguing and uncomfortable.

Have a hearing defect that caused so much strain that he withdrew from the attempt to listen.

Have emotional conflicts; his daydreaming might be a harmless way of relieving tension or a way of avoiding the task of facing reality and resolving his difficulties.

Each of these possibilities was considered in the light of the information already available. The group decided to make a further study of the boy. They realized that nothing is accomplished by merely driving a symptom out of sight.

METHODS OF DEALING WITH BEHAVIOR PROBLEMS

Punishing, scolding, taking away privileges, and further restricting the child's behavior often intensify the very conditions that gave rise to the problem. Far more effective methods are necessary. If possible, the child's feelings should be channeled into acceptable ways of behaving. Baruch suggested that the child's needs be met, even though belatedly, and that outlets for his feelings of resentment, anger, or fear be provided (13, p. 116, 1949).

Court and clinic methods

When a juvenile delinquent is brought to court, the judge may (1) dismiss the case, (2) put him under the supervision of a "Big Brother" or other responsible adult, (3) put him on probation, or (4) assign him to temporary care in an institution or commit him to a state institution. Evidence as to the efficacy of treatment of delinquency is not encouraging. However, children with the following characteristics are most likely to profit by clinical guidance: chronological age below fifteen years, normal or superior intelligence, school placement on a par with mental age. The importance of the early discovery and treatment of behavior disorders is evident.

Group methods

Hope for the prevention of serious maladjustment lies in the home care of infants and preschool children and in public school education. Pediatricians and physicians should take more responsibility for the psychological aspects of maternal and infant care. They are strategic persons in helping a child get off to a good start. As the child grows older, in an autocratic home, overrestriction of freedom often gives rise to tension and hostility. In the laissez-faire home or classroom, he is allowed to do as he pleases. With completely unrestricted freedom some children become anxious; others become bored. Their behavior is so aimless that they accomplish little. In the democratic group, the teacher helps the children to appraise the situation, asks for their suggestions, and assists them when necessary; relations are friendly and co-operative and much creative and original work is accomplished.

The dynamics of a group are complex. Often two or three members wield the dominant influences. They change the attitudes of other members without themselves being changed. Children on the fringes of the group—those not chosen by others—tend to "leave the field." They seem somewhat immature, unwilling to co-operate, unable to pay attention. They need to be helped to make some special contribution toward achieving the group goal.

Some children and young people are much more susceptible to group influence or contagion than are others. Their conduct improves under the stimulus of a socially minded group and, by the same token, deteriorates under bad influence. They cheat in one class but not in another. A child's behavior cannot be fully understood unless his relation to teacher and pupils is known.

There is social security in belonging to several groups. Success in one helps to neutralize failure in another. Thus one is able to maintain some self-esteem. For example, a boy who was very sensitive about his inferiority in a reading group became a better swimmer than many of the boys who surpassed him in reading. Success in swimming gave him confidence to cope with his reading problem. In a summer reading center one boy did not improve in reading until the middle of the term, when he suddenly gained prestige in the group by attending a big-league baseball game.

By providing a satisfying present experience, the group helps the individual to reduce his anxiety about the past. Having brought his anxiety out in the open, having recounted it to the group, and having

shared experiences, he often finds the past event less important and disturbing. Sometimes the group shows an individual that he no longer
needs to put up a front of "big guy stuff." When he finds that other behavior, more acceptable to himself and others, is approved, he will drop some
of his defenses. When a child gains status in the group, establishes interpersonal relations, and is accepted as an equal, he becomes a stronger,
more secure person; he gains strength through belonging. He is disciplined
through goal-directed activity. Thus he builds inner controls and self-
esteem.

Discipline

SON: Did you beat me when I was a child?
FATHER: Yes, for your own good.
SON: Then why shouldn't I beat you, if beating does a person good? Besides a
    father deserves to be beaten much more than a child does. He has less ex-
    cuse for doing wrong.

Effective discipline redirects the child's energy and aggressive impulses into constructive channels and helps him to reach, through his own
efforts, goals that seem to him worthwhile. Viewed as progressive control
by which he learns to meet the demands of the social situation, discipline is
essential to growing up.

The main features of effective discipline have been described in previous chapters and need only a brief review here:

1. Effective discipline is directed toward the underlying sources of the
difficulty, not toward its symptoms. One would hardly whip a child for feeling
inferior, even though his sense of inferiority manifested itself in disturbing behavior, nor would one detain after school a child whose restlessness was caused
by fatigue. In most instances the occasion for punishment disappears when the
cause of the difficulty is discovered.

2. Discipline, in the mental-hygiene sense, looks toward the future; it is
not concerned with expiation for a past offense. Preadolescent children may
profit by thinking in advance about the consequences of certain courses of
action.

3. It associates freedom with responsibility and with acceptance of the
natural consequences of one's act. For example, three boys who selected a
vacant lot in which to play ball recognized the justice of having to pay for the
large pane of glass that they broke. They earned the money or took from their
banks the amount needed to repair the damage.

As the child grows older, his attitude toward discipline changes; he
resents, more and more, corporal punishment—the use of force by someone who has superior power. Scolding and nagging are especially annoy-

ing to children of this age. They acquire great facility in ignoring these manifestations of adult authority. One twelve-year-old invariably returned an absent-minded yes to his mother's incessant admonitions, without the slightest intention of acting upon her suggestions. "Please don't begin to preach," one twelve-year-old girl begged. Threats are seldom worth the breath it takes to utter them; children rarely consider them of much importance.

The person best fitted to deal with the child's behavior problems is the one who knows him best and has his respect and affection. Such a person will use the highest level of appeal that will work. He may appeal to the rules of conduct accepted by the child's group and to the child's own capacity for self-control. Between the extremes of thoughtful consideration for others and fear of unpleasant consequences, lie many other incentives to wholesome behavior: personal advantage, approval of others, satisfaction to be derived from increased skill and successful activity, service to the group, and development of the kind of character one wants to have.

The following quotation from Arnold Bennett's *The Old Wives' Tale* illustrates the vacillating type of discipline frequently found:

He [Cyril] had apparently finished his home-lessons. The books were pushed aside, and he was sketching in lead-pencil on a drawing-block. . . .

Constance [his mother] put a hand on his shoulder. "Finished your lessons?" she murmured caressingly.

"Yes." And after a pause: "Except my arithmetic. I shall do that in the morning before breakfast."

"Oh, Cyril," she protested.

It had been a positive ordinance, for a long time past, that there should be no sketching until lessons were done. In his father's lifetime Cyril had never dared to break it.

He bent over his block, feigning an intense absorption. Constance's hand slipped from his shoulder. She wanted to command him formally to resume his lessons. But she could not. She feared an argument; she mistrusted herself. And, moreover, it was so soon after his father's death!

"You know you won't have time to-morrow morning!" she said weakly.

"Oh, mother!" he retorted superiorly. "Don't worry." And then, in a cajoling tone: "I've wanted to do that stag for ages."

She sighed and sat down in her rocking chair. . . .

When he had finished [his supper], he refilled his glass with water, and put it next to his sketching-block.

"You surely aren't thinking of beginning to paint at this time of night!" Constance exclaimed, astonished.

"Oh yes, mother!" he fretfully appealed. "It's not late."

Another positive ordinance of his father's had been that there should be nothing after supper except bed. Nine o'clock was the latest permissible moment for going to bed. It was now less than a quarter to.

"It only wants twelve minutes to nine," Constance pointed out.

"Well, what if it does?"

"Now Cyril," she said, "I do hope you are going to be a good boy, and not cause your mother anxiety."

But she said it too kindly.

He said sullenly: "I do think you might let me finish it. I've begun it. It won't take me long."

She made the mistake of leaving the main point. "How can you possibly choose your colors properly by gas-light?" she said.

"I'm going to do it in sepia," he replied in triumph.

"It mustn't occur again," she said.*

Persistence and negativism may be allied traits in preadolescents. If so, it would be undesirable to suppress negativism to the point of discouraging persistence.

SPECIAL PROBLEMS

Inattentiveness

Inattentiveness has many possible underlying causes. Too often teachers and parents label an inattentive child "lazy" and go no further in their diagnosis.

Among the factors that may contribute to inattentiveness in any particular situation are the following:

1. Physical defects such as poor hearing or vision.
2. Illness, pain, or bodily discomfort.
3. Fatigue, which may reduce the child's ability to concentrate.
4. Hunger, which may be responsible for the inattention of some children who come to school without breakfast.
5. Inability to grasp the meaning of what is being taught; too often children are blamed for inattention when they are quite unable to comprehend what is going on.
6. Lack of interest; when the work is too easy, there is no incentive for the well-informed, alert child to pay attention.
7. Undefined purpose; the child's activity is aimless.
8. Preoccupation with matters that seem to the child more important than schoolwork; some event at home, some imaginary event, sex fantasies.

In view of these complex factors it is obvious that each case of inattention must be treated according to the combination of causes involved.

* Arnold Bennett, *The Old Wives' Tale* (educational ed.; Garden City, N.Y.: Doubleday & Co., Inc., 1928), pp. 259-261. Reprinted with permission of Doubleday & Co., Inc. and of "The Owners of the Copyright."

Problems relating to sex

In our culture questions about sex are frequently suggested to pre-adolescents by pictures in newspapers and magazines, by motion pictures, and by new companions. Unsatisfied curiosity about sex may lead to surreptitious discussions during recess or on the way to school, to circulation of obscene notes and pictures, and even to mutual inspection and exploration. Older boys, especially, are likely to engage in homosexual play and masturbation. If skillfully handled, these sexual stirrings need not cause disturbed sexual behavior (11, 1955).

Children of this age are less likely to express curiosity to parents. The adult can best secure and keep the child's confidence by being honest with him in feeling as well as in facts, by taking time to talk things over, and by having realistic knowledge of the child's world. One mother lost the confidence of her daughter on the last point. "I don't talk things over with her," the girl said, "because she never suggests anything that works."

Timing is important. Boys and girls should have learned the essential facts about sex bit by bit during their early years before they have acquired information from undesirable sources. They also need the information before events like menstruation occur and before the emotional problems of adolescence overwhelm them. The first step is to find out what is already in the child's mind. Specific emotional problems and undesirable sexual habits should be dealt with individually, but some problems may be discussed in small groups. Except under unusual conditions, a separate course in sex education is not advisable. Some children may prefer to get the facts from books. The basic facts of social hygiene are presented simply and directly in a number of books (34, 1953; 92, 1956; 140, 1956) and are pictorially presented in several films.

Social hygiene, however, is not mainly a matter of facts; it involves feeling more than thinking. The object of sex education is to make children "more able to give and receive love in all their human relationships." (101, 1956) It takes an emotionally mature person to handle it effectively. A child deeply troubled about sex is more disturbed than ever if he gets the impression that it is a taboo subject.

Stealing

It is helpful to think of degrees of honesty, that is, stages in the development of honest behavior. To label a child a thief is neither descriptive nor helpful. The underlying difficulty may be constant even though the child may be dishonest in different ways. A fifth-grade boy who steals a dollar from the teacher's desk cannot properly be labeled a dishonest child. He may be honest in many other ways. Why did he fail in that one situation? What can the parent or teacher do about it?

One cause may be an underdeveloped sense of the meaning of possession, which should have been built up in the preschool period. Children of school age need experience in working for their possessions, in buying them with money they have earned. This helps them to recognize the rights of others to the possessions *they* have earned. Children need to be taught to feel responsibility for possessions held in common and to know that "finding is not keeping."

Another reason why children steal is that they know of no other means of obtaining certain things they need. Sometimes they need food. Hunger is a powerful urge. Stanley Hall said a good table is one of the best preventives of stealing. Sometimes a child feels the need of clothing or money in order to maintain his standing in the group and thus satisfy his strong desire for social approval. Stealing may represent an urge to show off or to win friendship by having something to give to others.

Sometimes stealing is an attempt to relieve tension; it is clearly related to mental conflict. It may arise from many motives—from jealousy, from conflict over sex experiences, from revenge, from a desire to injure a person toward whom one feels hostile. For example, one boy in a family of seven began to steal. All of the other children were a credit to their father, who was prominent in boys' welfare work. The father had put this one boy under the care of an older brother. Resenting his father's lack of personal attention, the boy unconsciously resorted to stealing in order to bring shame to his father.

Frequently the cause may be traced back a number of years. Stealing may first have been tried as an experiment; the theft remained undetected; nothing happened. No dissatisfaction was attached to the act. It was therefore repeated. To overlook real stealing is to encourage it. On the other hand, its importance should not be exaggerated.

Kleptomania—the desire to steal objects for no rational end—is sometimes found among children. Youngsters with this obsession may steal objects of no value. One girl stole the belts of other girls' suits. Twenty-three belts which were of no possible use to her were found in her possession.

An important underlying cause of dishonesty, detected by special tests of honesty, is lack of inhibition. The child who steals is frequently one who has never learned to refrain from doing anything he desires to do.

The treatment of Peter illustrates a method of recognizing the fault without unduly magnifying it. Peter hid in his locker a purse which belonged to a little girl. The teacher

. . . took Peter to his locker, showed him the purse, and asked him if he knew to whom it belonged. Peter said that he did not. She then asked him if he knew who put it there, and he said no. Miss Henton (the teacher) then said, "Well, I know to whom the purse belongs, Peter. It belongs to Alice. Now wouldn't you like to give it back to her?" Miss Henton reported afterward that at her suggestion of restitution, a really childlike smile broke on Peter's face for the first time since he had been in the school. He had often been caught in misdemeanors and punished, but this was his first experience in being caught and helped out of his plight legitimately. He said he would like to return the purse, and did so at once.*

At all ages false accusation should be avoided.

Pupil self-government is a group preventive approach. Mowrer (114, 1939) reported the results of a plan of modified self-government, which helped to put a group of children from four to twelve years of age back on the path of normal development. The utilitarian value of socially acceptable behavior was pointed out. If children took things that belonged to others, no one's possessions would be safe. As the group took over more and more responsibility for its own conduct, the children's attitude toward the staff changed. They no longer regarded the teachers as enemies to be outwitted or placated, but as consultants who could help them achieve their goals. There was a marked decrease in the number of infractions with which the staff had to deal. The expert worker tries to understand the real meaning of the behavior to the child; he observes when and where and how he steals; he tries to discover what purpose stealing serves and what experience in the child's past has led him to gain this end through stealing.

When a child is exposed to immoral conduct or to oversevere discipline, or when he lacks parental support in developing self-control, it is sometimes necessary to find a more suitable home for him. This is especially difficult when the child is emotionally attached to a parent who is an immoral influence. A younger child may be helped to form new ties; an older child, through counseling or group therapy, may gain insight into his past and present relationships.

* Helen T. Wooley, "Case Study, No. II, Peter: The Beginning of the Juvenile Court Problem," *Journal of Genetic Psychology*, XXXIII (March, 1926), p. 20. Quoted by permission.

Lying

In all grades from the fourth to the twelfth there are children who consistently tell the truth and others who tell falsehoods whenever faced with a trying situation. Why do the untruthful ones lie? Intelligence tests have shown that it is not always because these children cannot think clearly or in abstract terms. In most instances, tests of moral judgment have indicated that it is not because they lack moral discrimination. The child's behavior can only be understood by a study of the conditions under which it occurred.

Knowledge of the specific causes of lying is a prerequisite to preventing it. At this age a child may lie to the parent or teacher when he would not lie to a member of his own gang. His standards of truth, based on community interest in the gang, might well be broadened to include the school and the home. Fear of social disapproval is at the basis of conventional lies, many of which children have observed adults using. The actions of adults have a much greater effect than the advice they give young people. Fear of physical pain or deprivation fosters lies in situations in which the child is in want or in danger. For example, one child said: "Once I lied to my mother; she told my father and I had to lie again because I was so frightened." Fear lies at the basis of many children's falsehoods. One investigator found that more lies are told by children from homes in which the punishment is severe. Suggestibility is another important factor in lying. Very frequently children will tell a lie before they stop to think, especially if the question has been worded in such a way as to suggest a particular answer.

Innumerable situations in everyday life favor lying. One boy reported that his "mother was so fussy that he could only avoid her plaguing him by telling lies." Frequent lying suggests that the child may be under too much pressure to achieve or to attain adult standards. Lying may show that he is concerned about meeting teachers' or parents' expectations. Adults should help children to learn better ways of meeting everyday situations and crises.

What can be done about lying? One can sometimes check the habit of lying by detecting a child's first attempts and by helping him realize that advantage rarely comes of it, i.e., that there are usually better ways of meeting situations and that lying usually makes a bad situation worse. A teacher or parent who is easygoing or indifferent about detecting falsehoods may help to strengthen the lying habit. A habit of moral courage needs to be built up. An appeal may be made to children's admiration of this kind of fearlessness; the relationship between physical courage and moral courage should be pointed out. The story about George Washington and his colt, which is a favorite with children of this age, illustrates two types of bravery, fearlessness in riding the colt and fearlessness in telling his mother the truth about the colt's sudden death.

Lying should be treated as part of the child's total adjustment. If a child lies about his own or his father's accomplishments in order to make an impression on someone, he should be helped to find other ways to satisfy his desire for approval and recognition. If a child tells lies through fear of consequences, his home and school relations should be considered. A very suggestible child may lie without really meaning to. He should not be hurried in his answers, but encouraged to think before he speaks.

Cheating

Why do children cheat? Is it because they do not know any better? Probably not. In Hartshorne and May's classic experiments (65, 1928) little relation was found between moral knowledge and conduct. Is cheating due to lack of intelligence? Bright children as well as dull children sometimes cheat, although cheating, under present school conditions, is more prevalent among the mentally retarded and the scholastically incompetent. Cheating may represent lack of inhibition. Children who cheat have been found to be unusually suggestible. Children sometimes cheat as an experiment. When there is a sporting chance of "getting away with something," some exuberant children will take it, unless the morale established in the classroom is effective enough to counteract the tendency.

Some classrooms promote cheating by placing an exaggerated emphasis on the importance of marks. Some children's fear of failure is so intense that they use any means to prevent it. In many schools the record of the individual's achievement, study habits, and results on standardized tests is replacing teachers' marks. Instead of or in addition to the school report cards, teacher and parents confer about the child's all-round development (143, 1955).

Smoking

Curiosity, imitation, desire to "do as the Romans do," or to increase self-esteem, may lead to smoking toward the end of this period. The same impulses may just as well lead to interest in nature study, science, reading, or to participation in worthwhile clubs, teams, and societies. If his playmates are interested in Scouts, 4-H Club, or similar activities, a boy is not so likely to learn to smoke. As with lying, adult practices and children's relations with adults are important determinants of the child's attitude and behavior. Smoking may be presented as a foolish waste of money which could be spent for things wanted very much.

Fighting

Michael Pupin, the great physicist who rose from immigrant to inventor, recounts a number of fights he had as a boy. One of them, on the day he landed in America, was with a boy bigger than himself who made fun of his shabby appearance. He says he has been fighting ever since. Every vigorous personality is a fighter. Theodore Roosevelt comes to mind immediately. Browning writes, "I was ever a fighter. One fight more, the best and the last." The tendency to fight is a motive force too valuable to be repressed; it reinforces other drives in overcoming difficulties. Boys should not be forbidden to fight, but taught when to fight and what is worth fighting for.

If two fifth-grade boys on the playground start fighting, what should the teacher do? One experienced teacher offered to referee the fight and see that the rules of the game were observed. This prevented any serious physical injury, and the teacher found that the boys' anger frequently evaporated and they stopped fighting. If there is little danger of serious injury, noninterference is advisable. Children need practice in settling their own disputes. If they pass through a stage of conflict in this period, they are likely to arrive at the conviction that physical combat is not so good a way of settling disputes as coming to a peaceful understanding with one's enemy. Casual but specific comments by the teacher help children to interpret their experience of fighting.

Careful planning prevents unnecessary squabbling. Plenty of interesting work and play, games with definite rules that everyone knows, opportunity to take initiative, and abundance of space help to reduce bickering and quarreling. Athletic contests use up fighting energy. Baseball, football, tug-of-war, volleyball, hockey, and other team games are also valuable in developing co-operation and loyalty.

EMOTIONAL ADJUSTMENT

The various degrees of emotional intensity have been described in Chap. 16 and the beneficial effect of mild emotion recognized. Preadolescents express their emotion in different ways. One child may become pale in anger, another flushed. A preadolescent may respond to frustration and difficulty by withdrawing or resorting to other ways of escape, by engaging in uncalled-for aggression, or by making an active endeavor to solve the problem.

Fear

Fear is a natural response to a situation with which one is unable to cope. It has its roots in feelings of inadequacy and worthlessness. Parents and teachers can help children meet social situations more constructively and successfully, and to win status and real acceptance in their groups. If a child is socially awkward and afraid, he should be placed, if possible, in small congenial groups of children, some of whom feel adequate in social situations. As children grow older, their fears tend to become more imaginary; they tend to become increasingly afraid of things that might happen. During the preadolescent, adolescent, and adult years fear may take the form of timidity, stage fright, or social withdrawal. Intelligence alone does not cast out fear, though superior children may conceal their fears more successfully than mentally retarded children.

Anger

Anger is an aggressive response to difficulty. It is the opposite of fear, which is retreat. Boys and girls in this age period are frequently blocked and thwarted. An outburst of anger often results from an accumulation of irritations, none of which appears to be sufficiently provocative by itself. To the adult who is not aware of this sequence of experiences, the child's anger seems unreasonable. Preadolescents appear to go through a period of open resistance. If unskillfully treated, they may become obstinate. During these years a certain amount of resistance is a normal sign of growth; it represents the child's attempt to meet his needs.

Anger may be manifested in various ways. Frustration caused by failure in schoolwork may come out in the form of dislike for the teacher, imaginary triumphs over the person who is disliked, or thoughts of dying and being mourned. The treatment of anger becomes more and more difficult as its expression becomes less natural and overt.

The response of an adult to a child's anger should be sympathetic, but objective. To respond to anger with anger is to intensify the problem. This does not mean that an adult should never show indignation. There is a place for righteous wrath. But it should be directed against the act, not against the child. Parents and teachers can help the child to create a social environment for himself in which it is possible for him to love instead of hate.

Jealousy

Jealousy contains some elements of both fear and anger. The jealous child doubts his own abilities. His wishes are thwarted; he feels defeated; he fears losing the affection he has and resents anyone else's getting the attention he desires. In order to minimize jealousy, invidious comparisons should be avoided. Neither parents nor teachers should have "pets"; it is a mistake to show favoritism with children. Showing dislike for the jealous child and attempting to make him feel inferior will only intensify his feelings.

This does not mean that the jealous child should not be expected to recognize superiority in other children. Children notice one another's work. Gifted children may make other children more keenly aware of their limitations. Therefore, it is necessary for each child to obtain a realistic idea of his own capacity and to acknowledge frankly that there are certain things he cannot do and be. At the same time he should focus his attention on his assets—on what he *can* do. This attitude should replace jealousy of others. When a child's level of aspiration is too high, he must be helped to lower his goals.

CONCLUDING STATEMENT

Middle childhood lies between two spurts of growth. It is a relatively calm, outgoing period, in which children are eager to learn. They should be accepted as they are and as they can become. Although the past and the future enter into their thoughts and feelings, they live in the present. And the best preparation for the future is to live most fully in the present.

Questions and Problems

FOR CLASS DISCUSSION OR STUDY GROUPS

1. Study two children, one who is reported to be a "problem" and one who is recognized as a fine all-round child. What conditions seem to have given rise to these different kinds of development?

2. One principal told his teachers never to leave anything around which the pupils might steal. Do you approve of this policy? Give reasons for your approval or disapproval.

3. When is a problem not a problem in the negative sense, but a necessary phase of growing up? Give examples.

4. Which is better: to look for problems in children or to focus attention on positive aspects of growth? Why?

5. The cause of a child's behavior at any one time may be broadly considered as the total residue of interaction between his heredity and environment up to that time. Is this concept of causation in opposition to the approach of considering various physical, intellectual, and social factors in a child's behavior?

6. Try to translate some common behavior problems into positive forms; for example, discuss stealing from the preventive aspect, sex as a phase of normal development, fighting as a way of channeling aggressive impulses.

7. As an example of a description of procedures, thoughtfully evaluated, read Mowrer's description of a plan of modified self-government. Compare this type of investigation with a control-group type of experiment with respect to degree of generalization possible and practical help in dealing with behavior problems.

Chapter 19

CHILD-STUDY AND GUIDANCE

OF ELEMENTARY-SCHOOL PUPILS

The task of understanding his pupils is an intrinsic part of a teacher's work. Morrison's significant statement presents a new concept of teaching: "The teacher should spend half his time in studying pupils as individuals and the other half of the time doing what that study shows to be desirable and necessary." During the first few weeks of school every teacher should devote time to "learning" his pupils—learning about their readiness for the work of his grade, their physical needs, their interests, and their unique personalities.

The educator with the guidance point of view sees every child as an individual with special potentialities, capacities, talents, and needs. He sees the school as a place in which children's potentialities are discovered. He makes changes in educational objectives and in instructional materials and methods, as they are needed to develop these potentialities. In such a school, gifted children develop their special abilities and talents for serving society as well as for achieving their own happiness, and handicapped children capitalize their assets and find joy in work. In the process of child study and guidance everyone has a part: administrator, classroom teacher, parents, specialists, special classes, summer camps, clinics, and community agencies and organizations. The influence of parents persists during the school day and throughout the school years.

Child study involves much more than knowing what a child does. It involves understanding why he does it, how he feels about it, and what the behavior means to him. Moreover, child study is focused not on the child exclusively but on the interaction between the child and other persons—on dyadic and group relations. It is important to recognize the subtle interplay of forces between the child and the adults in his environment. The person studying the child also seeks to understand himself—why he behaves as he does with the child, why the child's behavior pleases or annoys him, how his attitudes and behavior affect the child. In this sense,

456

the adult is a participant observer. Guidance is interwoven with child study of this kind.

An intensive study of one or two children gives a teacher a better understanding of his class as a whole. Understanding of children's behavior is the basis for guidance. The teacher takes his cues from the child. Understanding prevents the adult from taking hasty action, from doing something merely to relieve his own feelings.

Child study should lead to self-appraisal by the child. As the child grows older he can gain more and more understanding of himself—of his strengths and weaknesses. Self-knowledge is basic to self-guidance.

MAJOR METHODS OF CHILD STUDY

Many of the modern methods of child study can be successfully used by teachers and parents; others require some special training; still others require the co-operation of specialists in different fields. The major methods may be listed as a scale ranging from the simplest to the most technical:

1. Observation of parents and child together, or of the child alone or in a group of children in everyday situations; free-play and other informal activities offer ideal opportunities to make significant observations.

2. Observation in controlled experimental situations.

3. Compilation of a developmental history and record of family background.

4. Study of the child's oral and freely written responses, his art products, and his handwork.

5. Techniques that elicit information about his feelings and relationships —incomplete sentences, incomplete stories, pictures and stories to which children are asked to respond, "three wishes," and similar projective-type ma terial.

6. Talks with the child and with the parent.

7. Sociometric techniques.

8. Dramatization and role-playing.

9. Standardized and teacher-made group tests.

10. Standardized individual tests.

11. Projective techniques.

12. Clinical study.

13. Medical and neurological examination.

Methods of synthesizing information from many sources—cumulative record, case study, case conference—are, of course, essential. The wider and deeper the teacher's background of experience and knowledge, the more effectively he will see what is important and the more acutely he will interpret what he sees. To interpret accurately it is important to know the situation in which the child makes a given response and to avoid reading one's own personality, wishes, or beliefs into the child's behavior. Many books deal, in varying degrees of comprehensiveness, with techniques of understanding children (14, 1956; 44, 1956; 113, 1956; 126, 1957; 128, 1941; 141, 1949; 144, pp. 311-453, 1953).

Observation

Observation is a way of studying a child directly; the child may not even be aware that he is being observed. At the same time the teacher can observe his own influence on the child's behavior.

To be of greatest value, observations should be selective and significant. Too often teachers note trivial incidents, or only behavior that attracts attention because it is negative. Although it is difficult to know just what behavior is most significant in an individual case, certain kinds of information are generally important:

What first impression does the child make? Does he have a winning way, or are his mannerisms and personal habits likely to repel people?

Is he well enough to be in school; what signs of health or of disease does he show? (105, 1947)

What is his self-concept—his idea of himself? Does he seem to think of himself as inferior, worthless, inadequate? Does he feel that he is understood? Is he more self-centered than children of his age usually are? Is he dissatisfied with his appearance, his school ability, his social ability?

How does he respond to thwarting, disappointment, criticism? By getting angry, discouraged, or depressed; or by using failure and criticism as a means of learning how not to fail that way again? How does he handle his difficulties? Under what conditions does he go to someone for help, cry or become angry, give up without trying, or persist until he succeeds?

How does he work? Reluctantly, or with real interest and enjoyment; usually alone or with others; for a reward or because of joy in the work itself? Does he complete the tasks he begins and the duties for which he is responsible? Under what circumstances?

When he has succeeded, does he then talk about his success, busy himself with other work, repeat the act he has just performed successfully?

How does he play? Is he relaxed and spontaneous? Does he play alone or with others, with older or younger children, or with contemporaries? Are most things fun for him? With what toys does he play? How does he treat pets?

How co-operative and helpful is he? Does he share his books and toys?

How does he get along with other children? What is his behavior in

Is adolescence becoming a less turbulent, less rebellious period?

Do modern adolescents face the future with confidence, diffidence or despondency?

groups? Does he understand and show awareness of the feelings of others? How do other children treat him? Does he accept and work for group goals?

What are his major satisfactions and interests?

What is his relation to strangers? To other adults? Is he overdependent, hostile, friendly, or indifferent?

What are his assets and special abilities? How good are his vocabulary, understanding of number, power of attention, ability to see relations? What are his liabilities and difficulties? How well does he read?

What does he do when nothing has been planned for him? Does he frequently go to the reading table? Does he show initiative in finding something worthwhile to do? Does he work on it until it is finished? Does he create new ideas?

Does he understand and accept reasonable rules and standards of conduct?

To what is the child reacting? To a baby brother or sister, to the children in his class who do not accept him, to his teacher, to conflict between his parents, to a mother who really does not love him? What are the issues in his life? How can he be helped to meet them constructively?

How is the child's environment stimulating him, giving him satisfaction, frustrating him, affecting his approaches to adults and other children?

Some situations offer much greater opportunities than others for understanding children. The free-play of a six- or seven-year-old child usually reflects his inner world of feeling and meaning. Teachers and parents may obtain glimpses of this inner world by watching the child at play. For example, when a little boy was playing in the sand under the supervision of a person with whom he had a good relation, his play was constructive. But when his parents, to whom he was antagonistic, showed interest in his sand-play, he began throwing stones and making holes instead of building castles and ships as he had done previously.

One way of getting into the children's world is through listening to their spontaneous conversation. Before class or at a party their conversation flits from television and radio programs and movies to food likes and dislikes, to classmates, jokes, and other topics.

When a parent brings the child to school, the teacher may learn much by observing them together. For example, the good relation which a teacher observed between one father and his son turned out to be the most positive factor on which to build. In the health examination, physicians and nurses have similar opportunities for valuable psychological observations of mothers and children.

Home visits offer opportunities to observe the physical environment of the child as well as the family relations. For example, the following observation of two brothers at play showed a somewhat unhealthy situation; the older one dominated the younger and constantly tried to prove his superiority.

The children are making houses in the sand.
TOMMY (the older): This is my house and you can make your own.
ARTHUR: All right.
TOMMY: I have a garage on mine, and you're too small to have one.
ARTHUR: I can have one, too (and proceeds to make one).
TOMMY: That's wrong. (Takes away Arthur's stick and rubs out his sand house. A scuffle follows. Later they begin to play ball.)
TOMMY: You can stand over there . . . further back. (Children play ball until Tommy loses interest. He throws the ball far away and makes Arthur get it. Later Tommy begins singing.)
ARTHUR: I can sing it, too (and joins in).
TOMMY: That's no good. . . . You keep quiet.

Tommy continued to order Arthur around and to criticize everything he did.

Occasionally a teacher may wish to see how a child responds to a controlled situation. For example, he may show each child the same picture and ask the same question about it, or give each child the same errand to do, being careful to state the directions in exactly the same words. Thus he can compare one child's behavior with that of other children of the same age.

Much can be done to improve the quality of anecdotal records, behavior diary-records, summaries of observation, and ratings. The following anecdotal record illustrates accurate, objective recording of observation of a boy in the fourth grade, whose IQ was 78 and whose academic achievement was on a second-grade level:

While the teacher was explaining a new process in arithmetic Jerry gazed around the room, played with a pencil and eraser on his desk, found a piece of paper and drew a picture on it. The class was assigned some written work and the teacher gave Jerry a sheet of paper on which were simple exercises in subtraction. As she began to explain the work Jerry looked at the paper, then at the work of the pupils near him and remarked in an angry tone, "This is not fourth-grade work." The teacher ignored the remark and continued with her explanation. Jerry paid little attention. In the twenty minutes that followed he worked one problem, and that one incorrectly.

Later, in a conference with the counselor, the teacher said that this was typical of Jerry's attitude when she attempted to provide work on his ability level.

This single observation raised the question why. Other techniques would be necessary in order to understand what the boy's behavior meant to him, and why he did not respond to individual help.

A series of anecdotal records frequently gives clues as to patterns of behavior and attitudes, as in the following record of Don, eleven years old and in the sixth grade.

October 12. Don was slowly finishing his reading workbook after the others had gone out to play. He said to the teacher: "I'd rather do good work in the slower group than always be behind in this group."

October 15. Don came later and tried to take his seat without being seen. The teacher said, "What made you so late this morning, Don?" Don answered: "I stayed in bed late because I was too tired to get up."

October 16. Don quit playing ball in the middle of the game. The boys were angry at his desertion. The teacher took him aside to talk to him. He was crying. She said, "I was sorry to have you stop playing before the game was finished. Didn't you feel well?" Don said, "I was tired. I had a headache and we were losing anyway. The teams were uneven. Peter wasn't playing hard on our side either."

October 19. Before school Don had a fight with a fourth-grade boy about his size. The children said Don started it; he said he was fighting because he felt like it. Don had been out late three nights a week at square dances, which he enjoyed very much. On the basis of these observations and other information the teacher talked with the parents about Don's loss of weight and the evidences he showed of fatigue and irritability. He stopped going out on school nights.

October 23. While the children were finishing lunch Don said, "Miss B——, couldn't we take the Victrola downstairs and spend part of our noon hour doing square dances?" The teacher agreed that was a good idea, but wondered if the school had the right records. Don said he could borrow some from Mr. A—— who had charge of the evening square dances. This he did, and thenceforth Don square-danced at noon instead of late at night. The teacher also visited Don's home and talked with his mother about his diet and sleep habits. From then on the anecdotes showed that Don made a marked improvement in physical energy, and developed a more co-operative attitude.

Teachers' summaries of their observations frequently show personality fault lines that go uncorrected year after year; there are also marked differences in the quality of teachers' summaries of children's behavior:

SECOND-GRADE TEACHER: Small, but very energetic, somewhat immature, gets into tempers, but gets over them quickly. Gets along pretty well with others, but is too ready to pick fights. Mother is oversolicitous. He is directed too much at home.

THIRD-GRADE TEACHER: Bob has made well over a year's progress. Has good study and work habits. Is immature for the grade and gets into difficulties with other children because of lack of judgment. Must be kept busy.

FOURTH-GRADE TEACHER: Bob is an excellent student.

FIFTH-GRADE TEACHER: Bob is socially and physically immature and has a negative attitude. For example, when a group of children were enthusiastically discussing a play that another class had given, Bob said, "Oh, I didn't like this play." Teacher: "Why not, Bob?" Bob: "Oh, just 'cause it wasn't any good." Teacher: "Was there anything you did like about it?" Bob: "The costumes weren't bad." Later, when another child suggested that they write the players a letter to tell them how much they liked the play, Bob said, "Do we *have* to write the letter?"

The fifth-grade teacher had been giving Bob opportunities to make constructive criticisms. She pointed out the positive elements in his criticism, showed how a valid negative comment can be used constructively, and invited him to say what he liked about a given situation. She encouraged him to bring some of his books from home to share with his classmates, and, in various other ways, helped him to win the recognition and friendship of the other children.

A teacher's observation may be guided by a good rating scale. *The Vineland Social Maturity Scale*, developed by Edgar A. Doll (36, 1947), is a pioneer attempt to quantify social behavior. It considers 117 socially significant items of behavior "arranged approximately in the order of their development." If a child is habitually mature in any one of these respects, he rates a plus score; if he is habitually immature with respect to any item, he is rated minus; and if his behavior fluctuates on any item, he is scored plus-minus ($\pm$). In the total score, allowance is made for items which cannot be assessed under the limitations of the evironment.

Observation and rating do not end with a description of behavior. It is important to know the personal and social consequences of any given behavior: Does it make the child feel more inferior or more secure? Does it improve the morale of the group? Does it have a detrimental effect on others? Is it constructive or destructive? For example, a child who prefers solitary pursuits like reading, and does not participate actively in the group, may have a constructive influence. Another child who shows similar introverted tendencies may slyly cause disturbances in the group.

There is often a discrepancy between test results and teachers' ratings of children's intelligence. Three explanations for this discrepancy might be given. The first is that many teachers are not skillful in observation. To correct this fault, they may be given more instruction and practice in observation and rating. The second possible explanation arises from the fact that a rating scale cannot give a dynamic picture of a child's mental ability since it involves a listing of traits, each considered separately. It is difficult to construct a complete picture from fragments of behavior rated separately. A descriptive summary is usually more useful in that it presents a pattern or Gestalt. A third explanation is that many average and superior children are actually functioning below their mental capacity in everyday situations. To the observer they may give the impression of retardation; whereas tests reveal their potential ability.

Developmental history and family background

By understanding a child's past, the adult is better able to guide his future development.

Although it is difficult for parents to give accurate information about all the aspects of their child's development, the teacher may learn much from them about a broken home, periods of unemployment and want, the child's illnesses and accidents during infancy and early childhood, his daily schedule, his interests and activities, his playmates, his quickness to learn, his relations with adults and children in the family circle.

The most important outcome of the first contact with parents is a friendly relation. Once this relation is established, the parent will volunteer much helpful information. On the other hand, no information is worth getting at the cost of antagonism. Both parent and child should be encouraged to present the situation in their own way, and their reticences should be respected. In the course of a conversation, answers may be obtained to questions that have an important bearing on the child's school adjustment.

More objective information on home background may be obtained from measures of socioeconomic status. For example, the Burdick Apperception Tests suggest items to observe in a home visit. The Sims Score Card consists of a series of questions such as "Have you a telephone in your home?" Pupils answer these questions after the teacher has explained them carefully. Scales have also been devised for measuring occupational status, which is probably the best single indication of general socioeconomic level. Among these are the Barr Occupational Scale, which assigns values of from 0 to 20 to each of 121 occupations. The Minnesota Scale for Occupational Classification, devised by Goodenough from previous scales, includes farming. All of these classifications emphasize the intellectual requirements of each occupational level.

Knowledge of home conditions helps teachers to give individual children the experiences they need. Take the case of nine-year-old Dick, for example. His disturbed behavior became quite understandable in the light of facts about his home relations:

Dick's home environment was created largely by his mother, who was highly unstable and unpredictable. Her treatment of the child fluctuated with changes in her mood, and was influenced by spasmodic attempts to apply child psychology. Dick lacked the sense of security that arises from definite limits, consistently maintained. The mother's nervous breakdown presented a baffling situation for the young child. Her dissatisfaction with herself as a person and her feeling of frustration at becoming a mother instead of a successful business woman also entered into her relationship with the child. She tried too hard to fit herself into a pattern instead of finding within herself the best pattern to develop.

The father failed to take a positive part in the situation. Although he had good reasons to seek help—a mentally ill wife and a seriously disturbed child—he did not take advantage of a counseling service. However, there was some evidence of a good relation between Dick and his father, even though the father said that he felt more comfortable with his younger son than with Dick. The younger brother was another very important factor in the case. Dick fought with him and gave some evidence of intense jealousy in the play interview.

Dick's previous experiences also helped to explain his present behavior. Toilet-training was apparently begun too early. The mother made feeding an issue by her emotional response to his refusal to eat. She spoon-fed him until he was seven years old. That he allowed her to do so may indicate that he felt either hostility or a desire for closer contact with her. According to the mother's report, he began to walk and talk earlier than the average. This evidence of precocity was in line with test results. When he was disciplined by his father he brooded over it. Through unskillful handling, a relatively simple tonsilectomy became a traumatic experience.

The school reinforced rather than mitigated these unfavorable home conditions. Teachers took an attitude of negative expectancy toward Dick. One teacher was reminded of a boy like Dick who had been a serious problem. Despite his superior mental ability, he was not doing well in his present class.

Dick's behavior in the medical examination was unusual. A nine-year-old is ordinarily interested in the examination and enjoys it as a new experience. Dick shuddered when he listened to his heart beat and inquired anxiously about how the heart works. During the examination he said, "I'm just skin and bones; my stomach's no good. Maybe I've got T.B.; mother's friend died of it." Actually, although he showed some indications of malnutrition and throat infection and of being generally under par physically, he had no serious physical defects.

The results of individual and group tests showed an intelligence level of around 130 IQ. The vocabulary and mental activity which he displayed in response to the Thematic Apperception Test pictures were in line with his rating on the intelligence tests. Although killing, dying, and ghosts entered into many of his Thematic Apperception Test stories, this is not particularly abnormal, since many nine-year-olds fill their minds with such images by listening to radio and television programs. Half of Dick's stories had happy endings, and half had unhappy endings.

The most positive factors in the situation seemed to be the boy's high intelligence and his good relation with his father. Possibly counseling would give the father a clearer idea of his role and lead him to increase his beneficial contacts with Dick. Both parents might help Dick by modifying their behavior toward him, even though they could not change their fundamental personalities. A change of teachers or of the present teacher's attitude toward Dick would be another means of making the environment easier for him to handle. Skillful play therapy would help the boy appreciate his potentialities and learn to cope with his difficult environmental conditions.

Children's products and personal documents

Dated samples of their schoolwork. "By their works ye shall know them." Everything that a pupil writes, says, draws, paints, or makes is potential child-study material. It is also a permanent record of accomplishment. Dated samples of writing, spelling, composition, arithmetic, drawing, and other kinds of work will show progress in penmanship, vocabulary, sentence structure, clarity of expression, general information, computation, and creative expression. A skilled person may obtain indications of a child's emotional adjustment from his dramatic play, the things he makes, his dreams and original stories, his paintings and drawings. In his drawing, the school child, concerned with the outer world, tries to represent reality and to reproduce it convincingly for others. Creative expression may release unexpected capacities, build self-confidence, and satisfy unconscious wishes, fears, and fantasies. From time to time, the teacher and the pupil can study dated samples of the pupil's work to note progress in communication and personal development.

Daily schedules. The way in which children spend their time is often most revealing. They may keep a detailed twenty-four-hour record of all activities, or merely note time expenditures at certain times of day. An example of the latter method is the child's record of his social activities outside of school (100, 1948). The following excerpt illustrates this type of record:

I got home at four. From four to six-thirty I practiced. I had dinner and washed the dishes. At seven-thirty I started my homework. By nine-thirty I was in bed. The things I do are pretty much routine.

Some daily schedules show close parental supervision and insistence upon study, special instruction in music and dancing, and other supervised activities. In other situations the children seem free to associate with a variety of friends and to initiate their own activities. Daily schedules are of little or no value unless the children (1) are stimulated to write freely; (2) record their activities accurately, chronologically, and in detail; and (3) are assured that their schedules will be kept confidential. Samplings that comprise one or two days at a time, taken over a period of several weeks, are less burdensome and more representative than schedules kept consecutively for one or two weeks.

Autobiographies, themes, and open-end questions. If adults only knew what children were thinking and feeling! One way of getting into this "inner world of childhood" is through children's autobiographies and other personal documents. In the upper elementary grades some children express their feelings more frankly in writing than in a face-to-face conversation. Although they are usually not interested in writing an autobiography or other lengthy personal document, they will write briefly and frankly on topics like the following (100, 1948):

> The things I wish for most.
> What I most like to do.
> What I dislike most.
> What I admire in other people.
> What I like about myself.
> What I dislike about myself.
> What others like about me.
> What others dislike about me.
> What makes me mad.
> How I feel when I get my report card.
> Changes I would like to see in my home.
> How I was punished and for what.
> How children get to be important in my neighborhood.

Topics of this kind introduced occasionally when children seem ready to write freely about themselves may relieve their tensions as well as yielding pertinent information about the way each child views his world.

One fifth-grade class, at the close of a discussion on report cards, agreed to think through for themselves these three questions:

> 1. In what things do I honestly think I have improved during this year?
> 2. In what have I done my best work this year?
> 3. In what do I most need to improve?

The sentence-completion method. The incomplete sentence may be used and interpreted in various ways. Children may use the incomplete-sentence technique as a safety valve. Hymes (72, p. 30, 1949) suggested the following:

> Once I was very angry because . . . .
> Once I was very much afraid . . . .

One time I didn't think it was fair when . . . .
Once I got mad because . . . .

The following are other incomplete sentences that have evoked significant responses:

One thing I wonder about is . . . .
Sometimes I have been afraid when . . . .

In response to "I wish . . . ," one child wrote, "my parents paid attention to me when I did something good."

Teachers may use the method to gain understanding of children, in the same way that they seek to understand a child's comments in class, in an interview, or in a written composition. The responses may be evaluated by research workers as positive, negative, or neutral; categorized, as in content analysis; fused into patterns, as in sequential analysis; or interpreted deeply by a skilled clinician who detects hidden feelings and conflicts.

This technique has the advantage of being indirect; incomplete sentences do not suggest answers as many direct questions do. Children may express certain attitudes and feelings without having their attention directly called to these areas. For example, Harris and Tseng (60, 1957) used the sentence-completion technique to reveal children's attitudes toward peers and parents. Four sentences—"Most boys_____," "Most girls_____," "My father_____," and "My mother_____"—embedded among others referring to school and to other childhood experiences, evoked the children's attitudes toward their parents and toward other children.

A variation of this approach is the incomplete-story technique. A story or a description of an episode gives children a realistic basis for discussing what children and adults should do under the circumstances. One teacher read to some fifth-grade children a story about the antagonism between a "good little girl" who did everything to please the teacher, and a natural leader from a lower socioeconomic level. At the end of the story the children answered three questions:

1. Who do you think was to blame for the fight—Marie, Helen, both, neither?
2. How do you think the story should end? What do you think the teacher should do? What would be the fairest thing for her to do?
3. Have there been times when you thought you were punished unfairly? Tell about one or more of these times. Don't mention any names but tell just what happened and how you felt.

The fifth-grade children expressed widely different views about the situation presented in the story.

In personal documents such as these, children express their wishes; their self-concepts; their attitudes toward their homes and neighborhoods, their groups, their teachers. They reveal the ways in which they are beginning to look at life. Children's free responses help to explain their observed behavior, their performance on standardized tests, and their remarks in interviews.

Interest and personality questionnaires. Interest is an ally of learning and should be considered in any adequate attempt to understand a child. It is doubtful, however, whether one can obtain significant information by submitting a checklist of items to children. Individuals of all ages tend to check items that they think will make a good impression. Docile children aim to please; dull children tend to check items without fully realizing their meaning. Moreover, a child's interests change with changes in the situation, the group, or the instruction. However, despite these limitations, the questionnaire has been used extensively in the study of children's interests.

Personality inventories for studying the emotional adjustment of elementary-school children, as screening devices, may detect individual children who need special help. Used as a clinical instrument, their separate responses may yield clues. However used, the results of paper-and-pencil personality tests should be supplemented by observation and interpreted with caution and psychological insight.

Standardized tests

Tests of intelligence and achievement are widely used for studying school children under standard conditions in which they put forth their best efforts. Group tests are usually given in the fall, beginning at grade three or four. Teachers, counselors, and principals who want to study tests and measurements will find a number of books on this subject (4, 1954; 28, 1949; 52, 1954; 157, 1955; 160, 1954). These books answer such questions as, Why test? Which tests? How interpret and use test results? What other methods of appraisal are promising? Persons with some background in the theory and practice of measurement turn to Buros' comprehensive *Mental Measurement Yearbook* (25, 1959) to obtain a critical appraisal of a wide range of psychological tests.

Trends in the measurement of children's mental abilities are toward development of tests having both verbal and quantitative scores, toward analysis of mental ability according to various factors—notably as in Thurstone's seven primary mental abilities, and toward synthesizing the results of different tests so that they form patterns or profiles. Trends in achievement-testing are toward more emphasis on broader educational objectives, use of a wider variety of instruments, better interpretation and use of test results, and basic research on the laws and principles underlying the learning of each subject.

Intelligence tests. As a check on and supplement to the teacher's informal appraisal of children's scholastic aptitude, intelligence tests are very useful. It must be admitted that intelligence tests have been misinterpreted and misused, but the same could be said about almost any instrument or scientific invention. Few teachers and administrators fully understand the assumptions underlying intelligence tests, or carry out the modifications of curriculum and instruction that the results suggest to be desirable. However, the fact that an instrument has been misused and misinterpreted in the past is no logical reason for dispensing with its potential usefulness in the future. The following are several cautions to observe in the use of intelligence tests:

1. Intelligence-test scores or IQ's should not be given to parents, when there is any possibility that parents will misinterpret them, and draw erroneous inferences that lead them to reject or nag or exploit their children.

2. Test results should always be interpreted in the light of all the information made available by continuous study of the child in natural situations; the psychometric approach should be reinforced by the clinical. In interpreting group-test results, the tester should realize that in the case of emotionally disturbed and unco-operative children and of those with reading disability, the scores probably do not represent their true mental ability.

3. No important decision should be based on the results of a single test.

4. The teacher should take a positive attitude toward test results, seeking to discover potentialities that the child may develop.

In many school systems intelligence tests are given in alternate years, beginning with grade three or four. The following are a few tests which have been widely used in this way:

Henmon-Nelson Test of Mental Ability, for grades 3-8 and 7-12, Houghton Mifflin Company, Boston, and Psychological Corporation, New York

Kuhlmann-Anderson Intelligence Tests, for grades 4, 5, 6, 7, and 8, Educational Test Bureau, Minneapolis and Psychological Corporation, New York

Otis Quick-Scoring Mental Ability Tests, Intermediate Examination, for grades 4-9, World Book Company, Yonkers-on-Hudson, New York

Pintner General Ability Tests, for grades 4-9 and 9 and above, World Book Company, Yonkers-on-Hudson, New York

School and College Ability Tests, five levels from grade 4 to college freshmen and sophomores, Educational Testing Service, Princeton, New Jersey

Thurstone Tests of Primary Mental Abilities, Science Research Associates, Chicago

Verbal ability is stressed to a greater degree by some tests of intelligence than by others. Thus children who come from superior schools or homes where there is emphasis on verbal expression have an advantage on certain tests—for example, the Henmon-Nelson.

More dependable information about a child's mental ability may be obtained from individual tests administered by trained persons who have a background of psychological knowledge. Two individual tests of intelligence that are widely used in this country are the Revised Stanford-Binet Scale and the Wechsler Intelligence Scale for Children. The latter makes possible a more complete analysis, in that it measures a child's success in ten different types of mental tasks. It yields both a verbal IQ and a performance IQ. Mental age is a useful index of the individual's brightness, in that it directs teachers' attention to the mental tasks which different children can do.

Especially useful for children who have a reading or language handicap are the performance tests, such as the Revised Arthur Performance Tests. The directions for these tests are given orally or in pantomime, and many of the responses are oral. The performance tests measure a somewhat different kind of ability than do the verbal tests. Whereas the latter favor children from homes in which language skills are emphasized, the performance tests favor children from homes in which the stress is on solving practical nonverbal problems. Verbal and performance tests used together constitute a "culturally fair" measuring instrument (see Chap. 13). All these tests need expert interpretation and follow-up.

In individual testing the examiner has an excellent opportunity to study factors which may affect a child's score, such as emotional states, personality traits, and reactions to the testing situation. He should note whether the child is slow to learn and to make associations, but accurate when sufficient time is allowed; whether he makes quick but superficial associations, and has difficulty in grasping abstractions; whether he performs poorly on both learning and motor tests; whether his mental functioning is facile and adequate in simple situations but incapable of more difficult levels of achievement. The child's age, experience, background, and schooling, the quality of his daily functioning in mental tasks, and his physical condition and defects should likewise be taken into account in the interpretation of test results. For example, a retardation of two years at six years of age is more serious than a retardation of two years at sixteen.

Tests should be repeated at intervals during the child's educational journey in order to obtain a cumulative picture of his probable mental ability. In general, positive results on a single test can be regarded as indicating the presence of the trait tested at the time of testing, while negative results do not necessarily indicate its absence. The results of a single intelligence test should be regarded as a sample, not as a final judgment of the child's ability.

Achievement tests. Standardized tests of achievement survey children's knowledge and supplement teachers' informal tests. The best tests are based on sound educational objectives and attempt to measure the individual's ability to use facts in thinking. The following batteries are a few of the vast number available:

Iowa Every-Pupil Tests of Basic Skills, for grades 3-5 and 5-9, Houghton Mifflin Company, Boston

Metropolitan Achievement Tests, for grades 1-3, 4-6, and 7-8, World Book Company, Yonkers-on-Hudson, New York

Sequential Tests of Educational Progress, Level IV, for grades 4-6, also three other levels up to and including college sophomores, Cooperative Test Division of the Educational Testing Service, Princeton, New Jersey

Stanford Achievement Tests, for grades 1-9, World Book Company, Yonkers-on-Hudson, New York.

Wise interpretation of the results of standardized achievement tests requires a knowledge not only of the possible limitations and values of various types of tests, but also of many factors related to pupils' achievement. Suppose the median grade score on a comprehensive achievement test for all seventh-grade pupils in a school system was 1.5 grades above the grade norm of 7.7. At first glance it would seem that these schools were doing superior work. However, this could not be stated positively until additional information was considered: What percentage of the pupils are seriously retarded? How many pupils drop out before the seventh grade? Have the teachers been focusing their attention on bringing the slightly-below-average pupils up to standard at the expense of the superior and very slow children? To have the classes make a good showing on the tests, have teachers been drilling on test-type questions to the neglect of other important learning? Is the school term longer than the average? Have the pupils had a great deal of practice in taking standardized tests? Was the test given under standard conditions? What is the potential learning ability of these pupils compared with that of the general population? How do their cultural advantages compare with those of the groups on which the test was standardized? All this information and more is necessary if one is to interpret standardized test results accurately.

The results of any standardized test may be plotted on a profile chart. This enables both teacher and child to see at a glance the strengths and weaknesses in his school achievement.

Special techniques

The teacher may use other special techniques to elicit certain kinds of information or to reveal certain feelings. The following kinds of pictures are being used with children as a basis for classroom and clinical observation:

Pictures of thirteen schoolroom situations were presented by Biber and Lewis (17, 1949) to first- and second-grade children. In their responses to these pictures, the children revealed their feelings about teachers and their life in school.

The children's form of the Rosenzweig Picture Frustration Study, published in 1948, is used with individual children from four to nine, and in groups above the age of nine. There is one form and it is untimed.

A picture test to detect anxiety in young children (151, 1944) consists of twelve colored drawings, each displaying a situation familiar to four-, five-, and six-year-old children. The central figure with whom the child is expected to identify has a blank head in which the child inserts either a "sad" or a "happy" face, according to his response to the situation. The examiner also records any verbal responses which the child may make. The "anxiety score" is the percentage of pictures to which the child gives a "sad" face. Children enjoy this test and seem to identify themselves closely with the situation. Teachers in kindergarten and primary grades may give this test or use similar pictures from magazines to sense situations in which a given child is anxious or afraid.

The interesting Pictorial Guess Who technique (62, 1948) enabled kindergarten children to show a social responsiveness to other children which they could not put into words. The test consists of a series of line drawings of children, each illustrating a particular behavior or personality trait, as, for example, a child slapping another, a child sucking his thumb, or a child hugging another. The investigator showed a child a picture and said, "This is a picture of someone at school—who do you think it is?" If the child named a member of the group the investigator asked, "What is _____ doing?" There was a high percentage of correspondence between the children's responses and the teachers' descriptions of the same pupils.

A character picture test was used to investigate children's preferences among types of behavior ordinarily regarded by adults as "good" or "bad." On each page of four pictures the children were asked to put a cross on their preferred picture, two crosses on their second choice, and three crosses on their third choice. A teacher could use this idea in an informal way with his own collection of suitable pictures. Or he could ask the pupil to describe a picture showing a child in any one of various situations, and to tell what the child is thinking and what he himself would think in such a situation. From these responses the adult may obtain important leads or clues to follow up in an interview. When the same pictures are shown a few weeks later, children tend to respond in much the same way, though the details of their verbal comment are different. The value of this technique lies in the child's expression of feeling—what he feels as he tells the story—not in the accuracy with which he describes the picture.

Since children reveal themselves to some extent in everything they do, much may be inferred about their attitudes and personalities from observation of their behavior. To obtain deeper insight into their inner worlds of feeling and meaning, projective techniques have been used by persons with clinical background and special training. These techniques offer a dynamic approach to understanding the individual personality. Instead of setting the subject to a specific task, the examiner presents vague materials to which he responds in his own unique way. In the permissive play-therapy situation the child has opportunity to use the play material in any way he desires; through this experience it is hoped that he will gain a better understanding of himself and begin to have more positive feelings about himself and others. The Rorschach test, the Children's Thematic Apperception Test, and the Draw-a-Person technique are frequently used in the psychological analysis of children's personality (21, 1956).

Health appraisal

In schools where special health services are limited, the teacher may make certain screening tests in addition to his daily observation. Among the items to be checked are height and weight, posture, vision, and hearing. The teacher uses the tests for appraisal and referral; he never makes a medical diagnosis on the basis of his own observation and testing. Keeping a record of a child's height and weight helps teachers and parents to understand his growth pattern. An individual height-weight record card, properly filled out, is of interest to pupil, teacher, and parent.

Boys and girls are interested in using the hand dynamometer to test the strength of the forearm. Posture tests, such as the shadow picture, or the posture silhouette, also arouse interest and have educational value.

Observation of the child at play shows how effective his bodily adjustment is when he is in action. To correct poor posture one must give attention to underlying causes such as fatigue, poor nutrition, or illness.

The testing of vision and hearing is most important; poor vision or hearing handicaps a child in much of his school learning. The improved Snellen Chart, the Massachusetts Vision Test, or other vision screening tests are being used in the schools. Detailed directions for vision-testing can be obtained from the National Society for the Prevention of Blindness, 1790 Broadway, New York 19, New York. A scale devised at the Merrill-Palmer School yields a clear picture of deviations in trends of growth and development (78, 1955).

One of the most important functions of the school nurse is to help the teacher acquire skill in observing children, in making screening tests, and in keeping a developmental health record for each child. On the other hand, the nurse gains valuable information from the teacher that helps her to understand the child's health better. Another important part of the nurse's work is with parents; no one has a better opportunity than she to establish co-operative home-school relations. Although parents may be on the defensive about a child's achievement or behavior, they are almost always approachable when it is a question of health. When special welfare or medical services are needed, the nurse can usually obtain them through local or state social or health agencies. Her role as assistant to the physician in the health examination of the child is clearly recognized.

The school physician serves children who do not have a family physician. His examinations have educational importance; they lead the child, the parent, and the teacher to take a favorable attitude toward medical and dental care and toward preventive measures. The physician also performs many other functions such as insuring a healthful school environment, supervising the summer roundup, developing functional health records, and supplying health information to parents and teachers. In addition to filling out the usual technical items on the cumulative health record, the physician should also write a brief nontechnical appraisal of the child's health status, as well as recommendations for improving it. The fact that only a low percentage of defects are corrected may indicate failure by the school to give the medical information to the persons responsible for making the correction, or it may show that medical care in the community is inadequate. Everyone concerned with the health of children can work together to promote a higher level of physical efficiency for every child.

Talking with parents and children

Talking with parents is one of the most fruitful methods of gaining understanding of the child's family relations, and of helping parents to understand themselves and their children better. The following are excerpts from interviews with a mother at a child guidance clinic:

Esther, a seven-year-old child, was so limited in intelligence that she had not been accepted in the public school. The mother said she knew her daughter was slow, but felt that she would profit from school attendance. The family consisted of father, mother, a three-year-old boy, and Esther. The family doctor had told the mother that the child would be normal within two years. In the first interview the mother gave details about the child's early development. According to the mother, Esther sat up alone at nine months, walked a few steps at twelve months, but did not say words until four years of age. At seven, the child spoke very indistinctly in short phrases. The mother concluded by saying, "She can't be so stupid if she could learn all that."

WORKER: You know all these facts so well.

MOTHER: Yes, it has been preying on my mind. It just worries me so I can't think of anything else.

WORKER: Is her father concerned, too?

MOTHER: No, he thinks that Esther is all right. (Hesitantly) Can it be that slowness is inherited?

WORKER: That is possible.

MOTHER: My husband says he was awful stupid as a child.

WORKER: He had a hard time in school?

MOTHER: Yes, he had a terribly hard time; he was real stupid; he did not talk much until he was seven. Some of our relatives were slow, too, in the beginning but they got along all right. So I think Esther will, too.

WORKER: What about Esther's brother?

The mother gave evidence that the younger child was bright. Near the end of the interview she said, "If it should turn out that she really can't go to school and cannot learn to read or write, what then? What happens to children like that?"

The worker mentioned special schools but indicated that a child might have to wait a long time to get in. She also told of children who could not meet the demands of regular school and became nervous and unhappy.

MOTHER: I'm so glad you said that. I've always felt I was keeping something from her that she ought to have had. . . . Perhaps you can help me so I won't have to worry so much; you don't know how I worry.

WORKER: You would worry naturally. I'm sure we can gain understanding of Esther and meet her needs better. You have been very helpful today.

In subsequent interviews the mother further clarified her feelings about the child, began to understand that neither she nor her husband should feel guilty, and intellectually accepted the fact that Esther's IQ was probably below 40 and that she would never attain average mental ability. Yet she had great difficulty in emotionally accepting Esther's retardation. At every session she brought up instances of any slight improvement, which she interpreted as meaning that the child would eventually become normal in intelligence.

Through her contacts with both child and mother the worker accomplished the following objectives:

1. To get as exact an estimate as possible of the child's mental capacity through observation in play sessions, as well as through the use of appropriate tests.

2. To establish a strongly supportive relation with the mother and relieve her sense of guilt about the child's mental deficiency.

3. To help her analyze her contradictory statements and focus attention on the positive aspects of the situation—for example, on what the child could do.

4. To help her make concrete and reasonable plans for Esther's training.

5. To help provide a more favorable home environment for the younger, normal child.

The skillful interviewer listens. He encourages the parent to think through the situation; he makes suggestions only when the parent needs them and is ready to accept them. He speaks the parent's language. At the end of the interview the parent has a sense of something accomplished; he does not leave still confused, not knowing which way to turn.

Although teachers have neither the time nor the skill to conduct a series of therapeutic interviews, in their informal contacts they can help parents gain more understanding of their children and provide a more favorable home environment for them. Parents, in turn, can help teachers to understand the child more fully and meet his needs more adequately in school.

Talking with a child is one way of finding out what his behavior means to him. In trying to explain it to himself, the preadolescent also clarifies his conduct for the teacher. From casual conversations with the child, teachers learn much about the way the child views his world. For example, when a first-grade child tells "tall tales," the teacher is interested in knowing why the child needs to resort to fantasy; the reason is more important than the behavior per se. If his fantasies are concerned with imaginary possessions or exploits, or with the imagined prestige of his family, neglect and lack of self-esteem may be indicated. In his fantasies the child often describes his world as he would like to have it. Further observation of the child in school and at home often reveals conditions in his life that should be changed—lack of toys and pets, physical neglect, emotional rivalry with another child in the family, incidents in school that make him feel left out or unwanted, strong unsatisfied interests, lack of skills possessed by most other children of his age. Casual conversations that arise out of the child's normal activities are more fruitful at this age than formal interviews. Many children respond better to play techniques than to interviews. They prefer action to words; they are not so introspective as adolescents.

Sociometric techniques

In any classroom there are patterns of social relations. To improve these relations, the teacher needs to understand the network of associations in the group and know how it influences the pupils' personal and social development.

The teacher may gain knowledge of complex inter-pupil relationships by means of observation, group discussion, casual conversation, and sociometric techniques. Direct observation shows which children are usually the center of an activity, which are helped by others, which are always on the fringes, what roles individual members play. Skillful interviewing may throw light on the basis for these various groupings; case studies indicate the characteristics and backgrounds of the children who are chosen by many, and of those who are not chosen or who are rejected. The sociometric test shows how a given child would like to relate himself to others and how they feel toward him. It blueprints the present group structure. At the same time it may raise questions about motives underlying the choices and values that affect the children's interaction (76, p. 11, 1948).

The following suggestions for administering the sociometric test and making a sociogram are condensed from Jenning's monograph (77, pp. 203-224, 1950):

1. Make the conditions of choice vivid and important enough to "elicit a genuine response"—describe situations in which the children's choices will actually make a difference to them: for example, choosing persons to sit with in class or in the lunchroom, to work with on a committee, to play with, to go on a trip with.
2. Make it clear that the choices will actually be used, that no one but the teacher will see the results, that everyone will be given at least one of his choices and more if possible.
3. Give out small blank slips of paper on which the children are asked to write their own names and the names of their choices, numbered 1, 2, and 3, 1 being the first choice. Children in the primary grades who cannot write may tell their choices to the teacher out of hearing of the other children.
4. If tensions are known to exist, it may be useful to ask the children to name also any boy or girl with whom they would prefer not to work or who

might prefer not to work with them. No specific number of rejections is asked for.

5. Take the action indicated by the choices as soon as possible.

6. Make a sociogram in order to study further the interrelations and to "trace the networks of feeling" in the group. This graphic device shows clearly which pupils are not chosen, chosen by few, chosen by many, and overchosen. It also shows the patterns of relations between boys and girls. (In one sixth-grade class there were no mutual choices between boys and girls.) If the range of choice is wide enough, almost every child will choose or be chosen by someone.

Interest in sociometry has become widespread since this technique of studying social relations was developed by Moreno and Jennings. Even in the primary grades the teacher may learn much about children's social relations, transitory as they are, through the simple device of asking each child whom he would like to sit near, eat lunch with, or associate with in other ways. The configuration may be temporarily distorted by a recent incident: one child may have given a party; another may have done something that annoyed many of the other children. However, the teacher can use this method effectively to supplement his observation of interpersonal relations in the group.

Without an appreciation of the positive attractions that children feel for one another, teachers often err in guiding interpersonal relations. Instead of capitalizing on pupils' preferences, they sometimes try to separate friends and break up cliques. Understanding of the interactions in the classroom helps teachers to use the group as an instrument for personal development. For example, after making a sociometric study, the teacher may arrange for "isolates" to work on committees with pupils whom they have chosen, and on topics closely related to their interests. He may give a child some appropriate responsibility in which he can gain recognition and appreciation for his service—in one instance, a physically handicapped boy who was interested in photography was chosen team photographer, and his pictures were exhibited.

Dramatization and role-playing

Children of this age enjoy any kind of dramatization. They act out simple jingles, take the parts of characters they read about, dramatize their father's work, and spontaneously play the roles of people in real life situations. In a first-grade class the teacher gradually introduces situations in which the children reveal their feelings about conditions and relations important in their development. The more real and concrete the situation is made, the more effectively will each child play his role. Sociodrama skillfully conducted (77, pp. 260-285, 1950) helps children to release tensions and to build more healthy attitudes; through it the children gain practice in working out techniques of social relations.

Synthesis of information from many sources

The teacher gains understanding of a child in much the same way as the artist develops his conception of a new painting; his first general impression is gradually filled out by details as his perception grows broader and deeper. As he accumulates knowledge about a child, the teacher sees how he is progressing along certain lines, and becomes aware of his need for guidance. It is better to study each child's development continuously than to wait until a problem or crisis arises and then try to work back to its complex causation.

Cumulative records. Much of the teacher's observation is never recorded; he uses it immediately in helping a child choose the best way of handling a present situation. But surely the teacher cannot expect to keep in mind all the significant information about each child's development. Therefore, the effective teacher makes brief sketches of children's typical or exceptional behavior, records interviews with a parent or a child, collects samples of the child's work, and keeps tests that he has taken. All of these pieces of information he slips into the child's folder as he obtains them. Periodically, perhaps two or three times a year, the teacher should try to synthesize and interpret the accumulated information, see trends, and make recommendations for each pupil.

In using records passed on by other teachers, it is important to remember that (1) the child is changing and growing, (2) the record gives only a small sample of the child's total behavior, and (3) the record often tells as much about the teacher as about the child.

Case study. The case study continues from where the cumulative record leaves off; it is more detailed, more complete, and gives more understanding of the dynamics of the child's development. Case studies, especially of young children, should be family-centered.

Case conference. The case conference, in which teachers and specialists who have had contact with a particular child get together to pool their information and make interpretations, justifies the time it takes. Not only does it synthesize apparently disparate aspects of an individual child's development; it also enlightens both teachers and specialists. It is an effective form of in-service education.

Perceptive interpretation and synthesis of information from many sources require a wealth of knowledge and experience. For example, the effect of a broken home is difficult to interpret. It is true that children referred to clinics and courts usually show a much larger percentage of broken homes in their case histories than does the general school population; in certain cases the proportion is as high as 30 per cent. But whether a broken home contributes to maladjustment depends upon the interpersonal relations and other factors in the total situation. There are many kinds of broken homes; some harm children much more than others. Many children from broken homes present no marked behavior disorders. The broken home is only one of a number of related factors that create personality difficulty in children. Divorce or separation is often merely the culmination of a long process of family disintegration. Cruelty, poor methods of discipline, and immorality in the home can exert a more devastating influence than a broken home per se.

Clinical study. The clinical study of a child differs more in degree than in kind from that made by a teacher; it is more intensive; it deals more thoroughly with underlying causes. Teachers and parents should become acquainted with the clinical services available to their children. If a child fails to respond to the sound "mental-hygiene first aid" given by the teacher, referral for clinical study and treatment is indicated. Referral requires skill on the part of the teacher, since both child and parent are often loath to accept psychological or psychiatric services. Their reluctance, usually the result of a misconception about such services, is dispelled when they understand that a psychiatrist or a mental-hygiene clinic helps normal people to live more abundantly.

GUIDANCE OF SCHOOL CHILDREN

Despite their growing independence, school children still need their parents' guidance. This is basic to their adjustment in school. At school the administrator, the teacher, and the specialist all contribute as a team to the individual development and guidance of children. Their respective roles will now be briefly discussed.

Parental guidance

There are numerous excellent books on how parents can help their children grow up. Of special help are the publications of, and the study groups sponsored by, the Parent Education Project, University of Chicago; the *National Parent-Teacher* magazine, and the program of the National Congress of Parents and Teachers; the pamphlet series of the Child Study Association of America; the Public Affairs Pamphlets; the Children's

Bureau publications; and the *Better Living Booklets* of Science Research Associates.

Of first importance is a favorable emotional milieu for each child. All children need to feel that they belong to a family group; they need real jobs to do and the satisfaction that comes when they have completed them. They need faith as well as food, a close relation with their parents as well as clothing, shared experiences as well as shelter. The following quotation illustrates these needs:

> Mélanie [the mother] bent her head; her light breath stirred the tuft of pale hair, gently, with love.
> "I'm glad it's a boy," she said. "Un beau garçon comme son papa, n'est-ce pas?" she added, in a proud whisper for the baby alone to hear.
> "Do you like boys best?" Cosette [the six-year-old foster child] said casually, fiddling with the ribbons on the lace pillow, in a way she was told not to do.
> Mélanie glanced at her. Her eyes danced as she said very gravely:
> "But naturally, little silly. I have already a girl, voyons! What would I do with another?"
> "*Oh!*" said little Cosette, her mouth open. She seemed struck with this idea, then her spirits soared and soared. She greeted Soeur Bernarde with a beaming smile and went, without fuss, into the garden. There was no longer any need to cling to the Flower Room on such a lovely day, now she was *sure* they needed her. It just made all the difference.*

As children grow older, parents tend to grow less indulgent and more restrictive. The decisions the older child makes are more important, his mistakes more serious, his life-space much wider. The parent wants to protect him from harm and errors. It is also true that the preadolescent's independence may make the adult feel less secure. Sometimes it has an ego-deflating effect, though the parents want the child to become more mature even at their own expense. It is helpful for parents and teachers to see children as people in the process of becoming; to see their behavior as an expression of some need; to look for what is right rather than what is wrong in their behavior. School children want parents who can and will maintain reasonable rules and standards. Wise parental guidance helps children to grow up, but does not create undue anxiety or antagonism.

Parent child-study groups help parents to take a more relaxed attitude toward their problems and to look at their role as parents more objectively. Groups can be arranged as part of a family night at school, church, or recreation center, when the whole family have supper and then play and

---

* Oriel Malet, *My Bird Sings* (Garden City, N.Y.: Doubleday & Co., Inc., 1946) p. 154. Quoted with the permission of Doubleday & Co., Inc. and Faber & Faber Ltd.

study together. In Reading, Michigan, the older children kept house for a day while their parents and the preschool children went to a conference at the school; the local factory released fathers, with regular pay, to attend all or part of the conference.

Parents and teachers may study child development together. Kawin (85, 1950) described parent-teacher study groups which from time to time presented the results of their study to the community. In these public programs, teachers, parents, and children all participated. To make them more interesting to the public they used skits, movies, role-playing, and other techniques.

The role of the administrator in guidance

The administrator's main task is to provide a school environment in which each child can reach out toward the realization of his most acceptable self. More specifically, his role is to (1) provide the equipment and materials that children need, (2) develop policies of promotion, marking, and scheduling that are conducive to learning, (3) select new teachers who are qualified by personality and eager to grow in their guidance responsibilities, (4) help all teachers improve their understanding and guidance of children, and (5) establish constructive home-school relations. By arranging conferences with mothers and by publishing practical articles in the local paper about the transition from home to school, the principal can help parents make the first days of school easier for little children. The effective administrator releases the creative energy of all who work with him. If he is to attract and hold well-qualified teachers, he may have to enlist community co-operation in improving teachers' living and working conditions.

The role of the teacher in guidance

There are four main avenues for teacher guidance: guidance through teacher-child relations, guidance through the environment, guidance while teaching, and guidance through personal conferences with individual pupils and parents outside the classroom.

The most important guidance takes place through the teacher's friendly, understanding relation with each child. This beneficial teacher-pupil relation has its roots in a genuine, deep, psychological acceptance of each child—a belief that each child is valuable, no matter how he looks or acts, and that every child has unrealized potentialities. Such was the attitude of one rural teacher who, when asked to list her gifted children, said, "All my children are gifted."

Children should feel that the teacher understands them and is "all for them." (167, 1949) When they have been absent he says, "We're so glad to have you back," not, "Have you made up all the work you've missed?" He makes allowances at certain times when children are under special strain owing to an unemployed or alcoholic father, a sick mother, a quarrel with a friend, a long illness, a new and strange situation to meet. As he comes to understand the complex forces and motives operating within the child and in his environment, he treats a particular incident as part of a larger pattern. He appreciates the ways in which a child is trying to meet his own needs, and expresses the approval he feels. In trying to meet the emotional needs of every child, the teacher often has to give extra affection to one child without causing the others to feel that the child is "teacher's pet."

Recognition of children's feelings can be accompanied by a friendly firmness with respect to behavior. The teacher may say, "I know just how you feel about having to put away your paints now. But this is something you have to do anyway; we're all leaving the room now." In this way the child learns to accept limits and necessary restrictions, but with the assurance that his friend, the teacher, understands how he feels. If the feeling is genuine it will be expressed in many different ways. By means of his friendly relation to children, the teacher himself lives more abundantly.

Guidance through the environment is another basic aspect of the teacher's role in guidance. The following are a few of the ways in which the teacher uses or modifies the environment to meet individual needs:

Provides a progression of experiences in which each child can engage wholeheartedly and successfully, and will obtain the social experiences, the knowledge and skills he needs, and the opportunity to develop his special talents and abilities.

Gives the child opportunities to set realistic and challenging goals for himself, decide on ways to reach them, and begin to make progress toward them.

Accepts children's occasional need to rebel, but firmly maintains limits desirable for both the individual and the group.

Guidance while teaching goes on all during the school day. Most important is guidance in learning. That is the teacher's main responsibility. Children appreciate the strict teacher. Some classroom guidance is developmental—it is necessary for all children; some may be considered as "mental-hygiene first aid." A few examples follow:

Encourages a child to go ahead on his own initiative without unnecessary interference with his activities; expects him to become increasingly self-directing.

Adjusts the demands of the environment to the individual child; considers optimum timing for different tasks (166, 1957).

Holds group discussions in which children can freely express their feelings, discover how others feel, and learn how others have successfully solved similar problems. The teacher accepts and builds on each child's contribution, however slight: "Mary has an idea we can use." He encourages children to be helpful to others and to express their appreciation of others' work and contributions.

Calls the child's attention to what he can do; gives constructive suggestions; helps him to learn from failure.

Since the large majority of teachers have had little or no special preparation for their guidance responsibilities, the principal must supply in-service education. He will give his support to child-study groups (23, 1956), workshops, institutes, case conferences, study groups, and other professional aid that teachers request. He will encourage them to take courses in mental hygiene, child development, child psychology, counseling, case work, group work, and related areas and techniques. Internships in child-guidance centers offer an especially rich experience, though they are limited to a small number of teachers. Outstanding in their effectiveness are the child-study groups developed and described by Prescott (126, 1957).

Specialists in guidance

A child guidance bureau that serves the school system, a guidance co-ordinator or consultant for the schools of a district or county, a counselor for every one or two large elementary schools—these supply the specialized guidance services needed at the present time. Specialists have four main functions: (1) to help teachers improve the quality of their guidance, (2) to work with individual pupils and parents referred to them, (3) to suggest desirable changes in the curriculum and in administrative policies, and (4) to be familiar with community resources and use them to extend the schools' services. By working with teachers individually on cases referred to them, by conducting case conferences and voluntary child-study groups, by administering tests and interpreting test results, by supplying the visual aids and information that teachers need, by giving demonstrations of group discussions and interviews with pupils and parents, the specialists in guidance will gradually help all the teachers to improve their counseling and group work.

In interpreting case-history data, teachers need the help of specialists in guidance. The school counselor or a member of the child-guidance department may go over each pupil's record with the teacher-counselor to interpret it and make recommendations. In case-conferences, teachers may learn what kind of information is most significant for the child's development, what it means, and what the school can do about it. Fortunate is the teacher who can work with members of a child-guidance staff—the psychiatrist discusses the causes of the pupil's maladjustment as revealed in the psychiatric interview; the educational psychologist interprets the case in relation to the pupil's school background, the results of standardized tests, and the available opportunities for remedial teaching and group therapy; and the social worker discusses the influence of the child's social environment.

SELF-UNDERSTANDING AND SELF-GUIDANCE

Without making children prematurely introspective, adults can help them to appraise themselves realistically. If children learn in the elementary-school years to recognize their strengths and limitations—especially their strengths—they may avoid many false steps as they move into adolescence. All of them can anticipate greater maturity; they can recognize that growing up involves both greater freedom and greater responsibility. With the help of a teacher or counselor, they can begin to make appropriate educational plans. The health examination offers an opportunity for the child to appraise himself physically with reference to participation in sports, and with respect to general health and vitality. Evidence of his social success—or lack of it—is forced upon him by the frank acceptance or rejection of his peers. In schoolwork he has many objective evidences of accomplishment or failure.

However, information is not enough. There should be interviews in which the child's own record of his progress and the teacher's additional information are interpreted and synthesized into a meaningful pattern that changes year by year. Fault lines, too, can be noted—those personality and behavioral trends that should be modified during these flexible years. Toward the end of the elementary-school years certain values and goals begin to take more definite shape; they may still be somewhat vague, but they are real.

CONCLUDING STATEMENT

Preadolescence is perhaps the most difficult period for parents and teachers. Adults have a decreasing importance in the lives of these children, who are now most concerned about gaining status with their peers. They occasionally indulge in childish behavior, but they now evaluate it and often abandon it for good. Preadolescents put adults in their proper place with little sympathy; they show little understanding of how it feels to be a rejected parent or a rebuffed teacher. It is well to get these new relationships out in the open. Parents and teachers can live through this period; children must live through it in order to pass on to their next stage of development.

Recognizing the child's need to "put away childish things," they will treat him with respect and understanding. They will recognize that appeals and threats that used to be effective now infuriate or embarrass him. It humiliates him to be treated as a baby. If the adults recognize and respond to the child's need to sort out his childish ways of behaving and build a more mature personality, if they will realize how important it is to him that he win the respect and loyalty of his age group, if they will serve as a sure resource in time of need, they will help him emerge into adolescence as a more mature, responsive, and self-confident person.

School education can avoid the two extremes of (1) catering exclusively to children's interests and (2) forcing them to learn "what is good for them." It can help them to set standards by which they can measure their own conduct. They are eager to know and to do; they have unbounded energy that can be channeled into useful learning. Out of their spontaneous self-direction, they will develop worthwhile interests if the environment is favorable.

Questions and Problems

FOR CLASS DISCUSSION OR STUDY GROUPS

1. In a class of forty elementary school children, how many of the detailed child-study and guidance procedures could a teacher actually use? To do a good job of understanding individual children, what change must the teacher make in the ordinary concept of teaching?

2. How does child study aid children's learning?

3. Collect detailed descriptions of teachers' guidance while teaching.

4. Interpret and synthesize the information on the cumulative record of an elementary-school child. Point out gaps and deficiencies in the record. What other information would you like to have?

5. Study and guide one child, using as many of the methods suggested in this chapter as seem appropriate.

6. Read some good examples of detailed case studies, noting the kind of information obtained, its interpretation and synthesis, its bearing on the child's development.

7. Plan a classroom method of facilitating self-appraisal by pupils at or above the fourth-grade level.

8. Evaluation of child development programs and procedures is greatly needed. Read Brandt and Perkins' collection of evaluative studies of a child study program (23, 1956) to find out what methods were used, and what evidence of the effectiveness of the program was obtained.

*Bibliography**

1. ABERNETHY, ETHEL MARY. *Relationships between Mental and Physical Growth.* ("Monographs of the Society for Research in Child Development," Vol. I, No. 7.) Washington, D.C.: National Research Council, 1936. 80 pp.

2. AMATORA, SISTER MARY. "Developmental Trends in Pre-Adolescence and in Early Adolescence in Self-Evaluation," *Journal of Genetic Psychology,* XCI (September, 1957), 89-97.

3. AMERICAN FRIENDS SERVICE COMMITTEE. *Books Are Bridges.* Philadelphia: The Committee, 1957. 64 pp.

4. ANASTASI, ANNE. *Psychological Testing.* New York: The Macmillan Co., 1954. 682 pp.

5. ANDERSON, HAROLD H., JOSEPH E. BREWER, and MARY FRANCES REED. "Studies of Teachers' Classroom Personalities. III. Follow-up Studies of the Effects of Dominative and Integrative Contacts on Children's Behavior," *Applied Psychological Monographs of the American Psychological Asso.,* Vol. XI. Stanford, Calif.: Stanford Univ. Press, 1946. 156 pp.

6. APPEL, KENNETH E. "Psychiatry and Human Relations," *Understanding the Child,* XVIII (January, 1949), 3-8.

7. ARMSTRONG, CHARLES M. "How Do Children Grow?" *New York State Education,* XLIII (December, 1955), 181-183.

8. ASSOCIATION FOR SUPERVISION AND CURRICULUM DEVELOPMENT OF THE NEA. *Toward Better Teaching, a Report of Current Practices.* ("1949 Yearbook.") Washington, D.C.: National Education Assoc., 1949. 282 pp.

9. AUSTIN, MARY C., and GEORGE G. THOMPSON. "Children's Friendships: A Study of the Bases on Which Children Select and Reject Their Best

* All references referred to in the text are included in the bibliography. The single-starred references (*) are specially recommended for their practical suggestions; those double-starred (**) are specially recommended for their technical and research emphasis.

Friends," *Journal of Educational Psychology*, XXXIX (February, 1948), 101-116.

10. Ausubel, David P., and others. "Perceived Parent Attitudes as Determinants of Children's Ego Structure," *Child Development*, XXV (September, 1954), 173-183.

11. Bakwin, Harry. "Disturbed Sexual Behavior in Children and Adolescents," *Journal of Pediatrics*, XLVI (June, 1955), 729-730.

12. Banning, Evelyn I. "Social Influences on Children and Youth," *Review of Educational Research*, XXV (February, 1955), 36-47.

13. Baruch, Dorothy W. *New Ways in Discipline*. New York: Whittlesey House, 1949. 280 pp.

**14. Bayley, Nancy. "Child Study Technics," in "Twenty-Five Years of Educational Research," *Review of Educational Research*, XXVI (June, 1956), 280-281.

**15. ———. "Individual Patterns of Development," *Child Development* XXVII (March, 1956), 45-74.

16. Bedoian, Vagharsh H. "Mental Health Analysis of Socially Over-Accepted, Socially Under-Accepted, Overage and Underage Pupils in the Sixth Grade," *Journal of Educational Psychology*, XLIV (October, 1953), 366-371.

17. Biber, Barbara, and Claudia Lewis. "An Experimental Study of What Young Children Expect from Their Teachers," *Genetic Psychology Monographs*, XL, No. 1, 3-97.

18. Blewitt, D. B. "An Experimental Study of the Inheritance of Intelligence," *Journal Mental Science*, C (October, 1954), 922-933.

19. Board of Education of the City of New York. "The Pupil's Role in Unit Development," *Strengthening Democracy*, IX (January-February, 1957), 1, 3-8.

20. Bonney, Merl E. *Popular and Unpopular Children, A Sociometric Study*. ("Sociometry Monographs," No. 9, 1947.) 80 pp.

21. Bosquet, Kennison T., and Walter C. Stanley. "Discriminative Powers of Rorschach Determinants in Children Referred to a Child Guidance Clinic," *Journal of Consulting Psychology*, XX (February, 1956), 17-21.

22. Bowers, Mary E. "Experiences Enrich Writing," *National Education Association Journal*, XXXVII (April, 1948), 211.

**23. Brandt, Richard M., and Hugh V. Perkins. *Research Evaluating a Child Study Program*. ("Monographs of the Society for Research in Child Development," Vol. XXI, No. 1, Serial No. 62, 1956.) 96 pp.

24. Burk, Sophie. "Attitudes and Behavior of Emotionally Disturbed Children Who Are Retarded in Reading." (Unpublished doctoral thesis.) New York: Teachers College, Columbia Univ., 1956. 135 pp.

**25. Buros, Oscar. *The Mental Measurement Yearbook* (5th ed.). New Brunswick, N.J.: Rutgers Univ. Press. (To be published in 1959.)

26. CASSEL, ROBERT H. *The Vineland Adaptation of the Oseretsky Tests.* ("Training School Bulletin 46," Supplement 1-32, May, 1949.)

27. COHEN, ALBERT K. *Delinquent Boys: The Culture of the Gang.* Glencoe, Ill.: The Free Press, 1955. 202 pp.

28. CRONBACH, LEE J. *Essentials of Psychological Testing.* New York: Harper & Bros., 1949. 475 pp.

29. DALES, RUTH J. "A Method for Measuring Developmental Tasks: Scales for Selected Tasks at the Beginning of Adolescence," *Child Development,* XXVI (June, 1955), 111-122.

30. DAVIDSON, HELEN H. *Personality and Economic Background. A Study of Highly Intelligent Children.* New York: King's Crown Press, 1943. 192 pp.

31. DE HAAN, ROBERT F., and ROBERT J. HAVIGHURST. *Educating Gifted Children.* Chicago: Univ. of Chicago Press, 1957. 275 pp.

32. DENNIS, WAYNE. "A Cross-Cultural Study of the Reinforcement of Child Behavior," *Child Development,* XXVIII (December, 1957), 431-438.

33. DE MORAES, ANNA MARIA M. *Psychopedagogical Research on the Solution of Arithmetic Problems.* Paris: J. Vrim, 1954. 139 pp.

34. DE SCHWEINITZ, KARL. *Growing up; the Story of How We Became Alive, Are Born and Grow Up* (3d ed.). New York: The Macmillan Co., 1953. 73 pp.

35. DILLON, HAROLD J. *Leavers; Major Early School Educational Problem.* New York: National Child Labor Comm., 1949. 94 pp.

36. DOLL, EDGAR A. *Vineland Social Maturity Scale.* Minneapolis: Educ. Test Bureau, 1947.

37. ———. "What Is a Moron?" *Journal of Abnormal and Social Psychology,* XLIII (October, 1948), 495-501.

**38. DYER, HENRY S., ROBERT KALIN, and FREDERIC M. LORD. *Problems in Mathematical Education.* Princeton, N.J.: Educ. Testing Service, 1956. 50 pp.

39. ERIKSON, ERIK. "Sex Differences in Play Configurations of Preadolescents," *American Journal of Orthopsychiatry,* XXI (October, 1951), 666-692.

40. ESTES, W. K. *Annual Review of Psychology.* Edited by Paul R. Farnsworth and Quinn McNemar. Vol. VII. Stanford, Calif.: Annual Reviews, Inc., 1956. Pp. 1-38.

41. ESTVAN, FRANK J. "The Relationship of Social Status, Intelligence, and Sex of Ten- and Eleven-Year-Old Children to an Awareness of Poverty," *Genetic Psychology Monographs,* XLVI (August, 1952), 3-60.

42. FAY, TEMPLE, and EDGAR A. DOLL. "Organic Impairment Simulating Mental Deficiency," *American Journal of Orthopsychiatry,* XIX (January, 1949), 112-119.

43. FINLEY, CECILE B. "The Social Opinions Inventory as a Measure of Social Maturity," *Child Development,* XXVI (June, 1955), 81-90.

44. FLANAGAN, JOHN C. *Teacher's Guide for the Personal and Social Development Program.* Chicago: Science Research Associates, 1956. 63 pp.

45. FLORY, CHARLES D. *The Physical Growth of Mentally Deficient Boys.* ("Monographs of the Society for Research in Child Development," Vol. I, No. 6.) Washington, D.C.: National Research Council, 1936. 119 pp.

46. FORSHAY, ARTHUR W., and KENNETH D. WANN. *Children's Social Values.* New York: Teachers College, Columbia Univ., 1954. 323 pp.

47. FRANK, JOSETTE. *Comics, Radio, Movies—and Children.* ("Public Affairs Pamphlet," No. 148.) New York: Public Affairs Comm., Inc., 1955. 28 pp.

*48. FREEMAN, FRANK N. *Teaching Handwriting.* ("What Research Says to the Teacher," No. 4; Department of Classroom Teachers and American Educational Research Association of the NEA.) Washington, D.C.: National Education Assoc., 1954. 33 pp.

49. GALLAGHER, JAMES J. *A Comparison of Brain-Injured and Non-Brain-Injured Mentally Retarded Children on Several Psychological Variables.* ("Monographs of the Society for Research in Child Development," Vol. XXII, No. 2, Serial No. 65, 1957.) Lafayette, Ind.: Purdue Univ., 1957. 79 pp.

50. GORDON, IRA J. *The Teacher as a Guidance Worker.* New York: Harper & Bros., 1956. 350 pp.

51. GRAY, HORACE. "Prediction of Adult Stature," *Child Development,* XIX (September, 1948), 167-175.

52. GREENE, HARRY A., ALBERT N. JORGENSEN, and J. RAYMOND GERBERICH. *Measurement and Evaluation in Secondary School* (2d ed.). New York: Longmans, Green & Co., Inc., 1954. 690 pp.

53. GRITZNER, FLORENCE A. "Why Parents Annoy Us; A Little Survey," *National Parent-Teacher,* LI (May, 1957), 29-31.

54. GRONLUND, NORMAN E. "Sociometric Status and Sociometric Perception," *Sociometry,* XVIII (May, 1955), 122-128.

55. GROSSMANN, BEVERLY, and JOYCE WRIGHTER. "The Relation between Selection-Rejection and Intelligence, Social Status, and Personality amongst Sixth Grade Children," *Sociometry,* XI (November, 1948), 346-355.

56. GRUENBERG, SIDONIE. *The Wonderful Story of How You Were Born.* Garden City, N.Y.: Doubleday & Co., Inc., 1952. 38 pp.

57. HANSZEN, MYRA W., and WILLIAM G. HOLLISTER. "Teaching Human Relations through Spontaneous Pupil Play Writing and Play Acting," *Understanding the Child,* XXV (October, 1956), 103-110.

58. HARRELL, LESTER E., JR. *A Comparison of the Development of Oral and Written Language in School-age Children.* ("Monographs of the

Society for Research in Child Development," Vol. XXII, No. 3, Serial No. 66.) Lafayette, Ind.: Purdue Univ., 1957. 77 pp.

59. HARRIS, DALE B. "How Student-Teachers Identify Responsibility in Children," *Journal of Educational Psychology,* LXV (April, 1954), 233-239.

60. HARRIS, DALE B., and SING CHU TSENG. "Children's Attitudes toward Peers and Parents as Revealed by Sentence Completions," *Child Development,* XXVIII (December, 1957), 401-411.

61. HARRIS, DALE B., and others. "Personality Differences between Responsible and Less Responsible Children," *Journal of Genetic Psychology,* LXXXVII (September, 1955), 103-109.

62. HARRIS, ESTHER K. *The Responsiveness of Kindergarten Children to the Behavior of Their Fellows.* ("Monographs of the Society for Research in Child Development," Vol. XI, No. 2, Serial No. 43, 1946.) Washington 25, D.C.: National Research Council, 1948. 184 pp.

63. HARTLEY, RUTH E. *Sociality in Preadolescent Boys.* New York: Teachers College, Columbia Univ., 1946. 117 pp.

64. ——— and ROBERT M. GOLDENSON. *The Complete Book of Children's Play.* New York: Thomas Y. Crowell, 1957. 462 pp.

65. HARTSHORNE, HUGH, and MARK A. MAY. *Studies in the Nature of Character. I. Studies in Deceit.* New York: The Macmillan Co., 1928.

66. HAVIGHURST, ROBERT J., MYRA Z. ROBINSON, and MILDRED DORR. "The Development of the Ideal Self in Childhood and Adolescence," *Journal of Educational Research,* XL (December, 1946), 241-257.

67. HAWKES, GLENN R., LEE G. BURCHINAL, and BRUCE GARDNER. "Pre-Adolescents' Views of Some of Their Relations with Their Parents," *Child Development,* XXVIII (December, 1957), 393-399.

68. HILDRETH, GERTRUDE. *Child Growth Through Education.* New York: The Ronald Press Co., 1948. 437 pp.

69. HONZIK, MARJORIE P. "Sex Differences in the Occurrence of Materials in the Play Constructions of Pre-Adolescents," *Child Development,* XXII (March, 1951), 15-35.

70. HORN, ERNEST. *Teaching Spelling.* ("What Research Says to the Teacher," No. 3.) Washington, D.C.: National Education Association, 1954. 32 pp.

*71. HYMES, JAMES L., JR. *A Pound of Prevention: How Teachers Can Meet the Emotional Needs of Young Children.* New York: New York State Comm. on Mental Hygiene, 1947. 63 pp.

*72. ———. *Teachers, Listen, the Children Speak.* New York: New York State Comm. on Mental Hygiene of the State Charities Aid Assoc., 1949. 44 pp.

73. IOWA TESTS OF BASIC SKILLS. Boston: Houghton-Mifflin Co., 1956.

74. JENKINS, R. L., and LESTER HEWITT. "Types of Personality Structure Encountered in Child Guidance Clinics," *American Journal of Orthopsychiatry,* XIV (January, 1944), 84-95.

**75. JENNINGS, HELEN HALL. *Leadership and Isolation; A Study of Personality in Inter-Personal Relations* (rev. ed.). New York: Longmans, Green & Co., Inc., 1950. 349 pp.

*76. ———. *Sociometry in Group Relations: A Work Guide for Teachers.* Washington, D.C.: American Council on Education, 1948. 85 pp.

*77. ———. "Sociometric Grouping in Relation to Child Development," and "Sociodrama as Educative Process," in *Fostering Mental Health in Our Schools,* pp. 203-224, 260-285. ("1950 Yearbook of the Association for Supervision and Curriculum Development.") Washington, D.C.: National Education Assoc., 1950. 320 pp.

78. JERSILD, ARTHUR T. *In Search of Self.* New York: Teachers College, Columbia Univ., 1952. 141 pp.

**79. JERSILD, ARTHUR T. "Emotional Development," in Leonard Carmichael (ed.), *Manual of Child Psychology* (2d ed.), pp. 833-917. New York: John Wiley & Sons, Inc., 1954. 1295 pp.

80. JERSILD, ARTHUR J., and RUTH TASCH. *Children's Interests and What They Suggest for Education.* New York: Teachers College, Columbia Univ., 1949. 173 pp.

81. JONES, HAROLD E. *Motor Performance and Growth.* Berkeley, Calif.: Univ. of California Press, 1949. 181 pp.

82. JONES, MARY COVER, and NANCY BAYLEY. "Physical Maturing among Boys as Related to Behavior," *Journal of Educational Psychology,* XLI (March, 1950), 129-148.

**83. JONES, VERNON. "Character Development in Children—an Objective Approach," in Leonard Carmichael (ed.), *Manual of Child Psychology* (2d ed.), pp. 781-732. New York: John Wiley & Sons, Inc., 1954. 1295 pp.

84. KATZ, MARTIN R. *You: Today and Tomorrow.* Princeton: Educational Testing Service, 1958.

85. KAWIN, ETHEL. "Teachers and Parents, United," *Survey,* LXXXVI (April, 1950), 194-196.

86. KLUCKHOHN, CLYDE, and HENRY A. MURRAY. "Personality Formation: the Determinants," in Clyde Kluckhohn and Henry A. Murray (eds.), *Personality in Nature, Society, and Culture.* New York: Alfred A. Knopf, 1955. 701 pp.

87. KROGMAN, WILTON MARION. *A Handbook of the Measurement and Interpretation of Height and Weight in the Growing Child.* ("Monographs of the Society for Research in Child Development," Vol. XIII, Serial No. 48, 1948.) Evanston, Ill.: Northwestern Univ., 1950. 68 pp.

88. KRUGMAN, MORRIS. "Reading Failure and Mental Health, *Journal of the National Association of Women Deans and Counselors,* XX (October, 1956), 10-12.

89. LANDECK, BEATRICE. *Time for Music—a Guide for Parents.* ("Public Affairs Pamphlet," No. 260.) New York: Public Affairs Comm., Inc., 1958. 20 pp.

90. Langford, Louis M., and Oscar W. Alm. "A Comparison of Parent Judgments and Child Feelings Concerning the Self-Adjustment and Social Adjustment of Twelve-Year-Old Children," *Journal of Genetic Psychology*, LXXXV (September, 1954), 39-46.

91. Lassner, Rudolph. "Annotated Bibliography on the Oseretsky Tests of Motor Proficiency," *Journal of Consulting Psychology*, XII (January, 1948), 37-47.

92. Lerrigo, Marion L., and Helen F. Southard. *Sex Facts and Attitudes.* New York: E. P. Dutton & Co., Inc., 1956. 88 pp.

93. Lichtenstein, Arthur. *Can Attitudes Be Taught?* ("Studies in Education," No. 21.) Baltimore: The Johns Hopkins Press, 1934. 89 pp.

94. Lippitt, Ronald, and Ralph K. White. "The Social Climate of Children's Groups," in Roger C. Barker, Jacob S. Kounin, and Herbert F. Wright, *Child Behavior and Development*, pp. 485-508. New York: McGraw-Hill Book Co., Inc., 1943. 652 pp.

95. Lowrey, Lawson G. "Education as a Factor in Personal Adjustment," in *An Educational Philosophy for Exceptional Children*, pp. 15-20. ("Proceedings of the Spring Conference on Education and the Exceptional Child of the Child Research Clinic of the Woods Schools," Langhorne, Penn., May, 1947.) 53 pp.

96. McCandless, Boyd R., and Alfred Castaneda. "Anxiety in Children and Social Status," *Child Development*, XXVII (December, 1956), 385-391.

97. McDonald, Margherita, Carson McGuire, and Robert J. Havighurst. "Leisure Activities and the Sociometric Status of Children," *American Journal of Sociology*, LIV (May, 1949), 505-519.

98. McIntosh, W. John. "Follow-up Study of One Thousand Non-Academic Boys," *Journal of Exceptional Children*, XV (March, 1949), 166-170.

99. McKenna, Helen V., Peter R. Hofstaetter, and James P. O'Connor. "The Concepts of the Ideal Self and of the Friend," *Journal of Personality*, XXIV (March, 1956), 262-271.

100. Marburg, Francis W. "Studying the Child's Social World," *Journal of Educational Sociology*, XXI (May, 1948), 535-543.

*101. Martin, Alexander Reid. "Do We Teach Our Children Too Much about Sex?" *McCall's Magazine*, LXXXIV (October, 1956), 39 and 102, 104.

102. Melton, Arthur W. "Present Accomplishment and Future Trends in Problem-Solving and Learning Theory," *American Psychologist*, XI (June, 1956), 278-281.

103. Menninger, William C., and others. *How You Grow Up.* New York: Sterling Publishing Corp., 1957. 160 pp.

104. Metropolitan Life Insurance Company. *America's Children*, 1956, pp. 1-7.

105. ———. *What Teachers See*, 1947. 32 pp.

106. Millard, Cecil V., and John W. M. Rothney. *The Elementary School Child; a Book of Cases.* New York: The Dryden Press, 1957. 660 pp.

107. Mitchell, Adelle H. "The Effect of Radio Programs on Silent Reading Achievement of Ninety-One Sixth Grade Students," *Journal of Educational Research*, XLII (February, 1949), 460-470.

108. Moreno, Jacob L. "Organization of the Social Atom," *Sociometry*, X (August, 1947), 287-293.

109. Morgan, Joy Elmer. "Alone in Its Field," *National Parent-Teacher*, LI (November, 1956), 25.

*110. Morris, Glyn. *Practical Guidance Methods for Principals and Teachers.* New York: Harper & Bros., 1952. 266 pp.

111. Morse, Lucia Burton. "Young Pegasus," *Progressive Education*, V (January-February-March, 1928), 51-61.

112. Morton, R. L. *Teaching Arithmetic.* ("What Research Says to the Teacher," No. 2.) Washington, D.C.: National Education Assoc., 1953. 33 pp.

113. Moustakas, Clark E. *Teacher and the Child; Personal Interaction in the Classroom.* New York: McGraw-Hill Book Co., Inc., 1956. 265 pp.

114. Mowrer, O. H. "Authoritarianism vs. 'Self-Government' in the Management of Children; Aggressive (Anti-Social) Reactions as a Preparation for Citizenship in a Democracy," *Journal of Social Psychology*, X (February, 1939), 121-126.

**115. Munn, Norman L. "Learning in Children," in Leonard Carmichael (ed.), *Manual of Child Psychology*, pp. 374-458. New York: John Wiley & Sons, Inc., 1954. 1295 pp.

*116. National Society for the Study of Education. *Juvenile Delinquency and the Schools.* Edited by Nelson B. Henry. ("Forty-seventh Yearbook of the National Society for the Study of Education," Part I.) Chicago: Univ. of Chicago Press, 1950. 352 pp.

117. ———. *Learning and Instruction.* Edited by Nelson B. Henry. ("Forty-ninth Yearbook of the National Society for the Study of Education," Part I.) Chicago: Univ. of Chicago Press, 1950. 352 pp.

118. ———. *Spiritual Values in the Elementary School*, pp. 5-252. (Twenty-sixth Yearbook; Bulletin of the Department of Elementary School Principals," Vol. XXVII, No. 1, September, 1947.) 351 pp.

*119. Newman, Ruth G. "The Acting-Out Boy," *Journal of Exceptional Children*, XXII (February, 1956), 186-90+.

120. Ogilvie, Mardel. *Speech in the Elementary School.* New York: McGraw-Hill Book Co., Inc., 1954. 318 pp.

*121. Ojemann, Ralph H. *Personality Adjustment of Individual Children.* Washington, D.C.: National Education Assoc., 1954. 32 pp.

122. Parsons, Talcott. "Age and Sex in the Social Structure of the United

States," in Clyde Kluckhohn and Henry A. Murray, *Personality in Nature, Society, and Culture,* pp. 363-375. New York: Alfred A. Knopf, 1953. 701 pp.

123. Peterson, Ruth C., and L. L. Thurstone. *Motion Pictures and the Social Attitudes of Children.* New York: The Macmillan Co., 1933. 75 pp.

124. Pope, Benjamin. "Socio-Economic Contrasts in Children's Peer Culture Prestige Values," *Genetic Psychology Monographs,* XLVIII (November, 1953), 157-220.

125. Pratt, Karl C. "A Study of the Fears of Rural Children," *Journal of Genetic Psychology,* LXVII (December, 1945), 179-194.

126. Prescott, Daniel A. *The Child in the Educative Process.* New York: McGraw-Hill Book Co., Inc., 1957. 502 pp.

127. Rasmussen, Carrie. *Speech Methods in the Elementary School.* New York: The Ronald Press Co., 1949. 340 pp.

*128. Redl, Fritz. *What Should We Know About a Child?* Washington, D.C.: American Council on Education, 1941. 33 pp.

*129. Redl, Fritz, and David Wineman. *Controls from Within.* Glencoe, Ill.: The Free Press, 1952. 332 pp.

130. Ross, Clay C. *Measurement in Today's Schools* (3d ed.). New York: Prentice-Hall, Inc., 1954. 485 pp.

131. Rudman, Herbert C. "The Informational Needs and Reading Interests of Children in Grades IV through VII," *Elementary School Journal,* LV (May, 1955), 502-512.

132. Russell, David H. *Children's Thinking.* New York: Ginn & Co., 1956. 449 pp.

133. ———. *The Dimensions of Children's Meaning Vocabularies in Grades Four Through Twelve.* Berkeley, Calif.: Univ. of California Press, 1954. Pp. 315-414.

134. ———. "A Second Study of Characteristics of Good and Poor Spellers," *Journal of Educational Psychology,* XLVI (March, 1955), 129-141.

135. San Diego County Schools. *Reading—Grades One Through Eight; Course of Study.* San Diego, Calif.: Office of the Superintendent of Schools, 1956.

136. Sanford, R. Nevitt, and others. *Physique, Personality and Scholarship: A Cooperative Study of School Children.* ("Monographs of the Society for Research in Child Development," Vol. VIII, No. 1, 1943.) 705 pp.

137. Scheinfeld, Amram. "The Mortality of Men and Women," *Scientific American,* CXCVIII (February, 1958), 22-27.

138. Shaw, Ruth F. *Finger-Painting and How I Do It.* New York: Leland Brent Publishing Co., 1947. 47 pp.

139. Sheviakov, George V., and Redl, Fritz. *Discipline for Today's Chil-*

dren and Youth. Washington, D.C.: National Education Assoc., 1956. 64 pp.

140. Strain, Francis B., and Chester L. Eggert. *Framework for Family Life Education; A Survey of Present Day Activities in Sex Education.* Washington, D.C.: American Assoc. for Health, Physical Education and Recreation, 1956. 117 pp.

141. Strang, Ruth. *Counseling Techniques in College and Secondary School* (2d ed.). New York: Harper & Bros., 1949. 302 pp.

142. ———. *Group Work in Education.* New York: Harper & Bros., 1958. 309 pp.

143. ———. *How to Report Pupil Progress.* Chicago: Science Research Associates, 1955. 47 pp.

144. ———. *The Role of the Teacher in Personnel Work* (4th ed.). New York: Teachers College, Columbia Univ., 1953. 491 pp.

145. ——— and Bracken, Dorothy K. *Making Better Readers.* Boston: D. C. Heath & Co., 1957. 367 pp.

146. Stratemeyer, Florence B., and others. *Developing a Curriculum for Modern Living* (2d ed.). New York: Teachers College, Columbia Univ., 1957. 740 pp.

147. Strickland, Ruth C. *A Study of the Possibilities of Graphs as a Means of Instruction in the First Four Grades of Elementary School.* New York: Teachers College, Columbia Univ., 1938. 172 pp.

148. Sullivan, Harry Stack. *The Interpersonal Theory of Psychiatry.* New York: W. W. Norton & Co., Inc., 1953. 393 pp.

149. Swenson, Esther J., and Charles G. Caldwell. "Spelling in Children's Letters," *Elementary School Journal,* XLIX (December, 1948), 224-235.

150. Tanner, J. M., and Barbel Inhelder, (eds.). *Discussions on Child Development.* ("Proceedings of the World Health Organization Study Group on the Psychobiological Development of the Child.") 2 vols. New York: International University Press, 1957. 240 pp. and 271 pp.

151. Temple, Rita, and Elizabeth W. Amen. "A Study of Anxiety in Young Children by Means of a Projective Technique," *Genetic Psychology Monographs,* XXX, No. 2 (November, 1944), 59-113.

152. Terman, Lewis M., and Maud A. Merrill. *Measuring Intelligence.* Boston: Houghton Mifflin Co., 1937. 460 pp.

153. Terman, Lewis M., and Melita H. Oden. *The Gifted Child Grows Up.* Stanford, Calif.: Stanford Univ. Press, 1947. 448 pp.

**154. Terman, Lewis M., and Leona E. Tyler. "Psychological Sex Differences," in Leonard Carmichael (ed.), *Manual of Child Psychology* (2d ed.), pp. 1064-1114. New York: John Wiley & Sons, Inc., 1954. 1295 pp.

155. Thelen, Herbert A. "Group Dynamics in Instruction: Principle of Least Group Size," *School Review,* LVII (March, 1949), 139-148.

**156. Thompson, Helen. "Physical Growth," in Leonard Carmichael (ed.), *Manual of Child Psychology* (2d ed.), pp. 292-334. New York: John Wiley & Sons, Inc., 1954. 1295 pp.

157. Thorndike, Robert L., and Elizabeth Hagen. *Measurement and Evaluation in Psychology and Education.* New York: John Wiley & Sons, Inc., 1955. 575 pp.

158. Thrasher, Frederic M. *The Gang; A Study of 1313 Gangs in Chicago* (2d ed.). Chicago: Univ. of Chicago Press, 1936. 605 pp.

159. Tolor, Alexander, and Belle Tolor. "Judgment of Children's Popularity from Their Human Figure Drawings," *Journal of Projective Techniques,* XIX (June, 1955), 170-175.

160. Torgerson, Theodore L., and George S. Adams. *Measurement and Evaluation for the Elemenetary-School Teacher.* New York: The Dryden Press, 1954. 489 pp.

161. Traxler, Arthur E. *Techniques of Guidance* (rev. ed.). New York: Harper & Bros., 1957. 374 pp.

162. Van Riper, Charles, and Katharine G. Butler. *Speech in the Elementary Classroom.* New York: Harper & Bros., 1955. 182 pp.

163. Volberding, Eleanor. "Out-of-School Behavior of Eleven-Year-Olds," *Elementary School Journal,* XLVIII (April, 1948), 432-441.

164. ———. "Out of School Living of Eleven-Year-Old Boys and Girls from Differing Socioeconomic Groups," *Elementary School Journal,* XLIX (February, 1949), 348-353.

165. Walker, Edward L. "Learning," in Paul R. Farnsworth and Quinn McNemar (eds.), *Annual Review of Psychology,* pp. 113-138. Vol. VIII. Stanford, Calif.: Annual Reviews, Inc., 1957.

166. Walters, James, Francis I. Stromberg, and Geraldine Lonian. "Perceptions Concerning Development of Responsibility in Young Children," *Elementary School Journal,* LVII (January, 1957), 209-216.

167. Washburn, Ruth W. *Children Know Their Friends.* New York: William Morrow & Co., Inc., 1949. 192 pp.

168. Wattenberg, William W. "Eleven-Year-Old Boys in Trouble," *Journal of Educational Psychology,* XLIV (November, 1953), 409-417.

169. ———. "Ten-Year-Old Boys in Trouble," *Child Development,* XXVIII (March, 1957), 43-46.

170. Watts, A. F. *The Language and Mental Development of Children.* London: George G. Harrap & Co., 1944. 354 pp.

171. Whitley, Harold E. "Mental Health Problems in the Classroom," *Understanding the Child,* XXIII (October, 1954), 98-103.

172. Whyte, William F. *Street Corner Society; the Social Structure of an Italian Slum* (2d ed.). Chicago: Univ. of Chicago Press, 1955. 366 pp.

173. Witty, Paul. "An Analysis of the Personality Traits of the Effective

Teacher," *Journal of Educational Research*, XL (May, 1947), 662-671.

174. ———. "Some Results of Eight Yearly Studies of TV." *School and Society*, LXXXVI (June 21, 1958), 287-289.

175. Yearbook of Education: Guidance and Counseling. Edited by Robert King Hall and Joseph A. Lauwerys. New York: World Book Co., 1955. 644 pp.

176. Zeligs, Rose. "Social Factors Annoying to Children," *Journal of Applied Psychology*, XXIX (February, 1945), 75-82.

Films for Child Study

Angry Boy. International Film Bureau. 33 minutes. 1951. Produced by Alexander Hammid and Irving Jacoby. The hidden hostility in a child which is expressed in terms of stealing. With the help of a child-guidance clinic it is traced back to its source. (*See also* other films in the series sponsored by the Mental Health Film Board.)

Being Different. McGraw-Hill. 11 minutes. Produced by the National Film Board of Canada. A thirteen-year-old boy faces the problem of pursuing his genuine interest or conforming to the opinion of his friends.

Children Growing Up with Other People. British Information Services. 30 minutes. 1948. Shows development of self-reliance and awareness of other people in children.

Children Learning by Experience. British Information Services. 40 minutes. 1948. Produced by British Ministry of Information. Observation of children in the process of learning.

From Ten To Twelve. McGraw-Hill. 26 minutes. 1957. Produced by National Film Board of Canada. Discusses how the emotional and physical development of children from ten to twelve years manifests itself in their behavior and attitudes.

Near Home. International Film Bureau. 25 minutes. 1946. Produced by British Information Services. A film about good teaching. The class studies the community.

The Quiet One. Exclusive distribution by Athena Films, 165 West 46th Street, New York, N.Y. 67 minutes. 1950 Prize-winning film showing the emotional rehabilitation of a delinquent boy.

Part Six

PREVIEW OF

ADOLESCENCE

*That night, lying in bed, I could not help wishing
that there wasn't so much sadness in growing up. It was
all so confused in my mind. There had been the long,
long days of being young and not wondering about tomorrow at all and thinking in a strange, forgotten child's
world. There were days when my thoughts were as mild
as feathers and even an hour seemed like a long time.
Then suddenly it was like turning a sharp corner—you
were older and the things that counted when you were
young didn't count any more at all, and looking back,
you couldn't even see them. Growing up crowds your
mind with new thoughts and new feelings so that you
forget how you used to think and feel.*

MAUREEN DALY, *Seventeenth Summer*
(New York: Dodd, Mead & Co., Inc., Copyright
1942 by Dodd, Mead & Co., Inc.), p. 179.
Quoted with permission of Dodd, Mead & Co., Inc.

Chapter 20

TRANSITION FROM

CHILDHOOD TO ADULTHOOD*

Adolescence is a significant segment of an individual's development. During this period—"the reconstructing teens"—usually between the ages of twelve and twenty-one, the majority of boys and girls in the United States become physiologically mature, i.e., capable of having children; they become adults in physical appearance; they approximate mental maturity. They are in a state of becoming. During these years they increase in independence and responsibility, take a greater interest in the other sex, and become more concerned with the work of the world and the meaning of life. They want and need opportunities to think through questions and problems, make decisions, and take responsibility. Underlying most of the developmental tasks of this transitional period is a striving for long-term goals, even when this necessitates relinquishing the pleasures of the moment.

Adolescence is an "in-between period." Teen-agers vacillate between childish and grown-up behavior. In our culture there are no coming-of-age primitive rites by means of which adults say to adolescents, "Now you're a man." Parents are ambivalent in their attitudes; in the morning they say, "You're big enough to help me with this," and the same evening, "What do you mean by borrowing the car—you're just a kid." Thus the youngsters are facing two ways and are being pushed in two directions at once. They live in two overlapping life spaces.

Adolescence is a vulnerable period of life. The ratio of environmental demands and hazards to the individual's ability to deal with them is high. The very instability of this period, however, offers an opportunity for reorganization and reorientation. It is the golden opportunity for counseling.

---

* The purpose of this chapter is merely to invite further study of the adolescent stage of development. Some of the many books devoted entirely to this period are listed at the end of the chapter.

There is no typical adolescent. Despite the fact that common ways of dressing and behaving give an appearance of uniformity to any group of adolescents, each boy or girl has an individuality of his own. Moreover, the same individual will at different times act in inconsistent ways. No research has been sufficiently broad in its sampling nor deep in its analysis of adolescent behavior to warrant much generalization.

Whether an adolescent makes a good adjustment depends a great deal on the way in which his personality has developed through his previous experiences. A child who feels insecure tends to cling to old ways of meeting life's situations; he is afraid to venture upon new experiences and relations. Consequently he is less likely to progress without strain to the next stage of development. The effects of errors in early-childhood upbringing may not become evident until they are uncovered by the increased strain of adolescent adjustment. Stored-up hostility, feelings of rejection, a sense of unworthiness or inferiority, an unrealistic level of aspiration, a "loss of self"—all these have their roots in early childhood and may be reinforced and intensified by elementary-school experiences. The child who from his early years has accepted dependency on his parents for the sake of obtaining security is likely to have feelings of reluctance or guilt in breaking his close ties with them. On the other hand, the child who from early years has gained security through voluntary dependence and gradual self-realization has been preparing for the more complete independence of adulthood. The individual who has fought his way to independence and prestige throughout childhood may continue the struggle during adolescence; however, he may adopt adult independence with ease.

In a sense, the past in its entirety influences the present and the future.

The adult with a capacity for true maturity is one who has grown out of childhood without losing childhood's best traits. He has retained the basic emotional strengths of infancy, the stubborn autonomy of toddlerhood, the capacity for wonder and pleasure and playfulness of the preschool years, the capacity for affiliation and the intellectual curiosity of the school years, and the idealism and passion of adolescence. [29, p. 345, 1957]

If all of these components of personality have been achieved along the developmental path, they should culminate in a sense of integrity. The individual may not have achieved an ideal pattern of life. However, if it is the best pattern he can achieve and he has accepted responsibility for it and developed a respect for the lives of other persons, and if he has acquired the quality of loving kindness, then he has achieved integrity in the best sense of the word.

DEVELOPMENTAL TASKS OF ADOLESCENCE

The four major problems of adolescence, stated so many years ago by Leta S. Hollingworth, have been substantiated by subsequent research. To these four Havighurst (10, pp. 33-63, 1952; 11, 1956) has added several more in his list of developmental tasks. The following is a composite list based on many sources (24 pp. 279-280, 1957):

1. Achieving emotional independence from parents and other adults. This includes the right to make more decisions and take more responsibility. Helpful to this end are part-time work experience and increased economic independence. This goal should be achieved with the minimum of emotional wear and tear on the adolescent and his parents, and without the adolescent's losing the security of a loving relationship. He should achieve a balance between independence and a mature kind of dependence.

2. Establishing satisfying and constructive relations with both boys and girls. This implies taking a constructive attitude toward persons with different interests, abilities, and backgrounds; it requires accepting one's own masculine or feminine role without feelings of inferiority; it involves learning ways of making oneself attractive to the other sex; and it arouses interest in preparing for marriage and family life.

3. Choosing and preparing for a vocation. Adolescents are greatly concerned about finding a suitable vocational field. They should develop sufficient flexibility to modify their choice in accordance with changes in economic conditions and in their own interests and abilities. Their immediate task is to choose and complete successfully an appropriate educational program.

4. Building deeply personal social, ethical, and spiritual values—a functional philosophy of life to guide their behavior.

5. Understanding and accepting themselves—understanding the physical changes that are taking place, assessing and accepting their intellectual capacities, recognizing their limitations, but focusing attention on their assets.

6. Developing the interests, concepts, and skills necessary to civic competence and socially responsible behavior: self-control and self-discipline, critical but constructive judgment, hobbies including intelligent reading and listening.

7. Reaching forward toward maturity in all areas of living—a maturity that must be achieved by constantly setting immediate goals to be accomplished.

In the study of adolescence it is well to start with the biological changes and endeavor to understand their relation to the behavior of the individual as he tries to adjust to the personal and social demands of his environment. These physical and physiological changes intensify the adolescent's awareness of himself and of his relations to others.

TRENDS IN ADOLESCENT DEVELOPMENT

Physiological maturity marks the beginning of the adolescent period. In the United States approximately half of the girls become capable of bearing children between the ages of twelve years, six months, and fourteen years, six months. Boys mature, on the average, a year or two later. Even within the normal range, the variation is wide. Some reach puberty as early as nine years; others as late as eighteen. Boys and girls should be encouraged to welcome this change as an essential part of life—a necessary preparation for their respective masculine and feminine roles.

Physical maturity is attained during the adolescent period. After the growth spurt, which is a prelude to puberty, boys and girls continue to grow in height and weight, and with respect to calcification of the wrist bones and other parts of the body until they reach adult proportions. Boys continue to grow in height and weight during the college years; they attain their maximum stature, on the average, at about nineteen years, but continue to increase in weight. Girls tend to reach their maximum height during the high-school years. The growth patterns of individuals vary according to the age of attaining puberty. Although the development of an adolescent cannot be precisely predicted it may be sympathetically observed. It is encouraging to a short boy to know that about a third of those who are initially classified as "short" have reason to expect a rating of "medium stature" at a later examination. The late-maturing boy may be handicapped by feelings of physical and social inadequacy because his physical development has not kept pace with that of other boys of his chronological age. Delayed adolescence may not be disadvantageous if the youngster has a number of other slow maturers with whom to associate. Teachers can help adolescents to understand their growth cycle, the physical changes associated with it, and the difficulties arising from them.

Mental maturity, as measured by intelligence tests of aptitude or power for doing increasingly difficult mental tasks, may be attained in the twenties. However, horizontal growth—increase in knowledge, experience, and judgment—may continue throughout life. Excellent summaries of facts about the mental development of adolescents and the ways of measuring it may be found in the books listed at the end of this chapter. Persons in school or college or in occupations requiring the use of verbal and mathematical ability tend to continue to grow in these mental abilities. The growth of mental abilities depends a great deal on the extent to which these are used (34, 1948).

On scholastic aptitude tests, high-school boys are generally superior to girls, but they seem to be more variable, i.e., there are more gifted and more extremely retarded boys than girls.

Adolescence is not accompanied by a new birth of intellectual powers. An individual tends to follow his developmental trend rather than to shift into a different pattern of mental growth during adolescence. Relatively few children shift to a markedly higher mental level, as, for example, the maladjusted child who initially tested low but is subsequently freed from emotional blocks, or the intellectually deprived child later placed in a much more stimulating environment.

Scholastic achievement during adolescence depends still more on circumstances; the attitude of the group toward scholastic achievement is an important factor. Success is relative. It depends upon the relation between the individual's accomplishment and the goal that he has set for himself. If he falls short of his level of aspiration he has a feeling of failure; if he surpasses it he experiences success, unless he recognizes that he had set the goal much too low. Moreover, the will to learn is complicated by other motives and drives that stem most frequently from personal relations.

Emotional maturity is indicated by the individual's growth in inner control or conscience and ability to accept inevitable frustrations and to meet life situations in constructive ways. It is indicated by his satisfaction in being of service to others and by his adaptability to changing conditions. New conditions and responsibilities challenge the mature individual.

Adolescents, however, have much to contend with; they must revise their body image, modify their parent-child relations. They lack status; they are neither children nor adults. They are often less mature emotionally than physically. They may not know what is expected of them. They ask themselves such questions as, "Where do I belong?" "Am I as grown up as others of my age?" Emotional outbursts are common to those who feel uncertain of their status regardless of their age. The long duration of this period of indeterminate status is very trying. Adolescents need to experience success in channeling their emotional energy into creative and constructive activities.

Falling in love is a sign of emotional maturity; it indicates the ability to feel for and give to another person. It is another stage in the emotional progression whose previous phases were infantile self-love, the close family attachments of early childhood, later childhood friendships, and preadolescent loyalty to the group or gang. Genuine love of another person may foster an interest in the welfare of all members of the community.

However, many problems stem from adolescent love relations. Certain psychological conditions are necessary to actualize the potential sex drive inherent in the sex hormones. The practice of "heavy petting" excites the emotions and arouses the desire for sexual intercourse. The recommendation arrived at by one group of college girls—"Practice moderation in petting, not total abstinence"—would appeal as reasonable to the majority of adolescents. Premarital love affairs are prevalent, reaching a peak of frequency between sixteen and twenty years of age.

Understanding of sex as a normal part of life should be acquired long before adolescence. However, since many high-school students have not obtained accurate information, remedial work must be done. The best approach is to answer the students' questions directly in personal conferences and to find places in the curriculum where social education may naturally be given: in biology; in social science; in literature, especially through a study of biographies and novels dealing with emotional and sexual problems; in home economics; in art; and in social activities. To introduce sex education indiscriminately might prematurely stimulate youngsters who are not ready for the experience. A number of colleges are developing effective courses in the broad aspects of family life.

Strong impulses are not easily stifled. Lacking the stimulus of contact with the opposite sex, the love impulse may find expression in masturbation or homosexual relationships. Prolonged segregation of the sexes, as in so many homes and schools where the child's contacts are almost exclusively with one sex, may decrease normal interest in the opposite sex. Adolescent "crushes" are most prevalent in girls' schools and girls' camps. Normally this form of attachment does not persist as a habit, although it may be troublesome for the teacher or camp counselor. Crushes are more intense than ordinary friendships; they are quite different from the experience of intimacy described earlier; they more frequently involve jealousy and are exclusively between two persons, thus shutting out other friends. A boy's attachment to an adult may take the form of hero worship; it may indicate a need for affection or for a concrete ideal of what he may become. The adult should treat such attachments kindly but avoid becoming emotionally involved.

Social maturity is closely related to emotional maturity, and involves increased social sensitivity. This sensitivity influences the way in which the adolescent perceives social situations and, consequently, the way in which he behaves. Social maturity involves extension and improvement of social relations. At University High School (28, 1937) a clubhouse established for the girls and boys and their friends as part of the University Adolescent Study, made no appeal to the children in the seventh grade, who were more interested in team games or in individual activities. In the eighth grade the pupils were at first interested in coming to the clubhouse for classes in photography, interior decorating, dramatics, and shop work; later in the year they increasingly used the clubhouse as a place for unorganized social contacts with both sexes. By the time they had reached the ninth grade, they were using the clubhouse as a place in which to work out their own social relationships. Their desire for group approval motivated many of their activities. The clubhouse gave them an opportunity to try out various types of response and to eliminate those which appeared to lessen their own popularity and those which they saw used by others unsuccessfully. Some pupils who had not previously been socially successful with their own sex gained acceptance through their popularity with the opposite sex.

During the period of gaining social acceptance, adolescents seem to consider adults an impediment. They avoid them if possible, especially those who want to dominate and those who do not understand the situation and the group's ways of thinking and acting. Though the presence of a possessive parent is considered a hindrance, the presence of an understanding club sponsor is accepted. After passing through this phase, the same boys and girls may seek the companionship of adults and talk with them as man to man. At best, adults have only an imperfect understanding of the younger generation; they should be ready to learn from youth.

The preadolescent's identification with his peer group paves the way for developing intimacy with the other sex. Achieving such intimacy naturally leads to interest in marriage and family life, in producing and caring for children of one's own. It may also be manifested in a broader interest in other people's children and in creative activities.

Girls usually begin to show social awareness and interest in the opposite sex a year or two earlier than boys; they often succeed in stimulating a reciprocal interest in the boys, whom they refuse to leave alone. This difference in social maturity creates a difficulty in the junior high school; approximately two thirds of the girls are in the postpubescent stage while an equal number of boys are still prepubescent in attitudes and behavior.

The social behavior of adolescents is to some extent related to the social status of their families. However, it is all too easy to assume a causal relation between social class and certain factors such as cliques, recreation, school-leaving, or placement in jobs. Actually there may be a number of interrelated causes operating simultaneously: mental ability, disposition, personal appearance, or other underlying conditions distinct from social class per se. Social barriers are often broken down when adolescents from several socioeconomic levels work together toward worthwhile goals. By means of this interaction children learn ways of thinking, feeling, and acting which prepare them for "upward mobility." (22, 1949) Much may be done in school subjects to help adolescents gain an understanding of how human personality develops and why people behave as they do.

Many adolescents desire to render social service and find many opportunities to do so. "Education as community improvement" gives every pupil a chance to help make his local school and community more healthful, safe, beautiful, and productive. Those who make satisfactory adjustments with their families and age-mates appear to become most interested in the welfare of the larger social group. Development of character and personality is largely a by-product of the experience of living together. It is caught, not taught.

Attainment of religious security and maturity involves the development of values, a philosophy of life, and an orientation to the universe. Religious adjustment is related to other aspects of life, especially to human relations. The church supplies an appropriate place to worship and a quiet time in which to view one's life in relation to something greater—an ideal, a goal, or God. The social aspects of worship give a sense of belonging, of sharing a common purpose.

The foundations of religion are laid in childhood; later experiences may cause early religious attitudes either to wither or to mature. A gifted youngster expressed the following attitude toward religion:

I go to church regularly. Religion is an essential part of everyone's life but the services fail to impress me and through the week I forget about religion entirely. The chief reason I go to church is that my parents want me to go. I believe in life after death chiefly because that belief was taught to me as a child and I have never had the initiative to doubt it. I am almost afraid to think about that question for fear I will come to a negative conclusion and I really want to believe in such an after-life.

To some extent, however, a sound philosophy of life grows out of knowledge, as well as out of personal experience. History, science, literature, philosophy, and theology, all contribute to the development of an adolescent's understanding of the nature of the universe and of his place in it. Successful living demands a certain conformity to the mores and customs of the culture. Laws must be obeyed. Common purposes, attitudes, and ideals are woven into a "moral imperative" that guides conduct.

Appel's rules for effective living suggest these paths toward maturity:

"To use one's abilities effectively and with enthusiasm."
To work toward worth-while ends.
To cooperate with others.
To tolerate frustration.
To persist in effort.
To take responsibility.
To show love for something beyond oneself. [1, 1949]

The mature personality finds a worthy purpose or goal, which is an important unifying factor in life in that it influences decisions and guides conduct. The integrated personality is built in life situations that demand wholehearted attention to the task in hand. Any experience that is constructive, vital, challenging, and appropriate for an adolescent helps him to develop a mature personality. Integration of personality is only approximate; it is never completely achieved. An adolescent has a number of potential selves. He needs to develop the concept of his most acceptable and attainable self. Failure to achieve a satisfactory integration of conflicting tendencies or too great a discrepancy between one's level of aspiration and one's achievement may result in negativism, delinquency, mental disorder and insanity, alcoholism or drug addiction, or suicide. Negativism is a manifestation of insecurity—a crude attempt to maintain one's ego. Delinquency, mental disorder, and insanity withdraw the person's energy from constructive activities. Drunkenness and drug addiction are other forms of withdrawal from "the emotional hardships of life." Suicide sometimes represents the ultimate form of withdrawal, when pain or utter lack of satisfaction in life becomes too intense to endure.

Vocational maturity is a clearly recognized major goal of adolescence. As the student goes through high school, he becomes more and more concerned with choosing, preparing for, entering, and progressing in an occupation. The following quotation from a high-school student is probably typical of the attitude of many adolescents:

My problem is what am I going to do when I get out of school, and that will be this June, I hope! I haven't the vaguest idea what I would like to do or work at. I have had several jobs but none of them appealed to me. What would I do to find out what kind of work I would like and could do well? Where would I go to do this and when? . . . I know people usually know what they are going to do before they get out of school, but I don't. I like to hunt, fish, swim, and play football but I can't live on that the rest of my life.

Vocational development is not a simple matter of finding a specific vocation; it involves the individual's self-concept and is often complicated by conflicting family attitudes. Society frequently intensifies the adolescent's problems of vocational adjustment. In wartime, adolescents are expected to grow up quickly because youth are needed to bear the brunt of war. During an economic depression adults try to prolong youngsters' childhood; they do not want children to grow up quickly and take adults' jobs. Consequently young people who would make a successful adjustment in industry are sent back to schools where they have a record of failures. About half of the out-of-school youth, fourteen to nineteen years of age, surveyed in Louisville, Kentucky, in 1949, said that their principal reason for discontinuing their education was dissatisfaction with some aspect of school (6, 1949).

Mental level is not the only determinant for occupational choice and success. Physical appearance, social intelligence, emotional development, and other personality factors must be considered. The most difficult adolescents to place vocationally are those who are emotionally unstable as well as mentally defective. The most frequently reported reason for failure to get a job is lack of education. The most frequent reason for losing a job is not being able to get along with people. Try-out and other work experiences contribute to the training in versatility and adaptability, which is a requirement for vocational success in a changing world.

Educational guidance is basic to vocational guidance. If a pupil has developed his educational potentialities he will be prepared to specialize in a vocation when the time comes. Adolescents' selection of courses may be complicated by (1) an earlier emotional attachment to an unsuitable course of study, (2) inadequate appraisal of their scholastic aptitude, (3) the complexity of the factors that influence learning, (4) inadequate curricular offerings, and (5) the parents' desire that their children study subjects associated with a certain social status.

Decisions about higher education face every high-school pupil. Many pupils have ambitions that are far beyond their mental ability; others have mental ability that is superior to their ambitions. Ever greater financial resources for going to college are being made available to able learners. Accordingly, it is important that boys and girls who are likely to profit by further education be identified early. The next task is to choose the college or other educational experience that is most appropriate for the individual. There is enormous variation in the mental caliber of the student bodies in different institutions of collegiate rank. In one year the median scores of different colleges on the American Council Psychological Examination covered a range of from 90 to 249.

UNDERSTANDING ADOLESCENTS

The social-psychological approach is the best method of studying adolescents because it considers all the forces that influence the individual on his road to maturity. It gives a complete developmental picture of parent-child relations and shows how they are operating in the present; it considers the adolescent's role in his family; it emphasizes the totality of the adolescent's experience, and considers each incident as having a dynamic relation to the total personality. The family-centered or the community-centered case study, which views the adolescent in his environment, is the best present method of understanding the adolescent as a whole. To the case study all the methods and techniques described in previous chapters may contribute.

TOWARD EMOTIONAL MATURITY

Adolescence should be viewed as an opportunity. Since the teen-ager is in a state of unstable equilibrium, he can gain a new and more hopeful orientation in spite of unfavorable childhood experiences. Even though his early experiences have led him to expect the outside world to be hostile and threatening, and even though he goes out to meet it with defensive tactics that have worked fairly well in the past, he may, in an environment where he feels understood and accepted, learn that the whole world is not necessarily bent on defeating him and that he can dispense with his defensive mechanisms. Even though he has developed an attitude of hopelessness and defeatism, he may gradually achieve a measure of self-esteem by experiencing success in some corner of his life. Adolescence is a most fruitful period for learning techniques of living. The mature adolescent is one who has learned to use his emotional energy in constructive ways, to lose himself in worthwhile tasks, to change conditions or to change his attitude toward them, and to adapt to situations he cannot modify. He has learned to relate himself to others and to take a constructive attitude toward them. Since he has gained an understanding of himself, he no longer acts blindly. The happy adolescent is one who feels that, despite some ups and downs, he is successfully achieving maturity.

Questions and Problems

FOR CLASS DISCUSSION OR STUDY GROUPS

1. Study several adolescent boys and girls with whom you have established a confidential relationship. Note their development toward maturity and try to see the world through their eyes.

2. Ask a group of adolescents to write their autobiographies or life histories, including not only the chronological events but also interpretations of them.

3. Have a panel of teen-agers discuss the kind of guidance they want from adults.

4. As an example of an elaborate control-group experiment, read Glueck and Glueck's *Delinquents in the Making* (9, 1952). Note the factors on which the two groups were equated. On which characteristics studied was the delinquent group differentiated from the non-delinquent group?

5. List specific situations you have met in dealing with adolescents in which you felt the need of more understanding. Gather from your readings suggestions which will help you to act more wisely in such situations.

6. What new tendencies have you noticed in adolescents today which make them somewhat different from the adolescents described in books on the psychology of adolescents? Is there as much evidence of turbulence, of antagonism toward parents? Are today's adolescents less fearful of growing up? (30, 1957).

7. What are the characteristics of early and of late adolescence? How may the differences be explained?

Bibliography*

1. APPEL, KENNETH E. "Psychiatry and Human Relations," *Understanding the Child*, XVIII (January, 1949), 3-8.

2. AUBREY, J. (ROUDINESCO). "Severe Maternal Deprivation and Personality Development in Early Childhood," *Understanding the Child*, XXI (October, 1952), 104-108.

   * All references referred to in the text are included in the bibliography. The single-starred references (*) are specially recommended for their practical suggestions; those double-starred (**) are specially recommended for their technical and research emphasis.

**3. AUSUBEL, DAVID P. *Theory and Problems of Adolescent Development.* New York: Grune & Stratton, 1954. 580 pp.

4. BROOKS, ALICE R. "Integrating Books and Reading with Adolescent Tasks," *School Review,* LVIII (April, 1950), 211-219.

5. COLE, LUELLA. *Psychology of Adolescence* (4th ed.). New York: Rinehart & Co., Inc., 1954. 712 pp.

6. DILLON, HAROLD J. *Early School Leavers.* New York: National Child Labor Comm., 1949. 94 pp.

7. GARDNER, GEORGE E. "The Mental Health of Normal Adolescents," *Mental Hygiene,* XXXI (October, 1947), 529-540.

8. GESELL, ARNOLD, FRANCIS L. ILG, and LOUISE AMES BATES. *Youth: the Years from Ten to Sixteen.* New York: Harper & Bros., 1956. 542 pp.

**9. GLUECK, SHELDON, and ELEANOR GLUECK. *Delinquents in the Making.* New York: Harper & Bros., 1952. 214 pp.

10. HAVIGHURST, ROBERT J. *Developmental Tasks and Education.* New York: Longmans, Green & Co., Inc., 1952. 100 pp.

**11. ———. "Research on the Developmental-Task Concept," *School Review,* LXIV (May, 1956), 215-223.

12. HEALY, WILLIAM, and AUGUSTA F. BRONNER. *New Light on Delinquency and Its Treatment.* New Haven, Conn.: Yale Univ. Press, 1936. 226 pp.

13. HOLLINGWORTH, LETA S. *The Psychology of the Adolescent.* New York: Appleton-Century-Crofts, Inc., 1928. 259 pp.

**14. HORROCKS, JOHN E. "The Adolescent," in Leonard Carmichael (ed.), *Manual of Child Psychology* (2d ed.), pp. 697-734. New York: John Wiley & Sons, Inc., 1954. 1295 pp.

**15. HURLOCK, ELIZABETH B. *Adolescent Development* (2d ed.). New York: McGraw-Hill Book Co., Inc., 1955. 590 pp.

16. IOWA TESTS OF EDUCATIONAL DEVELOPMENT. Grades 8.5—13-5. Chicago: Science Research Associates.

17. IVES, VIRGINIA, MARGUERITE GRANT, and JANE H. RANZONI. "The 'Neurotic' Rorschachs of Normal Adolescents," *Journal of Genetic Psychology,* LXXXIII (September, 1953), 31-61.

*18. JERSILD, ARTHUR T. *Psychology of Adolescence.* New York: The Macmillan Co., 1957. 438 pp.

*19. JOSSELYN, IRENE M. *The Adolescent and His World.* New York: Family Service Assoc. of America, 1952. 124 pp.

20. KUHLEN, RAYMOND G. *The Psychology of Adolescent Development.* New York: Harper & Bros., 1952. 675 pp.

21. LANDIS, PAUL H. *Understanding Teen-Agers.* New York: Appleton-Century-Crofts, Inc., 1955. 246 pp.

22. MACDONALD, MARGHERITA, CARSON McGUIRE, and ROBERT J. HAVIGHURST. "Leisure Activities and the Socioeconomic Status of Children," *American Journal of Sociology,* LIV (May, 1949), 505-519.

23. MEAD, MARGARET. *From the South Seas: Studies of Adolescence in Primitive Society.* New York: William Morrow & Co., Inc., 1939. 304 pp.

24. PRESCOTT, DANIEL A. *The Child in the Educative Process.* New York: McGraw-Hill Book Co., Inc., 1957. 502 pp.

25. SEGEL, DAVID. *Intellectual Abilities in the Adolescent Period; Their Growth and Development.* ("Bulletin 1948, No. 6, Federal Security Agency, Office of Education.") Washington, D.C.: Government Printing Office, 1948. 41 pp.

26. SEIDMAN, JEROME M. (ed.). *The Adolescent; a Book of Readings.* New York: The Dryden Press, Inc., 1953. 798 pp.

27. SOROKIN, PITIRIM A. *The American Sex Revolution.* Boston: Porter Sargent, 1957. 186 pp.

28. STOLZ, HERBERT R., MARY COVER JONES, and JUDITH CHAFFEY. "The Junior High School Age," *University High School Journal,* XV (January, 1937), 63-72.

29. STONE, L. JOSEPH, and JOSEPH CHURCH. *Childhood and Adolescence,* pp. 268-345. New York: Random House, 1957. 456 pp.

*30. STRANG, RUTH. *The Adolescent Views Himself, a Psychology of Adolescence.* New York: McGraw-Hill Book Co., Inc., 1957. 581 pp.

31. ———. *Educational Guidance: Its Principles and Practice.* New York: The Macmillan Co., 1947. 268 pp.

32. SULLIVAN, HARRY STACK. *The Interpersonal Theory of Psychiatry,* pp. 263-310. New York: W. W. Norton & Co., Inc., 1953. 393 pp.

33. SUPER, DONALD E. *Psychology of Careers; an Introduction to Vocational Development.* New York: Harper & Bros., 1957. 362 pp.

34. VERNON, PHILLIP E. "Changes in Abilities from 14 to 20 Years," *Advancement of Science,* V (April, 1948), 138.

35. WATTENBERG, WILLIAM W. *The Adolescent Years.* New York: Harcourt, Brace & Co., 1955. 510 pp.

36. ZACHRY, CAROLINE B., and MARGARET LIGHTY. *Emotion and Conduct in Adolescence.* New York: Appleton-Century-Crofts, Inc., 1940. 563 pp.

Films for Child Study

Adolescent Development. McGraw-Hill. A series of eight films illustrating the later stages in development toward maturity.

        Meaning of Adolescence
        Physical Aspects of Puberty
        Age of Turmoil
        Social-Sex Attitudes in Adolescence
        Meeting the Needs of Adolescents

Discipline During Adolescence
Emotional Maturity
Social Acceptability

Feelings of Depression. National Film Board of Canada. Black and white. 30 minutes. 1950. The story of 30-year-old businessman John Martin, of how he became depressed, and of the factors which precipitated his depression.

Kid Brother. Mental Health Film Board. 25 minutes. 1957. Explores some of the hidden emotional forces behind excessive drinking and other teen-age "acting out."

Preface to a Life. New York Department of Mental Hygiene, Albany, N.Y. 28 minutes. 1950. Portrays the effect of parental attitudes, expectations, and behavior may have upon the growing child's eventual life adjustment.

Toward Emotional Maturity. McGraw-Hill. 11 minutes. 1955. To help adolescents understand and control their emotions, the film gives an illustration of an eighteen-year-old girl, faced with a decision deeply involving her feeling for both a boy and her parents.

Chapter 21

PATTERNS AND PRINCIPLES OF

CHILD DEVELOPMENT

The theory running through this book integrates many points of view. It recognizes the biological basis of behavior—the constitutional factors, the chemistry of the body, the nutritional condition, physical characteristics and effects of serious illness. It takes into account the inter-action of these biological factors with the environment and the way in which the individual has learned to perceive himself and his environment.

THEORY

Of all the environmental factors, the most influential are the inter-personal relations in the home, school, and community. "Social contacts are a biological necessity." Even the physical, and much more, the psychological development of children is modified by the family's and the social groups' expectations of the child and, as he grows older, by the individual's goals and values.

Several stages or phases or epochs of sequential growth are recognized. These, however, are not distinct and separate building blocks, fitted into a set pattern of child development. There is much overlapping of characteristics in consecutive stages. There is much variation in the chronological ages at which an individual passes from one stage to another. Each transition from one stage to another represents not only hazards to growth but also opportunities to correct personality faults. The child is always in the process of becoming.

Yet in a sense "the child is father to the man." The present and future build on the past. Each competency gained paves the way for further progress. The individual's developing concept of himself tends to persist and to resist change. Many individuals tend to maintain throughout life

516

a generally persistent and pervasive core of personality that is unique to each. For this reason, the development, from earliest years, of the child's concept of himself—how he views himself and how he feels about himself—is of crucial importance. This self-concept develops as he demonstrates to himself his growing competence and as he absorbs his parents' and peers' appraisal of him.

His learning takes place in a relationship. At the beginning of life, the child's relation with his mother influences his learning along all lines. Gradually other relationships—with father, brothers and sisters, grandparents, and other people in the home—are interwoven with mother-child relationship. As the child grows older, relationships with other adults and children enter into his life. From the frank responses of their playmates, children in later preschool and early elementary-school years learn how their behavior affects other people, and they modify it accordingly. During preadolescence, chums may correct faults resulting from earlier childhood experiences. Adolescent years offer opportunities for sorting out childish ways of behaving and for forming new relationships.

Within the matrix of these personal relationships other factors are influencing the child's learning. Among these are his health and vitality, his urge to be active physically and mentally, and his curiosity. As soon as he acquires speech, the magic power of words, generalizations that guide learning, and thoughts of the future give him a sense of direction and purpose. All these psychological forces, interacting with environmental stimuli, enter into the learning sequence of drive-clue-response-gratification or reduction of tension.

Much learning takes place in the child's attempt to cope with anxiety or conflict by trying to change the conditions that are causing the conflict. Freud seems in conflict with learning theory in that neurotic behavior, though not rewarding, persists. However, it may be immediately rewarding by temporarily reducing the tension caused by inner conflicts. Moreover, it represents the only way the child has found of coping with a threatening, fear-arousing situation. The child's behavior at any moment is a resultant of several forces—his native predispositions, the situation that he faces, and the response patterns he has built up to that time.

Each child has a pattern of growth unique to him. The concept of growth as a sequence of changes allows for wide individual difference within a culture and among cultures.

PRINCIPLES AND PRACTICES

A few guideposts emerge quite clearly:

1. Infants and children need someone to love them. But love alone is not enough; understanding guidance, too, is necessary.

2. Behavior characteristic of a child and of a parent will change with advancing stages of maturity. Children need different conditions at different stages of their development.

3. It is important to distinguish between problems of growing up and problems interfering with growing up. A child's behavior should be interpreted in the light of his pattern of needs and experiences.

4. Growth is a process having its ups and downs and fluctuations.

5. In the swing from extreme permissiveness to coercion on the part of parents and teachers, the kind of permissiveness based on individual needs should not be discarded.

6. For the sake of the child, as well as for the comfort of adults, reasonable limits to the child's behavior should be set and firmly held. Children need and respect reasonable limits; they feel more secure when these limits are firmly held. Permissiveness, support, and firmness are all needed at times.

7. Physical, dietary, and chemical causes may underlie emotional disturbance.

8. A developmental history may throw light on behavior that is otherwise inexplicable.

9. Failure to learn and other frustrations may produce aggression or self-defeating modes of behavior that tend to persist.

10. Neither parent nor child are totally responsible for the child's growth; it is a shared responsibility.

11. Methods appropriate to emotionally sick children cannot be applied indiscriminately to classroom situations; the distinction between psychotherapy and education should be recognized.

12. To listen to children and learn from them is far better than to label them.

13. An individual's perception of himself and his world largely determines his behavior.

14. No one—child or adult—is expected to be perfect; "mistakes are to learn from."

RESEARCH NEEDED

Extensive experiments with animals have yielded hypotheses to be tested further by observation of the behavior and experience of children and by laboratory experiments with children of different ages under natural conditions. At present few such experiments have been reported. The results of experiments in life situations could be applied more directly than the results of experiments conducted in artificial laboratory situations. Some problems in child development can be approached only by the longitudinal method, for example, the study of individual patterns of mental growth and their relation to personality (6, 1958).

Observation and introspection are both useful. For example, the critical incident technique, described by Flanagan and his associates (3, 1954) involves asking the child or parent to describe one or more instances of a specific kind of behavior, such as instances in which the child has been praised. From the analysis of many specific incidents, the investigator or teacher arrives at certain generalizations. The critical incidents may be obtained in interviews or in writing.

Parents' attitudes toward children may be studied by asking children to give their perception of their parents' attitudes and behavior. Since people respond to a situation as they perceive it, children's perception of their parents' attitudes may be a more direct and significant way of getting this information than by asking the parents directly.

The clinical approach as used by a highly insightful person like Piaget is a rewarding method.

To understand the intellectual mechanism used in the solution of problems and of determining the mechanism of reasoning, . . . we used a method which is not standardized, a clinical method, a method of free conversation with the child. We encouraged each child, as far as possible, in a way which was not comparable to that used with the preceding child. That is why, personally, I am always very suspicious of statistics on our results. Not that I dislike statistics . . . but to make statistical tables on children when each was questioned differently appears to me very open to criticism. [7, p. 89, 1953]

Dyadic relations is another fruitful field of study. Instead of focusing attention on the individual, the researcher studies the interaction between two or more individuals.

To relate accurate observations made in early childhood to personality pattern in later years is a type of research that should be valuable, insofar as mental health may be promoted by creating conditions in childhood that will develop favorable predispositions and correct early maladjustment.

Research in child development seems to be moving in several important directions. Recognizing the uniqueness of each child, research is swinging away from the purely statistical study of many children and entering a descriptive phase in which more complex variables are taken into account. In developmental studies such as those reported by Nancy Bayley, individual patterns clearly emerge. The comprehensive scientific study of the person-as-a-whole is the best present method of studying patterns of personality. How to make generalizations from a large number of such studies and how to study complex and subtle, cause and effect relationships within a case study is an important next step.

Bibliography

METHODS OF CHILD STUDY

1. ANDERSON, JOHN E. "Methods of Child Psychology," in Leonard Carmichael (ed.), *Manual of Child Psychology* (2d ed.). New York: John Wiley & Sons, Inc., 1954. 1295 pp.

2. BRANDT, RICHARD M., and HUGH V. PERKINS. *Research Evaluating a Child Study Program.* Society for Research in Child Development, Inc., Vol. XXI, No. 1, Serial No. 62, 1956. 96 pp.

3. FLANAGAN, J. C. "The Critical Incident Technique," *Psychological Bulletin*, LI (July, 1954), 327-358.

4. JACKSON, EDITH B., and ETHELYN H. KLATSKIN. "Rooming-in Research Project: Development of Methodology of Parent-Child Relationship Study in a Clinical Setting," *The Psychoanalytic Study of the Child*, V (1950), 236-274.

5. McCARTHY, DOROTHEA. "Trends in the Psychological Appraisal of Children," *Child Development*, XXVI (September, 1955), 213-222.

6. SONTAG, LESTER W., CHARLES T. BAKER, and VIRGINIA L. NELSON. *Mental Growth and Personality: A Longitudinal Study.* Society for Research in Child Development, Inc., Vol. XXIII, No. 2, Serial No. 68, 1958. 143 pp.

7. TANNER, J. M., and BÄRBEL INHELDER. *Discussions on Child Development.* 2 Vols. New York: International Universities Press, Inc., 1953. 240 pp. 1954. 271 pp.

SELECTED BOOKS

ON CHILD DEVELOPMENT

ALMY, MILLIE. *Child Development.* New York: Henry Holt & Co., Inc., 1955. 490 pp.

ANDERSON, JOHN E. *The Psychology of Development and Personal Adjustment.* New York: Henry Holt & Co., Inc., 1949. 720 pp.

**ANNUAL REVIEW OF PSYCHOLOGY. Paul R. Farnsworth and Quinn McNemar (eds.). Stanford, Calif.: Annual Review, Inc. Yearly volumes.

BARKER, ROGER G., and HERBERT WRIGHT. *Midwest and Its Children.* Evanston, Ill.: Row, Peterson & Co., 1954. 532 pp.

**BLAIR, ARTHUR W., and WILLIAM H. BURTON. *Growth and Development of the Preadolescent.* New York: Appleton-Century-Crofts, Inc., 1951. 221 pp.

BOSSARD, JAMES H. S. *The Sociology of Child Development* (rev. ed.). New York: Harper & Bros., 1954. 788 pp.

*BOWLBY, JOHN. *Child Care and the Growth of Love.* London: Penguin, 1953. 190 pp.

*BURTON, WILLIAM H. *The Guidance of Learning Activities; A Summary of the Principles of Teaching Based on the Principles of Learning* (2d ed.). New York: Appleton-Century-Crofts, Inc., 1952. 737 pp.

**CARMICHAEL, LEONARD (ed.). *Manual of Child Psychology* (2d ed.). New York: John Wiley & Sons, Inc., 1954. 1295 pp.

**CRUICKSHANK, WILLIAM M. (ed.). *Psychology of Exceptional Children and Youth.* Englewood Cliffs, N.J.: Prentice-Hall, Inc., 1955. 594 pp.

*CUTTS, NORMA E., and NICHOLAS MOSELEY. *Teaching the Disorderly Pupil in Elementary and Secondary School.* New York: Longmans, Green & Co., Inc., 1957. 170 pp.

ERIKSON, ERIK H. *Childhood and Society.* New York: W. W. Norton and Co., Inc., 1950. 397 pp.

FREUD, SIGMUND. *A General Introduction to Psychoanalysis.* New York: Liveright Publishing Corp., 1935. 412 pp.

* Examples of practical treatment.
** Examples of more technical and research emphasis.

521

Gesell, Arnold, and Frances L. Ilg. *Child Development*. 2 Vols. New York: Harper & Bros., 1949. 403 and 475 pp.

Gruenberg, Sidonie M. (ed.). *Encyclopedia of Child Care and Guidance.* Garden City, N.Y.: Doubleday & Co., Inc., 1954. 1016 pp.

Hurlock, Elizabeth B. *Child Development*. New York: McGraw-Hill Book Co., Inc., 1956. 703 pp.

*Ilg, Frances L., and Louise B. Ames. *Child Behavior*. New York: Harper & Bros., 1955. 364 pp.

*Jenkins, Gladys G., Helen Schacter, and William W. Bauer. *These Are Your Children* (expanded ed.). Chicago: Scott, Foresman & Co., 1953. 320 pp.

Jersild, Arthur T. *Child Psychology* (4th ed.). Englewood Cliffs, N.J.: Prentice-Hall, Inc., 1954. 676 pp.

Josselyn, Irene. *The Happy Child: A Psychoanalytic Guide to Emotional and Social Growth*. New York: Random House, 1955. 410 pp.

Lane, Howard A., and Mary Beauchamp. *Human Relations in Teaching*. Englewood Cliffs, N.J.: Prentice-Hall, 1955. 353 pp.

Mental Health and Infant Development. ("Proceedings of the International Seminar Held by the World Federation for Mental Health at Chicester, England"; Edited by Kenneth Soddy.) New York: Basic Books, Inc., 1956. 299 pp.

*Millard, Cecil V., and John W. M. Rothney. *The Elementary School Child; A Book of Cases*. New York: The Dryden Press, 1957. 660 pp.

*Moustakas, Clark E. *The Teacher and the Child; Personal Interaction in the Classroom*. New York: McGraw-Hill Book Co., Inc., 1956. 265 pp.

*Murphy, Lois B. and others. *Personality in Young Children*. 2 Vols. New York: Basic Books, Inc., 1956. 424 and 267 pp.

Mussen, Paul H., and John J. Conger. *Child Development and Personality*. New York: Harper & Bros., 1956. 569 pp.

National Society for the Study of Education. *The Education of Exceptional Children*. ("Forty-ninth Yearbook of the National Society for the Study of Education," Part II.) Chicago: Univ. of Chicago Press, 1950. 350 pp.

————. *Education for the Gifted* ("Fifty-seventh Yearbook of the National Society for the Study of Education," Part II.) Chicago: Univ. of Chicago Press, 1958. 420 pp.

————. *Learning and Instruction*. ("Forty-ninth Yearbook of the National Society for the Study of Education," Part I.) Chicago: Univ. of Chicago Press, 1950. 352 pp.

Olson, Willard C. *Child Development*. Boston: D. C. Heath & Co., 1949. 417 pp.

*Prescott, Daniel A. *The Child in the Educative Process*. New York: McGraw-Hill Book Co., Inc., 1957. 502 pp.

**The Psychoanalytic Study of the Child. New York: International Universities Press. Many volumes.

*Redl, Fritz, and David Wineman. *Controls from Within*. Glencoe, Ill.: The Free Press, 1952. 332 pp.

Rogers, Dorothy. *Mental Hygiene in Elementary Education*. Boston: Houghton Mifflin Company, 1957. 497 pp.

*Sears, Robert R., and others. *Patterns of Child Rearing*. Evanston, Ill.: Row, Peterson & Co., 1957. 549 pp.

Selye, Hans. *The Stress of Life*. New York: McGraw-Hill Book Co., Inc., 1956. 324 pp.

*Spock, Benjamin. *Baby and Child Care* (Cardinal Giant ed.). New York: Pocket Books, Inc., 1957. 627 pp.

Stewart, Robert S. *Children and Other People; Achieving Maturity Through Learning*. New York: The Dryden Press, 1956. 276 pp.

Stone, L. Joseph, and Joseph Church. *Childhood and Adolescence*. New York: Random House, 1957. 456 pp.

Sullivan, Harry Stack. *The Interpersonal Theory of Psychiatry*. New York: W. W. Norton & Co., Inc., 1953. 393 pp.

*Valentine, Charles W. *Parents and Children*. New York: Philosophical Library, 1955. 212 pp.

PAMPHLETS OF SPECIAL VALUE

TO PARENTS AND TEACHERS

AUERBACH, ALINE B., with assistance of FAITH B. LAURSEN. *The Why and How of Discipline*. New York: Child Study Assoc. of America, 1957. 39 pp.

ESCALONA, SIBYLLE K. *Understanding Hostility in Children*. Chicago, Ill.: Science Research Associates, 1954. 48 pp.

FOSTER, CONSTANCE J. *Developing Responsibility in Children*. Chicago: Science Research Associates, 1953. 48 pp.

FRANK, LAWRENCE K. *Individual Development*. Garden City, N.Y.: Doubleday & Company, Inc., 1955. 52 pp.

GUDRIDGE, BEATRICE M. *Happy Journey—Preparing Your Child for School*. Washington, D.C.: Department of Elementary School Principals, National School Public Relations Association, 1953. 32 pp.

HORN, ERNEST. *Teaching Spelling*. Washington, D.C.: National Educational Association, 1954. 32 pp. (See other pamphlets in this series on other school subjects: National Education Association, "What Research Says to Teachers.")

HYMES, JAMES L. J. *A Pound of Prevention: How Teachers Can Meet the Emotional Needs of Young Children*. New York, N.Y.: New York State Comm. on Mental Hygiene, 1947. 63 pp.

———. *Teacher, Listen, the Children Speak*. New York, N.Y.: New York State Comm. on Mental Hygiene, 1949. 44 pp.

KAWIN, ETHEL. *A Guide for Child-Study Groups*. Chicago: Science Research Associates, 1952. 72 pp.

MENNINGER, WILLIAM C., and others. *How You Grow Up*. New York: Sterling Publishing Corp., 1957. 160 pp.

———. *Self-Understanding—A first Step to Understanding Children*. Chicago: Science Research Associates, 1951. 48 pp.

NEISSER, EDITH G. *Children in the Family; Rivals and Friends*. New York: Teachers College, Columbia Univ., 1951. 60 pp.

NEW YORK STATE DEPARTMENT OF HEALTH. *The Gift of Life*. New York, N.Y.: Mental Health Materials Center, Inc., 1953. 32 pp.

NORTHWAY, MARY L. *What Is Popularity?* Chicago: Science Research Associates, 1955. 47 pp.

OJEMANN, RALPH H. *The Child's Society—Clubs, Gangs and Cliques.* Chicago: Science Research Associates, 1953. 48 pp.

OLSON, WILLARD C., and JOHN LEWELLEN. *How Children Grow and Develop.* Chicago: Science Research Associates, 1953. 48 pp.

OSBORNE, ERNEST. *How Can Your Child Learn About Work?* New York, N.Y.: Mental Health Materials Center, Inc., 1954. 28 pp.

PUNER, HELEN W. *Helping Brothers and Sisters Get Along.* Chicago: Science Research Associates, 1952. 48 pp.

RIDENOUR, NINA A. *Building Self-Confidence in Children.* Chicago: Science Research Associates, 1954. 47 pp.

ROSS, HELEN. *Fears of Children.* Chicago: Science Research Associates, 1952. 49 pp.

SHEVIAKOV, GEORGE V., and FRITZ REDL. *Discipline for Today's Children and Youth.* Washington, D.C.: National Education Association, 1956. 64 pp.

STRANG, RUTH. *Helping Children Solve Problems.* Chicago: Science Research Associates, 1953. 48 pp.

WELFARE AND HEALTH COUNCIL OF NEW YORK CITY, Central Harlem Street Clubs Project. *Working With Teen-Age Gangs.* New York, 1950. 162 pp.

WITTY, PAUL. *Helping the Gifted Child.* Chicago: Science Research Associates, 1952. 48 pp.

WOLF, ANNA W. M. *Helping Your Child to Understand Death.* New York, N.Y.: Child Study Assoc. of America, 1958. 63 pp.

———— and MARGARET C. DAWSON. *What Makes a Good Home?* New York, N.Y.: Child Study Assoc. of America, 1956. 34 pp.

WOLF, KATHERINE M. *The Controversial Problem of Discipline.* New York, N.Y.: Child Study Assoc. of America, 1953. 35 pp.

AUTHOR INDEX

SUBJECT INDEX